Entrepreneur® Magazine

ENCYCLOPEDIA *of* ENTREPRENEURS

Published:

Bringing a Product to Market
Guide to Integrated Marketing
Human Resources for Small Businesses
Making Money with Your Personal Computer
Small Business Legal Guide
Starting a Home-Based Business
Starting an Import/Export Business
Successful Advertising for Small Businesses
The Entrepreneur Magazine Small Business Advisor
The Entrepreneur Magazine Small Business Answer Book
Guide to Professional Services
Guide to Raising Money
Organizing and Promoting Seminars
Encyclopedia of Entrepreneurs

Entrepreneur® Magazine

ENCYCLOPEDIA *of* ENTREPRENEURS

Anthony and Diane Hallett

John Wiley & Sons, Inc.
New York • Chichester • Weinheim • Brisbane • Singapore • Toronto

This text is printed on acid-free paper.

Published by John Wiley & Sons, Inc.

Library of Congress Cataloging-in-Publication Data:

Hallett, Anthony, 1956-
The Entrepreneur magazine : encyclopedia of entrepreneurs / by Anthony & Diane Hallett.
p. cm. —(The Entrepreneur magazine small business series)
Includes index.
ISBN 0-471-17536-6 (cloth : alk. paper)
1. Businesspeople—United States—Biography—Dictionaries.
I. Hallett, Diane, 1955- , II. Entrepreneur (Santa Monica, Calif.) III. Title. IV. Series.
HC102.5.A2H35 1997
338'.04'092273—dc21
[B] 97-21816
CIP

Printed in the United States of America

10 9 8 7 6 5 4 3 2 1

Credits for photos are listed on pp. 499–500.

To our daughters, Amanda Elizabeth Hallett and Andrea Marie Hallett

Acknowledgments

Diane and I are deeply indebted to literally hundreds of people who have helped bring this book to press.

This project actually started back in the mid-1980s. I had the good fortune of working at the Western Pennsylvania Advanced Technology Center, operated by the University of Pittsburgh and Carnegie Mellon University, where Roger Ahlbrandt and Carol Balliet turned me loose in the exciting world of entrepreneurial development. My interest in the culture of entrepreneurship grew with the help of my coworkers and other colleagues, including David Castaldo, Barry Denk, Bob Gleeson, Joe Carr, Lisa Sossong, Tom Canfield, Randy Fraas, Joe Kirk, Bob Logue, and Tim Parks.

No one, however, did more to shape my appreciation of entrepreneurship than Dr. Walt Plosila who, at the time, was a Pennsylvania Commerce Department official and an architect of the state's Ben Franklin Partnership. Walt, now the director of the North Carolina Alliance for Competitive Technologies, instilled in me (and most everyone else who came in contact with him) an enthusiasm for entrepreneurship, and there is no greater champion of entrepreneurs.

The research for this book took more than three years, and through the kindness and participation of hundreds of people, our home office quickly filled with books, photographs, and archival materials capturing the history of the country's greatest entrepreneurs. We are deeply indebted to the family members, archivists, librarians, and other employees at the companies and foundations founded by the great entrepreneurs featured in this encyclopedia. We are also grateful to the staff at the B.F. Jones Memorial Library in Aliquippa, Pennsylvania, for all their help throughout this project.

Everyone has a great idea for a book, but very few make it to publication. If not for our editor, Ruth Mills, this book would be nothing more than a good idea. Ruth, Monika Jain, and many others at John Wiley & Sons, along with Chris Furry and the folks at North Market Street Graphics, have been valuable partners on this project and we'll be forever indebted to the entire team.

The home stretch of this ambitious project became quite challenging, and we are especially grateful for the support provided by Chuck Betters and Pascal Nardelli, two of Pittsburgh's most successful entrepreneurs. We also received much-needed support and prayer from Joni and Jim Witter, Diane and Alex Robenski, Mel and Jim Rosenkranz, Cindy and Rob Prokop, and the entire family at Prince of Peace Episcopal Church.

We also would like to express our gratitude to Howard Raymond Hallett, as well as Randy Adams, Larry Chiappetta, Al Scelp, Mark Tiberio, and Steve Zdinak.

Finally, we'd like to thank our family. My mother, Barbara Boggs Hallett Novak, worked tirelessly at our side throughout the project—making copies, stuffing envelopes, conducting research, and even writing entries. My stepfather, Larry Novak, spent many evenings alone while we burned the midnight oil. Last but not least, Diane and I thank our daughters, Amanda and Andrea, for sacrificing valuable time with their parents and the family computer in the interest of meeting deadlines.

—Anthony M. Hallett

Introduction

The *Encyclopedia of Entrepreneurs* is a comprehensive reference that presents biographical information on hundreds of the greatest entrepreneurs in American history. Each entry presents essential information about the entrepreneur, including family history, education, company and product history, and major accomplishments. This information will be useful to a broad range of users—from those preparing research papers to those interested in inspirational or entertaining reading.

In the mid-1980s, my wife, Diane, and I decided that an encyclopedia of great entrepreneurs would serve as a valuable first step for people wishing to learn more about the art of entrepreneurship. Moreover, it would be a useful research tool to provide a published record of achievement for the featured entrepreneurs.

Identifying individuals who would be included in the *Encyclopedia* proved to be no small task. We asked the governors of all 50 states, more than 200 business and professional trade associations, nearly 100 chambers of commerce, more than 100 public and private business assistance agencies, and more than 200 colleges and universities to provide suggestions. This resulted in a list of nearly 2,500 candidates.

We then mailed inquiries to these individuals or their companies, families, or foundations. Nearly 1,500 responses poured in. We then spent nearly three years obtaining as much information as possible directly from the participating organizations, working closely with public relations and media specialists, librarians, archivists, and company historians.

Our objective has been to prepare profiles of the most interesting entrepreneurs that we have encountered during this project and to provide the most accurate information possible by going directly to the source. Where possible, we have studied authorized biographies and company histories. We therefore have confidence that the entries in this book quite accurately reflect each entrepreneur's family history, education, company and/or product development, and major accomplishments.

The *Encyclopedia of Entrepreneurs* is extremely user-friendly: It includes two alphabetical indexes to help you easily find the information you need. The first index lists the companies and many products that are showcased in the book, which is helpful if you don't know the name of the founder. For instance, if you need information on Carnival Cruise Lines, you might not know that Ted Arison was the company's founder. With this index, you could look up Carnival Cruise Lines and easily find the location of the correct entry in the book. Whether you're a student, professor, or an entrepreneur yourself, this encyclopedia should be a very useful and easy-to-use reference.

The second index lists the name of each entrepreneur who is profiled in the book. Although the book is already organized alphabetically by entrepreneur, this index is helpful because some companies were founded by several entrepreneurs, but are alphabetized only under the name of the primary founder. For example, suppose you're looking for information about Adolphus

Busch (of Anheuser-Busch). Busch would not be found under the *B*s, but rather, he would be found under the *A*s, in the entry for Eberhard Anheuser, his partner. With this helpful index, you can simply look up Busch and flip to the correct page.

You will no doubt think of several successful entrepreneurs who are not included in this premier edition. Those who are included rank among the best-known and most successful entrepreneurs, but the list is by no means complete. Several of those contacted are quite modest about their success and asked not to be profiled, and we have honored their requests. However, we have started files on literally hundreds of others, which we intend to follow up on while you enjoy this first edition.

—Anthony M. Hallett

Wallace C. Abbott

[Abbott Laboratories]

Wallace C. Abbott was born to Luther Abbott, a Vermont farmer, and his wife Wealtha Barrows. He worked on the family farm and, at age 20, being only an elementary school graduate, set out to obtain a formal education. Within a few short years he was a promising graduate of the University of Michigan Medical School.

In 1888, Abbott purchased a medical practice and drugstore in Ravenswood, Illinois, for $1,000. While building his practice and drugstore, the highly inquisitive and energetic doctor could be seen responding to house calls on his Beckley-Ralston bicycle.

Abbott was particularly dissatisfied with the liquid medication that was popular. He was intrigued with the work of Belgian-born surgeon Adolphe Burggraeve, which focused on the "active principles" of drug plants. Dr. Burggraeve isolated the alkaloid (or active part) of drug plants, compressing it into small granules or pills. This could be given in modest doses without distaste or discomfort to anyone, even children.

Initially, Abbott purchased and dispensed the granules. However, he was unhappy with their slow disintegration and, true to his impatient demeanor, began to manufacture his own pills in the kitchen of the apartment behind his drugstore. His first-year sales of $2,000 were impressive, considering it was actually an incidental business behind his medical practice and drugstore.

Dr. Abbott has been described as a man possessing "good health, relentless optimism, unstoppable energy, and a reasonable disregard for debt." He openly discussed his ideas with a mix of intellectualism and quick wit. At the same time, he couldn't shake his intense curiosity about medicine or his nagging desire to find better ways of treating the sick and injured.

By 1890, Abbott's granule business was quickly growing. He expanded his business into a two-story house near the drugstore, where his parents and sister Lucy increased output. The first nonfamily member was hired at $6.00 per week. Sales grew to $8,000—a 400 percent increase in two short years.

In 1894, sales reached $29,000 and Abbott made a key acquisition—the *Alkaloidal Clinic*—a medical journal. He quickly increased the size of the magazine from 12 to 36 pages, filling it with his wit and wisdom, letters, and advertisements. Within two years he purchased an entire building to house the publication, complete with 15 typesetters and pressroom workers.

The magazine grew through unorthodox marketing. If a doctor couldn't afford the $1.00 per year subscription price, Abbott offered a deal: "If times are hard, Doctor, and you can't spare the dollar, hustle around and get us three new subscriptions and we'll advance you one year." The *Alkaloidal Clinic* grew to a monthly circulation of 20,000, making it the fourth most widely read medical and surgical journal in the country.

Abbott formally incorporated the Abbott Alkaloidal Company in 1900, and even with sales of $125,000, he continued to respond to house calls on his bicycle. However, in the ensuing years he was forced to cut back on his medical practice and attend to the flourishing pill and publishing operations. After a disastrous fire in 1905, Abbott rebuilt the plant and, despite his long-standing policy, hired a sales force.

The magazine was renamed the *American Journal of Clinical Medicine,* and the annual subscription cost was raised to $1.50. Advertising costs were raised and the publication carried such prestige that in 1909 Abbott traded one year of advertising for his first car, a Waverley, and a few hundred dollars in cash.

At the height of World War I, the U.S. government was unable to obtain desperately needed pharmaceuticals on which German companies held patents. Due to the adversarial relationship, the medications could not be obtained from Germany. That situation led to the passage of the Trading With The Enemy Act, which authorized the Federal Trade Commission to license American firms to produce German products.

Even with this protection, the manufacturing process required risky product research. Abbott rose to the challenge and conducted the necessary research to provide the drugs in demand. This transformed Abbott into a long-term research-driven firm.

Dr. Abbott died on July 4, 1921, at the age of 63. He had built a million-dollar business empire on his faith that the practice of medicine could be greatly improved through innovative pharmaceuticals.

Dr. Abbott can lay claim to one of the most unique methods of personnel recruitment: delivering babies whom he later employed! James F. Stiles Jr. was brought into this world in 1892 by Dr. Abbott, and 21 years later Stiles secured a job with the company as a packer in the shipping room. He rose to the position of company treasurer and, eventually, to chairman of the board.

One hundred years after Wallace Abbott started manufacturing pills in his kitchen, Abbott was ranked as a Fortune 100 company, with revenues exceeding $4 billion.

SOURCE: *The Abbott Almanac: 100 Years of Commitment to Quality Health Care,* Benjamin Publications, Elmsford, NY, 1987

Joseph A. Albertson

[Albertson's, Inc.]

Joseph Albert Albertson was born on October 17, 1906, in Yukon, Oklahoma, one of four sons of Earl and Rhoda Albertson. Three years later Earl, a farmer and horticulturist, moved his family to Caldwell, Idaho.

Albertson graduated from high school in 1925 and studied business at the College of Idaho in Caldwell. In chemistry class he became acquainted with Kathryn "Kay" McCurry, whom he later married. While in college, Joe worked as a janitor, but the money wasn't enough. He left college after two years and took a job as a clerk at a local Safeway grocery store.

Joe's career moved quickly at Safeway. Before his 12-year career with Safeway ended, Joe was managing more than a dozen stores and learning every phase of the retail business. Joe and Kay married in 1930, and their daughter, Barbara Jean, was born in 1933.

However, Joe Albertson wanted to own a store, designed to his specifications. In 1939, he formed a partnership with L. S. Skaggs, a fellow Safeway employee, and Tom Cuthbert, an accountant. Joe used his life's savings of $5,000, plus a $7,500 loan from his aunt, to make up his share of $12,500. His aunt elected to have stock instead of monetary repayment. Upon her death, its value had risen to $750,000.

On July 21, 1939, the trio opened their first Albertson's Food Center in Boise, Idaho. Shoppers were greeted by a fresh bakery, an automatic doughnut machine, one of the first magazine racks in the country, and double-dipped ice-cream cones called "Big Joe" that cost a nickel. The store netted a $10,000 profit in the first year, and Joe quickly opened two more stores in 1940, in Nampa and Caldwell. By the end of the second year, total sales exceeded $1 million.

At the end of World War II, Joe opened a fourth store in Emmett, Idaho. Shortly thereafter, Joe and his colleagues elected to dissolve the partnership, and in December 1945, he incorporated the company as Albertson's Corporation. In 1946, he opened yet another store, this one in Idaho Falls. He also built a complete poultry operation that would eventually produce more than 8 million pounds of poultry annually.

Joe stuck with his rapid-growth formula. By the end of 1948 he opened seven more stores, including the first outside of Idaho, in Vale, Oregon. In 1949 he opened the Dutch Girl Ice Cream Plant, which became an early trademark for ice cream and bakery products. He next expanded into Washington, and by the end of 1950 he had 16 stores in operation.

During this time he experimented with expanding retail sales in clothing, shoes, bedding, appliances, and furniture. But this experiment was phased out after four short years. In 1957, he purchased a small pharmacy known as Sugarhouse Drug, in Salt Lake City. From that point forward, Joe incorporated pharmacies into his grocery stores, complete with sundries and cosmetics, wherever possible.

By the beginning of 1960, Albertson owned 62 supermarkets, five drugstores, and one department store. Combined sales approached $70 million, and profits reached nearly $2 million. Through expansion and acquisitions in states from Wyoming to California, Joe Albertson ended the 1960s owning 200 stores in nine states, employing 8,500 people.

The 1970s witnessed still more expansion. In 1978, Albertson consolidated all administrative and financial operations in a new building in Boise, Idaho. By the end of the decade, the company had grown to 365 stores, 25,000 employees, and annual sales in excess of $2 billion.

Joe Albertson died on January 20, 1993, in Boise, Idaho. Joe and Kathryn Albertson were generous people. Perhaps their best-known philanthropy involved the College of Idaho, where they met decades earlier, which has been renamed Albertson College of Idaho.

SOURCE: Albertson's company archives

Charles C. Alderton, Robert S. Lazenby, Wade B. Morrison

[Dr Pepper Company]

Wade B. Morrison was born on August 19, 1852, at Christianburg, Virginia. After graduating from the Philadelphia College of Pharmacy, he accepted a job in a drugstore in Rural Retreat, Virginia, owned by Dr. Charles T. Pepper. Morrison became attracted to Dr. Pepper's beautiful young daughter, but had his hopes dashed when his employer told him to stay away from her.

Heartbroken, the 19-year-old pharmacist picked up his belongings and moved to Texas. In 1880, he married Carrie B. Jeffress of Round Rock, Texas. Two years later, the couple moved to Waco, Texas, where Morrison landed a job with John Castles, owner of a small drugstore. Morrison became a partner in the venture and, upon buying out Castles, changed the name of the store to Morrison's Old Corner Drug Store.

Charles Courtice Alderton was born on June 21, 1857, at Brooklyn, New York, the eldest of five children born to English immigrant parents. After attending college in Stowmarket, England, young Alderton headed west to the University of Texas at Galveston, where he attended medical school. Upon receiving his M.D., he married Lillie E. Walker of Galveston, Texas, and in 1884 moved to Waco, taking a job as a pharmacist at Morrison's Old Corner Drug Store.

While working at the drugstore, Alderton noticed that customers quickly tired of the beverage flavors offered at the soda fountain. He mixed a variety of fruit extracts from the fountain and, through trial and error, eventually devised a distinct-tasting blend that both he and owner Morrison enjoyed. They shared the beverage with customers, and soon people were coming to the drugstore to try "Doc Alderton's drink." The two later renamed the drink Dr Pepper after Morrison's meddling former employer.

In time, customer demand for the drink was causing a problem at the drugstore: There simply wasn't enough room to make the syrup and fill all the orders. Then one of the store's patrons, Robert S. Lazenby, offered a solution. Lazenby, an experienced beverage chemist, was the founder and owner of Circle "A" Ginger Ale in Waco.

Robert Sherman Lazenby was born on September 12, 1866, in Johnson County, Texas. His father, Henry Clay Lazenby, was a Virginia native who had served as an officer under General Robert E. Lee. Shortly after Robert's birth, his parents moved their four sons to Waco. Robert, who studied pharmacy, launched his Circle "A" Ginger Ale company at age 18.

Lazenby was excited about the potential of Dr Pepper, and the men formed a new company, The Artesian Manufacturing & Bottling Works. Lazenby assumed responsibility for mixing and bottling their new Dr Pepper drink (which from the beginning has been marketed as "Dr Pepper"—minus a period). They acquired a trademark for "Dr Pepper Phos-Ferrates."

Sales of Dr Pepper, delivered by teams of horses and wagons, spread quickly throughout Texas. However, the drink was given a real boost with the exposure it received at the 1904 World's Fair and Exposition in St. Louis. Along with the introduction of the hamburger and the french fry, the entire world embraced the new soft drink with the exotic taste.

Charles Alderton didn't maintain a close relationship with the Dr Pepper venture. In 1894, he left Morrison's operation to become the chief chemist for the Behrens Drug Company of Waco, a position he held for 19 years. He next worked as a salesman for Eli Lilly & Company for six years before joining the Red Arrow Laboratories (eventually the Southwestern Drug Company), where he served as a chemist until his retirement in October 1938 at the age of 79. He died two years later on May 29, 1941.

Wade B. Morrison stayed in the drugstore business a total of 42 years. He became one of Waco's most respected businessmen and community leaders. Morrison died on July 23, 1924, at the age of 72.

Robert Lazenby continued to direct production and sales of Dr Pepper until his retirement in 1925, at which time he was succeeded by his son-in-law, J. B. O'Hara. Lazenby died on April 17, 1941, at the age of 74.

SOURCE: Company publication, *Dr Pepper: King of Beverages,* by Dr Pepper Company and Taylor Publishing, two-volume set

James A. Allison, Carl G. Fisher

[Allison Gas Turbine]

The Allison family was quite enterprising. In 1840, James M. and Julia Allison left England and immigrated to Greene County, Indiana, where James became proprietor of several riverboats. The family later moved to Michigan, where James established a grocery store.

James's son, Noah, worked for his father for several years before launching Allison & Nixon, a knitting and hosiery manufacturer. Noah also founded a credit company, a publishing house, and an international discount-coupon company. Upon Noah's untimely death, his wife Myra became the proprietor of the business and their three sons were made directors. However, son James Ashbury Allison (born August, 1872) didn't stay with the family business long.

Carl Fisher was Jim Allison's closest friend. Fisher was the consummate entrepreneur, taking up venture upon venture. He had a bicycle shop, which he promptly parlayed into an automobile dealership in 1904. Percy Avery, a man familiar with Fisher's enthusiasm for new business, approached Fisher that same year with an idea. Early automobiles were equipped with kerosene lamps. The newer lights that burned acetylene from a generator were brighter, but they were also dangerous.

Avery developed an idea for compressing and storing acetylene in a small steel cylinder. Fisher immediately contacted Allison, and the three men launched the Concentrated Acetylene Company in September 1904, with total capitalization of $10,000. The company's offices were located in Fisher's automobile dealership. Despite periodic explosions at their manufacturing plant, the business was quickly successful. In 1906, Avery left the business, and the remaining founders changed the name to the Prest-O-Lite Company.

One year after the formation of their company, Fisher, Avery, and their friends attended the Labor Day car races at the Indiana State Fair. The group immediately organized a 24-hour race that would, of course, feature their acetylene lamps for night driving.

The November race was a huge success, drawing participants from around the country. In the late hours after the race concluded, someone suggested that the event would be even better if it were held on a real paved and banked track. The idea stuck and, in 1909, Allison, Fisher, and two other men put up $72,000 for farmland and built their motor speedway. On May 30, 1911, the first Indianapolis Speedway 500-Mile International Sweepstakes Race was run. Allison and Fisher also went on to establish several racing teams.

In 1917, Allison and Fisher sold their 30,000-share controlling interest in Prest-O-Lite for $9 million, but Allison retained some Prest-O-Lite stock. The two men then started spending considerable time in Florida, and soon they were buying property. Allison built a hospital in North Miami Beach, an aquarium in Miami, and a large home on Biscayne Bay's Star Island.

On August 3, 1928, James Allison died suddenly at the age of 55. The previous weekend he had married his second wife at Carl Fisher's Long Island home. During a subsequent train trip to Indianapolis, Allison became ill and within days died of bronchial pneumonia.

Today, the lamp company built by James Allison and Carl Fisher still exists as Allison Gas Turbine Company.

SOURCE: Allison Gas Turbine Company archives

John B. Amos

[American Family Life Assurance Company]

After building a modest savings account through his law practice, John Amos followed a lifelong dream and in 1955 established a small insurance company in Columbus, Georgia. Among his many innovations was cancer insurance, which propelled the company through America and into Japan. Today, his American Family Life Assurance Company (AFLAC) is the world's largest provider of supplemental health insurance.

John Beverly Amos was born on June 5, 1924, in Enterprise, Alabama. At the age of 11, he sold his first insurance policy. He devised a plan that would pay 10¢ for a cigarette burn on the foot and 15¢ for a nail puncture. His only customer was his nine-year-old brother, who paid a weekly premium of a nickel.

At age 31, John Amos realized his dream. He, his wife Elena, and their two children moved from Florida to Columbus, Georgia, where he established his first insurance company. He chose Columbus because, at the time, it wasn't home to any other insurance company. He was soon joined by his two brothers, Bill and Paul, and their father Shelby, who had sold insurance in Dallas, Texas, for two years.

Their company, the American Family Life Assurance Company of Columbus (AFLAC), was officially launched in November 1955. To raise the $300,000 in necessary capital, the Amos family sold stock door-to-door to the Georgia residents on an installment plan—50¢ down and 50¢ per week. Within four months, the money was raised.

The company first offered inexpensive life insurance, with some premiums costing only 10¢ per week. In time, the company switched directions, selling its weekly premium business to another company and concentrating on health and accident coverage. Then John Amos developed an innovative product—cancer insurance. AFLAC offered simple, inexpensive policies to cover the expensive treatment that clients faced if they developed cancer.

Many people ridiculed John's program. What would he do when a cure was found? John researched the topic thoroughly and became convinced that a cure was not in the foreseeable future, so he moved forward with marketing the policies. His 150 licensed agents sold more than 5,800 cancer insurance policies in 1958. The following year, they expanded into Florida and more than doubled the number of agents. By the end of 1964 there were 150,000 policies in effect.

By the early 1970s, AFLAC was selling in 42 states, and John Amos started looking beyond the border. He took a long trip through Japan and became convinced that the Japanese standard of living would soon be equal to that in America. His visit was during the damp, rainy month of April, and he noticed many people wearing masks to prevent the spread of the flu virus. This convinced him that the health-conscious Japanese would be interested in his cancer insurance.

He faced an uphill battle. The Japanese government was not anxious to grant an American insurance company permission to sell policies. Moreover, there was a cultural fear of cancer in Japan. Many people wouldn't even discuss the subject aloud because they associated it with certain death.

Undaunted, John Amos worked his way through the bureaucratic maze and, in 1974, was granted a license to conduct business in Japan. He estimated that first-year sales would be nearly $3.5 million. They actually reached $25 million. That same year was important in America, too. The company's stock became publicly traded, and AFLAC opened its new 18-story American Family Center in Columbus.

John Amos died in 1990. His brother and AFLAC cofounder, Paul Amos, assumed the position of chairman of the board. By then, AFLAC had annual revenues of over $2.5 billion and assets of nearly $7 billion. Today the company insures more than 40 million people worldwide (including more than 20 percent of Japan's population) and has total assets of more than $25 billion.

SOURCE: AFLAC company archives

Arthur E. Andersen

[Arthur Andersen & Company]

Arthur Andersen, orphaned at age 16, built what is today one of the largest accounting firms in the world.

In 1882, Norwegian immigrant John Andersen and his Danish-born wife Mary emigrated to the United States with their two young sons. Two more sons were born after their arrival, including Arthur Edward Andersen, born in 1885. That same year, the family returned to Oslo, Norway.

The family, now including six children, returned to the United States in 1889, eventually settling in Chicago, Illinois, where the last two of eight Andersen children were born. Tragically, both of Arthur's parents died young: Mary Andersen died in 1896 at the age of 38 and John Andersen died in 1901 at age 44. Subsequently, the four younger Andersen children were scattered with various relatives, and 16-year-old Arthur and his three older brothers were left on their own.

Having completed only eight years of school, Arthur was determined to finish his education. Working as a mailboy for the manufacturing firm of Fraser & Chalmers by day, he attended night classes and graduated from Chicago's Atheneum High School in 1903. Within three years he was promoted to assistant to the controller of Fraser & Chalmers and had married Emma Barnes Arnold.

Andersen became interested in the field of public accounting and, in 1907, left his comfortable position for a job with Price Waterhouse at a lower salary. A year later, at age 23, he became the youngest certified public accountant in the state of Illinois. Driven to constant improvement, Andersen enrolled at Northwestern University in 1908 and, because of his academic success, was soon asked to teach night school classes, filling his evenings as both student and teacher.

Andersen accepted a position as controller for the Uihlein family businesses in Milwaukee in 1911, but rather than move from Chicago he opted for a 180-mile-per-day commute. A year later, key members of Northwestern's business program left, and the university offered the 27-year-old Andersen the position of assistant professor and head of the accounting department. He accepted and immediately reorganized the department and developed new course material, all while maintaining his full-time job in Milwaukee.

In 1913, Andersen and another Price Waterhouse employee purchased a small public accounting practice for $4,000 and renamed it Andersen, DeLany & Company. The partners and their staff of seven worked out of two rooms in Chicago's Harris Trust Building.

From this beginning, Andersen sought to compete with the large, established accounting firms. His strategy was to take a comprehensive, quality-centered approach that went beyond number crunching. He wanted his clients to understand the impact the finances were having on their businesses.

The small business experienced rapid growth for several reasons. External factors were favorable: World War I fueled manufacturing growth, and concurrently the federal government passed legislation such as the Clayton Act and established the Federal Trade Commission. All of this resulted in an increased demand for sound financial management assistance.

Internally, Andersen insisted that a high-quality operation would result in corporate success. He elected to employ full-time professional staff members rather than seasonal help. Drawing from his relationship to academia (by 1915 he was granted a full professorship at Northwestern), the firm became one of the first to recruit college and university graduates. All new employees were taught the company adage (which Andersen was given by his mother at an early age): "Think straight and talk straight."

In 1918, Clarence DeLany, Andersen's well-liked and highly respected partner, amicably left the firm, which was renamed Arthur Andersen & Company. Andersen soon diversified from the audit business, establishing, for example, the Industrial Engineering group in 1918 "to show the strong or weak points in company position or management [and to] correct such weak spots." The strategy paid off, as revenues increased from $67,700 in 1916 to $322,000 in 1920. By 1921 the firm opened a Washington, D.C., office.

Arthur Andersen died on January 10, 1947, at the age of 61. Upon Andersen's death, the 25 partners met and most voted to dissolve the partnership. However, a small group opposed the move, including 39-year-old Leonard Spacek. In the absence of a clear successor to Andersen (Arthur Andersen Jr. had previously left the firm), Spacek rose to the occasion and led the continued growth of Arthur Andersen & Co., which, known today as Arthur Andersen LLP, has offices worldwide.

It is interesting to note that after Andersen's death it was discovered that his great-grandfather was the first recognized public accountant—*authorized accountant,* as they call it in the north European countries—in Denmark.

SOURCE: Arthur Andersen & Company archives

Eberhard Anheuser, Adolphus Busch

[Anheuser-Busch Companies]

Eberhard Anheuser (born 1805) was a successful soap manufacturer in St. Louis. In 1860, a small brewery that he financed was on the brink of failure, and reluctantly, Anheuser purchased the interests of other minority investors and became a brewer.

Adolphus Busch was born on July 10, 1839, in Kastel, Germany, the second-youngest of 22 children born to Ulrich Busch, a prosperous merchant and innkeeper. His mother, Barbara Pfeiffer Busch, was Ulrich's second wife.

Adolphus immigrated to St. Louis, Missouri, in 1857, via New Orleans and the Mississippi River. In 1859 he opened a wholesale commission house that came to be known as Adolphus Busch & Company.

In 1861, Busch married Eberhard's daughter, Lilly Anheuser. The couple had 13 children, 9 of whom lived to adulthood. Their third-born, August A. Busch, would eventually take over the reins of the family business.

Adolphus Busch continued to build his company and even served with the Union army. In 1864, however, Eberhard persuaded Busch to help manage the brewery. By 1869, Busch became Eberhard's partner, and within ten years the firm was renamed Anheuser-Busch Brewing Association and Busch was named its president. On May 2, 1880, Eberhard Anheuser died.

Busch dreamed of building and supplying a national beer market. His first step was to create a network of railside icehouses that would cool railcars of beer in shipment. By the late 1870s, he had successfully applied the pasteurization process to beer, and the icehouses gave way to refrigerated freight cars.

In 1876, Busch and his close friend Carl Conrad collaborated on a new beer that they labeled Budweiser. Today, the "King of Beers" is the number one seller in the world and is still brewed to the exact standards employed more than 100 years ago. Twenty years later he launched Michelob, which quickly became (and continues to be) the leading superpremium American beer.

Busch, a master marketer, opened the brewery to the public. He insisted on using only the finest horses to draw his shiny red-and-green beer delivery wagons through city streets. The tradition is kept alive by the famous Budweiser Clydesdales which make hundreds of appearances each year.

Busch also actively pursued other business interests. He was president of the South Side Bank and the Manufacturers Railroad Company. He founded the Adolphus Busch Glass Manufacturing Company, the St. Louis Refrigerator Car Company, and the Busch Sulzer Brothers Diesel Engine Company. He also owned a controlling interest in five brewery plants and six hotels (including the Adolphus in Dallas, which opened on October 6, 1912) and was an investor in more than 30 businesses in the United States and Europe.

Adolphus Busch died on October 10, 1913, at the family villa in Langenschwalbach, Germany. Through his final years, Adolphus had left most of the day-to-day operations to his son August A. Busch Sr., who assumed control of the company upon Adolphus's death.

August led Anheuser-Busch through the trying years of World War I, Prohibition, and the Depression. It was during these years that Anheuser-Busch experimented with diversification. Under the leadership of August A. Busch Jr., the company became active in diversification into family entertainment, real estate, can manufacturing, transportation, and sports.

Today, Anheuser-Busch is under the leadership of August A. Busch III, the fourth generation in the business. He has increased beer operations while continuing expansion into other areas, including the acquisition of Sea World. The company is now the world's largest brewing organization, one of the largest theme-park operators, the second-largest U.S. manufacturer of aluminum beverage containers, and the world's largest recycler of used aluminum beverage containers. Sales exceed $12 billion per year, and the company employs more than 23,000 people.

SOURCE: Anheuser-Busch Companies archives

Ted Arison

[Carnival Cruise Lines]

Ted Arison was born on February 24, 1924, in Tel Aviv, Israel. He attended the American University in Beirut, but his education was interrupted by the outbreak of World War II. Arison enlisted with the British Army and fought in Italy and Germany, attaining the rank of sergeant major.

When Arison's father died not long after the war, Ted assumed management of the family shipping business. In the early 1950s, the business was sold, and Arison launched his own fleet of cargo ships under Panamanian and Honduran flags. After the Korean War, he sold his interests and moved to the United States.

Arison spent the next 12 years pursuing a number of business interests, particularly in air cargo. He again sold his interests and moved, this time to Miami, Florida. Not long after his move, Arison came to the rescue of a passenger shipping company that was in financial trouble. He and an old friend, Norwegian ship owner Knut Kloster, then launched Norwegian Caribbean Lines.

In 1972, Arison led an investment team that negotiated a $6.5 million financing deal to operate the *Empress of Canada,* which he renamed the *Mardi Gras.* The venture was dubbed Carnival Cruise Lines, and the *Mardi Gras* was rushed into service. On the ship's maiden voyage, it ran aground on a sandbar outside the Port of Miami. Its image tarnished, the *Mardi Gras* was steaming toward bankruptcy.

Facing mounting problems, Arison offered to acquire full equity in the troubled venture for $1 in cash and assumption of a $5 million debt. The offer was accepted, and Arison moved quickly to change the image of cruises, which until then was summed up as "trips for the newlywed or nearly dead." He added activities, creating a festive environment, and targeted advertising toward vacationers of all types.

The *Mardi Gras* quickly was fully booked on a regular basis. Encouraged with the success, Arison purchased a second ship, the *Carnivale,* formerly the *Empress of Britain.* Two years later, he purchased the 38,000-ton *S.A. Vaal,* which, after a $30 million refurbishment, was renamed the *Festivale,* the largest and fastest Miami-based vessel that sailed the Caribbean. All of these original ships are now retired from Carnival Cruise Lines.

Carnival entered a period of shipbuilding, launching the *Tropicale,* the *Holiday,* the *Jubilee,* and the *Celebration* during the 1980s. In 1990, the firm launched its first superliner, *Fantasy,* a 70,000-ton, 2,044-passenger ship that was built at a cost of $225 million. The fleet has since grown to six superliners.

Arison brought professional basketball to Miami in 1988, becoming the majority owner of the Miami Heat. In the early 1990s, he retired from active management of his companies, reclaimed his Israeli citizenship, and returned to his birthplace, Tel Aviv. Today, Carnival Cruise Lines is the largest cruise line in the world, with 11 ships.

SOURCE: Carnival Cruise Lines archives

Thomas M. Armstrong

[Armstrong World Industries]

Following his investment in a small cork plant, Thomas Armstrong quit his full-time job to help his partner. Tragically, the partner died, leaving an inexperienced Armstrong with a growing business. Through hard work and an occasional lucky break, he established the Armstrong Cork Company, now known as Armstrong World Industries, as one of the world leaders in cork and household products manufacturing.

Thomas Morton Armstrong's parents had emigrated from Londonderry, in Northern Ireland, to Manhattan a few years before his birth. When Tom was four, the family moved to Pittsburgh, Pennsylvania. By age 12, young Armstrong was working in a rope factory. He later became a shipping clerk for a bottle manufacturer, where he had his first contact with cork.

In 1860, Armstrong was approached by John D. Glass to invest in a small cork-cutting business. Cork, which had to be imported, could not be shipped profitably to Pittsburgh. Yet Glass thought the city was large enough and was well positioned to be a good distribution point for regions west of the Appalachian mountains. The 24-year-old Armstrong agreed and invested $300, keeping his day job and visiting the shop in the evenings.

Life for Armstrong changed quickly after launching the new venture. Later that year, he married Martha Jane Porter. Then the Civil War broke out, throwing the cork business into disarray. Armstrong had to raise more money for the venture, and he even found $1,000 to buy a new cork-cutting machine. When the business showed signs of growth, Armstrong quit his job and joined Glass full-time. Then, in 1864 John Glass died unexpectedly.

Armstrong filled the void by recruiting new faces, including his brother, Robert D. Armstrong, who was a banker and early supporter of the venture. Thomas pioneered quality control by putting his name on bags of cork, which provided customers with a place to go if the cork was not up to standards. Unhappy with the industry practice of "let the buyer beware," Tom Armstrong adopted his own motto: "Let the buyer have faith."

Just when the market was growing comfortably for Armstrong, Brother & Company, a new market innovation known as the Mason jar displaced the need for cork. Shortly thereafter, the spring stopper took the place of cork in soda water bottles. Armstrong blamed himself, stating that he should have foreseen the developments, and he vowed never to let market changes sneak up on him again.

The company had another big change in 1878. Robert Armstrong passed away, and Thomas was joined by his 17-year-old son, Charles D. Armstrong, and another brother, Andrew J. Armstrong. The company was still struggling, making cork deliveries throughout Pittsburgh by wheelbarrow until it had enough money to afford a horse and wagon.

The work paid off. Within ten years, the firm employed more than 200 people, and with annual sales of $450,000, Armstrong was one of the world's largest cork manufacturers. The growth continued into the 1890s, when Armstrong brought together seven cork manufacturers to form one company: The Armstrong Cork Company. Three of the seven, who were in the small, central Pennsylvania community of Lancaster, merged into the Lancaster Cork Works.

Thomas Morton Armstrong died in May of 1908. The previous year, his company had surpassed 1,000 employees and sales of $5 million. He was succeeded by his son, Charles, who soon divided the company into three divisions, including the Linoleum Division, which was centered in Lancaster. In 1929, the company's headquarters was moved from Pittsburgh to Lancaster. Armstrong World Industries is still based in Lancaster, Pennsylvania, and has annual sales in excess of $2 billion.

SOURCE: Company publication, *Let the Buyer Have Faith: The Story of Armstrong,* by William A. Mehler Jr., 1987

Mary Kay Ash

[Mary Kay Cosmetics, Inc.]

Mary Kay Wagner (Ash), the youngest of three children, was raised in Hot Wells, Texas. When she was seven years old, her father returned home after spending three years in a sanatorium for treatment of his tuberculosis. He remained an invalid throughout her childhood. Her mother, a restaurant manager in nearby Houston, was left as the sole source of support for the family.

Mary Kay's older brother and sister were not living at home. Since her mother worked long hours, Mary Kay was left to care for her father, cook and clean, and do most of her own shopping. Each note that her mother left for her ended with "Honey, you can do it," which the young lady took to heart and has carried with her throughout life.

Upon her graduation from high school, Mary Kay's family didn't have enough money to send her to college. At age 17, she married a local radio personality and musician. By the time he was called to serve in World War II, the couple had three children. Mary Kay supported the family during the war, and shortly after her husband's discharge from the service the couple divorced.

To support herself and her children, Mary Kay became a direct sales representative for Stanley Home Products, frequently holding three home demonstration parties daily, earning $10 to $12 at each one. She once was awarded a "Miss Dallas" ribbon for successful recruitment of new dealers, an experience that convinced her that recognition for achievement was as important as financial incentives.

In 1963, Mary Kay retired from her direct selling career with Stanley Home Products. She soon decided to write a book that would provide insight to help women survive in a male-dominated business world. However, the project turned into an ingenious plan for her own dream company that was based on the Golden Rule: Treat others as you would want them to treat you.

While still selling Stanley products in the 1950s, Mary Kay met a woman who made her own skin care lotion. The woman's father had worked as a hide tanner who, until his death at age 73, had amazing skin tone and elasticity, which he attributed to constant exposure to tanning lotion. His daughter experimented with the formula and eventually developed creams and lotions gentle enough for women's skin.

In September 1963, Mary Kay and her 20-year-old son, Richard, launched Mary Kay Cosmetics in a Dallas storefront. Using her life savings of $5,000, she purchased some used office furniture, supplies, and the rights to the skin care products owned by the tanner's heirs. Another son, 27-year-old Ben, contributed his $4,500 savings and eventually left his job in Houston to join the family business. Her daughter Marilyn also worked at the company during the early years.

Mary Kay created a unique sales method where a well-educated consultant provides instruction to a small group of customers. In the beginning, she recruited a force of nine beauty consultants who sold the Basic Skin Care Set—five products in small jars. First-year sales nearly reached $200,000, which quadrupled to $800,000 the following year. In 1964, Mary Kay held the first companywide convention in her warehouse because the company couldn't afford to rent a hotel.

Drawing on her longtime belief in the importance of personal recognition, Mary Kay instituted a recognition and awards program that continues to this day. Successful beauty consultants were presented with jewelry, dream vacations, and even cars for their success and achievements. Soon, the Mary Kay pink Cadillac became a common sight in neighborhoods across the country. By 1966, sales reached $1 million.

Today there are more than 475,000 independent Mary Kay beauty consultants in 25 countries. Global retail sales for 1996 exceeded $2 billion. Mary Kay Ash created an unparalleled business opportunity for women that today has delivered career flexibility, unlimited earnings potential, and recognition to hundreds of thousands of women worldwide. Her determination and commitment to helping women develop and succeed in business is what ultimately has made Mary Kay, Inc., among the most admired and respected companies today.

SOURCES: Mary Kay Cosmetics archives; Mary Kay Ash, *Mary Kay,* HarperCollins, 1981, 1987, 1994

Samuel Austin

[The Austin Company]

Samuel Austin was born on June 16, 1850, in England. Sixteen years later, he was bound as an apprentice to a carpenter in the village of Orton Waterville until his twenty-first birthday in 1871. When the apprenticeship was complete, Austin moved to a more urban setting in search of steady work. The following year, word spread to England about the Great Chicago Fire, including reports that a great deal of work was available for craftsmen to rebuild the city.

Several of Austin's coworkers agreed to make a spring voyage to America, but when the day arrived to depart, only Austin showed up. Disappointed but not discouraged, he boarded the boat and made the 16-day voyage, though he did not know any of the other passengers and had no one waiting for him in America.

After arriving in New York, Austin headed for Cleveland, Ohio, where he visited with friends of some of his English acquaintances. There was plenty of work available in Cleveland, so Austin abandoned his Chicago plans and went to work near his hosts. He returned to England briefly in 1873, but then made the trip back to Cleveland where, in 1874, he was married.

The family moved to England again for two years, then returned to Cleveland for good in 1878. Austin went back to work for his old employer, J. Vining. Later that year, a local physician asked Austin to build a small addition onto his home. Austin did such a good job that subsequent contracts followed.

In 1889, Austin was awarded a contract to build a bank. It was his first commercial undertaking, and he worked quite hard at the project, believing it would be an opportunity to showcase his quality to other businesspeople who had accounts at the bank. His efforts paid off, and he was soon swamped with opportunities to build offices and factories.

Within six years, Austin had developed a strong reputation for commercial projects. In 1895, he was awarded the contract to build Cleveland's first electric lamp factory. That same year, he accepted a contract to build a wool factory in Chicago, his first work outside Cleveland.

Austin's son, Wilbert, graduated from Case School of Applied Sciences (now part of Case Western Reserve University) in 1904 with a degree in engineering, and the firm was named The Samuel Austin & Son Company. Father and son blended their talents and were soon offering engineering and construction services under one roof. This approach soon became known as "The Austin Method" throughout the industry.

As the company grew, they were able to accept larger contracts. By 1916, they reorganized as The Austin Company and were bidding on jobs throughout the country. Austin retired as president in 1925 and was replaced by Wilbert. Samuel Austin died in 1936. Tragically, Wilbert died in a plane crash four years later.

Today, Austin has nearly 1,000 employees and annual sales of more than $1 billion.

SOURCE: The Austin Company archives

R. Stanton Avery

[Avery Dennison]

Stan Avery left social work to join a small company that made adhesive labels. When the company went out of business, Avery's enthusiasm for the innovative product remained. He and his wife launched a small business making and marketing Avery's patented self-adhesive labels to local gift shops. Over time, the Avery Dennison Corporation became a leading manufacturer of self-adhesive labels and related office products. More significantly, Avery's invention of a label that could stick without moisture or heat established a global industry.

The first Avery to arrive in America was Christopher Avery, landing in Boston in 1640. His son, James, later built a house in Groton, Connecticut, which became the center of the Avery family for the next 300 years. In 1891, Oliver Perry Avery left Connecticut and traveled to Grand Junction, Colorado, where he married Emma Dickinson, the daughter of a local minister. One of their children, Ray Stanton Avery, was born on January 13, 1907, in Oklahoma City. The family later moved to California.

Avery's father and brother taught him to use a printing press at an early age. Throughout high school and college, he printed dance programs, invitations, and business cards, experience that came in handy later in life.

When young Avery entered Pomona College, his unconventional side emerged. During his junior year, he rented an abandoned chicken coop for $5 a month, which he renovated into living quarters. Originally a psychology major, Avery thought it was intellectually dishonest to refer to that field as a "science." He was eventually granted a degree in something called "Cultural Synthesis."

During college, Avery volunteered at a social service agency called the Midnight Mission. He graduated during the heart of the Great Depression and went to work for the Los Angeles County Department of Charities. Once each month, he returned to the Pomona campus to participate in general discussions at the home of a former teacher, Professor Russell Story. There he met H. Russell Smith, a man who would later figure prominently in Avery's business.

In 1933, Avery left his county job and went to work for the Adhere Paper Company, a small firm that was marketing masking tape cut into crude adhesive labels. Stan was able to fashion a primitive machine that made better labels, and the firm expanded into other lines, including removable "Funeral" signs that were placed on automobile windows.

The company soon failed, however, and Avery was jobless. Another friend from college owned a floral shop, and soon Avery was packing flowers from 4:00 A.M. until 11:00 A.M. Thereafter, he retired to a loft above one of the floral refrigeration units, where he had fashioned another self-adhesive label machine. Avery proved to be a prolific inventor, registering 18 patents over four decades.

In June 1935, Avery and his fiancée, Dorothy Durfee, launched their own business, which they called Kum-Kleen Products. Dorothy, an elementary schoolteacher, kicked in the $100 capital. Soon the couple was offering gift shops 1,000 removable, self-adhesive labels for a dollar. Two months later, they were making enough money to get married.

Sales for the first six months totaled $1,391, and Avery quit his job at the flower shop at the beginning of 1936 and hired his first full-time employee. More sales and employees followed. To keep things simple, Avery paid all his employees $15 per week and paid himself $20 per week.

Through the late 1930s, Avery perfected his labels, making them much easier to peel off from the backing. He also renamed the venture the Avery Adhesive Company. In 1940, the five-year-old firm recorded sales of $71,857. Sales increased significantly during World War II, as the American military found considerable value in Avery's adhesive labels.

At the close of the war, Avery surveyed his 50-employee company and decided he needed a professional business manager. He called upon Russ Smith, his old friend from Dr. Story's discussion group. Smith had built a solid resume of project management in private and public service. Avery eventually sold one-third of the company to Smith, and the pair led Avery through phenomenal growth over the next two decades.

In the mid-1970s, Avery and Smith turned over management of the corporation to longtime Avery executive Charles D. Miller, who successfully established the company as an office products giant and global leader in self-adhesive materials and label-converting technology.

Today, Avery Dennison is a multibillion-dollar corporation with 16,000 employees in 36 countries.

SOURCES: Avery Dennison archives; David L. Clark, *Avery 1935–1985: The First Fifty Years,* Avery International Corporation

Jesse Aweida, Juan Rodriguez, Zoltan Herger, Tom Kavanagh

[StorageTek]

After building a successful career at IBM, Jesse Aweida developed a business plan for a new start-up company that could build computer storage products. He enlisted the help of three coworkers, Juan Rodriguez, Zoltan Herger, and Tom Kavanagh, and in 1969 launched Storage Technology Corporation. Today, StorageTek (as it is now known) is a $1.2 billion market leader.

In 1952, Jesse Aweida emigrated from Saudi Arabia. After graduating from Swarthmore College in Pennsylvania with a bachelor's degree in mechanical engineering, he joined IBM at Poughkeepsie, New York, where he helped develop their first transistorized computers. He also attended night classes at Syracuse University and in 1960 earned his M.S. degree. In 1966, he was promoted to senior engineer and transferred to IBM's Boulder, Colorado, facility, where he worked on advanced computer tape drive development.

While working on computer storage products, Aweida became focused on the size of the market. IBM's sales projections increased from 4,500 units to 50,000 in two short years. Convinced that there was room for a new company, he raised $250,000 from a New York venture capital firm and established his own business in 1969.

The company, Data Storage Devices, was actually founded by Aweida and three fellow IBM employees—Zoltan Herger (a Hungarian immigrant), Juan Rodriguez (a Cuban immigrant), and Tom Kavanagh (a Pennsylvanian). The company, located in rented space above the Aristocrat Steak House in Boulder, soon faced its first dilemma. The business name conflicted with the registered trade name of another company. The founders renamed their company Storage Technology Corporation (more familiarly, StorageTek), a name they trademarked in 1984.

The company's first product, the 2450/2470 nine-track tape drive, shipped in 1970, four months ahead of the schedule established in Aweida's business plan. Other products soon followed, including a magnetic disk subsystem (1973), semiconductor add-on memory (1975), and printers (1980). In addition to phenomenal domestic growth, the company moved into international markets in the 1970s. By 1981, it was earning over $600 million annually and employed 13,000 people.

By 1981, StorageTek found itself in a spirited competition with IBM. When IBM had to postpone bringing its newest disk product to market, customers turned to StorageTek for its model 8650. Revenues in 1982 surpassed $1 billion, and StorageTek was on a roll. The company made the decision to build and ship as many units as possible before IBM could catch up, but the work became sloppy and customers started to return equipment.

After StorageTek piled up large bills for capital upgrades and materials, IBM launched a reliable, better model. Customers dumped defective StorageTek equipment (and their accompanying invoices) and turned back to IBM. In 1984, the company filed for Chapter 11 bankruptcy protection. Aweida stepped down as CEO; Kavanagh had left the company in 1975; Rodriguez and Herger left shortly after the Chapter 11 filing.

After leaving StorageTek, Aweida founded another start-up, Aweida Systems, to build and market storage systems. Another former StorageTek employee, Ron Vitullo, built Aspen Peripherals about the same time. Soon, Aweida and Vitullo merged their companies. Then, in 1989, they sold the venture to StorageTek, after which Aweida launched Aweida Ventures Management. He and his wife, Maria, parents of five children, still live in the Boulder area.

After leaving StorageTek, Juan Rodriguez founded Exabyte Corporation, a successful computer peripheral company. He has also founded a company called Datasonix and has taught classes at the University of Colorado. In 1984, Zoltan Herger founded Cherokee Data Systems, Inc., of Boulder, Colorado. Tom Kavanagh founded NBI in Boulder and later became chairman and CEO of Cadis, Inc., a software company.

StorageTek emerged from bankruptcy protection on July 28, 1987. In 1990, the company topped $1 billion in sales. Today, the company continues to build on their established product line of computer storage products.

SOURCE: Storage Technology Corporation archives

James Baker, Edmund Baker, Walter Baker

[The Walter Baker Chocolate Company]

The Walter Baker Chocolate Company is the oldest business in America with a record of having made the same type of product continuously in its original location. The story begins on September 5, 1739, with the birth of James Baker at Dorchester, Massachusetts, the great-great-grandson of Richard Baker, who arrived from England on November 28, 1635.

After graduating from Harvard in 1760, James Baker began to study for the ministry. Two years later, he decided to take up medicine while teaching in the Dorchester school district, the first public, tax-supported school system in America. Later, he abandoned his medical practice and opened a general store, which he named Dr. Baker's Corner.

In the fall of 1764, John Hannon, a penniless Irish immigrant, pointed out to Baker that no one had yet launched a chocolate-making venture in the new world and that such an enterprise would do well. Dr. Baker agreed, leased a grist- and sawmill, and put up the capital for equipment and supplies. In March of 1765, the company started grinding the first chocolate made in North America.

The company quickly prospered until tragedy struck. While traveling to the West Indies in search of cocoa beans in 1779, Hannon was lost at sea. Dr. Baker assumed full ownership and management of the plant and started making a blend that he called Baker's Chocolate. In 1791, James's son Edmund was admitted as a partner in the business, and upon James's retirement in 1804, Edmund assumed control of the company.

In 1818, the third generation of the Baker family entered the business. Walter Baker, Edmund's son, was given a partnership and assumed control upon Edmund's retirement in 1824. Walter Baker was successful in further expanding the family chocolate business. In 1833, Walter Baker's Breakfast Cocoa could be found in the Salem, Illinois, general store owned by Abraham Lincoln and William Barry. Walter Baker later introduced German's Sweet Chocolate, named in honor of Walter's former coachman, Samuel German, who had developed the product.

After being held by the Baker family for more than a century, the company was sold in 1883. It was later reorganized as Walter Baker & Company, and the new owners continued to build the chocolate product line. In 1927, the Postum Company, which later became General Foods, purchased the company.

SOURCE: Kraft Foods archives

Melvin Baker, Joseph Haggerty, Clarence Williams

[The National Gypsum Company]

In the 1920s, three former coworkers reunited to manufacture a brand of gypsum board that was superior to all competing products. Today, the National

Gypsum Company is the second-largest producer of gypsum wallboard in America.

Melvin Baker was born in 1885 to Scotch-Irish parents who farmed rented land in eastern Tennessee. After completing grade school, Baker was determined to attend college. He wrote to the president of Carson-Newman, a small Baptist College in Jefferson City, Tennessee, and asked if he could work at the school in exchange for tuition, room, and board. His offer was accepted, and his father and stepmother delivered him to the college in the horse-pulled family buggy and handed him $10.50.

After three years, Baker withdrew from the college and attended business school. He soon moved to Chattanooga, Tennessee, and accepted the only job that he was offered, an assistant to an auctioneer. However, the job provided young Baker with keen insight into the process of selling and buying hardware.

Before long, Baker accepted a job with the Willer Manufacturing Company of Milwaukee as a traveling salesman. His territory included the Carolinas and Virginia, and after three years, he was able to establish a small savings account.

In 1911, Baker called on Beaver Products of Buffalo, New York, manufacturers of a revolutionary wallboard called Beaver Board. Baker, sensing that the product had a good future in the construction market, was hired as a salesman under Joseph Haggerty, the company's vice president of sales.

Baker's enthusiasm for the product was not unfounded. It was a good product, and Baker was soon peddling Beaver Board wherever a sale could be made. He once shared the following story:

> I was in Charleston, West Virginia, when we had an inquiry from a coal mine operator way back in the mountains. The only way to get there was on a coal train and then stay overnight and return on the same train the following afternoon. After getting the order, the next morning the superintendent loaned me his dog and gun, and I killed some grouse. While back in the hills, I was closely questioned by a man named Hatfield. I later learned they were feuding with another family named McCoy.

Joseph Haggerty was impressed with Baker's performance and brought him into the Buffalo home office as a sales manager. After World War I broke out, Beaver Board sales were brisk, particularly sales to the military to build barracks. However, during the war Baker and Haggerty watched helplessly as their chief competitor, United States Gypsum, proved to the military that its gypsum board was lighter and safer than Beaver Board.

In 1920, 45-year-old Joe Haggerty talked management into building a small plant in nearby Batavia, New York, to experiment with gypsum board. Haggerty developed and patented a promising process of adding starch to the gypsum mixture. But Beaver Products lost interest in the entire project. Haggerty, feeling betrayed and discouraged, retired a year later.

Clarence Williams, age 43, was the vice president in charge of production for Beaver in 1920. Both Baker and Williams, like Haggerty, felt that gypsum wallboard would soon replace Beaver Board. Despite the loss of Haggerty, they convinced Beaver Board president William MacGlashen to purchase one of the larger existing gypsum plaster companies.

Unfortunately, MacGlashen insisted on control of the company and structured the financing to meet that goal. Rather than raise equity funds, he elected to borrow the start-up money in an untraditional way. He told the bank he would sell $6 million in bonds and use the proceeds to pay off the loan. He then gave the bonds to the underwriting bank. Tragically, before he was given the loan or sold the bonds, the bank failed, and the bonds became part of the bank's listed assets. That meant that MacGlashen was $6 million in debt to the bank's creditors, even though he was never given any money.

By 1922, Beaver was in trouble. Williams accepted a job with Universal Gypsum. Baker, now 37 years old and married, had lost his job and his life savings. However, he eventually was hired by a Chicago underwriting firm and was quickly earning a good living.

One day in 1925, Baker bumped into his former boss, Joe Haggerty, while on business in Buffalo. Haggerty invited Baker to return home with him to see the new gypsum wallboard formula that he had invented. In the Haggerty kitchen, Joe poured powdered gypsum, ground-up newsprint, and starch into his wife's mixer, explaining that the wood fibers in the newsprint added strength and the whipping process made it lighter. He poured the mixture on a cookie sheet and baked it in the oven a few moments. After picking up the freshly baked wallboard, Baker was convinced that Haggerty had a winner.

Shortly thereafter, Haggerty bumped into Clarence Williams. Joe described his perfected wallboard and complained that the big manufacturers had exclusive access to the gypsum supplies. Williams countered with some good news: "I've just located a deposit near here that should support a plant for fifty years—and I put an option on it!" The National Gypsum Company was launched on August 29, 1925, complete with a source of raw material (courtesy of Williams), a secret formula (courtesy of Haggerty), and a master salesman (Baker).

Operations started at Clarence Center, New York, in late 1925. The partners scrapped more than a quarter million dollars' worth of material until they were satisfied with the process. To differentiate itself from competitors, National Gypsum elected to distribute its wallboard exclusively through lumber dealers, creating the image of a prestige product.

They backed their advertising claims of superiority with a certificate, printed on gold-colored bond stock, offering $5,000 to anyone who could prove their claims weren't true. Dealers started referring to the certificate as a "gold bond," whereby the product name evolved into Gold Bond Wallboard. The name stuck, and the company's gypsum board to this day is sold under the Gold Bond label.

The Gold Bond Wallboard was quickly a market success. However, the company hit tough times just as fast. Joe Haggerty died in 1928, and not long after that Clarence Williams's health failed and he retired from the company. (He died five years later.) The responsibility to navigate the critical early years of the company was left to Melvin Baker, just one year before America entered the Great Depression, followed by World War II.

Despite the challenges, Baker was able to keep the company afloat. He bought up idled companies during the Depression. He operated military manufacturing facilities during the war. By 1945, Baker correctly predicted that the returning soldiers would cause an explosive demand for new houses and for National's gypsum board. By 1950, he had captured nearly 30 percent of the domestic gypsum business.

In 1993, National Gypsum relocated its corporate headquarters from Dallas, Texas, to Charlotte, North Carolina, where it was consolidated with the company's Gold Bond Building Products gypsum wallboard division. One year later, the company was acquired by Delcor, Inc., a wholly owned subsidiary of Golden Eagle Industries. National Gypsum achieved record sales in 1996 and, in early 1997, announced plans to build a new wallboard manufacturing plant at Shippingport, Pennsylvania.

SOURCE: Marc Bockmon, *Turning Points: The National Gypsum Company Story,* Taylor Publishing Company, Dallas, 1990

Earl E. Bakken, Palmer Hermundslie

[Medtronic, Inc.]

Earl E. Bakken was born in 1924 in Minneapolis, Minnesota. As a boy, Bakken read all the *Popular Mechanics* he could get his hands on. He was also fascinated with Mary Shelley's *Frankenstein,* going so far as to fashion a working human robot. He used a hot water bottle for the lung and even rigged his robot to smoke cigarettes.

After graduating from high school, he served in the United States Air Force as a radar maintenance instructor until 1946, when he enrolled in the University of Minnesota. After earning a bachelor of electrical engineering degree in 1948, he studied electrical engineering and mathematics at the University of Minnesota Graduate School.

While attending graduate school, Bakken would frequently spend time at Minneapolis's Northwestern Hospital, where his wife-to-be worked as a medical technologist. When the equipment malfunctioned (which was frequently), staff members would coax Bakken into making repairs.

Soon, Bakken and Palmer Hermundslie, who was married to Bakken's wife's sister, became convinced that opportunities existed in the medical equipment market. In 1949, Bakken left graduate school and Hermundslie quit his job at a lumber yard, and the men launched Medtronic in a 600-square-foot, three-car garage. A potbellied stove that sat in the middle of the garage provided the only heat during Minnesota's cold winters.

The early months were difficult. One month the firm grossed exactly $8 in sales. Slowly, the firm represented more product lines, and sales picked up. Most of the company's activity during the 1950s involved the sale and service of other companies' products. However, the men continued to innovate several products and spent considerable time with the doctors and nurses at their client hospitals.

In 1957, Bakken was asked by the University of Minnesota Medical School to innovate a portable, external cardiac pacemaker. He returned to his shop and in a matter of weeks built a working model that was tested and quickly embraced by the hospital. Within three years, Medtronic was established as a premier manufacturer of medical equipment.

In 1960, the company launched another successful product. After reading about a new, transistorized, implantable pacemaker, Hermundslie flew his plane to Buffalo, New York, to meet with the inventors. They signed a contract at the airport giving Medtronic exclusive rights to build and market their Chardack-Greatbatch implantable pulse generator.

Over the next several decades, Medtronic made several other critical innovations, passing the $100 million annual sales mark in 1975. Today, Medtronic is the world's leading developer and manufacturer of therapeutic medical technology. Annual sales are nearly $2 billion, and the company employs some 10,000 people worldwide.

SOURCES: Medtronic, Inc., archives; William T. Harper, "Insights Into Creativity," *Focus, the Newsletter of the American Creativity Association,* November/December, 1990

Howard L. Baldwin

[Baldwin/Cohen Productions and Pittsburgh Penguins]

Over the past three decades, Howard L. Baldwin has had an impact on literally millions of sports and cinema enthusiasts throughout the world. Upon graduating from the Salisbury School, Howard Baldwin played baseball at Boston University. After serving with the United States Marines, he secured a job with the Philadelphia Flyers professional hockey franchise, serving first as the business manager for a minor league affiliate, then later as head of the Flyers' sales and promotion staff.

In 1972, 30-year-old Baldwin and a partner purchased a franchise in the upstart World Hockey Association known as the New England Whalers. Two years later, he moved the club into the new Civic Center Coliseum in downtown Hartford, Connecticut, and renamed the team the Hartford Whalers. In 1979, the 37-year-old Baldwin was instrumental in the merger between the WHA and the National Hockey League. Thereafter, he served as the managing general partner of the Hartford Whalers until the club was sold in 1988.

Baldwin continued to serve in various advisory capacities to the NHL until November 1991, when he and two partners purchased the Pittsburgh Penguins NHL franchise from Edward J. DeBartolo. Since acquiring the club, the Penguins won three division titles and one Stanley Cup championship. In 1993, Baldwin added the (Russian) Central Red Army hockey team to the Penguins organization.

Baldwin is also a partner in Baldwin/Cohen Entertainment, a movie production company based at Universal Studios. His company has produced a number of feature films, including *Sudden Death, From the Hip,* and *Spellbinder.* In 1995, the growing company entered into a formal affiliation with Universal Studios.

His wife, Karen Baldwin, is an actress and is closely involved with Baldwin's ventures. Karen, in fact, created the original script for *Sudden Death.*

SOURCE: Pittsburgh Penguins archives

Lucius L. Ball, William C. Ball, Edmund B. Ball, Frank C. Ball, George A. Ball

[Ball Brothers Manufacturing Company]

Shortly after Frank and Ed Ball started their tin can business, they were joined by their three brothers. Expanding into glass, the Ball brothers quickly achieved success manufacturing Mason jars. The Ball Brothers Manufacturing Company then diversified into related ventures throughout the twentieth century. Today, the Ball Corporation ranks among America's largest companies.

It took nearly two centuries for the families to meet one another, but the Ball and Bingham families followed very similar paths. Both migrated from England to America in the 1600s, served in the Revolutionary War, lived in New England, and then moved to Canada.

Curiously, both families returned to the United States in the nineteenth century. In 1834, William and Marcy Ball moved their nine children through Buffalo, New York, and into Trumbull County, Ohio. Six years later, the Binghams made an almost identical move. The two families finally met. Lucius Styles Ball, a farmer and part-time inventor, married Maria P. Bingham, an attractive and industrious schoolteacher.

The couple had two daughters and five sons: Lucina in 1847, Lucius L. in 1850, William C. in 1852, Edmund B. in 1855, Frank C. in 1857, Frances in 1860, and George A. in 1862. The success of the Ball brothers is attributed to their close relationship, for which, as stated by Frank Ball in his memoirs, their mother was to be credited:

> Her chief ambition was to bring up her children with good, strong minds and bodies with right ideals and true Christian principles. She urged us to always stick together and help each other; it was through her influence and her advice that we five brothers have been associated in business throughout life.

In 1863, the family loaded their belongings onto a wagon and set out for a farm near Niagara Falls, New York, owned by George Harvey Ball, Lucius's younger brother. "Uncle George" was a renowned Baptist preacher from Buffalo who would eventually be a factor in founding the company.

Lucius S. Ball died in early 1878. Lucius L. Ball, the eldest son at age 28, William, age 26, and George, age 16, continued to work the family farm. Frank and Ed, the more aggressive of the five brothers, moved to Buffalo with their Uncle George in search of a business enterprise that the family could build.

They failed in their first two ventures, making containers for the fish-packing industry and a rug-cleaning business. But Buffalo was a bustling, growing community rich with opportunity and optimism. Undismayed, they purchased a small, unprofitable shop in 1880—the Wooden Jacket Can Company—that made oilcans.

Frank, a natural salesman, quickly acquired business in Toledo, Indianapolis, Detroit, St. Louis, and many other cities. Before long they were in new, larger quarters that could accommodate their rapid growth. Soon the other three brothers moved to Buffalo and joined the operation. They expanded their product line in tin cans, and eventually they started selling glass containers made elsewhere in New York.

It didn't take long for the Ball Brothers Glass Manufacturing Company to make the first of many strategic moves: Rather than buy the glass containers, they established their own manufacturing facility. Soon, Ball Brothers glass was selling faster than it could be made, and the facilities were expanded. By 1886, they were producing "Mason jars," named for John L. Mason who invented the functional canning jars.

As production increased, so did production costs. The discovery of natural gas in Pennsylvania, Ohio, and Indiana caught the attention of the brothers, and Frank Ball took to the road to investigate. While traveling throughout Ohio, he received an invitation from a Mr. James Boyce to visit Muncie, Indiana. Despite having no prior acquaintance with either the man or the town, Frank decided to see what the town had to offer.

Throughout the early 1880s, towns like Muncie eagerly drilled for natural gas. The discovery of reserves meant economic success, and those cities fortunate enough to have a good supply offered industrialists free gas and cheap land in exchange for building factories. Muncie, Indiana, was one of those fortunate towns, and James Boyce, a local entrepreneur, was its loudest cheerleader.

In July 1887, Frank struck a deal with Muncie officials. The city provided $5,000 to help the company move, a gas well, and seven acres of ground for the factory. Within a year the plant was built and the Ball Brothers became one of several manufacturers to open new plants in the Indiana community.

By 1904, the Ball brothers not only had a large, modern plant at Muncie, but through internal growth and acquisition they also were operating plants in Converse, Fairmount, Loogootee, Marion, and Swayzee, Indiana; Belleville, Illinois; and Coffeyville, Kansas.

Unhappy with the volatile zinc market (zinc was used to cap their jars), Ball Brothers established a zinc melting and rolling facility in Muncie. This venture resulted in the creation of the zinc division, and eventually into the production of batteries. The company also created a rubber division to manufacture the rubber rings used in the fruit jars. As with other ventures, the rubber division took on a life of its own and pursued other market opportunities.

In 1910, Ball Brothers started using corrugated paper to ship its jars. Not only was this lighter than the wood crates, it was also less expensive. Drawing on their successful formula of self-manufacture, the brothers purchased a paper company in 1916, not only to supply their own needs, but to allow entry into a new, diversified market.

The brothers made numerous other investments. One of their largest ventures outside the family business involved an investment in the diversified empire of Oris P. and Mantis J. Van Sweringen. These two brothers had accumulated a vast railroad empire—28,000 miles of railroad—that included the Chesapeake & Ohio, the Chicago & St. Louis, the Erie, the Wheeling & Lake Erie, and others. It also included steamship lines, trucking companies, coal mines, hotels and resorts, and trolley lines.

In 1935, the Van Sweringens were near default of a $40 million note from J.P. Morgan & Company. George Ball led the bailout and secured control of the organization, leaving the Van Sweringens in charge of operations. Shortly thereafter, both Van Sweringens died, and George was forced into an active position with the organization. In 1937, he transferred all his stock in the venture into the newly established George and Frances Ball Foundation. The foundation subsequently sold the stock.

The Ball family has been very generous. For 90 years, the family has made significant contributions to historic preservation, medicine, youth organizations, and educational religious organizations.

Perhaps the best-known philanthropic venture of the Ball brothers is Ball State University. In the early 1900s, Muncie's only college had difficulty getting established. In 1917, a court ordered that the school be sold at a public auction. The best bid was placed by the Ball family, who promptly acquired more land and erected two buildings. In 1918, the school was reopened under the name Eastern Division of Indiana State Normal School in Terre Haute. Eventually, the name was changed to Ball State University.

William Ball, the first brother to pass away, died in 1921. Ed died in 1925. Lucius, the oldest boy in the family, died in 1932. He was the least active of the brothers in the business. Once Ball Brothers became self-sufficient, Lucius pursued a lifelong dream and, at the age of 40, became a physician.

In 1943, at the age of 85, Frank C. Ball died. He had been president of the company since its founding 63 years earlier. George A. Ball, the youngest and only surviving brother, then became president at age 80. George died in 1955 at the age of 92. His wife died in 1958, the last of her generation of the Ball family.

Edmund F. Ball, the son of Edward, entered the family business in 1928. After serving in the military during World War II, Ed returned to the family business and in 1948 succeeded his uncle George as the third president of Ball Brothers. By this time, the company had experienced an uncharacteristic decline in profits and productivity. Through a series of turnaround efforts, Ed renewed the company's strengths and expanded into high-technology markets, including a lucrative aerospace venture.

SOURCES: Frederic A. Birmingham, *Ball Corporation: The First Century,* The Curtis Publishing Company, Indianapolis 1980; Ball Brothers Foundation archives

Charles R. Bard

[C.R. Bard, Inc.]

At the turn of the century, Charles Russell Bard, a successful importer of French silks, was afflicted with acute tuberculosis. During a trip to Europe, he encountered a medicine called *Gomenol,* derived from the eucalyptus tree, which relieved his urinary discomfort. Upon inquiry to the French manufacturer, Bard found that the company had no distributor in the United States. By 1898, Bard had secured exclusive distribution rights for Gomenol, a product that remained with his company until World War II.

Through his marketing efforts, Bard became acquainted with many American urologists. One physician, Dr. James Garner of Buffalo, New York, asked if Bard could track down a French manufacturer of a new ureteral catheter. Once again, Bard arranged to become the American distributor of a French product. In 1907, at age 55, Bard officially launched a new enterprise, C.R. Bard, Inc., to market his urology-related product line.

In 1915, shipments from Europe became unpredictable because of the onset of World War I. That same year, a man named Morgan Parker scoured the New York telephone directory for surgical instrument distributors. Parker had just successfully introduced his new surgical scalpel to the American College of Surgeons and was anxious to find someone who could market his blade. His second call was to Bard, who agreed to put up $500 and office space as his part of their venture, the Bard-Parker Company, Inc.

The pair originally had their knife manufactured by an Ohio company. However, in 1922, Parker decided he wanted to expand operations and manufacture the scalpel in-house. Bard disagreed and, in 1923, the men dissolved their partnership, with Parker paying Bard $28,000 for his share of the business.

Bard, in his 70s, was ready to retire from the catheter business as well. In 1926, he sold the business for $18,000. He continued to serve as a consultant to the company until 1932. Charles R. Bard died in May, 1934.

Today, C.R. Bard, Inc., designs, manufactures, and markets disposable medical, surgical, diagnostic, and patient care devices, including urological products and coronary angioplasty catheters. The company employs nearly 8,700 people, with annual sales in excess of $1 billion.

SOURCE: C.R. Bard, Inc., archives

William B. Barnett

[Barnett Banks, Inc.]

Following the establishment of a successful bank on the Kansas frontier, William Barnett moved his family to Jacksonville, Florida, where his ill wife could enjoy a better climate. In 1877, he established his first bank in Florida. Today, Barnett Banks ranks among America's largest financial institutions.

William Boyd Barnett settled in Hiawatha, Kansas, in 1857. Thirteen years later, he and two partners established the first bank in that region of the state, Barnett, Morrill & Company. Five years later, while visiting his son in Jacksonville, Florida, he became intrigued with the growth potential of Florida and was convinced that the favorable climate would be good for his wife, who suffered from neuralgia.

Barnett returned to Kansas, sold his share of the bank and, on March 17, 1877, moved his family to Jacksonville. Two months later, at age 52, he established the Bank of Jacksonville with $43,000 in capital. The start-up had three employees: Barnett, his son Bion H. Barnett, and a clerk. At the end of their first year in business, deposits totaled only $10,000. Over the next few years, however, business grew steadily, boosted by the award of several state banking contracts.

In the late 1800s, banks were susceptible to a wide range of community and economic influences. In 1888, a yellow fever epidemic swept through the region, bringing business to a standstill. Barnett and three clerks actually contracted the disease, and only Barnett survived. By the end of the epidemic, three-fourths of Barnett's loans had become delinquent. However, the only account that wasn't settled was for $50, since the account holder had died without leaving an estate.

Deposits in Barnett's bank passed the $1 million mark in 1893, and the bank continued to grow despite national financial panics in 1893, 1907, and, of course, the Great Depression that started in 1929.

William B. Barnett died in October 1903 at the age of 79. He was succeeded by his son, Bion Hall Barnett. Five years later, Bion Barnett rechartered the firm as The Barnett National Bank of Jacksonville and orchestrated several decades of growth. He continued to report to his office until he turned 93. He lived to be 101.

The founder's other son, also named William, was also active in the family bank for some time. His son, William R. Barnett (the founder's grandson), devoted much of his life to the bank, eventually serving as president and chairman prior to his 1973 retirement. His son, William B. Barnett (the founder's great-grandson), maintains the family tradition by serving as an officer with the bank. Today, Barnett Banks rank among the top 25 in the entire country.

SOURCE: Barnett Banks, Inc., archives

Francis A. Bartlett

[The F.A. Bartlett Tree Expert Company]

Francis A. Bartlett developed a love for vegetation while growing a vegetable garden on his family's farm. He pursued his interest through college and quickly established his own tree care service. Through hard work and devotion to the industry, the F.A. Bartlett Tree Expert Company has grown to be one of the largest tree service companies in America.

From his birth, Francis Bartlett was ahead of his time. On November 12, 1882, a doctor in Belchertown, Massachusetts, arrived at Cold Spring Farm to oversee the delivery of a baby to the Bartlett family. By the time the child was delivered, however, the season's first blizzard prevented the doctor from returning to town until the following day, at which time the birth of Francis Alonzo Bartlett was recorded as having taken place on November 13.

Francis "Frank" Bartlett grew up on the family farm with two sisters and two brothers. Frank was responsible for the vegetable crops for the family, which he sold door-to-door from a spring wagon. Part of his earnings went to support the family, and part he was permitted to save.

Frank was a diligent student, walking three miles daily to Belchertown High School, from which he graduated in 1901. His interest in plants led him to enroll in Massachusetts Agricultural College, now known as the University of Massachusetts at Amherst. By his junior year, Bartlett became quite interested in botany and horticulture. He graduated in 1905 with a B.S. degree in Agriculture.

Because of his outstanding academic performance, Bartlett was given a position with the Hampton Institute in Virginia to teach horticulture and supervise the institute's nursery and orchards. He was also hired as a consultant to the Oasis Farm and Orchard Company of Roswell, New Mexico, which was establishing an orchard of approximately 20,000 trees.

Bartlett, however, had his heart set on working with shade trees. In 1907, he called on Harold L. Frost, a graduate of Massachusetts Agricultural College. Frost, the owner of Frost Insecticide Company, had helped several men enter the tree business, and they, in turn, purchased his insecticides. They formed The Frost & Bartlett Company, and 25-year-old Frank Bartlett took up residence near the railroad station in White Plains, New York.

The early sales by F. A. Bartlett were made rather casually. He would take a train to neighboring towns, walk the streets striking up conversations, and eventually make some sales. As soon as he had enough contracts in hand, Bartlett would hire a crew and supervise their work while continuing his sales walks in nearby neighborhoods. In his first year he made several sales in Westchester County, New York, in neighboring Connecticut towns, and in the Hudson Valley. Within a year he expanded as far south as New Jersey and Philadelphia, and into upstate New York.

In 1909, Bartlett moved his company to Stamford, Connecticut, which had much better access to his stronger markets. He rented a small building and sold agricultural tools and supplies from the front, while storing his pumps, tree care equipment, and Frost insecticides in the back. His rapid success enabled him to buy out Frost's share of the partnership, and he even had enough money to purchase a bright red Buick.

Within a year, Bartlett started hiring men into key positions, such as sales, operations supervision, and business management. This enabled Bartlett to devote more attention to the study of trees and insects, experimentation with trees, and other related pursuits. In 1913, he started publishing *Tree Talk,* a magazine that carried a variety of articles about the care of trees.

The company experienced sustained growth throughout that decade, converting from a production-oriented tree surgery firm into a tree care company whose purpose was to improve and save trees through scientific knowledge. This philosophy was reflected in 1920, when the company was incorporated in the state of Connecticut as The F.A. Bartlett Tree Expert Company.

Bartlett started opening regional field offices in cities such as Philadelphia in 1920, Boston in 1921, Westbury in 1923, and several others. By 1928, there were offices in at least 11 cities. The company also developed important innovations: in 1920 a fertilizer designed specifically for trees and in 1921 an electric drill to clean out tree cavities. The company also established The Bartlett School of Tree Surgery in 1923 to conduct formal employee training. Research was so important to Bartlett that, in 1927, he established the Bartlett Tree Research Laboratories and funded a full-time staff.

The Depression that started in 1929 had a dramatic effect on Bartlett's company, not only because of the lack of work, but also because of competition for labor from the federal government. Under President Franklin Roosevelt, the Works Progress Administration was paying tree trimmers $1.20 an hour, while firms like Bartlett's were paying their employees only 75¢ per hour. In an attempt to halt the loss of employees, Bartlett and Martin Davey of the Davey Tree Expert Company were able to schedule a one-minute meeting with President Roosevelt. Shortly thereafter, the government wage was reduced to 80¢ per hour.

As the Depression waned, Bartlett was once again improving his company. In 1933, he offered clients a lifetime guarantee on the treatment of trees. A year later he perfected a method of force-feeding trees with liquid fertilizer under pressure. This was further enhanced with the development of a spray gun in 1935.

However, when World War II broke out, the company was once again facing a challenge. Most of the able-bodied tree climbers were drafted for the war effort, and communities couldn't afford tree service. The company, however, was able to secure work camouflaging military installations here in America.

Bartlett detached himself from most aspects of the business in 1937, naming Orville Spicer as president. Francis Bartlett lived to the age of 81. He died on November 21, 1963. Upon Spicer's retirement in 1961, Robert A. Bartlett, the son of the company's founder, assumed the post. In 1974, the third generation of Bartletts assumed the top spot in the company when Robert A. Bartlett Jr. was elected president.

Today, The F.A. Bartlett Tree Expert Company has offices stretching from San Francisco to London. The Bartlett Tree Research Laboratories are still a very important component of the company. Their primary workplace is a carefully planned 100-acre site in Charlotte, North Carolina.

SOURCE: The F.A. Bartlett Tree Expert Company archives

Burton Baskin, Irvine Robbins

[Baskin-Robbins]

Irvine Robbins was born in 1917, the son of a Tacoma, Washington, dairy farmer. As a teenager, young Robbins worked in his father's ice cream and dairy store, where he took note that people visited the store to buy ice cream and to take a break. "It wasn't like making a trip to the pharmacy or the grocery store," he recalled, "it was a small, affordable but very pleasurable luxury."

He soon made another observation while selling ice cream and other dairy products to retail stores. Their interest was in selling a lot of products, be it ice cream, bread, or brooms. To give his ice cream an edge, Robbins would stay up late at night preparing exotic ice cream flavors and attention-grabbing signs. However, he would no sooner place a sign in a grocer's store than another vendor would move it.

Upon his discharge from the military in 1945, Robbins (shown at left) needed to find a venture to support his wife and young child. Since his teen years, he had conceived the idea of a store that would sell a wide variety of his exotic flavors of ice cream and nothing else. People could come in and enjoy a break, just the way they did in Tacoma.

Unable to find a suitable store, Robbins decided to take a brief vacation in Los Angeles. While driving along a street in Glendale, he spotted a store for rent. The setting seemed to be suitable for an ice cream business, so he invested his $6,000 in savings from the military and an insurance policy and, on December 7, 1945, opened his first store—Snowbird—which featured 21 flavors. Encouraged by the initial success, he quickly added two more stores.

Meanwhile, Burton Baskin (below left) was building ice cream experience in another part of the world. Born in 1913, the Chicago native worked as a PX operator in the southwestern Pacific Islands of New Hebrides (now Vanuatu) during World War II. After obtaining an ice cream freezer from an aircraft carrier, the enterprising Baskin created a variety of flavors from local tropical fruits.

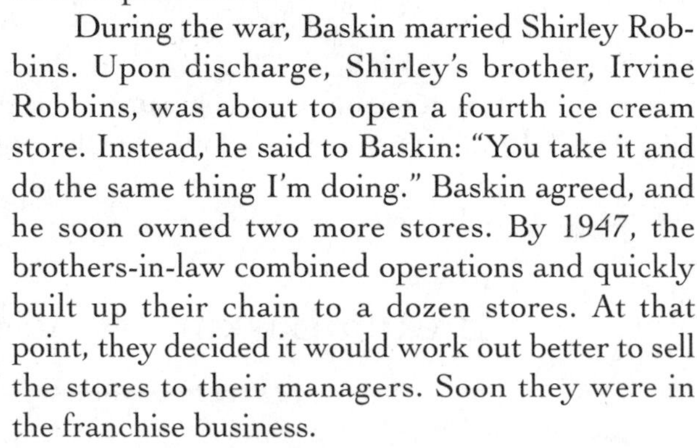

During the war, Baskin married Shirley Robbins. Upon discharge, Shirley's brother, Irvine Robbins, was about to open a fourth ice cream store. Instead, he said to Baskin: "You take it and do the same thing I'm doing." Baskin agreed, and he soon owned two more stores. By 1947, the brothers-in-law combined operations and quickly built up their chain to a dozen stores. At that point, they decided it would work out better to sell the stores to their managers. Soon they were in the franchise business.

The founders decided to rotate their clever, exotic flavors on a monthly basis to maintain customer interest. As a further marketing incentive, they presented 31 flavors—one for every day of the month. The concept caught on, and Baskin-Robbins continues to use its "31 flavors" branding even though they have offered more than 700 different ice cream flavors.

Baskin-Robbins grew from that handful of stores in the late 1940s to nearly 100 stores in 1960 to nearly 1,200 by the end of that decade. In 1967, the founders sold Baskin-Robbins to United Brands. Six months later, Burton Baskin died unexpectedly at the age of 54. Robbins remained with the company until his retirement in 1978. Today, Baskin-Robbins, a wholly owned subsidiary of Allied Domecq PLC, has 2,700 stores nationwide and 1,700 internationally.

SOURCES: Baskin-Robbins archives; "Why Irvine Robbins Likes Ice Cream," *San Fran-*

cisco Chronicle, August 29, 1979, from *Meet the Makers: The People Behind the Producer,* by Scott Cohen, St. Martin's Press, 1979

Frank Batten Sr., Samuel L. Slover

[Landmark Communications, Inc.]

At age 20, Samuel Slover became business manager for a failing newspaper, the *Knoxville Journal,* in his native Tennessee. He was unable to turn the company around; the paper fell into bankruptcy two years later, and Slover assumed nearly $40,000 in obligations.

In 1900, Slover moved to Virginia and soon concluded that the state was in need of high-quality newspapers. Unable to secure funding to acquire his own newspaper, he quickly built a reputation for selling advertising for existing companies. When offered half interest in a Newport News newspaper on the condition he pull it out of the red, he succeeded and acquired his first profitable enterprise.

Slover applied his successful formula in Richmond and Petersburg, and then turned his sights to Virginia's Hampton Roads region, built around Norfolk and Virginia Beach. Through a series of acquisitions and mergers, he built what is now the *Virginian-Pilot.*

As Slover approached retirement age, he was content with his hard-earned newspapers and, rather than seek expansion, focused on sharing the fruits of success with his employees. Additionally, the *Virginian-Pilot* became the foundation for an even more successful media empire orchestrated by another member of his family, Frank Batten.

Frank Batten was born on February 11, 1927, at Norfolk, Virginia. Frank's father died while he was quite young, and his uncle, Samuel Slover, stepped in to look out for the boy. The two developed a father-son relationship that lasted for several decades.

Batten benefited from a strong educational background, including Culver Military Academy, the University of Virginia, and the Harvard Graduate School of Business Administration. Upon graduation, he served with the Merchant Marine in World War II, then later as a Naval reserve officer.

Batten's newspaper career started while he was still a student, filling in as a newsroom copyboy during summer vacations. After college and military service, he became a reporter for the *Norfolk Ledger-Star* and later worked in the advertising and circulation departments of that paper and the *Virginian-Pilot.* In 1953, he was appointed vice president of the newspapers, and one year later, 27-year-old Batten was named publisher. Eventually, Slover passed complete control of the company to his nephew.

With the newspaper business serving as a firm foundation, Batten entered the cable television industry in 1963 by acquiring cable franchises in North Carolina and West Virginia. Other media-related acquisitions followed: the *Greensboro Daily News,* the *Greensboro Record,* and WFMY-TV in 1965; the *Roanoke Times & World-News* in 1969. To manage these new ventures, Batten founded Landmark Communications.

In 1982, Batten entered into national cable programming when he launched The Weather Channel. Today, it is seen by over 60 million households. In 1992, Landmark acquired The Travel Channel from Trans World Airlines. Today, Landmark employs more than 4,500 people in 20 states and Europe. Annual revenues are nearly $600 million.

Frank Batten and his wife, Jane, have three children. Their son, Frank Batten Jr., serves as executive vice president of Landmark Communications.

SOURCE: Landmark Communications, Inc., archives

Eddie Bauer

[Eddie Bauer, Inc.]

Eddie Bauer, through excellent marketing insight and a commitment to quality, parlayed his love of sports and outdoors into a multimillion-dollar company.

Eddie Bauer was born October 19, 1899, on Orcas Island in Washington's Puget Sound. He was the last of six children born to Russian-German immigrants Jacob and Mary Catherine Bauer who had arrived in Seattle ten years earlier with two Russian rubles (about $1) in their pockets. In 1897 they moved to Orcas Island, rich with wildlife and abundant fishing, and became farmers.

At age five, young Eddie became enthusiastic about the hunters and anglers he would encounter. His family moved again to a nearby dairy that his father was hired to run. Eddie began clipping advertisements from the Sears and Montgomery Ward catalogs for hunting and fishing items he intended to someday purchase.

At age eight, about the time his father bought him his first rifle (a model 1890 Winchester .22 Special Caliber), Eddie's Uncle Lesser immigrated from Russia and moved in with the family. Eddie would remember the stories his uncle told about life as a Russian Cossack in the Russo-Japanese War of 1904. He wrote, "I remember my dad saying that if it hadn't been for those down-lined coats the Cossacks wore, my uncle would have froze to death." This would later influence his use of goose down in the manufacture of clothing and sleeping bags.

Eddie pursued work as a caddie at a local golf course at age ten. Soon he was not only caddying, but also performing odd jobs for some of Seattle's leading families. This provided him with a relatively good income as well as a wealth of contacts that would help him later in life.

Jacob and Mary Bauer separated in 1913, and Eddie moved with his mother back to Seattle. He immediately secured a part-time job with the sporting goods store Piper & Taft, working an hour before school and three hours after school each day and all day Saturday. Still, the 14-year-old outdoor enthusiast was able to establish a reputation as a master fisherman and, later, an accomplished tennis racquet stringer and tennis player.

In 1920, Ed made his move. With a $500 loan co-signed by his father, he opened up Eddie Bauer's Tennis Shop. With his good reputation among the Seattle socialites, the business was profitable from the start, despite the short work year. Each year after Labor Day, he would hang a sign that read, "Eddie Bauer has gone hunting—Back February 1," and would travel the Northwest hunting and fishing.

Eventually the store was expanded to include all sorts of sporting goods for hunting, fishing, and golf. He implemented the ultimate customer satisfaction policy—total satisfaction or a full refund—that exists to this day.

On February 21, 1929, Eddie married Christine "Stine" Heltborg, a beautiful woman he had met on a grouse-hunting trip. Stine operated her own beauty shop in Seattle, but spent nearly as much time in the outdoors as Eddie did. The couple was passionate about the outdoors and one another, and their marriage lasted until their deaths. They had one son, Eddie Christian Bauer, born in 1938.

Being active skiers, the Bauers started importing skis from Norway for the store. Later they developed specialty departments, such as Eddie Bauer Tackle Makers. Stine was in charge of all women's apparel.

If an item was in demand and couldn't be found, the Bauers found a way to make it themselves. They were successful first with badminton shuttlecocks. And in 1935, Ed undertook a project that would eventually make Eddie Bauer an internationally known name. After being caught in a drenching, freezing rain while fishing, he designed a down-lined jacket that became an instant success.

Within a year he had 16 design patents for quilted clothing and, because he served as both manufacturer and distributor, business flourished. He then added sleeping bags to the product line and launched the Eddie Bauer Expedition Outfitters mail-order division.

A shortage of sleeping bags for American troops during World War II became a bonanza for the company. Eddie personally financed the acquisition of a four-story building that became a manufacturing center, eventually supplying the armed forces with more than 100,000 sleeping bags per year. He also made backpacks, parkas, and pants that became popular among the troops. The "Eddie Bauer" labels sewn into the clothing—agreed to by the military at the insistence of Eddie—would later prove to be a stroke of genius.

The end of the war coincided, for several reasons, with the end of prosperity for Eddie Bauer sporting goods. Partly, the years of hard work were taking a physical toll on Eddie, who suffered from an intense back injury.

Enter William F. "Bill" Niemi Sr., the fifth child of Finnish immigrants Frank and Hannah Niemiaho. After serving in the Navy, Niemi purchased a Seattle cabaret and built a thriving business. Bill, his wife, and children became friends with the Bauers.

When the Bauer businesses (and Eddie's health) went into decline, Bill sold his nightclub and entered into a partnership with Eddie. Bill immediately implemented changes at the store and paid down debt. By 1951, Eddie Bauer officially abandoned the retail store business and became dedicated to mail order. Eddie's health and adrenaline returned, and the two men quickly built (or rebuilt) the business. Catalog sales increased from $50,000 in 1953 to

$500,000 in 1956, buoyed by sales to former military people who remembered the Eddie Bauer outfits from the war.

By 1960 two new partners were brought into the fold: Eddie C. Bauer, a graduate of the University of Washington, and William F. Niemi Jr., a graduate of Harvard and the Massachusetts Institute of Technology. The two father-and-son teams continued to build the company until the Niemis bought out the Bauer's 50 percent of the business in 1968 for $1.5 million.

Under the leadership of Bill Jr., the company was acquired by General Mills in 1971, who financed rapid growth in both mail-order business and the establishment of retail stores. Bill Jr., the last link to the business grown by the Bauer and Niemi families, left the company in 1975. In May 1988, Eddie Bauer was purchased by Spiegel, Inc., for $260 million.

Eddie Bauer died on April 18, 1986, at the age of 86. His companion of 56 years, Stine, had died two weeks earlier of pancreatic cancer. The Bauers built an empire from their beloved hobbies. By living the life of sports enthusiasts, they and their employees ensured that only high-quality products were sold to customers, a practice that still continues to be at the heart of the company's philosophy.

SOURCE: Robert Spector, *The Legend of Eddie Bauer,* Greenwich Publishing Group, Inc., Lyme, CT, 1994

Russell H. Baumgardner

[Apogee Enterprises, Inc.]

In 1949, Russ Baumgardner, a self-described "lousy lawyer," made a $10,000 investment in the Harmon Glass Company in Minneapolis, Minnesota. From this single store, he established Apogee Enterprises and built it into the nation's largest curtain-wall contractor and architectural glass fabricator and second-largest retailer of replacement automobile glass.

Russell H. Baumgardner was born on September 4, 1918 in St. Paul, Minnesota. He left home at age 12 during the early days of the Depression to avoid being a burden to his family. He worked a number of odd jobs through the years, including farm laborer, cook, janitor, and bottle collector for bootleggers. Yet he never neglected his education.

After earning his bachelor's degree in 1940 from Macalester College, Baumgardner entered the United States Army. While serving in the European theater, he achieved the rank of major and was awarded the Bronze Star for valor. After the war, he attended George Washington University in Washington, D.C., and earned his law degree in 1948. He then returned to the Minneapolis–St. Paul area and entered private law practice.

Harold Burrows was a delivery truck driver and glass installer. While making a delivery to Western Windshield, one of Minneapolis's largest auto glass shops, he was struck by the sight of employees too busy to answer the ringing telephone. To Burrows, this signaled a lucrative business. He recruited two associates, and with $3,000, the partners established the Harmon Glass Company on July 12, 1949.

The company had $50,000 in sales its first year. When it came time to expand, the founders landed on the doorstep of Russ Baumgardner, attorney at law, who liked the enterprise and invested $10,000. He quickly became involved in the business, and when one of Burrows's partners left and the other died, Baumgardner purchased their shares. By 1952, he abandoned his law practice and joined the company full-time.

Through acquisition, expansion, and advertising, the company grew quickly. By 1957 the partners established a new subsidiary named The Glass Depot for wholesale sales. By the end of the year, annual revenue from combined operations reached $800,000.

Russ Baumgardner was convinced that building a business hinged on giving employees the encouragement to grow. He hired talented people, then gave them the freedom to perform to their fullest potential. However, as the company grew and capable employees joined the business, the last original partner called it quits. In 1963, Harold Burrows decided to retire. His stock was sold to other Apogee employees, and Harold headed for the northern woods of Minnesota.

The company continued to buy other firms and expand operations. By 1968 annual sales reached $4 million, and in November of that year Baumgardner purchased Wausau Metals Corporation, a Wisconsin window manufacturer. By 1972, Baumgardner had created a holding company, named Apogee Enterprises, and had taken the new company public. Two years later, sales reached $18 million.

Apogee pressed forward through the 1970s with a focus on increasing sales. By 1981 sales reached $106 million. Employment rose from about 400 in 1972 to nearly 1,700 in 1981. However, the company experienced erratic profit growth, leading to an unusual memo from Baumgardner: "Cut back on sales . . . pay attention to profit margins." The company had actually expanded product lines and territories faster than they were able to manage the growth. Fortunately, Baumgardner put on the brakes before serious consequences were felt.

Baumgardner's adjustment was well timed. By the time he retired as chairman of Apogee on June 28, 1988, sales exceeded $300 million and the company employed more than 5,000 people. He had succeeded by taking many small risks, pursuing opportunities that others ignored, and properly controlling corporate growth.

Failure at Apogee was looked upon as an investment for future success. Baumgardner said, "I have a high tolerance for mistakes. When there's a failure, we look at it as an experiment and ask, 'What are we going to do next time?' Then we close the books and just let it heal."

Russell Baumgardner died on January 5, 1994. In 1996, Apogee Enterprises' sales exceeded $900 million.

SOURCE: *Windows of Opportunity: Apogee Enterprises, Inc. 1949–1989,* Apogee Enterprises, Inc., 1989

John J. Bausch, Henry Lomb

[Bausch & Lomb]

John Jacob Bausch was born on July 25, 1830, at Gross Suessin, Württemberg, Germany. He left his home at age 18 and moved to Bern, Switzerland, where he accepted a job with an optical shop. The following year he immigrated to the United States and spent the next few years traveling through New York state in search of an opportunity in the optical field.

In 1853, Bausch opened his own optical goods shop in Rochester, New York, and featured eyeglasses, magnifiers, microscopes, telescopes, opera glasses, and other products imported from Europe. That same year he found a scrap piece of Vulcanite rubber on the street and, after some experimentation, fashioned it into eyeglass frames. As Bausch's growing business required more capital, he borrowed $60 from his good friend, Henry Lomb, with the stipulation that if the business was successful, Bausch would bring in Lomb as a partner.

Like John Bausch, Henry Lomb was a German immigrant. He was born on November 24, 1828, at Burgham, Hesse-Kassel, Germany, and later immigrated to the United States, eventually settling in Rochester, New York. Shortly after making his loan to Bausch, the company grew so quickly that he accepted Bausch's offer for a partnership. The company's eyeglasses, made from the hard rubber frames with imported lenses, quickly became a strong seller.

When the Civil War erupted, Lomb answered the call for service and joined the 13th Regiment of the New York Volunteers. Over the next two years, he quickly rose in rank to sergeant, lieutenant, and finally captain. He was discharged from duty in 1863 and rejoined Bausch, who had developed the first power lens-grinding machine in the country. Because of the shipping blockade in effect during much of the Civil War, demand for the small company's products flourished.

During the decade following the Civil War, Bausch and Lomb moved away from retailing to focus on manufacturing. Their store was sold in 1864, and a small manufacturing shop was established in Rochester while, two years later, Lomb established a New York City sales office. Under the direction of Bausch, the company made eyeglasses, nose frames, watchmakers' and engravers' loupes, magnifiers, and many other products. In the 1870s, they manufactured their first telescope.

Throughout the 1870s and 1880s, second-generation Bausch and Lomb family members became active in the business. Like his father, Edward Bausch became an accomplished inventor and was the recipient of several important patents. The company developed a strong line of scientific and industrial microscopes, and these and its other products, including successful binoculars, flourished. By 1900, Bausch & Lomb employed 1,000 workers.

Henry Lomb died on June 13, 1908, three months after the company was formally organized as Bausch & Lomb, Incorporated. In 1912, John Bausch's son William became active in glass manufacturing, and through his work, Bausch & Lomb became a major producer of optical-quality glass. During World War I, the company supplied nearly two-thirds of the military requirements for glass used in binoculars, telescopes, gun scopes, and searchlights.

John Jacob Bausch died on February 24, 1926. The company continued to produce optical glass products over the next several decades. In the early 1950s, they introduced plastic eyeglass frames, and the following decade they introduced contact lenses. Today, Bausch & Lomb is a world leader in eye care, with annual sales of nearly $2 billion.

SOURCE: Bausch & Lomb corporate archives

John Bean, John D. Crummey, Will C. Anderson

[FMC Corporation]

In the latter part of the nineteenth century, John Bean and Will Anderson were successful inventors and entrepreneurs in California's fertile Santa Clara Valley. Although they didn't work together, Bean sold his spray pumps and Anderson sold his prune equipment to local farmers. Bean's grandson, John Crummey, eventually brought their companies together into one corporation, which was named the Food Machinery Corporation and later FMC.

John Bean was born in 1821 in Maine. He later moved to Ohio, where he became a successful inventor of several products, many of which had to do with farm implements and pumps, including the Buckeye Force Pump, the first deep-well pump ever made. After selling the Buckeye Pump for $25,000 and a 25¢-per-pump royalty, the 62-year-old Bean retired and purchased a ten-acre almond ranch in Los Gatos, California.

His retirement wasn't permanent. James Lick, the California philanthropist who financed the Lick Observatory, had imported some diseased fruit trees from China. As the disease spread, trees around the entire valley were infected by scale. Bean became frustrated with the insecticide sprayers that could deliver the spray only in short bursts. In less than one year, Bean had designed and patented a continuous-flow pump.

The elderly Bean eventually convinced his son-in-law, David C. Crummey, to move to California to market the pump. Thus, Crummey became the first president of the Bean Spray Pump Company, which achieved modest success over the next 30 years.

When David's son, John D. Crummey, graduated from high school, he enrolled at Stanford University. The family pump business was not generating any profits, so young John had to work odd jobs to pay for room and board. On weekends he bicycled home, some 16 miles, so he could work on Saturdays collecting water bills. Eventually, John Crummey quit school and joined his cousin, Roy Bean, in a bicycle shop venture.

In 1901, John Crummey accepted his father's invitation to return home and take control of the floundering pump company. John quickly found the reason for poor sales. When his grandfather, John Bean, invented the pump, most of the field work was done by Chinese workers, who liked the horizontal pump. Later, as Caucasian Americans were more involved with spraying, they favored vertical pumps.

Crummey called his 82-year-old grandfather out of retirement once again to redesign the pump. Bean's new design, which was drawn on the bottom of a shoe box, produced 120 pounds of pressure, far superior to anything else on the market. Crummey put the new pumps into production and personally delivered them into the countryside on his bicycle.

In May, 1904, John Crummey, his father, and a handful of investors formally incorporated the Bean Spray Pump Company. Within one year the company had tripled its capitalization. The company experienced a setback when the plant suffered extensive damage during the 1906 San Francisco earthquake. However, one year later it was twice the size it was in 1905.

The company advanced into wagon-mounted sprayers powered by gasoline engines. Sales in 1909 totaled $117,000, and within six years exceeded $400,000. In 1915, Bean established a second manufacturing facility in Michigan. A local newspaper covered the opening by reporting: "The large number of beans grown in Michigan should provide a fine opportunity for the Bean Spray Pump Company." Crummey immediately recognized that the company name was misleading, causing some people to think they only made sprayers for bean plants.

About the same time that John Bean and his son-in-law were establishing their pump business, the Santa Clara Valley orchards were producing bumper prune crops. Subsequently, there was a backlog of prunes that needed processing for market. This provided an opportunity for a local inventor, Will Anderson.

Will Anderson was one of seven children born to John and Mother Anderson in Worthington, Indiana. In 1863, the family moved to California in a covered wagon. Tragically, John Anderson died in an accident not long after they arrived. Will's mother later remarried a widower who also had seven children. The combined families lived modestly raising sheep and cattle.

Will moved off the farm at age 12, supporting himself by working on local ranches. This life of hard labor planted the desire in young Anderson to invent mechanical devices that would lessen the burden on farm workers. He moved to the Santa Clara Valley and built harvesting equipment. Eventually, he built a mechanical prune dipper that revolutionized prune processing, thereby reducing the backlog.

By 1897, the Anderson Prune Dipper Company was manufacturing a variety of equipment for drying and packing prunes. Down the street, the Barngrover-Hull Manufacturing Company was serving the same market. The competitors eventually found themselves in a legal battle over patents, which was resolved by merging the companies. Will Anderson assumed the post of president of the new company, named Anderson-Barngrover. The company had strong growth and, by 1920, had annual sales of $2 million and employed 300 people.

When David Crummey died on May 27, 1928, he was succeeded as president of the Bean Spray Pump Company by John Crummey. John immediately renamed the firm the John Bean Manufacturing Company to better reflect the nature of the business. He also cast his eye toward his next-door neighbor, Frank Burrell, who was the manager of Anderson-Barngrover. Crummey suggested to Burrell that the two companies would make a good match, and in less than 24 hours, they formalized an agreement. The new company maintained the John Bean Manufacturing Company name until 1929, when it was renamed the Food Machinery Corporation and, eventually, FMC.

FMC expanded into other agricultural-related lines throughout the 1930s. When the United States entered World War II, FMC supplied a wide range of military products, including amphibian vehicles known as the Alligator and the Water Buffalo. This vaulted FMC into the military supply business that is still a major component of the company.

Today, FMC is one of the world's leading producers of chemicals and machinery for industry, agriculture, and government, serving five broad markets: industrial chemicals, performance chemicals, precious metals, defense systems, and machinery and equipment. FMC operates 115 manufacturing facilities and mines in 24 countries, generating nearly $5 billion in annual sales.

John Crummey, grandson of John Bean, died in November, 1976, at the age of 98.

SOURCE: *Growing Orbit: The Story of FMC Corporation,* published by FMC Corporation, 1992

Leon L. Bean, Leon A. Gorman

[L.L. Bean, Inc.]

Leon Leonwood Bean was born on October 13, 1872, in Greenwood, Maine, the fourth of six children born to Benjamin Warren Bean and Sarah Swett Bean. A year after L.L.'s birth, Benjamin abandoned farming and became owner of the Mount Abram Hotel in nearby Locke's Mills. He later sold the hotel and returned to farming, but tragedy struck in 1884 when he and his 41-year-old wife, Sarah Bean, died four days apart, leaving Leon an orphan at age 12.

Young Leon spent his teen years hunting, fishing, and trapping while attending Kents Hill School and working on a farm. While in his early 20s, he worked with his brothers in shoe and clothing ventures. In 1898, he married Bertha Porter, the daughter of a Freeport carpenter whose family was prominent in Maine's shipbuilding industry. The couple had three children: Lester Carleton, born in 1900; Charles Warren, born in 1901; and Barbara, born in 1907.

By 1906, the L.L. Bean Clothing and Shoes store appeared in Freeport, the newest among the Bean ventures. Bean's store grew steadily as residents from bordering states were drawn to Maine for hunting, fishing, and vacationing. Leon Bean soon recognized a need for a light, comfortable, waterproof hunting boot. In 1911, he designed a pair of boots that combined rubber bottoms with leather tops. He made up and sold 100 pairs for $3.50 each. Unfortunately, the design was flawed and 90 pairs were returned and the money was refunded. Undaunted, Bean took the design to the U.S. Rubber Company in Boston and his Maine Hunting Shoe was soon in production.

By 1915, Bean had shifted the emphasis of his company completely toward the sports enthusiast. Portland's suburban directory listed the business as "Maine hunting specialties, clothing, and shoes." His mail-order business grew substantially, boosted by targeted catalog mailings to nonresidents who purchased Maine hunting licenses. Through the 1920s, Bean expanded his retail product line into camping and fishing equipment, as well as some larger items such as canoes. By 1924, sales exceeded $135,000 and the company had a staff of 25 employees.

By the 1930s, Bean was actively manufacturing many of the products he sold. The company was officially incorporated in 1934, and it not only survived the Depression, it prospered, surpassing the $1 million sales mark in 1937. However, the decade brought personal loss. Bertha Bean, L.L.'s wife, died in 1939. A year later his brothers Ervin and Henry died.

World War II brought shortages of material and leisure activities, but Bean compensated by producing war goods, including specialized footwear for combat soldiers. He also married his second wife, Lucille Claire Boudreau, who had been his nurse during a series of eye operations. Despite the challenges of world conflict and a new marriage, Bean published his first popular book, *Hunting, Fishing, and Camping,* in 1942.

Sales at L.L. Bean approached $2 million by 1950. While his focus was on product quality and not growth, he did institute some changes. At his wife's insistence, he added a women's department in 1954. Also, he purchased the Small-Abbott moccasin factory, his first and only acquisition. He also opened his factory salesroom to business 24 hours per day, 365 days per year.

Leon Arthur Gorman was one of three children born to Bean's daughter, Barbara (Bean) Gorman. After graduating from Bowdoin College in Brunswick, Maine, Leon Gorman served as a lieutenant on a destroyer in the United States Navy. He joined the business in 1961, and for the next seven years was able to learn the business firsthand from his grandfather.

Leon L. Bean died on February 5, 1967, at the age of 94. Within one year, Leon Gorman was appointed president of the company, which recorded sales that year of just under $5 million. Over the next three decades, Gorman led the company through tremendous growth in manufacturing, marketing, and distribution.

Today, L.L. Bean, Inc., is still based in Freeport, Maine. Its primary retail store, also in Freeport, remains open 24 hours per day, 365 days per year, and attracts more than 3.5 million visitors annually. The company sells more than 16,000 different products and circulates nearly 115 million copies of its 24 different catalogs each year. Total sales now exceed $900 million annually.

SOURCES: L.L. Bean, Inc., archives; William David Barry, *L.L. Bean, Inc.: Outdoor Sporting Specialties,* The Anthoensen Press, Portland, ME, 1987

Charles Beckman

[Red Wing Shoe Company]

Charles Beckman was born in Germany in 1856. In 1873, the 17-year-old immigrant made his way to the small Minnesota town of Red Wing, where he found a job at the Trout Brook Tannages. Beckman and the tannery's 38-year-old founder, S. B. Foot, became friends. In 1883, Beckman established a retail shoe store in Red Wing with Foot providing the financing.

Over the next 20 years, C. Beckman & Company sold more than 500,000 pairs of boots and shoes. Then Beckman grew restless and became intent on manufacturing shoes rather than just selling them. In 1905, he organized the Red Wing Shoe Company and raised enough capital to start construction on a new factory.

As work progressed on the plant, Beckman tried to sell his retail store. Over time, he became discouraged with what he considered to be low offers and, eventually, decided to maintain ownership himself. When the first Red Wing shoes were manufactured, they were sold to the C. Beckman & Company shoe store. Two years later, he was able to find a buyer for the store, allowing Beckman to devote full attention to his factory.

Beckman, a natural salesman, spent more time on the road than behind his desk. Once, while bound for Kansas City, his train collided head-on with another train, throwing the car off the tracks and destroying Beckman's shoe samples. Unharmed by the crash, Beckman collected his wits and hopped on another train to Salt Lake City, where he knew he could make sales without his sample case.

By 1907, the Red Wing shoe catalog offered 81 different pairs of shoes and boots. One year later, he added a two-story addition to the factory, allowing Red Wing to add a line of highly durable "welt-constructed" shoes. Continuing his focus on the farm market, Beckman introduced a line of "Manure Proof" shoes, which he claimed would not crack from contact with manure or become hard after getting wet.

Suffering from declining health, the 55-year-old Beckman retired from active service with Red Wing in August, 1911. On October 21, 1912, Charles Beckman died. By 1919, leadership of the company had passed to J. R. Sweasy.

Today, Red Wing Shoe Company employs nearly 1,800 people in manufacturing plants in Red Wing; Potosi, Missouri; and Danville, Kentucky. The company offers more than 200 styles of footwear through more than 4,000 Red Wing Shoe dealers.

SOURCES: Red Wing Shoe Company archives; Patrice A. Marvin and Nicholas C. Vrooman, *Heart and Sole: A Story of the Red Wing Shoe Company,* Red Wing Shoe Company, 1986

Walter H. Beech, Olive A. Beech

[Beech Aircraft Corporation]

After Walter Beech built a modest airplane manufacturing firm, he married his office manager, Olive, and merged his company with Curtiss-Wright. Walter and Olive soon missed the excitement of having their own company and launched the Beech Aircraft Company, which grew into one of America's best-known aircraft manufacturers.

Walter Herschel Beech was born on January 30, 1891, in Pulaski, Tennessee, the son of Cornelius Beech and Tommie (Hay) Beech. Early on, he displayed a mechanical aptitude and an interest in flying. At age 14, he fashioned a glider from a wooden frame and his mother's new bedsheets. The contraption didn't fly, but the interest remained.

After graduating from Giles College, Beech became a salesman for a Minneapolis automobile company. While in Minnesota, he and a friend purchased a wrecked Curtiss biplane, which they reassembled and flew. At that moment, airplanes became the center of Beech's life.

Beech served as a flight instructor for the Aviation Section of the U.S. Army Signal Corps from 1917 through 1920. Upon discharge, he toured the country as a barnstorming pilot at air shows, becoming familiar with a wide range of equipment and flying techniques.

In 1921, Beech accepted a job with a Wichita, Kansas, airplane manufacturer as a test pilot and demonstrator. Two years later, the Swallow Airplane Manufacturing Company was reorganized and Beech became a principal of the firm. In 1924, Beech resigned from the company in protest of their use of wood (he favored metal) to manufacture airplanes. He then launched a new aircraft company, named Travel Air, in a 900-square-foot corner of an old planing mill.

The first Travel Air, an open-cockpit model, took flight in 1925. He was soon filling commercial orders and, in his spare time, organizing and competing in air shows. After producing more than 200 biplanes, Beech turned to monoplanes in 1927. The monoplanes proved to be even more successful, and Beech was producing 1,000 planes annually by 1929.

Olive Ann Mellor was born on September 25, 1903, at Waverly, Kansas. Olive showed an early financial aptitude, opening a bank account by age 7 and writing checks by age 11. In 1917, her family moved to Wichita, where Olive attended the American Secretarial and Business College. In 1924, she became the twelfth employee hired by Walter Beech's Travel Air. The other 11 were male pilots. On February 24, 1930, Walter and Olive were married.

Just prior to their marriage, Beech merged Travel Air into the Curtiss-Wright airplane conglomerate. The newlyweds moved to New York City, where Walter became vice president in charge of sales for Curtiss-Wright. However, city life and big corporations didn't appeal to the couple. In April 1932, at the height of the Great Depression, Walter and Olive Beech moved back to Wichita and launched the Beech Aircraft Company, with Walter serving as president and Olive as secretary-treasurer.

In a small, closed-down factory, Walter, Olive, and a small staff designed and built a five-seat, closed-cabin biplane with the feel of a luxury sedan. On November 4, 1932, their first Beechcraft was presented at the Wichita Municipal Airport. Orders soon followed, and the couple moved their manufacturing operations back into the old Travel Air plant.

To promote their growing company, Walter entered a Beechcraft in the 1936 Bendix Transcontinental Speed Dash. At Olive's insistence, two female pilots were recruited: Louise Thaden and Blanche Noyes. These women not only won the race, beating their nearest competitor by 45 minutes, but set a new transcontinental speed record for women.

Walter and Olive Beech had two daughters, born in 1937 and 1940. Following their arrival Beech entered into a period of phenomenal growth. In 1938, the company had about 200 employees and sales had just reached $1 million. In 1940, World War II brought a number of military contracts, pushing the backlog of orders to $22 million in 1940 and $82 million in 1941. Employment jumped to 4,000 by 1942. In the midst of this period, Walter Beech became ill and was hospitalized nearly a full year, leaving Olive to run the company while tending to their two daughters.

After the war, the couple turned their attention back to the commercial market. However, by 1950, hostilities erupted in Korea and Beech Aircraft geared up once again for military contracts. Then, on November 29, 1950, Walter H. Beech died unexpectedly of a heart attack, and his 47-year-old widow, Olive, took the reins of the company. In the ensuing years, she led the company into rapid expansion in the aerospace industry.

In January 1968, Olive Beech retired as president, but remained on the board of directors. In February 1980, Beech Aircraft merged with Raytheon Company, and Olive Beech became a director of Raytheon. A few years later, she retired from the boards of Beech Aircraft and Raytheon. Olive Ann Beech died on July 6, 1993, at the age of 89.

SOURCE: Beech Aircraft Corporation archives

William H. Belk, Dr. John M. Belk

[Belk Brothers Department Stores]

William Henry Belk, better known as "Mr. Henry," started his first store in 1888. Soon afterward he invited his younger brother John to forgo a career in medicine and join him in retail sales. John agreed, and soon a second store was opened in Charlotte. From this humble beginning the Belk Brothers Company grew to one of America's largest department stores.

John Belk immigrated to the United States from England in the eighteenth century. He soon acquired considerable land in Johnston, Lincoln, and Mecklenburg counties in North Carolina and raised a large family. A descendant, Able Nelson Washington Belk and his wife Sarah (Walkup) Belk had three boys. The second-born was William Henry Belk, born June 2, 1862, in Lancaster County, South Carolina.

The young family faced tragedy that was all too common during the Civil War. In the early spring of 1865, word reached the family that Union troops were marching toward Charlotte from Savannah, and the Belk homestead lay directly in their path. Fearing that they would kill the man of the house, young Abel Belk decided to hide in the woods until the troops had passed. Thomas M. Belk, four years of age, William Belk, nearly three, and their infant brother, John Montgomery Belk, watched with their mother as Abel headed for the woods. Tragically, Union troops under the command of General William T. Sherman, soon found and drowned Abel Belk.

Henry Belk knew from a very early age that he wanted to be a merchant. He later stated that the inventory of country stores and the interaction between shopkeepers and farmers fascinated him. By 1876, 14-year-old Henry set out to earn a living. Despite the fact that his mother had remarried, Henry had assumed the role of eldest Belk in the family due to the death of both his grandfather and older brother a year earlier.

He landed a job with B. D. Heath, a merchant in Monroe, North Carolina, for $5 per month. He remained with Heath for 12 years, eventually becoming the second-in-command after mastering all the shopkeeper's responsibilities.

After securing a modest start-up loan, 25-year-old Henry opened his own store on May 29, 1888. From his experience in retailing, he introduced three principles that were revolutionary in rural North Carolina at that time: First, he sold only on a cash basis. While this was contrary to the practice of carrying farmers on credit until harvest, the idea proved to make sense for both Henry and his customers. Second, he placed a retail price on his merchandise rather than bartering with customers. Third, he offered to take any merchandise back and refund a customer's money, no questions asked.

These innovations paid off, and business grew steadily through Henry's hard work and integrity. Optimistic about the future, Henry convinced his younger brother John, by this time a physician, to abandon medicine and join him in the store. The Belk Brothers Company would last until John's death in 1928.

In 1893, a chance meeting with an in-law led to an arrangement that would eventually sweep the Belk name throughout the South. Alex Kluttz, the husband of the brothers' first cousin, Alice Jane Walkup, dropped by the store. The Kluttz family had been poor, and Henry was impressed with Alex's honesty and optimistic demeanor. Soon Henry offered Kluttz a deal—the brothers would set him up in business in his hometown of Chester, South Carolina, and the Belks would take a stake in the store.

Kluttz accepted, and the first "branch" was created. The venture was successful, and the brothers struck a similar deal a year later, setting up Reece P. Harry as co-owner and manager of a store in Union, South Carolina.

Their biggest move came on September 25, 1895, when they opened their fourth store in Charlotte, North Carolina. Henry moved to Charlotte and personally controlled the store, which grew to be the hub of the Belk organization, while John stayed in Monroe and managed the flagship store. Henry worked diligently to ensure that shoppers in the Carolinas received the same level of service offered by northern retailers such as John Wanamaker and Marshall Field.

By 1915 they had a total of 16 stores operating. Ten years later there were 44. Most of the stores involved co-ownership, as reflected in the name: Matthews-Belk in Gastonia, Belk-Harry in Salisbury, Williams-Belk in Sanford, Hudson-Belk in Raleigh, and many others. The Belks also made considerable investments in local manufacturing and other businesses. All of their expansion and investments were made out of a strong belief in the people in their corner of America and a faithful conviction that the entrepreneurial spirit will breed success.

Henry Belk invested so much of his time into the building of his company that he had little time for anything else, including a family. Finally, on June 9, 1915, at the age of 53, Henry married Mary Lenora Irwin, the daughter of a prominent Charlotte physician. The couple would eventually have five sons and a daughter, all of whom became active in the business.

Henry experienced two tragic losses while leading the company through further expansion. On March 21, 1928, John Belk died at the age of 62. Henry and John worked in harmony their entire adult lives, together opening a total of 51 stores. John, preceded in death by his wife, left behind seven daughters.

A few years later, on March 9, 1932, Henry's mother died. Sarah Walkup Belk Simpson had lived 95 years. Up to the end of her life, Henry remained loyal to his mother. He would make the trip from Charlotte to Monroe every Sunday to attend church services with her. With the number of Belk stores approaching 90, Henry had outlived his parents and both his brothers.

On February 21, 1952, Henry died at the age of 89. While he had orchestrated the founding of more than 300 department stores, William Henry Belk is remembered more for what he did for local churches and communities than for his personal business success. All told, Henry and his brother helped establish more than 300 Presbyterian churches and manses. He was a strong supporter of education, making lasting contributions to Queens College in Charlotte and Davidson College in Davidson, North Carolina.

SOURCES: Belk Brothers archives; LeGette Blythe, *William Henry Belk: Merchant of the South,* The University of North Carolina Press, Chapel Hill, NC, 1950, 1958

Donald J. Bell, Albert S. Howell

[Bell & Howell Company]

After meeting at a parts store, Donald Bell, a movie projectionist, and Albert Howell, a projector repairman, launched a company to build and repair motion picture equipment. Within 12 years, Bell and Howell dominated the industry with their movie equipment.

Donald J. Bell was born in 1869 at Jamestown, Ohio. In 1896, Bell went to Chicago and was hired as an usher in the Schiller Theatre. He was fascinated with the Lumiere Cinematograph that projected the moving pictures, and he soon talked his way into the position of assistant operator at a discount wage.

Projection equipment operators worked not only in theaters, but anywhere that an audience could be booked to see a movie. Bell's first assignment as a projectionist was in Waukegan, Illinois, where he mounted his equipment on a platform supported by beer barrels from a nearby saloon. The projector drew so much power that the nearby streetlamps dimmed drastically while the movie was playing.

Bell's boss held authority with the local railroad, which afforded him access to machinist's tools. Working in the railroad powerhouse, Bell tinkered with the movie equipment and made modifications to improve efficiency. While buying projector parts at the Crary Machine Works, Bell was introduced to another man who shared his interest in projection equipment: "Bert" Howell.

Albert Summers Howell was born in 1879 on a farm near West Branch, Michigan. At age 11, his family moved to another farm, near a lumber camp in Indiana. There, young Howell busied himself repairing farm and lumbering machinery. In 1895, the family moved to Chicago, where he landed a job as an apprentice mechanic with Miehle Printing Press Company.

Howell attended night school and eventually graduated from the Armour Institute of Technology (today known as the Illinois Institute of Technology) as a mechanical engineer. He then moved through several jobs, building car-sealing machines, berry-box machines, and even animal traps. At last he began work in a machine shop that built and repaired motion picture equipment. In 1906, Howell was awarded his first patent for a framing device for the Kinodrome 35mm Theatre motion picture projector.

After the two Crary patrons, Bell and Howell, were introduced, Donald Bell immediately saw the potential for pooling their resources. The Bell & Howell Company was incorporated on February 17, 1907. The new venture was housed in a 30- by 60-foot lab that soon employed 18 people. During the first year of business, most of their revenue came from repairs.

Within a year, however, the pair had innovated a film perforator, a camera, and a continuous printer, all based on 35mm width. This became the start of an industrywide 35mm film standard. In 1910, they presented their first cinematograph camera, made entirely of wood and covered with black leather. Two years later, they launched an improved camera, the model 2709. When Walt Disney animated *Snow White and the Seven Dwarfs* in the 1930s, he used a Bell & Howell 2709 that had been manufactured in 1914.

In 1914, the partners moved to a new building, and within three years employment rose to 85. By the end of World War I, nearly every Hollywood movie producer was equipped with Bell & Howell equipment. In fact, as late as 1942, it was estimated that 90 percent of the motion pictures made in the entire world were cut on Bell & Howell perforators.

During its first decade, Bell & Howell had been dominated by Donald Bell, who was ten years older than Howell and more involved with the administrative and marketing duties. Howell, on the other hand, had been the inventive genius behind the company's new products. In fact, Albert Howell was granted nearly 150 patents over his lifetime.

By the end of 1917, Bell had become dissatisfied with some of the administrative policies of the company, which led to a dispute with Howell and several managers. Bell agreed to sell his interests to the others for a little over $180,000. Though his name has remained part of the company, Bell moved to New York, then later to California, and never again played a role in the Bell & Howell Company.

Albert Howell remained with the company for the next three decades. The company grew in the 1930s with the help of a growing educational market and the advent of talking motion pictures. In the 1940s, Bell & Howell supported the war effort with advanced optical equipment and training-film equipment.

Albert S. Howell died on January 3, 1951.

SOURCE: Bell & Howell Company archives

Judson M. Bemis

[Bemis Company, Inc.]

Judson Moss Bemis was born on May 18, 1833, at Fitchburg, Massachusetts, the third son born to Stephen and Miriam Thurston (Farwell) Bemis. When he was five years old, the Bemis family moved to the Western frontier, first by wagon to Buffalo, then steamship to Detroit, and again overland, passing Fort Dearborn (later renamed Chicago) and settling on a 120-acre farm at Light House Point.

Young Judson lived the life typical of farm children, which centered on helping with the work and, when possible, attending school. His mother died while Judson was still a young boy, and his father eventually remarried. When the elder Bemis grew tired of farming, he joined the California gold rush. His wife thereupon leased the farm to another family, and Judson moved to a neighboring farm, working for $12 a month and board. He later moved in with an uncle until his father returned from his unsuccessful venture in California.

In 1852, 19-year-old Judson Moss moved to Chicago and, for the next six years, loaded lake steamboats for a shipping company. By 1858, he had built up modest savings and decided to form his own business. His cousin, a Chicago bag maker, pledged some surplus equipment for the venture.

In December 1858, the 25-year-old Bemis rented a small loft in St. Louis, Missouri, and opened for business as J. M. Bemis & Company. His first order was for 200 half-barrel sacks. The client was so satisfied with the quality of the work that he permitted Bemis to use him as a reference for future work, which came slowly.

At the time, there were no directories of manufacturers available. To find new customers, Bemis went to the levee each morning to observe the unloading of flour. He would examine the shipping crates and note the name and locations of the flour mill, then return to his shop and prepare letters soliciting their business.

Bemis was soon joined by his cousin, Edward Brown, and the firm was renamed Bemis & Brown. Brown then moved to Boston, Massachusetts, to handle the purchase of cotton goods. By the end of the Civil War, however, Bemis bought out his business partner and was then joined by his older brother, Stephen, and the name was changed once more, this time to Bemis Brother & Company.

In 1870, Judson Bemis left the St. Louis plant in Stephen's hands and moved to Boston, where for the next 15 years he devoted himself to obtaining material and administering the business. By 1880, they had established another branch factory in Minneapolis, Minnesota. This was followed by plants in Omaha, Kansas City, San Francisco, New Orleans, Houston, New York, and several other locations, including Winnipeg, Canada. By 1920, the company was operating plants in 15 cities.

In November 1866 he married Alice Cogswell, and the couple eventually had three children. Judson Moss Bemis died on April 6, 1921, at the age of 88. His son, A. Farwell Bemis, succeeded him as president of the company, which had been renamed Bemis Brother Bag Company. Farwell's sons, F. Gregg Bemis and Judson Bemis, later became third-generation CEOs, retiring in 1965 and 1978, respectively.

Today, Bemis makes packaging machinery, pressure-sensitive products (such as self-adhesive labels), and is the largest flexible-packaging manufacturer in North America, with 8,500 employees and $1.4 billion in revenue.

SOURCE: Bemis family archives

Vincent H. Bendix

[Bendix Corporation]

Vincent Bendix transformed an interest in automobiles into a multimillion-dollar empire. After his first venture of building cars failed, Bendix invented the electric starter. After introducing safe brakes to American automakers, he became known as the "King of Stop and Go." His company, The Bendix Corporation, became a leading supplier of automobile and aviation parts.

Vincent Hugo Bendix was born on August 12, 1881, in Moline, Illinois, the oldest of three children born to Reverend Jann and Anna Bengtson, both immigrants from Sweden. They later changed the family name to Bendix and moved to Chicago.

When he was 16 years old, Bendix left home and moved to New York City, where he worked as an elevator operator and, later, in a variety of odd jobs that exposed him to electricity, stenography, and accounting. He also attended night classes in engineering and was a motorcycle enthusiast.

After seeing an "auto buggy," Bendix was convinced that his future was in the emerging automotive industry. He moved to Chicago and secured a job with Holsman of Chicago, one of the leaders in the auto buggy industry.

Once Bendix was confident that he had sufficient experience, he designed the Bendix Motor Buggy and started his own company. He contracted with the Triumph Motor Company of Illinois, to assemble the vehicles. Within two years, 7,000 of the vehicles were built and sold. However, the venture was short-lived, going bankrupt in 1909.

Bendix was not discouraged with the outcome of his first company. Within a year he was at the drawing board, intent on developing a method for starting cars without having to crank the engine. He developed a push-button starter and, for the next three years, engineered improvements while trying to find a buyer.

Finally, he reached an agreement with the Eclipse Manufacturing Company of Elmira, New York, who agreed to build the starters and pay a royalty to Bendix. The 1914 Chevrolets were the first cars to use the starters, and more than 5,500 units sold that year. The improvement over the hand crank was obvious, and it didn't take long for sales to skyrocket. Encouraged by this success, Bendix looked for a place to build a manufacturing plant and experiment with other ideas. He selected South Bend, Indiana, because it sat midway between Chicago and Detroit, the two automotive centers of America.

The next new Bendix product emerged from a 1922 tragedy. Bendix's father was standing on a Chicago street corner when a car equipped with defective brakes struck and killed him. Later that year, Bendix acquired manufacturing rights to the Perrot braking system built in France. Within a year, he introduced his Bendix four-wheel brakes, which quickly found their way into 25 percent of American cars.

The name of the company was changed to The Bendix Corporation in 1924, and Vincent Bendix started selling his stock to the public. This boost of cash, combined with a flood of revenue from starters and brakes, launched Bendix on a buying binge. He purchased interests in Stromberg Carburetor, Bragg-Kliesrath (which made vacuum boosters), and several other companies. He moved most of his acquisitions to South Bend, and the small factory grew into an immense manufacturing complex, with nearly 25 acres of space under one roof.

Bendix paid little attention to the Depression. In 1931, 20 new products were introduced to the market. He remained committed to being a manufacturer of automobile *parts*, and not complete automobiles. However, he turned his attention to other corners of the transportation industry, and aggressively moved into train, boat, and airplane parts. He acquired Pioneer Instrument Company and several other manufacturers of aircraft parts, which evolved into Bendix Aviation Corporation.

One of the most familiar consumer items that sported the Bendix label was not even made by Bendix. In 1936, two young entrepreneurs built an automatic washing machine. They struck a deal with Vincent Bendix, who allowed them to name the company Bendix Home Appliances, Inc., and to name the machine the Bendix automatic washer. For this, Bendix Aviation was given 25 percent of the company, which at one point controlled more than 50 percent of the automatic washer market.

Vincent Bendix didn't limit his ventures to the parts business. Upon moving his plant to South Bend in the early 1920s, Bendix didn't relinquish his extensive social club memberships in Chicago. The entire fourth floor of the South Bend office building amounted to his personal chambers, complete with a cook, a maid, a butler, and a barber. In addition to his own mansion, originally built for Clement Studebaker Jr. in 1910, Bendix purchased an ocean-front estate in Palm Beach and a posh New York apartment. He also purchased the Potter Palmer mansion and the entire block south of Lake Shore Drive in Chicago for $3 million in 1928.

This indulgent lifestyle, coupled with questionable management skills, eventually caught up with Vincent Bendix. By 1938, he was essentially powerless at his own company, having gradually sold off all of his stock, predominantly to General Motors. Once GM realized the company was losing a quarter million dollars a month, they had Bendix removed from the daily operations of the company. By 1942, Bendix had severed all ties with the company.

Vincent Bendix didn't fare any better in his personal life. His net worth, once estimated to be $50 million, sank to $1 million by 1939, with liabilities reaching $14 million. Bankrupt and unable to protect his assets, Bendix stood helplessly by as everything he had accumulated over the years was seized by creditors. This marked the second fall of Vincent Bendix, although this one was much more severe than the loss of his 1907 automobile venture.

Incredibly, Bendix had one more burst of energy left in him. In 1942, Bendix, now in his early 60s, went to New York and formed Bendix Helicopter, Inc., to develop a four-passenger helicopter sedan. Within three years the venture reportedly made more than $1 million for him. However, Vincent Bendix didn't have enough time to work his magic a third time. He died on March 27, 1945, at the age of 63. He was cremated and buried in Grace Memorial Cemetery in Chicago.

SOURCE: Rebecca Wolfe, "The Splash and Splendor of Vincent Bendix," *St. Joseph Valley Record,* Northern Indiana Historical Society, fall 1990

Michael L. Benedum

[Benedum-Trees Oil Company]

A humble man from humble beginnings, Michael L. Benedum left his small West Virginia hometown in search of an opportunity. After working briefly in the Rockefeller organization, he entered a partnership with Joe Trees. Seventy years later, he was known as one of the most successful oil and gas wildcatters in America.

Michael Late Benedum was born in 1869 in Bridgeport, West Virginia, the fourth of five children born to Emmanuel and Caroline Benedum. His father, a cabinetmaker, served as the town's mayor.

In 1890, Benedum boarded a train to Parkersburg, West Virginia, seeking employment. As the trip progressed, all the seats filled, and Benedum offered his seat to a gentleman who boarded at the Wilsonburg stop. The man accepted, but insisted that Benedum sit on the arm and talk. The man was John Worthington, head of the land-and-lease department of the South-Penn

Oil Company, a Rockefeller subsidiary. By the time the train arrived in Parkersburg, Michael Benedum was its newest employee.

This chance encounter marked the beginning of Benedum's lifelong quest for oil and gas. By 1897, Benedum had learned enough about the business to be self-sufficient. He met Joe Trees, an engineer and geologist, who also had talent and ambition. They soon had a major strike in Crawford County, Illinois. In 1900, they launched their lifelong partnership, the Benedum-Trees Oil Company. In 1907, they established their headquarters in Pittsburgh, acquiring a building on Fourth Avenue, which they renamed the Benedum-Trees Building.

Benedum was one of America's most successful wildcatters throughout the first half of the twentieth century. His last big strike occurred in Texas in 1948, and the site was eventually named the Benedum Field.

While Benedum was not formally educated, he became a trusted adviser to public leaders, including President Franklin D. Roosevelt. He never ventured far from oil and gas, however, once observing: "I've always lost money whenever I fooled with anything but oil."

In 1896, Benedum married Sarah Lantz of Blacksville, West Virginia. The couple had only one child, Claude Worthington Benedum, born in 1898. Claude's life ended tragically during an influenza epidemic in 1918 while he served in the U.S. Army in World War I. Ironically, Graham Trees, Joe Tree's son and Claude's school classmate, was killed in action in 1918 at the age of 20.

Michael Benedum died in 1959 at the age of 90. He was an active man, still searching for oil (in Alaska) almost up until his death. He was deeply religious and quite active in the Methodist church, while at the same time, he was a pioneering businessman unafraid of risks. He was modest, naming his son after the man who gave him his start in the oil business and then naming his foundation after his deceased son.

Michael and Sarah Benedum established their foundation in 1944 with a small contribution and named it in honor of their late son. Not long after Michael Benedum's death, distributions from his estate brought the foundation's assets to more than \$60 million. Today, the market value of the assets of the Claude Worthington Benedum Foundation exceeds \$200 million. Since its inception, the foundation has distributed more than \$150 million through more than 5,000 grants.

SOURCE: Claude Worthington Benedum Foundation archives

William R. Besserdich, Bernard A. Mosling

[Oshkosh Truck Corporation]

Unable to sell their four-wheel-drive technology to existing manufacturers, William Besserdich and Bernard Mosling started building their own trucks. They soon moved their business from Clintonville to Oshkosh, Wisconsin, where the Oshkosh Motor Truck Manufacturing Company quickly became a leading truck manufacturer. Today the company is a world leader in manufacturing large trucks.

In 1916, William Besserdich and Bernard Mosling were co-owners of two patents for improving four-wheel-drive capability. They approached Case, Ford, Packard, Studebaker, and others, but met with only rejection.

Undaunted, the two launched the Wisconsin Duplex Auto Company on May 1, 1917, in Clintonville, Wisconsin. Besserdich went to work on designing a prototype, while Mosling raised $250,000 in start-up capital. Later that year, the company relocated to Oshkosh, Wisconsin, and became the Oshkosh Motor Truck Manufacturing Company.

Its first truck, affectionately dubbed Old Betsy, was built in a Milwaukee machine shop. It incorporated both of the founders' patented improvements in four-wheel-drive technology and quickly became a marketing tool for raising capital. Their first product line, the Model A, featured a 72-horsepower Herschel-Spillman engine and a frame manufactured by the A.O. Smith Company. The truck retailed for about $3,500, and sales skyrocketed from 7 trucks in 1917 to 142 in 1920.

In 1920, the company built a larger production plant in Oshkosh, which opened with about two dozen employees working on the Model A. This vehicle became quite popular, reaching speeds of 20 miles per hour and having a hauling capacity of 2 tons. This was followed by the 3.5-ton-capacity Model B and the 5-ton-capacity Model F, all of which appealed to contractors, loggers, and government road crews.

Besserdich was never completely active in operations and resigned as president in 1922. He was replaced by Mosling, who by 1925 had introduced the Model H, which included double-reduction axles. The new trucks were far superior to any two- or four-wheel-drive vehicles on the market and quickly became a favorite for snow removal. While Oshkosh employees moaned at the first sight of falling snowflakes, Bernard Mosling affectionately called them "pennies from heaven."

The company survived the Depression and adapted its trucks to new uses, such as hauling milk. Mosling, however, had relinquished the title of president to focus his attention on boosting sales to cash-poor companies and municipals.

The lean years passed by the mid-1930s, and by the outbreak of World War II, Oshkosh factories were working overtime. Not only did Oshkosh build highly celebrated military equipment, it also had to fill orders at home for snow removal equipment to expedite the movement of military goods from manufacturing centers to the battlefield.

In 1944, Mosling returned to his previous position as president and led the company through another period of great growth. He adapted military vehicles for use in rough environments such as mines and oil fields. The company was also quick to enter the cement mixer market, capitalizing on the tide of domestic building projects. Still later, the company started building fire and rescue trucks.

Bernard Mosling remained as president of the company until 1956, when his son John assumed the role.

SOURCES: David Wright and Clarence Jungwirth, *Oshkosh Trucks: 75 Years of Specialty Truck Production,* Motorbooks International, Osceola, WI 1992; Oshkosh Truck Corporation archives

William E. Bindley

[Bindley Western Industries, Inc.]

Drawing on his family background in pharmaceutical wholesaling, William Bindley developed a plan to penetrate the drugstore-chain market. Starting with one employee and one truck in 1968, he built Bindley Western Industries into a $5 billion pharmaceutical giant.

William E. Bindley was born on October 6, 1940, in Terre Haute, Indiana. His father managed the family business, E.H. Bindley & Company, a small pharmaceutical supply firm that was founded by his great-grandfather in 1865.

After Bindley graduated from Purdue University in 1961 with a degree in industrial management, he elected to take a job with Brunswick Corporation rather than move into the family business. He later took a job with Controls Company of America, where he stayed until 1965, at which time he agreed to join his father at the pharmaceutical company.

In his spare time, Bindley started developing real estate in Aspen, Colorado, under the name Bindley Western Industries. However, it was not enough to satisfy his entrepreneurial drive. He was determined to manage something bigger than the small firm that had supported his family for more than a century.

In the 1960s, drugstore chains were just starting to hit stride, and Bindley saw an opportunity to sell to that market in addition to the mom-and-pop stores that were the family's existing customers. However, his conservative father was not inclined to let young Bill tamper with the business. Although his father was very supportive of Bill establishing a new company, he wasn't willing to lend him any money.

Selling equity in his Terre Haute home and Aspen real estate, Bindley raised $50,000 in start-up funds. In 1968, he used the basement of E.H. Bindley & Company, along with one employee and one truck, to launch his company. Bud Hook, president of Hook's Drug Store chain, allowed Bindley to conduct an intensive study of his business, from purchasing through sales. Bindley used the research to develop a plan that would enable him to supply Hook's with pharmaceuticals at a better rate than the company had previously been paying, and Bindley Western was off and running.

As it turned out, the drug wholesaling industry grew rapidly, and so did Bindley Western. William Bindley's commitment to customer service, willingness to accept thin profit margins, and automated distribution have enabled the firm to be the fifth-largest drug wholesaler in America, with annual sales exceeding $5 billion. What is particularly impressive is that the company employs about 800 workers, which translates into average annual sales of about $6 million per employee.

Bindley continues to serve as chairman and chief executive officer of Bindley Western. He resides in Carmel, Indiana, with his wife Mary Ann. The couple have three grown children. Bindley is active in educational and community affairs, serving as a board member of the Citizens Speedway Committee for the Indianapolis 500 race, the Indianapolis Convention and Visitors Association, the Indiana State Chamber of Commerce, the Indianapolis Entrepreneurship Academy, and many other groups. He is an avid skier and is a trustee and member of the executive committee of the United States Ski Team.

SOURCES: Dennis Hamilton, "Managing the Margins," *Indianapolis C.E.O.*, June 1991; Bindley Western Industries archives

Edwin Binney, C. Harold Smith

[Binney & Smith Inc.]

Edwin Binney and C. Harold Smith formed a partnership in the late nineteenth century to continue the business started by Binney's father. The company soon diversified into various markets and perfected the manufacture of wax crayons in various colors, giving birth to Crayola crayons.

Joseph W. Binney was born in England in 1836. He immigrated to Shrub Oak, New York, in 1860 and in 1864 founded the Peekskill Chemical Works in nearby Peekskill. Three years later he established an office in New York City to coordinate sales of his pharmaceutical charcoal and lampblack (a black pigment), as well as paint and imported colors. Joseph Binney, after building a successful business, retired in 1885 and passed the organization to his son Edwin and his nephew C. Harold Smith.

Edwin Binney (facing page, left) was born in 1866 and, upon graduating from school, joined his father in the family business. C. Harold Smith (facing page, right), Joseph's nephew and Edwin's cousin, was born in London in 1860 and, after serving in various capacities while traveling the world by sea, Smith came to New York in 1879.

The pair developed a unique color additive known as *carbon black*, which was blacker and stronger than any black pigment on the market. It quickly became the main ingredient in printing ink, stove and shoe polish, marking inks, and black crayons.

The cousins complemented each other well. Smith, outgoing and well traveled, became the chief salesperson for the company and established strong business relationships throughout the world. Meanwhile, Binney handled marketing in the United States as well as all administrative functions.

Around 1900, Edwin Binney struck a deal with a North Carolina businessman who owned a considerable soapstone supply and was looking for a grinder. Binney purchased a water-powered stone mill on Bushkill Creek near Easton, Pennsylvania, to fulfill the contract. As a bonus, the mill was near substantial deposits of slate, which Binney used to make high-quality pencils.

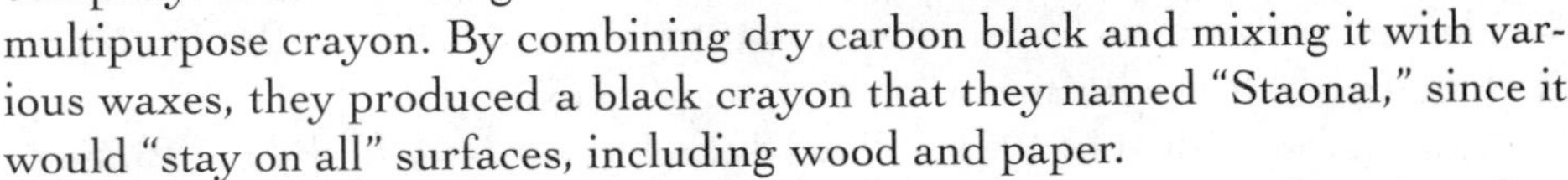

While peddling the pencils to schools, Binney & Smith salespeople witnessed the poor-quality chalk used on blackboards. Through experimentation, the company soon developed a high-grade chalk that didn't produce dust when erased. It became a successful product, buoyed by the Gold Medal it won at the 1902 St. Louis Exposition.

At the same time, the company was refining a multipurpose crayon. By combining dry carbon black and mixing it with various waxes, they produced a black crayon that they named "Staonal," since it would "stay on all" surfaces, including wood and paper.

With pencils and the new chalk, sales reps once again took notice of an opportunity in the schools. Colored wax pencils being used by the students were of poor quality. Only artists were able to afford the high-quality imported colored wax pencils. The partners realized their success with black crayons could be duplicated in various colors, and experimentation was once again active at the Easton plant.

By 1903, Binney & Smith had developed a line of colored crayons. Edwin Binney's wife Alice, a schoolteacher, coined the name Crayola by joining *craie,* the French word meaning chalk, with *ola,* from oleaginous, meaning oily. The term was well chosen because the crayons are, to this day, made mostly of colored pigment and paraffin wax, an oil derivative.

The early crayons were made in small batches, stirred and poured by hand. After drying, they were sent to the upper floor of the factory where a legion of young women hand-rolled the labels onto the crayons, much the way cigars were labeled. Next they were hand-packed into boxes and then placed into wooden shipping crates. By 1904 the company was producing 16 different-colored crayons. A box of 8 sold for a nickel, and a box of all 16 colors sold for a dime.

The company had another significant success during the early 1900s. Automobile tires were generally built around a canvas carcass, to which was applied a tread mixture made of rubber, zinc oxide, and other chemicals to give it strength. This process yielded all-white tires that lasted about 5,000 miles.

The B.F. Goodrich Company of Akron, Ohio, had developed a new tire, built around a carcass made of heavy cotton cords instead of canvas, that lasted considerably longer than other tires. In an attempt to distinguish the new tires from the old, Goodrich added Binney & Smith carbon black, a product sold by the Pigment Division. As a bonus, it was discovered that the material added strength to the tire.

In late 1911, Goodrich placed an order for 1 million pounds per year of carbon black to a startled Binney & Smith salesman, who immediately transmitted the news to Harold Smith in New York. Smith himself traveled to Akron and finalized the contract, despite the fact that he had to organize all the company suppliers into a new company, the Columbian Carbon Company. Eventually, the Binney & Smith holding in Columbian and its Pigment Division were sold off.

C. Harold Smith lived the rest of his life in New York City with his wife and two children, a son, Sidney, who joined the company in 1912 and became chairman of the board of directors in 1935, and a daughter, Bertha. Smith was the consummate world traveler, maintaining friendships throughout the world. As the company grew, Smith documented his travels and outlined business philosophies in four books that he personally wrote.

Edwin and Alice Binney were a quiet, artistic couple. Very early in their marriage they moved to Connecticut, and thus Edwin became one of New York City's earliest commuters. They purchased and renovated a pre–Civil War plantation in North Carolina and maintained citrus groves in Florida. The Florida venture grew so large, in fact, that to handle his crops, Binney organized the Indian River Refrigeration Terminal Company.

Harold Smith died in 1931, followed three years later by Edwin Binney. The cousins combined their various talents with hard work to build a company that became recognized around the world. The Crayola brand name is now recognized by 99 percent of Americans. The 1991 Landor Image Power Survey ranked Crayola 51st of all world brands in terms of the brand's recognizability and consumers' esteem for the brand.

Today, Binney & Smith is owned by Hallmark Cards, Inc., of Kansas City, Missouri. The company employs more than 2,500 people worldwide who make an average of 5 million crayons each day, as well as a host of other products. Since Binney & Smith first developed the Crayola crayon, more than 100 billion have been sold.

SOURCES: Binney & Smith Inc. archives; *The Story of a Rainbow: Binney & Smith,* Binney & Smith Inc., 1961

Clarence Birdseye

[Birds Eye Frozen Foods]

Clarence Birdseye was born on October 9, 1886, in Brooklyn, New York, one of eight children born to Clarence F. and Ada (Underwood) Birdseye. While young Clarence was in his teens, the family moved to Montclair, New Jersey.

After graduating from high school, Birdseye entered Amherst College, where he studied entomology, ornithology, mammology, and other sciences. However, lack of sufficient family funds forced him to leave college in 1910. He was able to obtain a job as a naturalist with the U.S. Department of Agriculture's Biological Survey, collecting specimens of animal and bird life in New Mexico and Arizona.

Birdseye had met Eleanor Gannett in Washington, D.C., but his poor financial condition precluded thoughts of marriage at that time. When he learned that there was good money to be made in fur trapping in Canada, Birdseye secured a job with the Hudson Bay Trading Company, and one year later, he struck off on his own, setting up operations on the Atlantic Coast of Labrador.

Within three years, he was making enough money to support a family and, on August 21, 1915, married Eleanor. The couple moved back to the isolation of Labrador, where they lived for the next two years. He then landed a job as a purchasing agent for the U.S. Housing Corporation and later as an assistant to the president of the U.S. Fisheries Association.

In 1922, Birdseye launched his first private seafood venture, a wholesale fish distributorship located in lower Manhattan. The highly perishable nature of fish became very frustrating to Birdseye, and even his costly practice of packing fish in dry ice was not foolproof. From his days in Labrador, he recalled that fish that were quickly frozen tended to retain a fresh taste when later cooked.

Birdseye invested $7 in salt, ice, and an electric fan and started experimenting with rapid freezing techniques in the corner of a New York City ice plant. Soon, a successful freezing process was identified, and Birdseye was able to find financial support for a Manhattan plant. However, one of the backers fell into personal bankruptcy, sidetracking the venture.

In 1924, the company was successfully restructured, and the owners decided that Gloucester, Massachusetts, would be a more appropriate location. By 1925 the company, called General Foods Company, was producing frozen haddock fillets packed in plain cardboard boxes.

Birdseye sold the company to the Postum Company in 1929, but he remained on the payroll through 1934 as he continued to perfect his frozen food technology. Postum renamed the business the Birds Eye Frosted Food Company, and the Postum Company changed its corporate name to General Foods Corporation later in 1929.

Birdseye spent the next 25 years working on new inventions, such as a reflecting lightbulb, an electric fishing reel, and a recoilless harpoon for whale hunters. Working in his kitchen, he developed a new process for dehydrating foods. He and his wife also wrote a book on wildflowers.

Clarence Birdseye died on October 7, 1956, at the age of 69. At the time of his death, he owned nearly 300 patents.

SOURCE: Kraft Foods, Inc. archives

Melville R. Bissell, Anna Bissell

[Bissell Inc.]

Melville and Anna Bissell had a problem in their small crockery shop in Grand Rapids, Michigan. The daily shipments of china and glass were packed in protective sawdust, which promptly worked its way into the shop's carpet. Melville was an avid tinkerer, and in 1876 the first Bissell carpet sweeper was built for a market of one—his wife Anna.

Customers who witnessed the sweeper in action started asking where they could purchase the device. Convinced that a market existed, the room above the shop became Melville's production facility. Anna took to the streets and sold the sweeper to retail outlets.

Sales climbed steadily, and in 1883 the Bissells purchased two local sweeper companies (primarily for their management talent) and built a five-story brick factory. No sooner was the new factory producing when a fire in a neighboring building spread to Bissell's facility and burned it to the ground. Melville and Anna mortgaged their home and personal property to restore the plant, and it was quickly back in production.

A second tragedy was not far behind. A new Bissell model proved defective, and Melville was forced to recall and destroy the entire output at a loss of $35,000. However, the recall only strengthened Bissell's reputation for integrity and reliability, and the company became a dominant force in sweepers.

Then a third tragedy struck. In March of 1889, the 45-year-old Melville Bissell contracted pneumonia and was dead within a week. Anna Bissell didn't miss a beat. She assumed Melville's job and became one of America's first female corporate chief executives, a job she would hold into the 1920s. Anna quickly introduced Bissell sweepers to the international market. Queen Victoria endorsed Bissells for her palace, and English housewives referred to their sweeping chores as "Bisselling" the carpet.

When American homes were wired with electricity, Anna was reluctant to enter the market of electric-powered vacuum cleaners. Just as that market started to gain popularity in the early 1930s, the Depression interrupted its momentum because families couldn't afford the luxury of such appliances. Thus, Anna's hesitation had saved the company considerable research and production costs.

Melville R. Bissell Jr. succeeded Anna in the 1920s. He was succeeded by his nephew, Melville R. Bissell III in 1953, who was succeeded by John M. Bissell. The company expanded into floor care products, such as Bissell Rug Shampoo and the lightweight Shampoomaster.

SOURCES: Bissell, Inc., archives; *Great American Brands*, by David Powers Cleary, Fairchild Publications, 1981

S. Duncan Black, Alonzo G. Decker Sr.

[The Black & Decker Corporation]

S. Duncan Black and Alonzo G. Decker were both born and raised in rural Maryland communities outside Baltimore during the late 1800s. Decker, whose father died when he was seven, was forced to quit school after the seventh grade to help support the family. His first job was ladling molten brass in a foundry. Through the intercession of his girlfriend, who later became his wife, Decker landed a less taxing job with Boyden Air Brake.

Because of his remarkable engineering aptitude, he was soon transferred to the engineering department of the parent company, National Composotype. There he was assigned to an engineering team that produced an automatic type-molding machine. At age 22, Decker was being sent across the country to demonstrate and install the machine, and he was even sent to England to negotiate foreign distribution with Lord Northcliffe, who promptly offered $1 million for manufacturing rights.

Decker delivered the offer to his employer and, full of optimism, got married. Unfortunately, National Composotype didn't act quickly on the matter, and Lord Northcliffe lost interest. The fiasco discouraged Decker, who promptly quit and took a job as an $18 per week engineer at Rowland Telegraph Company, where he met Black.

S. Duncan Black had a much easier childhood than Decker. He completed elementary school and attended a high school that was academically on par with many colleges. Upon leaving the school, Black was hired by the Rowland Telegraph Company to trace engineering drawings. Decker joined the company in 1906, and the two men, both age 23, became close friends.

Although both men were exemplary employees, there was little room for advancement for Black in sales or for Decker in engineering. When Rowland refused to meet the $25 per week offer of another company, Decker quit. One of his loyal customers encouraged Decker to start his own company, promising to steer as much business as possible his way.

Encouraged by the support, Decker opened his own shop and tried to persuade Black to join him as a partner. Black, who was married with three children, was initially reluctant to jeopardize a secure income. However, when Rowland cut his sales commission, Black gave Decker's offer serious consideration.

In the fall of 1910, Black and Decker each put up $600 and, with $3,000 from other investors, launched The Black & Decker Manufacturing Company. Black raised his share by selling his Model T Ford to Decker's father-in-law. Decker raised his by mortgaging his house. Their first products, manufactured to the designs and specifications of others, included a milk bottle cap machine, a vest-pocket adding machine, a postage stamp splitting and coiling machine, machinery for the U.S. Mint, a candy-dipping machine, a shock absorber, and a cotton picker.

Despite this early success, the partners wanted to develop their own proprietary products that would appeal to a broad market. Their first such product was a lightweight air compressor for the automotive aftermarket, which was well received. Their second product, however, became something of a signature product that defined the company: a portable ½-inch electric drill with a patented pistol grip and trigger switch. The drill, which was introduced in 1917, can now be viewed at the Smithsonian.

While Decker engineered their products, Black was a progressive salesman with an eye toward national advertising. In the 1920s, two buses were converted into schoolrooms on wheels to tour the United States and offer product demonstrations to salesmen and plant operators. The company also moved beyond American borders, forming subsidiaries in Canada in 1922 and Britain in 1925.

During the Depression, the company bought a six-passenger airplane and transformed it into a flying showroom for power tools used in reconditioning aircraft engines, and these products were taken directly to the end users. After surviving the rigors of the Depression and World War II, Black & Decker expanded beyond the industrial and professional power tool markets and became the world's major manufacturer of consumer power tools.

S. Duncan Black served as president of Black & Decker from 1910 until his death on April 15, 1951, at the age of 68. He was replaced by his longtime partner, Alonzo G. Decker, who served as president until his death on March 18, 1956.

Today, Black & Decker is a diversified worldwide manufacturing and marketing company with annual sales of nearly $5 billion and a net market value of more than $3 billion. Products include portable electric power tools, lawn and garden products, household products, security hardware, plumbing products, and commercial and industrial products.

SOURCE: The Black & Decker Corporation archives

Isaac E. Blake

[Conoco, Inc.]

After making and losing a small fortune in the Pennsylvania oil industry, Isaac Blake moved to Utah and established a petroleum marketing firm. Through growth and merger, the company became Conoco.

Isaac E. Blake was born on August 4, 1844, in Bolton, Canada, one of eleven children born to American parents. His father was a Methodist Episcopal minister who was killed in the Civil War while serving as a battlefield chaplain.

Not long after the war ended, young Isaac moved to Pennsylvania to pursue oil exploration. By 1869, 25-year-old Blake was clearing as much as $100,000 annually selling crude oil. However, the oil business was highly speculative, and soon Blake lost his entire savings and inventory.

By the mid-1870s, Blake had settled in Ogden, Utah, where he was determined to enter the less-volatile marketing end of the oil business. In 1875, he led a group of investors in founding the Continental Oil and Transportation Company, with the following objectives: "in the main the producing, purchasing, refining, transporting, selling and delivering and dealing in petroleum, and in all its products of every kind."

Blake's venture achieved success in marketing oil products in the eastern United States. His product line consisted of coal oil, kerosene, candles, axle grease, and even some nonpetroleum products such as lard and paints. He was soon looking for opportunities further west, and in the late 1870s he established two more companies: the Pacific Coast Oil Company and the Continental Oil and Transportation Company of California.

While in California, Blake introduced several clever innovations, including the first railroad tank car, which included two large oil storage tanks placed at either end of a dry storage compartment. He also introduced a horse-drawn tank wagon. His California ventures quickly became petroleum suppliers serving Rocky Mountain mining communities. He was also a major exporter of products to the Hawaiian Islands, Samoa, and Japan.

In 1885, Blake sold his interests, and Continental was merged with John D. Rockefeller's Standard Oil Company. In 1913, when the Supreme Court dissolved Standard Oil, Continental was spun off as an independent entity once again. The company continued to grow and, in 1919, merged with the Maryland Oil Company, which had been founded by Ernest W. Maryland.

In 1979, the corporate name was changed to Conoco. Today, Conoco is an integrated, international petroleum company employing 16,000 people and operating in 30 countries around the world. Headquartered in Houston, Texas, Conoco is the energy subsidiary of DuPont.

SOURCE: Conoco, Inc. archives

Henry W. Bloch, Richard Bloch

[H&R Block Corporation]

The Bloch family has a long history as American pioneers. Henry and Richard's paternal grandfather traveled west as a scout for Kit Carson, eventually settling down and opening a general store along the Kansas-Nebraska border. His son (Henry and Richard's father) was a successful Kansas City attorney who refused to accept any partners, claiming it would add to his business and detract from his family time.

As he was finishing his degree at the University of Michigan, Henry W. Bloch was drafted into the military. Following a tour of World War II combat duty with the Eighth Air Force, Henry enrolled in and attended Harvard, where he developed an interest in operating his own business. He later returned to his native Kansas City.

Henry's interest in business persisted, and within a year he and his brother Leon established a company to provide advertising, bookkeeping, accounting, and legal services for small businesses. The first year of the venture was not encouraging, and Leon left the company to attend law school.

At his mother's urging, Henry brought his younger brother Richard into the business. As a favor, they prepared their clients' income tax returns, and soon others in the neighborhood sought them for income tax preparation assistance, for which they charged $5. Although they made $1,800 by doing 300 returns during the tax season of 1954, both brothers were exhausted from the long workdays and were prepared to discontinue tax services.

One of their many customers worked at the *Kansas City Star.* He convinced Henry and Richard to take out two small ads the following tax season. If it didn't generate substantial business, the brothers would drop the business. The timing of the experiment proved critical. The Internal Revenue Service (IRS) had decided to discontinue their longtime practice of assisting taxpayers in preparing their returns. Additionally, the Bloch brothers' newspaper ad ran the day after most people received their W-2 forms. Their small office was flooded with clients, and that year the Blochs grossed $25,000 preparing tax returns.

Henry and Richard were convinced they had identified a lucrative market, and the H&R Block Company was officially established. They decided to use *Block* spelled with a *k* because of peoples' tendency to mispronounce their last name as "blotch."

Predictably, early opposition came from accountants and attorneys who felt the Blochs were challenging their domain. Despite this complaint, the Blochs felt that their target customers were the millions of Americans who prepare their own taxes and that wealthy people with complicated taxes would continue to patronize accountants and attorneys.

They established a New York office for the following tax season and grossed $56,000. Their formula for success has been constant since the early years: "Do the finest possible work; charge fairly; and stand behind the work." Any client who was audited by the IRS could count on H&R Block to stand with them through the process. This policy has generated considerable name recognition and repeat business over the years.

In 1957 they began to franchise the business so they could expand rapidly. One of their most innovative marketing moves was a deal struck with Sears in 1973. In exchange for a percentage of sales, H&R Block was permitted to staff booths inside hundreds of Sears department stores.

Educating their employees (and the general public) is of paramount importance to the company. Each fall, the company conducts training classes throughout the country. Nearly 100,000 people now pay the modest tuition for the course, and a great many return each year to keep abreast of changes in the tax code. The company also prepares tax guides that are sold to the general public through bookstores.

Starting in the late 1970s, H&R Block expanded the company through the acquisition of other promising companies. Probably the best known of these is CompuServe, which was purchased in 1980 for stock and cash totaling $23 million. CompuServe, then a ten-year-old computer time-share company, now boasts annual revenue of nearly $500 million. Also in 1980, the company added Hyatt Legal Services to its holdings, although it has subsequently been spun off.

Today, H&R Block has sales from its Tax Services division approaching $1.1 billion and total sales approaching $2 billion. Henry W. Bloch still serves as chairman of the board of directors.

While Henry provided creative, stable leadership, Richard Bloch had always been considered the more aggressive of the brothers. At age 9 he purchased a manual printing press and started doing small jobs for his school, and by age 12 the business was doing so well that he acquired three automatic presses and was doing work for several Kansas City schools. After graduating from high school, Richard sold his printing business to an Iowa college.

In March 1978, Richard Bloch was diagnosed with terminal lung cancer. However, following extensive treatment, he is in remission and celebrated his 70th birthday in February 1996. He left active involvement with the company and in 1979 established the R.A. Bloch Cancer Foundation. He wrote three books on conquering cancer, copies of which are sent free to every public library in America and to anyone requesting them.

SOURCES: H&R Block Corporation archives; Thomas Goldwasser, *Family Pride: Profiles of Five of America's Best-Run Family Businesses*

Rose Blumkin

[Nebraska Furniture Mart]

Rose Blumkin joined her husband in America two years after he fled Russia to avoid serving the czar during World War I. The couple owned various small stores in Iowa and Nebraska until Rose's interest in furniture led to her founding of Blumkin's, which was later renamed the Nebraska Furniture Mart.

Rose Gorelick was born on December 3, 1893, in the small Russian-Jewish village of Schidrin, near Minsk, Russia. Her father was a rabbi, and her mother operated a small grocery store. The couple and their eight children lived in a two-room log cabin, sleeping on straw mattresses. As a young girl, she heard villagers' tales of relatives who had emigrated to America, where they had not only escaped the czar's Cossacks, but had also found rewards for hard work.

At age six, Rose went to work in her mother's store, picking up whatever education she could over the next several years. At age 13, she left home to find a better way to help support her family. She walked barefoot 18 miles to the nearest train station and, with the equivalent of 4¢ in her pocket, knocked on more than two dozen shop doors in the next town until she found a job. By the time she was 16, she was promoted to shop manager, supervising six married men.

Four years later, Rose married Isadore Blumkin, a shoe salesman. When World War I broke out, the Blumkins wanted to leave Russia. They had only enough money for one to leave, so Isadore left for America to avoid service in the czar's army.

Rose stayed behind and opened a small grocery store, and by 1917, she had saved enough money to join her husband. She took a train to the Chinese-Siberian border and convinced a border guard that she was on a shopping expedition and would bring him a bottle of vodka if he would let her pass. The guard agreed, and Rose was soon aboard a peanut boat bound for America.

An immigrant aid organization and the American Red Cross helped her find Isadore in Fort Dodge, Iowa. The couple was reunited and, for the next two years, operated a laundry and junk store. However, Rose was unable to grasp the English language. Frustrated, they moved to Omaha, Nebraska, into an established community of hundreds of Russian- and Yiddish-speaking immigrants.

In 1919, the Blumkins opened a secondhand clothing store. Within three years, they had saved enough money to help bring the rest of Rose's family to America. Over the next several years, Rose and Isadore raised three daughters and a son.

When the Depression hit, sales at the family store dropped steadily to a trickle. Rose, who had been staying home to raise the children, became active in the business again. She later recalled: "I know how to make money. . . . You buy a box for $10, sell it for $11. . . . Everybody else makes 40 to 50 percent. It's too much!" Rose printed 10,000 circulars offering to dress any man from head to toe for $5. The next day the store sold $800 worth of merchandise.

Rose, known affectionately in Omaha as "Mrs. B," became interested in furniture. She started taking customers into local wholesalers and letting them pick out what they wanted. She then purchased the furniture and resold it at a 10 percent markup. While this was well below the 50 percent markup charged by established retailers, Mrs. B's enterprise went unnoticed because of the low volume.

In 1937, Mrs. B borrowed $500 from her brother and rented a 3,000-square-foot basement storeroom, which came to be known as the Nebraska Furniture Mart. Sales grew steadily, and other retailers started taking notice. They complained to the wholesalers, who in order to protect their longtime customers refused to sell to Mrs. B. Undaunted, Mrs. B traveled to other cities, buying furniture at discount or wholesale prices that still allowed her to undercut her competitors in Omaha.

The Nebraska Furniture Mart continued to grow, but it had its share of setbacks. Isadore Blumkin died in 1951. Sales slumped during the Korean War. At one particularly low ebb, Mrs. B rented the Omaha City Auditorium and held a massive three-day sale. The promotion brought in $250,000, and from that day forward Mrs. B. was no longer in debt.

Mrs. B and her son, Louie Blumkin, continued to build the business until, in September, 1983, another successful Omaha entrepreneur, Warren Buffett, bought 90 percent of the company's stock for $55 million. Mrs. B remained active until 1989, when she quit after a dispute with her grandchildren.

At the age of 95, she launched Mrs. B's Warehouse, building it on an 11-acre site next door to the Nebraska Furniture Mart. Within two years, she was eating away at the market share she spent so many years building with the Nebraska Furniture Mart, still being operated by family members. In 1991, her point had been made, and Mrs. B sold her new venture to Nebraska Furniture Mart.

On December 3, 1993, Rose Blumkin celebrated her 100th birthday. Today, the Nebraska Furniture Mart companies enjoy annual sales of nearly $270 million.

SOURCES: Nebraska Furniture Mart archives; "The Life and Times of Rose Blumkin, An American Original," *Omaha World-Herald*, December 12, 1993

William E. Boeing

[Boeing Airplane Company]

William E. Boeing was an active lumberman in the Pacific Northwest who became fascinated with airplanes. In 1915, he started a small plant to build airplanes, and this eventually grew into the Boeing Company. He also started an airline transport company that grew into United Airlines, and he assisted in founding a manufacturing company that became United Technologies.

William Edward Boeing was born on October 1, 1881, in Detroit, Michigan. After receiving an education in America and in Switzerland, he entered Yale University. However, he was anxious to follow the path of his father, a German immigrant, who was a wealthy and successful lumberman in midwestern United States. In 1903, Boeing left Yale and moved to the Grays Harbor area of the state of Washington, where he quickly built his own successful timber business.

In 1910, 28-year-old Boeing traveled to Los Angeles to see firsthand the flying machines that he had heard so much about. He developed a love of airplanes on the spot as he watched fliers from the Glenn Curtiss company compete in air races against Frenchman Louis Paulhan. By 1915 he was taking flying lessons from Glenn Martin, founder of Martin-Marietta.

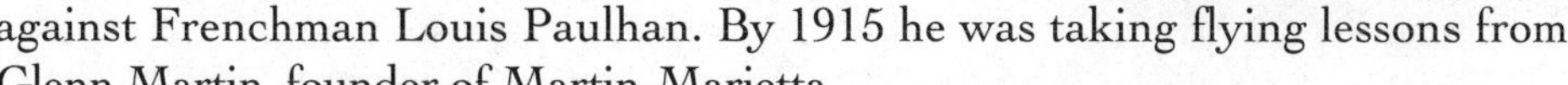

Boeing befriended Lt. Conrad Westervelt, a Navy engineer stationed near Seattle. Soon Westervelt designed a twin-float seaplane, which they named the B&W (for their last names). Boeing then leased a large hangar, hired a crew of 21 shipwrights, carpenters, cabinetmakers, and seamstresses, and built two of the biplanes with wood, linen, and piano wire.

The planes were finished in June 1916. Impatient when the test pilot was late for the maiden flight, Boeing took the controls himself, gunned the engine, and lifted off for a quarter-mile trip. Despite losing Westervelt due to a military transfer before the planes were finished, Boeing was excited with the promising airplane design and pushed forward. On July 15, 1916, 34-year-old William E. Boeing incorporated his small operation as Pacific Aero Products. Soon afterward he changed the name to Boeing Airplane Company.

Boeing was unable to attract much attention to the planes and sold them to the government of New Zealand. Undaunted, he expanded his brain trust by hiring one of the few aeronautical engineers in the country and recruiting recent graduates from local universities. He guaranteed a loan to cover the $700 per week payroll (wages ranged from 14¢ per hour to $300 per month) while a second plane, the Model C, was designed and built.

This time, luck was with him. The United States had entered World War I and needed airplanes. After purchasing two Model C planes for tests, the Navy placed an order for 50 more.

The prosperity was short-lived. By 1919, the war had ended and there was a glut of used war airplanes on the market. The enterprising Boeing tried to revive the sliding company. On March 2, 1919, he and another pilot flew to Canada, picked up a pouch of Canadian mail, and returned the next day to Seattle. This was the first international airmail flight into the United States.

Yet the market was not ready to support that venture, and burdened with an empty 50,000-square-foot factory, Boeing started building boats and furniture to keep the company in business. He also secured some contracts to refurbish World War I planes, and maintaining his faith in the future of airplanes, he built his third model—dubbed the B-1—in his spare time.

Finally, in 1921, Boeing was awarded a contract to build 200 MB-3A pursuit planes for the United States Army. Subsequent contracts solidified Boeing as one of the country's largest airplane builders, and by 1928 the number of employees had reached 800. Propelled by the growth, Boeing listed his company on the New York Stock Exchange.

In 1927, Boeing pursued another opportunity. The United States Post Office announced its intention to subcontract all transcontinental airmail routes. Boeing and his staff designed the Model 40A, designed to carry passengers and 1,000 pounds of mail. He was awarded the San Francisco–Chicago mail route and soon added the Seattle-to-Los Angeles route. By 1928, his new company, Boeing Air Transport, was flying a quarter of the airmail in the United States. Through sales and acquisitions, this company eventually became United Airlines.

William Boeing later became involved with the formation of the United Aircraft and Transport Corporation, a holding company that brought together the Boeing Airplane Company and Boeing Air Transport with Pratt & Whitney, Chance Vought, Hamilton Propeller Company, Stearman, and Sikorsky.

In 1934 the government proclaimed the venture a monopoly and ordered it to split up. As a result, United Aircraft was broken into three parts: United Airlines, United Technologies, and the Boeing Airplane Company. William E. Boeing resigned as chairman of the board, retiring at the age of 52 and thereafter devoting himself to breeding horses.

William Edward Boeing died on September 28, 1956, at the age of 74. Despite the fact that he was active in the aviation industry for only 18 years, he was a major factor in developing a mature aerospace and defense industry.

SOURCE: Boeing Corporate archives

Hector Boiardi

[Chef Boyardee]

After learning to cook in his family's restaurant business in Italy, Hector Boiardi immigrated to America and worked in several well-known hotel kitchens until opening his own restaurant in 1924. Satisfied customers frequently asked for take-home dinners, which eventually became a successful sideline. By the 1930s, he had originated a nationally marketed take-home Italian pasta and sauce dinner, which he named Chef Boyardee.

Hector Boiardi was born in Piacenza, Italy, in the late 1800s into an Italian family who had been active in the food and hospitality business for many generations. At age 11, he started his apprenticeship to become a chef. Boiardi emigrated to America six years later to join his older brother, Paul, who was the maître d'hôtel at the Plaza Hotel in New York City.

After working at the Plaza, Boiardi worked in kitchens at Claridges, Rector's, the Ritz-Carlton, and the Hotel Greenbriar in West Virginia. At the age of 24, he was hired to head the kitchen at the new Hotel Winton in Cleveland, Ohio. Because he was so young, Boiardi decided to grow his trademark mustache to help him look more authoritative.

Three years later, in 1924, Boiardi and his wife, Helen, opened their own Cleveland restaurant: Il Giardino d'Italia. Patrons had to pass through the kitchen to get into the dining room. As they departed, many asked for portions of his delicious sauce to take home. Boiardi gladly filled empty glass milk bottles. When the customers complained that their meals didn't taste the same at home, Boiardi started to send along uncooked pasta and his special blend of imported grated Parmesan cheese.

A food broker named Bill Swayze, a loyal patron at Boiardi's restaurant, made a suggestion to the chef: Why not market the take-home spaghetti dinners nationally? Swayze arranged a demonstration for truck drivers in the food distribution business, and after Boiardi cooked a spaghetti dinner in a truck garage, the drivers flooded him with orders.

By 1928, Boiardi opened a separate processing plant for his sideline business. He also reluctantly changed the name of his product to *Boyardee* because customers had trouble pronouncing his last name. After outgrowing two more plants, Boiardi looked for a new home.

In 1938, he acquired an empty silk mill in the central Pennsylvania community of Milton, where he could be close to fertile soil that yielded high-quality crops. Upon his arrival in Milton, Boiardi immediately contracted with local farmers for 1,000 acres of tomatoes, and within months the new plant was producing spaghetti dinners. Shortly thereafter, World War II broke out and the plant was converted to prepare food for soldiers. Boiardi later said that his greatest challenge was to convert carloads of ham and eggs into palatable field rations for our troops.

After the war, Boiardi was approached with an offer from American Home Foods to purchase Chef Boyardee, and on February 1, 1946, the sale was completed. But that didn't end Boiardi's involvement, and he remained a consultant to the company for 33 years, until his death in 1985 at the age of 87.

In 1996, Hicks, Muse, Tate, and Furst, a leading private investment firm, together with C. Dean Metropoulos & Company, its food industry management affiliate, acquired American Home Food Products. The company, now called International Home Foods, Inc., continues to manufacture Chef Boyardee prepared pastas. In 1997, the company is projected to have sales of over $1 billion, of which an estimated $400 million are expected to come from Chef Boyardee products.

SOURCE: International Home Foods, Inc., archives

Edwin G. Booz, James L. Allen, Carl L. Hamilton, George A. Fry

[Booz Allen & Hamilton, Inc.]

Building on the master's thesis he prepared at Northwestern University, Edwin Booz launched a one-man firm to prepare "investigations and inquiries" into the management practices of Chicago businesses. He was later joined by two other Northwestern alumni, James Allen and George Fry (who later left the company), as well as a lumber executive named Carl Hamilton. Eventually, Booz Allen & Hamilton became one of the most respected management consulting firms in the world.

Edwin George Booz (photo at left) was of Pennsylvania Dutch and English descent, the fifth of seven sons born to Thomas H. and Sally (Spencer) Booz. His mother died when he was only four years old. Despite the hardships that followed, Booz received a bachelor's degree in economics and a master's degree in psychology from Northwestern University. His master's thesis, "Mental Tests for Vocational Fitness," established the foundation for his company and lifelong pursuit.

While in graduate school, he worked for 16 months as an advertising statistician for *Woman's World,* a large Chicago-based magazine. The man who hired him was so impressed with Booz's work that he urged him to establish his own business. Upon graduation in 1914, Booz took the advice and hung out his shingle. His early work was performing investigations into the market conditions of various industries.

When World War I broke out, Booz was drafted into the U.S. Army, where he served in various clerical and information support positions. By the end of the war, Booz was a major in the inspector general's department, where he was constantly reorganizing and perfecting the way that the military managed its affairs.

In 1919, the 30-year-old Booz returned to Chicago and opened the Edwin G. Booz Business Engineering Service. To establish his firm, Booz took out a modest loan with a local bank, where his talents were spotted by Sewell Avery, one of the bank's directors. Avery, who organized the United States Gypsum Company, soon contracted Booz to analyze his own management structures and to identify efficient improvements.

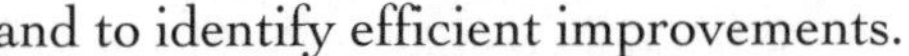

In 1925, Booz was joined by his first associate, George Fry, who was another Northwestern graduate. The two men worked for several respected companies, including the *Chicago Daily News.* By 1929, there was plenty of work but not enough money to hire another employee. Along came James L. Allen (pictured left), a 25-year-old Northwestern graduate who passed up several good job offers to become an associate.

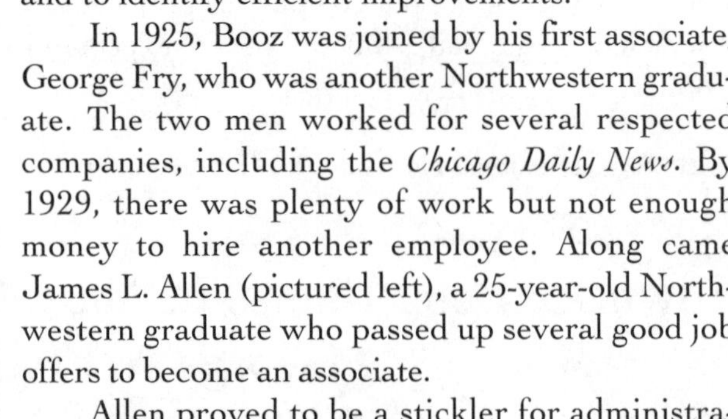

Allen proved to be a stickler for administrative detail, which served the clients well but was not appreciated internally. Booz focused on the work of clients and paid less attention to in-house systems, which mortified Allen. In the early

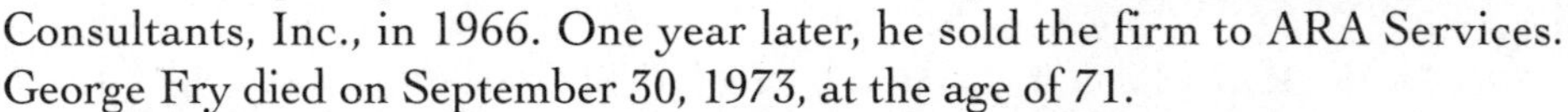

1930s, Allen left the firm and went to work with a local duplicating-machine company, and Carl A. Hamilton (photo right), a 47-year-old marketing whiz from Weyerhaeuser enterprises, joined Booz and Fry.

Two years after he left the firm, Allen decided to return. In 1936, Edwin Booz renamed the firm Booz, Fry, Allen and Hamilton. The list of clients continued to grow, and many were well beyond the Chicago area. During World War II, the firm was closely involved with a number of sensitive military projects.

During the war, George Fry decided to strike out on his own. He left the firm in 1942 and formed George Fry & Associates, renamed Fry Consultants, Inc., in 1966. One year later, he sold the firm to ARA Services. George Fry died on September 30, 1973, at the age of 71.

Upon Fry's departure in 1942, the firm was renamed once again, this time as Booz Allen & Hamilton. Sadly, Carl Hamilton died of a heart attack on May 27, 1946, at the age of 58. Edwin Booz, however, had changed the name of the firm for the last time, and the memory of Carl Hamilton was kept alive in the firm's name.

By 1947, the company was busy servicing the postwar economy, with more than 100 employees and annual sales of $2 million. The 1950s started with another tragedy when Edwin G. Booz, founder of the firm, died on October 14, 1951, at the age of 64. This left Jim Allen as the sole remaining original partner, a role he would maintain for the next four decades.

The company had built a secure international reputation by the end of the 1950s. *Time* magazine called the firm "the company doctors" and "the world's largest, most prestigious management consulting firm." In 1977, the company surpassed $100 million in annual revenues and passed $500 million in 1990. Today, Booz Allen & Hamilton employs more than 7,000 people and has annual revenues of over $1.2 billion.

SOURCES: Booz Allen & Hamilton, Inc., archives; *Booz Allen & Hamilton: Seventy Years of Client Service, 1914–1984,* by Jim Bowman, 1984

Gail Borden

[Borden, Inc.]

After frequent moves, business ventures, and other life changes, Gail Borden discovered a method of removing water from milk, enabling it to last for long periods without spoiling. The product came to be known as Eagle Brand Condensed Milk and made Borden a household name.

Gail Borden was born on November 9, 1801, on a 250-acre farm in Norwich, New York, the eldest of seven children. His ancestors had immigrated from England to Massachusetts in 1637. Gail, like many Bordens before him, learned the trade of surveying at a young age.

The Borden family moved to Kentucky when Gail was 13, and he helped his father lay out the town of Covington. Soon afterward, the Bordens moved to the territory of Indiana, where Gail attended school for 18 months. It would be the only formal education he ever received.

By 1822, Borden was teaching school and doing surveying in Mississippi. In 1826, at age 24, he was appointed as the official surveyor for Amite County, Mississippi. Still restless, Gail and his new wife joined his brother Tom in Texas, where he continued surveying. He also founded a newspaper, the *Telegraph and Texas Register,* which remained in business for more than 40 years. He became a voice of American dominance. His two newspaper partners fought in the war against Mexico, while Gail roused support by proclaiming, "Remember the Alamo!"

After the Republic of Texas was created, Gail moved his family to Galveston, where he was active in surveying, tax collecting, and real estate sales. He became one of the town's elders, and in keeping with his strong Baptist faith, relentlessly chased gamblers and other unsavory characters from the city. He also laid out the town of Houston, angling North Main and South Main Streets such that residents would enjoy the Gulf breeze coming out of the southeast.

Borden married his first wife, Penelope Mercer, in Mississippi in 1828. The couple had seven children. A year after her death in 1844, he married Azuba F. Stearns. This marriage was dissolved in 1854. In 1860 he married his third wife, Emeline Eunice Church, whom he preceded in death.

Gail eventually became fascinated with the creative process of invention. When his first wife died of yellow fever in 1844, he designed a building that would be refrigerated with ether through the summer. He suggested all Galveston citizens should live in the building during the summer to avoid the plague that spread during these hot months. Unfortunately, no one accepted the offer.

Borden also designed his "Terraqueous Machine," which was a modified Conestoga wagon equipped with sails. Theoretically, wind could propel it on land or on sea. The one and only field test was made in the Gulf of Mexico with many of Galveston's leading citizens on board, but after the machine upset and the dignitaries barely escaped drowning, plans were scrapped. Borden also designed a boat with oars that were to be powered with steam, but this never made it off the drawing board.

Turning his attention away from his mechanical failures, Borden experimented with removing water from food and beverages. His first food product was the "meat biscuit," which was made by boiling meat, filtering the resulting broth, and removing the water. This extract was then mixed with flour and baked. The biscuit was nutritious and long lasting; it even won a gold medal at the Great Council Exhibition in London in 1851. Despite modest sales, the meat biscuit failed in the marketplace because it simply tasted bad.

He next devised a method of condensing 6½ gallons of apple cider into 1 gallon. The molasses-like liquid could then be reconstituted by adding water. He also concentrated coffee, ½ teaspoonful of which, when added to water, would make a strong cup of coffee. While the cider venture was dropped, the instant coffee was marketed by Borden's company until the late 1920s.

Throughout his life, Borden was alternately wealthy and broke. Prior to the failed meat biscuit venture, he enjoyed a net worth of about $100,000 in 1850. Six years later, all his holdings were mortgaged to the limit, and his net income was about $30 per month. Undaunted, he pushed forward. "I don't lose half as much sleep on account of the loss of my property as I shall in perfecting my inventions," he said. "The one will soon be forgotten while the other may last for generations."

Despite his optimism, Borden was broke and was forced to return to New York with his children, who were sent to live with various relatives. Nearly at rock bottom, Borden came up with another idea. While returning from London, he witnessed several young babies in misery because of the lack of milk. As many as four children died on the trip.

Haunted by their suffering, Borden was determined to apply his condensing process to milk. However, his early experiments in a friend's New York City basement produced milk that tasted burnt. While visiting his children in 1853, Borden happened to stop at a Shaker colony in New Lebanon, New York, and observed the Shakers boiling fruit and maple syrup in airtight vacuum pans at low temperatures. Borrowing the idea (and one of their copper pans), Borden was able to produce a sweet-tasting condensed milk. Jubilant, he applied for a patent and started planning a new venture.

However, Borden would once again face adversity. First, the patent office turned back his application three times. It wasn't until August 19, 1856, that U.S. Patent Number 15,553 was awarded to him for the "concentration of sweet milk and extracts." Next, his poor business record (and threadbare personal appearance) worked against him, and he was forced to shut down his first plant in Wolcottville, Connecticut.

Once again, Borden found an answer while traveling. In 1857, he happened to be seated on a train next to a New York banker named Jeremiah Milbank. Upon hearing the story of the condensed milk, Milbank arranged for a large loan and newspaper publicity. Borden launched the New York Condensed Milk Company and opened a factory in Burrville, Connecticut. (In 1899, long after his death, the company was renamed the Borden Company in his honor.)

By 1859, annual sales reached nearly $50,000. Two years later his condensed milk was put into service by the Union Army during the Civil War. Gail Borden's lifelong pursuit finally paid off. Several competing products appeared, including one called Borden's, forcing Gail Borden's company to adopt the name Eagle Brand Condensed Milk.

Gail Borden died on January 11, 1874, in Borden County, Texas, southeast of Lubbock. (The county *and* the county seat of Gail were named in his honor.) He was buried ten days later in Woodlawn Cemetery, New York. At his direction, the following words were carved on his tombstone: "I tried and failed, I tried again and again and succeeded."

John Gail Borden, his youngest son, succeeded him as president. His oldest son, Henry Lee Borden, eventually became the third company president. One of John Gail Borden's sons, Lewis M. Borden, was the last director of the Borden company with the name of Borden. The grandson of Mary Jane Borden (Gail Borden's daughter), Marcus Munsill, was the last direct descendant of Gail Borden to serve on the board of directors. Marcus died in 1956.

In his lifetime, Gail Borden, a deeply religious man, helped establish Baylor University and supported various ministers, missionaries, and Protestant students. He also helped establish and finance numerous Protestant churches.

SOURCE: Borden, Inc., archives

Amar G. Bose

[Bose Corporation]

As a teenager in Philadelphia, Amar Bose, the son of an Indian immigrant, established a successful radio repair business. In 1947, he entered the Massachusetts Institute of Technology as a freshman, and he hasn't left yet. In addition to his academic profession, he researched audio technology and launched his own company that designed and marketed a revolutionary speaker system. Today, Bose is the world's largest manufacturer of component-quality loudspeakers and is one of the best-known names in the world in audio equipment.

Amar G. Bose grew up in Philadelphia, Pennsylvania, the only child of a salesman and a schoolteacher. Bose's father had been forced from his native India while helping Gandhi wrestle the country from British rule. The elder Bose pumped gas and washed dishes while working his way through Temple University. He maintained a role in the struggle for Indian independence and frequently welcomed Indian revolutionaries into his home.

The Bose family faced prejudice because of their dark skin color as well as financial struggles. At age 13, Amar decided to help with the money problems. He learned to repair radios, and when World War II broke out and many of the city's repairmen enlisted in the military, there remained a significant demand for local repair service. Bose enlisted many hardware stores to advertise for radio repairs and paid them a 10 percent commission for all referrals. Soon, he ran one of the largest repair services in Philadelphia.

Bose earned his B.S. (1952), M.S. (1952), and Sc.D. (1956) in electrical engineering at the Massachusetts Institute of Technology. Upon graduation in 1956, Bose was appointed to the position of assistant professor of electrical engineering at MIT. As a graduation present to himself, Bose set out to buy a good stereo system. However, he was disappointed in the quality of sound reproduced by the speakers available at that time.

Amar Bose, the consumer, transformed himself into Dr. Bose, the researcher. He and his grad students launched an exhaustive research project into *psychoacoustics,* the study of sounds as perceived by the human ear. They discovered that more than 80 percent of the sound that reaches a listener at a concert has first bounced off the ceiling, walls, and even the floor.

Bose surmised that one problem with speakers was that they were pointed directly at the listener. To correct this, he designed a speaker that reflected the sound rather than aiming it, and he proceeded to patent his new audio technologies. Unwilling to give up his teaching position at MIT, he hired one of his students, Sherwin Greenblatt, who was not only the company's *first* employee, but for the first year of operation he was the *only* employee. Today, Greenblatt is the company's president.

In 1968, the company unveiled its first product: the Bose 901 direct/reflecting loudspeaker. Not only were sales brisk in the early years, the speaker is still a best-seller today. More innovations followed, and in 1972 Bose introduced the first professional loudspeaker for performing musicians. Soon the Bose name became synonymous with high-quality sound.

Bose is a research-driven company that is not afraid to invest literally millions of dollars into an unproven technology. In 1979, General Motors approached Bose with a problem. Car stereos were of such poor quality that customers were ordering them without radios, then purchasing high-quality systems from electronics dealers. Without a commitment from GM to actually buy a finished product, Bose invested $13 million and four years into the development of car stereo systems. The risk paid off handsomely.

In 1994, after nine years of research, Bose introduced the Auditioner audio demonstration system, which enables designers to hear what a public place will actually sound like before it is built. Over the years, Bose has also made a considerable investment in stereo sound technology for televisions, noise-reducing headsets for air travel, and related applications.

In addition to his role as chairman and technical director for the Bose Corporation, Dr. Amar Bose retains his faculty appointment as professor of electrical engineering and computer science at MIT. Bose continues to be a privately held company, with sales in excess of $700 million. The company reinvests all profits into research and operations.

SOURCES: Bose Corporation archives; Jane Ammeson and Will Crockett, "Sound Is Golden for Dr. Bose," *Northwest Airlines Compass Readings*, February 1991

Samuel A. Boyd

[Stardust Hotel and Casino]

After losing his father at age 10, Samuel A. Boyd went to work at a soda fountain. Later his family moved to California, where Boyd worked on the boardwalk and, eventually, on gambling ships. When World War II broke out, Boyd moved his family to Las Vegas, where he worked at casinos in various capacities. Eventually, he became an owner of several of Las Vegas's best-known casinos, including the Sahara and the Stardust.

Samuel Addison Boyd was born on April 23, 1910, at Enid, Oklahoma, the fourth of six children born to William and Lotta (Cope) Boyd. Both the Boyd and Cope families were of Irish, Scotch, and English descent and had moved to the Oklahoma Territory in the 1890s, where Bill Boyd operated a small freight and taxi service and Lotta was a hat maker.

Shortly after the death of his father, 10-year-old Sam Boyd landed his first job at a local drugstore, where he worked at the soda fountain while standing on a box to see over the counter. In 1923, the family moved to Albuquerque,

New Mexico, then to Monterey Park, California, where Sam helped to support the family by selling oranges and lemonade.

The family moved once more, to Long Beach, California, where 17-year-old Boyd earned 10¢ an hour hawking games of chance on the boardwalk. There he met Mary Teresa Neuman, a Salt Lake City native, whom he eventually married.

In 1928, Boyd's boss sent him to work on a gambling ship anchored off the California coast. Soon, Boyd was running bingo games, dealing blackjack, throwing dice, and spinning the roulette wheels. From 1935 to 1940, his job frequently took him to Hawaii, where he helped establish bingo games.

Boyd returned to California in 1940, and in addition to running bingo parlors on offshore gaming ships, he worked for the Rendezvous Ballroom in Newport Beach. There, he gave an up-and-coming bandleader named Stan Kenton his first break.

When World War II broke out, the offshore gaming industry folded because of the obvious dangers at sea. The 31-year-old Boyd, his wife, and their only son headed for Las Vegas, Nevada, population 8,200. They arrived on Labor Day weekend, 1941, with about $30.

Both Sam and Mary Boyd landed jobs at the Jackpot Club, although one year later Mary turned her attention to raising their son. Sam was drafted and served in the U.S. Army from 1944 through 1946. Upon discharge, he was hired as a dealer at the Savoy Club. One year later, he was a pit boss at the El Rancho Vegas. He then moved to Lake Tahoe and Reno for three years, returning to Las Vegas in 1951 as a pit boss at the Thunderbird Hotel.

At age 42, Sam Boyd invested $10,000 to become a partner at the Sahara Hotel. For the next 20 years, he worked in various capacities at Sahara-owned properties. He also purchased The Wheel in nearby Henderson, renaming it the Eldorado Club. This was the first of the Boyd-owned casinos. In 1974, Boyd started building a string of casinos. His first was the Hotel Nevada and Casino. One year later, Sam Boyd's California Hotel and Casino opened, marking the beginning of The Boyd Group. In 1979, they opened Sam's Town Hotel and Gambling Hall, followed by Sam's Town Gold River in 1984. In 1984, The Boyd Group purchased the Stardust and the Fremont Hotel and Casino from Trans-sterling Corporation.

Samuel A. Boyd died on January 15, 1993, at age 82.

SOURCES: Stardust Hotel archives; Elaine Kartzmann, *Sam Boyd: Nevadan, An Informal Biography of a Las Vegas Gaming Innovator,* edited by Stanley W. Paher

Herbert W. Boyer, Robert A. Swanson

[Genentech, Inc.]

Herbert W. Boyer received his bachelor's degree in biology and chemistry in 1958 from St. Vincent College in Latrobe, Pennsylvania. He then was awarded his master's (1960) and doctorate (1963) degrees from the University of Pittsburgh.

In the early 1970s, Dr. Boyer, then a professor at the University of California at San Francisco, and Dr. Stanley Cohen of Stanford University pioneered a new field called *recombinant DNA technology.* The scientists have been honored for this and other achievements over the past two decades, including the 1996 award of the Lemelson-MIT Prize, the world's largest cash prize for American invention and innovation.

Robert A. Swanson, a 29-year-old venture capitalist, was intrigued with the work of Dr. Boyer. Swanson had received his B.S. and M.S. degrees from the Massachusetts Institute of Technology and had developed a good familiarity with both science and finance.

Swanson contacted Boyer and expressed an interest in learning more about the new technology. Boyer was predictably busy, but agreed to give young Swanson ten minutes. The two stepped out for a beer, and Swanson then laid out his vision for a private company that could commercialize Boyer's work. The ten-minute meeting lasted three hours, and by the end of it, Genentech—an acronym for *genetic engineering*—had been launched, with each founder contributing $500.

Swanson soon arranged significant venture funding, and Genentech was in business. During the 1970s, the company reached some impressive milestones: It produced the first human protein in a microorganism, cloned human insulin, and cloned the human growth hormone. Genentech marketed the first recombinant DNA drug, human insulin, through a licensing agreement with Eli Lilly in 1982.

The following year, Genentech received approval for Protropin, used for children with growth hormone inadequacy. It was the first recombinant pharmaceutical product to be manufactured and marketed by a biotechnology company. Several other innovations followed, including Activase, used to dissolve blood clots in heart attack patients, and Pulmozyme, used to treat cystic fibrosis.

In 1990, Genentech and Roche Holding Limited of Switzerland completed a $2.1 billion merger. Today, Genentech employs nearly 3,000 people, most of whom work on the sprawling 82-acre campus near San Francisco. Annual revenues are nearly $1 billion.

SOURCE: Genentech, Inc., archives

Caleb D. Bradham

[Pepsi-Cola Company]

Caleb Bradham, a young pharmacist in New Bern, North Carolina, began experimenting with soft drinks in 1893. Friends and shoppers sampled them at his drugstore soda fountain. His most popular formula, known as "Brad's Drink," was a unique combination of carbonated water, sugar, vanilla, rare oils, and cola nuts.

On August 28, 1898, he renamed his popular drink "Pepsi-Cola." It was quickly embraced by consumers, and Bradham elected to devote all his attention to building a business around this new soft drink. In 1902, he formed the Pepsi-Cola Company and secured a trademark. Within a year he had moved from his pharmacy into a leased warehouse and sold nearly 8,000 gallons of Pepsi syrup. A year later he purchased a building in New Bern and started selling 6-ounce bottles of Pepsi. Sales quickly reached 20,000 gallons per year.

Encouraged by the initial success, Bradham started expanding his operations, and in 1905 he established franchises in Charlotte and Durham, North Carolina. Within two years, he had granted 40 franchises, the Pepsi trademark was registered in Canada and Mexico, and sales exceeded 100,000 gallons of syrup. By 1908, Bradham had converted his horse-drawn delivery carts to motor vehicles.

The 1920s proved to be catastrophic for Bradham, and Pepsi was nearly lost forever. The price of sugar reached 26¢ per pound in 1920, and Bradham gambled that the price would continue to rise. He purchased large blocks of sugar stock, only to watch the price plummet to 2¢ per pound by the end of the year.

Bradham attempted to counter his huge losses by borrowing cash, selling off assets, and issuing additional stock. Yet by the end of 1921 Pepsi was insolvent and its bottling network collapsed, with only two plants remaining open. In 1923, the company was declared bankrupt and the assets were sold to a North Carolina company who, in turn, sold the operation to a Wall Street broker for $35,000.

Five years later, the company was bankrupt again and was acquired in 1933 by Charles G. Guth. He later moved the entire Pepsi-Cola operation to Long Island City, New York. (Corporate headquarters would later be moved to Manhattan, and then in 1970 the world headquarters were moved to Purchase, New York.) Finally, in 1934, Pepsi-Cola regained popularity and sales started to increase. That same year, Caleb Bradham died.

Today, Pepsi is one of the most popular soft drinks in the world. The Pepsi-Cola Company has built an incredible food empire around its drink and now owns several popular restaurants, including Kentucky Fried Chicken and Taco Bell. Annual sales are nearly $10 billion.

SOURCE: Pepsi-Cola Company archives

Paul Brainerd

[Aldus Corporation]

Paul Brainerd was born on November 17, 1947, at Medford, Oregon. He received a B.S. in business administration from the University of Oregon and an M.S. in journalism from the University of Minnesota. While in college, he served as editor in chief of the *Minnesota Daily* and the *Oregon Daily Emerald.*

Upon graduation, Brainerd went to work for the *Minneapolis Star Tribune,* where he implemented various computer projects. Brainerd then joined Massachusetts-based Atex, Inc., a manufacturer of dedicated publishing systems for newspapers and magazines. Atex maintained a small office in Redmond, Washington, that was devoted to integrating personal computers as workstations for its systems.

At Atex, Brainerd served in several capacities, including vice president of customer service and product management. When Atex decided to close the Redmond office, Brainerd convinced five of the engineers to join him in a new venture. In 1984, Brainerd put up his money and, with the other engineers, launched Aldus Corporation.

The company set out to develop a new generation of page-composition software that would allow users to perform page layout and design functions on desktop computers. Brainerd coined the term "desktop publishing" for this new technology, and as the money started to run out, he took to the road with a prototype and a business plan.

Brainerd called on nearly 50 venture capital firms in search of backing. Many, perhaps most, didn't even bother to read the business plan. A company dedicated to software was risky business in the early 1980s, and this software appeared to be particularly limited since few companies employed their own desktop publishers.

Investment money was, however, readily found in the rapidly expanding hardware market. Apple Computer was particularly interested in finding software that would enhance its hardware. Apple agreed to invest in Aldus, who in 1985 released its first version of Aldus PageMaker software for use with the Apple Macintosh computer and LaserWriter printer. As PageMaker became available for other operating systems, a broader range of users surfaced, and as this market grew, Aldus became the most recognized name in personal computer–based desktop publishing.

Brainerd served as Aldus's president for ten years, retiring from the company in 1994 when Aldus merged with Adobe Systems. Today, Paul Brainerd devotes most of his time to the Seattle-based Brainerd Foundation, where he serves as president. The foundation is committed to the protection and restoration of the environment in the Pacific Northwest.

SOURCE: Brainerd Foundation archives

William A. Breyer

[Breyer Ice Cream Company]

In 1866, William Breyer was out of work. The country was still recovering from the Civil War, and many people were uncertain about their future. Breyer decided to try his hand at making and selling ice cream, a relatively new dairy product made from cream, pure cane sugar, fresh fruits, and other natural flavorings.

Working from the kitchen in his home in Philadelphia, Pennsylvania, Breyer sold his ice cream to neighbors and people in neighboring communities. As his reputation grew, he experimented with different flavors and ingredients. Eventually, he purchased a horse and wagon to make deliveries. He mounted a large dinner bell on the wagon, which announced his approach to eager customers.

By 1882, Breyer had saved enough money to open his first retail ice cream shop, and soon people were traveling from neighboring communities to visit the Frankford Avenue store. It was such a success that he quickly opened five more retail stores in Philadelphia and also increased the number of horse-and-wagon delivery teams.

It took William Breyer 16 years to build his highly popular Philadelphia enterprise. Sadly, Breyer died late in 1882. His wife, Louisa, assumed control of the business, and with the help of sons Frederick and Henry, the family business continued to grow.

By 1904, the company had built two manufacturing plants to supply the demand for its ice cream. By 1907, Louisa and Frederick had both passed away, leaving Henry as the sole owner of the family business. In 1908, he formally incorporated the business as the Breyer Ice Cream Company. He instituted a corporate pledge that is still embraced by the company: Each container of Breyer's product will include the highest-quality natural ingredients and will be the best ice cream available.

The company was producing 1 million gallons annually by 1914. Henry expanded beyond the Philadelphia market, and in 1924, he built the largest ice cream manufacturing facility in the world, followed by additional plants in New York (1925) and New Jersey (1927). In the late 1920s, the company was incorporated into the National Dairy Products Corporation and was soon selling more ice cream than any other producer in the United States.

The Depression of the 1930s and Henry Breyer's death in 1936 had a devastating effect on the company. Sales were disappointing and unpredictable. By the 1960s, Breyer's ice cream was sold only in ice cream parlors, soda fountains, and other service establishments.

By the early 1970s, the National Dairy Products Corporation had purchased another popular ice cream maker, Sealtest, and merged it with Breyer's. The company also was renamed Kraftco Corporation, which was shortened to Kraft, Inc., in 1976. Kraft revived Breyer's as a retail product, and it has since regained its position as a favorite ice cream, the oldest name brand still produced in the United States.

SOURCE: Breyer's Ice Cream Company archives

Stephen F. Briggs, Harold M. Stratton

[Briggs & Stratton Corporation]

As a college student at South Dakota State College, young Stephen Foster Briggs developed a six-cylinder, two-cycle engine that he hoped to market to the new automobile industry. A coach at the college, Bill Juneau, maintained a farm next door to Harold Mead Stratton, a successful grain merchant, whom he introduced to Briggs. When Briggs graduated in 1907, he and Harold Stratton launched Briggs & Stratton.

The early days were a mix of optimism and disappointment. Briggs's six-cylinder engine proved too costly to manufacture profitably. The partners' second product was a complete automobile called the Superior. However, after building two touring cars and one roadster, they exhausted their money.

They were not, however, out of the automobile supply business. In 1910, Briggs was granted a patent for a gas engine igniter that included an induction coil, an interruption mechanism, and a distributor in a single device. The company started selling them to the bigger car manufacturers, including Ford, who soon had Briggs & Stratton building ignition and horn-button assemblies.

This entry into the electrical parts market carried the company well into the 1920s. By that time, the company had annual sales in excess of $4 million and nearly 1,500 employees. By 1924, Briggs & Stratton was also manufacturing automobile locks, and within five years, it was supplying 75 percent of the locks in America.

Despite the success with other products, Briggs maintained an interest in finding applications for small electric motors. As early as 1919, the company acquired the rights to a device known as the Motor Wheel, which was simply a wheel with a small engine attached. Briggs fashioned a 2-horsepower Briggs & Stratton engine onto the device and adapted it for use on bicycles. The company sold about 25,000 of these units before selling the rights to another company.

The company also experimented with home appliances. From 1918 through 1922, the partners built the Briggs & Stratton Frigerator with Alfred Mellowes, who had earlier founded the company that became Frigidaire. They also innovated small engines that could be attached to washing machines, which became their major market for cast-iron engines until World War II.

Stephen Briggs is probably best known for his contributions to agriculture and lawn care products. As early as 1920, the company was supplying utility engines to a Columbus, Ohio, manufacturer of garden cultivators. By the late 1940s, Briggs & Stratton was one of the country's largest manufacturers of small gasoline engines for home and farm use. Ultimately, "Briggs & Stratton" and "lawnmower" were nearly synonymous.

Stephen Briggs served as president of the company from its incorporation in 1909 until 1935, when he was named chairman of the board. He then split his time between Briggs & Stratton and the Outboard Marine Company until 1948, when he moved on to Outboard Marine full-time. Stephen F. Briggs died in 1976.

Harold M. Stratton served as vice president of the company from its founding until his death in March 1962. His son, Frederick P. Stratton Sr., served as board chairman in the early to mid-1970s, and his grandson, Frederick P. Stratton Jr., was appointed chairman and chief executive officer in 1986. Today, under his leadership, Briggs & Stratton continues to be a world leader in supplying gasoline engines for outdoor power equipment, with annual sales of nearly $1.3 billion.

SOURCE: Briggs & Stratton Company archives

Norman Brinker

[Chili's Grill and Bar; Steak & Ale]

After serving in the military, being a member of America's 1952 Olympic Team, and working his way through college, Norman Brinker went to work at the new Jack-In-The-Box Restaurant chain. Soon he launched his own restaurant, Steak & Ale, which he eventually sold to Pillsbury. After directing restaurant operations for Pillsbury, he took the helm of a new restaurant called Chili's, which he has built into an international, multichain business.

Norman Brinker was born on June 3, 1931, in Denver, Colorado, the only child of Kathryn and Gene Brinker. Upon graduating from high school in Roswell, New Mexico, Brinker attended the New Mexico Military Institute, where he earned a position on the United States International Equestrian Jumping Team.

In 1952, he enlisted in the United States Navy. However, he maintained his love for sports, and that same year, he served on the United States Olympic Equestrian Team. Two years later, he joined the U.S. Modern Pentathlon Team and competed in the World Championships in Budapest, Hungary.

Upon discharge from the Navy, Brinker worked his way through San Diego State University by selling cutlery door-to-door and managing his own clothing import business. Upon graduation in 1957, he went to work for the Jack-In-The-Box restaurant chain founded by Robert Peterson, who at that time had only seven outlets.

In February 1966, Brinker opened his own restaurant, Steak & Ale, in Dallas, Texas. With innovations such as the salad bar, the restaurant became an instant success and grew quickly. By 1971, the 28-outlet company offered its stock to the general public. Five years later, with 109 restaurants, Steak & Ale merged into The Pillsbury Company. Brinker remained active and, in 1982, was named president of the Pillsbury Restaurant Group of Burger King, Steak & Ale, Bennigan's, and Poppin' Fresh restaurants.

After being introduced to a new restaurant named Chili's in 1983, Brinker bought into the company and quickly became the chairman and CEO. Under his leadership, the company grew from 28 outlets to more than 500 restaurants in six chains, employing more than 44,000 people. The largest chain, Chili's Grill and Bar, is one of America's leading casual dining chains with over 400 restaurants.

Brinker has not only faced business adversity, but personal adversity as well. In 1955, he married Maureen Connolly, a three-time Wimbledon and U.S. National Tennis Champion, and the couple became parents of two daughters. In 1969, at the age of 34, Maureen died of cancer. Brinker's second marriage, in 1981, was to Nancy Goodman. Having lost her sister to breast cancer, Nancy has been active nationally with cancer-related research and service organizations. Norman and Nancy reside in Dallas, Texas.

SOURCE: Brinker International, Inc., archives

George W. Brown

[Brown Group, Inc.]

George Warren Brown was born on March 21, 1853, on a farm near Granville in northern New York. As a young man, he not only plowed and harvested the fields, but he also sold muskrats he'd trapped and fruit from his father's orchard in neighboring villages.

Brown graduated from Bryant, Stratton & Cornell's Business College in Troy, New York, at the age of 19. The following year, in 1873, he moved to St. Louis, Missouri, and went to work for his brother, Alanson, a partner in the retailer Hamilton-Brown Shoe Company. The 20-year-old shipping clerk was promptly promoted to traveling salesman, and within four years he led the company in sales.

Convinced that St. Louis could become a major shoe center, Brown became active in the trade. He was elected first president of the St. Louis Shoe Manufacturers and Jobbers Association. With $7,000 in savings, he was eager to be a part of that growth.

Unable to convince his brother to join him in a manufacturing venture, 25-year-old Brown entered a partnership with Alvin L. Bryan and Jerome Desnoyers to make ladies' shoes. Bryan, Brown and Company hired five skilled shoemakers from New England who brought their own tools with them. The operation admirably produced 150 pairs of shoes daily, resulting in first-year sales of $110,000.

In 1885, Alvin Bryan sold his share of the business, which was renamed Brown-Desnoyers Shoe Company. Sales that year reached $500,000. In 1893, Jerome Desnoyers retired, leaving 40-year-old Brown in complete control, and the company was renamed the Brown Shoe Company.

A cartoonist of the day, Richard Fenton Outcault, had created a trio of newspaper comic characters named Buster Brown, his dog Tige, and his sister, Mary Jane. In 1904, Brown Shoe Company purchased rights to use the character, giving birth to Buster Brown Shoes. The company immediately launched a promotion using midgets, all dressed as Buster Brown and accompanied by a dog, who toured the country.

Shipments surpassed $4 million annually by 1900. By 1907, Brown Shoe Company had five factories in St. Louis and opened its first out-of-town plant in Moberly, Missouri. In 1913, the company was listed on the New York Stock Exchange. Two years later, Brown moved into the newly created position of chairman of the board. In the following years, the company was awarded large military contracts to supply footwear during World War I.

George Warren Brown died on December 13, 1921. Today, the Brown Group is a large international producer of consumer products for men, women, and children. Brown owns, in addition to Brown Shoes, several other established companies, including the Wohl Shoe Company and the Hedstrom furniture company.

SOURCE: Brown Group archives

Herman Brown, George Brown

[Brown & Root, Inc.]

After his employer went bankrupt, young Herman Brown was granted the company's modest assets in lieu of nine months' wages. He promptly recruited his brother and brother-in-law to join the venture and launched a successful road-building company. The company, Brown & Root, Inc., grew to become one of the world's largest providers of engineering, construction, project management, facilities operation and maintenance, and environmental services.

In 1914, 22-year-old Herman Brown faced a dilemma. His Freestone County, Texas, employer, a small road builder, went bankrupt, indebted to Brown for nine months' pay. As settlement, Herman was given the firm's assets—18 mules, four scrapers, a pair of plows, six wagons, and a few tents. All had liens placed against them. Brown had no choice but to go into the contracting business.

The timing of events proved to be a blessing for Brown. Two years after going into business, the federal government passed the Federal Road Act. One year later, Texas established a Highway Commission. America was investing huge sums of public money into highway development.

Herman Brown married Margaret Root of Georgetown, Texas, in 1919, and recruited her brother Dan into the company. The name was changed to Brown & Root and has remained so to this day, despite the fact the Dan Root died ten years after the venture was launched. Herman also was able to persuade his brother George, a graduate of Colorado School of Mines, to join the firm.

The company accepted almost any contract that was available, building roads, levees, and even railroad beds. Over time, the Austin-based company secured larger contracts, such as highways and bridges. In 1926, George established a branch office (which eventually became the center of the company's business) in Houston, Texas.

The growth of the company was severely stunted by the Depression. Construction jobs were virtually nonexistent, and Brown & Root clung to what little business it could muster. Finally, the cloud lifted in 1936 when they were awarded the contract to build the Marshall Ford Dam (now known as the Mansfield Dam) near Austin, Texas. This job not only provided a much-needed infusion of operating capital, it also opened the doors to large international projects.

The company entered the shipbuilding business in an unusual way. During World War II, George Brown called on the Navy and offered to build a shipyard in Houston. Twenty-four hours later, the Browns signed a contract to build not only the shipyard, but also a number of ships, despite the fact that no one in the company had ever seen a ship built before. Nonetheless, Brown Shipbuilding put 25,000 people to work and turned out more than 350 combat ships before the end of the war.

Over the next 15 years, Brown & Root continued to expand into engineering- and energy-related markets around the world. With failing health, Herman Brown looked to sell the company in the early 1960s. In

December 1962, shortly after Herman Brown died, the Halliburton Company purchased Brown & Root.

Today, Brown & Root continues to operate as a subsidiary of Halliburton. The company provides services to refining, chemical, and other process-related industries; the energy industry, including onshore and offshore oil and gas development; and transportation, water, contract mining, electric power, and manufacturing industries, including pulp and paper, pharmaceutical, and automotive. The company has over 40,000 employees serving some 3,000 diverse industrial and governmental clients in 60 different countries.

SOURCE: Halliburton Company archives

John M. Browning

[Browning Firearms]

As a young boy, John Browning spent time in his father's gunsmithing shop, learning to repair all makes and models of firearms. At age 25, he built his first rifle, the Single Shot, which eventually was licensed to Winchester. Browning went on to become one of America's greatest firearms designers, developing some 80 weapons.

Captain John Browning was one of America's early settlers, arriving in 1622 aboard the *Abigail.* Several generations later, Jonathan Browning was born on the family farm in Tennessee. Because of the perils of the frontier, settlers seldom ventured far from their homes without being armed. Naturally, there was a great demand for experienced gunsmiths, and by the time he was 19, Jonathan Browning fit the mold. After building a successful business in Tennessee, Jonathan moved his family to Illinois, where he befriended an attorney who was destined for a place in American history: Abraham Lincoln.

In 1840, Jonathan joined the Mormon church, and when violent opposition chased the members from Illinois, Jonathan and his family moved to Utah territory and maintained a close personal relationship with Brigham Young. At age 28, Jonathan Browning had a wife and five children. After converting to Mormonism, which at the time endorsed polygamy, he married two more women. Altogether, Jonathan had 22 children, the last of which was born when Jonathan was 71 years old.

Jonathan's second wife, Elizabeth (Clark) Browning, delivered John Moses Browning on January 23, 1855, in the city of Ogden in Utah territory. Elizabeth gave birth to his brother, Matthew Sandifer Browning, nearly five years later. Of Jonathan's 22 children, only John and Matthew were born to Elizabeth.

At age seven, young John helped his father in the family tannery and learned what he could about gunsmithing. Three years later, he built his first crude rifle from spare parts and was soon working on projects in his father's workshop.

One day in 1878, while the 23-year-old Browning was looking over a complicated rifle he was repairing, he said in disgust that he could build a better gun. His father walked by and said, "I know you could, John Moses. And I wish you'd get at it. I'd like to live to see you do it." Soon, he finished his first gun, the Single Shot, which he presented to his father just before his death in 1879.

That same year, young Browning married Rachel Teresa Child. John and his brother Matt soon built their new gun shop and went to work manufacturing the Single Shot. John, at age 25, supervised a small workforce of young men, most of whom weren't yet 20 years old. It wasn't long before the shop was doing a modest but steady gun trade.

In 1883, T. G. Bennett, the vice president and general manager of the Winchester Repeating Arms Company, was given one of Browning's guns. Bennett was so impressed with the quality that he hopped a train to Utah to track down this new, unfamiliar gun design. The two soon reached an agreement, launching a long association between the two firms. Browning's first rifle was renamed the Winchester Model 1885 High Wall. This was followed by more than 40 additional guns.

In 1902, however, Browning developed a firearm that was too revolutionary for Winchester: an automatic shotgun. It was quickly picked up by two other manufacturers, including Remington Arms. This was followed quickly by other innovations: the semiautomatic Government Colt 45, the BAR rifle, the .30- and .50-caliber machine guns, and even a 37-mm aircraft cannon.

Altogether, he was issued 128 patents that have produced more than 80 separate firearms. Not long before he died, John Browning was asked which of his guns was the most profitable. He said that it was his first gun, the Single Shot. When reminded that he made only $8,000 from it, he replied: "But is was a big eight thousand. They don't come that big anymore. . . . It made me so rich that I've never worried about money since. It gave me eight thousand dollars' worth of certainty that I could invent things for which people would pay large prices."

John Moses Browning died the day after Thanksgiving, 1926, at the age of 71.

SOURCES: Browning archives; *John M. Browning: American Gunmaker,* by John Browning and Curt Gentry, the Browning Company, 1994

James E. "Ed" Broyhill, Thomas H. Broyhill

[Broyhill Furniture Industries]

James Edgar "Ed" Broyhill and his older brother Thomas Hamilton "Tom" Broyhill were active in the North Carolina timber industry in the early 1900s. Each went a separate way for many years, but eventually joined forces to build several companies that were consolidated as Broyhill Furniture Industries.

In the early 1800s, a Revolutionary War veteran named James Broyhill moved from his native Virginia to northwestern North Carolina, into an area now known as Wilkes County. He was the earliest-known ancestor of Isaac Broyhill, born June 1, 1850 in a Moravian Falls farmhouse. Isaac and his nine brothers slept in a loft above the only room in their house. His parents and three sisters slept in the room below.

In 1876, Isaac Broyhill married Margaret Parsons, also a descendant of a Revolutionary War soldier. The couple eventually owned a farm at the base of the Brushy Mountains, halfway between Lenoir and Wilkesboro. They had eight children, including Thomas Hamilton Broyhill, born in 1877, and James Edgar Broyhill, born in 1892.

In addition to working the farm, Isaac owned the town's only grinding mill and molasses mill, and the 10 percent in-kind payments of grain and molasses supplemented the food provided by Broyhill's chickens, cows, and hogs. All the Broyhill children worked hard at Isaac's enterprises.

The oldest son, Tom Broyhill, worked himself into the lumbering business at the turn of the century. By the time he was in his early 20s, Tom was operating two sawmills and was emerging as a successful businessman in the community.

James E. Broyhill, known by everyone as "Ed," was still a young boy. However, he worked hard on the family farm as well as in the local lumber industry, where he'd pull logs from the woods into logging camps, rake sawdust at the sawmills, and even cut timber. He attended the Boomer area one-room schoolhouse until the age of 18, by which time he received the equivalent of a fourth grade education.

By 1913, Ed had decided that farming wasn't a good future and that he would earn his high school diploma. So, at age 21, he enrolled in the Appalachian Training School (now Appalachian State University) in Boone, North Carolina, a small town built on the site of one of Daniel Boone's hunting camps. Unfortunately, Ed was drafted into World War I before he could complete his fifth and final year.

Ed was discharged from the Army in 1918. The 26-year-old soldier had no high school diploma, no job, and few clothes. He had, however, picked up a valuable skill in the service—typing. His brother Tom, then in his mid-40s, by this time owned several ventures, including a small manufacturing concern known as the Lenoir Furniture Company. Ed started working at Tom's factory and, using his typing skills, became a valued member of the office team.

Lenoir Furniture, and Ed's role in the company, grew at a steady pace. Within a year he was making sales calls. By 1921, Ed was secure enough to marry Satie Hunt, the daughter of a successful timberman. They would eventually have four children—Allene, Paul, James, and Bettie.

While it became clear that Tom Broyhill was satisfied with his station in life, Ed Broyhill had ambitions of his own. In addition to his duties at Tom's factory, Ed started selling life insurance in the evenings and during weekends, providing him with additional capital that would soon be useful.

In 1926, Ed was presented with an opportunity. The Bernhardt Chair Company, supplier of chairs, rockers, and benches to the Lenoir Furniture Company, burned to the ground. In his mid-30s with several years furniture experience, Ed decided the time was right. He mortgaged his house and, with $5,000, founded the Lenoir Chair Company.

The former J.A. Allen Blacksmith and Buggy Shop was transformed into Ed's first shop. Chair frames were finished upstairs in the buggy shop, where a single spray booth was in operation. They were then upholstered next door in the blacksmith shop. Soon after Ed opened his shop, a small ironing board factory across the street became available. He purchased the woodworking machinery for $500 and agreed to rent the building. This quickly put Ed into the frame-making business, as well.

The Lenoir Chair Company had nearly $200,000 in sales in 1927 during its first full year. While the new enterprise grew, Ed continued working at Tom's company. But there were obvious differences between the two ventures. Tom Broyhill had no interest in expanding his company, and so life at the Lenoir Furniture Company was uneventful. However, over at the Lenoir Chair Company, Ed continued to seize opportunities for expansion, constantly pushing his cash position to the extreme. While he never missed a payroll or a banknote, there were last-minute scrambles on more than one occasion.

Ed and Tom added to their furniture expansion with the purchase of the Harper Furniture Company, makers of bedroom suites, secretaries, and desks. The line complemented the Lenoir Furniture and Lenoir Chair lines, and the price was right.

Their second acquisition came in 1932, during the Depression. The Newton Manufacturing Company in nearby Newton, North Carolina, became available through bankruptcy. The 50,000-square-foot plant and full line of machinery were purchased for the bargain price of $12,500. Tom, in his mid-50s, viewed the purchase as a real estate investment and was content to let the plant sit idle. Ed, in his early 40s, saw it as an opportunity to expand, and within two years it resumed operations. He renamed it Lenoir Chair Company Number Two and quickly bought out Tom and two other investors in the venture.

In 1936, Tom had a heart attack and subsequently elected to reduce his business activities. Ed diligently consolidated many of the existing operations and invested considerable time developing efficient plant management and sales forces.

However, he was soon restless for new opportunities. In 1941, the McDowell Furniture Company of Marion, North Carolina, producers of low- and medium-priced bedroom furniture, became available. As Ed negotiated a purchase, the Conover Furniture Company, producers of kneehole desks, also was on the market at a bargain price. Ed took the plunge, and for $100,000 he was the proud owner of two more plants. He traveled to Florida where Tom was vacationing and gently broke the news to his brother. Tom shook his head gravely and diagnosed Ed as being "out of his mind."

Ed's next move was to consolidate his six plants under a new banner: the Broyhill Furniture Factories, which was later changed to Broyhill Furniture Industries. The company continued to grow steadily. At the close of World War II, Ed implemented a high-quality sales training program that revolutionized Broyhill's approach to marketing.

In 1946, Ed Broyhill's son-in-law, Bill Stevens, joined the company and was followed by Ed's sons, Paul in 1948 and James in 1950. All three became active in running the company, although in 1961 James was elected to the United States Congress.

Today, Broyhill is recognized as one of America's most popular furniture manufacturers.

SOURCE: William Stevens, *Anvil of Adversity: Biography of a Furniture Pioneer,* Kingsport Press, 1968

Lucien N. Brunswig, Emil P. Martini Sr.

[Bergen Brunswig Corporation]

Lucien Brunswig and Emil Martini envisioned successful pharmaceutical enterprises, but in different centuries and on opposite sides of the country. Brunswig, a French immigrant, launched his wholesale empire during the late 1800s in California. Martini started his in New Jersey after World War II. Through rapid growth, Martini's company, the Bergen Drug Company, acquired the Brunswig Drug Company, forming the Bergen Brunswig Corporation.

Lucien Napoleon Brunswig was born in 1854 in the French village of Montmedy. His father was a country doctor, and young Brunswig grew up with a desire to maintain the family tradition of helping the sick and injured. Looking for better opportunity, Brunswig left France in 1871 and, at the age of 17, immigrated to America.

By the time he was 21, Brunswig had opened his own pharmacy in the small town of Atchison, Kansas. A few years later, he rode the railroad until the tracks literally ended in Fort Worth, Texas. He checked into a rundown hotel, where he witnessed two cowboys arguing in the lobby. Later that night, he awoke to gunfire coming from either side of his pitch-black room. When daylight came, he realized that his room was directly between the rooms of the cowboys, who continued their argument by firing salvos at each other through the flimsy walls.

Fort Worth proved to be an ideal location for Brunswig's enterprise, which included both a retail drugstore and wholesale drug business. Being at the end of a railroad line, the settlers and storekeepers to the west came into town for supplies. Success came quickly, and Brunswig soon opened another store in New Orleans.

In 1888, Brunswig moved to Los Angeles, California, and established a new wholesale apothecary with a partner, F. W. Braun. Two years later, they added a second division in San Diego. In May, 1907, Brunswig bought out his aging partner and reorganized the business as Brunswig Drug Company. He then set out to expand the venture into Arizona, Utah, and Nevada. He also started to manufacture his own pharmaceuticals and cosmetics

Lucien N. Brunswig died on July 17, 1943. Two years later, the company moved into a new headquarters building in Vernon, California. The size of the company was fueled by the 1949 acquisition of Coffin-Redington, a well-known pharmaceutical company founded in San Francisco during the gold rush.

On the other side of America, Emil Martini was building his own pharmaceutical empire.

Emil P. Martini Sr. was born on December 9, 1903, in New York City, and his family moved to New Jersey while he was quite young. He graduated from the New Jersey College of Pharmacy in 1923 and, in 1928, opened his first retail pharmacy in Hackensack, New Jersey. Two years later, he opened a second store. The Depression stymied further growth, but by 1937 Martini had opened his third store.

Martini enjoyed success in the field, and in 1947, he and some acquaintances established a wholesale drug company named the Bergen Drug Company after their home county (Bergen County, New Jersey). The enterprise was launched in a modest 2,000-square-foot converted garage. In less than a decade, the business was thriving and serving New Jersey, New York, and Connecticut.

Emil P. Martini died in 1955 and was succeeded by his son, Emil P. Martini Jr., who orchestrated the 1969 purchase of the Brunswig Drug Company. Today, the Bergen Brunswig Corporation is the nation's largest supplier of pharmaceuticals to the managed-care market and the second-largest wholesaler to the retail pharmacy market. The company employs nearly 5,000 people and has annual sales of more than $9.9 billion.

SOURCE: Bergen Brunswig Corporation archives, *Centennial Sampler: 1888–1988*

Eliphalet A. Bulkeley

[Aetna, Inc.]

An attorney by education, Eliphalet Bulkeley became an active business organizer and trustee. While he founded or cofounded several banks, insurance companies, and other business ventures, he is best remembered as the founder and architect of the Aetna Insurance Company.

Eliphalet Adams Bulkeley was born on June 20, 1803, at Colchester, Connecticut, to John C. and Sally (Taintor) Bulkeley. The small town, located near Hartford, was founded by his great-great-grandfather, Gershom Bulkeley. Gershom's father, Peter Bulkeley, was a nonconformist English minister who emigrated with his followers from Woodhall, England, in 1635 and founded the town of Concord, Massachusetts.

Bulkeley graduated from Yale Law School in 1824 and, after serving an apprenticeship with Judge William J. Williams (the son of a signer of the Declaration of Independence), moved to Selma, Alabama, where he practiced law for two years. In 1830, he returned to Concord to marry Lydia S. Morgan, with the intention of returning to Selma or possibly moving to the exciting Western frontier.

His wife-to-be, however, was quite comfortable with New England life and announced that the wedding plans would proceed only if Bulkeley dropped any notion of moving. The couple married on January 31, 1830, and settled in East Haddam, Connecticut, where Bulkeley took over the law practice of a retiring judge.

Bulkeley was not only a good lawyer, he was a creative organizer. He soon helped to form the East Haddam Bank and became its first president. He also gained an interest in the Willimantic Linen Company, a thriving cotton thread manufacturer. By 1846, the successful businessman moved into the insurance industry as the president of the newly founded Connecticut Mutual Life Insurance Company. In 1850 he became a vice president of the highly respected Aetna Insurance Company, a 30-year-old fire insurer. At Aetna, he headed the newly formed Life Annuity Department. In 1853 the department was spun off as an independent corporation, the Aetna Life Insurance Company, and Bulkeley assumed the post of president. One year later, the family moved to Hartford, where he established the Hartford County Savings Association.

While much of his attention was focused on his growing insurance business, he continued to launch other ventures. In 1857, he founded and became the first president of the Aetna National Bank of Hartford. He also became a director and part owner of the Hartford Eyelet Company and the American Silver Steel Company.

Bulkeley also maintained an active political life. In 1834, he had been elected to the State Assembly, and four years later he was elected a state senator. He also was a member of the local school board and even served as its commissioner. From 1849 through 1855 he served as a judge of the Hartford City Court and later was elected alderman of his ward.

Bulkeley was characterized as a rather formal businessman, although he faced tragedy in his personal life. His firstborn child, Mary, died at the age of two after an accidental fall. Later in life, all three of his sons served in the Civil War, and his oldest, Charles, was killed in battle on February 13, 1864.

Eliphalet Bulkeley reported to his Aetna office every day right up until his death. On February 6, 1872, he suffered a stroke while working at his desk. The following day he slipped into a coma and died on February 13, 1872, at the age of 68.

In 1879, Eliphalet's son, Morgan Gardner Bulkeley, became Aetna's third president, a post he held until 1922. Morgan led the company to phenomenal growth: By the time of his death there were more than 2,000 employees and nearly $210 million in assets. He also continued his father's tradition of diverse public and private service, being named the first president of the National (baseball) League and serving two terms as Connecticut's governor.

SOURCES: Aetna, Inc., archives; Robert Pierce, *Aetna Historical Monographs, No. 1, The Story of Its Founding*, Aetna Insurance Company, 1951

W. Atlee Burpee

[W. Atlee Burpee Company]

After dropping out of the University of Pennsylvania Medical School, W. Atlee Burpee decided to go into the seed business. He was fascinated with horticulture, particularly the art and science of producing improved lines of flowers and vegetables. In 1876, he launched the W. Atlee Burpee Company, one of the world's most famous providers of seeds.

In 1876, 18-year-old W. Atlee Burpee borrowed $1,000 from his mother and established the W. Atlee Burpee Company to discover, develop, and market the highest-quality vegetable and flower seeds available. From his first day of business, he guaranteed satisfaction for one year from date of purchase with a promise of replacement seeds or a full refund.

In his second year in business, Burpee introduced a new cabbage variety he called Surehead. It was a tremendous improvement over the tough, chewy cabbages of those days, and it became an instant success. He also introduced Burpee's Iceberg Lettuce, Burpee's Stringless Green Pod Bush Bean, and Burpee's Fordhook Bush Lima Bean, all of which became longtime best-sellers.

In 1888, Burpee established Fordhook Farms in Doylestown, Pennsylvania, as an experimental farm to test and evaluate new varieties of vegetables and flowers and to produce seeds. His commitment to research continued, and 20 years later he established Floradale Farms in Lompoc, California, to test cool-weather crops.

Burpee maintained a relentless search for good seeds. It is estimated that he traveled, on average, 30,000 miles annually throughout America and Europe, looking for seeds that would produce superior flowers and vegetables.

He was also an innovator who took chances. In 1900, Americans didn't eat yellow corn, which was grown for farm animal feed. A farmer in Greenfield, Massachusetts, came across a delicious sweet yellow corn, but guarded the seeds closely. Burpee purchased a handful of kernels, which he promptly started to market under the name Golden Bantam Sweet Corn. Facing resistance to yellow corn, Burpee worked a deal with market gardeners to throw in a few ears of the Golden Bantam with the white corn they sold. That was enough to open the market for yellow corn.

By 1915, Burpee was the largest mail-order seed company in the world, distributing more than 1 million catalogs annually. That same year, Burpee's health declined, and he died on November 27, 1915. His 22-year-old son, David Burpee, assumed the position of president, and held that post for the next 55 years. David Burpee died on June 24, 1980, at the age of 87.

SOURCE: W. Atlee Burpee and Company archives

Dick Cabela, Mary Cabela, Jim Cabela

[Cabela's, Inc.]

In 1961, Dick and Mary Cabela started selling trout flies from their kitchen. Joined by Dick's brother Jim two years later, Cabela's, Inc., has grown to one of the largest international mail-order retailers of sporting goods in the world.

Brothers Dick and Jim Cabela grew up in an entrepreneurial family in Chappell, a small town in western Nebraska. Their parents, A. C. and Marion Cabela, owned a furniture store in Chappell. Their grandfather, James Cabela, owned a furniture store in Brainard, Nebraska.

While in Chicago on family furniture business in 1961, 25-year-old Dick Cabela purchased a large quantity of trout flies at a price well below what was being charged back in Nebraska. He returned home and placed an ad in the Casper, Wyoming, newspaper, marketing the flies at 12 for $1. Dick and his wife Mary soon were operating a lucrative side venture, and when Dick's brother Jim returned home from the Coast Guard in 1963, he was recruited into the business.

The first marketing and administration office was Dick and Mary's kitchen, and their first warehouse was a shed in the backyard. In 1964, the business was moved to the basement in Dick and Jim's parents' furniture store, and a year later the company was formally incorporated and moved into a former USDA building across the street. They opened a retail business to supplement catalog sales, primarily because neighbors were constantly wandering into the building and asking to purchase items from warehouse shelves. In 1967, they traded the USDA building for the Chappell Legion Hall.

Cabela's small mail-order business continued to grow, and the brothers searched for even larger facilities. In 1968, they were able to purchase a vacant John Deere building in nearby Sidney, Nebraska. Deere had earlier donated the property to a local hospital that, in turn, was anxious to find a buyer before property taxes came due. Within a year, the four-story, 50,000-square-foot building was put into service.

As the company entered the 1980s, it became clear that additional facilities were once again needed. In 1986, Cabela's purchased a former Rockwell plant in Kearny, Nebraska, as the headquarters for its telemarketing operations and a second retail store.

In response to limited warehouse space, the brothers obtained three buildings on the former Sioux Ordnance Depot grounds in 1990. They added another five depot buildings in 1992, which provided warehouse space equal to ten football fields.

The centerpiece of the Cabela organization is its 75,000-square-foot retail store, built in 1990 on a 45-acre site that includes a 4-acre pond and an RV parking lot with water hookups and waste disposal facilities. The ceiling inside the building reaches 52 feet above the door, providing room for a 30-foot-high simulated mountainside housing 40 small and large game mounts, including bear and deer. Altogether, more than 700 mounts are distributed throughout the store. There are also four 2,000-gallon aquariums stocked with trout, game fish, and most freshwater species found in North America. The store also houses a restaurant, an art gallery, and an office of Cabela's travel agency, Outdoor Adventures.

Cabela's markets 60,000 different products. Four times each year, the company ships 45 million catalogs throughout the United States and 95 other countries. *Sports Afield Magazine* calls the Cabela's catalog the "*Oxford English Dictionary* of outdoor wishbooks."

SOURCE: Cabela's, Inc. archives

Asa G. Candler, John S. Pemberton

[The Coca-Cola Company]

The Coca-Cola Company was built by marketing a refreshing soft drink concocted in the late 1800s by Dr. John Pemberton, an Atlanta pharmacist who created the drink after considerable experimentation. He and three colleagues formed a company to produce and market the drink, but success was nominal. Asa Candler, an enterprising businessman in the pharmaceutical field, purchased control of the soft drink and quickly established Coca-Cola as a national product.

John Stith Pemberton was born in Knoxville, Crawford County, Georgia in 1833. After obtaining a degree in Pharmacy, he opened a pharmacy in Columbus, Georgia. In 1853, he married Miss Anna Eliza Lewis. During the Civil War, he organized Pemberton's Cavalry and served as a captain under General Joe Wheeler.

In 1869, Pemberton moved to Atlanta and formed the firm of Pemberton, Wilson, Taylor, and Company. For the next 18 years the company manufactured pharmaceutical compounds, including Globe of Flower Cough Syrup, Triplex Liver Pills, and Indian Queen Hair Dye. In the early 1880s, Pemberton became interested in finding a distinctive beverage that could be made from syrup and carbonated water and sold at soda fountains.

By May 1886, Pemberton's drink was unveiled at an Atlanta soda fountain. Pemberton, Frank M. Robinson, and two others formed the Pemberton Chemical Company to manufacture the drink. Robinson is credited with selecting the name "Coca-Cola" and, drawing from elaborate Spencerian script, creating the flowing trademark identification that is still used today.

The venture was not successful because Dr. Pemberton didn't have the resources to properly finance marketing and production. This was complicated by Pemberton's failing health, and within a year he decided to sell the company's assets.

Asa Griggs Candler was born on December 30, 1851, near Villa Rica, Georgia, one of 11 children born to Samuel Charles and Martha Beall Candler. He grew up on the family farm in a disciplined Christian environment. Family finances prevented him from pursuing his interest in medicine, and by 1861 Candler had the equivalent of five years of education.

As the Civil War drew to a close, General Sherman's troops decimated the Candler farm and small family store. The Candler's only remaining asset was a small amount of cotton they were able to hide in the woods. As the family rebuilt their farm and store, Asa attended school for two more years.

Candler became an apprentice to two physicians in Cartersville, Georgia, in July of 1870. By day he handled a wide array of tasks in their pharmacy and by night he studied Latin and Greek in his small room at the rear of the store. After nearly three years, Candler gave up hope of becoming a doctor and headed for Atlanta to establish a pharmacy career.

In July 1873, 21-year-old Candler arrived in Atlanta with $1.75 and proceeded to walk the streets looking for a job. One of his stops was a drugstore owned by John Pemberton, but there were no jobs available. By nine o'clock that evening, however, he had landed a job in a drugstore owned by George Jefferson Howard.

Candler worked diligently for Howard, and about four years later he was ready to set out on his own. At age 25, he formed the partnership of Hallman and Candler, Wholesale and Retail Druggists, and in less than a year he took another big step: On January 15, 1878, he married Lucy Elizabeth Howard, daughter of his former employer. The couple eventually had five children.

In 1881, Candler bought out his retiring partner and continued to expand the business. In 1883, Candler made an acquisition. Dr. John Pemberton had formed the Pemberton Chemical Company to pursue work on his soft drink. Pemberton's old firm, the manufacturer of pharmaceutical products, went out of business, and Candler purchased the remaining inventory.

Another interesting contact between Candler and Pemberton occurred in 1886, when it appeared that Pemberton's drink was gaining momentum. Daniel B. Candler, Asa's nephew, was employed in his uncle's business. One day he received an order for 1 quart of Coca-Cola syrup. Daniel went to Pemberton's building and found the doctor's son, Charles Pemberton, mixing a batch in a three-legged pot in the backyard. Charles filled a quart bottle, for which Daniel paid 65¢. This is believed to be the first wholesale distribution of Coca-Cola.

By 1887, John Pemberton was in failing health and had decided to sell off the business. One year later, on August 16, 1888, he died at his home in Edgewood, near Atlanta. His son, Charles M. Pemberton, died only six years later, and John's wife, Clifford, died in 1909.

Asa Candler purchased a one-third interest in the Coca-Cola venture on April 14, 1888, just four months before Pemberton died. On April 22, 1891, he completed the acquisition of the remaining two-thirds. The total cost of these transactions, giving Candler complete ownership of Coca-Cola, amounted to $2,300. In addition to the formula for Coca-Cola, Candler brought one of Pemberton's finest assets, Frank Robinson, into his business.

By 1891, Candler was grossing about $100,000 annually through his pharmaceutical business and his various proprietary products. In his heart, he felt that his refreshing soft drink had limitless potential. So, at the age of 40, Candler sold off his other interests and moved the operations of Coca-Cola into two floors of a building, above a saloon, pawnshop, and secondhand clothing store. By February of the following year the company had formally incorporated as The Coca-Cola Company.

Sales grew, and the company moved to an old, three-story residence at the corner of Ivy Street and Auburn Avenue. In 1894, Candler sent his nephew Daniel to Dallas to establish their first branch factory. A year later, factories were opened in Chicago and Los Angeles. The company established a large warehouse in Philadelphia in 1897, and one year later a new Coca-Cola office building and factory was opened on the corner of what is now known as Coca-Cola Place in Atlanta.

Sales of Coca-Cola syrup increased from 25 gallons in 1886 to 214,000 gallons in 1898. In 1900 the figure increased to 370,000 gallons. When Frank Robinson retired from the company in 1914, sales were approaching 7 million gallons annually.

Asa Candler, at the age of 66, essentially retired from operations in January 1916. In his retirement he dedicated much of his time to community affairs. As a child, Candler had hoped to become a doctor, but family circumstances stood in the way. He desperately wanted others to have the opportunity that he did not have, and therefore he focused much of his attention on education, particularly on Emory University. Asa Candler died on March 12, 1929, at the age of 78.

Today The Coca-Cola Company is the global soft drink industry leader. Its 32,000 employees produce 12.8 billion cases of soft drinks each year in 200 different countries.

SOURCE: The Coca-Cola Company archives

William W. Cargill

[Cargill, Inc.]

William Wallace Cargill was born on December 15, 1844, one of five children born to William D. and Edna E. (Davis) Cargill. His father, a sea captain, was born in the Orkney Islands of Scotland and immigrated to America in the late 1830s. In 1856, the family moved to Janesville, Wisconsin, one of the frontier's growing grain centers.

At about age 21, young William Cargill moved to Conover, Iowa, and entered into a partnership with H. C. Marsh, an experienced businessman nearly twice his age. In addition to their lumber and hardware trade, the company of Marsh & Cargill became active in the grain storage business. It was rather inexpensive to establish grain storage warehouses, and as was common practice, Cargill extended his holdings by participating in several partnerships.

By 1867, Marsh & Cargill established facilities in Austin, Minnesota. The following year, 24-year-old Cargill married Ellen T. Stowell and the couple established a home in Austin. In 1869, their first child, William Samuel Cargill, was born. William W. soon established two more warehouses west of Austin in the town of Albert Lee, Minnesota. Shortly thereafter, the family relocated to Albert Lee.

More warehouses and other investments followed, although most seemed to involve new partners, often family members. He also established a friendship with Jason Easton, a well-known banker and railroad investor, and the two made several investments together.

With an eye toward opportunities in Chicago and Milwaukee, William W. Cargill moved his family to La Crosse, Wisconsin, in 1875, where he and his wife spent the rest of their lives. From this new location, he managed his considerable grain holdings. He also became interested in new technology, purchasing rights to use many of the newest innovations in farming and grain processing.

In 1880, Cargill built a huge grain elevator, capable of holding 50,000 bushels, along the railroad tracks at La Crosse. Fed by his warehouses to the west, this was his first strategic terminal that facilitated transport to the eastern markets. At about the same time, he continued to diversify his holdings by purchasing two flour mills in Minnesota. He also established grain and seafood operations in Green Bay, Wisconsin, and even operated a small tugboat.

Across the street from the Cargill's home lived another family, named MacMillan, that has figured prominently in the company. The Cargill and MacMillan children played together, a fondness that continued into adulthood. The oldest Cargill child, William Samuel, married a MacMillan cousin in 1892. Three years later, his sister Edna married John, one of the MacMillan children. For the next five generations, the Cargill and MacMillan families have controlled Cargill.

In the 1890s, William W. Cargill brought together many of his holdings under two umbrella organizations called the W. W. Cargill Company and the Cargill Elevator Company. He suffered a stroke in 1904 that slowed him briefly, but he eventually resumed his hectic pace for the next several years. William W. Cargill died on October 17, 1909.

Today, Cargill is one of the largest companies in the United States, with annual sales approaching $50 billion. The company is still privately held, primarily by descendants of the Cargill and MacMillan families.

SOURCES: Cargill, Inc. archives; Wayne Broehl, *Cargill: Trading the World's Grain,* University Press of New England, 1992

Curtis L. Carlson

[Carlson Companies, Inc.]

Curtis LeRoy Carlson was born on July 9, 1914, in Minneapolis, Minnesota, the third of five children of Charles and Leatha Carlson. Charles had immigrated to America from Sweden with his family at age three and was raised on a farm in east-central Minnesota. Leatha was born on a Wisconsin farm to a Swedish mother and Danish father.

After working for a grocery wholesale company, Charles Carlson opened his own grocery store in Minneapolis. His hard work and long days eventually paid off, and the family earned a comfortable living from the store. Young Curt Carlson launched his own enterprising career at age ten, delivering the *Minneapolis Journal.* He also farmed out several of his newspaper routes to his brothers—realizing a profit from each of them. Over the years, he supplemented his newspaper earnings by caddying, shoveling snow, mowing lawns, and, or course, helping at the family store.

After high school, Carlson paid his own tuition at the University of Minnesota, and upon graduation in 1937 with a bachelor's degree in economics, he accepted a sales position with Procter & Gamble at a monthly salary of $110. The job enabled him to become quite familiar with grocery store owners in the greater Minneapolis area, and his name was soon working its way toward the top of the sales rep rankings. By the time he was 23 years old, he was selling more soap west of the Mississippi than any other Procter & Gamble salesperson.

Despite the success, Carlson was becoming restless for a business venture of his own. He had married Arleen Martin, a classmate from the University of Minnesota, and the couple eventually had two daughters. One day, Arleen and Curt were given coupons by a downtown Minneapolis department store that could be redeemed for cash. He was intrigued by the concept and developed a plan for retail grocers—his clients—to use trading stamps as a sales incentive for food sales.

He borrowed $55 in capital and, in 1938, Carlson launched the Gold Bond Stamp Company, selecting the word "Gold" to denote value and "Bond" to denote security. At first, he worked around his Procter & Gamble job, plowing the proceeds of his modest sales back into the business.

Eventually, his diligence paid off. Gold Bond trading stamps were sold by Carlson in 1953 to one of the largest wholesale grocery chains in the nation—Super Valu—which operated hundreds of large supermarkets across the Midwest. Super Valu was the first major supermarket food chain in the nation to use trading stamps. Carlson's successful volume increases for the small food stores had paid off and would now be tried by a big supermarket chain operation.

Almost overnight, Gold Bond trading stamps became a household word for Americans. "It was an idea," Carlson would later say, "whose time had come!"

During the 1960s, the trading stamp business had grown to such a phenomenal extent that further growth projections were impossible. Nineteen out of the top twenty food chains were issuing trading stamps and 50 percent of all gasoline stations were giving stamps on purchases. It was a time to review the present and anticipate the future of trading stamps.

As a result of some strategic planning, Carlson began to diversify his capital into other businesses including real estate in the western suburbs of Minneapolis—part of which would be the future home of his Carlson Companies World Headquarters which opened in 1989.

Among his diversification was the purchase in 1962 of the nationally known Radisson Hotel in downtown Minneapolis. This marked the beginning of the expansion of the Radisson name, first in Minnesota and then throughout the United States and Canada. Today, there are more than 320 Radisson Plaza Hotels, Suite Hotels, Hotels, Inns, and Resorts throughout the world.

Later, Country Hospitality Inns & Suites as well as Country Kitchen International and TGI Friday's restaurants joined the Hospitality Group. Today, there are more than 615 restaurants around the world bearing the TGI Friday's, Italianni's, Friday's Front Row Sports Grill, Friday's American Bar, and Country Kitchen name.

This diversification into other businesses, besides trading stamps, prompted the changing of the name of his company from the Gold Bond Stamp Company to Carlson Companies, Inc. in 1973.

Today, the Carlson Companies is an international conglomerate of more than 100 service businesses including Radisson Hotels Worldwide, Friday's Hospitality Worldwide and Country Hospitality Worldwide; Carlson Marketing Group, Inc.; Carlson Wagonlit Travel; and the Carlson Travel Network, including A.T. Mays in the United Kingdom. The original Gold Bond Stamp Company is now part of the Carlson Marketing Group which specializes in sales promotion/marketing, loyalty and incentive programs—all making up the cornerstone of Carlson's entrepreneurship.

In April 1986, Carlson gave a personal gift of $25 million to his alma mater, the University of Minnesota. Shortly thereafter, the university's School of Management was renamed the Curtis L. Carlson School of Management. Among the school's many honors is its perpetual ranking as one of America's best academic programs in the study of entrepreneurship.

In 1989, Carlson moved its world headquarters into a glistening, new 15-story Twin Towers complex in the City of Minnetonka—just ten minutes from downtown Minneapolis. The new building anchors a 310-acre, $650 million development called Carlson Center, which within a decade will become a "city within a city."

SOURCES: Carlson Companies, Inc. archives; Curtis L. Carlson, *Good as Gold: The Story of the Carlson Companies,* the Carlson Companies, 1994

LeRoy T. Carlson Sr.

[Telephone and Data Systems, Inc.]

LeRoy T. Carlson was born on May 15, 1916, in Chicago, Illinois, the youngest of three children of Axel and Gerda Carlson. His father had immigrated from Sweden six years earlier, and young Carlson was raised in a predominantly Swedish neighborhood on the city's south side. During the Great Depression, he assisted with family finances by purchasing fruits and vegetables at the Farmer's Market before dawn and selling them door-to-door through the day.

Upon graduation from high school, Carlson first attended Morgan Park Junior College, then the University of Chicago, paying his expenses by selling the *Encyclopaedia Britannica* and *McCall's* magazine and by serving as the Illinois district supervisor of *Newsweek.* He worked his way through Harvard University Graduate School of Business by organizing a laundry route to service the more affluent students.

When World War II erupted, Carlson enlisted in the U.S. Army and was soon named accountant in charge of the Army Ordinance motor pool in Detroit, Michigan. He later established the accounting control system for building and operating two automobile and truck manufacturing plants. In 1943, he was sent to India to establish a motor rebuilding and assembly plant. Carlson returned to Chicago on leave during the Christmas season in 1944 to marry Margaret Deffenbauch, then returned to Calcutta until the spring of 1946.

Upon discharge from the Army, Carlson was hired as an administrative assistant to Joseph Kennedy at the Chicago Merchandise Mart. By 1950, he grew restless for his own company and acquired the Suttle Equipment Company in Lawrenceville, Illinois. The company, which produced printed forms and other supplies for independent telephone companies, had fallen on difficult financial times after the death of its founder. In a relatively short time, Carlson nursed Suttle back to profitability.

While the postwar economy expanded, antiquated telephone service—including operator-assisted dialing and party lines shared by a dozen or more families—was still the rule in rural America. Carlson recognized this as an opportunity and, in 1956, acquired the Calvert City (Kentucky) Telephone Company. Encouraged by his initial success in Calvert City, he launched an acquisition campaign across the country, bringing telephone companies, directory publishers, and manufacturers under an umbrella organization known as Telephones, Inc.

After selling Telephones, Inc., in 1964, Carlson looked for new opportunities in the communications field. By late 1968, he had acquired ten small, independent telephone companies in Wisconsin. On January 1, 1969, he launched Telephone and Data Systems, Inc., to provide centralized support and management for his holdings, which serviced about 25,000 customers.

Carlson's early success in Wisconsin enabled him to quickly expand, first in Wisconsin, then into New England, and finally throughout the country. By 1978, he had diversified into cable television. In 1980, American Paging, Inc., was organized and, within seven years, placed 100,000 pagers into service in 31 major metropolitan markets. Another subsidiary, United States Cellular Corporation, was launched in 1984 and quickly expanded into dozens of markets.

Carlson's son, LeRoy T. "Ted" Carlson Jr., assumed the post of president in 1981, the same year the company went public, and in 1986, 70-year-old LeRoy Carlson Sr. passed the title of CEO to his son. Today, Telephone and Data Systems has annual sales of nearly $1.2 billion and 7,000 employees.

SOURCE: K. C. August, *TDS: The First Twenty Years*, Telephone and Data Systems, Inc., 1989

Andrew Carnegie

[Carnegie Steel Company]

Like his father and grandfather, William Carnegie earned a modest living as a weaver at Pattiemuir, Scotland. In 1830, he moved to Dunfermline where he met and later married Margaret Morrison. On November 25, 1835, their first child was born and, following custom, was named after his grandfather, Andrew. Four years later, a daughter named Ann was born, but she died in 1841. In 1843, their third and last child, Tom, was born.

Business conditions turned sour for William, and in 1848, the family sold their possessions and set sail for Pennsylvania, where members of Margaret's family had already established a new life. Three months later, the 12-year-old Andrew Carnegie and his family arrived in Pittsburgh and promptly took up quarters in a rent-free bungalow behind his aunt's home. William rented a loom and made tablecloths, which he sold door-to-door, and Margaret started making shoes.

To help with family finances, Andrew quit school, and soon he and his father both went to work in a local textile plant. He later accepted another job that paid better—$2.00 per week—tending the boiler in a factory basement. One day young Carnegie was asked to help make out the bills for the company, and he quickly saw the opportunity to become more successful. During the winter months of 1848 and 1849, he traveled to downtown Pittsburgh three nights a week to receive instruction from an accountant.

The following spring, Carnegie switched jobs again, this time becoming a messenger for a Pittsburgh telegraph company. He was still only 13 years old, but despite the danger of running the city streets, the Carnegie family needed the 50¢ per week pay raise. Young Carnegie took great delight in his new job, which gave him the opportunity to learn all the businesses in Pittsburgh as well as the important businesspeople. Within a few years his income skyrocketed to $20 monthly, and he became the primary source of support for the family.

In 1852, the Pennsylvania Railroad opened a new line between Altoona and Pittsburgh, and the local assistant superintendent persuaded 17-year-old Andrew Carnegie to operate as his personal secretary and telegraph operator. The job provided him with keen insight of the railroad industry and introduced him to business finance. In 1856, he borrowed money and purchased his first stock. When it later produced a $10 dividend, Carnegie was overwhelmed with the fact that he earned money "without the sweat of his brow."

By the time he was 24 years old, Carnegie was appointed superintendent of the western division of the Pennsylvania Railroad. When oil was discovered in nearby Titusville, Pennsylvania, in 1859, Carnegie made a significant investment. He also invested in a railroad car builder and the Keystone Bridge Company. In 1861, he and a friend formed the Freedom Iron Company, his first iron manufacturing venture. Five years later, the plant converted to a Bessemer steelmaking plant.

After a European tour in 1872, Carnegie became convinced that steel producers would flourish in the coming decades. Over the next three years, he built a new plant—the J. Edgar Thomson Steel Mill—which became the largest and most modern Bessemer plant in the United States. In 1892, he organized his holdings into the Carnegie Steel Company, which was easily the largest and most profitable steel empire in the world.

In February 1901, the 65-year-old Carnegie sold his interests to the newly formed United States Steel Company, backed by financier J. P. Morgan. The sale made him one of the world's richest men, and he spent the rest of his life devoted to responsible philanthropy. Among other projects, he built more than 2,800 libraries and placed nearly 7,700 organs in churches.

Carnegie married Louise Whitfield, the daughter of a successful New York merchant, in April, 1887. Andrew Carnegie died on August 11, 1919.

SOURCE: Joseph Frazier Wall, *Andrew Carnegie,* University of Pittsburgh Press, 1989

Frank Carney, Dan Carney

[Pizza Hut, Inc.]

Growing up in an enterprising family, Dan and Frank Carney were not strangers to hard work and pursuing opportunity. While attending Wichita State University in the 1950s, the young men were offered a good deal on leasing a restaurant with the suggestion that pizza was an up-and-coming menu item. Within two years of opening their Pizza Hut restaurant, the brothers opened at five more locations before franchising their unique concept.

Frank and Dan Carney were two of twelve children born to owners of a small, Wichita, Kansas, grocery store. They were raised with strong work ethics, holding jobs with the family store and with other local merchants.

While attending college, 25-year-old Dan Carney was approached by the woman who owned the building that housed the family grocery store. She owned an adjacent property that was about to become vacant and thought it would be the ideal location for making pizza. She had read a story about how well pizza was selling in New York City and felt that it would sell well in Wichita, too.

Dan invited his younger brother, 19-year-old Frank Carney, to join him in the venture. When the two Wichita State University students showed up to meet with the landlord, each thought the other would write the check for the $155 lease payment. The surprised brothers realized that neither had enough money to cover the cost.

They huddled with their family and borrowed $600 from the insurance fund left by their late father. The money was enough to cover the lease and buy paint and some used restaurant equipment, tables, and chairs. Then the brothers turned their attention to another problem. Neither knew how to make pizza. In fact, Frank had only eaten it once in his entire life.

Their sister told them that a neighbor, John Bender, knew how to make pizza. They contacted him and received an invitation to his apartment, where the brothers ate what would become the first Pizza Hut pizza. Bender later told the brothers that when they first contacted him he was able to remember the recipe for the sauce but not the dough, so he substituted a recipe for French bread, which in essence became the foundation for Pizza Hut's original thin and crispy pizza.

Dan and Frank had one other matter to attend to: They didn't have a name for their business. The sign above the door said "B & B Lunchroom," and they didn't have enough money to make a new sign. When they added the word "Pizza" to the sign, there was only room for three more letters. When Dan's wife suggested the building resembled a hut, they had found their word. In 1958, Pizza Hut served its first pizza.

The first real crowd to visit the restaurant came after a Wichita State football game. After the second game, they knew they had a winner. Within six months the loan was repaid and they opened a second shop. Within a year they opened four more. The venture became a challenge to the brothers, who continued to pursue their college degrees, but were finding less and less time for studies.

They decided to franchise their next restaurant to Dick Hassur, the manager of their busiest store. With a $2,500 loan from the Carneys, he opened the first franchise in Topeka, Kansas. Soon, people from throughout Kansas and Oklahoma were requesting franchises, which the Carneys awarded to most anyone who could afford one.

Problems soon surfaced, however. The franchised Pizza Huts were being opened in all sizes and shapes, and many quickly experienced financial problems. By 1961, the brothers realized that the key to success was uniformity among franchisees and soon adopted a number of quality control standards. They also designed an innovative building, complete with large picture windows, which debuted in Colorado Springs, Colorado, in 1965.

In the late 1960s, they had more than 250 franchised stores in addition to their original six company-owned stores. In 1969, they took the company public, giving them the resources to spread Pizza Hut throughout the country. They quickly added 200 more company-owned stores.

Not long after the company went public, Dan Carney announced his retirement from the business that outgrew him. In 1972, Frank Carney replaced his older brother as president and chief executive officer. Within four years, there were 2,000 Pizza Hut restaurants.

In 1977, Frank Carney orchestrated the sale of Pizza Hut to PepsiCo. He was named to PepsiCo's board of directors, but later resigned to pursue other restaurant interests.

SOURCES: Carney family archives; Carrie Shook and Robert Shook, *Franchising: The Business Strategy That Changed the World*, Prentice Hall, 1993

Thomas Carvel

[Carvel Corporation]

Thomas Carvelas was born in 1908 in Athens, Greece. At age 4, his family, including six brothers and sisters, immigrated to Connecticut. They later moved to Manhattan where Thomas (now Carvel) held a number of jobs, including a drummer in a Dixieland band, a test driver for Studebaker, and as a helper in his older brother's auto body shop.

When he was 26, Carvel was diagnosed with tuberculosis and was told he would only live three months. To help improve his health, Carvel decided to work in the country. He borrowed $15 from his girlfriend (whom he later married) and purchased his inventory from a Bronx supplier. He packed his ice cream in salt and ice, and took to the country.

One day, his ice cream wagon blew a tire next door to a pottery shop in Hartsdale, New York. Faced with a melting inventory, Carvel started selling his ice cream right there along the roadside. Business was so good that he remained at the same spot all summer, carefully living on a $2 per week budget. By the end of the year, he had enough money to buy the pottery store, which he converted to his first ice cream stand.

During World War II, Carvel assisted the war effort by serving food at Fort Bragg, North Carolina. Because of material shortages, he had to repair old ice cream equipment, fashioning a machine that would provide mixed ice cream on demand. After the war, he perfected his equipment and started selling it to other vendors. As a shrewd businessman, Carvel was often consulted by the owners of ice cream stands for business advice.

Because of the demand, Carvel started charging consulting fees. Eventually, he decided to franchise his ice cream operation, since he was already providing the equipment and business expertise. By 1950, 21 independently owned stores were operating under the Carvel name.

Carvel became personally involved with company advertising in 1955. After paying a New York radio station $150 for saturation coverage of the opening of a new store, the disc jockey gave vague directions to the location. Carvel was incensed, concluding that "if they can screw up a commercial, I can, too. And I work cheaper . . ." From that time forward, Carvel cut thousands of his own unrehearsed radio commercials, characterized by his scratchy voice.

The impressive growth of Carvel Ice Cream was attributed to two keys. First, Tom Carvel insisted that franchises use only high-quality, Carvel products. He spent considerable time in court dealing with vendors who used cheap substitutes. Second, he focused on his famous ice cream cakes, insisting that they set Carvel apart from other ice cream companies.

Carvel, like most entrepreneurs, saw opportunities come and go. In the 1950s, a friend of his who sold multimixers for the Prince Castle Corporation asked Carvel to invest in his start-up company, a chain of hamburger stands. Carvel passed on the investment, but did provide his friend with a sample franchise agreement and insight into how to build low-cost, all-glass-front buildings. That friend was Ray Kroc, who had purchased the rights to franchise the fast-food restaurant founded by the McDonald brothers.

In 1989, Carvel sold his company to Investcorp, an international banking concern, for a reported $80 million. Less than a year later, Tom Carvel died at age 84. He and his wife had no children of their own, but the couple was quite close to the families of their friends and employees.

Today, Carvel has annual sales in excess of $200 million through more than 500 franchised stores and more than 2,000 supermarkets.

SOURCES: Carvel Corporation archives; Walter K. Taylor, "The Marvel of Carvel," *Westchester Illustrated*, March, 1981

Jerome I. Case

[Case Corporation]

In 1633, John Case left his comfortable life in Aylesham, England, behind and traveled across the ocean to join the growth in the Massachusetts Bay Colony. His great-great-grandson, Caleb Case, married Deborah Jackson, a relative of future president Andrew Jackson. The couple had seven children, including Jerome Increase Case, born on December 11, 1819, at Williamstown, New York.

Young Jerome had a childhood typical of nineteenth-century farm families: He threshed wheat and walked to school. When he was 16, he and his father attended a local demonstration of a groundhog wheat thresher, patented in England, that could do more work in an hour than a person could do in a day. Caleb was so impressed he not only bought one, he became a dealer.

Over the next five years, Jerome offered threshing services to neighboring farms. During these years, young Case became convinced that, while this particular machine was helpful, an improved machine could truly revolutionize farming. By 1840, Wisconsin Territory had become a major producer of wheat, promising opportunity for those who dared to venture to the frontier.

The future became clear to Case. He loaded up six groundhog threshers and headed west in 1842, selling five of them along the way. He settled in the growing town of Rochester, Wisconsin, and contracted with local farmers to perform threshing services. With two new acquaintances, he also started working on his own thresher-separator. Within two years, the device was put into service.

Encouraged by the utility of his machines, Case decided to manufacture and sell them rather than doing the actual work himself. When the town council balked at granting him rights to waterpower for a factory, Case packed up and moved to Racine. There, he found a more receptive audience and quickly established a plant along the Root River.

It took Case only three years to build a much larger facility for his company, which he named the Jerome Increase Case Machinery Company. One year later, in 1848, he added another story to his plant. By that time he was the largest employer in the city, a distinction the company holds to this day.

Case was producing about 100 threshers a year, which provided a sufficient living for the founder to start a family. In 1849, he married Lydia Ann Bull. The couple had seven children, four of whom lived through childhood.

The company continued to expand, but there were considerable challenges. In the early days, there was no railroad to transport the equipment, only crude roads that, in poor weather, were useless. On one occasion, Case sold six threshers in Iowa that didn't arrive at their destination until after harvest season. Instead of making $1,000 in sales, he was forced to pay nearly $250 in delivery charges.

Case handled his own sales for many years and, when necessary, made the repairs as well. On one occasion, a farmer from Faribault, Minnesota, experienced trouble with his separator, and Case mechanics were unable to correct the problem. Case, who was then 65 years old, personally visited the farmer. By nightfall it became clear that even the founder couldn't correct the problem.

Frustrated, Case doused the machine with gasoline and lit it afire, then left the farm. The next day, a new machine was delivered to the farmer.

The company was reorganized in 1863 as J. I. Case & Company, with three new partners. After the Civil War ended, Case introduced new equipment to the entire country, and sales continued to climb. By 1870, the company was offering a steam-powered thresher that was built on a wagon and pulled by a team of horses. Through the next several decades, Case & Company offered a line of steam traction engines.

Jerome Increase Case died on December 22, 1891, at the age of 73. Today, the Case Corporation, still based in Racine, is a leading designer, manufacturer, and distributor of construction and agricultural equipment. Annual sales are nearly $5 billion.

SOURCE: Case Corporation archives

James E. Casey

[United Parcel Service]

James E. Casey was born on March 29, 1888, the oldest of four children born to an innkeeper and gold prospector in the small mining community of Candelaria, Nevada. While he was still an infant, the family moved to the boomtown of Seattle, Washington. However, the family's fortunes weren't much better, and with his father in failing health, young Casey had to quit school at age 11 to help support the family.

Casey's earliest job was delivering packages for a department store at a monthly salary of $2.50. He also worked as a messenger for a telegraph company, and at age 15, Casey and two fellow messengers started their own service. After two years, Casey sold his share and moved to Nevada briefly to prospect for gold.

In 1907, at the age of 19, Casey returned to Seattle and, with a partner and $100 in capital, established the American Messenger Company. Their quarters, provided by his partner's father, were a 6- by 17-foot room in the basement of a saloon. Because few people owned telephones in those days, Casey's company delivered messages received through Seattle's two telephone companies, along with trays of food and anything else that a messenger could deliver.

To compete against the more established services in town, Casey offered 24-hour, seven-day-per-week service. Six messengers initially walked or rode streetcars, but the young firm soon purchased a small fleet of bicycles and motorcycles. After being in business only one month, the partners were contracted by a local clothing store to deliver packages, and soon, package delivery became the focus of the company.

After merging with a competitor in 1913, monthly revenues topped $2,000. That's when Casey put his first delivery truck into service. Casey and his partners borrowed enough money to purchase a new Model T Ford, whereupon they removed the body and placed a custom-built truck body on the chassis. The new vehicle, which could haul 50 packages, became an instant success, and additional growth followed.

Their first delivery truck was painted red. When the partners purchased a second truck, they painted it yellow because Casey had been told that the color yellow attracted the most attention. However, as they picked up more business from department stores, they realized that their clients weren't particularly happy to have it appear obvious that they were contracting for delivery service. A local carriage painter was consulted, and he recommended a shade known as "Pullman brown," which was used for Pullman railroad cars. The partners agreed, and the color has stuck with the company.

By 1915, their Merchants' Parcel Delivery had a fleet of four trucks, five motorcycles, and 20 foot messengers. Two years later, Casey's original partner sold his share back to the company and entered the insurance business. In 1919, Casey purchased a delivery company in Oakland, California. Another firm in San Francisco was named Merchants Parcel Delivery and, since this was too close to his own company's name, he decided to rename his entire organization United Parcel Service.

United Parcel Service entered the Los Angeles market in 1922 and, within five years, was established in San Diego, San Francisco, and Portland. Casey moved into New York City in 1930, securing contracts with Lord & Taylor and James McCreery & Company, then with other department stores who were happy to give up in-house delivery service. He then moved into other cities, including Cincinnati (1934), Milwaukee (1938), and Chicago (1940).

At the end of World War II, Casey decided to make delivery service available to everyone, not just department stores. He also developed special package-handling equipment that would increase the efficiency of his service.

James E. Casey died on June 6, 1983, at the age of 95. He was a lifelong bachelor. Today, United Parcel Service has nearly 340,000 employees worldwide, with annual revenues of more than $22 billion.

SOURCES: United Parcel Service archives; *Puget Sound Business Journal,* April 2–8, 1993

Joel O. Cheek

[Maxwell House Coffee]

Joel Owsley Cheek was born on December 8, 1852, in Burkesville, Kentucky. When he turned 21, he left the family farm and traveled by raft along the Cumberland River to Nashville, Tennessee, where he was hired as a traveling salesman for a wholesale grocery company.

At about the same time, Colonel John Overton opened an elaborate Nashville hotel that he named The Maxwell House in honor of his wife, whose maiden name was Harriet Maxwell. The hotel quickly became famous for its fine cuisine and lavish hospitality, and The Maxwell House became *the* place to stay while traveling through Nashville.

Of all the products that Cheek peddled, coffee held most of his interest. As he traveled from village to village, he developed plans for blending his own brand of coffee. He was eventually granted a partnership in the grocery firm that he worked for, which meant that his travel days were over. With his free time in Nashville, he started experimenting with coffee blends. In 1882, he quit the partnership and established a full-time coffee business.

Over the next decade, Cheek built his coffee business while continuing to experiment with new blends. In 1892, he developed a particularly fine blend that he considered to be so rich that it was suitable for a hotel like The Maxwell House. He approached the management of the hotel, who agreed to serve it to customers for a trial period. Soon, everyone seemed to be talking about the wonderful Maxwell House coffee.

One satisfied customer was Theodore Roosevelt, President of the United States. While visiting Nashville in 1907, a hostess asked him if he would like another cup of the Maxwell House coffee. "Delighted," responded the president, "It's good to the last drop!" This response was later adopted by Maxwell House as its long-running slogan.

The success of the coffee blend contributed to a rapid growth of Cheek's partnership, the Cheek-Neal Coffee Company, that he operated with John W. Neal. Other innovations followed, such as Maxwell House tea, which was introduced in 1917.

On August 1, 1928, the Postum Company acquired the Cheek-Neal Coffee Company for approximately $40 million, changing its name to the Maxwell

House Products Company. One year later, Postum changed its name to General Foods Corporation.

Joel Cheek died on December 13, 1935, at the age of 83. The original Maxwell House hotel was destroyed by a fire on December 25, 1961.

SOURCE: Kraft Foods, Inc. archives

Robert A. Chesebrough, Theron T. Pond

[Chesebrough-Pond's, Inc.]

During the mid-1800s, Theron Pond was scouring patches of witch hazel trees in New York, while Robert Chesebrough was scraping residue from oil rigs in western Pennsylvania. Both men dedicated their lives to the resulting concoctions, although their enterprises grew quite independent of one another. Building on the success of Pond's Extract and Chesebrough's Vaseline, the two companies merged in 1955 to form Chesebrough-Pond's.

In 1846, Theron T. Pond was interested in developing an improved formula for witch hazel, a popular skin treatment extracted from witch hazel trees. (Witch hazel trees had another popular use: Their branches were used as divining rods to locate water underground.) In time, Pond perfected a formula for a mixture he called Pond's Extract.

Eventually, sales were so good that Pond moved his distillery from Utica, New York, to Chester, Connecticut, an area that was rich with hazel trees. He shipped his extract in barrels by schooner to a bottling plant in Brooklyn, New York. In 1888, the distillery and bottling plant were moved to a new, combined facility at Clinton, Connecticut.

Over the next several decades, cosmetics and other toiletries were added to the company line, including Pond's cold cream and vanishing cream (1907). Buoyed by strong advertising campaigns, Pond's was a leading U.S. manufacturer of skin creams by the 1920s.

While Theron Pond was making his witch hazel, another innovative gentleman was busy developing another popular skin-care product. Robert Augustus Chesebrough, a 22-year-old Brooklyn, New York, chemist, listened with intrigue to the stories coming from Titusville, Pennsylvania.

A new oil strike had created a boomtown in the small, western Pennsylvania community. But Chesebrough wasn't interested in oil. There was a rumor that a residue accumulated on the pump rods held miraculous healing powers. Curious, Chesebrough took a trip to Titusville and collected a sample. Working tirelessly in his lab, he was able to reduce the goo to a white jelly that, indeed, seemed to help heal cuts and blisters.

Chesebrough named his new ointment Vaseline, a combination of the German word for water and the Greek word for olive oil. He passed out samples to Brooklyn construction workers, instructing them to try it on burns and cuts. Soon, orders were pouring in from the city. Then he started loading horse-drawn wagons and sending them throughout New England. By 1880, Vaseline was stocked on medicine shelves throughout the country.

The Chesebrough Manufacturing Company Consolidated merged into Rockefeller's Standard Oil empire in 1881. However, in 1911, it was spun off again as an independent corporation. The company grew through new product innovations, including Vaseline Hair Tonic and, per government request, Vaseline sterile burn dressings.

On July 1, 1955, well after the deaths of Robert Chesebrough and Theron Pond, the two companies merged into Chesebrough-Pond's, Inc. Over the next three decades, the company grew into an international manufacturer of a range of personal care products. Key acquisitions included Pertussin Cough Syrup (1956), Prince Matchabelli (1958), Cutex nail care products (1960), and Q-tips (1962). In 1987, the company merged into Unilever.

SOURCE: Chesebrough-Pond's USA Company archives

Don Clayton

[Putt-Putt Golf Courses]

Don Clayton was born on August 30, 1925. By 1954, the 28-year-old Clayton was a hard-driving insurance salesman, supervising 11 agents at his successful agency in Fayetteville, North Carolina. He was also feeling desolate, alone, and constantly on the verge of breaking into tears. His physician concluded he was on the verge of something else—a nervous breakdown—and told him to spend a month away from the office.

Clayton agreed, and a few days into his vacation took a trip to a local miniature golf course with his father and brother. Rather than relax, however, Clayton quickly became agitated with the course, which he later described as being made of "dirt and goat's hair." His brother pointed out to Clayton that, if he didn't care for the course, he had 30 days off to build one that was more to his liking.

The project proved to be not only therapeutic, it was the beginning of an empire. Clayton returned home and quickly designed holes on 3- by 5-inch index cards. He went to his father's house, which had a larger living room than his own home, and experimented on the living- and dining-room rugs, concluding that 30-foot putting distances would be about average. That same night, Clayton called the owner of a vacant lot and arranged to lease it for $100 per year.

The next morning, Clayton went to the local unemployment office and hired several laborers. They went to the empty lot and, using stakes and a ball of twine, laid out the holes that were drawn on the index cards. Twenty-one days and $5,200 later, he was ready to open for business. He named his venture Putt-Putt Golf.

Clayton estimated that perhaps 60 customers might show up for his June 21, 1954, opening. By closing time, nearly 200 people had paid 25¢ each for a round of Putt-Putt golf, providing opening-day revenues of nearly $50. The following day, almost 350 people came, and revenues exceeded $85. Clayton's father teased, "That's it, son. Everybody in town's played this here game now. The fad is over." The following night, almost 750 people showed up.

Actually, the daily revenue kept increasing. At the end of the first month in business, Clayton had averaged nearly $200 each day. He paid off the entire construction costs, plus the first year's rent on the property. He then returned to his insurance job, but at a much more relaxed pace. His mind was on the Putt-Putt course.

One evening the line was so long that an embarrassed Don Clayton got on the public address system and invited everyone to come one week later to play on a second, brand-new course that would be open. He quickly hired three shifts of laborers and spent $7,200 on the new course, which registered sales of $366 on opening day.

Clayton was quickly convinced that if one course was so successful in Fayetteville, then his courses would probably enjoy similar success in any town. He bought out his early investors and, within two years, opened eight Putt-Putt courses. By the third year, 44 courses were open, and Clayton's insurance business was relegated to a sideline operation. Over the next several decades, Clayton learned the art of franchising. By 1976, there were 1,300 Putt Putt courses around the world.

He and his wife Patricia had a daughter, Donna, and two sons, Don S. and Nash. Don Clayton died on April 17, 1996, at the age of 70. Today, Putt-Putt Golf & Games operates complete fun centers in addition to Putt-Putt golf courses. Clayton's daughter, Donna Clayton Lloyd, serves as chairman of the board of directors.

SOURCES: Putt-Putt Golf Courses archives; William Barry Furlong, "The Uphill Course of Putt-Putt Golf," *The Saturday Evening Post,* October 1980

Bennett Cohen, Jerry Greenfield

[Ben & Jerry's Homemade, Inc.]

After experimenting with various jobs and colleges, high school buddies Ben Cohen and Jerry Greenfield decided to open an ice cream parlor in Burlington, Vermont. Their unusual ice cream flavors, made with fresh Vermont milk and cream, quickly became a local favorite. Today, Ben & Jerry's ice cream is appreciated by a growing international audience.

Bennett Cohen and Jerry Greenfield were born four days apart in Brooklyn, New York, in 1951. They eventually met in a junior high gym class and, sharing an aversion to running track, soon became buddies.

Ben's first job working with ice cream came during high school, when he drove an ice cream truck through local neighborhoods. Upon graduation, Ben attended Colgate University, but within two years he dropped out and returned to the ice cream truck. After studying pottery and jewelry making at Skidmore College, Ben worked at a variety of jobs, including as a McDonald's cashier, a

Pinkerton security guard, a night cleaner at Jamesway and Friendly's, a night-shift clerk at Bellevue Hospital, and a taxi driver.

Jerry graduated from high school with a National Merit Scholarship and enrolled at Oberlin College in Ohio to study premed. He later recalled that his favorite course was "Carnival Techniques," where he learned the sledgehammer-and-brick trick that would eventually become legendary at Ben & Jerry's. It involved suspending Ben, known to employees as "Habeeni-Ben-Coheeni," between two chairs and placing a cinder block on his bare belly. Jerry, wearing a pith helmet, would then smash the cinder block with a sledgehammer without harming Habeeni.

After graduating, Jerry wasn't accepted into medical school, so he moved back to New York into Ben's apartment and worked as a lab technician. A year later, still unable to get into medical school, Jerry moved to North Carolina for two years, then decided to move back north with Ben and establish a business.

Ben, by this time, was working in the Adirondack Mountain region of New York, teaching crafts to emotionally disturbed children. Reunited and eager to build a business, Ben and Jerry decided to open an ice cream parlor. (They passed up a bagel shop because the equipment was too expensive.) After receiving As in a $5 correspondence course in ice cream making from Penn State University, they selected Burlington, Vermont, as a good place to locate because of the college crowd and lack of competition.

Ben & Jerry's Homemade Ice Cream Parlor opened in May 1978 in a gas station renovated for $12,000, of which $4,000 was borrowed. Jerry made the ice cream in the early days and experimented with rich, unusual flavors, while Ben reached out to the local community with his socially conscious business concepts. The ice cream soon became a local favorite and its reputation started to spread.

In 1980, the partners rented space in a vacant textile plant and started packing their ice cream in pints. Ben would then load them in his Volkswagen Squareback wagon and peddle them to small grocers in the area. A year later, their first franchise store opened on Route 7 in Shelburne, Vermont.

Jerry moved to Arizona with his wife, Elizabeth, while she completed her Ph.D. program. They returned to Vermont in 1985, and Ben and Jerry promptly took their ice cream to a national market in their "Cowmobile," a modified motor home from which they handed out free samples. Unfortunately, the Cowmobile caught fire and burned in Cleveland, Ohio.

By introducing unusual flavors, such as Cherry Garcia, named in honor of the late Grateful Dead guitarist, Ben & Jerry's Ice Cream quickly became known throughout the country. By 1985, the company's annual revenues were nearly $10 million. One year later, they doubled to $20 million.

The phenomenal growth and success of Ben & Jerry's led to the unavoidable quest for a professional chief executive officer. However, Ben and Jerry conducted an unusual search. They sponsored a "YO! I Want To Be CEO" contest and invited anyone interested in the job to submit a 100-word essay application. After sifting through 22,000 applications, the founders hired Robert Holland, a former McKinsey & Company partner.

Today, Ben & Jerry's achieves nearly $160 million in annual sales. Ben serves as chairperson of the board and Jerry as vice chairperson. Both are active members of Businesses for Social Responsibility, an organization that works to promote socially responsible business practices. The company maintains a "Joy Gang," composed of employees who devise weird and exciting ways to keep people smiling, such as Ben & Jerry's "Weird Hat Day."

SOURCE: Ben & Jerry's Homemade, Inc. archives

Nehemiah M. Cohen

[Giant Food, Inc.]

Soon after immigrating to the United States, Nehemiah Cohen established three small grocery stores in Lancaster, Pennsylvania. Following the industry trend toward large supermarkets, Cohen and a partner opened their first large grocery store in Washington, D.C., in 1936. Through aggressive expansion, he built Giant Food, Inc., one of America's largest grocery store chains.

Nehemiah Myer Cohen was born on September 10, 1890, in the city of Jerusalem. After graduating from the Yeshiva, he was ordained a rabbi and accepted a teaching position in the small village of Rishon le Zion, near the Mediterranean coast. In 1908, at the age of 18, he married Naomi Halperin. The couple had three children: Emanuel in 1910, Israel in 1913, and Lillian, who was born in 1926 in the United States.

In 1914, Cohen traveled to England to gain insight into modern farming and construction, which could be put to use in his village. He soon found himself in a dilemma. Turkey, which at the time ruled his homeland, was at war with England. Cohen was not allowed to return to his village, nor was his family permitted to leave. Shortly thereafter, World War I erupted, leaving Cohen completely cut off from his family.

Cohen decided his best course was to continue his studies in the United States until he could be reunited with his family. In 1915, he arrived in Carnegie, Pennsylvania (near Pittsburgh), and earned income as a rabbi, teacher, and *Schochet,* preparing meat according to Jewish dietary laws. This led to the opening of a small meat market.

By the time the war ended, Cohen had become attached to the United States. He was reunited with his family in 1921, and they settled in Lancaster, Pennsylvania. Building on the experience gained in his small market, Cohen operated a small grocery store with Naomi, Emanuel, and Israel. Through diligence and hard work, the family opened two more stores.

During the Great Depression, Cohen became convinced that the best strategy for survival was to establish a large supermarket, require all sales to be in cash, and add the lowest markup possible. He discussed the plan with a friend, Samuel Lehrman, the owner of a successful food distributorship, and the two established a partnership.

On February 5, 1936, 45-year-old Cohen and his partner opened their first superstore in Washington, D.C. The venture was an immediate success and more stores were opened in the District of Columbia, Virginia, and Maryland.

The company continued to grow. When Samuel Lehrman died in 1948, Cohen assumed the position of president.

By the mid-1960s, the chain included 75 stores with annual sales in excess of $200 million. Cohen, in his 70s, took the title of chairman of the board and assumed a less active role in the company. In 1977, Joseph Danzansky was elected chairman of the board and Cohen took the title of "Honorary Chairman and Founder." His youngest son, Israel, was elected president and chief operating officer. Two years later, upon Danzansky's death, Israel also assumed the post of chairman of the board.

Following complications from an automobile accident, Cohen died on June 5, 1984, at the age of 93. At the time of his death, Giant had 16,000 employees, 132 stores, and annual sales exceeding $2 billion, making it America's 12th-largest retailer.

Cohen never lost sight of his roots. Until the late 1970s, he continued to visit his homeland regularly and contributed much of his time and money to the struggling state of Israel.

SOURCE: Giant Food, Inc. archives

Arthur A. Collins

[Collins Radio Company]

Arthur Andrew Collins was born on September 9, 1909, at Kingfisher, Oklahoma. His father, Merle Collins, was a successful businessman and farmer who applied mass production and modern management philosophies to farming. His strategy was to form units of independent farms that would cooperate with crop plantings and rotations, thereby providing the maximum efficient yield. As a result, the Collins Farm Company grew to include 60,000 acres in 31 Iowa counties.

Young Arthur Collins became interested in wireless radio communication before his tenth birthday. He and a friend often rigged crude radio equipment and once attached equipment to a 60-foot antenna that promptly routed a thunderbolt into the friend's basement. They moved what was left of the equipment to Collins's house, where they rebuilt it and were soon listening to transmissions from the U.S. Navy station in Arlington, Virginia.

Collins's passion for radios only grew stronger. When the Federal Radio Commission (now the Federal Communications Commission) started regulating amateur radio communications in 1923, 14-year-old Collins promptly passed the test and became a licensed operator. His father initially had reservations about the hobby, but eventually recognized its merit and started supplying him with more sophisticated equipment.

By the time he was 15, Collins had befriended John Reinartz, a German immigrant who gained fame in the electronics world by building a tuner for his radio that would allow changing radio frequencies manually and making adjustments to ensure optimum receptions. In early 1925, Reinartz accompanied an expedition to Greenland whose crew included Navy Lieutenant Commander Richard E. Byrd. While the Navy had trouble receiving transmissions, Collins picked the crew up quite clearly and made daily treks to the local telegraph office to pass along the expedition's findings to Washington.

After graduating from high school, Collins studied electronics at Amherst College, Coe College, and the University of Iowa. He and two friends took their hobby on the road in 1927, rigging a truck with shortwave radio equipment and driving through America's Southwest, while chatting with the Navy and friends back home.

In 1930, Collins married Margaret Van Dyke and promptly turned their home's basement into a workshop and laboratory. Within a year, the 23-year-old electronics whiz was building and selling radio transmitters. He later told *Forbes* magazine: "I picked what I was interested in and looked for a way to make a living."

The market, to this point, was dominated by hobbyists who pieced together systems at home, often resulting in a cluttered room and unreliable equipment. Collins built not only organized components, but also pretested, highly reliable equipment. Customers responding to his modest classified advertisements in *QST* magazine were consistently satisfied, and by 1933 Collins had to move his growing operations into a nearby plant.

Also in 1933, he formally incorporated his eight-employee firm as the Collins Radio Company. When Admiral Richard Byrd set sail that year for the South Pole, he carried Collins's radio equipment because of the 1925 experience. However, for the next two years, Collins's primary focus was the amateur market.

Slowly the commercial and government markets took notice. In 1935, Firestone Tire and Rubber purchased a transmitter for its operations in Liberia, Africa. Within three years, Collins was supplying police departments in several states with radio equipment and soon began selling to commercial radio stations. Concurrently, the company developed a new transmitter called the *Autotune,* which enabled aircraft pilots to maintain contact with air traffic on multiple frequencies. By 1937, Braniff Airways had equipped its entire fleet with Autotune radios.

None of the advances, however, provided a surge in business as great as World War II. By 1940, Collins had about 150 employees. Buoyed by military orders, that number jumped to nearly 1,200 in two short years, and peaked at more than 3,300 by 1945. The postwar economic growth provided considerable opportunity for the company in industries such as construction, public safety, aviation, and entertainment. Employment dropped to about 2,000 in 1950, but surged to nearly 11,000 in less than a decade.

The Collins Radio Company was acquired by Rockwell International in 1972. Arthur Collins resigned his post on the board of directors and launched a new venture, Arthur A. Collins, Incorporated. Arthur Collins died in 1987.

SOURCES: Collins Division, Rockwell International archives; Ken C. Braband, *The First 50 Years: A History of Collins Radio Company and the Collins Divisions of Rockwell International,* Rockwell International, 1983

Samuel Colt

[Colt Manufacturing Company]

Samuel Colt was born July 19, 1814, in Hartford, Connecticut. His mother died when he was only six years old, leaving behind six children. His father had made and lost considerable money in West Indies trade ventures. However, young Colt and his siblings weren't deprived in childhood, most likely because of his grandfather, a successful banker.

Colt was an intelligent and colorful individual, even as a child. He took apart his first gun at age seven. At age 15 he designed a crude underwater explosive device, which he detonated during a town celebration, dowsing onlookers with a wave of mud and water. One year later, while on a trip at sea, he conceived the idea of a revolving firearm by staring at the ship's rotating paddle wheel. He refined the design and, in 1832, was awarded a patent.

A gifted showman, Colt spent four years raising money for his venture billing himself as "Dr. Coult of Calcutta," giving lectures on laughing gas throughout North America. Proceeds were given to gun manufacturers, who built several prototype rifles, shotguns, and pistols. In 1836, he organized the Patent Arms Manufacturing Company in Paterson, New Jersey. His five-shot "Paterson" pistol was popular with soldiers fighting the Seminole Indians in the Florida Everglades, but lack of sales closed the company in 1842.

However, Colt was soon presented with another opportunity. In 1845, Sam Walker of the Texas Rangers needed a reliable weapon to help maintain order in Texas. Walker approached Colt and asked if he could produce a revolver. Colt, who had lost his manufacturing facilities, turned to young Eli Whitney Jr., son of the inventor of the cotton gin. Together, they produced the early models of Colt's revolvers at Whitney's plant near New Haven, Connecticut.

Colt designed the six-shot "Walker" gun for the Rangers. The first of the initial order of 1,000 guns from the Colt Patent Fire Arms Manufacturing Company were delivered to Captain Walker four days before he was killed in action.

By 1848, Colt was operating in a new factory at Hartford, which soon employed nearly 1,400 people who produced 150 revolvers each day. By introducing interchangeable parts and mass production, Colt quickly became a wealthy man. He personally led sales trips into the West during the California Gold Rush. By 1855, demand was so high that he purchased an additional 250 acres of land and built a spectacular Armory.

Colt's ventures weren't limited to guns. He also invented an electrically controlled naval mine and in 1843 laid a submarine electrical cable from New York City to Coney Island. Such ventures secured Colt's role as one of the country's early defense industry entrepreneurs.

Colt married rather late in his business career, wedding Elizabeth Jarvis of Middletown in 1856. A few years later their only child, Caldwell, was born. Samuel Colt's health declined at an early age. He died on January 10, 1862, at the age of 47. The Colt estate is still active today. The bigger part of the estate became the city-run Colt Park, which includes a statue of Colt. Sections of the old armory serve as offices and studios.

SOURCE: Robert L. Wilson, *The Colt Heritage,* Simon & Schuster, 1939

Moses H. Cone, Ceasar Cone

[Cone Mills Corporation]

In 1846, 17-year-old Herman Kahn immigrated to America from his native Bavaria, Germany, and took up residence with his sister and brother-in-law in Richmond, Virginia. To fit in with his new community, he changed the spelling of his last name to Cone and went to work at his brother-in-law's general store.

Within five years he was a partner, and the operation was moved to Jonesboro, Tennessee. In 1856, Cone married Helen Guggenheimer, and they eventually had 13 children, including sons Moses and Ceasar. The family moved again in 1870 to Baltimore, Maryland, where Moses and Ceasar went to work for their father's enterprise.

For the next 12 years, Moses and Ceasar traveled from Maryland to Alabama, selling their leather goods, tobacco, and groceries. Because money was scarce, many of their southern customers bartered with textiles rather than cash, which the brothers then resold. Soon, it became apparent to them that there were few cotton factories in the south.

Sensing an opportunity, they invested $50,000 in the C. E. Graham Manufacturing Company of Asheville, North Carolina, in 1887. The following year, 31-year-old Moses and 29-year-old Ceasar helped support two more North Carolina mills at Salisbury and Minneola. By 1900, they controlled the Minneola plant, which made flannels, sports denims, and corduroy until it closed in 1988.

Along with their own plants, the Cone brothers established a selling agency that eventually represented nearly 90 percent of the southern cotton mills. This venture opened up new markets and fueled rapid growth in the industry.

Ceasar Cone was especially confident in the role that denim would play in building America. In 1896, he led the family effort to build a denim mill in Greensboro, North Carolina. He named the venture Proximity Cotton Mills, because it was located in close proximity to the cotton fields. In 1902 the brothers opened their White Oak mill which, by 1910, was supplying one-third of the world's denim.

Moses Cone died unexpectedly on December 8, 1908, at the age of 51, leaving the mills and export company in the hands of Ceasar, who by 1912 had become one of the leading figures of the southern textiles industry and launched yet another mill, the Proximity Print Works. By the end of the following year, the Cone family owned part or all of seven textile mills.

Ceasar Cone died on March 21, 1917, at the age of 58. Fortunately, Cone family members and other capable administrators were able to maintain management of the company and sustain its growth. In 1945, most of the Cone holdings were restructured under a single company, and three years later the name was changed to the Cone Mills Corporation.

Today, Cone Mills is a public company traded on the New York Stock Exchange. It is still the world's largest producer of denim and the leading manufacturer of yarn-dyed and chamois flannel-shirting fabric, as well as the largest commission printer of home fabrics in the United States. Annual sales exceed $700 million.

SOURCES: Cone Mills Corporation archives; company publication, *Cone: A Century of Excellence*

John E. Connelley

[J. Edward Connelley Associates]

John Edward Connelley was born on August 15, 1925, in Pittsburgh, Pennsylvania, and grew up in the city's North Hills. His parents died when he was 16 years old, forcing him to abandon plans for college and take a job in a coal mine to support his four brothers and sisters. To earn extra money, he put on boxing gloves and climbed into the ring.

Connelley became interested in politics and served a term as a congressional assistant, leading to his own unsuccessful bid for Congress. He was, however, appointed to the Allegheny County Sanitary Authority, a post he held for 25 years. During that time, his most important project involved cleaning up Pittsburgh's three rivers, which had long been abused by the region's steel industry.

The experience convinced him that there were recreation opportunities on the rivers, and in 1958 he launched a 100-passenger river excursion boat that he named the *Gateway Clipper.* Two years later, he added a 400-passenger boat that served a complete dinner for about $3. The events, food, and entertainment eventually became more sophisticated, and guests lined up for gourmet dinner cruises with the Pittsburgh Symphony.

Connelley expanded his riverboat operation in Pittsburgh to include several vessels. He also acquired the Sheraton Hotel at Station Square on Pittsburgh's south side, adjacent to the docks for his riverboats.

Nearly two decades after establishing his Pittsburgh venture, Connelley acquired the Chelsea Pier on the west side of Manhattan and established World Yacht dinner cruises, a venture that was later sold. His next riverboat enterprise started in Davenport, Iowa, where he launched the President Casino company and acquired the Blackhawk Hotel. The company later established gaming enterprises at Biloxi, Mississippi, and St. Louis, Missouri.

However, riverboat operations are only part of the Connelley empire. He has long been active in the "incentive marketing" industries, orchestrating promotional campaigns for a wide range of clients, including more than 4,000 banking institutions nationwide.

One program, called "Apples for the Students," mixes supermarket promotions with the distribution of Apple computers to schools in the United States and abroad. Another is a venture with Chevrolet called "Driving for Education," and his newest educational partnership program is "Investment in Education" for the banking industry.

Connelley, a devout Roman Catholic, has a long history of supporting the Catholic church. In the Pittsburgh region, he has assisted numerous Catholic charities and schools, including the establishment of a business school focusing on entrepreneurship at Duquesne University. At the Vatican City in Rome, he financed Doma Sanctae Marthae, a 132-suite residence hotel near the Sistine Chapel, to accommodate visiting dignitaries.

Because of his track record with marketing partnerships and his relationship with the Vatican, Connelley has recently been awarded exclusive marketing rights to world famous reproductions of the Vatican Museum and Sistine Chapel. His newest company, Pittsburgh-based Treasures, Inc., will manage the program.

Today Connelley, in his early 70s, still oversees the day-to-day operations of his vast business empire, which employs several thousand people.

SOURCE: J. Edward Connelley Associates archives

Marquis M. Converse

[Converse, Inc.]

Marquis Converse descends from a noble ancestry that traces directly to Edward III of England, who reigned from 1327 to 1377. The first Converse to immigrate to America was Edward Converse, born in Wakerley, England, in 1590, and who sailed to Massachusetts with the Puritans in 1630. Marquis's father, Peter Mills Converse, spent most of his life farming in New Hampshire.

Marquis Mills Converse was born on October 25, 1861, in Lyme, New Hampshire. In 1880, he was hired at the Boston department store Houghton and Dutton, rising to the post of general superintendent within six years. He then returned to New Hampshire and purchased a general store, which he sold in 1890.

Converse returned to Boston and, with a partner, formed Converse and Pike, wholesale rubber boot merchants. He later took a position with the Beacon Falls Rubber Shoe Company. When his employer was acquired by U.S. Rubber, Converse decided it was time to launch his own company.

In 1908, he organized the Converse Rubber Shoe Company, using $100,000 of his own funds and $250,000 invested by others. A plant was built at Malden, Massachusetts, and by 1910 the company employed 350 people and made 4,000 pairs of boots and rubbers daily.

The work was seasonal, and Converse routinely laid off most of his workers from Christmas until the spring. By 1915, however, he was able to offer year-round employment through the manufacturing of canvas tennis shoes, which could be sold in the spring and summer. Sales that same year reached $1.5 million and increased to $2.5 million just one year later. By 1918, Converse had over 2,000 employees working in more than 4 acres of factory space.

Encouraged by the success of his shoes, Converse started making tires in 1915 after catching wind of a rumor that Harvey Firestone was going to build a rubber-shoe plant in Massachusetts. As long as hard-rubber tires remained popular, Converse was, in fact, able to competitively manufacture and sell tires.

However, in the 1920s, a new balloon technique was introduced from Europe, and Converse wasn't able to convert his technology to build reliable tires and inner tubes. Soon his defective tires were being returned as fast as they were shipped. Converse stubbornly refused to abandon his tire operations, even when they became a drain on the profitable shoe and boot business. In 1928, the Converse Rubber Shoe Company fell into receivership.

Marquis Mills Converse died in 1930 at the age of 69. In 1929, a local businessman named Mitchell Kaufman purchased the ailing company, but his leadership was short-lived. Kaufman was an avid sportsman, and while hunting in Maine in November 1930, he was separated from his companions in a snowstorm and died.

Converse then passed to the Stone family, who owned the company for the next 40 years. After going through subsequent ownership changes, Converse was spun off from its most recent parent company, Interco, as an independent, publicly traded company in 1994. Today, the company produces a variety of footwear products—basketball, children's, cross-training, and active-casual—that are distributed through more than 9,000 retailers.

SOURCE: Converse, Inc., archives

Scott Cook, Tom Proulx

[Intuit, Inc.]

After earning a B.A. degree in mathematics and economics from the University of Southern California and a master's degree in business administration from Harvard University, Scott Cook went to work for Procter & Gamble in marketing and brand management. Four years later, he joined the well-known consulting firm of Bain & Company.

In the early 1980s, Cook was having a problem at home. Both he and his wife were using their personal checking account, but they weren't doing a very good job of keeping their records coordinated. Cook, a novice personal computer user, evaluated the checkbook management software that was on the market and found them all to be cumbersome and difficult to understand. Digging a little deeper, he found that only 4 percent of the people trying the software actually used it, and that the return rate to retailers was nearly 50 percent. His marketing instincts told him that an opportunity existed.

Unlike most modern rapid-growth computer companies, Intuit wasn't launched with venture capital. In fact, Cook couldn't get a second meeting with any venture firms that listened to his pitch. Undaunted, he cashed in his various savings accounts, borrowed from his parents, maxed his credit cards, and mortgaged his house. Eventually, he was able to piece together $350,000.

For Cook to develop his package, he obviously needed a computer programmer. He decided to post recruiting posters throughout the campus at nearby Stanford University. When he visited the campus, he asked a passing student, Tom Proulx, for his opinion on where the posters would attract the most attention. Proulx, an engineering student with proficient computer skills, told Cook that he didn't have to look any further.

Cook was obsessed with developing a simple, inexpensive family financial management program. While Proulx worked on the code, Cook called literally hundreds of households to find out what consumers would want from such a package. They were determined to create a software product with a user-oriented interface that anyone could apply intuitively, hence the name of their new company: Intuit.

Working in Cook's Palo Alto, California, basement the pair was able to complete the first version of Quicken in 1984. As part of their prerelease testing, they sat several women from the Palo Alto Junior League in front of computers and cut them loose with the program. Cook and three colleagues watched carefully, but didn't offer any assistance.

Proulx noted the basis of each problem or uncertainty that surfaced, and he quickly modified the program. The founders were convinced that if a purchaser or reviewer would encounter the same problem, they'd never use the product again. Proulx got the bugs worked out, and Quicken hit the market.

Initially, the founders attempted to market their software through banks. This quickly proved unsuccessful, leaving Intuit in a tight spot. Cook's initial investment was running so low that he wasn't sure how he'd pay his seven employees; the venture capital firms were still not impressed, and the software retailers weren't interested in a new product that wasn't backed by a massive advertising campaign.

Cook scrambled to sell what inventory he could through a few more banks. By 1986, he had saved about $125,000 from sales, which he invested in an advertising campaign that he put together himself. The ads and the product hit the market in time for the Christmas season, and Quicken sales skyrocketed. By 1990, more than 1 million copies were sold by a sales force of only two people. Cook succeeded in building a company around a low-cost, high-quality product backed by a comprehensive technical support structure.

Intuit has grown rapidly by developing new products as well as by acquisitions. In 1992, Intuit unveiled QuickBooks, a business accounting package designed for small businesses. Two years later, the company acquired ChipSoft, Inc., a leading developer of PC tax-preparation software. Then, in 1994, Intuit acquired Parsons Technologies, the software company built by dynamic entrepreneur Bob Parsons. One year later, they acquired GALT Technologies, developer of the NETworth mutual fund information network.

The company went public in March 1993, and current annual sales are in excess of $500 million. Intuit's flagship product, Quicken, has over 8 million users, which translates into about 70 percent of the market share for home financial management software.

SOURCES: Intuit, Inc. archives; Sean Silverthore, "Four-Star Service," *PC Week* magazine, March 25, 1996; John Case, "Customer Service: The Last Word," *Inc.* magazine, April, 1991; *PC Week* magazine, March 25, 1996; *Inc.* magazine, April 1991

Ira J. Cooper, Claude E. Hart, John F. Schaefer

[Cooper Tire & Rubber Company]

Ira James Cooper was born in 1874, the only son of John W. and Elizabeth Cooper, and was raised in western Ohio with his younger sister, Amy. In the early 1880s, Cooper started working in his father's blacksmith shop shoeing horses, but soon realized that he didn't have the size or strength to work with the heavy plow horses and mule teams.

Cooper turned his attention to business and, in the early 1890s, graduated from the Miami Jacobs Business School in Dayton, Ohio. He moved to Chicago and in 1894, was hired as a bicycle salesman for Morgan & Wright. This led to a job selling the new rubber-cushioned tire for buggies and, eventually, pneumatic tires for automobiles.

By 1912, Cooper had returned to Ohio and established the I. J. Cooper Rubber Company in Cincinnati. The tire and auto accessory wholesale firm quickly opened nine retail stores throughout Ohio, Indiana, and Tennessee in what Cooper considered "the center of the best automobile population in the country."

Sales for the Cooper Rubber Company reached $4.7 million in 1919, and the Cooper catalog—which listed more than 15,000 car accessories—was considered one of the most complete in the country. That same year, Cooper organized The Cooper Storage Battery Manufacturing Company in Madisonville, Ohio, to supply the considerable demand for automobile replacement batteries.

While Cooper was expanding his business holdings, Claude E. Hart and John F. Schaefer were building their own enterprise in Akron, Ohio. In 1914, these brothers-in-law purchased the M&M Manufacturing Company, which made tire patching and repair kits. The venture grew quickly since a tire's lifetime barely reached 5,000 miles and most automobile owners were buying five tires each year.

In 1915, Schaefer and Hart expanded into the retreading business by forming the Giant Tire & Rubber Company to make rebuilt (retreaded) tires. Within two years they required larger quarters and moved into the vacant Toledo-Findlay Tire Company plant in Findlay, Ohio. Cooper was an investor in Giant and, by 1920, had helped the company expand into the production of new tires, which were primarily distributed through Cooper's retail stores.

On March 11, 1920, the Giant Tire & Rubber Company merged with the I. J. Cooper Rubber Company and The Cooper Storage Battery Manufacturing Company to form The Cooper Corporation. Initially, Cooper was named president, Hart vice president, and Schaefer secretary. One year later, a second plant was added, and the company manufactured a complete line of rubber products, including new and rebuilt tires, inner tubes, carriage tires, and rubber goods for radio equipment.

Hart and Schaefer remained with The Cooper Corporation for the next four decades, while Cooper moved into new ventures. In 1930, Cooper formed a holding company, called the Master Tire & Rubber Company, that combined The Cooper Corporation, Giant, and The Falls Rubber Company of Cuyahoga Falls, Ohio. That same year, Cooper expanded his interests to include the Biltmore Manufacturing Company of Cincinnati, which made automotive seat covers.

In 1941, Ira J. Cooper died at the age of 67. He was survived by his wife of 28 years, Florence Warrick Johnson Cooper, and his son, Ira J. Cooper Jr. Five years later, the board of directors of Master Tire voted to change the name to Cooper Tire & Rubber Company.

SOURCE: Cooper Tire and Rubber archives

Adolph Coors

[Adolph Coors Company]

Adolph Coors was born in 1847 in Barmen, Prussia, a city that would later become Wuppertal, Germany. Adolph's father, Joseph Coors, was a master flour miller. He moved his family to the nearby city of Dortmund to find work two years after Adolph's birth. At age 14, young Adolph found his life's passion. He began working as an apprentice at the Henry Wenker Brewery in Dortmund. It was here that he began to learn the craft of the brewery business.

In 1862, one year after Adolph began his apprenticeship, tragedy struck the Coors family: Adolph's mother and father both died, and at age 15 he had to support himself. His position at the brewery was now his only means of survival. To earn extra money, he started working nights as the brewer's bookkeeper.

After war erupted in Germany during the spring of 1868, Adolph stowed away on a ship headed to the United States. Upon arrival, he supported himself with various jobs, including bricklayer, stonecutter, and fireman. Coors soon decided to journey west, where he found a job in Naperville, Illinois, at the

Stenger Brewery. After working there for about two years, he again headed west and settled in Denver, Colorado.

In 1872, Coors purchased a partnership in a Denver bottling company and, within one year, acquired full ownership. He spent his Sundays—his only day off—roaming through the valley of Golden, Colorado. The abundant, clear, cool springs drew him, and he knew it was the place he wanted to start his brewery.

In 1873, just before Colorado became the 38th state, Coors joined with Jacob Schueler, a prosperous Denver businessman, to establish the Golden Brewery. The business grew rapidly and, when production reached 3,500 barrels in 1880, Coors was able to buy out his partner and repay him his initial $18,000 investment.

Shortly after the brewery was under way, Coors launched another company called Colorado Glass Works and began manufacturing glass bottles. He also found his bride, Louisa Weber of Denver. They married in 1879, and by 1893 they had six children.

Coors' brewery continued to prosper, reaching 17,600 barrels in 1890 and 48,000 barrels in 1900. He continuously reinvested his profits in the brewery and traveled in search of more efficient production equipment to keep the brewery competitive in the industry.

In 1914, Prohibition came to Colorado and all three of Coors's sons scrambled to keep the company in business. Colorado Glass Works had since become Coors Porcelain Company, and Coors had purchased a cement manufacturing plant as well. These two operations helped keep the family afloat.

The company used its brewery equipment to make near beer, and sold the alcohol by-product to hospitals and drug companies. It also made malted milk, which is produced by essentially the same process as malting barley to produce beer. The venture became so successful that the company maintained its malted milk line until 1955, long after the repeal of Prohibition in 1933.

Although Adolph Coors died in 1929, before the end of Prohibition, he lived long enough to know that his company would survive in the hands of Adolph Coors Jr., his eldest son. Adolph Jr. sought expansion, and in the six years following the repeal of Prohibition he expanded the company's market to include ten western states. It was during this time that the famous Coors slogan—"Brewed with Pure Rocky Mountain Spring Water"—was introduced.

During World War II, new challenges arose for Coors. The brewery began producing beer for the government, setting aside half of all beer produced for military troops. However, it contained less alcohol, hence the term *3.2 beer.* Sales continued to climb after the war, reaching 1 million barrels in 1955.

Coors made the transition from a regional to a national brewer during the 1970s and, by 1985, broke ground for a new packaging facility in Virginia's Shenandoah Valley. Five years later, the company purchased a second eastern brewery in Memphis, Tennessee.

The 1990s have been prosperous for Coors. Under the direction of Peter Coors, the founder's great-grandson, Coors has become the third-largest brewer in the nation and began international expansion distributing Coors into more than 30 foreign markets. Today, Coors sales exceed 20 million barrels annually at the world's largest single-site brewery.

SOURCE: Coors Brewing Company archives

Tom Corson, Claude Corson, Keith Corson

[Coachmen Industries, Inc.]

Claude Corson, an Air Force veteran and rising sales manager in Elkhart, Indiana, dreamed of owning a business with his brothers. Drawing from his interest in the emerging recreational vehicle (RV) industry, he scouted the Middlebury area, just east of Elkhart, for a suitable location. In April 1964 he negotiated a lease for a 55- by 85-foot building, which formerly housed a farm implement dealership, for $80 per month.

Claude's brother Tom Corson was 37 years old. After serving with the U.S. Navy, he spent 17 years with an investment company. Having experienced 11 transfers during his career climb to the level of assistant vice president, Tom was anxious to sign on to the family venture.

The third Corson brother, Keith, was a production manager at a refrigeration manufacturer in Elkhart. He had served in the U.S. Marines and attended the University of Wichita (now Wichita State). He, too, was interested in putting his skills to work for the family.

Claude was the first full-time employee of the company, which was capitalized with an initial investment of $700. Within one month of moving into their new quarters, Claude, with help from his wife, Sue, and brother Keith, completed their prototype model. At about the same time, Tom was traveling along the Ohio Turnpike and was intrigued with a roadside motel named Coachman.

After modifying it to the plural Coachmen, Tom suggested the name to his brothers, who quickly agreed to adopt it. However, they weren't sure exactly what direction their company would take, so they listed the name as Corson Car and Coach Company. By September of 1964, Keith joined Claude full-time, and the brothers worked 16 hours per day, seven days per week for months.

Tom's wife, Dorothy, and Keith's wife, Janice, both nurses, started working part-time at Coachmen. The family environment even encompassed Pete, the Dalmatian watchdog that eventually became part of the company logo. Legend has it that the Corsons taught Pete to distinguish between dealers (buyers) and nuisance salespeople. When the salespeople called, Pete would chase them off with a threatening growl.

The first line of trailers, known as the Coachmen Cadet, boasted a spacious floor plan with generous cabinet, storage, and counter space. This became a hallmark of Coachmen, and annual sales increased from $23,600 in 1964 to $3 million in 1967. A luxury model was soon added that quickly outsold the standard model. Other innovations in design and marketing soon followed, including the Caravan Club for Coachmen owners.

In 1965, Tom resigned his position with the investment company and became the third full-time brother at Coachmen. The brothers quickly added another building and acquired the Quonset Hut, producer of truck covers and campers.

Today Coachmen has annual sales in excess of $330 million and employs nearly 2,500 people who manufacture more than 16,000 RVs each year under the trade names Coachmen, Travelmaster, Viking, and Shasta.

SOURCE: Coachmen Industries archives

Joshua L. Cowen

[Lionel Corporation]

Joshua Lionel Cowen was born in New York City on August 25, 1877, the eighth of nine children born to Hyman and Rebecca Cohen. (The family changed the spelling of their last name between generations.) Hyman had immigrated to America after building a successful hat-making business in England. Rebecca, in addition to raising the children, maintained a successful piece goods store.

Young Cowen showed an early aptitude for invention. In high school, he fashioned an electric doorbell, but he didn't pursue commercialization of the device after being told by his instructor that nothing would replace a knock at the door. After graduation, he enrolled at and dropped out of City College and Columbia, then became an apprentice for an electrical firm.

He left that job to work for Acme Electric Lamp Company, where he developed his own dry cell battery. In 1899, he was granted his first patent, for a battery device that would ignite photographers' flash powder. His work caught the attention of the U.S. Navy, who contracted with him to assemble land mines. In 1900, Cowen was granted a second patent for improvements to his explosive fuses. With the patents and Navy experience under his belt, Cowen was ready to launch his own business.

In September 1900, 22-year-old Cowen and another Acme employee named Harry Grant established the Lionel Manufacturing Company (taken from Cowen's middle name) to "engage in the manufacture of electrical novelties." They produced fuses, small low-voltage motors, and electrical novelties, while Cowen invested his considerable inventive talents at finding a new product that could be readily marketed.

In 1901, Cowen was struck by the idea of building an electric car that could ride along a track in a circle. He envisioned the placement of these cars in store windows, where they might call attention to the other merchandise featured in the window. However, shoppers became more interested in the car itself, which quickly became a strong seller. He quickly fashioned it into an electric train, and by 1903 Cowen was distributing his first Lionel train catalog.

The success gave Cowen the security to start a family. In 1904, Cowen married Cecelia Liberman, whom he had met on a crowded trolley. The couple had two children, Lawrence and Isabel, both of whom would eventually serve with the company.

By 1910, the New York City manufacturing plant was unable to keep up with demand. Cowen moved the company to a new factory in New Haven, Connecticut. By 1920, annual sales had increased to nearly $850,000 and employment topped 700. Four years later, the company had to move to an even larger facility in Irvington, New Jersey.

As with nearly every company in the United States, the Great Depression had a devastating effect on Lionel. Few people could afford to spend their money on toys and hobbies. By 1934, however, Lionel teamed up with Walt Disney to produce a Mickey Mouse handcar. One million of these items were sold for $1 each. A year later the Steam Whistle was introduced. The two innovations are credited with saving Lionel during the Depression.

In less than a decade the company faced another obstacle: World War II. By 1942, all train production at Lionel was halted. Fortunately, the company was able to manufacture navigation and communication equipment for the armed forces, keeping the factory open. After the war, Cowen passed day-by-day control to his son, Lawrence Cowen, who was named Lionel's president. Joshua Cowen died on September 8, 1965.

By the late 1950s, Joshua retired from the business, and shortly thereafter, Lawrence Cowen sold Lionel to a group of investors headed by Roy Cohn, Joshua's great-nephew. The company was next owned by General Mills through the 1970s and 1980s. In the mid-1980s, General Mills combined the Lionel operations with its Kenner Toys and Parker Brothers Games, and manufacturing operations were eventually moved to Mount Clemens, Michigan.

In 1986, Detroit real estate entrepreneur Richard P. Kughn purchased Lionel and formed the current company, Lionel Trains, Inc. The company was sold again in 1992 to Wellspring Associates, LLC, and a new company, Lionel LLC, was established. Today the company employs 600 people and offers more than 350 different products.

SOURCES: Lionel Corporation archives; Ron Hollander, *All Aboard,* Workman Publishing, New York, 1981

John Cowles Sr.

[Cowles Media Company]

John Cowles was born on December 14, 1898, at Algona, Iowa, the fifth of six children born to Gardner and Florence Call Cowles. In 1904, his father took control of the *Des Moines Register and Leader* and moved the family to Des Moines, Iowa.

After graduating from Harvard University and serving in the U.S. Army during World War I, Cowles took a job with his father's newspaper as a reporter. In 1923, while assigned to Russia, he covered the rise to power of Joseph Stalin. Later that year, he returned home and married Elizabeth Morley Bates of Oswego, New York, on July 18. The couple eventually had two sons and two daughters.

In 1935, backed by his family, Cowles purchased a money-losing afternoon daily in Minneapolis, *The Star.* He revised the editorial direction of the newspaper, added more colorful stories, and increased the use of photography. As a result, circulation doubled within four years. In 1939, Cowles acquired his chief competitor, *The Journal,* and two years later he purchased *The Tribune,* essentially giving him control of the Minneapolis newspaper market.

The strong-willed editor and publisher kept a close eye on his writers, frequently sending them torn-out pages from the paper filled with red notes. When an article reported: "Of the 663 students at a local college, 361 were male and 212 were female," Cowles note demanded: "What sex were the rest?"

Cowles served as president of his Minneapolis Star and Tribune Company for 33 years, until 1968. He then retained the position of board chairman until his retirement in 1973. John Cowles died on February 25, 1983, at the age of 84.

Today, Cowles Media Company is a multifaceted organization with annual sales of nearly $450 million. Its holdings include Minnesota newspapers and several magazines.

SOURCE: Cowles Media Company archives

Jenny Craig, Sid Craig

[Jenny Craig, Inc.]

After gaining 45 pounds during a difficult pregnancy, Jenny Craig joined a local gym and shed the pounds through hard work. The gym's owner, noticing her dedication and results, hired her as a manager. She later went to work for Body Contour, Inc., a chain of women's fitness centers owned by Sid Craig, whom she later married. After selling Body Contour, Sid and Jenny launched Jenny Craig, Inc., which has become one of the leading weight management companies in the world.

Sid and Jenny Craig were both born in 1932 (Sid on March 22 and Jenny on August 7) but in different countries. Jenny Guidroz was the youngest of six children in a Berwick, Louisiana, Depression-era family. Her father worked three part-time jobs, while her mother raised chickens and tended a large family garden. As a teenager, Jenny worked in a dental clinic and planned to become a dental hygienist.

She didn't complete school, however, instead marrying a race boat driver and giving birth to two daughters. After the birth of her second child, Jenny was unable to shed the 45 pounds that she'd gained during the pregnancy. Since she knew nothing about dieting, she joined a New Orleans gym and went to work. In addition to working out, Jenny read all the material she could find about weight loss and nutrition. Soon, the owner of the gym hired Jenny as a manager.

Sid was born in Vancouver, British Columbia, where his parents worked in a dress shop. His mother felt Sid should be in show business and pushed his career early in life, carting him off to dance lessons soon after he started walking. Sid eventually made it into television, working as an extra on the "Our Gang" comedies.

After graduating from Fresno State University in 1955, Sid joined the Navy, where he made extra money giving dance lessons at the local Arthur Murray studio. He soon acquired his own Arthur Murray franchise. Over the years he learned that women not only wanted to be good dancers, they wanted to be thin dancers. Intrigued with the potential of this new market, he sold his interest in the dance studio and opened Body Contour, Inc., a chain of women's fitness centers.

Back in Louisiana, Jenny had mortgaged her house and opened her own gym, which she eventually sold. But her interest in combining fitness with weight control continued, and in 1970 she accepted a job with Sid's Body Contour center that had just opened in New Orleans. By this time Sid and Jenny were both divorced and, over the years, a romance developed. The couple married in 1979.

Sid sold Body Contour to Nutri/System in 1982 at an attractive profit. It didn't take long for the couple to get the bug to open another chain. However, the sales agreement prohibited Sid and Jenny from competing with Nutri/System for two years in the United States. So the couple packed their bags and flew to Australia, where they established the Jenny Craig Weight Loss Program. After several months of cultural adjustment, the chain became successful, opening 50 centers by the end of the first year.

In 1985, the noncompete clause expired, and the Craigs quickly reestablished their presence in the United States by opening 14 centers in the Los Angeles area. Today, there are nearly 800 company-owned and franchised centers throughout the world, producing revenues of approximately $400 million annually. Sid (chairman) and Jenny (vice chairman) still work well into the evenings at their La Jolla, California, headquarters.

SOURCES: Jenny Craig, Inc. archives; Kathleen Hendrix, "Craig: A Southern California Entrepreneur," *Los Angeles Times,* March 4, 1990

Richard T. Crane

[Crane Co.]

Unable to find work in New York, Richard Crane took his foundry experience and moved to Chicago. After building a small shed next to his uncle's lumberyard, Crane started casting lightning rod tips and couplings for local customers. Soon he expanded into valves, machine tools, and steam systems. His company later entered the bathroom fixture business. Today, the Crane Co. is still one of the largest and most successful manufacturers of mechanical systems in the world.

Richard Teller Crane was born on May 15, 1832, at Paterson, New Jersey. To help support the family, young Crane went to work in a cotton mill at age 9, then in a Brooklyn foundry at age 15, where he learned to fashion and finish brass. After several other jobs, the panic of 1854 put him out of work. He decided to move to Chicago, where his uncle owned a successful lumber business.

Upon his arrival in Chicago in 1855, Crane convinced his uncle to let him build a small foundry on his lumberyard property. Soon the 14- by 24-foot wooden shed was complete, and 23-year-old Crane was serving as molder, furnace tender, metal pourer, casting cleaner, and salesman.

Business grew rapidly, and Crane summoned his brother Charles from New Jersey to join him in the venture. They quickly expanded into a new three-story building and were filling orders from Wisconsin, Kentucky, and even Iowa. Their biggest break came when the supplier for P. W. Gates, a local freight-car builder, couldn't fill an order for parts because of a copper shortage. Gates turned to Crane, who was able to find a supply of copper in Detroit. He personally made the trip and, upon return, promptly filled the order, which resulted in a longtime business relationship.

The Crane brothers became adept at manufacturing valves and systems that carried steam heat. Eventually, they started bidding on construction contracts for installing steam heat systems. Their two early contracts, the Cook County Court House and the Illinois State Penitentiary in Joliet, propelled them to national recognition.

They increased their line of manufactured products as well, such as brass fittings, plates, knobs, spurs, and wagon equipment. The growth of the railroad increased demand for their valves, pipe, brass castings, and engine trimmings. An early Crane brass valve was even found at Colonel Drake's historic oil field at Titusville, Pennsylvania.

After the Civil War, rebuilding initiatives throughout the country provided several new opportunities and challenges for the Cranes. Their first printed catalog appeared in 1866. Among the new product offerings were water pumps, bung bushings for beer barrels, ventilating fans, and fire hydrants. The company even started producing steam engines and, in 1867, entered the elevator business. Their elevator division eventually was sold off and became part of the Otis Elevator Company.

When Mrs. O'Leary's cow set off the Chicago fire in 1871, Crane was lucky enough to be located on the other side of town. The company escaped with no damage whatsoever and invested a considerable effort to rebuild Chicago's crippled infrastructure. That same year, Charles Crane retired from the business and sold his stock to Richard for $300,000.

Over the following decades, Richard Crane and his engineers developed and patented a number of products. In 1884, a wholesaler in Omaha, Nebraska, was unable to pay his bills, putting Crane reluctantly in the distribution business. However, the venture proved so successful that he soon established a second sales center in Los Angeles. He also started acquiring related manufacturing businesses throughout the country.

Richard Teller Crane died in January 1912 at the age of 79. His eldest son, Charles R. Crane, assumed the post of president for the next two years, and he was succeeded by his brother, Richard T. Crane Jr., who had some very bold ideas about the direction of the company.

When World War I ended, the United States experienced a strong consumer market that reacted to years of backed-up demand. Richard Crane Jr. decided to build a better bathroom for a country that was just getting used to indoor plumbing. Building on the company's experience with drab plumbing fixtures, Crane became quite involved with stylish design and sophisticated merchandising of toilets, vanities, and other bathroom fixtures. Soon the company was one of the leading bathroom manufacturers in the world.

SOURCE: Crane Co. archives; *Crane Company, 1855–1975: The First 120 Years*

Zenas Crane

[Crane & Co., Inc.]

Following the trade of his father and older brother, Zenas Crane established a small paper mill on the Massachusetts frontier at the beginning of the nineteenth century. The six generations of Cranes who followed have maintained the high-quality craftsmanship in paper and stationery manufacturing that Zenas established when he founded Crane & Co., Inc.

Zenas Crane's great-great-grandfather, Henry Crane, immigrated to Dorchester, Massachusetts, from England in 1648. Zenas's father, Stephen Crane, was a papermaker during the late 1700s, supplying paper for banknotes to Paul Revere. Crane's oldest son, Stephen Jr., followed his father's footsteps and became a papermaker. Zenas was born on May 9, 1777, in Milton, Massachusetts. 11 years younger than Stephen, Zenas worked in the paper business under the watchful eyes of his father and older brother.

In 1799, Zenas Crane left his home in Worcester, Massachusetts, on horseback in search of a good location to establish a paper mill. Two years later, at age 24, he settled on a location in Dalton, Massachusetts, and established his company with two partners, whom he later bought out.

Crane's first advertisement in the Pittsfield *Sun* asked area housewives to save their rags so that he could convert them into workable pulp for paper products. From this modest beginning, Crane never wavered from his high-quality, rag-based paper products, even when the less expensive wood-pulp method became popular.

In 1809, Crane married Lucinda Brewer, and the couple would eventually have nine children. When he married, he had actually left the paper mill to operate a general store, a venture that lasted nearly three years. However, by 1810, Crane was back in the paper business for good.

Once the mill was adequately serving the needs of local residents, Crane began looking for other markets. He served as plant manager and chief salesman for Crane & Company, spending considerable time on horseback or stagecoaches, followed by exhaustive work at the plant to fulfill the resulting orders.

In 1842, at the age of 65, Crane elected to retire from the business, and on June 29, 1845, Zenas Crane died. He had passed the torch to two of his sons, Zenas Marshall Crane and James Brewer Crane, the second of seven generations that would maintain the family business.

Not long after Zenas's death, his sons were able to secure a contract for making the paper on which United States currency is printed, a business that exists to this day. Dating back even further than that was considerable contract work making paper for financial bonds and securities. The company also has a long-established history of producing high-quality stationery.

Today, Lansing E. Crane, a sixth-generation family member, serves as the company's chairman, president, and CEO. The company has annual sales in excess of $165 million and employs about 1,300 people.

SOURCE: Crane & Co., Inc. archives; *The First 175 Years of Crane Papermaking,* by Wadsworth R. Pierce, 1977

Seymour R. Cray

[Cray Research, Inc.]

Seymour Roger Cray was born on September 28, 1925, in Chippewa Falls, Wisconsin. At an early age, he showed an interest in science, working with chemistry sets and radio gear in the family basement. During World War II, Cray served in several capacities, including a tour in Europe and an assignment in the Philippines, where he helped decipher Japanese codes.

In 1947, Cray married Verene Voll, and the couple eventually had three children. He enrolled at the University of Minnesota, earning a bachelor's degree in electronic engineering and a master's in applied mathematics in 1951.

Upon graduation, he went to work for Engineering Research Associates as a computer designer. Founder William Norris eventually sold his company to the Sperry Rand Corporation and, with Cray, launched a new computer venture, called Control Data Corporation, in 1957. At Control Data, Cray orchestrated the design and manufacture of the world's first supercomputer. Using transistors instead of vacuum tubes, the computer was an instant hit with the military and research laboratories.

In 1972, Cray left Control Data and established Cray Research at Chippewa Falls. The new company was organized for a single purpose: to build the world's most powerful supercomputers. Its first computer—the CRAY-1—was delivered in March 1976, and that same month, the company made its first public stock offering. A second CRAY-1 was ordered in May of 1976.

The company received its first commercial order in 1978, the same year it established an office in the United Kingdom. One year later, offices were also established in Japan and West Germany. By 1980, Cray Research was the world's undisputed leading supplier of high-speed scientific computers.

As development progressed on a new generation of Cray supercomputers in the mid-1980s, Cray personally reduced his administrative responsibilities to focus on product development. By 1989, he had organized the Cray Computer Corporation in Colorado Springs, Colorado. The venture eventually soured and ceased operations in 1995.

Undaunted, Cray established yet another company in 1996, SRC Computer. The Colorado Springs start-up was launched with only five people and Cray's typical optimism. Tragically, after being severely injured in an automobile accident near his Colorado Springs home, Seymour R. Cray died on October 5, 1996, at the age of 71. He was survived by his second wife, Geri (Harrand) Cray, whom he married in 1980.

Today, Cray Research continues to serve the high-end computing market. Four out of five supercomputer sites use Cray systems. Nearly every Defense Department lab has a Cray Research system, as do more than 160 universities throughout the world. In 1996, Cray Research merged with Silicon Graphics, Inc.

SOURCE: Cray Research archives

John C. Crean

[Fleetwood Enterprises, Inc.]

Initially a producer of venetian blinds, John Crean established Fleetwood Enterprises in 1950 as a manufacturer of low-cost housing. Through growth and diversification, Fleetwood is now the leading producer of manufactured housing, motor homes, and travel trailers in the country.

John Crean was born on July 4, 1925. Four years later, his parents moved their daughter and four sons from the family farm in Bowdon, North Dakota, to Compton, California. At the onset of World War II, 16-year-old John quit school and enlisted in the Navy, spending most of the war sailing the Pacific.

After returning to Compton, Crean married Donna Setterstrom, a salesperson at the local Sears store record counter, and they eventually had four children.

Two years after his marriage, Crean started a business assembling and selling venetian blinds to house trailer manufacturers. As the business progressed, he sharpened a vision of building low-cost, mass-produced housing. In 1950, he established Fleetwood Enterprises and built his first plant in Anaheim, California. The company prospered and quickly became one of America's leading housing manufacturers.

In 1964, Crean recognized an opportunity in the recreational vehicle (RV) industry. He acquired a small plant that produced Terry travel trailers. Fleetwood now operates 10 manufacturing plants that have built more than 800,000 travel trailers. In addition to the Terry name, Fleetwood's travel trailers are sold under the names of Avion, Mallard, Prowler, Savanna, Westport, and Wilderness. In 1989, the company acquired the Coleman folding trailer product line.

In 1969, the company added a line of motor homes. Today, five plants have built more than 325,000 motor homes under the names Bounder, Pace Arrow, Southwind, Flair, Discovery, American Eagle, American Dream, American Tradition, Tioga, and Jamboree.

Fleetwood, now a Fortune 500 company based in Riverside, California, went public in 1965 when annual sales were about $18 million. Today, sales are nearly $3 billion annually. The company employs approximately 18,000 people in 51 manufacturing plants and builds more than 68,000 recreational vehicles and 69,000 single-family homes each year. In all, Fleetwood Enterprises has built nearly 1 million homes since John Crean founded the company.

John Crean, who turned 71 in 1996, still holds the post of chairman of the board and chief executive officer. Donna Crean manages The Crean Foundation, which actively supports youth, cultural, and educational programs. Earlier in their careers, the Creans established the Rancho Capistrano Foundation for youth and church outings. In 1981, they donated the 96-acre Rancho Capistrano to Dr. Robert Schuller's Crystal Cathedral.

SOURCE: Fleetwood Enterprises, Inc. archives

Trammell Crow

[Trammell Crow Company]

Born into poverty, Trammell Crow quickly became adept as a real estate developer after serving in the Navy in World War II. In 1948, he established the Trammell Crow Company, which eventually grew into America's leading real estate developer and property manager.

Trammell Crow was born in 1914 in Dallas, Texas, the fifth of eight children. The family grew up poor, and conditions worsened when Trammell's father lost his job during the Depression. About the time he was 16 years old, Trammell realized that the family was truly poor. He later recalled how it affected him: "There was a dull pain, as you must know. Fortunately it was expressed in action, work, and thought, and not in resentment and self-degradation."

The Crow family grew up financially poor, but spiritually rich. His parents were strong Christians who believed in the literal inerrancy of the Bible. The family attended church every Sunday and prayed together on their knees nightly.

After graduating from high school, Crow worked as a runner, and later as a teller, at the Mercantile Bank in Dallas. He studied accounting in night classes at Southern Methodist University, became a certified public accountant, and joined the accounting firm of Ernst and Ernst. When World War II broke out, Crow joined the Navy as an accountant. By the end of his fifth year, he was discharged after reaching the rank of commander.

In 1942, while in the Navy, Crow married Margaret Doggett. Her family owned and operated the Doggett Grain Company, although her parents had died in an automobile accident years earlier. The Crows would eventually have six children. Upon his discharge from the Navy in 1946, 32-year-old Crow joined his wife's family business.

Margaret owned the building that the Doggett Grain Company shared with several other tenants. Soon after Crow started working there, the building's major tenant moved out. To fill the void, he persuaded a group of small rug manufacturers to lease the available space. By combining several businesses under the same roof, he had established his first *mart,* a marketing approach that would become something of a trademark for Crow.

Not long after that Crow became acquainted with John and Storey Stemmons, two brothers who owned about 11,000 acres of undeveloped land. He became interested in the new trend of one-story warehouses, and when one of the rug merchants he had attracted to the family warehouse expressed an interest in moving, Crow offered to build him a new warehouse on the Stemmons property, and in 1948 the Trammell Crow Company was officially launched.

However, Crow wanted to build warehouses that would set him apart from the competition. He designed the buildings so that the loading docks were located on the side or in the rear of the building, and he located the offices in the front of the building, complete with windows. He insisted on attractive carpeting and bathroom fixtures inside the building. Also, he provided attractive landscaping, complete with trees, flowers, and manicured lawns.

Encouraged by his success in filling three warehouses, Crow quickly started constructing more buildings, even before tenants were identified. Because the economy was booming and he didn't have time to attend to details, he often starting construction before the loan was even approved.

Trammell Crow was a man who had faith in the people he dealt with until they gave him a reason not to. In the few instances where people took advantage of him, he would simply quit doing business with them. His negotiations lasted minutes rather than hours, and he would sign contracts without first reading them. By following his instincts, Crow was the biggest warehouse builder in Dallas by the mid-1950s.

Crow's interest in marts continued to grow. At some point he started paying close attention to the nation's two major furniture marts—one in Chicago and the other in High Point, North Carolina. He was convinced that their hallways were too small, too dimly lit, and too crowded as people moved between showrooms.

Despite the fact that the furniture industry wanted no part of another furniture mart, Crow built the Dallas Home Furnishing Mart in 1957, followed later by the Dallas Trade Mart and, eventually, the Dallas Market Center Complex—over 9 million square feet of wholesale exhibit space. As with most of his properties, Crow himself designed most of the property and handed his drawings to architects to prepare formal blueprints. His inclusion of a large, open atrium in the Trade Mart is credited with establishing a trend in the use of such atriums in many American public buildings.

By the 1960s, Trammell Crow was an immensely wealthy man. However, those who worked with him described a humble, unpretentious gentleman who was warm and generous toward everyone with whom he came in contact. His office was a large, open floor, surrounded by secretaries and associates who were invited to listen in on his conversations and read his mail so that everyone would be aware of business activities.

The Trammell Crow Company was hardly a structured organization. Until the 1990s, it was actually a series of partnerships that eventually grew to more than 100 partners and more than 600 separate partnership agreements. His business increased through his trust in almost anyone who would propose a sensible real estate venture. Crow usually supplied the bulk of the cash and credit, and the partner or partners usually supplied the labor. Many of his partners were even allowed to sign his name to documents.

When Crow reached his 60s, he decided to turn over the day-to-day operations of the company to Don Williams. While Crow continued to maintain a presence in the office, he also spent time with some of his other investments. He entered the hotel business starting with the Loews Anatole, a $55 million venture, and subsequently founded the Wyndham Hotel chain.

Trammell Crow, now in his early 80s, is considered one of America's greatest real estate developers and property managers. He developed more than $15 billion worth of industrial, office, and retail projects. The Trammell Crow Company employs more than 2,500 people in 70 offices who manage 14,000 tenants occupying 230 million square feet of space.

SOURCES: Trammell Crow Company archives; Joseph Nocera, "The Eccentric Genius of Trammell Crow," *Texas Monthly,* August 1984

Thomas Crowley

[Crowley Maritime Corporation]

Starting with $80 and a love of boats, Thomas Crowley purchased his first rowboat and opened for business along a rough San Francisco wharf. Soon the rugged teenager was adding employees and more boats. Today, the Crowley Maritime Corporation is one of America's largest privately held shipping businesses.

On December 5, 1875, Thomas Bannon was born to Irish immigrant parents in San Francisco, California. When Tom was only 16 months old, his father died of tuberculosis. Later, another Irish immigrant named David Crowley married Tom's mother and adopted her two children, and Thomas Bannon became Thomas Crowley.

In 1890, 15-year-old Crowley quit school and took a job ferrying sailors on Whitehall boats for $5 a week. Whitehalls were 18-foot rowboats named after the New York City street on which they were first built. They were operated by one or two men, and were primarily used to transport groceries, captains, and crews between incoming boats and the shore.

Crowley launched his own company at age 17, investing his $80 savings in a used Whitehall. The business was highly competitive, and the first Whitehall to meet an incoming ship usually was awarded the right to provide service as long as the ship remained in port. He claimed a shack along San Francisco's Vallejo Street Wharf where he ate and slept, and this proximity allowed him to respond quickly to word of an incoming ship.

He soon had enough business to hire his first employee and immediately purchased a second boat. To beat competitors to incoming ships, he often hooked his Whitehalls onto departing vessels and rode to the entrance of the San Francisco Bay, where he would patiently await customers. By plowing profits back into his business, Crowley soon had a third Whitehall and, after hiring his younger half-brothers, incorporated his business as Thomas Crowley and Brothers.

The Yukon gold strike of 1896 provided Crowley with his first gasoline-powered boat. As ships returned from the Alaska boom region, their crews were eager to get rid of their arctic clothing. Crowley bought the furs and other clothes at a low rate and stored them in a warehouse. Eventually, he found a buyer, and the $900 profit provided a sizable down payment on a 36-foot gasoline-powered launch built by John Twigg & Sons. Soon he added six similar boats to his growing fleet.

Crowley's next expansion was into the scow business. Scows are bargelike, flat-bottomed boats that are ideal for hauling dry-bulk cargo, and they are particularly suited for river use. When an established scow company named Piper-Aden was put on the market, Crowley acquired it and quickly expanded services.

He soon added gasoline and steam-powered tugboats to his fleet and reorganized as the Crowley Launch and Tugboat Company. His motto became: "Anything, Anywhere, Anytime, On Water." To accommodate his growing business, he established the Crowley Shipyard along the Bay in Oakland.

In 1913, San Francisco hosted the Panama Pacific International Exposition to celebrate the opening of the Panama Canal. Crowley played an important role in the festival, not only helping with the logistics of moving construction equipment and materials, but in a new venture as well. He built two double-decker passenger boats that shuttled visitors to the U.S. battleship *Oregon,* which was anchored in the bay.

Crowley later moved into the Puget Sound region of Washington, as well as south into the Los Angeles area. Over the next several decades, Crowley grew into the strongest full-service freight and passenger organization on the West Coast.

Crowley's marriage to Louise Gade in 1910 produced four children, including Thomas Bannon Crowley, born September 3, 1914. After attending Stanford University for two years, the young Crowley quit school to enter his father's business and was soon active in all phases of the company's business. After Thomas Crowley died on August 4, 1970, at the age of 94, Thomas B. Crowley continued the pattern of growth, leading the company into new international markets.

Thomas B. Crowley died on July 7, 1994. The company remains a family- and employee-owned business, with annual sales exceeding $1.2 billion, a fleet of more than 400 vessels, and nearly 5,000 employees.

SOURCES: Crowley Maritime Corporation archives; Jean Gilbertson, *Two Men at the Helm,* the Crowley Maritime Corporation, 1993

Hugh Roy Cullen

[Quintana Petroleum Corporation]

Hugh Roy Cullen was born on July 3, 1881, in Denton County, Texas, to Cicero and Louise Beck Cullen. His grandfather was Ezekiel Wimberly Cullen, veteran of the Texas revolution, judge, and Texas state senator.

Cullen attended school for only a few years and started working at age 12. At the age of 17, he became a cotton buyer in Texas and Oklahoma. In 1904, at the age of 23, he established his own cotton business, later securing a seat on the Houston Cotton Exchange. He also became active in real estate.

Cullen married Lillie Cranz, the daughter of a Schulenburg, Texas, merchant and rancher on December 29, 1903. The couple had five children: Roy, Lillie, Agnes Louise, Margaret Ruth, and Wilhelmina Daisy.

By 1917, Cullen was ready to enter the oil business. He worked jointly with other independent contractors and established himself as a successful wildcatter. Cullen and James Marion West organized the South Texas Petroleum Company in 1928. Capitalized with $1 million, this venture earned more than $30 million in six years.

In 1932 Cullen organized the Quintana Petroleum Company, which was later incorporated as the Quintana Petroleum Corporation. His Houston-based company worked closely with other oil companies on projects such as the Pierce Junction Field and Blue Ridge Field in Harris County, the Thompson Field in Fort Bend County, and the Tom O'Connor Field in Refugio County.

His most important strike occurred in Humble, Texas, where he located the Yeagua sand, an oil-bearing stratum later found to exist from Mexico to Mississippi. Altogether, Quintana operated approximately 600 producing wells with an annual production of 8 million barrels of oil and 40 billion cubic feet of gas.

Cullen was well known for his philanthropy, both during his lifetime and, since his death, through the Cullen Foundation and various Cullen trusts. His foundation has donated nearly $100 million to the University of Houston.

Other substantial donations were made to hospitals, other colleges and universities, and community cultural organizations.

His generosity can be traced to his religious convictions. Dr. Clarence Manion, former Dean of Law at Notre Dame, summarized Cullen's Christian faith: "He has the most profound belief in God I have ever encountered. He follows his moral conscience more carefully than many a monk in a monastery."

Hugh Roy Cullen died in Houston on July 4, 1957.

SOURCES: The Cullen Foundation archives; *The National Cyclopedia of American Biography,* James T. White & Company, New York

Emmett J. Culligan

[Culligan International]

Emmett Joseph Culligan was born on March 5, 1893, at Yankton, South Dakota, one of four children born to John and Molly Culligan. When he was five years old, the family moved to Sioux City, Iowa. In 1902, John Culligan died suddenly, leaving Molly to care for her four children and John's elderly parents.

Emmett Culligan and his two younger brothers were sent to St. Thomas Academy in St. Paul, Minnesota. His brothers became doctors while Emmett, eager to seek his fortunes, dropped out of school and started repairing farm buildings. When he turned 21, he took his inheritance and purchased prairie land in southwestern Minnesota that was later sold at a substantial profit.

Culligan continued to buy and sell real estate, and by 1920 his holdings were valued at about $250,000. Confident with the success, he married Anna B. Harrington in December 1919. Two years later, as Anna was about to deliver their first child, the nervous father-to-be wandered through the halls of St. Joseph's Hospital in St. Paul. He found his way to the boiler room and struck up a conversation with the maintenance superintendent. Curious about two large tanks in the room, Culligan was told they held water for the boilers and laundry that had been softened using a mineral called zeolite. Culligan was so intrigued with the substance that he persuaded the superintendent to give him a coffee can full of the greenish-black zeolite.

The farm depression during the early 1920s proved devastating to the Culligan family, who watched as almost all their possessions were sold at a public auction. Culligan and his pregnant wife and daughter were left with only the farm, a cow, some pigs, and a flock of chickens. Still interested in the zeolite, Culligan landed a job selling water softeners, but this lasted only a short time until he was once again unemployed.

With about $3,000 in loans from his brothers, Culligan next launched the Twin City Water Softener Company. Encouraged by the discovery of a synthetic zeolite that would provide better profit margins, Culligan took over the family kitchen to concoct mixtures on the stove and dry them in the oven.

He concluded that it would be better to manufacture the synthetic gel in a warm climate, so he packed up his growing family, which now included four children, and moved to Phoenix, Arizona. The desert climate indeed proved favorable for the venture, but when the country fell into the Great Depression, the sale of water softeners ground to a halt.

Now with six children, the Culligans moved to Fort Wayne, Indiana. Discouraged with zeolite, Emmett Culligan launched a new enterprise to write, publish, and sell books by mail. His first and last book was *Life Begins with Marriage.* After the failed venture, he was hired by a Chicago company and moved his family to La Grange, Illinois, where Anna delivered their seventh child.

Predictably, Culligan quit his job after a disagreement. By this time, Anna was hospitalized with depression, and Emmett was unemployed with seven children to feed. He was, however, a man with a strong faith in God and a relentless obsession with zeolite. In 1936, with his last $50, he launched yet another company, the Culligan Zeolite Company, in a Northbrook blacksmith shop.

This time, the product caught on and Culligan water softeners became fast sellers. Within two years his first franchised dealership was established in Wheaton, Illinois. By the time World War II erupted, he had 150 dealers, and growth was even more impressive in the 1950s, when the world first heard a female calling out "Hey Culligan Man!" on radio advertisements.

Emmett J. Culligan died on June 3, 1970, at the age of 77, from complications after an automobile accident. Today, Culligan continues to be one of the world's leading manufacturers and distributors of water purification equipment, with annual sales of nearly $350 million.

SOURCE: *The People of Culligan: 1936–1986,* by Don Hintz, the Culligan Corporation

Nathan Cummings

[Sara Lee Corporation]

Nathan Cummings was born on October 14, 1896, in St. John, New Brunswick, Canada, to Lithuanian immigrant parents. Two years later, his mother died while giving birth to her second child. Nathan's father, David Cummings, later remarried and had four more children.

In the early 1900s, the Cummings family moved to Waltham, Massachusetts, where young Nathan attended elementary school and worked in his father's store. The family moved twice more, eventually settling in Montreal, Canada, where David Cummings opened a shoe store. Nathan, who had quit school after nine years, spent the next several years working for his father and with relatives in Boston and New York.

By 1912, Nathan had gained considerable experience in the shoe business and was granted a partnership in his father's venture. Within two years they opened a second store in Montreal. About the same time, Nathan sold a pair of shoes to a woman named Ruth Lillian Kellert, whom he married in 1919. The couple had three children.

Nathan Cummings grew restless for his own company and, in 1915, established another partnership to produce and market a white summer shoe. However, the company warehouse was located near a train yard, and the fallout of soot and grime ruined the entire inventory. The business was liquidated, and Cummings returned to work as a shoe salesman, eventually repaying his debts.

By the mid-1920s, Cummings was back in the shoe manufacturing business with another partner, whom he eventually bought out. He expanded the business by importing other goods, including rubber boots. However, the pressures of the Great Depression were too great, and in 1932 his second venture folded. Within two years, Cummings bounced back, this time buying a biscuit company, which proved successful enough for him to once again pay off debts.

Cummings sold the biscuit company in 1938 and moved his family to Baltimore, Maryland. The C. D. Kenney Company, a small importer of coffee and tea, was in financial trouble, and he arranged to revive it in exchange for stock. By 1941, the company was profitable and Cummings had purchased 100 percent ownership. Over the next four years he acquired several other grocery businesses in Illinois and Iowa, which he brought together to form the Consolidated Grocers Corporation in 1945.

His next acquisition has played a monumental role in the company's history. Charlie Lubin, a baker from Decatur, Illinois, and a partner had purchased three small bakeries in 1935. Despite the lingering Depression, they used only the finest ingredients for their baked goods and sold them at premium prices. As business grew, Charlie starting selling the goods under the label Sara Lee, named after his 8-year-old daughter. Cummings later acquired the company, and Lubin stayed on to direct the bakery division.

In 1968, Cummings purchased the Bryan Packing Company of Mississippi and was so impressed with John Bryan that he persuaded him to play an instrumental role in his company, which had been renamed the Consolidated Foods Corporation in 1954. Other acquisitions followed, including Electrolux, Fuller Brush, Hanes, Hillshire Farm, Jimmy Dean Meats, Coach Leatherware, Champion Products, and L'eggs hosiery.

The company had diversified well beyond foods and, in the search for a more appropriate corporate name, discovered a strong consumer recognition of its Sara Lee brand name. Thus, in 1985, the company was renamed the Sara Lee Corporation. In February of that same year, Nathan Cummings died at age 88. Today, the Sara Lee Corporation employs more than 100,000 people and has annual sales of nearly $15 billion.

SOURCE: Sara Lee Corporation archives

Clessie L. Cummins

[Cummins Engine Corporation]

Clessie Lyle Cummins was born on December 27, 1888, on a Henry County, Indiana, farm, the oldest of five children born to Francis M. and

Josephine Cummins. His father manufactured wooden barrel hoops made from elm, and to keep close to a plentiful supply, the family moved often. Young Cummins soon grew tired of the frequent school changes, and his formal education went no further than the eighth grade.

At age 12, he built a working steam engine by whittling out the patterns, persuading a local foundry operator to make the castings, and after converting his mother's sewing machine into a lathe (without her permission), machining the final parts. He eventually blew up the steam engine trying to coax more power from it.

After completing an apprenticeship program in a local machine shop, Cummins left home in 1906 to pursue opportunities in the automobile industry at Indianapolis. He was not a formally trained engineer, but was, however, universally regarded as a mechanical genius who needed no academic credentials and knew no boundaries. A temporary job as a chauffeur in 1910 for Will G. Irwin, a Columbus, Indiana, industrialist, led to a lifelong friendship, and Irwin proved to be a valuable financial mentor.

In 1912, Cummins and his brother-in-law took to the Ohio and Mississippi Rivers in a 16-foot boat with a used, 4-horsepower engine. The experience inspired him to develop a reliable oil-burning engine. With Will Irwin's support, Cummins opened an automobile repair shop and, between contract jobs, attended to the new engine whenever possible. World War I, however, put the plans on hold, as Cummins made gun parts for the U.S. Army.

Cummins launched the Cummins Engine Company in 1919. Throughout the 1920s, he innovated new, improved marine and generator engines. By 1928, he had completed his Model U, the first diesel engine with all working parts totally enclosed. The engine provided a foundation that helped the company hobble through the Great Depression.

After years of exhaustive research and development, not to mention a constant struggle for capital, the Cummins Engine Company finally became profitable in the late 1930s. However, Clessie Cummins didn't have the luxury of enjoying the moment. World War II erupted, and he was recruited as head of engine scheduling for the War Production Board.

Cummins retired as president in 1947, but continued to innovate new products and processes. While in his early 70s, Cummins conceived and pioneered a device known as the Jacobs Engine Brake, used by the majority of large off- and on-highway trucks. He licensed the idea to another company, and the product had an astounding impact on the industry.

Clessie L. Cummins died on August 18, 1968, at the age of 79. He had been granted a total of 33 patents, all but one of which applied to automobile engine and fuel system improvements. Three of the patents were issued after his death, and they involved a new engine configuration that he built and tested in his home shop.

SOURCES: C. Lyle Cummins Jr., "Clessie Cummins Imagineer," *Diesel Car Digest* magazine, 1978; C. Lyle Cummins Jr., "Diesels from the Woodshed," Society of Automotive Engineers, paper #700346, 1970

Cyrus H. K. Curtis

[Curtis Publishing Company]

Convinced that a magazine devoted to women's issues would be a hit in late-nineteenth century America, Cyrus Curtis founded the *Ladies' Home Journal.* The ensuing success led to his purchase of *The Saturday Evening Post* and several other magazines and newspapers. During his lifetime, Curtis Publishing Company grew into one of the largest magazine publishers in the world.

Cyrus Hermann Kotzschmar Curtis was born on June 18, 1850, in Portland, Maine. After a limited education, young Curtis worked as a clerk, errand boy, and salesman until, at the age of 13, he founded his first publication, a modest paper called *Young America.* By the time he was 22, Curtis was an experienced advertising salesman in Boston, where he founded *The People's Ledger,* which he published for six years.

In 1876, Curtis traveled to Philadelphia, Pennsylvania, to witness the Centennial celebration. He enjoyed the town so much that he took up residence there and went to work for *The Philadelphia Press.* His desire for autonomy, however, was too strong, and in 1879 he and a partner established the *Tribune and Farmer,* a four-page weekly that cost subscribers 50¢ per year.

After four years of moderate growth, Curtis surprised his wife by bringing home a copy of his weekly with a new column that targeted issues for women, a segment of the market that was virtually untapped. His wife, Louisa (Knapp) Curtiss, read the articles and laughed out loud.

Determined that he had the right idea but the wrong material, his paper started carrying a weekly section assembled by Louisa, who proved to be a much better judge of material for women. Soon the paper was signing up thousands of new subscribers. Optimistic about the market for a periodical for women, Curtis left the partnership and launched the *Ladies' Home Journal,* which at the end of the first year boasted 25,000 subscribers. By 1904, it surpassed the 1 million mark, the first magazine ever to reach so many subscribers.

In 1891, Curtis formally incorporated the Curtis Publishing Company and, in the following years, started looking for more ventures. In 1897, an opportunity crossed his desk. *The Pennsylvania Gazette,* which was founded by Benjamin Franklin in the late 1720s, had undergone changes at the hands of several owners. By the late 1890s, it had become a sickly periodical with a circulation of less than 2,000 and its name had been changed to *The Saturday Evening Post.* When the owner died, the magazine was offered for sale, and Curtis obliged by paying $1,000 to the publisher's heir. After putting nearly $1.3 million into the magazine, the nickel-per-copy publication finally became profitable. Circulation reached 700,000 in 1905 and surpassed 1 million the following year. By 1920, it had passed 3 million.

Curtis next turned to the growing magazine market for farmers. He acquired a periodical with a strong tradition: *Country Gentleman.* The stated circulation was 24,000, but after he purged delinquent subscribers from the list, the total stood at only 2,000. He again put his publishing genius to work. After releasing his first issue on July 6, 1911, the magazine grew steadily, and by 1940 it had 2 million subscribers.

Curtis didn't limit himself to magazines. In 1913, he founded the *Philadelphia Public Ledger*. Eleven years later, he acquired the *New York Evening Post,* and in 1930 he purchased the *Philadelphia Inquirer*. He retired from active service in 1932, and on June 7, 1933, Cyrus H. K. Curtis died a few weeks before his 83rd birthday.

SOURCE: Curtis Publishing Company archives

Glenn H. Curtiss

[Curtiss-Wright Corporation]

Glenn Hammond Curtiss was born on May 21, 1878, at Hammondsport, New York. His boyhood enthusiasm for bicycles and motorcycles led to an early career as a mechanic and avid racer of both. He built engines and, eventually, complete motorcycles in his modest shop, and in 1904 he was asked by Captain Thomas S. Baldwin to produce an engine capable of powering a dirigible.

His early ventures were apparently successful enough to start a family. He married Lena Neff in 1898, and the couple eventually had two sons, only one of whom lived beyond childhood.

Alexander Graham Bell took notice of Curtiss's early successes and, in 1907, invited him to be part of his Aerial Experiment Association. The small group, which Bell and his wife financed to help promote air flight, was based at Nova Scotia, Canada, and had met with limited success. Seeking warmer weather, the group moved to Hammondsport, where their "dromes," powered by Curtiss engines, were put into service.

On July 4, 1908, the group's third drome, piloted by Curtiss, flew for more than a mile at nearly 20 feet, which was considered a major success. Encouraged, the group conducted additional experiments, but disbanded a year later. Curtiss, still interested in building airplanes, cofounded the Herring-Curtiss Company with Augustus Herring.

Within two years, the company was in a financial struggle. Curtiss and his supporters blamed Herring for mismanagement and decided that bankruptcy was their only alternative. When the company fell into receivership, Curtiss was the successful bidder for most of the assets, which he reorganized as The Curtiss Motor Company in 1911.

The first Curtiss hydroplane was his Triad, which was sold for military uses to England, Russia, Germany, and Japan in 1912. The U.S. Navy worked closely with Curtiss over the next several years to develop "flying boats." By 1914, the Navy placed so many orders that some of the work was contracted to Allan and Malcolm Loughead (who later founded Lockheed) and to the Boeing Airplane Company.

During these years, Curtiss was dogged by lawsuits filed by Wilbur and Orville Wright over aircraft design. The rift was aggravated in 1912 when

Wilbur Wright died of typhoid fever. Not long afterward, the court ruled in favor of the Wright brothers. However, Henry Ford interceded and helped reopen the suit, which became entangled in the court system until the outbreak of World War I. Eventually, the patent issue died.

In 1916, Curtiss went public, and the organization quickly became the world's largest aviation company. During World War I, the company produced nearly 10,000 aircraft and employed 18,000 people at its Buffalo, New York, plant and 3,000 people at Hammondsport. In 1929, the Curtiss Aeroplane and Engine Company and the Wright Aeronautical Corporation merged to form the Curtiss-Wright Corporation. Glenn Hammond Curtiss died the following year on July 23, 1930, at the age of 52.

SOURCE: Curtiss-Wright Corporation archives

Harry D. Cushman, Robert A. Weaver

[Ferro Corporation]

Convinced that a unique market niche existed for applying porcelain coatings to the growing array of home and industrial products, Harry Cushman left his job with Armco to establish the Ferro Enameling Company. A year later, he formed a companion company with Robert Weaver. Eventually, the two merged and became Ferro Corporation, one of the country's leading specialty materials firms.

Harry D. Cushman was born in 1874 in Three Rivers, Michigan. After graduating from Albion College with a B.S. degree in chemistry, he married Beatrice Breckenridge in 1899 and moved to East Cleveland, Ohio.

In the early 1900s, Cushman went to work for the American Rolling Mill Company (Armco), selling enameling iron to the appliance industry in the Cleveland area. Over time, he visualized a market niche that would entail applying porcelain enameled finishes to iron products. Finally, on October 11, 1919, Cushman and some partners launched the Ferro Enameling Company with a $1,000 investment.

Early jobs included contract work for firms such as Toledo Scale and the Garland Stove Company. As business grew, Cushman saw the need to reach new markets, and when Robert Weaver approached him with a proposal for a new business venture, Cushman jumped at the opportunity.

Robert A. Weaver was born in 1890 in Bradford, Pennsylvania. Ten years later, his family moved to Lima, Ohio, then again to Kenton, Ohio, where in 1904 his father opened the Weaver Hotel. Upon graduation from Kenyon College in 1912, Weaver taught English and coached sports at DeVeaux College in Niagara Falls, New York. There, he married Agness May Tuthill in 1914.

Weaver changed careers, accepting a job with the Eclipse Stove Company (later The Tappan Company) in Mansfield, Ohio. After holding marketing positions with several ceramics companies, Weaver discussed a new venture with Harry Cushman. His plan was to create a separate sales company that would market Ferro's product line. In 1920, they launched the Ferro Enamel & Supply Company.

Over the next several years, business was brisk, and the founders looked for new markets. In 1926, they established a furnace engineering division to design and build turnkey facilities for enameling products. One of their earliest customers was the Delco Company, which later became the Frigidaire Division of General Motors.

The Depression caused the founders to rethink their policy of maintaining separate companies. In 1930, they merged them into a single entity: the Ferro Enamel Corporation. Through the resulting efficiencies, as well as foreign and domestic growth, Ferro survived the Depression, with sales increasing from about $2 million in 1930 to $5.5 million in 1940.

Harry D. Cushman died on May 31, 1930. Weaver was active with the company for the next several decades, leading it into diverse enterprises, including coatings, chemicals, and plastics. Robert A. Weaver died on December 5, 1976, at the age of 86.

Today, Ferro is a highly diversified international corporation with operations in 21 countries on five different continents. Annual sales are nearly $1.5 billion.

SOURCE: *Ferro: The First Seventy Years 1919–1989,* by the Ferro Corporation, 1990

Adrian Dalsey, Larry Hillblom, Robert Lynn

[DHL Worldwide Express]

In 1969, Adrian Dalsey, Larry Hillblom, and Robert Lynn (D, H, and L) founded DHL Worldwide Express as a service to shuttle bills of lading between San Francisco and Honolulu. Hillblom had used a college loan for his share of the initial investment into DHL. All three partners, as well as friends, carried their cargo in personal suitcases between destinations using airline tickets purchased with their credit cards.

The partners and early employees picked up and delivered packages in the San Francisco Bay area in their first company vehicle, a 1969 Plymouth Duster. As the work increased, DHL hired only applicants who owned a car and were willing to hop a plane at a moment's notice. When service was extended to the Philippines, Japan, Hong Kong, Singapore, and Australia, owning a passport also increased your chances of being hired.

The company's first employee was a Honolulu resident named Max Kroll. Max and his wife, Blanche, had served in the Peace Corps in India and were quite used to chaos and uncertainty. Frequently, their Hawaiian apartment became a makeshift motel for traveling couriers.

The service worked well because couriers kept all documents and packages in their possession throughout the trip. An unfortunate early consequence, however, was the suspicions raised by the arrangement. In fact, several calls were placed to the Federal Bureau of Investigation urging them to take a close look at the couriers. Everything, of course, was legitimate and the partners became friends with several of the agents.

The company did, however, face a struggle with other government agencies, including the Civil Aeronautics Board and the U.S. Postal Service. As a result, DHL became a global network of many small companies.

Despite the challenges, DHL continued to expand during the 1970s and 1980s, adding service to Europe (1974), Latin America (1977), the Middle East (1978), and Africa (1978), followed by the Eastern Bloc countries (1983) and the People's Republic of China (1986). With the emergence of the fax machine, DHL reorganized with a focus on nonfaxable packages.

Hillblom retired from the operations of DHL in the late 1970s, although he remained a major shareholder. He moved to Saipan, the main island of the commonwealth of the Northern Marianas, a U.S. possession acquired after World War II. He continued to be active in international business deals, including a $50 million investment in Vietnam real estate, a resort on Guam, and ranches in the United States.

Larry Hillblom died in a plane crash near the Pacific island of Saipan in 1995 at the age of 52. Only two years earlier, he had crashed his small Cessna on another Marianas island, losing an eye and puncturing a lung. Adrian Dalsey died on October 10, 1994, at the age of 80.

Today, DHL employs 40,000 people working from 14 hubs, 220 gateways, and 1,600 international offices. Of DHL's nearly $4 billion in annual sales, only about $900 million is generated in the United States.

SOURCE: DHL Worldwide Express archives

Charles A. Dana

[Dana Corporation]

Charles Anderson Dana was born on April 25, 1881, in New York City, the only child of Charles and Laura Parkin Dana. After graduating from the Cutler School in New York City, he received his undergraduate degree from Columbia University in 1902, and his M.A. in international law from Columbia two years later.

Upon graduation, Dana was first employed by the law firm that represented the Pennsylvania Railroad, then with another firm specializing in corporate law. He then received an appointment to the staff of the New York City district attorney. Concurrently, he was elected to three terms in the New York Legislative Assembly.

Dana's early experience wasn't limited to law. He served with the New York National Guard for 11 years. For recreation, he frequently visited the Corralitos Ranch in Chihuahua, Mexico, spending days on horseback rounding up cattle and eating his meals from a chuck wagon.

In 1914, 33-year-old Dana was presented with an opportunity. The Spicer Manufacturing Company of Plainfield, New Jersey, had a strong product line serving the automotive market, but found itself in financial difficulty. Within two years, Dana was at the helm of the company and, with the help of General Motors' Charles Nash and others, was able to restore the company to profitability. Nash, who served as president and general manager of General Motors, later established the Nash Motors Company.

The timing of Dana's venture was fortunate. The demand for automobiles and trucks was rapidly rising, providing Dana with a ready market. The key was to develop efficient manufacturing operations, a talent that young Dana brought to the venture.

Dana also found the U.S. government to be a good client. Much of his time was spent on trains between the Plainfield headquarters and Washington, D.C.; some trains were so crowded that Dana had to sit on trunks in the baggage car.

Through growth and acquisition, Spicer Manufacturing grew considerably under the direction of Charles Dana. He negotiated the purchase of Snead & Company, a Jersey City manufacturer, while riding on a steamer between Cleveland and Detroit. On another occasion, he found himself in a railcar with the owner of a forge that was for sale. They arrived at a deal and Dana wrote on the margin of a newspaper: "I hereby purchase the plant from you for $3 million."

In 1946, the company name was changed to Dana Corporation. Today, Dana has annual sales in excess of $7.5 billion and employs nearly 43,000 people worldwide.

SOURCES: Dana Corporation archives; The History Factory

William H. Danforth

[Ralston Purina Company]

Unhappy with the seasonal income that came from selling bricks, William Danforth established a horse and mule feed business because, in his words, "animals must eat year-round." From these humble beginnings, Danforth built the Ralston Purina Company, well known for the "checkerboard square" symbol.

William H. Danforth was born on September 10, 1870, the son of a small merchant in Charleston, Missouri. He grew up a sickly farm boy in southeastern Missouri swamp country. In his early school days, he was "dared" by an inspiring teacher to overcome his problems and become the healthiest kid in the class. Throughout his life, Danforth would use the word "dare" as a challenge for those around him to be the best that they could be.

Danforth became a salesman in the brick business upon graduating from Washington University in St. Louis in 1892. (Danforth's grandson, also named William H. Danforth, would eventually become the chancellor of Washington University.) Unhappy with the seasonal nature of the brick industry, he discussed other ventures with two church friends, George Robinson and William Andrews. Following his father's advice to "get into a business that fills a need for lots of people—something they need all year round and in both good and bad times," the trio hit on an idea: horse and mule feed.

At the time, feed stores were as common as gas stations are today. Other than hay, the only two types of feed were corn, which frequently caused fatal cases of colic, and oats, which were costly. So, the group formed the Robinson-Danforth Commission Company in 1894 with a capitalization of $12,000. They mixed their special formula with shovels on the floor of a back room. It was then put into 175-pound sacks and sewn shut by hand.

Danforth was the chief buyer and salesman. During harvesttime, he visited mills and grain elevators throughout the North and Midwest. He would then travel by horse and boat between St. Louis and New Orleans, selling the horse and mule feed. Sales grew briskly, and within two years Danforth was president of the company, which had moved to a new location with milling machinery.

The same year that he launched his company, Will Danforth married Miss Adda Bush. The couple had two children, Dorothy and Donald. Donald would later become president and chairman of the board of Ralston Purina.

On May 26, 1896, William Andrews sold his share of the company to Danforth, making him the majority shareholder. The next afternoon, the worst tornado in the history of St. Louis struck, completely destroying the mill. Undaunted by the tragedy, Danforth marched into a local bank and borrowed $25,000 to replace the uninsured mill.

By 1898, Danforth was manufacturing and selling a whole wheat cereal. From the company slogan, "Where purity is paramount," he labeled the cereal *Purina.* During this time, a Dr. Ralston was professing the virtues of healthy living to a following that exceed 800,000. In his book *Life Building,* Dr. Ralston recommended a whole wheat cereal, similar to Purina. Danforth approached Ralston to endorse Purina, and he agreed, provided it was named Ralston Wheat Cereal. The name stuck and in 1902 the company was renamed the Ralston Purina Company.

At about the same time, Danforth wanted to develop a distinctive look for his products. He thought about his early days working in his father's store. There was a Mrs. Brown who would make clothes for the entire family from the same bolt of checkerboard cloth. When the Browns came into town shopping, Mrs. Brown would have no trouble locating her children when it was time to go home. Danforth picked up on the idea, and the Ralston Purina Company has used the checkerboard as its trademark ever since. The company is even headquartered in "Checkerboard Square."

Always a patriot, Danforth headed for Europe during World War I. At 48, he was too old to enlist, so he served as YMCA secretary for the troops of the Third Army Division. While there, he became intrigued with the way the troops enthusiastically responded to the call for "chow." Once back in the states, Danforth changed the term "feed" to "chow," a word that in the 1950s would resurface in company pet foods such as Purina Dog Chow. After World War I, Danforth visited England and was introduced to a type of feed containing several ingredients that were pressed into small cubes. This, too, was quickly adopted back home, introducing pellet-form feed into the industry.

William Danforth was well known for his strong support of Christian faith, healthy living, and personal achievement. His basic philosophy was the "Four Square" life. Drawing his familiar checkerboard, Danforth would write "Physical" along the left side, "Mental" across the top, "Social" along the right side, and "Religious" at the base. He said that a person's ingredients for life are a body, a mind, a personality, and character, all of which must grow in balance with each other.

Danforth shared his philosophies freely, through informal conversation, formal speeches, and even books. In fact, he wrote no fewer than 14 books during his lifetime, the most famous of which is *I Dare You!* More than 1.75 million copies of the book, now in its 32nd printing, have been distributed.

In 1924, Danforth organized the American Youth Foundation. Still active to this day, the AYF has been actively involved in training young men and women in Christian principles, responsibility, and leadership. The organization established Camp Miniwanca on a 300-acre campsite near Shelby, Michigan. For more than 30 years, up to the time of his death, Danforth spent his summers at the camp, where he met, counseled, and inspired thousands of young people.

The Danforth Foundation was formed in 1927 as an educational philanthropy dedicated to improving quality of life through programs directed at young people. The foundation is still quite active today in inspirational projects for young people.

On January 19, 1932, at the age of 62, Danforth turned control of the company over to his son, Donald, who had joined the company in 1920. From that point forward, William Danforth occupied himself with foundation and community activities.

Danforth was a man of traditions. He and a group of friends started a custom of meeting and singing Christmas carols on Christmas Eve, 1909. The group grew each year, and soon they were collecting gifts for the Children's Aid Society. In 1924, the group was formally named the Christmas Carols Association and Danforth became the organization's president. At age 85, William Danforth died on Christmas Eve, 1955, while awaiting the arrival of a group of Christmas carolers.

Today Ralston Purina is among America's largest companies. In addition to its food products, the company owns the Eveready Battery Company and Continental Baking Company.

SOURCE: Ralston Purina Company archives

Jasper N. "Jack" Daniel

[Jack Daniel Distillery]

Jack Daniel entered the whiskey business at the ripe age of ten in Lincoln County, Tennessee. Through his diligent marketing efforts and commitment to quality, Jack Daniel's continues to be one of America's most popular whiskeys.

Jasper Newton "Jack" Daniel was born on September 5, 1846, the last of ten children born to Calaway and Lucinda Daniel. His mother died five months later.

Calaway later remarried a woman who didn't get along well with Jack. So, at the age of six, he left home and moved in with a neighbor, "Uncle Felix" Waggoner and his family. A year later, he moved again, this time into the home of Dan and Mary Jane Call.

Dan was a diversified Tennessee entrepreneur. In addition to being a preacher, he owned a general store and a mountain distillery. Jack became a valued assistant, learning the trade from Dan and learning writing and mathematics from Mary Jane. When Jack was ten years old, Dan made him a full partner in the still. Jack expanded the business by purchasing a wagon and a team of mules and delivering the whiskey to other country stores.

The secret to Dan Call's whiskey resided with the operation's first distiller, a slave named "Uncle Nearest" Green. He made whiskey the "Lincoln County way." It starts with natural iron-free water from local limestone springs. The whiskey is a sour mash whiskey, using only natural fermenting, with no chemicals to induce fermentation. It is then filtered through 10 feet of sugar maple charcoal. This leeching process creates its distinctive taste.

In 1859, a spirited female evangelist named Lady Love toured central Tennessee, preaching against the use of alcohol. She captivated Dan, who shortly thereafter broke the news to Jack that he would be getting out of the whiskey distillery business.

Jack was quite upset at the prospect of closing the business. He consulted Uncle Felix, telling him that Dan's plan to abandon the whiskey business would interfere with Jack's childhood dreams of becoming "one of the best distillers in all the world." Uncle Felix shared the best advice he could muster, telling Jack, ". . . if you don't take care of your future, nobody else will do it for you." Thirteen-year-old Jack Daniel proceeded to buy out Dan Call, and Uncle Felix agreed to endorse all legal documents that Jack was too young to sign.

The Civil War opened new markets for Jack in Huntsville, Alabama. However, the road leading to Huntsville was riddled with troops from both sides in search of food and enemies. Undeterred, Jack and his friends devised clever ways to hide whiskey in wagons, and his midnight distribution business in Huntsville proved to be a rich market for the new company.

Following the Civil War, Jack concluded that it would be best to find another home for the still. He settled on property known as Cave Spring Hol-

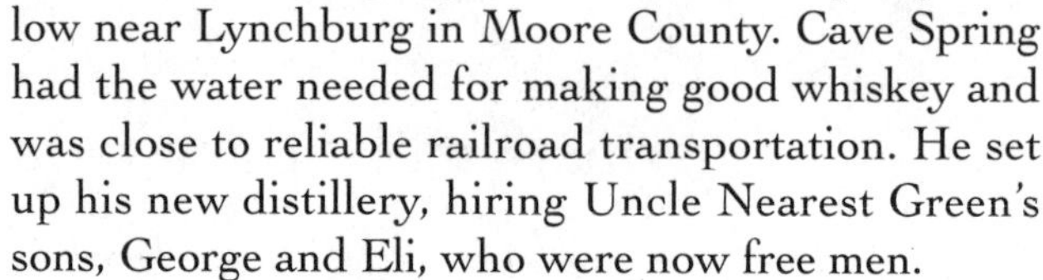

low near Lynchburg in Moore County. Cave Spring had the water needed for making good whiskey and was close to reliable railroad transportation. He set up his new distillery, hiring Uncle Nearest Green's sons, George and Eli, who were now free men.

In 1862, the federal government approved taxation to control whiskey making and first targeted the Confederate states for enforcement. When the feds swept into town, Jack met them with a smile and registered his business as the Jack Daniel Distillery. It is now recognized as the oldest registered distillery in America.

On his 21st birthday, Jack decided he needed a new image. The successful businessman disappeared for a few days, only to return wearing what became his trademark attire: a linen shirt, silk vest, bow tie, knee-length frock coat, and a high-rolled planter's hat. For the rest of his life Jack would wear no other type of clothing.

In 1885, Jack hired an able young man named Bill Hughes to handle the still operations. Two years later, Jack hired his nephew, Lem Motlow. Lem was as talented as Hughes and was soon promoted to manager. With the company in able hands, Jack was left to travel and market his whiskey.

Jack was uncomfortable for many years with the various brand names he attached to his whiskey. While discussing business with a friend who owned a chain of seven stores, Jack inquired about the key to the man's success. The merchant described his strategies of buying in quantity and other techniques. Somehow Jack associated his own vow to always follow the Lincoln County process for making whiskey with the merchant's tale of his seven successful stores. Returning to the still later that day, Jack announced his new brand name: "Jack Daniel's Old Time No. 7."

Jack's famous square bottle was introduced in 1895. Although round bottles were easier to pack in crates, Jack insisted on special bottles for his special whiskey. The square bottles, symbolic of Jack being a "square dealer," remain to this day.

Jack Daniel was highly respected for his fairness, kindness, and generosity. His whiskey was among the finest available and needed no paid advertising or sales reps. The 1904 St. Louis World's Fair presented Jack's No. 7 the gold medal for the finest whiskey in the world. It became the whiskey of choice at John Overton's Nashville hotel, the Maxwell House, renowned for its excellent coffee.

Jack stepped aside in 1907 and let his nephews Lem Motlow and Richard Daniel handle the day-to-day operations of the distillery. In 1910, feeling that he was not up to the challenge of prohibition forces, he signed the distillery over to them. Jack died on October 9, 1911, at the age of 65.

Lem Motlow and the other Daniel family members continued to nurture Jack's distillery. Lem continued at the helm until his death in 1947. His four sons assumed control and became known as the "shirtsleeves brothers" of Tennessee whiskey fame. In 1956, the burden of alcohol taxes convinced the family to sell the company to Brown-Forman of Louisville, Kentucky, who made few changes to the operation.

Jack Daniel's slogan, "Every day we make it, we'll make it the best we can," remains with the distillery to this day.

SOURCES: Jack Daniel Distillery archives; Ben A. Green, *Jack Daniel's Legacy,* Rich Printing, Nashville, 1967; Pat Mitchamore, *A Tennessee Legend,* Rutledge Hill Press, Nashville, 1992

John Davey

[Davey Tree Expert Company]

Rising above poverty on a farm in England, John Davey immigrated to the United States at the age of 27. He pursued his lifelong interest in horticulture and trees, extolling the virtues of proper tree care to anyone who would listen. Eventually, he even wrote a book on the subject. His business, The Davey Tree Expert Company, has grown from humble beginnings to one of America's largest tree service companies.

John Davey was born to a poor peasant family in Somersetshire, England, in 1846. Growing up nearly in serfdom, Davey excelled as a herdsman. Yet he preferred to work with plants and eventually studied horticulture, floriculture, and greenhouse management. He also taught himself to read using the Bible, a hymnal, and a dictionary.

In 1873, 27-year-old Davey immigrated to Warren, Ohio, and secured a job as a caretaker for a private school. Still hungry for an education, he bartered his own labor for classes such as Latin and astronomy. After marrying a local woman he had met at church, Davey opened a small nursery for additional family income.

Davey moved his family to Kent, Ohio, in 1880 and accepted a job as the caretaker for Standing Rock Cemetery. He quickly transformed the neglected cemetery from a public embarrassment into a beautiful park. It became his laboratory and training ground, and residents often found him climbing the largest and sickest trees, cleaning and disinfecting tree cavities.

Appalled by the lack of attention to the landscape in America, Davey became consumed with replacing "tree butchery with tree surgery." He became an avid lecturer (and critic) wherever he found an audience. This culminated in 1901 with his self-published science book called *The Tree Doctor.*

Requests for Davey's services grew as fast as his reputation. In 1909, he formally incorporated the business as The Davey Tree Expert Company. The company adopted as its motto the phrase that Davey was constantly hounded with by his father in England: "Do it right or not at all." Within two years, the company was operating in 31 states and Canada.

Upon the death of John Davey in 1923, his son Martin assumed the position of president. Martin Davey, who had joined his father in the business in 1907, not only guided the company through the Depression and World War II, he also served four terms in the U.S. Congress and two terms as governor of Ohio. Martin's son, Martin L. Davey Jr., served as company president from 1946 through 1961, and he remained on the board of directors until 1983.

John Davey's other sons also played prominent roles in the business and community. Paul Davey was a creative inventor, securing 50 patents for the business. Wellington Davey was also resourceful, founding the Davey Tree Surgery Company in California in 1928, expanding the operations to the West Coast.

On March 15, 1979, ownership of the company passed from the Davey family to the Davey employees. Today, nearly 50 percent of the company's 6,000 employees participate in the employee stock ownership plan (ESOP). Revenue in 1995 exceeded $230 million. The company headquarters is on a 35-acre campus across the street from Standing Rock Cemetery, where John Davey is buried and Davey field-workers are still trained.

SOURCES: Davey Tree Expert Company archives; Sue Gorisek, "A Man Ahead of His Moment," *Ohio Magazine,* October 1992

Davre J. Davidson, William S. Fishman

[ARAMARK Corporation]

After building separate companies in the food vending business, Davre Davidson of California and William Fishman of Illinois combined their companies in 1959 to form Automatic Retailers of America, also known as ARA.

Davre J. Davidson was born in 1911 in Portland, Oregon. His family moved to Duluth, Minnesota, in 1915, then to San Pedro, California, in 1928. He attended Long Beach Junior College in California for one year and was accepted by the University of Southern California. However, the pressures of the Depression forced him to withdraw from school in 1930 to help manage a retail store owned by his family.

In 1934, 23-year-old Davidson purchased a few penny peanut vending machines. Two years later, he founded a small food vending business in Los Angeles on $500 of borrowed capital. His first major account was with a Douglas Aircraft plant in Santa Monica, and the first week's receipts totaled $7.56. His first warehouse was the backseat and trunk of his 1932 Dodge. By 1939, the business had grown large enough for his brother Henry to join him, and the firm was called Davidson Brothers. The company grew significantly during World War II by providing food and refreshment services to California's busy defense plants.

Halfway across the country, William S. Fishman was building his own food service company. Fishman was born in Clinton, Indiana, in 1916, and grew up in the southwestern Indiana town of Princeton. He earned his bachelor's degree in political science from the University of Illinois at Urbana in 1936. By the age of 22, he was running a wholesale candy and tobacco distributorship with $4 million in sales, and in the late 1930s he entered the vending business where, coincidentally, Fishman's big break was to land a contract with the Douglas Aircraft plant in Chicago.

Davidson and Fishman became acquainted and developed a close friendship. By 1959, they decided that their long-term goals were quite similar, and by joining forces they could quickly establish themselves as leaders in the food service industry. Their new company was incorporated as Automatic Retailers of America (ARA).

They felt that the logical extension of their operation would be manual food service. Many of their existing clients operated cafeterias that competed with their vending operations. They found an answer in The Slater Company, a Philadelphia-based company that was founded on the campus of the University of Pennsylvania in 1926 as a food service for fraternity houses. In the early 1930s, Slater obtained its first industrial client and, by the 1950s, was serving several colleges and hospitals.

Davidson and Fishman acquired Slater for $15 million in 1961, then established Philadelphia as the corporate headquarters for ARA. The acquisition provided the balance they were looking for: ARA was 95 percent vending and Slater was 98 percent food service. Along with the company came experienced managers that filled key positions.

The pair quickly realized that the cumulative expertise in food service was easily transferable among their three markets—business and industry, schools and colleges, and hospitals. The predominant commonality involved the unique challenges that came from serving two distinct sets of clients: one being the company or organization that contracted with them to provide the service and the other being the employees or students that ultimately purchased the goods. Confident that their formula for success could be applied in a number of markets, the two set their sights on expansion.

In the mid-1960s, the partners noticed the trend toward shorter workweeks and increased vacation time. They formed the Araserve Division to focus on sports stadiums and arenas, golf courses, amusement and theme parks, convention centers, and state parks. In 1967, they acquired Air La Carte, a preparer of meals for in-flight dining, and in less than ten years they were serving nearly 7 million meals on 220,000 flights. Also, through Aero Enterprises, they opened airport concessionaire services, including newsstands, gift shops, cafeterias, and cocktail lounges.

Their entry into the distribution of newspapers and periodicals was launched in 1968 with the acquisition of the Washington, D.C., District News Company. In less than ten years, ARA subsidiaries were distributing 300 million newspapers, periodicals, and books to 20,000 retail outlets.

In 1973, ARA entered the nursing care market with the acquisition of National Living Centers. In only four years the company grew to 166 health care facilities with a total of 19,000 beds. The partners' expansion included bus companies, gourmet restaurants, and coffee services. In their first two decades in business together, they acquired an unbelievable total of nearly 300 firms.

The pair shared responsibilities throughout the company's history. Davidson served as chairman, president, and chief executive officer from the beginning. He passed responsibility to Fishman gradually, first with the title of president in 1964, then the post of chief executive officer in 1975. In 1977, Davidson retired from the day-to-day operations of the company and Fishman was named chairman of the board. Fishman continued to serve as president until 1977 and as chairman and chief executive officer until 1984.

William Fishman was a licensed pilot who literally flew from site to site. When on the ground, he was usually seen behind the wheel of his company car, while his uniformed chauffeur sat in the passenger seat. He was widely known as an unpretentious and generous man. One evening a receptionist with a faulty watch locked up and went home too early, trapping Fishman in his office. The gracious founder shrugged it off with a smile and had a new watch delivered to her the next morning.

Davidson has been married to his wife Charlotte since 1938. They have one son, Harold. Fishman's first wife, the former Clara Sylvan, died in 1980. The couple had three sons, Alan, Fred, and David. After Clara's death, he married Selma Demchick Ellis. William S. Fishman died on June 15, 1991, at the age of 75.

Davidson and Fishman have long philanthropic histories. In 1982, they established the Fishman/Davidson Center for the Service Sector at the University of Pennsylvania's Wharton School. Davidson has served as a trustee and honorary professor at the University of Southern California and held positions with several community and youth groups. Fishman was instrumental in setting up a series of schools throughout Israel to train craftspeople. He also was the catalyst for the creation of the Museum of American Jewish History on Independence Mall in Philadelphia.

In 1994, ARA was faced with mounting pressures from corporate raiders looking to take over profitable companies. In response, the company took control of its own destiny with a management buyout that placed 40 percent of ARA in company hands. This ensured the continuance of Davidson and Fishman's entrepreneurial dream.

After a decade of unparalleled growth, in October 1994 ARA officially changed its name to ARAMARK. This name reflects the company's successful heritage while solidifying its image in the managed services industry as the mark of quality. In 1996, the employee-owned company generated over $6 billion in annual revenue and employed more than 150,000 people at 11 locations around the world.

SOURCE: ARAMARK Corporation archives

Edward J. DeBartolo Sr.

[The Edward J. DeBartolo Corporation]

Edward J. DeBartolo was born on May 17, 1909, in Youngstown, Ohio, in a poor immigrant neighborhood known as Smoky Hollow. He was christened Anthony Paonessa Jr. after his natural father, who at age 26 had died two months before Edward's birth. His mother, Rosaria (Villani) Paonessa, later married an immigrant from southern Italy named Michael DeBartolo. As a teenager, he adopted the named Edward, after his uncle, and changed his last name to DeBartolo in honor of his stepfather.

In 1914, Michael DeBartolo started building concrete steps on the fronts of his neighbors' homes. Over time, the business grew to include small commercial structures, such as Sinclair service stations, and even commercial rental properties. Edward DeBartolo worked alongside his stepfather while attending high school. Upon graduation, he enrolled at Notre Dame, but continued to work the midnight shift at construction sites in northern Indiana while attending classes through the day.

After graduating with a degree in civil engineering, DeBartolo returned to the family construction business in Youngstown. He also started building houses as a sideline until the outbreak of World War II, at which point he enlisted in the U.S. Army, achieving the rank of second lieutenant. He was assigned to the Army Corps of Engineers, where he became adept at aerial topography.

After the war, DeBartolo returned once more to Youngstown and resumed his construction activities. In 1949, he built eight small retail stores alongside a grocery store in suburban Youngstown. He was encouraged by the public response and started developing similar sites, even though the banks were reluctant to put up money for the unusual developments.

Throughout the 1950s and early 1960s, The Edward J. DeBartolo Corporation built more than 50 shopping centers throughout six states and Canada. And when enclosed shopping centers, which eventually became known as *malls,* came into vogue, DeBartolo raised larger amounts of money, often through the sale of his existing shopping centers, and started building malls. By 1970, he was one of the top 50 builders in America.

In addition to his success as a developer, DeBartolo became active in the sports market. In 1959, he purchased the Thistledown horse racetrack in Cleveland, Ohio, followed by the Balmoral track near Chicago and Louisiana Downs at Shreveport. He also purchased the five-time Super Bowl winner San Francisco 49ers professional football club.

In 1977, DeBartolo acquired a one-third interest in the Pittsburgh Penguins professional hockey club and, the following year, bought out the remaining partners. Under his ownership, hockey eventually became a popular sport in Pittsburgh, and in 1991 the club won its first Stanley Cup. The following year, he sold the club to Howard Baldwin.

Edward J. DeBartolo died on December 19, 1994, at the age of 85. He and his wife, Marie, whom he met while directing traffic at a construction site, had two children, Edward J. DeBartolo Jr. and Denise DeBartolo York, who today oversee the real estate, sports, and entertainment empire. By the time he died, DeBartolo had developed more than 100 million square feet of commercial real estate.

In 1996, some of the company properties were merged with the Simon Property Group, forming the new Simon DeBartolo Group.

SOURCE: Edward J. DeBartolo Corporation archives

John Deere

[Deere & Company]

John Deere was born on February 7, 1804, and spent his childhood in Middlebury, Vermont, where he received a common-school education and served a four-year apprenticeship learning the blacksmith trade. He began his career in 1825 and quickly established an outstanding reputation for his work, particularly his highly polished pitchforks and shovels.

In 1836, as business conditions worsened, Deere traveled by canal boat, lake boat, and stagecoach to Grand Detour, Illinois. The town had such a strong demand for a blacksmith that Deere opened a forge two days after his arrival. His wife, Demarius (Lamb) Deere, and their four children soon joined him.

The young blacksmith learned quickly of the serious problem encountered by the area's farmers. The cast-iron plows of the East were not designed for the rich Midwestern soil, which stuck to plow bottoms and had to be removed with a stick by the farmer. Plowing was slow, laborious, and discouraged many farmers. Recognizing the need, Deere built a uniquely designed polished-steel plow—after much trial and error—that cleaned or "scoured" itself as it moved through the soil.

The steel plow became a side business for Deere's blacksmith shop. During 1839, he sold only ten plows. However, as word of the new plow spread and demand began to build, Deere reversed the normal sales procedure of the time and started building plows *before* they were sold.

As plow sales increased, transportation of raw materials and finished goods to and from Grand Detour became a problem. Deere consequently moved his operation to Moline, Illinois. Soon after moving, he arranged for a shipment of special steel to be transported to Moline from England via waterways. The steel began arriving in 1846 and was ready for use at his new plow factory, which opened in 1848 on the banks of the Mississippi River. By the time Deere & Company was incorporated in 1868, plow production had reached 13,000 per year.

John Deere died in Moline on May 17, 1886, at the age of 82. During his later years, he was active with the company and the community, and even served a term as mayor of Moline in the 1870s. In 1857, Deere had turned over control to his 21-year-old son, Charles, who ran the company for nearly 50 years.

During 1910 and 1911, Deere acquired companies that manufactured wagons, drills, hay tools, and manure spreaders. The most controversial purchase—strongly debated by the board of directors at the time—was the Waterloo Gasoline Engine Company in Waterloo, Iowa, in 1918. For the price of $2.2 million, the facility that produced the Waterloo Boy tractor was purchased, and Deere was instantly in the tractor business. The complex eventually became the John Deere Tractor Works.

William Butterworth, a son-in-law of Charles Deere, succeeded Charles in 1907 and proceeded to centralize many of the company's functions, expand Deere's crop-harvesting business, and acquire additional equipment lines. Charles Deere Wiman, a grandson of Charles, assumed leadership of the company in 1928 and served in that role until 1955. William Hewitt—married to John Deere's great-great-granddaughter Patricia Wiman—then became president and later chairman.

Today, Deere operations include several John Deere Health Care centers, one of the 25 largest credit organizations in the United States, several engineering and manufacturing units located in 10 countries, and a worldwide sales organization marketing agricultural, construction, and lawn-care equipment, plus engines and service parts, in over 160 countries. The company employs 34,000 people worldwide.

SOURCE: Deere & Company archives

Michael Dell

[Dell Computer Corporation]

Michael Dell was born on February 23, 1965, in Houston, Texas, and quickly became familiar with the world around him. At age 8, Dell applied for a high school equivalency diploma, and he got his first checkbook at age 9. At age 12, he got a resellers license and conducted a nationwide stamp auction, typing out a nine-page catalog with one finger. He netted a $2,000 profit from the venture, and the following year started speculating in gold, silver, and stocks at age 13. He purchased his first computer, an Apple II, at age 15 and immediately tore it apart and put it back together.

In high school, Dell sold subscriptions to the *Houston Post* by tracking down new households through marriage licenses. He hired some high school friends to go to the county courthouses and copy the names and addresses of people who had recently purchased marriage licenses. He then sent the couples a personalized letter, offering a two-week subscription, and most signed up after the trial period.

Working two days a week selling newspapers, Dell made $18,000 by the time he was 17 years old and became the *Post*'s top salesperson. Dell's father recalled: "He knew what he wanted to do with his money. He wanted to buy a BMW. We went down to the dealership—I had to sign for it—and he paid for it in cash."

In 1983, Dell enrolled at the University of Texas at Austin to study biology. While in school, he noticed that local computer dealers were receiving more IBM PCs than they could handle. He arranged to purchase surplus computers from the stores at cost, then added features such as more memory and larger disk drives. He advertised in small one-column ads, offering the computers at 10 to 15 percent below retail, literally selling from the trunk of his car.

Dell hid his enterprise from his family initially, but when sales reached $50,000 per month, he broke the news. His parents agreed to let him sell computers during his summer vacation, but if it didn't work out he'd return to school and study medicine. On May 3, 1984, with $1,000 in savings, 18-year-old Michael Dell launched the Dell Computer Corporation. He opened an office and continued with his winning formula. His first month's sales exceeded $180,000. Within four months, the company was manufacturing and selling its own computers.

Determined to succeed, Dell worked 18-hour days. In January 1986, the company reported annual sales of $34 million. Eighteen months later, on the day that Dell would have graduated from college, annual sales had increased to $70 million. As the company grew and the founder was cast into a management role, he never lost his passion for the technology. On one occasion, the engineering team had to literally throw him out of his own building in the middle of the night because they couldn't make progress with "the boss" looking over their shoulders.

Dell attributes his astonishing success to his direct-marketing strategy, which eliminates costly retailers or distributors. Every computer is built to customer specification after an order is received, resulting in low inventory costs.

However, the market didn't automatically respond to yet another mail-order house. Dell invested considerable effort to differentiate his company from the thousands of easy-come, easy-go ventures by getting his computers in front of industry analysts and writers.

Today, the Dell Computer Corporation is the world's leading direct marketer of computer systems and, in fact, is one of the world's largest computer manufacturers. The company employs more than 10,000 people worldwide. More than 90 percent of its sales are made to businesses and government agencies.

Still in his early 30s, Michael Dell is one of the most established CEOs in the computer industry. Dell, his wife, and their four children reside near Austin, Texas.

SOURCE: Dell Computer Corporation archives

D. J. De Pree

[Herman Miller, Inc.]

After working for Michigan Star Furniture Company, a small Michigan furniture enterprise, for 15 years, D. J. De Pree (along with his father-in-law) purchased the business and renamed it The Herman Miller Furniture Company. The company weathered the Depression by replacing bulky, ornate furniture with sleek, modern lines. They later entered the office and medical markets, and today Herman Miller is recognized as America's second-largest contract manufacturer of office furniture.

D. J. De Pree was born on July 31, 1891, in Zeeland, Michigan. After graduating from high school in 1909, he went to work for the Michigan Star Furniture Company as an office assistant. The company's principal business at the time was the manufacture of Princess Dressers for Sears, Roebuck & Company.

De Pree was a devout Christian and avid reader of the Bible, *American Boy* magazine, and other morally conscious publications. One day he came across an article titled "How to Plan Your Day." It so affected the young man that he soon was able to finish a day's work by his lunch break. While he wasn't particularly fond of accounting, he spent the rest of his day studying the subject because the federal income tax had just been established and he felt it would be an important topic on which to be knowledgeable.

In 1914, De Pree married Nellie Miller, also from Zeeland. Her father, Herman Miller, was a successful businessman known for his Colonial Clock Company. De Pree continued to work for Michigan Star until, in 1923, he and his father-in-law gained controlling interest in the company. De Pree renamed the company The Herman Miller Furniture Company in honor of his father-in-law, who was well known in the community as a man of honesty and integrity.

The early years of Herman Miller were uneventful. De Pree continued to make pretty much the same products that Michigan Star had made. In fact, he later recalled that the entire furniture industry in the 1920s was bland and not very innovative. By 1930, the Depression had taken its toll on the underfinanced furniture company. Even De Pree was convinced his business was near bankruptcy.

Fighting for survival, De Pree met with the renowned New York designer Gilbert Rohde, who presented his ideas on what modern furniture should look like. Rohde noted that houses were being built with smaller rooms and that smaller, lighter, more versatile furniture was needed. De Pree embraced Rohde's recommendations and immediately created a modern furniture line. Sales quickly took a turn for the better, and Herman Miller furniture became quite popular.

De Pree later orchestrated another revolutionary change in the company. A longtime and valued employee (who had held a millwright's job) suddenly died. At the funeral, De Pree was intrigued to hear about the man's interests and personal accomplishments. He was astounded that he knew so little about this special man who had worked so many years for the company.

De Pree came to recognize that all his employees were extraordinary in some way. He became determined to create a special work environment for his people and, in 1950, secured the services of Carl Frost, a Michigan State University psychology professor, to design a plan for employee participation, known as the Scanlon Plan, whose guiding principles are still in effect at Herman Miller.

In the 1960s, De Pree moved into two new markets: the *Action Office* system of furniture for offices and the *Action* system of hospital and laboratory equipment. In time, the office furniture would become, to many people, better known than the company's home furniture. Actually, by the 1990s Herman Miller was developing clever lines of furniture for people maintaining offices in their homes.

Today, De Pree's sons, Hugh and Max, are retired from the daily operations of the business, but both maintain the title of CEO emeritus. Herman Miller is still based in Zeeland, Michigan, and continues to enjoy record-breaking success in the marketplace, with annual sales exceeding $1.2 billion.

SOURCE: Herman Miller, Inc., archives

Richard M. DeVos, Jay Van Andel

[Amway Corporation]

After growing up near each other in the same city, attending the same high school and college, embarking on a sailing adventure, and building several businesses together, Jay Van Andel and Rich DeVos launched an innovative direct-selling company in 1959. Over the next three decades, Amway Corporation grew into one of the largest privately owned corporations in America.

Jay Van Andel and Richard M. DeVos were both born in Grand Rapids, Michigan—Van Andel on June 3, 1924, and DeVos on March 4, 1926. They both attended Grand Rapids Christian High School and Calvin College. The two were separated during World War II, when both served in the Army Air Corps, but at different posts.

After the war, the two high school friends teamed up to launch their first business, a flying school and commercial air charter service in Comstock Park, Michigan. They added one of the area's first drive-in restaurants a short while later.

In 1948, they sold off their businesses, bought a schooner, and set out from Connecticut for a one-year cruise to the Caribbean and South America. In March 1949, the schooner sank off the coast of Cuba, and a passing American freighter rescued the pair and delivered them safely to Puerto Rico. They continued their journey through South America.

In August of 1949, DeVos and Van Andel returned to Michigan, eager to launch another business. They formed the Ja-Ri Corporation to import and distribute general merchandise. Through Ja-Ri, the pair became distributors of Nutrilite.

After building a highly successful Nutrilite business, they felt that a much broader product line could be sold directly to the American public. In 1959, they founded Amway and worked from the basements of their neighboring homes in the first year. Their first product was L.O.C. Multi-Purpose Cleaner, which helped them reach $500,000 in sales their first year.

In 1960, they moved their business into a repair garage along the Grand River in Ada, Michigan. They prepared a far-reaching distribution plan that would encourage distributors to grow by not only merchandising products, but also by sponsoring others to become distributors. Their modest list of distributors grew quickly, totaling 80,000 by 1968 and 250,000 by 1976.

Over the years, they have built a comprehensive product line. Distributors market more than 400 Amway-brand products and services, plus another 6,500 brand-name products and services, through Amway's Personal Shoppers Catalog. Amway also has expanded dramatically in international markets. Its first overseas affiliate, Amway Australia, opened in 1971, and today Amway operates in more than 75 countries and territories.

Amway is one of the largest privately owned companies in the United States. Annual worldwide sales are approaching $7 billion. The company has over 13,000 employees and more than 2.5 million distributors worldwide. Amway has grown considerably on the site of its first garage. In Ada alone, there are more than 80 buildings totaling 3.8 million square feet. Worldwide, Amway facilities total some 10 million square feet.

The partners both married Grand Rapids women at about the same time. Jay Van Andel married Betty Hoekstra in August 1952, and the couple had two daughters and two sons. Rich DeVos married Helen Van Wesep in February 1953, and the couple had one daughter and three sons. In 1989, DeVos and his four children purchased the Orlando Magic professional basketball team. The founders have retired from daily management of the company. Van Andel's son Steve now serves as chairman of Amway Corporation, and DeVos's son Dick now holds the post of president.

SOURCE: Amway Corporation archives

Charles Diebold

[Diebold, Inc.]

Charles Diebold and Fred Bahman founded the Diebold and Bahman Safe Company in Cincinnati, Ohio, in 1859. Diebold's first safe was sold to the Tell City Furniture Company in Tell City, Indiana, on June 25 of that year. Eight years later, Bahman left the company to form a partnership with Gustav Mosler, who had formed his own security company.

In 1871, Diebold gained national prominence as a result of the great Chicago fire. After the fire, it was discovered that 878 Diebold safes had withstood the fire's violent heat and had protected their contents. Word of this feat spread, and orders for Diebold safes grew faster than the company's manufacturing operation could handle.

That same year, another partner, Jacob Kienzle, had been added. Diebold & Kienzle moved to Canton, Ohio, with the support of 60 different community leaders, banks, and firms in Canton who advanced the company $50,000 in return for promissory notes. The initial production facility was purchased for $7,080 and began operations on July 4, 1872.

In 1874, the company added John W. Norris to the partnership and changed its name to Diebold, Norris and Company. Later that year, the Duncan Safe Deposit Company of San Francisco, California, ordered the first complete bank vault, measuring 30 by 25 by 9 feet and including 4,600 safe-deposit boxes. The total cost was $100,000. Eighteen train cars were used to move the unassembled vault and component parts from Canton to San Francisco. Installation was completed on May 7, 1875. However, the financial strains of the project drove the company into bankruptcy.

The Diebold Safe and Lock Company was formed on July 29, 1876. W. W. Clark served as the first president, and Charles Diebold was the first plant superintendent. Toward the end of the century and up to World War I, Diebold employed so many German immigrants that German was the company language, which gave the company the nickname "Little Germany."

Diebold geared all of its efforts toward war production during World War I, which provided a dramatic increase in sales and revenues for the company. Diebold provided armor plate for tanks and covers for U.S. artillery tractors. The company also provided the U.S. Army with 6- to 9-inch shell lathes and timing fuses for many of the shell types used.

During the 1930s, Diebold worked with the Lake Erie Chemical Company and developed a system to discharge tear gas in bank lobbies to assist banks in deterring the notorious John Dillinger and his gang. In 1943, the Diebold Safe and Lock Company changed its name to Diebold, Incorporated. One year later, former crime fighter, Eliot Ness, of "The Untouchables" fame, was elected chairman of the company's board of directors.

Today, in addition to its line of safes, Diebold is a major automatic teller machine (ATM) manufacturer.

SOURCE: Diebold, Inc., archives

Walter E. Disney

[The Walt Disney Company]

Walter Elias Disney was born on December 5, 1901, in Chicago, Illinois, the youngest of five children born to parents Elias and Flora (Call) Disney. His Canadian father, of Irish descent, operated a contracting business and later acquired a farm near Marceline, Missouri. When Walt was eight years old, the family moved again, this time to Kansas City, Missouri.

Young Disney soon established a paper route and later sold magazines and candy aboard the Kansas City–Chicago train. His interest in art also surfaced at an early age, and he provided weekly sketches to a local barber in exchange for a quarter or a haircut, whichever was needed most. While Disney was attending secondary school and evening art classes, World War I erupted and he had to drop out of both while he served as a Red Cross ambulance driver.

When the war ended, Disney returned to Kansas City and spent the next several years as a commercial artist with local advertising companies. During these years he became intrigued with cartoon slides and built a modest studio in his father's garage to produce local films. Eventually he developed an idea for a film that combined the talents of a young female actress and animated cartoon figures and, with $40, set out for Hollywood.

In 1923, Disney and his brother, Roy Disney, founded The Disney Brothers Studio and fashioned another garage studio to serve as the company headquarters. After raising modest investment capital, they produced a series of "Alice Comedies" based on Walt's animation idea.

In 1925, Disney married Lillian Marie Bounds, and the couple eventually had two daughters. Also during this period of the mid-1920s, Disney conceived the idea for his premiere character, Mickey Mouse, while reflecting on an incident where a real mouse visited his drawing board during his Kansas City days. In 1928, the first Mickey and Minnie Mouse film, *Steamboat Willie,* became an instant success.

In 1929, the Disney partnership was replaced with four businesses, including Walt Disney Productions, Walt Disney Enterprises, the Disney Film Recording Company, and Liled Realty and Investment Company. Walt Disney and his creative forces quickly adopted Technicolor into many of their new productions, and other characters were introduced, including Pluto, Goofy, and Donald Duck. In 1937, *Snow White and the Seven Dwarfs* premiered, the world's first feature-length animated film.

The Disney studios employed nearly 700 people by 1940. That same year, *Pinocchio* and *Fantasia* were released, followed by *The Reluctant Dragon* and *Dumbo* (1941) and *Bambi* (1942). After *Bambi* was completed, the new Burbank studios were transformed into troop barracks, supply facilities, and military training film production studios during World War II.

After the war, Disney grew as rapidly as the postwar economy. Mickey Mouse debuted on television in 1950. Two years later, Disney launched WED Enterprises to design and create his first theme park, Disneyland, which opened in 1955 in Anaheim, California. Walter Elias Disney died on December 15,

1966, at the age of 65. His brother and longtime associate, Roy Disney, died on December 20, 1971.

Today, The Walt Disney Company is a thriving entertainment conglomerate that owns film and television production studios, theme parks, and related companies. In 1996, Disney acquired Capital Cities/ABC, Inc.

SOURCES: Walt Disney archives; *Current Biography 1952*, The H.W. Wilson Company, New York

Ray Dolby

[Dolby Laboratories]

Ray Dolby was born in 1933 in Portland, Oregon. At the age of 16, he was working on various audio and instrumentation projects at Ampex Corporation in Redwood City, California. While attending Stanford University during the 1950s, he was responsible for developing the electronic aspects of the Ampex videotape recording system.

After receiving his B.S. in electrical engineering in 1957, Dolby moved to England as a Marshall Scholar, pursuing graduate study at Cambridge University. In 1961, he received his Ph.D. in physics, specializing in the research of long-wavelength X rays.

In 1963, Dolby accepted a two-year appointment as a United Nations technical adviser in India. Upon his return to England in 1965, he launched Dolby Laboratories with four employees. His first product, the S/N Stretcher, was developed to remove the hissing sound from audio tracks.

The following January, he made his first sale: Decca Record Company of London purchased nine A301 professional noise-reduction units. The first commercial recording session that used the Dolby equipment was with Vladimir Ashkenazy playing Mozart piano concertos.

Throughout 1966 and 1967, Dolby's noise-reduction units received good press coverage, and soon CBS, RCA, MCA, and others were ordering equipment, leading Dolby to establish an office in New York City in November 1967.

Dolby next adapted his technology to the film industry. In 1971, *A Clockwork Orange* became the first film to use Dolby noise reduction on all premixes and masters. The result established a new standard in the film industry, with Dolby sound technology soon becoming common with feature film production.

In January 1976, Dolby closed his original New York office and established a new corporate headquarters in San Francisco, California. He continued to use the London site for manufacturing and stationed engineering support in New York and Hollywood.

Today, Dolby's corporate headquarters are in San Francisco's historic Potrero Hill district. It remains a privately held company with approximately 300 employees worldwide.

SOURCE: Dolby archives

Reuben H. Donnelley

[R.H. Donnelley Corporation]

Reuben Hamilton Donnelley was born in Ontario, Canada, in August 1864, two months before his parents, Richard R. and Naomi Shenstone Donnelley, moved to Chicago. By 1873, Richard Donnelley was a partner in a successful printing business. After attending the University of Chicago, Reuben enrolled at The Bryant and Stratton Business College. In 1881, while still in school, he joined his father's firm full-time as a clerk and within four years was head of the canvassing department.

In 1882, Richard Donnelley finally established a printing firm of his own in Chicago and called it R.R. Donnelley & Sons, the direct predecessor of today's printing giant. Four years later, a contract was signed between the Chicago Telephone Company and R.R. Donnelley & Sons to publish the *Chicago Telephone Directory.*

The separate *Lakeside Annual Business Directory* developed at this time into a publication of equal importance. As an offprint from the city directory, this book was not unique in the basic information it provided, but it contained many special features not found in the city directory, such as an alphabetical listing of all the businesses and businesspeople in Chicago.

The telephone was still not widely used. Of the nearly 1,000 "Physicians and Surgeons" listed in the *Lakeside Business Directory* of 1885–1886, only 30 had telephones. Before Reuben Donnelley took over management of the directories, the business directory appeared very modestly each year in a cardboard cover with advertising on the front and back. After 1887, it was transformed into the familiar *Red Book,* bound in "brilliant red and gilt."

Reuben also developed *The Blue Book,* which first appeared in 1890. This was a directory of about 25,000 "carefully selected" residents, including those in the city's most fashionable neighborhoods and suburbs, as well as members of its clubs and philanthropic organizations. Although he denied that this was intended to be a social register, news releases announcing its appearance each year typically caused anxiety in certain circles over whether one would be included. In a list of residences by street, it specified "calling days," and the alphabetical list of individuals included the addresses of summer residences.

In 1892, Donnelley married Laura Thorne, daughter of the prominent Chicago family who helped found Montgomery Ward. The couple eventually had a son, Thorne, and a daughter, Eleanor. Three years later, Reuben resigned from the Chicago Directory Company and became a partner in a brokerage firm.

Knight, Donnelley & Company was initially successful, and Reuben Donnelley was chosen as a member of the governing committee of the Chicago Stock Exchange, becoming president of the exchange in 1901. In the second half of 1905, however, Knight, Donnelley & Company failed and went out of business, and Donnelley returned to the Chicago Directory Company.

A classified directory for New York City had been printed since 1901 by the Jersey City Printing Company and published by Alcolm Company. It was called the *Alcolm Red Book.* Reuben Donnelley purchased the rights to the directory and took on most of its staff. The following year, a much-improved *Manhattan Red Book* was printed on yellow paper with a red cover.

In 1917, the Chicago Directory Company was dissolved and The Reuben H. Donnelley Corporation was officially chartered. Headquarters were relocated in New York City, with a branch office in Chicago.

The passage of the Graham Act in 1921 ended competition in the telephone industry and, as a result, effectively ended competition in the directory industry as well. Since AT&T emerged with nearly 90 percent of the business, Reuben Donnelley soon became the largest independent sales agent for Bell System directories.

Concurrently, Reuben Donnelley directed the company into new directory areas, such as creation of *The Manufacturers and Distributors Directories* in 1921 and a Distribution Department. The directory distribution activities blossomed with the acquisition in 1920 of the National Delivery Service Company in Philadelphia. Direct-mail marketing was a natural outgrowth of the directory business since both were dependent on compiling lists of names and addresses. In 1922, the M&F Mailing Company in Nevada, Iowa, was acquired and became known as Donnelley Marketing.

Reuben H. Donnelley died on February 25, 1929. Due to the changing business environment, his successors would eventually shift the emphasis of the firm from a publishing operation to a full-scale sales organization. In 1961, R.H. Donnelley merged with Dun & Bradstreet.

SOURCES: Adapted from material published for R.H. Donnelley Associates, a book published privately on the occasion of the company's centennial, and subsequent research

Richard R. Donnelley

[R.R. Donnelley & Sons]

Richard Robert Donnelley, by age 13, was an apprentice printer in his native Hamilton, Ontario, Canada. His mother, Jane Elliott Donnelley, was a widow who supported her only son by taking sewing jobs. She proved to be an inspiration for young Donnelley, who was granted a partnership in the printing company while he was still in his teens.

In 1857, the 21-year-old Donnelley accepted a job with a printer in New Orleans, Louisiana, and once more worked his way into a partnership. However, when the Civil War erupted he returned to Hamilton, where he and a partner launched another printing venture with a total capitalization of $2.50.

By 1864, Donnelley had built a strong reputation in the printing trades and was offered a partnership in a growing business in Chicago, Illinois. He moved his wife, Naomi, and infant son, Reuben, to the United States. A second son, Thomas Elliott Donnelley, was born in 1868. By 1870, the firm of Church, Goodman, and Donnelley was one of the region's largest producers of books and periodicals. However, one year later the firm's new six-story building in the heart of

Chicago's business district (renamed the Lakeside Publishing and Printing Company) was leveled by the great Chicago fire.

Donnelley not only lost his business to the fire, but also most of his personal possessions as well. Despite the setback, he rebuilt a new building on the former site and was back in business with new partners by 1873. In 1875, Donnelley formed a publishing partnership called Donnelley, Loyd & Company to undertake publishing ventures outside the printing firm. Two years later, he refinanced the firm with two new partners under the name of Donnelley, Gassette & Loyd, with Donnelley as minority owner. By 1881, he had bought out his partners and was president and primary owner of the company.

Donnelley was a firm believer in separating the publishing and printing functions of his organization, so in 1880 he created the Chicago Directory Company to publish directories. In 1887, his oldest son Reuben was named president of the Chicago Directory Company. Later, Reuben took over this enterprise completely and changed the name to the the Reuben H. Donnelley Corporation, which was sold to Dun & Bradstreet in 1961.

In 1882, Richard Robert Donnelley (pictured above) reorganized the printing company as R.R. Donnelley & Sons Company. Over the next two decades, the company enjoyed considerable growth and was able to attract prestigious contracts, such as the 1895 contract to print the Montgomery Ward mail-order catalog.

Richard Robert Donnelley died in 1899. His younger son, Thomas Elliott Donnelley, assumed the position of president and ran the company until after World War II, at which time he passed control to his sons, Elliott and Gaylord, and his son-in-law, Charles Haffner Jr.

Today, R.R. Donnelley & Sons is still based in Chicago and maintains more than 200 office and production locations in 26 countries. Annual sales now exceed $6.5 billion and the company employs 38,000 people.

SOURCES: R.R. Donnelley & Sons Company archives; *The Printer: A Quarterly Publication of R.R. Donnelley & Sons Company,* fall 1989

John T. Dorrance, Arthur Dorrance, John Campbell, Abram Anderson

[Campbell Soup Company]

The Campbell Soup Company evolved from a small canning company founded by John Campbell and Abram Anderson into the world's leading producer of soup. It is interesting to note that John Campbell severed ties with the company nearly 100 years ago, well before Campbell's produced its first can of soup. Arthur Dorrance assumed control of the company and brought his nephew, Dr. John Thompson Dorrance, into the company. John Dorrance developed the soup line.

Abram Anderson was born in 1834. He trained as a tinsmith, spending several years installing roofs in Newark, New Jersey. He moved to Philadelphia in 1860 and started manufacturing refrigerators, which used tin components. Later he made tin cans, a relatively new innovation for food storage. Believing that tin cans held a better future than glass jars, Anderson moved across the Delaware River and, with $400, established a canning factory.

In 1869, Anderson acquired a new partner, Joseph Campbell, a traveling purchasing agent for a Philadelphia fruit-and-vegetable wholesaler. Campbell had grown up on a farm in Cumberland County, New Jersey.

The company grew quickly with the addition of Campbell, who introduced new products such as jams, jellies, apple butter, and mincemeat. However, by 1877, the two disagreed about the direction the company should take. Anderson was pleased with the status quo, while Campbell favored aggressive expansion. Unable to find a compromise, Anderson sold his share of the business to Campbell.

Anderson started another company that achieved some degree of success. His reputation as a canner opened up several opportunities. It is interesting to note that a horseradish packer from Sharpsburg, Pennsylvania, once sought out Anderson for advice and a loan. Anderson provided both to the young man, whose name was H. J. Heinz. After a reasonable period of time, Heinz had not made enough money to repay Anderson, and in lieu of the cash he offered a prized horse, which Anderson accepted.

Meanwhile, Campbell had taken on three new partners in his venture, one of whom was a wealthy timber and flour merchant named Arthur Dorrance. The new firm was called Joseph Campbell & Company, and it marketed a number of products around its most popular product, "Beefsteak Ketchup." The name of the company was changed to the Joseph Campbell Preserve Company in 1891. Three years later, Joseph Campbell retired and Arthur Dorrance became president of the company. Campbell died in 1900, ending all association of Campbell family with the company.

John Thompson Dorrance received his degree in chemistry from the Massachusetts Institute of Technology in 1895 and his Ph.D. in organic chemistry from the University of Göttingen in Europe. Passing up offers to teach at Göttingen, Columbia, Cornell, and Bryn Mawr, Dorrance urged his Uncle Arthur to hire him at the Campbell's plant. His uncle agreed and hired him at $7.50 per week.

John Dorrance had a vision for a new market. While living in Europe, he became accustomed to the Continental practice of eating well-seasoned soup with many meals. At the time, soups were not popular with Americans. In fact, Franco-American and Huckins were the only two companies in the United States that were selling ready-to-serve soups.

Dorrance believed there were three barriers to the market. The first was price. Soup, heavily laden with water, was expensive to ship to market. He solved this by developing a process to reduce most of the water, resulting in a condensed soup that could be shipped at a much lower cost.

The second barrier was taste. Recognizing that American housewives would not serve any meal that didn't taste good, Dorrance fine-tuned his products until their taste and quality were unquestionable. The third barrier was a bit more difficult to overcome. Americans simply didn't eat much soup. To create a demand for his product, Dorrance had to first create a market.

The first of Dorrance's soups were ready for the market in 1897. One of the original varieties was tomato, which to this day continues to rank among the top-selling items in American supermarkets. The distinctive red-and-white label was adopted in 1898 after a company executive attended the Cornell-Penn football game and was struck by Cornell's new brilliant red-and-white uniforms.

Dorrance personally took to the road to create a demand for his soups, and he found little resistance. His condensed soups, priced at 10¢ a can, were a bargain for homemakers. The high-quality soups, using all natural ingredients, were instantly popular with families of all economic levels. Production rose from ten cases per week the first year to 20 million cans a year by 1905, and the name was changed to the Joseph Campbell Company to reflect the expansion of product lines.

By this time Dorrance was convinced Campbell's could be the greatest soup company in the world. He sought to expand advertising and increase consumer demand. The "Campbell Kids," cartoon characters of plump, lovable children, appeared in advertisements. However, even more effective was the introduction of menus and cookbooks, which put an ever increasing number of meal suggestions (all of which included Campbell's soup) in the hands of housewives.

John Dorrance married Ethel Malinckrodt of Baltimore in 1906. The couple had four daughters and a son. Early in the marriage the couple moved to Cinnaminson, a beautiful New Jersey farm property that eventually became important to Campbell's farm research. Later they moved to an estate in Radnor, Pennsylvania. The family did not lead a lavish lifestyle. Family vacations were usually spent in Maine, but John Dorrance had few other interests.

As soup displaced older Campbell's products, Dorrance developed another successful product. Soup is made in two stages. First, *stock* is prepared, then *garnish* (meat, vegetables, etc.) is added. Each Monday, as stock simmered at the factory, most workers had very little to do. Taking advantage of available labor and cooking equipment, Dorrance started making pork and beans, which didn't require soup stock. Campbell's Pork & Beans sales skyrocketed. By 1914, soup sales totaled $5,738,200, while Pork & Beans sales totaled $2,283,036.

In 1915, an aging Arthur Dorrance decided to retire. His nephew John had singlehandedly engineered Campbell's growing soup industry, and he was the logical choice to succeed Arthur. On April 23, 1915, John purchased his uncle's shares for a little over $3.5 million, leaving John as sole owner of the Joseph Campbell Company. That same year, Campbell's acquired Franco-American, not so much for their line of soups, but more for their spaghetti and other pasta products.

Growth in the company was steady through the 1920s, with soup remaining the company's primary product. John Dorrance had realized his dream of building the largest soup company in the country, and probably the entire world. On December 5, 1921, he renamed the organization the Campbell Soup Company.

Dorrance continued to spend considerable time at Cinnaminson, the family farm, where he was working on September 21, 1930, the day that he died. At the time of his death, Dorrance's net worth was approximately $115 million, making him the third wealthiest man in America.

Upon the death of John Dorrance, his brother Arthur assumed the position of president. Arthur, like John, was an MIT graduate who had joined Campbell's in 1920. He remained in that capacity until his death in 1946.

Campbell's acquired other entrepreneurial companies, including C.A. Swanson & Sons in 1955, Pepperidge Farm in 1961, Godiva Chocolatier in 1966, Vlasic Foods in 1978, and Mrs. Paul's Kitchens in 1982. Today Campbell's has 47,000 employees. Soup is still a very important product, with more than 2.5 billion cans sold annually in the United States.

SOURCES: Campbell Soup Company archives; Douglas Collins, *America's Favorite Food: The Story of Campbell Soup Company,* Harry N. Abrams, Inc., 1994

Charles H. Dow, Edward D. Jones, Clarence W. Barron

[Dow Jones & Company]

Charles Henry Dow (photo below) was born on November 6, 1851, on a farm at Sterling, Connecticut, the only surviving child of Charles and Harriet Allen Dow. His family descended from Henry Dow, who immigrated from Ormsby, England, to Watertown, Massachusetts, in 1637. When young Charles was only six years old, his father died. After receiving an education in a one-room schoolhouse, 16-year-old Dow left home to serve as an apprentice printer and reporter for a regional weekly newspaper.

In 1869, Dow accepted a job with the *Springfield* (Massachusetts) *Republican* and quickly rose to the position of assistant editor. In 1875, he was hired as the night editor for the *Press and Star* in Providence, Rhode Island, but left shortly thereafter to join the *Providence Journal.* There he cultivated an interest in history and research, and was soon traveling through the West writing about mining operations and the problems faced by owners and miners.

Dow returned East and, in 1879, landed a job reporting on mining stocks for the *New York Mail and Express,* owned by Cyrus W. Field, then quickly moved to the Kiernan News Agency, another publisher on New York's Broad Street.

There he was permitted to hire an old friend from his Providence days, Eddie Jones.

Edward Davis Jones (at right) was born on October 7, 1856, in Worcester, Massachusetts. He had enrolled at Brown University in 1877, but dropped out in his junior year to accept a full-time job as a reporter with the *Providence Journal.* When Charles Dow became a reporter in New York's financial district, Jones joined him.

In 1882, Dow, Jones, and a third Kiernan employee named Charles Bergstresser launched their own reporting agency, named Dow Jones & Company, in a small basement office on Wall Street. Initially, they issued financial bulletins that were delivered by runners.

Within one year their business picked up, and they introduced their *Customers' Afternoon News Letter* summarizing the day's bulletins and providing an analysis of stock market activity and trends. In 1884, their modest publication started including the Dow Jones Average, a stock price index devised by Dow.

Five years later, Clarence Barron of Boston became their first out-of-town correspondent. That same year, their *Customers' Afternoon News Letter* was expanded from two pages to four and was renamed the *Wall Street Journal.* Throughout the 1890s, the partners built Dow Jones & Company into a respected organization. In 1899, Edward Jones retired from the partnership. In March 1902, the organization's first correspondent, Clarence Barron, acquired the company. Charles Dow remained on board, but died in December of that same year.

Clarence Walker Barron (below) was born on July 2, 1855, in Boston, Massachusetts, to Henry and Elana Barron. By the time he was 20 years old, Clarence was reporting business news for the *Boston Daily News.* He later moved to the *Boston Transcript* where, in 1875, he introduced the paper's first business section.

In 1887, 32-year-old Barron established the Boston News Bureau and soon began exchanging news with the *Wall Street Journal.* In 1896, he replicated the service in Pennsylvania, forming the Philadelphia News Bureau. Six years later, he purchased Dow Jones & Company from Dow and Bergstresser.

Barron's wife, Jessie Waldron Barron, a savvy businesswoman, actually oversaw the company for the next ten years. In 1912, however, Clarence assumed control. Nine years later, he launched *Barron's* weekly financial magazine. Clarence Barron died on October 2, 1928, at the age of 73.

Today, Dow Jones & Company is the world's premier business information publisher and media organization. In addition to the *Wall Street Journal* and its international editions, as well as electronic business information services, the company publishes *Barron's* and owns 19 daily community newspapers and several other media ventures.

Its electronic information services include Dow Jones Markets, a provider of real-time financial information to the international business community; Dow Jones News Service and other business newswires; and Dow Jones Interactive Publishing. Dow Jones also provides business television programming in the United States and abroad.

Dow Jones & Company has 11,000 employees worldwide and generates annual revenues of nearly $2.5 billion.

SOURCES: Dow Jones & Company archives; Lloyd Wendt, *The Wall Street Journal: The Story of Dow Jones & the Nation's Business Newspaper,* Rand McNally & Company, 1982

Herbert H. Dow

[Dow Chemical Company]

Herbert Henry Dow was born on February 26, 1866, in Belleville, Ontario, Canada, where his father, Joseph, was temporarily employed. The family returned to Birmingham, Connecticut, a year later. Joseph Dow was a master mechanic, an inventive engineer, and an expert machinist, and these traits were passed to his son.

Young Herbert once read that ostriches laid many eggs but seldom bothered to hatch them. He took it upon himself to design an incubator that would handle the job and, after 40 prototypes, finally devised a working system. He then built and sold these machines. This early experience—identifying a market niche, filling the need, then moving on to the next project—became a trademark of Herbert Dow.

At age 12, Dow's family moved to Cleveland, Ohio. Six years later, Herbert enrolled in the chemistry curriculum at the Case School of Applied Science (which later became Case Western Reserve). During his senior year, a well-driller provided the young researcher with a bottle of brine (fossilized seawater), a by-product of oil drilling. Vast deposits of brine were trapped in porous rock under Ohio and other Midwestern states.

Dow was inspired to invent a method by which bromine could be efficiently extracted from brine, and in 1889 the 23-year-old scientist established the Canton Chemical Company. The venture was undercapitalized, however, and closed within a year. In 1890, Dow received the backing of J. H. Osborn and established the Midland Chemical Company in Midland, Michigan, which was close to a ready supply of brine. This time he was successful and, by 1893, recorded a profit of more than $11,000. It was during this period (1892) that he married Grace Anna Ball, and the couple eventually had seven children.

Encouraged by his success, Dow turned his focus to the chlorine that was also extracted from brine. Convinced that chlorine could be used in diverse markets, he built a plant for making electrolytic chlorine. However, one hour after production began, the new facility blew up, prompting his backers to withdraw support.

Undaunted, Dow moved to Ohio in 1895 and launched the Dow Process Company with new investors. He then set out to electrolyze a saltwater solution to extract chlorine and caustic soda. Once again, however, his backers grew restless after a short period and the plant was closed after only six months of operation.

In 1896, the 30-year-old Dow returned to Midland, leased land from the Midland Chemical Company, and obtained bromine waste. This time, Dow was able to extract chlorine, and on May 18, 1897, the Dow Chemical Company was organized. Within one year a plant was built and bleach was being sold.

The Dow Chemical Company bought the Midland Chemical Company in 1900, putting Herbert Dow back into the bromine business. The photography industry was growing rapidly, and bromine was used in the manufacture of film. The use of chloroform as an anesthetic was also growing, and Dow became the first chemical company to produce it through a purely synthetic process. Another breakthrough came in 1916, when Dow developed synthetic indigo. Within five years, his indigo was being sold throughout the world.

Dow was quite active in the war effort during World War I, producing phenol for use in explosives, bromine for tear gas, mustard gas, and many other products. After the war, Dow focused on the development of inexpensive, synthetic phenol. Eventually, the company was producing half of the phenol used in the entire world.

Herbert Henry Dow died on October 15, 1930, at the age of 64. He was succeeded by his son, Willard Dow. At the time of Herbert's death, Dow Chemical was producing 150 products and had annual sales of nearly $20 million. Today, the company has annual sales approaching $20 *billion* and employs nearly 40,000 people.

SOURCES: Murray Campbell and Harrison Hatton, *Herbert H. Dow: Pioneer in Creative Chemistry,* Appleton-Century-Crofts, Inc., New York, 1951; Don Whitehead, *The Dow Story: The History of the Dow Chemical Company,* McGraw-Hill, 1968

William Dreyer, Joseph Edy

[Dreyer's Grand Ice Cream, Inc.]

In 1906, 18-year-old William Dreyer immigrated to the United States from his native Bremen, Germany. To cover the cost of the journey on the luxury steamer *S.S. Kaiser Wilhelm,* he worked as a galley boy. On the last night of the voyage, he was asked to make a special dessert. His concoction of fresh fruit, sugar, and gelatin drew considerable praise from the captain's table, and young

Dreyer knew that his future in America would have something to do with dessert.

Dreyer's first job in New York was making ice cream at a candy store. There he met a young German girl named Albina, and the two were soon married. The young couple set their sights on California and started the journey west, stopping briefly in Oklahoma City, where Dreyer sold refreshments at a nickelodeon. Eventually, they reached northern California, where he worked at a variety of ice creameries.

By 1921, Dreyer had established his own ice cream manufacturing venture in the California dairy country community of Visalia. Word of his award-winning ice cream spread quickly, and in 1926 he was recruited to run a large new plant in Oakland for National Ice Cream. In Oakland he met a local candymaker named Joe Edy.

Joseph Edy was born in Missouri and raised in Montana. In the 1920s, he and his wife Grace decided to join his brother in California. In 1925, Edy opened the doors to Edy's Character Candies Shop in Oakland. His high-quality candy quickly became recognized as among the best in the East Bay area, and he was soon operating six shops.

In 1928, Dreyer and Edy decided to join forces to manufacture high-quality ice cream. They secured a small factory and launched Edy's Grand Ice Cream—the "Grand" reflected their street address on Grand Avenue, an Oakland shopping strip. The partners worked well together, with Dreyer supervising the manufacturing process and Edy handling the marketing.

As America entered the Great Depression, Dreyer continued to experiment with new and better ways to make ice cream. One night while making chocolate ice cream, he decided to add walnuts and marshmallows, which he cut with his wife's good sewing shears. The flavor was an instant hit and, in reference to the tough economic conditions around the country, they named it *Rocky Road*.

More flavors followed, including Peppermint Stick, Hawaiian Mango, Rum Custard, and Toasted Almond. When World War II caused shortages of butterfat and cane sugar, the founders developed a popular line of sherbets.

In 1946, Dreyer and Edy dissolved their partnership. Edy wanted to focus attention on spreading his candy stores into Los Angeles and to build a new candy manufacturing plant. Dreyer, joined by his son, Bill Dreyer Jr., who had just returned from the war, focused on expanding the ice cream business, which was renamed Dreyer's Grand Ice Cream, Inc. In 1948, a new plant was opened and, for the first time, packages of Dreyer's ice cream were available in grocery stores.

Upon William Dreyer's retirement in 1953, Bill Jr. expanded the business further by opening a chain of Dreyer's diners in the Bay area. Unfortunately, the concept didn't work out and the company fell into financial troubles and was sold to key managers in 1963. The new owners refocused on supermarket sales and nursed the company back to financial health.

The business hit another ceiling in 1976 and, unable to find financing for expansion, the owners sold the business to Gary Rogers and Rick Cronk. With $28,000 of their own funds, the two new owners were able to arrange financing. The new owners ironed out production bottlenecks in the original plant and invested instead in building a direct store distribution system that today reaches most American consumers.

The rapid expansion of Dreyer's caught the attention of Kraft, who at the time owned the competing Breyers Ice Cream. Because of the similarity in names, Dreyer's agreed that any products sold east of the Rocky Mountains would not use the Dreyer's Grand Ice Cream label. When they finally moved into the Eastern market, they resurrected the original product label: Edy's Grand Ice Cream.

Today Dreyer's Grand Ice Cream, Inc., has nearly 2,500 employees and annual sales of nearly $800 million.

SOURCE: "History in the Making," Dreyer's Grand Ice Cream, Inc., 1997

David G. Drum

[Kampgrounds of America]

David G. Drum was born on March 7, 1923, in Rushville, Indiana, and was raised in Miles City, Montana. He served two tours with the U.S. Marines, first during the invasion of Okinawa during World War II, for which he was awarded a Purple Heart, then again as an infantry officer during the Korean conflict. In between, he earned a bachelor's degree in business from the University of Montana in 1947.

Drum was an enterprising man his entire life. His brother-in-law, an accountant named Bob Boorman, grew so tired of hearing the constant flow of business ideas that he automatically said no to everything that Drum proposed. In the decade between World War II and Korea, Drum sold oil, hearing aids, battery rechargers, hardware, and steel buildings. He also ran a farm and garden center, which inspired him to establish an anhydrous ammonia fertilizer business.

In 1962, Seattle served as host to the World's Fair, and the residents of Billings, Montana, geared up for the tourists who would be traveling through town. Some people suggested the town build a campground, but that was dismissed because the motel owners protested using tax money for a competing alternative.

Drum saw an opportunity and opened a campsite along the Yellowstone River south of Billings. For a $1.75 registration fee, surprised guests were given access to hot showers, clean bathrooms, and even a small store. Word spread quickly among travelers and the campground was an instant success.

Each evening, Drum visited the campsite to make sure guests were comfortable (and to make sure all the guests were properly registered). During these visits, Drum spent considerable time chatting with the campers. He soon became convinced that his campground was quite unique and could be successfully replicated in other areas.

Predictably, Boorman said no. Drum then recruited John Wallace, the regional manager of a gas company, who agreed. Together, they talked Boorman into joining them, and in 1962 the men launched their new campground company with a $1,000 loan. Originally, they were going to call it Indian Joe's Campground. The name didn't fit, so they next selected Campgrounds of America. Facing copyright complications, they changed it to Kampgrounds of America (KOA).

Using a Holiday Inn franchise agreement as a model, Drum and his partners compiled a franchise system and recruited a salesman. Within a year, KOA opened six campgrounds. In 1965, there were 33 in operation, and one year later the number exceeded 70. By 1970, KOA had established more than 300 sites.

As more sites opened, KOA customers were provided with even more amenities, including water, sewer, and electrical hookups, coin laundries, and a reservation system that held a place to stay at the next KOA down the highway. Many offered swimming pools and recreation facilities. To support its strong growth, the company made an initial public offering in 1969, followed by a second offering three years later. It later returned to private ownership.

Drum remained active in several public and private ventures after founding KOA. He served a term in the 1967 Montana state legislature as a representative of Yellowstone County and served as a member of the Montana Constitutional Convention in 1972. He also made an unsuccessful bid for the United States Senate. His private ventures included cattle ranching, cattle feedlots, apple orchards, and land development.

David G. Drum died on October 19, 1994, at the age of 71, and is survived by his wife, Dorothy, and three children. Today, Kampgrounds of America is the largest system of franchised campgrounds in the world, with more than 500 sites in the United States, Canada, Mexico, and Japan.

SOURCES: Kampgrounds of America, Inc., archives; John Neary, "Hotels with No Rooms Are Booming," *Life* magazine, September 29, 1972

Robert G. Dun, John M. Bradstreet, Lewis Tappan, Benjamin Douglass

[Dun & Bradstreet]

The Dun and Bradstreet Corporation, generally referred to simply as Dun & Bradstreet, traces its roots to a small 1841 start-up company in New York City founded by Lewis Tappan. Over the ensuing 15 decades, the company grew into the largest and best-known financial reporting and information company in the world. Curiously, Dun and Bradstreet controlled competing agencies, and neither man lived to see their companies merge.

Lewis Tappan was born in 1788 at Northampton, Massachusetts. At age 15, he left home to serve as an apprentice to a merchant who, in 1809, provided him with the funds to start his own venture in Philadelphia, Pennsylvania. By age 24, Tappan had built a successful business and was relatively wealthy.

In 1815, Tappan loaned his brother Arthur $12,000 to establish a silk-importing business in New York City. Within 11 years, the venture soured, and Lewis moved to New York to manage the business. The Tappans were strict Christians and insisted that employees "be home no later than 10 P.M. and go to church at least once a week." Within a few years the business was thriving. In 1835, the brothers grossed nearly $2 million. (At the time, the entire budget of the United States government was less than $18 million.)

Throughout his life as a merchant, Tappan was constantly confounded with the issue of extending credit to buyers, particularly those from the western frontier. These buyers would present letters of reference from local preachers or judges, and Tappan had to make a decision. He knew that liberal credit policies lost money, while tight credit policies lost business.

Tappan saw opportunity in this dilemma and, in 1841, launched The Mercantile Agency, one of the first credit reporting companies in the country. He developed a network of correspondents from different American cities who, twice yearly, would submit reports about local companies, including "their means, capital and character, the length of their residence in their present location, and their general mode of business as to cash or credit." Subscribers paid an annual fee to be included in the reports.

In 1849, the 61-year-old Tappan turned The Mercantile Agency over to a rugged entrepreneur named Benjamin Douglass. In 1832, at age 16, Douglass had been named a partner in his father's West Indian trading firm. Within six years, he established a retail trade in Charleston, South Carolina. Later, he moved to New Orleans, Louisiana, and became an active trader throughout the Mississippi and Ohio River valleys.

Douglass, at age 33, took over the agency when the railroad and telegraph was ushering America into a period of unparalleled growth. He established branch offices throughout the West and conceived a direct-mail list for subscribers. In 1851, he became the first credit reporter to be sued. Two Ohio men filed suit regarding an unfavorable credit report and, when Douglass refused to release the name of the reporter, he was jailed for 20 days for contempt of court.

The Mercantile Agency was not without competition. Across town, John M. Bradstreet launched a modest credit reporting company in 1849. Within eight years, he had identified the chief weakness of his competitor: the need for a client to physically come to the office to hear a credit report read aloud. Bradstreet conceived a hard-copy loose-leaf-bound system of credit reporting with special codes for items such as "making money," "not too much extended," and so forth. Douglass was critical of the exposure of the system, which involved documents that could be read by others who had no business seeing the information, but couldn't deny he was losing clients to Bradstreet.

In 1859, Douglass turned the agency over to R. G. Dun, his brother-in-law. Robert Graham Dun and his four brothers and sisters were raised on a small allowance left after their father's early death. Dun became a clerk in a large general store at age 16 and, within five years, was named partner. He later joined The Mercantile Agency at the request of his brother-in-law, Benjamin Douglass.

About the time that Dun assumed control of The Mercantile Agency, the company released a large, comprehensive reference book with clever features for end users. The book was highly successful and helped to restore much of the client base lost to Bradstreet. However, the Civil War broke out, which affected every credit reporter in the country. As revenues fell, Dun focused on compiling information on southern debt and the effect on New York merchants.

In the middle of the Civil War, John Bradstreet died and his son, Henry, took control of their agency. Dun took advantage of the opportunity and issued an improved reference book. In 1865, Dun invested $15,000 to establish the agency's first print shop. Nine years later, he placed the first commercial order received by the start-up Remington typewriter company for 100 typewriters at $55 apiece.

Dun built an empire while achieving considerable success. He changed the name of the agency to R. G. Dun & Company. His personal attorney and fishing partner was Chester A. Arthur, the 21st United States president. In fact, four other U.S. presidents worked as Dun & Bradstreet correspondents: Abraham Lincoln, Ulysses S. Grant, William B. McKinley, and Grover Cleveland. At the time of Dun's death in 1900, he had established offices throughout the world.

For the next 30 years, both companies had an unremarkable existence. By the early 1930s, however, the Depression had delivered a crippling blow to both agencies, and Arthur D. Whiteside entered the picture. In 1912, at the age of 30, Whiteside acquired his first credit reporting company. In 1930, Whiteside merged with R. G. Dun & Company and assumed the role of chief executive. He then turned his attention to Bradstreet. In 1932, Dun had revenues of $11.1 million compared to Bradstreet's $5.9 million. With little public fanfare, Whiteside orchestrated the March 9, 1933, merger of the two firms into The Dun & Bradstreet Corporation.

In 1961, the Reuben H. Donnelley Corporation became a wholly owned subsidiary of Dun & Bradstreet, and one year later Dun & Bradstreet acquired Moody's Investors Service. In 1984, Dun & Bradstreet merged with the A. C. Nielsen Company, creating the world's premier business information and market research organization. In 1996, Nielsen was spun off as an independent, public company.

SOURCES: Dun & Bradstreet archives; *Dun & Bradstreet and the Rise of Modern Business*

Éleuthère I. du Pont

[E.I. du Pont de Nemours & Company]

Éleuthère Irénée du Pont was born on June 24, 1771, in the Nemours district of the French village of Chevannes. His father, Pierre-Samuel du Pont, who was a successful economist and public official, added "de Nemours" to his last name to prevent being confused with two other du Ponts in the French Chamber of Deputies.

Tragically, Irénée's mother died when he was 14. Shortly thereafter, Samuel du Pont moved his two sons to Paris, where they hosted famous international guests such as Ben Franklin and Thomas Jefferson. Irénée's favorite visitor, however, was French scientist Antoine-Laurent Lavoisier. Irénée soon went to work at Lavoisier's gunpowder factory, and in 1791 he married Sophia Dalmas.

During the French Revolution, the gunpowder factory closed, and 23-year-old Irénée operated the du Pont family printing business. Political pressures overcame the family, and in 1799 Samuel, Irénée, and 11 other family members set sail for the United States on the *American Eagle,* which landed 91 days later (in 1800) at Newport, Rhode Island.

Irénée originally planned to move his wife and three children to Virginia, but balked at the soaring land prices. While looking for an opportunity, he had occasion to go target shooting with an American military officer and was surprised at the poor quality of gunpowder that was available. He researched the subject and found that American manufacturers weren't utilizing the advances made by the European companies.

He returned to France and raised funding for an American gunpowder plant. He then scouted for an appropriate location in the United States, eventually settling on a site along the Brandywine River four miles west of Wilmington, Delaware. In April 1802, he purchased the 95-acre Jacob Broom farm, moved his family into the two-story farmhouse, and started to build a factory.

Within two years, the factory was producing some of the highest-quality gunpowder in America. While first-year sales exceeded $15,000, Napoleon's battles in Europe helped the company grow quickly and, the following year, sales more than tripled to nearly $47,000. By 1911, *profits* were almost $47,000, and the War of 1812 accelerated the growth even faster.

Éleuthère Irénée du Pont died on October 31, 1834, at the age of 63. At the time of his death, du Pont's mills were producing 1 million pounds of gunpowder annually. He was succeeded by his son Alfred. By 1837, the original investors had been paid off and the du Pont siblings, three boys and four girls, were sole owners of the company.

The company passed through successive generations of control over the following decades, and gunpowder slowly played a reduced role. In 1913, Du Pont employed more than 6,000 people and derived 97 percent of its income from gunpowder. Under the leadership of Pierre-Samuel du Pont, a great-grandson of Éleuthère Irénée, it diversified into markets such as synthetic fibers and rubber, chemicals, cellophane, and paint. By 1939, Du Pont employed nearly 55,000 people, and less than 10 percent of its income was related to gunpowder.

Today, E.I. du Pont de Nemours & Company employs more than 140,000 people and has annual sales of nearly $40 billion.

SOURCE: William S. Dutton, *Du Pont: One Hundred and Forty Years,* Charles Scribner's Sons, 1942

William C. Durant

[General Motors Corporation]

In 1856, Henry H. Crapo, a prominent businessman from the whaling port of New Bedford, Massachusetts, moved to the frontier town of Flint, Michigan. Crapo, in his 50s, was involved with Michigan's lumber industries and wanted to be closer to his growing enterprise. One of Crapo's daughters, Rebecca, married William Clark Durant, a Boston banker, in 1855. The couple had a daughter, also named Rebecca, and a son, William Crapo Durant, born on December 8, 1861.

Not long after Henry Crapo died, Rebecca left her husband and moved her two children to Flint. There, young William Durant lived a comfortable life among uncles, aunts, and cousins, as well as respectable family wealth. A few months before he graduated from high school, 17-year-old Durant suddenly dropped out and announced his intention to work at the family lumberyard. Expecting an office job, he showed up for his first day of work smartly dressed. He was promptly sent to the yards to pile lumber.

As the lumber industry lost steam, two new industries emerged in Flint—carriage making and cigar manufacturing. Durant became successful in the cigar business and, at the same time, became active with the town's private water company. In 1885, at the age of 23, he married Clara Miller Pitt, and within five years the couple had two children, Margery and Russell Clifford.

In 1886, while walking to read water meters, Durant was stopped by a friend, Johnny Alger, who was driving an odd horse-drawn road cart. Durant accepted a ride and was amazed at the smooth ride made possible by the shock-absorbing springs in the cart's wheels. That night, Durant hopped a train to Coldwater and called on the manufacturer the next morning, announcing his interest in buying in to the venture. The owners offered the entire company to him, including their patent for the spring, for $1,500. Within days, Durant raised the money and, with his partner, J. Dallas Dort, moved the company to Flint.

Durant renamed the venture The Flint Road Cart Company. He took to the road exhibiting the cart to buyers and soon had orders for 600. Initially, he contracted another carriage maker to build them for $12.50 each. However, as business grew, the partners formed their own manufacturing company. By the 1890s, their holdings were reorganized as the Durant-Dort Carriage Company, which maintained four operating divisions.

In 1905, Durant acquired controlling interest of the newly reorganized Buick Motor Car Company and soon moved the operation to Flint. To support the venture, he persuaded Charles Stewart Mott of the Weston-Mott axle company to move his plant from Utica, New York, to Flint.

Encouraged by the success of Buick, Durant decided to orchestrate an industry consolidation. In 1908, he formed the General Motors Company. Over the next three years, he acquired the Olds Motor Works, the Cadillac Automobile Company, and the Oakland Motor Car Company, which later became the

Pontiac Division. He also purchased partial or complete control of a large number of automotive parts suppliers and manufacturers. At about the same time, he divorced his first wife and promptly remarried Catherine Lederer.

General Motors grew quickly, perhaps too quickly. By 1910, the company's banks had taken control of the organization and, at age 49, Durant had lost his company. Unshaken, Durant decided to back European auto racer and inventor Louis Chevrolet. In 1911, they launched the Chevrolet Motor Company in Detroit. Two years later, Louis Chevrolet left the organization and, one year later, Durant was able to take back General Motors.

In 1921, Durant once again lost control of General Motors and, at age 59, was once again unemployed. Predictably, he quickly launched another automotive company, named Durant Motors, Inc., at Flint. The company exploded onto the market, quickly amassing dealers and stockholders. However, the success was short-lived. The Great Depression proved fatal not only to Durant Motors, but to all of Durant's holdings. In 1936, he filed for bankruptcy, listing debts of more than $900,000 and assets of only $250.

However, the drive to survive never left Durant. In 1940, he opened North Flint Recreation, an 18-lane bowling center. One year later, he added a drive-in restaurant. It became his last venture. William Crapo Durant died on March 18, 1947, at age 85.

SOURCES: General Motors Corporation archives; Lawrence R. Gustin, *Billy Durant: Creator of General Motors,* William B. Eerdmans Publishing Company, Grand Rapids, MI, 1973

George Eastman

[Eastman Kodak Company]

George Eastman was born July 12, 1854, in Waterville, New York, to George Washington Eastman and Maria Kilbourn Eastman. That same year the senior George established Eastman's Commercial College in Rochester, New York. He also maintained a nursery business, but he sold it in 1860 and moved the family to Rochester. Tragically, George W. Eastman died two years later and left the family with few financial resources.

By age 14, George Eastman had assumed responsibility for the support of his mother and two older sisters, Ellen and Kate. He left school and started working at a local insurance company. In 1874, at the age of 20, he was hired as a junior clerk at the Rochester Savings Bank.

Three years later, George was planning a vacation to Santo Domingo. A coworker encouraged him to buy a photography outfit to make a record of the trip. George agreed, but was discouraged with the bulky equipment. The camera was the size of today's microwave ovens, and it required a heavy tripod. Photographic emulsion had to be spread over glass plates under the cover of a tent. Chemicals and even water needed to be carried. On top of it all, George was charged $5 to learn how to operate the equipment.

Eastman never did take the trip, but he became immersed in photography and obsessed with finding an easier way to take pictures. He began experimenting with homemade gelatin emulsions in his mother's kitchen during the evenings, often falling asleep on the kitchen floor. After three years of diligent work, Eastman found what he was looking for and patented not only a dry plate, but also a machine for preparing large numbers of the plates.

Forming a partnership in 1880 with Henry Strong, a local businessman who provided financial backing, Eastman launched his company on the third floor of a State Street building in Rochester in April. Together, they built the Eastman Dry Plate and Film Company. As the company grew, Eastman's vision of the company widened:

> The idea gradually dawned on me that what we were doing was not merely making dry plates, but that we were starting out to make photography an everyday affair . . . to make the camera as convenient as the pencil.

As Eastman worked to improve his photographic process, the young company faced its share of challenges. On one occasion, an entire batch of dry plates that were sold to dealers went bad, and Eastman had no choice but to replace them. "Making good on those plates took our last dollar," he later said. "But what we had left was more important—reputation."

In 1888, George Eastman wanted a catchy name for his camera. He professed to being partial to the letter "K" and tried several combinations of words and sounds until arriving at the term *Kodak*. It was a word entirely made up by the 34-year-old inventor and entrepreneur. He added a distinctive yellow background and secured a trademark.

Eastman released the first Kodak camera, costing $25, that same year. It had 100 exposures, and users would send the camera back to Eastman, who processed and developed the film and inserted new film for a $10 charge. The cameras sold well, and in 1892 the company was formally organized as the Eastman Kodak Company. A year later a six-story building was constructed to keep up with demand. By 1900, the company had expanded internationally, with distribution centers in Canada and throughout Europe.

The company grew rapidly because of its innovative cameras and film. However, its long-term sustained growth can be attributed to Eastman's long-term vision for the company. First, he insisted on continued research and development. Kodak was a technology-based company that would lose its market advantage if it rested on its laurels. Second, he recruited the best employees possible and compensated them well. In 1919, he distributed one-third of his own holdings, valued at $10 million, among his employees. Third, he reinvested profits back into the company and expanded into related markets.

Eastman was a champion of education, medicine, and the arts. He gave away an estimated $100 million over the course of his lifetime, including $20 million to the Massachusetts Institute of Technology. He invested considerable time and money between 1902 and 1905 designing and building his dream house.

Despite his success, he led a very private life. Few pictures were taken of the man who built an empire in the photography field. He could walk the streets of Rochester without being recognized.

When he retired in 1925 at the age of 71, Eastman spent more time in his North Carolina hunting cabin and European art galleries. He participated in African safaris in 1926 and 1928. Not long after returning from the second safari, he was diagnosed with a progressive and irreversible spinal disease. George Eastman died on March 14, 1932, at the age of 78. Upon his death, Eastman left the majority of his estate, including his house, to the University of Rochester.

Today the Eastman Kodak Company is one of the world's largest organizations, employing more than 96,000 people. Total sales in 1994 exceeded $13.5 billion.

SOURCE: Eastman Kodak Company archives

Joseph O. Eaton, Viggo V. Torbensen

[Eaton Corporation]

Joseph Oriel Eaton was born on July 28, 1873, in Yonkers, New York. His father, also named Joseph O. Eaton, was a talented portrait painter who counted among his subjects Abraham Lincoln and Herman Melville. At the time of his birth, young Joseph was actually named Harrison but, when his father died two years later, his mother renamed him in honor of her husband.

Eaton was raised in Cincinnati, Ohio, by his mother and grandmother. He was a good athlete and, after graduating from Williams College in Massachusetts, briefly played professional baseball. He next worked for an uncle in a Cincinnati bank, then moved to New York where he worked for another relative selling cigarettes on Broadway.

After a job with American Express, Eaton enlisted in the U.S. Army and served during the Spanish-American War. Upon discharge, he worked for a shirt and collar manufacturer in Troy, New York. In 1903, he moved to Bloomfield, New Jersey, to work for the Empire Cream Separator Company. One year later, he returned to Troy and opened his own business, the Interstate Shirt and Collar Company.

The business didn't work out well, but Eaton did start courting a young widow named Edith Ide French, and they were married in 1910. One year later, Eaton returned to Bloomfield, New Jersey, to pursue a business venture with Viggo Torbensen, who had developed an axle for the growing automotive market.

Viggo V. Torbensen was born in Copenhagen, Denmark. After attending Denmark's Naval Technical School, he went to England and worked as a machinist with the Midland Railway. At the age of 20, he immigrated to the United States and, after a series of plant jobs, organized Clay & Torbensen to manufacture steam yachts and launches.

In 1892, Torbensen read of the "horseless carriage" with great interest. He sold his business and moved to Europe and, for the next three years, studied and worked with French and German engineers. He returned to America and took a job in New York with a French company that was starting to manufacture cars.

Torbensen was granted his first patent in 1900 for his Torbensen axle. Shortly thereafter, he started his own company in Newark, New Jersey, building the Torbensen automobile. His focus remained the axle, and after he met Joseph Eaton, the two became convinced that there was a strong future in manufacturing heavy-duty truck axles.

Eaton and Torbensen launched the Torbensen Gear and Axle Company in Bloomfield, New Jersey, in 1911. During their first year in business, the company built seven handmade axles. The number increased to 31 the following year and nearly 250 in 1913. The demand was strong, but the partners recognized that they needed to be closer to the automotive centers of Cleveland or Detroit.

In 1916, the company was reincorporated as the Torbensen Axle Company in Cleveland, Ohio, where a new plant produced more than 10,000 axles in the first year of operation. In 1917, output more than tripled to 33,000 axles. Employment rose from five employees in 1916 to 500 in less than two years. Their best customer was the Republic Motor Truck Company, America's largest truck manufacturer.

As World War I escalated, Eaton and Torbensen sold their company to Republic. Both founders remained with the company until 1919, at which time they sold their stock and, with other partners, formed the Eaton Axle Company. Torbensen served with the new company until 1921, then left to form the

Torbensen Motor Car Company and, later, the VigTor Axle Company. Viggo Torbensen died in 1947 at the age of 88.

In the early 1920s, Eaton orchestrated the acquisition of The Standard Parts Company and his old company, Torbensen Axle, which was put back up for sale by Republic. The new firm, named The Eaton Axle and Spring Company, quickly built its holdings in several automotive markets. By 1926, Eaton was the largest manufacturer of automotive springs in the country. The company also built everything from heaters to gas caps.

Joseph Eaton died on May 15, 1949, at the age of 75. Despite his success in the automotive field, he never personally learned how to drive a car. He made one attempt with an early electric model, drove it into a wall, and vowed never to drive again.

Today, the Eaton Corporation has 54,000 employees working at 155 manufacturing sites in 26 countries. Still based in Cleveland, the company has annual sales of $7 billion.

SOURCE: Eaton Corporation archives, *The History of Eaton Corporation: 1911–1985*

Jack Eckerd

[Eckerd Corporation]

Jack Eckerd was born on May 16, 1913, in Wilmington, Delaware. As he grew into adulthood, he bypassed a job in his father's pharmacy and headed West to learn how to fly airplanes. While there, he became intrigued with the revolutionary marketing practices of West Coast pharmacies. After being presented with an opportunity to purchase three Tampa Bay pharmacies, he founded the Eckerd Corporation, a rapid-growth chain of self-service, discount pharmacies.

As a young man, Jack Eckerd wasn't sure if he wanted to join his father's small but successful chain of pharmacies that included three stores in Erie, Pennsylvania, and a handful of others in western Pennsylvania, Delaware, and North Carolina. In fact, Eckerd was interested in learning to fly and actually attended the Boeing School of Aeronautics.

While traveling in the West, Eckerd happened to shop in a large, new, self-service drugstore. He was so intrigued with this innovative marketing idea that he approached several of the customers, introduced himself, and asked what they liked about the store. Most stated their appreciation for a wide selection, low prices, and no sales pressures.

Eckerd was convinced the formula could be copied back East, but had nowhere to test his idea. He went to work in his father's traditional pharmacy, working in the three stores in the Wilmington, Delaware, area, hoping for an opportunity to emulate the West Coast stores.

Opportunity knocked in 1952. A telegram came across Eckerd's desk announcing three failing pharmacies for sale in Tampa Bay, Florida. He went down and quickly struck a deal to purchase all three stores for $150,000, which he raised from family members. The first three years were difficult, yet he remained intrigued with the concept of self-service for customers. Eckerd set about to make it a mainstay of his operation, and the idea eventually caught on.

Until 1958, Eckerd, his wife, and five children had continued to live in Wilmington. Dividing his time between the five Florida stores and his father's pharmacies, his thoughts drifted at times to a comfortable business in Florida that would provide him with the time and money to pursue leisure sports, such as fishing and golf.

Then, out of the blue, he was presented an opportunity to open five more stores in shopping centers being opened by Publix Supermarkets. He decided that he really wasn't interested in golf and called on his local banker. After reviewing his plans, the banker said he'd lend him money for only two more stores.

Eckerd left and walked across the street to a competing bank. The banker looked over his financials and said that he couldn't help him. With nothing to lose, Eckerd announced that his most valuable asset didn't even show up on the balance sheet: his employees. The banker, who was a regular customer at one of Eckerd's stores, reflected on the proposition for a few minutes, then stated, "Okay, let's go." With that, Jack Eckerd doubled the number of stores in his chain.

From that point forward, Eckerd grew with considerable efficiency. In 1961, with 15 stores and $7 million in annual sales, stock was offered to the public. Within three years, sales doubled and so did the number of stores, and in 1967 he opened his first out-of-state store in Georgia. One year later, he opened his 100th store as sales reached $81 million. In 1973, the company was barely 20 years old and it had sales of $334 million through more than 300 stores.

Jack Eckerd retired from the business in the mid-1970s, but he had set in motion a formula for management and growth that ensured the long-term success of his company. He said that, in time of war, the most successful officers were those who could be found in the trenches with their troops. Eckerd was much more comfortable walking through his stores and talking with employees and customers than in sitting in his office reading computer printouts. Today, the Eckerd Corporation has sales in excess of $9 billion through nearly 2,800 stores.

SOURCE: Eckerd Corporation archives

Thomas A. Edison

[General Electric Company]

Thomas Alva Edison was born on February 11, 1847, in Milan, Ohio. Seven years later, his family moved to Port Huron, Michigan, where young Edison fashioned his first chemistry laboratory in the cellar of the family home.

Amazingly, Edison's formal education lasted only three months while he was seven years old, followed by intense tutoring by his mother. At age 12, he established a candy and newspaper business on the train that ran between Port Huron and Detroit.

After he saved a station agent's young son from an oncoming train, the agent taught Edison telegraphy, and by age 17 he was traveling throughout the United States and Canada as a telegraph operator. By the time he reached 21, Edison was in New York, penniless. After fixing a broken telegraph machine, he landed a job with the Gold and Stock Telegraph Company.

The new job gave him the time and connections to create his first commercial invention, a universal stock ticker. Soon, Edison raised enough money to open a manufacturing laboratory in Newark, New Jersey, making stock tickers.

At age 29, Edison established his research laboratory at Menlo Park, New Jersey. Between 1876 and 1886, several important inventions were created, including the incandescent electric lamp, the carbon telephone transmitter, and the phonograph. His quest to light an entire city required a multitude of products, several of which Edison had to create himself. In fact, he established the Edison Machine Works in New York City to build his new creations.

On September 4, 1882, Edison opened the Pearl Street Station, the first central generating station supplying electric power to New York City. Four years later, he purchased the former McQueen Locomotive Works near Schenectady, New York, and in 1892 it became the headquarters of the newly formed General Electric Company.

After General Electric was under way, Edison turned his attention to phonographs, movies, and storage batteries. He had founded the Electric Storage Battery Company, known today as the Exide Corporation, near Philadelphia in 1888. Exide installed its first practical storage battery at Germantown Electric Light Company, and soon its batteries were powering streetcars, passenger cars, boats, and railroad switching signals.

Edison is credited with a number of World War I initiatives, including sound detection of guns and submarines, airplane detection, increasing the efficiency of torpedoes and submarines, and developing chemicals that were previously imported from Europe. Thomas A. Edison died on October 18, 1931, at the age of 84. At the time of his death, he had been granted patents for more than 1,000 inventions.

SOURCES: General Electric archives; Exide Corporation archives

Bob Evans

[Bob Evans Farms, Inc.]

Bob Evans's roots are 100 percent rural. He was born on May 30, 1918, in Sugar Ridge, Ohio, not far from Bowling Green. His parents, Stanley and Elizabeth Lewis Evans, owned a farm, a grocery store, and eventually a small chain of West Virginia markets. While Bob was still a youngster, the family moved to Gallipolis, Ohio, a small town on the Ohio River, where he worked in his father's store, mowed lawns, and delivered newspapers.

After attending high school in Gallia County, Ohio, and Greenbriar Military School in Lewisburg, West Virginia, Evans spent a year and a half in veterinary school at Ohio State University. In June 1940 he married Jewell Waters of Morganton, North Carolina, and they eventually had six children.

Upon returning from World War II, Evans opened a 12-stool, 24-hour truck stop—specializing in breakfasts—on the outskirts of Gallipolis. As a result of war shortages, he was unable to procure enough good-tasting sausage, so he began making it himself from the hogs on his family's farm.

Evans used his knowledge of meat, his packing-house experience, and a family recipe to produce an extremely high quality sausage. Customers enjoyed Bob Evans's sausage so much that he began selling it in 10-pound tubs. Despite the high price—52¢ per pound compared to his competitors 12¢ per pound—it became so popular that Evans decided to start his own sausage business. His persistent emphasis on quality followed him through all of his endeavors in the food industry.

In 1950, Evans borrowed $1,000 from the bank and his father and built a 28- by 40-foot building to use as his plant. He put large doors at either end so that it could be resold as a machinery shed if the sausage venture didn't work out. It was here, in a shed with three hogs, 40 pounds of pepper, 50 pounds of sage, and a handful of other products, that Bob Evans launched what would become a multimillion-dollar sausage business.

His earliest customers were in the hills of southern Ohio and West Virginia, including his father's grocery stores. Evans loaded his fresh sausage into his 1949 Studebaker pickup and made his rounds. He packed his product in large blocks of ice, for it would be several years before he could afford refrigeration. Seven years later, he enlisted additional financial backing and acquired an old packing plant in Ohio, allowing him to increase both capacity and territory.

While the sausage business was strong, Evans noticed that there was a steady trend toward dining out, and he decided to diversify. In 1962, he opened a small convenience restaurant called the Sausage Shop on the family farm where he lived with his wife and children. It quickly became the testing ground for the company's restaurant division. Here, the most successful recipes used were those of his wife, Jewell, a great southern cook.

Bob and Jewell, along with an architectural designer, traveled the Southwest looking for a suitable restaurant prototype that would be reminiscent of the farm. They decided on a barn-red exterior with white trim, which has been the company's signature edifice ever since.

Expansion of the restaurant and sausage businesses progressed quickly, but cautiously. Although Evans has been a peer and a friend of such industry giants as Colonel Harland Sanders—once franchising two Kentucky Fried Chicken restaurants on a handshake—he decided against franchising because he felt it would jeopardize his high standards. In fact, he has since stated that he "probably would not have gone public" if he had it to do over again.

Bob Evans retired as president of Bob Evans Farms on December 31, 1986, but it is still managed by family members. Today, the company owns 389 full-service restaurants, employs nearly 29,000 people, and produces over a million pounds of sausage each week. Annual sales are in excess of $800 million.

SOURCES: Bob Evans Farms, Inc., archives; Robbin Evans Chamberlain, Evans family history

Ole Evinrude, Bess Evinrude

[Outboard Marine Corporation]

Ole Evinrude was born on April 19, 1877, on a farm near Christiana, Norway, the oldest of 11 children born to Andrew and Beatta (Dahl) Evinrude. When Ole was five years old, the family immigrated to the United States, eventually settling on a farm in Cambridge, Wisconsin. His most vivid memory of his trip to America was his fascination with the engine room on the boat, and his mother and grandmother made numerous trips to pull him back to their cabin.

Young Evinrude was forced to leave school after the third grade and work on the family farm. He became an experienced mechanic and gained a reputation for helping neighbors repair machinery. His interest, however, was nearby Lake Ripley. By the time he was 16, Evinrude had hand-built an impressive sailboat. He quickly developed a business taking visitors on tours of the lake for 25¢ per person.

Over the next several years, Evinrude held a variety of jobs. He worked in local machine shops and in electric motor plants. He found a job with a gasoline engine builder and even worked in a Pittsburgh, Pennsylvania, steel mill. Eventually, he settled into a job as a patternmaker in Milwaukee with the E. P. Allis Company in 1900.

In his free time, Evinrude experimented with machines, which landed him in trouble with his landlady more than once. He became known as something of an eccentric in the neighborhood and was soon asked to move. One of the neighbors, 16-year-old Bess Cary, was intrigued with his machines, and when Evinrude explained that he was building a horseless carriage, she convinced her family to loan him a shed next to their home.

Over the next several years, Evinrude and various partners tried to launch an automobile company without success. Bess, by then a business school student, worked nights and weekends handling Evinrude's correspondence and books. In 1906, Ole and Bess were married, and one year later their only child, Ralph Evinrude, was born.

Ole Evinrude eventually abandoned his attempts to build a car and opened his own pattern shop. The business did a respectable trade and soon employed six patternmakers. Privately, Evinrude worked on an engine that could attach to a rowboat and propel it through the water. It wasn't the first such device built in America, but it was the first that anyone in Wisconsin had seen and created quite a stir at its trial run on Pewaukee Lake.

By 1909, Ole and Bess Evinrude were selling their 62-pound, 1½-horsepower engines for $62 each. With a $5,000 investment from a partner, the Evinrudes were able to increase their modest manufacturing capacity, and sales rose from 1,000 in 1910 to more than 2,000 the following year and nearly 10,000 by 1913. Employment at their plant rose above 300 and their company—the Evinrude Detachable Row Boat Company—was gaining popularity.

By 1914, Bess fell into poor health, and the Evinrudes decided to sell their share of the business for about $140,000. The family then spent the next five years touring America, first by car, then on the 42-foot cruiser that Ole designed and built. Eventually, Bess's health improved and Ole grew restless. He designed a new lightweight engine and took it to the owner of his old company, who wasn't interested. Evinrude decided to build it himself.

In 1920, Ole and Bess formed the Elto Outboard Motor Company. (The initials represented "Evinrude Light Twin Outboard.") The company sold more than 1,000 of the new motors the following year, and more than tripled its sales in 1922. By 1925, Elto sold 7,600 motors, second only to market leader Johnson Motors.

The old Evinrude company, with declining sales, was sold to a group of investors in 1922. They were unable to turn it around, and six years later they sold the company to Briggs & Stratton, a successful manufacturer of engines and automobile components. Stephen F. Briggs, the company's cofounder, became intrigued with the boat market and orchestrated a 1929 merger between the old Evinrude company, Elto, and a third company. The new organization was named the Outboard Marine Company.

Bess Evinrude's health once again worsened, and she died on May 13, 1933. Ole Evinrude was devastated by the loss and, at age 57, he died on July 12, 1934. Ralph Evinrude, age 27, was then named president.

Stephen Briggs also became more involved with Outboard Marine, and in 1935 he masterminded the acquisition of Johnson Motors, the industry's leader, who had fallen into receivership. The new company soon diversified into several markets, including refrigeration, compressors, and even lawn mowers.

SOURCES: Outboard Marine Corporation archives; Jeffrey L. Rodengen, *Evinrude Johnson and the Legend of OMC,* Write Stuff, FL, 1992

Erastus Fairbanks, Thaddeus Fairbanks, Joseph Fairbanks

[Fairbanks Scale]

Of the three Fairbanks brothers raised in early-nineteenth-century Brimfield, Massachusetts, Erastus was the oldest. He started his career as a schoolteacher in his hometown. In 1812, the 20-year-old moved to St. Johnsbury, Vermont, to study law. However, he found that his eyesight wasn't strong enough to read the fine print of the legal profession, so he returned to teaching, which he later left to work in a general store.

In 1815, Erastus's parents sold the family farm in Massachusetts and, with their other two sons, Thaddeus and Joseph, joined Erastus in St. Johnsbury, building a home and small mill alongside the Sleepers River. Thaddeus Fairbanks was an industrious mechanic and wagonmaker, who soon established a shop above the family mill where he tinkered with new inventions. In 1823, he built a foundry to manufacture two of these discoveries, a stove and an iron plow.

Erastus failed to achieve success in three separate store partnerships and decided to join his brother, forming the E. & T. Fairbanks Company in 1824. Within a few years, they formed a second company to participate in the booming market for hemp, which was used to make rope. Their second venture, the St. Johnsbury Hemp Company, purchased hemp from farmers, processed it through a machine invented by Thaddeus, then sold it by the ton to ropemakers.

The only way to weigh their products was the 2,000-year-old "Roman steelyard" method, which was unreliable with heavy loads. Thaddeus retreated to his shop and soon devised a new method to weigh loads, not with the old counterbalance weights, but with a series of levers that could be placed in a pit, allowing the load to be weighed at ground level. By 1830, he had improved the design considerably and took out a patent.

Joined by their younger brother, Joseph, the Fairbanks brothers opened their scale venture with $4,000, ten employees, and a new 25- by 60-foot shop in St. Johnsbury. The company also continued to make Thaddeus's stoves and plows.

Originally, the brothers thought that their Fairbanks Platform Scale could be used to weigh hay. However, they quickly adapted it to other uses, such as weighing carts and wagons. Before long, they found a host of applications—everything from postal scales to scales that could weigh canal barges—and orders were received faster than they could be filled. The Fairbanks Wagon Scales would dominate the market for nearly 100 years.

The growth of E. & T. Fairbanks was slowed during the Civil War. Through these years, the company made stirrups, artillery harness irons, brass trimmings, and other items for the Union forces. After the war, however, they were soon turning out 4,000 scales monthly. By the last years of the century, the company had accumulated 113 patents and was building more than 80,000 scales annually.

The most successful distributor of Fairbanks scales was Charles H. Morse, a native of St. Johnsbury and partner in the Chicago-based Fairbanks, Greeleaf & Company, whose territory included the midwestern and western states. Morse proved to be an excellent businessman and added other products to his line, such as windmills and pumps. In the early twentieth century his company outgrew Fairbanks. In 1916, Morse gained control of the manufacturer and changed the name to Fairbanks-Morse.

SOURCES: Fairbanks Scales archives; *Fairbanks Standard 150 Years*

Mansour Farah, James Farah, William Farah

[Farah, Inc.]

After building a successful retail store, Mansour Farah, a Lebanese immigrant, established a small shirt manufacturing company. Upon his death, Mansour's sons, James and William, dropped the company's previous label in favor of the family name, *Farah*, and greatly expanded the product line and manufacturing capabilities.

Mansour Farah was born in 1885 in Beskinta, Lebanon, a small village near Beirut. His family emigrated first to Canada, then south into the territory of New Mexico, where in 1905 Mansour launched a modest retailing venture. Ten years later, he married Hana Abihider, the second of 16 children born to a Greek Catholic Orthodox priest.

The Farahs had two sons: James Farah was born September 1, 1916, and William Frank Farah was born on March 15, 1919. In 1920, after studying shirt design in New York City, Mansour moved the family to El Paso, Texas, rented a 25- by 50-foot building, and started making shirts. His first product was a line of work shirts under the Apache label that sold for 35¢ each.

The business grew slowly over the next decade and even survived the crunch of the Depression. However, when the United States prison system started making and selling shirts with inmate labor, Farah decided to get out of the shirt business, and he started making a line of denim pants. By 1935, the plant was producing matching khaki shirts and pants.

Mansour Farah died on May 11, 1937, at the age of 52. James Farah, age 21, stepped into the position of president, while his 18-year-old brother William took charge of maintenance and mechanical problems. Hana Farah spent her days supervising the sewing-room operation.

As America entered World War II, William Farah enlisted in the United States Air Force three days before the attack on Pearl Harbor. While he piloted combat missions in Europe, James and Hana were busy manufacturing khaki uniforms for the U.S. Army. During the war, the company produced 359,000 consecutive pairs of military pants without having a single pair rejected.

Upon discharge after the war, William Farah married Betty Corcoran and resumed his role at the Farah Manufacturing Company. William and Betty eventually had four children—James Clifton, Kenneth Duane, Robert Norman, and Haleen. Several years later, James Farah married Virginia Husson, and the couple had two sons—Frank Nicholas and Clifford James.

As with most companies, Farah had to retool for the civilian market and reclaim its niche. It didn't take the brothers long to get back on track, and in 1949 they announced a new 116,000-square-foot manufacturing center. They also dropped their Apache label and, instead, decided to sell their own Farah label.

Tragically, James Farah became ill and died while at his office on January 30, 1964. William Farah assumed the helm of the company that, by 1965, was reaching annual sales of nearly $50 million.

SOURCE: Evan Haywood Antone, *William Farah: Industrialist,* Carl Hertzog, El Paso, Texas, 1969

Tom J. Fatjo Jr.

[Browning-Ferris Industries]

Tom J. Fatjo Jr. was born in Texas on September 25, 1940. Upon graduation from Rice University with a B.A. in accounting and economics in 1963, he launched his career as a certified public accountant with the international firm Deloitte, Haskins & Sells. In 1966, he and two colleagues formed their own accounting practice and quickly built a successful client base.

In 1967, while serving as the president of his neighborhood civic club in southwest Houston, Fatjo found himself in the middle of a crisis. The private garbage hauler who had been contracted to service the neighborhood had fallen on hard times, and the trash was piling up. While conducting an emergency meeting of club members, it occurred to Fatjo that the group might want to purchase and operate their own garbage truck. However, his suggestion not only was quietly rejected, one member said to him: "Why don't *you* buy a garbage truck and be our garbage man?"

The question kept Fatjo awake most of that night. At the end of the following day, he had worked up some financial projections that appeared encouraging. With three months of fees paid in advance by the homeowners and $500 of his own funds, American Refuse Systems was quickly put into service in early September 1966.

Fatjo kept his job with the accounting partnership while he and a helper picked up garbage twice weekly. Sensing an opportunity, he quickly lined up two more neighborhood contracts and combined their advance fees with fresh investment money from friends. The capital allowed him to buy two larger garbage trucks, and within a few months he was hauling trash for 5,000 homes.

By 1968, 28-year-old Fatjo had built annual revenues to nearly $1 million, and he cast his eye toward other markets. First, he decided to invest three weeks of his time traveling to different American cities to meet with the best refuse collectors in the business. By the time he returned home he not only had a bundle of good advice for his own firm, but he also had a rough idea of how to consolidate garbage haulers from coast to coast under a single umbrella organization.

Determined to build the largest and best solid waste company in the world, Fatjo assembled a business plan and set out once again across the country looking for acquisition and merger partners. One year later, not a single deal had been made. The problem, he soon identified, was twofold. First, he lacked sufficient credibility to interest the haulers. Second, his company was privately held, meaning that his stock didn't offer potential partners liquidity.

To compensate, he immediately recruited Lou Waters, a corporate finance specialist, to serve as the company's chairman. Next, they put together a package to purchase a modest-sized, publicly traded company called Browning-Ferris Machinery Company. They folded American Refuse System into their new acquisition, which they renamed Browning-Ferris Industries (BFI).

Fatjo wasted little time putting his plan into motion. In November 1969, he acquired his first company—in Cincinnati, Ohio—for a combination of cash and BFI stock. Four months later, the second acquisition was made. As the pace accelerated, he brought in an operations specialist named Harry Phillips to serve a president, while Fatjo continued to serve as a coexecutive with Waters and Phillips.

Over the next two years, they acquired more than 100 companies. By 1973, annual sales reached $300 million. Three years later, with that volume nearly doubled, Tom Fatjo resigned from active management, having succeeded in building BFI into the largest and best solid waste company in the world in less than ten years.

Fatjo has since been involved in a number of successful ventures, including the 1970 purchase of the Fannin Bank, the 1972 purchase of American Title Company, the 1974 founding of Mortgage Banque, Inc., and the 1976 purchase of the Criterion Group, a private investment management company. He also founded and developed The Houstonian and Houstonian Estates, a large fitness, preventive medicine, and meeting complex and adjacent luxury condominium.

In 1990, Fatjo founded Republic Waste Industries, Inc., in Atlanta, Georgia. He later sold his interest in Republic and acquired control of TransAmerican Waste Industries, a Houston-based environmental services company.

SOURCES: TransAmerican Waste Industries, Inc.; Tom J. Fatjo, Jr. and Keith Miller, *With No Fear of Failure,* Word Books, Waco, TX, 1983

Manny Fingerhut

[Fingerhut Companies, Inc.]

Manny Fingerhut was born on November 20, 1914, one of five children of Russian immigrants Herman and Eva Fingerhut. His parents landed in

Rhode Island in 1902 and intended to travel to Indianapolis to join relatives. However, due to Herman's trouble with the English language, they mistakenly purchased train tickets to Minneapolis. Once in Minneapolis, Herman established a small auto body repair and seat cover business.

Herman died while Manny was still a young boy, so Manny delivered newspapers to help support the family. When he graduated from high school in 1933 there was no money for college, and he took a job as a bookkeeper for a new car lot, eventually working his way to manager. After marrying Rose Nemer in 1938, Manny entered the U.S. Army and served in France during World War II.

After the war, Manny returned to the car business. Meanwhile, his brother William, just like their father Herman, had built a small business making seat covers. Car seats in the early days were not durable, and they easily tore or stained. William's seat covers were used to protect the original car seats or to cover them once they became worn.

William invited Manny to join him in the seat cover business, and in 1948 the brothers pooled their savings to launch Fingerhut, a company that manufactured and sold seat covers from a small garage in Minneapolis, Minnesota. William handled production, while Manny served as salesman and bookkeeper.

Within the first year of business Manny realized that trying to make personal sales calls was very limiting. While considering options to overcome this limitation, he received a tie catalog in the mail, prompting him to consider the value of selling car seat covers by mail.

To begin the mail-order business, Manny acquired a list of new car buyers in the Minneapolis area, designed a modest advertising circular, and mailed it out. Encouraged by the initial response, he expanded the list to other states. Within four years, the business converted to strictly mail-order, and annual sales approached $1 million.

By the early 1950s, Detroit was making higher-quality and better-looking automobile seats. In response, Manny encouraged development of a clear plastic suitable for seat covers. The attractive new seats could be seen while still being protected, and this led to a spectacular increase in seat cover sales.

In 1957, an agency that represented a number of manufacturers interested in marketing their products directly to consumers approached Fingerhut, who agreed to add electric drills, dishes, and other products to its direct-marketing mailings. The company's manufacturing business also expanded beyond seat covers. One of the early products was a waist-length coat with a vinyl exterior and a rayon lining called the *car coat.* Within nine years, 4 million car coats were sold annually.

William Fingerhut, who had retired to California in the late 1950s, sold his share of the business to Manny in 1967. In order to keep pace with marketing opportunities, Manny took the company public three years later.

In 1973, Fingerhut issued its first general-merchandise catalog, which incorporated several unrelated products. Up until that time, each piece of merchandise was marketed through individual mailings. Manny continued to introduce a number of new marketing concepts and techniques to the direct-mail industry, many of which are still in use today.

When Manny Fingerhut retired in 1978, annual sales were approaching $225 million and the company employed 2,800 people. By 1987, sales topped the $1 billion mark. Manny Fingerhut died on February 23, 1995, at the age of 80. Today, Fingerhut annual sales exceed $2 billion and the company employs approximately 10,000 people.

SOURCE: Fingerhut Companies archives

Paul B. Fireman

[Reebok International]

The history of Reebok can actually be traced back to England in the 1890s, when Joseph William Foster made the first pair of spiked running shoes. J.W. Foster and Sons quickly built an international reputation by making shoes for distinguished athletes, including Britain's 1924 Olympic track team featured in the movie *Chariots of Fire.* In 1958, two of Foster's grandsons started a companion company, Reebok, named after the African gazelle. The older company was later merged into Reebok.

Paul B. Fireman was born on February 14, 1944, in Cambridge, Massachusetts. He graduated from Tabor Academy in Marion, Massachusetts and attended Boston University. He and his wife, Phyllis, a classmate since junior high, have three children.

After attending college, Fireman went to work for his family's outdoor sports distributorship. While attending a sporting goods trade show in 1979, Fireman spotted Reebok shoes and was intrigued with their quality. He struck up a conversation with the owners of Reebok, who offered a high-quality $60 running shoe. Despite having no experience in shoe manufacturing or wholesaling, he convinced the Reebok company to grant him a license for American distribution. Pentland Industries, a British shoe distributor, was an early backer, taking a 56 percent stake in the company with a $77,500 investment.

By 1981, sales were a brisk $1.5 million. That year, Fireman was traveling in California on business and took notice of the aerobics craze that was sweeping the state. He personally witnessed women in sporting goods stores picking out fashionable athletic clothing, then reaching for black and white athletic shoes.

Fireman was convinced there was a way to combine fashion with performance in an aerobic shoe designed specifically for women. Rather than focus on celebrities for advertising, he called on aerobics instructors for input on the design and, of course, to try out the shoes (in front of their clients).

When the first line of the Freestyle was released, Fireman literally packed and shipped every pair. For four months, sales were flat. Then, suddenly, every store sold out. Fireman and his modest staff couldn't keep up with reorders. Sales grew at an astounding rate: $13 million in 1983, $307 million in 1985, $1.4 billion in 1987, $2.2 billion in 1990, and $3.3 billion in 1994.

After the successful entry of the Freestyle into the athletic shoe market, Fireman guided the company through this incredible growth with a mix of new product development and acquisitions. In 1984, Fireman and Pentland acquired Reebok of England for about $700,000. In the mid-1980s, they aggressively diversified their target markets to include men's sports and even the children's market under the Weebok and Reebok Kids labels.

Fireman also made two key acquisitions: the 1986 purchase of Rockport, a Marlboro, Massachusetts maker of walking and casual shoes, and the 1987 purchase of Avia, a Portland, Oregon maker of high-end athletic shoes. They also introduced the Greg Norman line of golf and casual sportswear, inspired by the man known worldwide as "the Shark." By the late 1980s, Fireman introduced an inflatable pump shoe that cemented Reebok's position in the male market.

Today, the revenues of Reebok exceed $3.5 billion annually. The Stoughton, Massachusetts based company employs nearly 6,500 people worldwide. Paul Fireman continues to serve as chairman, president, and CEO.

SOURCES: Reebok International Ltd., archives; Lois Therrien and Amy Borrus, "Reeboks: How Far Can a Fad Run?", *Business Week* magazine, February 24, 1986

Harvey S. Firestone

[The Firestone Tire & Rubber Company]

Harvey Samuel Firestone was born on December 20, 1868, on a farm near Columbiana, Ohio. Not long after graduating from Columbiana High School, he moved to Detroit, Michigan, and rose to the position of manager of a buggy company.

Driving the first rubber-tired carriage in Detroit, he demonstrated the improved riding qualities of his buggies. In 1896, he furnished a set of the rubber carriage tires to Henry Ford, who was then experimenting with his second model of a horseless carriage. That same year, Firestone went to Chicago to sell the carriage tires. However, by 1890 he realized that the horse and carriage were soon destined for replacement by the automobile, and he intended to be part of the new industry.

In 1895, Firestone married Idabelle Smith of Jackson, Michigan. They had five sons and one daughter, and all four of his sons eventually became leaders in the business.

At age 31, Firestone moved to Akron, Ohio, center of America's rubber industry, and established The Firestone Tire & Rubber Company on August 3, 1900. He started selling tires manufactured by others, but soon realized that in order to stock only top-quality tires he would have to set up his own factory. In 1903, he purchased an abandoned building and, with 12 employees and used equipment, started manufacturing Firestone tires.

In 1906, the company pioneered the manufacture of pneumatic tires, shipping 2,000 sets to the Ford Motor Company. Sales that year exceeded $1 million. Harvey Firestone's friendship with Henry Ford lasted his lifetime. Along with Thomas Edison and naturalist John Burroughs, they made frequent camping trips for nearly 20 years.

Firestone was a creative and dynamic leader. His company pioneered achievements such as the mechanically fastened straight-side tire, nonskid treads, truck and farm tractor tires, low-pressure balloon tires, and gum-dipping to insulate tire cords against internal heat. By the 1930s, Firestone was supplying one-fourth of the tires used in the United States.

Harvey Firestone died at his home in Miami Beach, Florida, on February 7, 1938, at age 69. At the time, the company he founded with a $20,000 initial capitalization had annual sales that exceeded $100 million. In 1990, Firestone merged with Bridgestone U.S.A., forming Bridgestone/Firestone, Inc., which today has 45,000 employees and annual sales of $6.5 billion.

SOURCE: Firestone family archives

Herman G. Fisher, Irving R. Price, Helen M. Schelle

[Fisher-Price, Inc.]

After working for a toy builder for four years, Herman Fisher wanted to build his own toy company. He teamed up with a financier named Irving Price and a toy retailer named Helen Schelle to launch Fisher-Price Toys in 1930. Despite the difficult early years during the Great Depression, Fisher-Price has become one of the most respected toy manufacturers in the world.

Herman Guy Fisher was born on November 2, 1898, in Unionville, Pennsylvania. Despite losing his father at age five, Fisher graduated from local schools and, in 1921, graduated from Penn State University with a degree in commerce and marketing. Fisher worked his way through college selling Fuller brushes, ushering in a local theater, and working in a local clothing store and steel mill.

Upon graduation, Fisher went to work for a bond company in its Rochester, New York, office. In 1926, he went to work for another Rochester firm, the Alderman-Fairchild Company, a manufacturer of paper boxes and games. Soon, the company spun off its toy operations as All-Fair Toys, which they established in Churchville, New York. Fisher served at vice president and general manager of the venture from 1926 until 1930.

In 1930, Fisher tried unsuccessfully to purchase All-Fair from its parent company. A mutual friend, Elbert Hubbard II, introduced Fisher to Irving Price, a retail veteran who was looking for a good investment opportunity. As mayor of East Aurora, New York, a small town near Buffalo, Price was also interested in bringing new business to his town.

Irving R. Price was born on September 21, 1884, in Worcester, Massachusetts. After graduating from Brown University, in 1905 he launched a 17-year career with the retail chain F.W. Woolworth and Company. In 1909, Price married Margaret Evans, a well-known illustrator and author of children's books.

Fisher and Price were joined by Helen Schelle, another well-established figure in the toy industry. Helen M. Schelle, born in 1893, had owned the Penny Walker Toy Store in Binghamton, New York, and was well connected in the toy industry. Schelle and Margaret Evans Price collaborated to design many of the company's early toys.

On October 1, 1930, with total capitalization of $100,000, Fisher-Price Toys started operations in East Aurora with 15 employees and a modest plant that cost the company $5,000. The first 149 toys were discarded because of imperfections. However, the company was able to correct the flaws and, by 1931, produced their first three-color catalog of 16 toys that they quietly dubbed the "Sixteen Hopefuls."

The Fisher-Price line was indeed a hit at the New York City Toy Fair later that year, and their first shipment went to Macy's Department Store. Over the next four years, despite the Depression, the company was able to establish a market share. Their first international sale was to Harrods of London in 1933.

In 1936, sales reached $250,000, and for the first time Fisher-Price made a modest profit of $3,000 (which was distributed among the employees in silver dollars). Two years later, the company launched its first blockbuster toy, the Snoopy Sniffer. Over the next 25 years, nearly 4.5 million of the toys were sold.

Fisher-Price, like most American manufacturers, became a manufacturer of military products during World War II. Among the items made at its facilities were ammunition crates and box supports, field service chests for two-way radios, rudders, and even wooden dustpans. By 1947, the plant was converted back to toy manufacturing and, due to years of growing demand for toys, employment quickly rose to more than 220.

Growth continued for the next two decades, fueled by the introduction of plastics into the toy-making process. In 1968, Fisher-Price found another hit product with its Little People line. This led the company into an unprecedented level of success that caught the eye of the Quaker Oats Company, which bought Fisher-Price in 1969.

Herman Fisher served as president and general manager of Fisher-Price from its founding in 1930 until 1966, then remained on the board until Quaker Oats acquired the company in 1969. Fisher had married Suzanne Edwina on September 24, 1932, and the couple had three children. Suzanne died in 1968, and Fisher subsequently married Elizabeth Abbott. Herman Fisher died on September 26, 1975, at age 76.

Irving Price died on November 23, 1976, at the age of 92. Helen Schelle retired from Fisher-Price in 1957 and moved to Piqua, Ohio, where she died on April 12, 1984, at the age of 91.

SOURCE: Fisher-Price archives

Richard T. Fisher Sr.

[Boston Whaler]

Richard T. Fisher was born on July 14, 1914, in Worcester, Massachusetts. He attended Harvard University, where he majored in philosophy and served as captain of the swim team. Upon graduation in 1936, he married Mary Holcombe, and the couple eventually had four children. The Fishers later divorced, and Richard married his second wife, Doris Carlson, who actively participated in the growth of the company.

As early as 1943, Fisher developed an interest in building a lightweight boat made from balsa wood. However, since the wood dented easily, he eventually abandoned the idea and focused on his electronics company, Sigma Industries, where he worked on a diverse range of products, including traffic light controls, stepper motors, and even toys.

Fisher's interest in lightweight boats resurfaced when he became familiar with Styrofoam. In 1955, he and an associate built a small sailboat from Styrofoam and epoxy glass resin. When the craft was ready, Fisher consulted his friend Ray Hunt, a designer who saw promise in the boat, and he recommended some design changes. Hunt also suggested that the company focus on outboards instead of sailboats.

In 1958, Fisher and his buddies were ready to show their first boat, a 13-foot model that featured a foam-filled cathedral hull, making the craft remarkably stable and virtually unsinkable. After a successful showing at the Boston Boat Show, he launched his company, originally known as the Fisher-Pierce Company, in Braintree, Massachusetts, with just two employees. The boats were well received, and the new company was soon building ten boats weekly.

The boat model was designated as a Boston Whaler. The "Whaler" part of the name was derived from sturdy, unsinkable construction that makes it worthy of reeling in a harpooned whale. The "Boston" part, of course, comes from the nearby port.

In 1961, Fisher found an ingenious gimmick to market his unsinkable boats. He demonstrated the unsinkability of his boats in a *Life* magazine advertisement that included a series of photographs, first of Fisher seated in a boat, then of the boat being sawed in half, and finally of Fisher motoring off in his half of the boat. An even more dramatic demonstration of the boat's buoyancy was later conducted by the Colombian Marine Corps, who fired over 1,000 rounds from .50-caliber and 7.62-mm machine guns into a 22-foot Boston Whaler, and the boat didn't sink.

In addition to this foam-core construction, Fisher and Boston Whaler introduced several innovations, including the first center-console design and the self-draining cockpit. The proven dependability of Boston Whaler boats have made them popular not only among sports enthusiasts, but also with military and public safety agencies—police, fire, and emergency medical services.

Fisher sold his company in 1969 to CML of Acton, Massachusetts. The name of the company was changed to Boston Whaler to capitalize on the name-brand recognition of its boats. CML sold the company to Reebok International in 1989. In 1993, Boston Whaler was purchased by Meridian Sports, Inc., which consolidated production to its Edgewater, Florida facility.

In 1996, Brunswick Corporation became the parent company. Headquartered in Lake Forest, Illinois, Brunswick Corporation is a multinational company serving outdoor and indoor active recreation markets with leading consumer products in fishing, camping, bowling, billiards, pleasure boating, and marine engines.

Richard T. Fisher Sr. died on September 25, 1995, at the age of 81.

SOURCES: Boston Whaler archives; Adam Fisher, "Unsinkable! Richard Fisher and the Boston Whaler," unpublished research paper

Henry M. Flagler

[Standard Oil Company]

Convinced that the oil industry was a good investment, Henry M. Flagler and John D. Rockefeller established Standard Oil of Ohio. Within ten years it was the dominant company in the industry, leaving Flagler a wealthy man. After reducing his role with the company, Flagler moved to Florida, where he saw an opportunity to establish a tourist trade. After establishing a luxury hotel in St. Augustine, he added nearly 650 miles of railroad tracks and a network of hotels that extended from Jacksonville to the Bahamas.

Henry Morrison Flagler was born on January 2, 1830, in Hopewell, New York, the son of a Presbyterian minister who, during the week, operated the family farm. Young Flagler left home at the age of 14, working his way west by canal and lake boat to Republic, Ohio, where he went to work for relatives who owned a general store. He was so diligent with the family enterprises that by age 22 he was a partner in the business and was financially secure when he married Mary Harkness in 1853.

In the early 1860s, salt was discovered in Michigan. To feed the demand for salt during the Civil War, Flagler invested $100,000 in a Saginaw salt venture. At the close of the war, the salt market collapsed, as did Flagler's small fortune. He covered his losses and moved to Cleveland, where he manufactured horseshoes and sold barrels to local oil companies.

Flagler was 30 years old when Edwin Drake struck oil in 1859 north of Pittsburgh. He had personally visited Drake's well at Oil Creek, surveying the bustling drill site from a nearby hill, and was convinced that oil would be a factor in his future. After the Civil War, Flagler and a friend he had met in the grain business, John D. Rockefeller, established a company to set new standards for the disorganized oil industry. Initially called Rockefeller, Andrews, and Flagler, the company was appropriately renamed the Standard Oil Company.

Within a few short years, Standard Oil of Ohio became America's leading oil company by either acquiring the small start-ups or putting them out of business. By 1879, Standard Oil controlled more than 90 percent of the refining capacity in the entire world. Flagler and his family moved to New York City and enjoyed society life.

However, Flagler's wife, Mary, fell victim to ill health and was advised to spend her winters in the warm Florida climate, which they did during the winter of 1878–1879. While Mary's health responded positively, Henry Flagler was appalled at the poor accommodations that existed in this beautiful state. As business matters pressed Flagler to spend more time in New York, Mary refused to travel to Florida alone. Her death in 1881 was a tragic blow to Flagler, who relinquished his role at Standard Oil and headed south.

In 1888, Flagler opened the Ponce de Leon Hotel in St. Augustine, Florida, at a cost of $2.5 million. Encouraged by its success, he opened two more hotels and established a modern rail connection between Jacksonville and St. Augustine. Other hotels followed in Ormond, Palm Beach, and Miami. He continued to push south, building a railway that connected the Florida keys and opening a steamship line to serve two more Flagler hotels at Nassau.

Henry Flagler died on May 20, 1913, at the age of 83. His estate was valued at more than $100 million.

SOURCES: David Leon Chandler, *Henry Flagler: The Astonishing Life and Times of the Visionary Robber Baron Who Founded Florida,* Macmillan Publishing Company, 1986; Lena Clarke, *The Flagler Story and Memorial Church,* Memorial Presbyterian Church Society, St. Augustine, FL, 1949

James A. Folger

[The Folger Coffee Company]

In 1635, 18-year-old Peter Folger of Norwich, England, immigrated with his parents to the Massachusetts Bay colony. Soon after his arrival, he married a woman who sailed on the same ship, Mary Morrell, and the couple eventually had eight children. While in their 40s, the Folgers moved first to Martha's Vineyard, then to Nantucket, where Peter served as schoolmaster, blacksmith, poet, and preacher. One of their daughters gave birth to a son who later became a prominent figure in American history: Benjamin Franklin.

Several generations later, Samuel B. Folger, a successful blacksmith, was a prosperous member of Nantucket society. There, James A. Folger (pictured here), the second youngest of Samuel's nine children, learned building skills at an early age. In 1848, shortly after gold was discovered on the West Coast, 14-year-old James set sail with two older brothers—Edward, age 20, and Henry, age 16. After traveling through the exotic and dangerous country of Panama, the boys finally landed in San Francisco on May 5, 1850.

The brothers agreed that Jim would remain in San Francisco and pick up whatever carpentry work was available, while the older two boys would travel to the gold mines. The following day a great fire burned five city blocks, providing plenty of work for Jim.

Soon, Jim was approached by 27-year-old William H. Bovee, a coffee roaster who needed help building a spice and coffee mill. Through his Pioneer Steam Coffee and Spice Mills, Bovee produced coffee ready for the pot: roasted, ground, and packaged in small tins. When Jim's brothers returned from the mines, Edward Folger and two partners established Cook, Folger & Company, a whale-oil company, and moved into quarters next door to the Pioneer coffee mill.

One year after arriving in San Francisco, Jim Folger loaded up a wagon with tools and Bovee's coffee and headed for the mountains. As he traveled, he found a little gold and sold all his coffee. With his money, he established a small store and during the next two years built a sizable following. He then sold the store for a profit and returned to San Francisco, where he worked in shipbuilding and hardware retailing ventures.

In 1855, Folger decided that his heart was in the coffee business, and he returned to Bovee's firm and made a modest investment. When Bovee decided to pan for gold on a large scale, he sold most of his interest in the business to Folger, who renamed the firm Marden & Folger. Bovee eventually lost $250,000 chasing gold, and he then lived the rest of his life as a successful real estate broker.

Folger's success in the coffee business allowed him, at age 24, to marry Ellen Laughren, who arrived from Burlington, Vermont, in 1858. They moved into a nice home across the bay, in Oakland, and started a family. The couple eventually had five children, two of whom died during infancy.

The end of the Civil War brought economic chaos, forcing Marden & Folger into bankruptcy. In response, Folger bought out his partner, changed the name of the firm to J. A. Folger & Company, and focused on selling more coffee. Although it took him nearly ten years, Folger was able to pay back every penny owed to his creditors.

James A. Folger died on June 26, 1889, at the age of 54. His oldest son, James A. Folger II, who had been with the family business for seven years, assumed the post of president.

SOURCE: The Procter & Gamble Company archives

Henry Ford

[Ford Motor Company]

The Ford family traces its roots to Ireland, where the first family members left for America in 1832. By the 1847, William Ford's family, poor potato farmers in southern Ireland, immigrated to the United States and joined family members who had already established farms near Dearborn, Michigan.

William helped with the family farm, which grew successful by selling goods in nearby Detroit, then later traveled the Midwest building wagon sheds and other stations for the rapidly expanding railroad system. In 1861, he married Mary O'Hern. Their first child died during childbirth, and one year later Henry Ford was born on July 30, 1863. Thirteen years later, his mother died at age 37, 12 days after giving birth to her eighth child, who also died.

At the age of 16, Henry Ford left home, walked nearly ten miles to Detroit, and went to work at the Flower Brothers' machine shop. Several months later, he took a job with the Detroit Dry Dock Company and supplemented his income by cleaning and repairing watches in the evenings.

In 1882, Ford returned to the family farm and became something of a resource for neighboring farmers. He repaired a Westinghouse portable steam engine, which he contracted to local farmers during the summer months. The experience led Westinghouse to hire him as a demonstrator and repairman in the southern Michigan region.

Ford married Clara Jane Bryant in 1888, and three years later the couple moved to Detroit, where Henry took a job with the Edison Illuminating Company. For the next four years Ford supervised the company's generating facilities and even established a small workshop on the premises for his own experiments. Once more, he worked evenings to supplement his income, this time at the YMCA teaching machinist classes.

In 1896, Ford happened to pick up a two-part article in *The American Machinist* magazine that described the process for building a simple gasoline engine. He and several of his friends went to work in the garage behind his house and, in June of that year, completed their Quadricycle, a curious-looking machine that used a doorbell as a warning horn. Nonetheless, the machine worked, and Ford was able to attract some investors for a new company, the Detroit Automobile Company.

The new company produced its first horseless delivery wagon in 1900. However, the firm closed its doors after only one year because the investors grew restless over the slow pace of production, which Ford attributed to his quest for quality. He quickly recovered and launched the Henry Ford Company that same year. But it, too, was forced to close in a matter of months.

The two closings in less than two years didn't discourage Ford. He quickly secured funding from celebrated cycling champion Tom Cooper to build racing machines. In 1903, after developing a breakthrough engine through another partnership and securing $28,000 in start-up funds, Ford was able to launch the Ford Motor Company.

Within one year, he was able to build and sell 658 of his Model A cars, and quickly introduced the Model B, Model C, and Model F. By 1908, Ford was convinced that the company's best strategy was to focus on the mass production of inexpensive cars. That year, he introduced his Model T and proceeded to sell 15 million of them over the next 19 years.

Henry and Clara Ford had only one child, Edsel, who was born on November 6, 1893. While attending school, Edsel would leave classes in the afternoon and join his father at the factory. Upon graduation from high school, he bypassed college and went straight to work with his father.

In 1915, at age 21, Edsel was appointed to the board of directors and four years later was named president. He died of cancer on May 26, 1943 at the age of 49. Henry returned from retirement to run the company until 1945, when he was succeeded by his grandson, Henry Ford II. Two years after his second retirement, Henry Ford died on April 7, 1947.

Today, the Ford Motor Company is the world's second-largest automobile and truck manufacturer and is active in a number of other industries, including glass, plastics, industrial machinery, insurance, electronics, and property development. Annual sales are nearly $140 billion, and the company has nearly 350,000 employees worldwide.

SOURCES: Ford Motor Company annual report; Robert Lacey, *Ford: The Men and the Machine,* Little, Brown & Company, 1986

John B. Ford, John Pitcairn Jr.

[PPG Industries]

Although John Ford started many companies across several states, none of his ventures grew as rapidly as the glass factory that he built with the financial backing and expertise of John Pitcairn. By mixing entrepreneurial flair with sound financial management, their company, Pittsburgh Plate Glass, grew to be one of the most successful producers of glass, paint, and chemicals in the world.

John Baptiste Ford was born on November 17, 1811, in the wilderness settlement of Danville, Kentucky, the third child of Jonathan and Margaret (Baptiste) Ford. Shortly before the birth of their fourth child, Jonathan left with a group of Kentucky Volunteers to serve in the War of 1812 and never returned. His fate was never known.

While serving as an apprentice to an abusive saddlemaker, 12-year-old Ford ran away to Greenville, Indiana, where he found work with another saddler. He later purchased the shop and supplied cavalry saddles and harness equipment during the war with Mexico. He also operated a local flour mill. On March 17, 1831, Ford married Mary Bower, who taught him reading, writing, and mathematics. The couple had seven children, but only two lived beyond childhood.

Ford sold his Greenville business ventures in 1854 and moved to New Albany, Indiana, where he established several new ventures, including a nail factory, an iron-rolling mill, a forge, a foundry, and a plow factory. He also produced a feed-cutting box for farmers. By 1859 he was building and selling steamboats and operating a fleet of riverboats, thereby obtaining the lifelong nickname of "the Captain."

It was Ford's son, Emory, who aroused an interest in glassmaking. He convinced his father of the strong market opportunities in containers, prompting Ford to establish J. B. Ford & Sons in New Albany with sons Emory and Edward to produce bottles and jars and, later, window glass. Soon, Ford sold off his other ventures to concentrate on glass products. By 1872, however, he lost the company because of financial difficulties.

In 1881, the 69-year-old Ford launched the New York City Plate Glass Company at Creighton, Pennsylvania, along the Allegheny River north of Pittsburgh. Not long after he started operations, he consulted with a man named John Pitcairn about using natural gas at the plant.

John Pitcairn Jr. was born on January 10, 1841, at Johnstone, Scotland. His family immigrated to Pittsburgh, Pennsylvania, in 1846, where his uncle had established a woolens business. On his 14th birthday, young Pitcairn went to work as an office boy at the Pennsylvania Railroad in Altoona. He spent the next several years in various railroad capacities, including providing security for a special passenger en route to Washington, D.C.: president-elect Abraham Lincoln.

In the late 1860s, Pitcairn held superintendent and general manager positions with several railroad companies. As his income grew, he made several key investments in coal and petroleum ventures, oil and gas production, mining, and banks. In August 1883, six months after Ford's facility started operating as the world's first natural-gas-fueled glass plant, the company was reorganized as the Pittsburgh Plate Glass Company, with Pitcairn and other new investors providing a much-needed cash infusion. Edward Ford was president of the new company, and brother Emory was secretary and treasurer.

John Ford was often described as a man who liked to establish new plants but not to run the business. Pitcairn was somewhat the opposite. He was an accomplished supervisor and financial genius, and the two men provided a good balance for one another. He eventually took the position of chairman and, upon Edward Ford's resignation in 1897, Pitcairn assumed the position of president. At the turn of the century, Pitcairn led the company into new fields such as chemicals and paint. John Ford never held an executive position with the firm.

With financial support from Pitcairn, Ford started a gas pipeline business that was later sold at a substantial profit. The pair built two more glass factories near Pittsburgh, at Tarentum and Ford City (named in honor of the Captain), both of which were later absorbed by Pittsburgh Plate Glass. Ford also established a soda ash plant in Michigan to supply glassmakers.

In 1897, Ford's two sons left Pittsburgh Plate Glass after disagreements over financial and marketing policies. Subsequently, Edward and his son John established The Edward Ford Plate Glass Company at Rossford, Ohio. Through a 1930 merger, the company became Libbey-Owens-Ford Glass Company.

Not long after the death of his wife in early 1897, John Ford sold his stock to Pitcairn and, at the age of 86, built yet another business: the Ford City Potteries. The venture was later sold and eventually became part of the Eljer Company. John Baptiste Ford died on May 1, 1903, at the age of 91.

Pitcairn didn't marry until he was nearly 43 years old. His 1884 marriage to Gertrude Starkey produced six children, four of whom lived to adulthood. John Pitcairn died on July 22, 1916, at the age of 75.

The company's name was changed in 1968 to PPG Industries. Today, PPG is a global producer of coatings, glass, fiberglass, and chemicals. It employs about 31,000 people and has annual sales exceeding $7 billion.

SOURCE: PPG Industries, Inc., archives

William Fox

[Twentieth Century Fox]

Wilhelm Fuchs, whose name was soon changed to William Fox, was born on January 1, 1879, in the small Hungarian town of Tulchva, the first of 12 children, 7 of whom died in infancy. Soon after his birth, his family immigrated to New York and moved into a tenement on the lower east side.

At the age of six, young Fox sold shoelaces, stove blacking, and candy on the streets of New York. At age 11 he quit school and went to work in the city's garment district to help support the family. On New Year's Eve 1899, he married Eva Leo, and the couple eventually had two daughters.

In 1903 he saw his first theater. Actually, it was a small storefront with folding chairs where, for a nickel, patrons watched short films cranked by hand through a lighted box and projected onto a white wall. He was so excited that he invested his entire savings—about $1,700—in his own 146-seat theater in Brooklyn, called The Comedy Theatre. He also formed The Greater New York Film Rental Company to rent films to other small operations once they had been shown in his own theater.

Within five years his operation had made $50,000, enabling Fox to open more than a dozen theaters in New York. Fox next launched a film company, Fox Productions, and in 1914 released his first film, *Life's Shop Window,* directed by J. Gordon Edwards (grandfather of the modern-era director Blake Edwards). The following year, he folded his production company into the Fox Film Corporation, which by 1916 had established a Hollywood studio.

Fox faced a formidable impediment to advancing in the film industry. Thomas Edison and several major companies involved with film had formed the Motion Picture Patents Company in 1909 to preserve their control over the production of film and film equipment. Subsequently, independent producers like Fox were effectively barred from success. Fox led antitrust efforts to loosen the grip of Edison and his colleagues and, in 1917, succeeded in prompting the government to open the industry to independent film producers and suppliers.

During World War I, Fox continued to make pictures from his studios in New York and Hollywood. He also launched Fox Newsreel to create news clips that were shown before feature films. The news clips quickly carried the Fox name to other nations, greatly enhancing name recognition among future customers.

By 1923, Fox had built a considerable filmmaking empire, including expensive studios and famous actors such as Tom Mix. That year, he purchased West Coast Theatre Chain, making him one of the world's largest theater owners. Two years later, he reorganized most of his holdings into two companies, Fox Film Corporation and Fox Theatres Corporation. He also acquired the Roxy Theatre in New York City, the world's largest theater at the time.

The mid-1920s marked the beginning of sound technology for films, and William Fox was a pioneer. He developed a process known as Movietone for recording sound on film, and with inventor Theodore Case he organized the Fox-Case Corporation. Their first sound applications were made with Fox Movietone News in 1926. Encouraged by its success, the partners soon added sound to their feature films.

By 1928, Fox had retreated from day-to-day management of the company and looked toward expansion. Over the next two years, he spent nearly $70 million to acquire control of the Loews organization, which included Metro-Goldwyn-Mayer. Disaster struck in 1929, however, when Fox was in a devastating automobile accident. While Fox was recuperating, the stock market crashed and, after a series of actions from stockholders and regulators, he lost control of the company.

William Fox died on May 8, 1952, at the age of 73. In 1935, five years after Fox left the studio, his company merged with Twentieth Century Pictures, forming Twentieth Century Fox Film Corporation. In the mid-1980s, Fox Corporation launched the Fox Television Network and in the 1990s added the Fox Sports Network.

SOURCES: Twentieth Century Fox archives

Alfred C. Fuller

[The Fuller Brush Company]

The descendants of Edward Fuller, a passenger on the Mayflower, migrated from Massachusetts in all directions. Nathan Fuller moved into Nova Scotia, Canada, in the mid-1700s and became a large landholder. Several generations later, Alfred Carl Fuller was born on January 13, 1885, in Welsford, Nova Scotia, the 11th of 12 children.

Life on the farm was difficult, and all the Fuller children were expected to be picking and selling berries by the age of ten. In January 1903, 18-year-old Alfred Fuller was given $75 and a King James Bible from his parents and sent to live with his three brothers and two sisters in Somerville, Massachusetts, a region that would offer the young man considerably more opportunity.

Fuller was hired as a trolley car conductor in Boston but, 18 months later, was fired when his car derailed. He was next hired by a wealthy family as a gardener and groom, but was fired for incompetence. Eventually, one of his brothers hired him as a wagon driver. However, he repeatedly delivered packages to wrong addresses and skipped important pickups, forcing his own brother to fire him.

His next move was to a brush factory as a salesman. Unsure of himself, he carried his sample case into the field, and although doors were slammed in his face he managed to sell $6 worth of merchandise, providing him with more money than he was used to making in a week. On this fateful day, January 7, 1905, six days before his 20th birthday, Alfred Fuller found his life's calling.

Fuller had two assets. First, he was accustomed to long hours of hard work. Second, he had a sincere interest in people. As he grew more experienced with selling brushes, he and his clients became involved with discussions about their cleaning needs, prompting young Fuller to think about new types of brushes.

Fuller settled on six unique designs, and on January 1, 1906, he started to manufacture them in the basement of his sister's home. He had built his own brush-twisting machine for about $15 and rigged spools to hold several coils of soft, galvanized wire of different gauges. He took to the road with his own brushes and, at the end of the week, counted sales of $65 and a profit of $42.15.

Encouraged by the success of his venture after four months, Fuller moved to Hartford, Connecticut, where he continued his operations with the same intensity as he had in Boston. He took orders through the day and made brushes at night. Housewives continued to help him innovate new products by describing their needs in detail, then trying out the special brushes that he subsequently made.

Fuller slowly added help. His first employee was 18-year-old Harry Linden, who quickly became adept at manufacturing. He also happened to strike up a conversation with James Bradley, a blind man who was connected with the Hartford Institute for the Blind. As part of their mission, they sold corn brooms and Bradley was somewhat an authority on the subject. He liked the feel of Fuller's brushes and asked if he could be a dealer, and his request was readily granted.

By 1908, Fuller had $2,000 in the bank and was making $75 weekly. The success enabled him to marry Evelyn Ells, who quickly became a colleague in the business and a traveling companion. However, the brushes were selling as fast as they could be made, and it became clear that reliable salespeople were needed. In 1909, he placed an advertisement in *Everybody's Magazine,* and within one month he had 260 dealers, each investing $17 for a brush kit.

The company was formally organized as The Fuller Brush Company in 1913. The first branch office was opened in Boston in 1915, and within three years nearly 100 more were opened. Perhaps the company's greatest marketing accomplishment occurred in 1922 when a salesman for *The Saturday Evening Post* coined the term "Fuller Brush Man" while preparing a new series of full-page Fuller ads.

Alfred Carl Fuller died on December 4, 1973, after The Fuller Brush Company had become part of the Sara Lee Corporation in 1968. By the beginning of the 1990s, a private investment group from Kansas had acquired the company. Today, more than 15,000 independent distributors and nine outlet stores sell Fuller products throughout the United States.

In October 1994, The Fuller Brush Company was purchased by CPAC, Inc., a Leicester, New York–based manufacturer of processing solutions and environmental compliance equipment for the worldwide imaging market. On April 1, 1995, CPAC licensed all rights to manufacture, distribute, and sell Stanley Home Products in the United States, Puerto Rico, and Canada. All of this work is now performed at the Great Bend, Kansas, facility.

SOURCES: Fuller Brush Company archives; Alfred C. Fuller, as told to Hartzell Spence, *A Foot in the Door: The Life Appraisal of the Original Fuller Brush Man,* McGraw-Hill, 1960

Harvey B. Fuller Sr., Elmer L. Andersen
[H.B. Fuller Company]

Harvey Benjamin Fuller was born in 1845 in Youngstown, Ohio. He launched his first business in Chicago, Illinois, in 1886. Convinced that an adhesive product would be successful, he purchased and repackaged glue under the name Fuller's Premium Liquid Fish Glue. One year later, he moved to St. Paul, Minnesota, the heart of America's flour industry.

Experimenting with different paste formulas in an iron kettle on his kitchen's wood-burning stove, Fuller developed a strong flour-based wallpaper paste. With a $600 investment put up by three local attorneys, he set up his one-man shop, and the Fuller Manufacturing Company was in business.

He supplemented his paste business by selling ink to local schools and bottled laundry bluing. Eventually, he sold a host of products to everyone looking for ways to attach labels, secure bundles, or fix broken items. In 1892, he made his first acquisition by purchasing The Minnesota Paste Company for $200.

Soon after he started in business, Fuller's oldest son, 18-year-old Albert, joined the business. The father and son team experimented with new products, eventually marketing their Cold Water Dry Wall Cleaner, followed by Cold Water Dry Paste. These products were dry compounds that were mixed with cold water at job sites, a great convenience to paper hangers that led to rapid growth of the company. By 1898, the small firm reached $10,000 in annual sales.

In 1897, Albert Fuller moved to Pennsylvania to establish his own adhesives business. Fuller's second son, Roger, joined the firm briefly, but he, too, left to pursue other interests. Fuller's third son, Harvey Jr., joined the company in 1909 and began to promote advertising and marketing strategies.

During World War I, Fuller provided labeling glue for the canned rations being shipped to Europe. He also created new adhesives for paper bag manufacturing, bottle labeling, box construction, and envelope production. Fuller kept his focus on making things that would "hold the world together." Several of his early customers are still major clients of H.B. Fuller—among them, The Minnesota Valley Canning Company, which today is known as Green Giant, and The Washburn-Crosby Company, now known as General Mills.

Harvey Fuller Sr. died in 1921, and he was succeeded by Harvey Jr. The company continued to grow slowly, reaching $157,000 in annual sales by 1929. Despite the Depression, the company exceeded $200,000 in sales by the mid-1930s under the leadership of their new sales manager, Elmer Andersen.

Elmer L. Andersen was born on June 17, 1909, in Chicago, Illinois. His father was a Norwegian immigrant who worked as a streetcar motorman. His mother was American born, but her parents were Scandinavian immigrants. At age nine, Andersen was stricken with polio and spinal meningitis and was told he would never recover. Nonetheless, through rigorous physical conditioning, he overcame virtually all effects of his illness.

However, a second tragedy struck the family five years later after they moved to Muskegon, Michigan. Both of Andersen's parents died within nine months of each other. Rather than split into foster homes, the four Andersen children banded together and went to work. Fourteen-year-old Elmer not only delivered newspapers, but he also wrote news articles. Additionally, the young entrepreneur carried luggage for travelers, sold products door-to-door, and sold snacks on local trains.

Andersen's two older brothers worked for a local school furniture manufacturer, but the owner wouldn't hire young Elmer because he didn't have sales experience. Determined to join his brothers, Andersen gained his experience by selling real estate while attending Muskegon Junior College. Two years later, in 1928, he was hired by the furniture company and assigned to the Minneapolis, Minnesota, region.

While working in Minnesota, the 19-year-old salesman enrolled in the University of Minnesota's School of Business Administration. Not long after that, he married Eleanor Johnson, a fellow student. He soon tired of the travel for his employer and, in 1934, went to work for the H.B. Fuller Company.

In 1941, Harvey Fuller Jr. was approached by a competitor with an offer to buy his company. Things were not good at H.B. Fuller. Two key employees had left the company and taken many customers with them. Moreover, Harvey Jr. was recovering from a stroke. As Andersen and Fuller discussed the buyout bid, Andersen offered to buy the company. The two men quickly came to terms, and the 32-year-old Andersen took control of the company and immediately launched an expansion campaign.

By 1946, the company surpassed $1 million in sales and was the sixth-largest producer of adhesives in the nation. Andersen opened more plants in California, Georgia, and elsewhere. The company benefited by the postwar boom in consumer products, and for many years H.B. Fuller Company was able to double in size every five years.

Elmer Andersen also led an active public life. He served as a state senator from 1949 to 1958, followed by a term as the governor of Minnesota from 1961 to 1963. After retiring from public life, Andersen returned to Fuller. In April 1971, his 35-year-old son, Tony, was named president.

By 1971, Fuller became a Fortune 1,000 company. Thirteen years later, it broke the Fortune 500. Today, the company employs more than 5,800 people worldwide.

SOURCE: H.B. Fuller Company archives

Frank E. Gannett

[Gannett Company]

The first Gannetts to immigrate to America arrived from Dorsetshire, England, during the 1630s. Several generations later, Frank Ernest Gannett was born on September 15, 1876, on a farm in New York's Finger Lakes region near the town of Bristol, the fifth of six children born to Charles and Maria (Brooks) Gannett.

At age nine, young Gannett took his first job as a newspaper carrier for the *Democrat and Chronicle* of Rochester, New York. His parents abandoned farming and opened a small hotel in Howard, New York. They made two moves to larger hotels, first in Wallace, then in Bolivar, during which time Frank continued to sell and deliver newspapers. He supplemented his income by harvesting crops and picking berries.

Gannett noticed that the immigrant Italian laborers were unable to address their mail home in English. For a small fee, he had rubber stamps made bearing the names and addresses of the workers' families in Italy. At age 12, he contacted a fertilizer company to see if it would be interested in animal carcasses that were found along roads and on farms. When the firm agreed to pay him 50¢ per 100 pounds, he organized a workforce of his peers, paying them with nickels and candy sticks.

When he was 15, his parents made yet another move, and young Gannett elected to stay behind and finish high school. He worked for another local hotel as a waiter and bartender until graduation, at which time he split his time as a bookkeeper between two firms. Then, in 1894, he moved to Ithaca after being awarded a scholarship to Cornell University.

While at Cornell, Gannett again waited on tables and took other odd jobs. He was appointed to the school newspaper, but soon started compiling and selling news items to newspapers in other cities. He also worked during summer breaks as an unpaid intern for the *Syracuse Herald.* Upon graduation, Gannett had saved more than $1,000 from his news business and was hired by the Syracuse paper for $15 per week.

The following year, Gannett accompanied Cornell president Jacob Schurman on a fact-finding trip to the Philippines. Upon return to the United States, he was hired as the city editor for the *Ithaca Daily News.* There he gained valuable experience in both producing and administering a daily newspaper. The job also provided him with exposure and he was recruited by a Pittsburgh, Pennsylvania, newspaper to serve as editor in chief.

The Pittsburgh position didn't work out, and in 1906 Gannett returned to New York looking for his next opportunity. He learned that the part owner of the *Elmira Gazette* was interested in selling his share of the newspaper for $20,000. Gannett was able to piece together $10,000 in cash and another $10,000 in notes, which the owner accepted. On June 6, 1906, 29-year-old Frank Gannett became part owner of his first newspaper.

One year later, he acquired the Elmira *Star* and merged it with the *Gazette* under the new name *Star-Gazette.* Five years later, he bought the Ithaca *Journal,* which he later merged with the Ithaca *News* to form the Ithaca *Journal-News.* Gannett and his partners then moved into the Rochester, New York, market, acquiring and merging the *Union and Advertiser* and the *Evening Times* into the Rochester *Times-Union.* In 1920, Gannett married Caroline Werner. The couple had two children, Sally and Dixon.

In 1924, Gannett incorporated the Gannett Company and bought out his two partners for $1 million each. He then accelerated his practice of buying newspapers and, in 1927, made his first two acquisitions outside New York state by purchasing the *Courier-News* in Plainfield, New Jersey, and the *Sentinel* in Winston-Salem, North Carolina. By 1943, he controlled 21 newspapers in 16 cities in four states.

Frank E. Gannett died on December 3, 1957, at the age of 81. Today, the Gannett Company is one of America's largest diversified news and information agencies, with 82 daily newspapers, including *USA Today,* the nation's largest daily newspaper. The company also owns 10 television stations, 11 radio stations, and a broad range of support companies. Gannett has more than 36,000 employees and annual revenues of nearly $4 billion.

SOURCES: Gannett Company archives; J. Donald Brandt, *A History of Gannett: 1906–1993,* Gannett Company, 1993

Edward G. Gardner

[Soft Sheen]

Edward George Gardner was born on February 25, 1925, in Chicago, Illinois, to parents Frank and Eva Gardner. Following his tour of duty during World War II, Gardner returned to Chicago and enrolled at Chicago Teacher's College, where he earned his bachelor's degree in education, followed by a master's degree from the University of Chicago in administration and supervision in 1954.

Gardner spent 14 years as an instructor and school administrator for the Chicago Public School System while maintaining a part-time sales venture. In the early 1960s, he became aware that African-American consumers and hair care professionals were dissatisfied with many of the products on the market.

Knowing that Black hair was physiologically different than other hair, Gardner and his wife, Bettiann, went to work in their basement to develop products for African-American salons. In 1964, they incorporated Soft Sheen Products, and their four children—Gary, Guy, Terri, and Tracy—comprised the company's first workforce.

After more than 12 years of growth, the company was able to move into a new 15,000-square-foot building on Chicago's South Side. In 1977, the company had 15 employees and annual sales of $500,000, primarily because of two brand lines—Soft Sheen and Miss Cool—which were sold to both retailers and salons.

Two years later, the company launched a breakthrough product called Care Free Curls, and annual sales soared to more than $40 million. Three years later, Gardner had to increase the size of his facilities to more than 50,000 square feet to accommodate more than 300 employees. He also moved into international markets, including Europe, Africa, and the Caribbean.

By the late 1980s, Soft Sheen had become one of the best-known Afro-American hair care products in the world. Also, with more than 620 employees and annual sales exceeding $70 million, the firm was one of the country's largest African-American-owned companies. Ed and Betty Gardner became cochairs of the Soft Sheen board, and son Gary was appointed president.

Today, annual sales at Soft Sheen hover at the $100 million mark. The company markets its products in more than 76 countries. Gardner's daughter Terri now serves as presiding officer and CEO.

SOURCE: Soft Sheen corporate archives

Roswell Garst

[Garst Seed Company]

Roswell Garst was born on June 17, 1898, in Coon Rapids, Iowa, the last of four children born to parents Edward and Bertha Garst. Edward was a successful merchant who had accumulated over 10,000 acres of land, and he named his son after a recent land purchase in Roswell, New Mexico.

Young Roswell was raised with a balanced exposure to school, religion, neighbors, and business. Most of his childhood responsibilities involved family farming activities. He later studied agriculture at four different colleges, but grew frustrated at each of them and didn't complete his degree requirements.

In 1921, Garst launched his first farming venture with the purchase of 16 cows, from which he supplied milk to a local creamery. That summer, he met Elizabeth Henak, a schoolteacher in Cedar Falls, Iowa, and the two were married the following year. Within two years, both of Garst's parents died and Elizabeth gave birth to the first two of five children.

Garst's modest business grew, and he was soon prominent in Coon Rapids social and business circles. However, in 1926, he hired a manager for his farm and moved his family to Des Moines, Iowa, where he launched a land development venture. He also cultivated a friendship with Henry Wallace.

Henry Agard Wallace was born in 1888 in Orient, Iowa. His father, a teacher and researcher, later moved the family to Ames and became associated with the agricultural college there. Soon, Henry made friends with an older student, George Washington Carver, who helped inspire a lifelong love of botany in young Wallace. In 1913, he began crossbreeding corn and, ten years later, established the Hi-Bred Corn Company.

Garst struck a deal with Wallace to produce and market the corn, then returned to Coon Rapids and planted 15 acres. When the first seed field came in, Garst loaded the corn into the back of his Buick, 20 bushels at a time, and peddled it to farmers. He soon raised additional capital by taking on a partner and forming the Garst and Thomas Hi-Bred Corn Company.

By 1933, Garst was producing 10,000 bushels of corn seed annually. A new processing system was added to the firm that year, only to be replaced by a new seed-processing plant two years later. Encouraged by local success, Garst moved into neighboring states. By 1938, nearly 900 salesmen were selling more than 100,000 bushels of corn in southwest Iowa, Nebraska, Missouri, Colorado, Kansas, and Oklahoma.

After World War II, Garst actively campaigned for America to send surplus agricultural products and technology abroad as a gesture of peace. In 1955, he visited the Soviet Union and developed a warm relationship with Nikita Khrushchev. The two exchanged visits in subsequent years. That same year, David Garst, his youngest son, began working for the seed company. Over the next 12 years, David tripled business volume and built the company into the third-largest seed corn supplier in the United States.

Roswell Garst died in 1977. Four years later, the franchise with the Pioneer Hi-Bred Corn Company ended and the Garst family acquired the interests of the Thomas family in the seed business. David Garst was then named president of the newly formed Garst Seed Company. With a new seed line, he restored the market share which had declined significantly. The family sold the business to ICI through transactions in 1985 and 1987.

SOURCES: Garst family archives; Harold Lee, *Roswell Garst: A Biography,* Iowa State University Press, 1984; *Letters From An American Farmer,* edited by Richard Lowitt and Harold Lee, Northern Illinois University Press, 1987

William H. Gates III, Paul G. Allen

[Microsoft Corporation]

William Henry Gates III was born on October 28, 1955, in Seattle, Washington. His first exposure to the computer was at Seattle's Lakeside High School in the late 1960s. The Mothers' Club voted to use proceeds from a rummage sale to purchase a computer terminal and to lease time on a remote mainframe computer. At the time, this was a relatively novel idea. He and his school buddy, Paul Allen (who was three years older than Gates), pushed the computer as far as the technology would let them.

In 1972, the teenagers came across a ten-paragraph article in *Electronics* magazine announcing that a young firm named Intel had just released its 8080 microprocessor. They found a telephone number for Intel, called it, and requested documentation on the chip. Surprisingly, a technical manual showed up in the mailbox. Soon the teenagers fashioned a crude device that could measure automobile traffic on highways. However, they were unable to generate any real interest in their Traf-O-Data machine.

The following year they headed for Boston. Gates entered Harvard and, across town, Allen found a programming job with Honeywell. In 1975, when Altair released its computer using an Intel 8080 microprocessor, Gates and Allen quickly ordered one and created some simple applications written in BASIC. Gates dropped out of Harvard, Allen quit his job, and Microsoft was born.

The pair moved to Albuquerque, New Mexico, because that's where MITS, the small company that sold the Altair computer, was based. As other companies entered the personal computer market, such as Apple, Commodore, and Radio Shack, Gates and Allen provided BASIC software for customers, who were predominantly hobbyists.

Business grew, and in 1979 the partners moved their company and 12 employees to Seattle. They quickly added more staff and limited their focus to inexpensive microcomputer software, a market that was rapidly growing and drastically underserved. By the following year, two more products were introduced: Microsoft FORTRAN and Microsoft COBOL.

That same year, IBM approached the founders and invited them to prepare special software that would drive its personal computers, known as IBM PCs. The result was MS-DOS (Microsoft Disk Operating System), which was bundled with the release of the PC in 1981. Within seven years Microsoft was the world's leading software company, and by 1990 annual sales exceeded $1 billion.

Today, Microsoft continues to be the world's number one provider of computer software. It employs more than 20,000 people in nearly 60 countries. Annual revenues are approaching $10 billion. Gates remains at the helm of Microsoft.

While he remains a major shareholder and member of the board of directors, Paul Allen left active management of Microsoft in 1983 to pursue other interests. His wholly owned companies include Asymetrix Corporation, Starwave Corporation, Bulcan Ventures, Inc., and the Paul Allen Group, Interval Research Corporation, and Ticketmaster Corporation. He also owns the Portland Trail Blazers professional basketball team and is a partner in the highly touted DreamWorks media company.

SOURCES: Microsoft archives; The Paul Allen Group archives; Bill Gates, *The Road Ahead,* Viking, 1995

David Geffen

[Geffen Records]

David Geffen grew up in New York City longing to enter the entertainment business. After graduating from high school, he moved to Los Angeles and within seven years was a successful agent for the William Morris Agency. Soon he launched Asylum Records, which he quickly sold to Warner Communications. In 1980, Geffen founded Geffen Records, which was sold ten years later to MCA in a transaction that netted Geffen more than $700 million.

Today, Geffen continues as head of Geffen Records while producing movies and Broadway shows.

David Geffen's childhood was strongly influenced by his mother, a Russian Jew who immigrated to America after the Russian Revolution. Geffen's father, a Polish immigrant, was somewhat of an intellectual drifter who traveled the world. His mother supported the family through a sewing business. She started by making corsets and brassieres for people in her New York apartment. The business grew into a small shop, where David and his brother ate many of their meals while their mother worked. "You have golden hands," she said to him, "Whatever you want to be, you'll succeed at." She taught her son a simple lesson for success in life: no envy, no jealousy, and no hate.

Geffen was convinced at an early age that he wanted to be part of Hollywood. As a child, he read everything about the entertainment industry that he could get his hands on. He once stayed in a movie theater all day, watching *Singin' in the Rain* over and over while his worried mother had the police looking for him. The day after he graduated from high school he moved to Los Angeles and found a job as an usher at CBS Studios, working *The Judy Garland Show, The Danny Kaye Show,* and *The Red Skelton Show.*

In his early 20s, he obtained a $55-per-week job in the mail room at the William Morris Agency. Geffen "enhanced" his resume by stating that he was a graduate of UCLA. Each day he checked the mail until correspondence from UCLA arrived contradicting his resume. He steamed open the letter, made appropriate changes that backed his claim, then confidently delivered the letter.

Within five years, Geffen became a $2-million-per-year agent at William Morris, representing musicians such as Crosby, Stills, Nash, & Young, Joni Mitchell, Janis Joplin, and others. While trying to sell an up-and-coming new artist named Jackson Browne to record producers, someone suggested that Geffen start his own label and produce Browne himself. Geffen took the advice and, in 1970, formed Asylum Records. He led the label to several fast hits with artists such as Linda Ronstadt and his close friend Joni Mitchell, whose song *Free Man in Paris* is based on the life of David Geffen. Two years later, he sold the company to Warner Communications for $7 million.

Geffen's next move was to Warner films, a stint that lasted only a short time. Within a year, Geffen was (wrongly) diagnosed with cancer of the bladder. He moved back East and buried himself in the New York social scene. By 1980, however, he found that the cancer diagnosis was incorrect. He threw himself back into the entertainment business by launching Geffen Records in 1980. The first three acts he signed to his new label were Donna Summer, John Lennon, and Elton John. He also launched a movie production company that made several movies, including *Risky Business* and *Beetlejuice,* and a Broadway theater company that put together shows such as *Cats, Dreamgirls,* and *Miss Saigon.*

Geffen built his company by empowering his employees and sharing the wealth. Every key executive became a millionaire, based on Geffen's philosophy of rewarding employees with more money than they expect and passing around the credit. A loyal personal secretary, upon her retirement, was given a check for $5 million. No one at Geffen Records, other than the president, had job titles.

One decade after founding Geffen Records, MCA purchased the company for stock worth nearly $550 million. Within months of the sale, Matsushita purchased MCA, increasing the value of Geffen's stock holdings to more than $700 million. Today Geffen is reportedly worth more than $1 billion. Yet he remains at the helm of Geffen records for an annual salary of less than $1 million (which is donated to his active foundation).

SOURCES: Patrick Goldstein, "David Geffen," *Rolling Stone* magazine, April 29, 1993; "David Geffen," *Playboy* magazine, September, 1994

Conrad M. Gentry, Donald F. Kenworthy

[Mayflower Transit]

Conrad M. Gentry, an Indiana grocer, was active in moving produce and grocer's supplies between the small Indiana town of Monrovia and Indianapolis. He soon invited his friend, truck salesman Donald F. Kenworthy, to join him in establishing a moving company. In 1927, they established the Mayflower organization.

Gentry and Kenworthy built their business by recruiting contract drivers. They would paint their Mayflower emblem on trucks that were then sold to contractors. They opened sales offices in various cities to solicit work for their contractors.

Two years later, Burnside Smith brought additional capital and business management to the group. Under Smith, the company built a network of household goods movers who had storage warehouses, allowing Mayflower to offer high-quality moving and storage services.

In 1940, the Interstate Commerce Commission granted Mayflower the first nationwide household goods operating authority certificate. World War II broke out and the company was soon recruited into the war effort, moving thousands of families of industrial and military personnel around the country.

Mayflower has enjoyed sustained growth and name recognition throughout its history. In 1976, the company issued its first public stock offering. During the 1980s, Mayflower added a Contract Services Division, primarily to provide contract school bus services.

In 1995, the Mayflower Group sold both operating divisions. Mayflower Contract Services, based in Overland Park, Kansas, was sold for $157 million to Laidlaw Transit. Mayflower Transit was sold for $90 million to UniGroup, the Fenton, Missouri, parent company of United Van Lines.

Today, both Mayflower and United operate as separate companies. Mayflower is the fourth-largest van line in America. It employs more than 1,500 people, utilizes more than 700 agents, and coordinates the activities of nearly 3,000 private operators to accommodate 165,000 moves each year.

SOURCE: Mayflower archives

Stephen Geppi

[Diamond Comic Distributors]

Stephen Geppi was born in the rough Little Italy neighborhood of Baltimore, Maryland, in the late 1940s. While working as a mail carrier for the United States Postal Service, Geppi started collecting, selling, and trading comic books as a hobby. Soon the hobby turned into a good-paying sideline, so he left the post office and opened a store. After growing a respectable retail business, he opened Diamond Comic Distributors and built it into the world's largest distributor of comic books and comic-related materials. He also is a part-owner of the Baltimore Orioles baseball club.

Geppi landed his first job at age nine, sorting comic books for a local retailer in the back of a liquor store. Life in the neighborhood was tough, but was even more challenging because of an absentee father. By the age of 13, Geppi was handling football pools to support his mother. He dropped out of school and, with his brother, scouted for opportunities.

At the age of 19 Geppi landed a $3.06 per hour job with the United States Postal Service. The job provided a secure and steady income for his young family. In 1972, while vacationing at the New Jersey seashore, Geppi's life took a turn. His nine-year-old nephew was reading a *Batman* comic book. Geppi leafed through the book and reminisced about his days in Little Italy.

The moment at the beach turned into a hobby for Geppi. He started buying old comics from people on his mail route. He attended shows around his work schedule. His buying, trading, and selling eventually produced more income than his postal job. Finally, in 1974, Geppi left the post office and opened his own shop.

An old blue Ford van served as the company fleet, while Geppi was the sole employee of the venture. He'd have to lock up the store to go on buying and trading trips. Then he would return with a truckload of comic books, which he would sort through and put up for sale or trade. Within eight years he opened up three more stores, including one in Baltimore's Inner Harbor tourist district.

Although retail sales and trading were his main business, Geppi picked up extra money distributing comic books to a handful of smaller stores. When his primary distributor moved to Florida and (eventually) experienced money problems, Geppi picked up pieces of the company and became an active distributor. He named his new company Diamond, taken from the diamond-shaped imprint used by Marvel Comics to identify nonreturnable merchandise.

Geppi proved to be an able distributor. His company grew nearly 50 percent annually as he swallowed up smaller competitors. Today, Diamond controls nearly half of the comic book distribution market with sales exceeding $200 million annually. The company has nearly 1,000 employees and 27 warehouses in three countries. And Geppi owns 100 percent of the company.

Stephen Geppi has expanded into ventures beyond comic books. At Ernst & Young's regional Entrepreneur of the Year banquet in Baltimore in 1993,

Geppi spoke with several people who were organizing a team to purchase the Baltimore Orioles. The venture appealed to the lifelong city resident and Oriole fan, who joined writer Tom Clancy and other investors by writing a check for his $5 million share.

Geppi also purchased one of America's oldest publications, the *Baltimore Magazine,* in 1994. This regional monthly publication has a circulation of 50,000, giving Geppi an opportunity to promote, entertain, and inform the city and suburbs. He has also launched other publishing ventures and opened Diamond International Galleries, devoted to comics, comic collectibles, and related art for high-end collectors from throughout the world.

SOURCES: Diamond Comic Distributors archives; Michael Warshaw, "From Mailman to Millionaire," *Success* magazine, June 1994

Louis Gerlinger Sr., George T. Gerlinger

[Willamette Industries, Inc.]

Louis Gerlinger Sr. was born in 1853 in Alsace, France. At age 17, he immigrated to the United States, settling in Chicago, Illinois. There, he was married and raised four children while building a successful store- and saloon-fixture business. At the age of 41, Gerlinger became intrigued with the Pacific Northwest. He sold off his holdings and moved his family to Portland, Oregon. He quickly acquired an interest in Clark County, Washington, timberlands and built the Portland, Vancouver & Yakima Railroad.

In 1900, Gerlinger sold off his Clark County properties and purchased 7,000 acres of timberland in Polk County, Oregon. To reach the hundreds of square miles of untouched Douglas fir and other high-grade timber, he incorporated the Salem, Falls City, and Western Railway one year later, and set out to build a railroad from the Willamette River at Salem to the Oregon coast.

George Theodore Gerlinger was born on January 15, 1876, in Chicago, Illinois, son of Louis and his wife, Sophia (Hollacher) Gerlinger. He was raised in Chicago and attended public schools. In 1897, the family moved to the Pacific Northwest. While his father had an early interest in railroads, George preferred logging and sawmilling and established a logging operation near Yacolt, Washington. In 1903, he married Irene Hazard, and the couple eventually had four children, two of whom died in infancy.

After losing his first logging venture to fire, George and some investors established The Falls City Lumber Company near his father's Oregon railroad. Concurrently, Louis Gerlinger acquired the Cone Lumber Company, which he folded into his railroad and timberland holdings, renaming the venture the Willamette Valley Lumber Company. During the first year of operation, 1906, the company employed 40 workers. By 1910, sales of lumber, slabwood, lath, shingles, and moldings exceeded $250,000.

George Gerlinger felt that commercial developers and government agencies could work in partnership for sound land management. Through his efforts, the state established the Board of Forestry in 1911. Two years later he was appointed to the Board of Forestry, a post he held until his death more than 30 years later.

By 1920, the Gerlinger family and another family, the Pittocks, were the sole owners of the Willamette Valley Lumber Company. When H. L. Pittock died, the Clark family, who were successful sawmill operators, purchased the Pittock stake and remained silent partners. By this time, the company owned more than 11,000 acres of timberland containing over 334 million board feet of timber. Net assets of the company exceeded $1.5 million.

Gerlinger continued his work with the Board of Forestry after his retirement from daily management at Willamette. He also became active with the National Lumber Manufacturers' Association, being elected president in 1944. George T. Gerlinger died in October 1948 at the age of 72.

SOURCES: Willamette Industries, Inc. archives; Catherine Baldwin Dunn, *Making the Most of the Best,* Willamette Industries, 1982 and 1994

Amadeo P. Giannini

[Transamerica Corporation]

Amadeo Giannini worked as a young man distributing produce throughout California. In 1904 he established a small bank named the Bank of Italy. Through time, his enterprise grew into the Bank of America and an affiliated venture known as Transamerica. At the time of his death, Giannini controlled the world's largest private banking system.

Amadeo Peter Giannini, known to his friends as "A.P.," was born on May 6, 1870, to Italian parents in San Jose, California. He obtained his first job at age 13 with a San Francisco produce commission house, where he worked well into his 20s traveling throughout California, buying produce from growers and distributing it to small retailers. He eventually became a partner in the firm, but sold his stake in 1901.

Throughout his young career, Giannini befriended many of California's small-business owners. He concluded that the owners, their communities, and the entire state would benefit if there were a bank system that focused on the small entrepreneur rather than wealthy, established customers.

On October 17, 1904, Giannini launched the Bank of Italy in the North Beach section of San Francisco with paid-in capital of $150,000. The bank reached out to the region's small-business community, promoting its business services and asking for their support. By the end of the first year, assets grew to $700,000. In 1907 Giannini opened his first branch office and in 1909 opened his first out-of-town branch in San Jose. At the close of that fifth year, the Bank of Italy had total resources of over $2.5 million.

His success in the West led Giannini to New York City, where in 1918 he established the Bancitaly Corporation, which soon absorbed five other local banks. Undaunted by federal regulators, he established Transamerica Corporation as a holding company not only for his banking interests, but also as a vehicle to enter into nonbanking activities. The new venture was a billion-dollar organization, thanks to the $850 million in Bank of Italy resources and $300 million in Bancitaly Corporation resources.

One of Giannini's first acquisitions with Transamerica was the Farmers' & Mechanics' Bank of Sacramento, California. However, the bank's owner insisted that Giannini also buy his other venture, Pacific National Fire Insurance. Giannini agreed, and immediately transformed all his bank managers into insurance agents, a practice consistent with his vision of owning "financial supermarkets." The action was short-lived, however, due to protests from independent insurance agents in California. The insurance segment of Transamerica was strengthened with the March 1930 acquisition of the Occidental Life Insurance Company of California.

At about the same time, Giannini sought to consolidate his California banks under a single roof. Maneuvering through a labyrinth of local, state, and federal regulations, he was able to merge all his California holdings into one entity, the Bank of America, in 1930. It was the fourth-largest bank in America (the top three were in New York City) in terms of deposits (approximately $1 billion) and first in terms of branches and number of depositors.

In the aftermath of the Depression, government regulation of banking was further tightened, particularly with respect to the rights of holding companies and interstate banking. In response, Transamerica spun off the Bank of America as an independent entity in July of 1937.

Giannini died on June 3, 1949 while still serving as chairman and chief executive officer of Transamerica. His son, Mario Giannini, had served as president of the Bank of America since 1936 and on Transamerica's board, where he was the last remaining link between the two organizations, until his own death in 1952.

Today, Transamerica is a diversified insurance, leasing, financial services, and real estate company. The company is based in its landmark Transamerica Pyramid, the tallest (48 stories) building in San Francisco. In 1968, the Bank of America became BankAmerica Corporation. Today, it serves customers through more than 1,900 offices in the western United States and in 36 other countries.

SOURCE: Transamerica Corporation archives, George H. Koster with E. Elizabeth Summers, *The Transamerica Story: 50 Years of Service and Looking Forward,* Transamerica Corporation, 1978

Orville H. Gibson

[Gibson Guitar Corporation]

Orville H. Gibson invented a new way to make a mandolin, and the company that bore his name eventually became the world's best-known maker of guitars, banjos, and basses, as well as mandolins.

Gibson was born in 1856 on a farm near the small town of Chateaugay, New York, within sight of the Canadian border, the youngest of five children. By 1881 he had moved west to Kalamazoo, Michigan. He worked as a clerk for several local businesses, including a shoe store and a restaurant. Surviving photographs indicate that he played guitar and was also involved in theatrical productions.

The most popular fretted instrument of the 1890s was the mandolin, the small eight-stringed relative of the lute. The standard instrument was an Italian "bowlback" style, with a body made of thin wooden ribs that were bent and then glued together. The top was a flat piece of spruce with a slight bend or break across the middle. It was a relatively fragile instrument with a delicate sound.

Gibson envisioned an entirely different type of mandolin, based on his belief that wood in its natural state—unstressed and unencumbered—would produce the purest tone. His patent, granted in 1898, stated his point clearly: "Heretofore, mandolins and like instruments have been constructed of too many separate parts."

He carved the rims and neck for his mandolin out of a single piece of wood (he preferred walnut). The back, also carved from a single piece, resembled a shallow bowl or plate. For the spruce top, he borrowed an idea from the violin, again carving (rather than bending) the top into an arched shape. The oldest surviving instrument made by Gibson is an unusual ten-string mandolin-guitar dated 1894.

By 1895, Gibson had quit his clerking jobs and had opened for business as a manufacturer of musical instruments. Working alone in a shop in his living quarters in downtown Kalamazoo, he began making "The Gibson" mandolins in two standard styles. His first style had a symmetrical, pear-shaped body outline that he called style "A"; his second model, the "F," had an ornate scroll on one bout of the body, and the body came to a point at three places.

Gibson's mandolins and guitars were louder and sturdier than any others of the day, and he was soon receiving more orders than he could fill. A mandolin teacher from New York state wrote to him with an order for 50 instruments, asking how much they would cost and when he could expect delivery. Gibson replied: "$100 each and 50 years."

Gibson obviously needed to his expand his production capability, and the opportunity to do so came in 1902 from five Kalamazoo businessmen. He granted them the right to use his name and his lone patent, and he agreed to consult and teach artisans how to build instruments, but he had apparently had his fill of the instrument business. Although he was given 60 shares of stock in the new Gibson Mandolin-Guitar Mfg. Co., Ltd., he was not a partner.

Within six months, Gibson's relationship with the company had deteriorated to the point that the board of managers (directors) resolved "O. H. Gibson be paid only for the actual time he works for the Company." A few months later, Gibson sold his stock in the company. The company paid him a royalty for the next five years and then, when that agreement expired, a yearly pension of $500.

By 1906, Gibson had listed himself as an inventor in the Kalamazoo directory, although there is no evidence that he invented anything else. His 1909 listing as a music teacher offers the only clue as to how he spent his years after the founding of the Gibson Company. He stayed in Kalamazoo long enough to see his namesake instruments become the standards of the industry. In 1911, Orville Gibson returned to New York, where he died in a sanatorium in Ogdensberg, New York, in 1918 at the age of 62.

SOURCES: Gibson Guitar Corporation archives; Walter Carter, "Gibson History"

George Giddings, Orin F. Lewis, Rueping Family

[Giddings & Lewis, Inc.]

Giddings & Lewis is the largest machine tool manufacturer in America. Its history can be traced to the Rueping Leather Company, which was established in Fond du Lac, Wisconsin, in 1854. Five years later, John Bonnell established a small machine shop across the street from Rueping. Over time, the Rueping family financed the growth of the company and, eventually, assumed management of the company for a period of time.

The Fond du Lac region of Wisconsin was a prosperous lumber industry center during the 1800s. Rough logs were floated along Lake Winnebago, then stripped, sawed, and prepared for shipping. John Bonnell's small machine shop served this growing industry from the corner of Doty and Rees Streets in Fond du Lac (which to this day is the site of Giddings & Lewis). In subsequent years, the operation continued to grow while passing through the hands of several owners and going through several name changes.

George Giddings was born in Sheboygan, Wisconsin, in 1852 and moved with his family to Fond du Lac 14 years later. He pursued farming until 1872, then worked in a flour mill for the next three years. In 1876, he joined Colonel C. H. DeGroat, a distinguished Civil War officer, as part owner of the machine shop. Two years later, he married Hattie Belle Hunter.

Orin F. Lewis was born in Warren County, New York, on August 17, 1832. In 1847, he relocated to Rosendale, Wisconsin, and engaged in farming and the selling of agricultural implements. He married Mary A. Murray on December 31, 1856, and the couple eventually had five children.

Bonnell's machine shop, known as the Novelty Iron Works, became DeGroat, Giddings & Lewis in the 1880s, when Lewis joined DeGroat and Giddings as an owner. The three focused on manufacturing sawmill machinery and steam engines, and they quickly established a national reputation for high-quality equipment. Eventually, DeGroat sold his interest to his partners who, in 1895, incorporated the business as The Giddings & Lewis Manufacturing Company.

At the close of the century, the lumber industry experienced a significant downturn. In response, partners Giddings and Lewis sold off their sawmill machinery line and focused on machine tools. Throughout the early history of

Giddings & Lewis, the Rueping family was busy building a business empire across the street.

William Rueping immigrated to America from Germany in 1853 and the following year established William Rueping & Sons, a small tanning business in Fond du Lac. One of William's sons, Frederick, was the original tanner in the venture. Frederick and his wife, Margaret Thuerwaechter Rueping, had six children. The oldest, F. J. Rueping, born January 26, 1867, would eventually play a prominent role in the growth of Giddings & Lewis.

After learning business and marketing through internships at various American and German companies, F. J. Rueping entered the family tanning business in 1888. By 1893, Frederick had purchased his brothers' interest in the business, leaving himself and F.J. as the sole owners. Shortly thereafter, Frederick's health failed and he retired from the business, passing control to his 26-year-old son. The name of the business was changed to the Fred Rueping Leather Company.

In 1906, George Giddings was in failing health and sold his share of Giddings & Lewis to Henry Rueping, F.J.'s uncle. Over the next several years, Henry obtained loans from Frederick Rueping to help expand the business. In a few years, however, the debts became significant and sales were sluggish.

After Frederick Rueping died, Giddings & Lewis owed considerable money to his estate, which refused to endorse further loans to the company. Some relief was provided by a surge in orders attributed to World War I. However, the remaining owners prodded one another to assume full ownership of the company.

Finally, in 1916, F. J. Rueping acquired the shares of the other owners and turned his attention to building the company. He quickly added an experienced management team and upgraded the product line. In 1920, the name of the company was changed to the Giddings & Lewis Machine Tool Company to more accurately reflect the product line. By 1929, the company was enjoying comfortable sales and was poised for another growth surge. A team of investors extended an offer to buy F.J.'s holdings and retire the debt owed to the estate of Frederick Rueping, which was accepted.

Today, Giddings & Lewis is not only the oldest machine tool company in America, it is also the largest, with annual sales of more than $700 million. The company has more than 4,000 employees worldwide.

SOURCE: Giddings & Lewis, Inc., archives

Henry Glade, Alva R. Kinney

[ConAgra, Inc.]

Henry Glade, the youngest of 12 children, was born in Hanover, Germany. A few years after his birth, his family immigrated to the United States. Tragically, his parents died in New Orleans, and the children were forced to travel alone on the Mississippi River to Jackson County, Iowa, where relatives were awaiting their arrival. Henry was raised by a sister and went to work at an early age in Dubuque, Iowa, where he was managing a grinding mill by the age of 14.

By the early 1880s, Glade moved to Nebraska and established a mill at Columbus. Shortly thereafter, he acquired another grain mill at Grand Island and promptly rebuilt it with a steam-powered roller mill. His ventures prospered over the next two decades and soon employed most of his family—although two of his sons first played professional baseball.

Henry Glade died in 1910, and shortly thereafter the business was reorganized as the Henry Glade Milling Company. Over the next ten years, the Glade family continued to operate the plant as smaller operators closed down. By the end of the decade, the company joined discussions with three other milling firms to discuss a merger. The effort was spearheaded by Alva Kinney, who operated the Ravenna Mills of Ravenna, Nebraska.

Alva R. Kinney was raised in the small town of Crete, Nebraska. After graduating from Doane College in 1897, he went to work at Crete Mills, a local milling company. After a brief career as a traveling salesman, Kinney and some associates purchased the Ravenna Mill in 1904. Over the next 15 years, he constantly upgraded the mill, which became quite successful.

In 1919, Kinney succeeded in consolidating the four companies under a new venture named Nebraska Consolidated Mills, and the following year he raised nearly $850,000 through a public stock offering. The company experienced growing pains in its first 15 months, losing nearly $115,000. However, Kinney was able to report a $174,000 profit at the 1922 stockholders' meeting.

Nebraska Consolidated Mills also made its first acquisition in 1922 with the purchase of the Updike Mill in Omaha. Other mills followed, including the Brown Mill at Freemont in 1926 and the Blackburn-Furry Mill at St. Edward in 1928. Kinney also maintained an ongoing rebuilding and renovation program so that none of the facilities fell behind the available technology.

One of the best examples of the company's innovative spirit is its Duncan Hines cake mix. Duncan Hines, a native of Bowling Green, Ohio, worked for a Chicago printing company during the 1930s. He and his wife frequented fine restaurants, and he kept notes on their experiences, which he shared with friends. Eventually, he published a book, *Adventures in Good Eating,* which went through 47 printings over the next 20 years.

At about the same time America came to associate the name Duncan Hines with "good eating," Nebraska Consolidated Mills developed a cake mix that tested well with the general public. The company convinced the successful gourmet to license his name to its mix, and in 1951 Duncan Hines Cake Mix was introduced. The company projected first-year sales of 100,000 cases, but within six months it had sold six times that amount. The Duncan Hines Division was later sold to Procter & Gamble.

By 1970, the company was a highly diversified food conglomerate that had outgrown its original name, and in 1971 the company adopted a new name—ConAgra. Today, ConAgra is the second-largest food processor in

America, with more than 90,000 employees worldwide and annual sales of nearly $25 billion.

SOURCE: Jane E. Limprecht, *ConAgra Who?*, ConAgra, Inc., 1989

Alexander Glass

[Wheeling Steel Corporation]

Alexander Glass was born and raised in the Ohio River town of Wheeling, West Virginia. His maternal grandfather, Thomas Harris, was an ironmaker in England who had immigrated to Wheeling, where he established a "hoop iron" factory. His father, Andrew Glass, was a cofounder of the La Belle Iron Works. While supervising the transportation of Missouri iron ore, the elder Glass became ill and died in St. Louis in 1872.

In 1873, 14-year-old Alexander Glass set out to help support the family. At the time, there were several small iron manufacturers in Wheeling, most of which focused on the production of cut nails. In fact, nearly one-third of all nails used in America were thought to have been made in Wheeling.

Young Glass went to work in the nail department at La Belle Iron Works, packing nails into kegs for $2.50 per week. Soon he was promoted to apprentice nail feeder, then to full-fledged nail feeder at the impressive salary of nearly $25.00 for a 60-hour workweek. Glass was able to save most of his money and, hoping for a better life, left the mill to attend the Iron City college at nearby Pittsburgh, Pennsylvania.

Upon graduation from a business program, Glass went to work for the post office. He quickly grew restless with the pace and longed for the excitement of manufacturing. Raising $1,000, he moved to Nashville, Tennessee, where he took over the lease of a paper mill. However, the unreliable water supply near the plant led to poor-quality paper, and Glass shut down the plant and moved back to Wheeling.

Two of the most powerful men in the Ohio Valley steel industry were brothers Samuel and Alexander Laughlin. Glass joined their Junction Iron company at Mingo Junction, Ohio, as a bookkeeper. Here, his natural organizational and financial management skills became apparent, and he quickly advanced with the company.

When the local economy soured in the late 1880s, Glass moved west to another steelmaking center—eastern Chicago and northern Indiana—where he worked in various management capacities. However, this venture didn't last, and Glass returned once again to Wheeling.

This time, he didn't apply for a job. In 1890, the 31-year-old Glass and two partners raised $10,000 and launched their own company, the Wheeling Corrugating Company. They located in facilities next to the Whitaker Iron Company, which supplied their sheets. Later, when the Whitaker and Laughlin companies jointly acquired a steel plant in Portsmouth, Ohio, Glass was invited to help build the enterprise.

Once Glass built both enterprises into strong companies, he turned his attention to consolidating other Wheeling-area plants. By 1920, Wheeling Corrugating, the Whitaker company, La Belle Iron Works, and Wheeling Steel and Iron were consolidated into a single company known as Wheeling Steel Corporation, and Glass was named chairman.

SOURCE: Company publication, Robert L. Plummer, *Sixty-Five Years of Iron and Steel in Wheeling*

Francis H. Glidden

[The Glidden Company]

After working in the family dry goods business and shipping business, Francis Glidden obtained a sales position with a New York varnish manufacturer. He was quickly promoted to manager of the Cleveland office. After learning all aspects of the business, Glidden established his own varnish and paint firm, which became The Glidden Company.

Francis Harrington Glidden was born on May 24, 1832, in New Castle, Maine. At age 14 he dropped out of school and went to work in his brother's general store. Three years later he joined the family shipping business, putting out to sea on a boat built by his uncle. Three years after that, Glidden decided that sea life was too rough. Among other difficulties he encountered was the loss of his left eye in an accident. So, in 1852, at age 20, he returned to the dry goods business. He married Winifred Kavanagh Waters of New Castle, Maine, in 1854, and the couple eventually had eight children.

The store failed, and in 1859 Glidden moved his wife and (at that time) two children to Alabama, where he entered the steamship business. The timing of the move was poor, as the Civil War broke out a year later. Glidden was forced into service for the Confederacy, wearing their uniform but unarmed, while his family was restricted to Mobile to guarantee of his good behavior.

At one point during the war, Glidden's ship was seized by General Polk at Lewis Ferry, where it was used with other boats to form a pontoon bridge for Polk and his 13,000 troops to evade the pursuit of Union General William T. Sherman. A few days after that, General Polk was killed by cannon fire. Glidden was able to return to his family in Mobile, where they sat through a constant barrage of cannon fire as the Union forces captured the city. Happily, the Glidden family returned to New England at the end of the war.

Upon returning to Maine in late 1865, 33-year-old Glidden once again was employed in his brother's dry goods store. Six months later, in April 1866, he was recruited by the firm of William Tilden & Nephew, an established varnish business in New York City, to serve as a salesman in the western states (which, at the time, included Ohio and Michigan). Two years later, the company established a permanent branch office in Cleveland, Ohio, and named 36-year-old Glidden as the manager. The Glidden family then established residence in Cleveland in December 1868.

At the time, Cleveland already had an established paint and varnish company that was founded by Henry Alden Sherman in 1860. He was joined by Edward Porter Williams in 1870, forming Sherwin-Williams with $2,000.

In March 1875, at the age of 43, Glidden entered into a partnership with Levi C. Brackett and Thomas N. Bolles, both from New York City, to produce their own line of varnish. The company, Glidden, Brackett & Company, was established in Cleveland with $20,000 capital. The company assets included two 150-gallon kettles, a horse and wagon, a one-story building, and one employee.

Within two years Brackett and Bolles had retired from the firm. Shortly thereafter, a member of the Joy family, into which Glidden's sister married, joined the firm, and by 1883 it incorporated as The Glidden and Joy Varnish Company. In 1892, William Joy sold his interest to Glidden, and in 1894 the name was changed to The Glidden Varnish Company.

By this time the company employed 18 workers and was producing a variety of products for finishing carriages, wagons, furniture, and pianos. In 1895 they introduced a colored varnish, and in 1903 Glidden introduced Jap-a-Lac, which quickly became an American favorite.

In 1902, Glidden reflected on his accomplishments. He was obviously a man driven to build a business and economic security for his wife and children. After several unsuccessful ventures in other fields, Glidden found success in varnish and paints. He made the following observation about the keys to entrepreneurial success.

> To be ambitious is a good qualification, when tempered with caution and system. Economy consists in looking after small details, as well as the larger ones. Honesty and Integrity should go hand in hand always, as they assure a good reputation, which is essential to all business enterprises, where permanency is to be desired, and attained, as it forms one of the important adjuncts to your capital. The respect of employees is also a factor in the operation of every industry. Seek to obtain good help, treat all with consideration, and a kindly recognition.

In 1905, fire destroyed his entire plant. He built another factory and resumed production. Sales reached $2 million annually, and Glidden opened branches in New York, Chicago, and St. Louis. In 1910, he acquired the Blackwell Varnish Company of Toronto, his first venture in Canada.

By 1917, Francis Glidden was 85 years old. Henry A. Sherwin had died the year before, and two of the directors of Sherwin-Williams had decided they were ready to run their own paint and varnish company. Within two years, Robert H. Horsburgh and Adrian D. Joyce formed a syndicate, bought out Glidden and his family, recapitalized the company at $2.5 million, and acquired 11 other paint and varnish manufacturers.

Francis H. Glidden died on September 24, 1922, at the age of 91. His elaborate residence, named Inglewood, is still occupied by his descendants. Glidden was personally involved with all phases of construction of this mansion in 1910, which was designed by his cousin, architect Edwin Glidden of Baltimore.

In 1967, The Glidden Company merged with SCM Corporation, producers of the Smith-Corona typewriters and Marchant calculators. In 1986, Imperial Chemical Industries (ICI) PLC of England acquired ownership, creating the world's leading paint manufacturer.

SOURCE: The Glidden Company archives

B. Thomas Golisano

[Paychex, Inc.]

B. Thomas Golisano was born and raised in Irondequoit, New York. After graduating from high school, he was hired by a Rochester, New York, bank to count bills deposited by local department stores. After three months, he enrolled at Alfred State Technical College to study business.

After graduation from college, Golisano held a number of positions at Monroe Savings Bank, Burroughs Corporation, and Electronic Accounting Systems. With the last employer, Golisano was introduced to contract payroll services that were provided to medium and large businesses in the Rochester area.

Golisano suspected the company could broaden its client list considerably by marketing its services to smaller businesses. He took a trip to the library and was astonished to discover that 98 percent of all companies have less than 100 employees. Convinced that an entire untapped market existed, he drew up a plan and presented it to his superiors. "Not interested," they said.

To 30-year-old Golisano, the news was more of an opportunity than a rejection. In late 1970, with $3,000 capital, he launched a small company named Paymaster and targeted Rochester's small-business community. His five-year goal was to sign up 300 clients.

At the end of the first year, he had 40. After a few years of hard work, all-night sleepovers in the computer room, and meeting his own payroll with a MasterCard, Golisano reached his goal. Five years after he launched the business, he was even able to write a paycheck to himself.

Starting in 1975, Golisano expanded his concept to other cities through six franchises and 11 joint ventures. Eventually, the system became too unwieldy, and in 1979 all the operations were brought together and incorporated as Paychex. Four years later, the company made its first public stock offering.

For the next decade, Paychex expanded so rapidly that it constantly appeared on *Inc* magazine's list of fastest-growing companies in the United States. Today, employment has reached 4,800, and the company serves nearly 250,000 clients nationwide. In fiscal 1996, Paychex generated $566 million in revenue.

In August, 1996, Paychex merged with National Business Solutions of St. Petersburg, Florida. The new Paychex Business Solutions division provides small businesses with employee benefit, human resource, and information services.

SOURCE: Paychex, Inc., archives

Benjamin F. Goodrich

[BFGoodrich Company]

Benjamin Franklin Goodrich was born on November 4, 1841, in the small farming village of Ripley, New York. He was orphaned at age eight and went to live with his mother's brother, John Dinsmore. Goodrich performed well academically and, at age 17, entered the Medical School of Western Reserve College (now Case Western Reserve) in Cleveland, Ohio, to study medicine.

At the outbreak of the Civil War, Goodrich enlisted with the 9th New York Cavalry. During the war he completed his medical studies at the University of Pennsylvania. He then transferred to the Medical Corps, and at age 19 he was appointed assistant surgeon in the Army of the United States.

Returning to New York after the war, Dr. Goodrich practiced medicine briefly before going into the real estate business with a partner. The turning point in his career came in 1869, when the partners traded real estate valued at $10,000 for stock in the small Hudson River Rubber Company at Hastings-on-Hudson, New York.

The company struggled financially, and Goodrich was convinced that the operation wouldn't be profitable in New York. Instead, he believed it should be moved west of the Allegheny Mountains, where adequate power, transportation, and labor could be found.

With encouragement—and loans—from several prominent residents in Akron, Ohio, Goodrich relocated his company to what would soon become the center of the world's rubber industry. On December 30, 1870, Goodrich purchased land along the Ohio Canal in Akron, Ohio. The company was reincorporated as Goodrich, Tew & Company, reflecting Goodrich's partnership with his brother-in-law, Harvey Tew.

The company's first building, opened in 1871, was a two-story rubber factory and single-story boiler room. The first products were fire hose and belting, but the plant was soon producing bottle stoppers, rubber rings for canning jars, tubing, billiard cushions, and other products.

The company's first-year revenues of $50,000, however, fell short of expectations, forcing Goodrich to borrow additional capital from local businessmen. Goodrich, Tew & Company almost failed again in 1874 in the midst of a severe nationwide depression. The company reorganized as B. F. Goodrich & Company, and in 1875 investor George Perkins backed an additional loan and assumed management of the company's finances. By the end of the decade, the company returned to prosperity.

Goodrich established a firm foundation for his company, but his health prevented him from witnessing its continuing growth and prosperity. In 1888, weakened by tuberculosis, he retired to Colorado Springs, Colorado. Less than a month later, on August 8, 1888, Dr. Benjamin F. Goodrich died of a hemorrhage at age 46.

By 1895, BFGoodrich was Akron's largest and most profitable employer. As other rubber companies settled in Akron, the city became the

"Rubber Capital of the World." The company was on its way to establishing its reputation as one of our nation's premier companies, with manufacturing operations, research facilities, and offices eventually located around the world. Today, BFGoodrich is a leading aerospace and specialty chemicals company.

SOURCE: BFGoodrich archives

William R. Grace

[W. R. Grace & Company]

William Russell Grace was born on May 10, 1832, to James and Eleanor Mary (Russell) Grace while they were on vacation in the village of Riverstown, near the Cove of Cork, Ireland. Young William was raised on the expansive family farm alongside his six brothers and sisters, as well as several cousins and neighbors.

At age 14, William grew restless and ran away to sea, eventually landing in New York City, where he became familiar with the shipping industry. Two years later, in 1848, he returned to the family farm in Ireland and enrolled in school. However, Grace had tasted the sea, and this interest continued. In 1850, he launched William Russell Grace & Co. to broker transportation for emigrants en route to America.

The following year, Grace accompanied his father to Peru, where William found work with a shipping business, John Bryce & Company in Callao. Within three years he was granted a partnership in the business, which expanded considerably. He also became involved with the marketing of guano (bird droppings), a prized fertilizer.

In 1859, Grace married Lillius Gilchrest, the daughter of a sea captain. Shortly thereafter, Grace, who suffered from Bright's disease, took his young bride back to Ireland. Tragically, two of the couple's three daughters died in infancy.

The family left Ireland in 1863 and stopped briefly in New York City. However, the country was still embroiled in the Civil War, so they sailed to Peru, where Grace reentered business with the Bryce firm. The association was once again short-lived. As the Civil War ended in America, Grace learned that considerable business opportunities were opening up. By 1866, the family was in New York City. Grace quickly launched shipping and real estate ventures and within seven years had amassed a $500,000 fortune.

In 1880, Grace was elected mayor of New York City as the city was recovering from a damaging corruption scandal. He served two successful terms during the early 1880s and would eventually be remembered as one of the finest mayors in the history of the city. Despite public pressure, Grace did not seek reelection in 1886. He wanted to devote more time to his business interests and his children, who by then included two daughters and a son.

Throughout the 1880s and 1890s, Grace replaced much of his fleet with steamships. His business ventures grew into three general categories: import/export, industrial, and transportation. His years in South America provided Grace with considerable contacts, and the bulk of the company's importing and exporting activities involved South American products such as coffee and cocoa beans.

Grace also took advantage of opportunities to launch a number of manufacturing ventures, primarily in South America. This included sugar and paper-making companies in Peru, nitrate soda mills in Chile, as well as several cotton mills, flour mills, coffee and cocoa plants, tin mines, and a host of other industries throughout the continent. Ocean transportation of both passengers and cargo remained the heart of Grace's empire, led by companies such as the Grace Line.

William Russell Grace died on March 21, 1904. He was succeeded by his son, Joseph Grace. In 1945, Joseph passed control to his son, J. Peter Grace. Today, W. R. Grace & Co. (which is no longer family owned or managed) is a leading global supplier of flexible packaging and specialty chemicals, with annual sales in excess of $3 billion and 18,000 employees worldwide.

SOURCE: Lawrence A. Clayton, *Grace: W. R. Grace & Co., The Formative Years 1850–1930,* Jameson Books, Ottawa, IL, 1985

Ted Gronlund, Dick Nellis, Charles Wall, Caswell Holloway

[Wood-Mode]

As America braced for World War II during the late 1930s, the priorities for material such as steel shifted toward the war effort. To four salesmen for Whitehead Monel Kitchens Company, the impact was intense. Ted Gronlund and Dick Nellis of New York, and Charles Wall and Caswell Holloway of Philadelphia, found themselves with nothing to sell.

Undaunted, the four were completely confident in their ability to build and market quality kitchens. In 1942, they purchased a small lumber mill in Kreamer, Pennsylvania, and started their new company: Wood-Metal Industries. For three of the founders, it would be a pursuit that consumed the rest of their lives. (Caswell Holloway left the organization in 1948.)

Although the war imposed restrictions on kitchen sales, the company took advantage of other opportunities presented by the military: building cook's tables, coops for the Army's carrier pigeons, shell cases, ladders, and signal corps equipment. Because of the special demands imposed by difficult climates such as the South Pacific, the company became quality conscious from its first day in business.

As the war closed, the founders were positioned to participate in the post-war building boom. A second plant in Beech Bottom, West Virginia, was acquired. Growth was so rapid that a new problem surfaced: the ability to obtain a reliable supply of high-quality lumber. The founders responded by obtaining timber rights on local land and building a sawmill, which provided most of the raw material that was needed during the housing boom of the 1950s. In fact, to this day most of the lumber used by the company comes from within a 100-mile radius of Kreamer.

In the mid-1950s the company faced an identity issue. It was still known as Wood-Metal Industries, yet not a single metal cabinet was made at the Kreamer plant. Moreover, the trend was definitely wood over metal in American homes. The employees were brought into the process, and a secretary in the sales department won a $50 award for coining the name "Wood-Mode."

The founders of the company continually pursued unique marketing campaigns. The well-known game show *The Price is Right* featured the company and offered a custom-built kitchen as a grand prize. Later, the company distributed their "Picturebook" of kitchen ideas, which soon put more than 40 pages of Wood-Mode cabinets on coffee tables throughout America.

What began as Harry Kreamer's planing mill in 1942 has been transformed into more than 1 million square feet of design, production, and warehouse space. Yet Wood-Mode continues to serve as one of the premier cabinet manufacturers in America while maintaining their small-town quality. Not only have the founders passed control on to their children and grandchildren, the workforce at the plant is filled with second- and third-generation employees.

SOURCE: Wood-Mode archives

Leroy R. Grumman

[Grumman Aircraft Engineering Corporation]

After serving as a pilot in the Navy, Leroy Grumman accepted a job with Loening, a builder of military planes. Rather than move after the company was sold, Grumman established the Grumman Aircraft Engineering Corporation in a run-down garage in Baldwin, Long Island. Grumman Corporation eventually grew into Long Island's largest company and one of the nation's leading aerospace companies.

Leroy Randle Grumman was born on January 4, 1895, in the small town of Huntington, New York to George T. Grumman, a New England carriage builder, and Grace Conklin Grumman. He grew up on Long Island and worked his way through Cornell University, where he received a B.S. degree in mechanical engineering in 1916. At Cornell he met Rose Werther, whom he married in 1921, and the couple eventually had four children.

When the United States entered World War I in 1917, Grumman enlisted in the U.S. Navy Reserve. Over the next several months, the military sent him to various training centers, including Columbia University and the Massachusetts Institute of Technology. A year later, he received his commission as an ensign and was assigned as a flight instructor for the bombing squadron at Pensacola, Florida.

After the war, Grumman was assigned to the League Island Naval Yard near Philadelphia, Pennsylvania. There, he met Albert and Grover Loening, two pioneer aircraft builders, who offered Grumman a job with their company. He readily accepted and became a test pilot of the planes that he personally helped to design and build. Eventually he became the general manager of their Loening Aeronautical Engineering Corporation in Manhattan, assuming responsibility for the design and development of military and civilian aircraft.

In 1928, a banking firm purchased the Loening organization. One year later, it was merged into the Curtiss-Wright conglomerate, and the Long Island operation was closed. Grumman and his fellow employees were told to move to Bristol, Pennsylvania, or lose their jobs.

On December 5, 1929, two months after the stock market crashed, Leroy Grumman elected to start his own business, the Grumman Aircraft Engineering Corporation. With about $15,000 of his own funds, $30,000 from the Loening brothers, and $15,000 from five other aeronautical engineers and businessmen, the company rented an abandoned garage in Baldwin, Long Island, and started repairing and servicing Loening aircraft. To keep its 15 employees (former employees of the Loening company) busy, the company made aluminum truck bodies during slow periods.

However, Grumman had his sights on military contracts. The Navy was intrigued with Grumman's retractable landing gear and awarded the company a contract to build two amphibian floats for $33,700. Grumman personally flew with the Navy test pilot on the maiden flight, launched from a battleship. The Navy was impressed and subsequently ordered 21 more planes.

The contract enabled Grumman to move to better facilities. In 1937, the company acquired an expansive track of land, including potato fields and a polo field, in Bethpage, Long Island. It raised a manufacturing plant, built its own runway, and immediately started design work on a new carrier-based fighter plane that would incorporate its retractable landing gear. Such an innovation would, by company estimates, increase the fighter's speed by 20 to 30 miles per hour.

Soon afterward, the Navy approached Grumman and asked if the company would put their retractable landing gear on planes built by other manufacturers. Grumman argued against that and, instead, secured a Navy contract to build the entire fighter. The plane, called the FF-1, was an instant success and led to a large contract.

Grumman also pursued nonmilitary markets. In the mid-1930s he introduced a line of luxury amphibian planes that came to be known as the "Grey Goose" that was popular to wealthy sports enthusiasts. By 1937, Grumman was able to offer stock in his growing company to the general public. His company had grown to nearly 800 employees, with sales approaching $5 million annually.

When America entered World War II, Grumman's facilities became very busy. Orders for his planes poured in, not only from the U.S. military, but from France, England, and even Greece. Orders were being placed for hundreds, even thousands, of planes throughout the war.

Grumman and his employees worked at a furious pace not only to build planes, but to design more efficient models. In 1941, Grumman successfully built a model with folding wings that would reliably lock into place when ready for combat. This enabled the Navy to store considerably more Grumman Wildcats, Hellcats, and Avengers on its aircraft carriers.

Altogether, Grumman built 16,945 combat aircraft and 628 utility aircraft during the war. The Eastern Aircraft Division of General Motors built another 13,473 Grumman-designed aircraft. Employment at the Bethpage plant had increased from 800 to more than 25,000 in four short years.

After the war, Leroy Grumman relinquished his role as president but maintained his position as chairman of the board. In the postwar years, Grumman continued to supply military markets, and eventually pursued opportunities in space with the National Aeronautics and Space Administration (NASA). He also led the company into nonmilitary markets, such as the production of crop dusters, and even nonaerospace products, such as aluminum canoes. By 1969, Grumman surpassed the $1 billion annual sales mark and employed more than 36,000 people.

Grumman resigned as board chairman in 1966, then left the board altogether in 1972, and died in 1982.

Northrop Grumman was formed in 1994 when Northrop Corporation acquired the Grumman Corporation. Also in 1994, the company completed the acquisition of Vought Aircraft, a major producer of military and commercial aerostructures. In 1996, the defense and electronics systems business of Westinghouse Electric Corporation was acquired, and the company now employs more than 47,000 people.

SOURCE: Grumman History Center archives

Charles Gulden

[Gulden's Mustard]

Charles Gulden was born on September 23, 1843, in New York City. By the age of 15, he was employed as an engraver. Two years later, he went to work for his uncle, who owned the Union Mustard Mills. After serving with a reserve regiment at Gettysburg during the Civil War, he returned briefly to his uncle's shop.

Gulden opened his own mustard company in 1867. He chose Elizabeth Street in New York for his shop, near the South Street Seaport, where he could easily obtain the mustard seeds and rare spices necessary to mix with vintage vinegars.

By 1883, Gulden's product line included 30 mustard varieties and other products, including olives, capers, cottonseed oil, catsup, and Warwickshire sauce. That year, he moved down the street into a six-story building.

Drawing from his earlier experience as an engraver, Charles Gulden once asked his brother: "Do you think it would help if we were to attach a spoon to each bottle of No. 6, no extra charge?" Soon, the Guldens were attaching fine, imported spoons to each bottle. He increased the visibility of his innovative idea by distributing a catalog of his products printed in color.

In 1891, Charles Gulden Jr. assumed control of the company. Upon his death in 1911, his brother Frank Gulden was named president. It remained under family control until 1962, when the founder's grandson—also named Charles Gulden—orchestrated its sale to American Home Foods Company. The company later became part of International Home Foods.

SOURCE: International Home Foods archives

Joyce Clyde Hall

[Hallmark Cards]

Determined to overcome poverty and a lack of formal education, Joyce Hall went to work as a door-to-door salesman at age eight. After learning the card business with his brothers, he moved to Kansas City and established himself as the region's premiere card distributor. Today, Hallmark Cards is one of the nation's largest privately owned companies.

Joyce Clyde Hall was born on August 29, 1891, in David City, Nebraska, the third of four children born to George and Nancy (Houston) Hall. On the day of his birth, his religious parents were so impressed with a visiting Methodist bishop named Isaac W. Joyce that they named their son after him, leaving Hall with a lifelong chore of explaining his first name.

At age eight, Hall went to work on a neighboring farm. One year later, he started selling cosmetics and soap for the California Perfume Company (which later became Avon). In 1902, his older brothers moved to Norfolk, Nebraska, and opened a bookstore. Soon, the rest of the family joined them, and young Hall went to work in the store for $18 a month.

When he was 16, Hall and his older brothers established the Norfolk Post Card Company. However, the local market couldn't support the venture, and young Hall set his sights higher. At age 18, he quit school, packed two shoe boxes full of postcards, and hopped a train for Kansas City. When he arrived, he secured a room at the YMCA and started calling on drugstores, bookstores, and gift shops.

He quickly outgrew the modest room at the YMCA and hired his first employee. Within a year, most of his family joined him in Kansas City, and by 1912 the Hall Brothers logo started appearing on greeting cards. The line was expanded, and Hall opened retail stores in Kansas City and Chicago.

In 1915, disaster struck when a fire wiped out his entire inventory, putting Hall $17,000 in the hole. One of the early Hallmark cards read: "When you get to the end of your rope, tie a knot in it and hang on." That's exactly what Hall did, and soon the family was back in business. By 1921, the business was growing steadily, and Hall married Elizabeth Ann Dilday. The couple later had three children.

As the company moved from the 1920s into the Depression and World War II, Hall focused on creating a public image for his growing business. First, he devised the phrase "A Hallmark Card," which replaced "Hall Brothers" on the backs of cards. By the 1940s the company had coined the phrase "When You Care Enough to Send the Very Best." He also started sponsoring radio and television shows. He was especially successful with his targeted-appeal "Hallmark Hall of Fame" series, featuring the works of Shakespeare, Ibsen, and many others.

His devotion to the fine arts was also reflected in his cards. He introduced cards by Grandma Moses and Norman Rockwell. Later, he started his "Hallmark Gallery Artists" line, including works from Leonardo da Vinci, Michelangelo, and others. He also established the International Hallmark Art Awards.

In 1966, Joyce Hall stepped down as chairman and was succeeded by his son, Donald J. Hall. Even in retirement, the founder continued to put in full days at the office when he wasn't vacationing. Joyce Clyde Hall died on October 29, 1982, at the age of 91.

SOURCE: Hallmark Cards, Inc. archives

Erle P. Halliburton

[Halliburton Company]

Erle P. Halliburton was born on September 22, 1892, in Henning, Tennessee. He attended school in nearby Ripley, completing elementary and high school in just eight years. His father died when young Erle was only 12, and his widowed mother and her six children were soon living in poverty.

Beginning at age 14, Erle held a number of jobs to help support the family, including locomotive operator, steam crane operator, and even salesman in Brooklyn, New York. In 1910, he enlisted in the U.S. Navy, where he was trained in engineering and hydraulics and operated the Navy's first motor barge. Upon discharge in 1915, he married Vida Taber in Riverside, California.

In 1918, Halliburton went to work for the Perkins Oil Well Cementing Company, which operated primarily in California. The company's owner had developed an innovative way to cement oil wells. Halliburton experimented once too often in his quest to improve the company's methods and was fired. He later claimed, "The two best things that ever happened to me were being hired, and fired, by Perkins."

Unemployed and broke, Halliburton moved to Wichita Falls, Texas. He borrowed a wagon and team of mules from a neighbor, and found a pump and some tools. After building a cement-mixing box, he launched his first business. Not long after that, in 1919, he raised $1,000 from four investors and opened for business as The New Method Oil Well Cementing Company.

Business was tough, however, and Halliburton eventually bought out the interest of his other investors and moved across the state line into Wilson, Oklahoma. Halliburton's wife later recalled her role in the early days. Not only did she raise the family and manage the household, she took orders for jobs, dispatched cementers to various sites, and took care of the employees when they were ill.

After landing a good contract in 1920, Halliburton purchased his first cement wagon and hired several employees, including the neighbor who loaned him the mules to start his business. A year later he moved the business to Duncan, Oklahoma, and put several trucks built by the Four Wheel Drive Corporation into service. Concurrently, he developed and patented several new products, including his highly efficient Jet Mixer for preparing cement in the field.

The Jet Mixer proved valuable in more than the field. Halliburton and his old boss, Almond Perkins, struck a deal. Halliburton was given the right to use Perkins's patented process, and Perkins was granted exclusive use of the Jet Mixer in California and surrounding states. The deal stayed in effect until

1940, when Halliburton bought Perkins Oil Well Cementing Company—the organization that had fired him 21 years earlier.

To feed a growing need for capital, Halliburton devised a creative strategy. He incorporated his 60-employee company as Halliburton Oil Well Cementing Company in 1924 and sold minority interest in the company to seven oil producers, including Magnolia Oil Company (later merged into Mobil), Texas Company (Texaco), Gulf Oil Corporation, Humble Oil (later merged into Exxon), Sun Oil Company, Pure Oil (later merged into Unocal), and the Atlantic Refining Company (Atlantic Richfield).

The capital and client base allowed Halliburton to expand rapidly. By 1932 he had 75 cementing units working in seven states. He reached for international markets, including Canada and South America. By 1938, the company was cementing offshore oil wells.

Halliburton experimented with other businesses as well. He organized Southwest Air Fast Express (Safeway), which offered to fly the mail at bargain-basement rates. His experience with the aeronautics industry paid off during World War II, when Halliburton secured contracts to build aviation equipment.

In 1947, poor health forced Halliburton to step down as president. A year later, the company made its first public stock offering, allowing the new management team to rapidly expand Halliburton operations. Erle Halliburton died on October 13, 1957. At the time of his death, his company had annual revenues of nearly $200 million and 10,000 employees.

Halliburton relocated its corporate headquarters from Duncan to Dallas, Texas, in 1961. One year later, the company made its largest and most significant acquisition, Brown & Root, Inc., a diversified and successful engineering and energy services company founded by Herman and George Brown.

Today, Halliburton continues to be a dominant force in the worldwide energy business, with annual revenues exceeding $6 billion. Many of the company's projects have an international impact. For example, in 1991 Halliburton teamed with fire-fighting companies in Kuwait to extinguish over 300 of the 647 blowout wells caused by Iraqi soldiers during the Persian Gulf war.

SOURCE: Halliburton Company archives

Brenton S. Halsey, Robert C. Williams

[James River Corporation]

When the Ethyl Corporation decided to get out of the paper business, two talented members of its management staff, Brenton Halsey and Robert Williams, offered to buy the modest division. Through internal growth and more than 40 key acquisitions and joint ventures in a little over 20 years, the James River Corporation has grown into one of the world's largest paper companies.

Brenton S. Halsey was born on April 8, 1927, in Newport News, Virginia. After graduating from the United States Merchant Marine Academy, he attended the University of Virginia, where he earned a bachelor's degree in chemical engineering. Upon graduation, he served with the U.S. Navy in the Korean theater, reaching the rank of lieutenant. He then embarked on a career in the paper industry, eventually reaching the post of president and general manager of Interstate Bag Company, a subsidiary of the Ethyl Corporation.

Robert C. Williams was born on January 24, 1930, in Cincinnati, Ohio. After receiving a bachelor's degree in mechanical engineering from the University of Cincinnati and an MBA from Xavier University, he served in various capacities at the Diamond International Corporation. In 1959, he went to work for Albemarle Paper Company, which also was affiliated with the Ethyl Corporation.

In the late 1960s, the Ethyl Corporation, based in Richmond, Virginia, focused on its plastics and petroleum markets, leaving the fate of its paper operations in question. Separately, Halsey and Williams approached upper management with plans to buy the specialty paper operations.

Ethyl encouraged the two men to join forces, and in 1969 they acquired the paper operations. They named their new company the James River Paper Company, after the historic river that bordered their headquarters. Their mill employed about 100 people and had annual sales of over $5 million.

The new venture was boosted by a contract with the AC Spark Plug company, which was experiencing problems with the paper stock in their oil filters. James River was able to develop a new paper that increased filter-line productivity and nearly eliminated filter waste. The company backed up its product by creating an in-house trucking operation that provided overnight delivery to AC, thus reducing inventory costs.

Over the next decade, James River doubled in size three times, making ten key acquisitions in specialty packaging and industrial papers, specialty printing papers, coated papers, and custom-coated industrial film products, raising annual sales to nearly $300 million. In 1980, the company acquired the Brown Paper Company, doubling in size once again, and entered into three new markets—sanitary paper, food and beverage service, and paperboard packaging products. Sales increased to nearly $600 million, and the company entered into the Fortune 500 ranks.

Encouraged by the performance of their acquisitions, the partners once again doubled the size of the company with the purchase of the Dixie/Northern assets from the American Can Company in 1982, which complemented the recent purchase of the Brown Paper Company assets. Now marketing popular brands such as Northern bathroom tissue, Brawny paper towels, and Dixie cups and plates, the entrance into these new segments became a major strategic focus.

The Dixie cup was innovated in 1908 by Hugh Moore, a 22-year-old inventor from Kansas. He had convinced the American Can Company to invest $200,000 in his Health Kup, as it was then called. The idea was to sell a drink of cool, pure water from a vending machine dispensed in a 5-ounce paper cup for one penny. The "penny vendors" with dispensers containing 100 paper cups and a 5-gallon jug of spring water were first placed in major railroad stations.

In 1986, James River purchased the San Francisco–based Crown Zellerbach company, doubling its size for the sixth time. Crown Zellerbach's history began in 1868, when Anthony Zellerbach arrived on the West Coast nearly penniless and settled on "paper jobbing" as his business. Working from a small room, he sold printing, writing, and wrapping paper remnants to customers in the city's printing district. Over the next five decades, his family built the business into a $27 million paper company. In 1928, the company merged with the Crown Willamette Paper Company and became known as Crown Zellerbach.

Today, James River Corporation, headquartered in Richmond, Virginia, is a leading marketer and manufacturer of consumer products, packaging, and business, printing, and converting papers. The company employs approximately 23,000 people at more than 60 manufacturing facilities worldwide, with annual revenue exceeding $5 billion.

SOURCE: James River Corporation archives

Louis H. Hamilton, Chester H. Beach

[Hamilton Beach Company]

In 1910, two friends combined their talents to launch a new venture. Louis Hamilton had acquired considerable business and financial experience. Chester Beach had quickly become a successful inventor of electrical motors and products. By successfully developing small AC/DC motors, the Hamilton Beach Company quickly became a leading manufacturer of home and commercial products.

Chester H. Beach was born on July 27, 1880, on a farm near Union Grove, Wisconsin. Throughout his childhood, he demonstrated a remarkable mechanical aptitude. Upon his marriage to Ella Koenig, the couple moved to Racine, Wisconsin, where Beach went to work first for the Standard Electric Company, and later for the Arnold Electric Company.

After working as a cashier for the Barry Steamship Line, Louis Hamilton accepted the job of advertising manager for Standard Electric, where he met Beach. In 1910, Hamilton and Beach, with financial backing from Standard Electric co-owner Frederick C. Osius, launched the Hamilton Beach Manufacturing Company. The business was built around the inventive genius of Beach, while Hamilton handled business and financial matters.

The key to their success was the perfection of the universal motor, which operated on either direct current or alternating current. The "battle of the currents" had been waged in the 1890s between Thomas Edison, who supported the use of *direct current,* and George Westinghouse, who pushed for *alternating current.* Westinghouse and AC eventually became the standard, although power companies continued to supply both well into the early 1900s.

The firm grew quickly as the Hamilton Beach product line became associated with soda fountains. Its first product was a small motor that powered soda fountain drink mixers that were used to make malted milks and milkshakes.

This was followed with juice extractors, bar mixers, electric drills, hair dryers, and many other products, and even a device that would wash 800 dirty glasses an hour using four motor-driven scrub brushes. Some of the products were made entirely by Hamilton Beach, while in other cases the company supplied its motors to other manufacturers.

The company's next big success came in 1912 with the unveiling of the Sew-E-Z, a small motor that replaced the foot treadle on sewing machines. An early advertisement stated: "Just place Sew-E-Z on your machine next to the wheel. Attach the plug to any electric light socket and place the little pedal on the floor. A slight press of your toe starts the wheel." This small engine was easily adapted to power other devices, such as fans, buffers, and food mixers.

Hamilton and Beach sold their interest in the company in 1913. Fred Osius continued to operate the company until 1922, when he sold it to the Scovill Company of Waterbury, Connecticut.

Hamilton and Beach soon launched their next venture, the Wisconsin Electric Company, to manufacture small engines for power tools. The company eventually made a complete line of products, including tool-post grinders, hand grinders, drill grinders, automatic drill heads, flexible-shaft tools, and fractional-horsepower motors.

The founders named their product line *Dunmore* because consumers could expect the tools to have "done more" than competing products. The name of the firm was eventually changed to The Dunmore Company.

Chester Beach had been awarded nearly 25 patents at the time of his death in 1934. Louis Hamilton served as president of Dunmore, then later as chairman of the board until his death in 1957, at which time he was succeeded by his son, Robert L. Hamilton. The company was later sold.

SOURCE: Hamilton Beach/Proctor-Silex archives

John K. Hanson

[Winnebago Industries]

John K. Hanson was born on June 22, 1913, in the small town of Thor, Iowa. Soon after his birth, his family moved to Forest City, Iowa, where his enterprising father built a number of successful businesses, including a funeral home, furniture and appliance store, International Harvester dealership, and automotive dealership.

As a teenager, Hanson was directed by his father to work at a new job each year to provide him with a number of job skills. After high school, Hanson graduated from Waldorf College in Forest City in 1932, and two years later he received his B.S. in mortuary science from the University of Minnesota. Upon returning to Iowa, Hanson married Luise Voss and assumed a role in the family business ventures. Over time, he assumed management of the companies and eventually purchased his father's stake.

Hanson was an avid outdoorsman and was active in economic development in Forest City. In 1957, he obtained a travel trailer dealership and quickly became enthusiastic about the new industry. Within two years, he and other Forest City leaders convinced Modernistic Industries, a California travel trailer manufacturing firm, to relocate to Iowa, and Hanson was named president of the venture.

Immediately, Hanson explored methods for improving the company's trailers. He introduced mass production to motor home assembly, and the company was renamed Winnebago Industries, Inc. (Forest City is the county seat of Winnebago County, Iowa.) The company quickly became a dominant presence in the industry. Today, Winnebago is one of the world's largest manufacturers of motor homes and a major employer in the state of Iowa.

SOURCE: Winnebago archives

Alfred Harcourt, Donald Brace

[Harcourt, Brace & Company]

Growing up in rural New York state, the paths of Alfred Harcourt and Donald Brace eventually crossed at Columbia University. The two quickly became friends and, after working for Henry Holt & Company, launched their own publishing house. Harcourt, Brace & Company quickly became one of the industry's most respected and successful publishers.

Alfred Harcourt and Donald Brace were both born in 1881 in the state of New York, but in different regions. Harcourt was born in Ulster County, part of the Hudson River valley. He was raised in a stone house that his family had owned since about 1720. His father, a fruit farmer, sold his goods in New York City.

By age nine, Harcourt had developed a passion for books. While absent from school for an entire year due to illness, he became obsessed with reading the works of James Fenimore Cooper, Mark Twain, and other great writers.

Donald Brace was raised in the Mohawk valley region, a historical region noted for battles during the French and Indian War and the Revolutionary War. His father owned and operated a modest newspaper in West Winfield, providing young Brace with typesetting and printing experience from the time he was 12 years old.

Both Harcourt and Brace entered Columbia University the same year and joined the editorial staff of the *Spectator*, the campus daily newspaper. There the two men met and quickly became friends. Upon graduation in 1904, they both secured jobs with the publisher Henry Holt & Company, Brace as a typographer in the production department and Harcourt as an editor in the trade department.

In time, Brace became the director of manufacturing and served as Henry Holt's assistant treasurer. Harcourt rose to director of the trade department, signing up an array of accomplished authors. However, in 1919 Harcourt left Henry Holt and, while contemplating his next job, was urged by author Sinclair Lewis to launch his own publishing house.

Harcourt eventually decided to open his own business and was quickly joined by his college pal Donald Brace. On July 29, 1919, Harcourt, Brace & Company opened for business with the founders and one employee, Ellen Knowles Eayrs, who later married Alfred Harcourt. They worked in a basement cubbyhole until the lease expired on the corset maker located on the first floor, at which time they moved to more comfortable quarters.

The company quickly released a number of books that had modest success. Louis Untermeyer's *Modern American Poetry* was released in December 1919. It remained a classroom textbook for more than five decades. The partners' first big find was a British economist who was preparing a book on the Paris Peace Conference. The writer, John Maynard Keynes, entered into an agreement with Harcourt to publish *The Economic Consequences of the Peace,* a masterful work that helped to launch Keynes to international recognition.

Meanwhile, the friendship between Harcourt and Sinclair Lewis grew stronger. For some time, Harcourt urged Lewis to write a book about small-town America. In July 1920, Lewis presented Harcourt, Brace & Company with the manuscript for *Main Street.* Harcourt was optimistic that the book would sell at least 40,000 copies. It actually sold more than 400,000 copies in hardcover alone.

The company published new American writers while maintaining its interest in British authors, adding people such as Virginia Woolf, T. S. Eliot, and Betrand Russell. Harcourt and Brace also turned their attention to textbooks, which proved to be a wise move. During the Depression, textbook sales remained rather steady, while the trade books took a beating. Among the successful books was a new language title published in 1941, the *Harbrace College Handbook,* which eventually sold several million copies.

In the 1940s, Alfred Harcourt became afflicted with cancer. He retired from the company in January 1942, but returned to service in 1948. He retired a second time in 1953 and died on June 21, 1954, at the age of 73. Ironically, Donald Brace died on September 20, 1955, also at age 73.

SOURCE: Harcourt, Brace, Jovanovich archives

Henry Harnischfeger, Alonzo Pawling

[Harnischfeger Industries, Inc.]

Starting with a small, cold machine shop, Henry Harnischfeger and Alonzo Pawling quickly established a reputation as creative and talented machinists. In time, they started building their own equipment, including overhead cranes and construction vehicles. Today, Harnischfeger Industries is a world leader in the manufacture of specialty equipment and vehicles.

Henry Harnischfeger was 16 years old when he left his native Germany in 1872 and sailed to New York City. He already had more than three years experience as a locksmith under his belt, a skill that he put to work for the next ten years as a locksmith and a machinist.

By 1881, Harnischfeger grew restless and moved to Milwaukee, Wisconsin, a bustling manufacturing center that was crying for skilled workers. It also had a large German population, which appealed to the young Harnischfeger. Upon arrival, he was hired as a foreman in a new sewing machine plant. There he met Alonzo Pawling, a Chicago-born patternmaker.

Within a few years, their employer fell on hard times and advised employees to look elsewhere for work. On December 1, 1884, 26-year-old Pawling and 28-year-old Harnischfeger launched Pawling & Harnischfeger with a handshake and little more. Their job shop was 26 by 50 feet, with heat provided by a single potbellied stove. The partners took turns climbing onto their building during the harsh Wisconsin winters to shovel snow off the sagging roof.

As the knitting business grew in Milwaukee, the P&H machine shop came to be recognized as expert in the design and repair of knitting machinery. These and other manufacturers sought out the partners to do a variety of jobs. Among their early clients was the E. P. Allis Company, which eventually became Allis-Chalmers.

In 1887, the company built an overhead crane controlled by three electric motors. The revolutionary idea quickly caught on, and P&H was swamped with orders from across the country. The business led quite naturally to the manufacture of related equipment such as hoists.

At the turn of the century, the country was in a construction boom. P&H observed the strenuous labor that was involved and became convinced that a mechanical solution could be found. They designed and built a ladder-type trench and manhole digger, driven by a steam engine and mounted on a wagon. Buckets descended vertically into the hole to scoop dirt and make a U-turn back out of the hole, where the dirt would be dumped to the side. This crude contraption launched the founders into an explosive market that included excavators and other construction equipment.

In 1911, ill health forced Pawling to withdraw from the partnership. Shortly thereafter, Henry Harnischfeger purchased Pawling's interest and reorganized the company as the Harnischfeger Corporation. However, out of respect to his partner, he retained the well-known P&H trademark. Pawling died three years later.

After World War I, Harnischfeger introduced the world's first gasoline-powered dragline, a truck-mounted machine that could be used for lifting, pile-driving, clamming, and dragging. Next came a shovel-type excavator mounted on crawlers, then a backhoe. These developments established the company as a world leader in construction equipment, increasing employment from about 100 in 1900 to nearly 1,500 by 1930.

Henry Harnischfeger died in 1930 and was succeeded by his son, Walter, who led the company into a period of growth and diversity. Harnischfeger started making welding machines and electrodes, diesel engines, road-building equipment, and even prefabricated houses. Walter's son, Henry, became president of the firm in 1959 and, during his tenure, he refocused the company on two core businesses: mining equipment and overhead cranes and hoists.

Today, Harnischfeger Industries is a leading producer of mining, material handling, and papermaking equipment. It has annual sales in excess of $2.8 billion and more than 17,000 employees worldwide. The company remains headquartered in Milwaukee, Wisconsin.

SOURCE: Harnischfeger Industries archives

George H. Hartford, George F. Gilman

[The Great Atlantic & Pacific Tea Company]

George Huntington Hartford was born on September 5, 1833, in Augusta, Maine. After working in a Boston dry goods store, Hartford moved to St. Louis, Missouri, and obtained employment in a store owned by George F. Gilman.

In 1859, Hartford and Gilman established a tea emporium in New York City, offering customers all types of tea blends at "cargo prices," which were nearly half the cost charged by tea retailers. They purchased tea at the New York dockyards and sold their product at about 2¢ per pound above cost.

The partners offered a shopping environment much richer than the general stores, featuring paneled walls, flowery tin ceilings, crystal chandeliers, checkout lines shaped like pagodas, and red and gold tea bins.

Their early merchandising program included the organization of "tea clubs" in different cities, offering even further discount rates and awarding club organizers with special incentives. They also targeted religious teetotalers and prepared colorful circulars that included special-interest news articles and even poems. A third method of distribution was an efficient horse-and-wagon network that reached rural customers.

On their tenth anniversary, the partners renamed their venture The Great Atlantic & Pacific Tea Company, which became known to most as simply the "A&P." By this time they operated ten stores in New York, Boston, and Philadelphia. In addition to a variety of teas, they started offering coffee under the Eight O'clock label, which today survives as the oldest existing, and the fourth most popular, coffee in America. By 1876, the company opened its 100th store, making it the first significant chain grocery store in the country.

When Hartford's 15-year-old son, also named George, joined the venture, he brought with him a friend who could make a high-quality baking soda. This became the first product manufactured under the A&P label. The same year that its baking soda was introduced, 1887, the company sales surpassed $1 million. Butter, sugar, and canned tomatoes and pears were soon added, fueling the growth of one-stop shopping.

At the turn of the century, the number of stores reached 200, and annual sales exceeded $5.6 million. George Gilman retired in 1878. George Hartford died on August 29, 1917.

The number of stores increased from 480 stores in 1912 to nearly 4,600 stores in 1920. At the start of the Depression in 1929, A&P had reached $1 billion in annual sales with 15,400 stores. Sales in fiscal year by A&P's 1,200 stores now exceed $10 billion.

SOURCES: A&P archives; *Supermarket News,* December 19, 1994

William R. Hearst

[The Hearst Corporation]

Spurning an offer to follow his father's success in mining and ranching, William Hearst pursued an education and a career in journalism. He gained experience at Joseph Pulitzer's New York *World,* then took the helm of the small *San Francisco Examiner.* After building the *Examiner* into a world-class newspaper, Hearst acquired and founded several other newspapers, magazines, and media companies. Today, The Hearst Corporation is one of the world's leading media organizations.

William Randolph Hearst was born on April 29, 1863, in San Francisco, California, the only child of George and Phoebe (Apperson) Hearst. His father had traveled West in a covered wagon in 1850 and acquired an interest in a mine that was found to be part of the Comstock Lode, the largest deposit of silver in the world. From this and other investments, the elder Hearst accumulated holdings in mining, timberland, and other properties.

In 1882, William Hearst entered Harvard, where he developed an intense passion for journalism. He subscribed to newspapers from around the country, studying each intensely for style, content, and appearance. His favorite was the *World* in New York City, owned by the famous newspaper publisher Joseph Pulitzer. When Hearst was expelled from Harvard for sending personalized chamber pots to all of his professors, he joined the staff of the *World* as a reporter.

Hearst returned to California in February 1887 and convinced his father to turn over control of the *San Francisco Examiner* to him. The elder Hearst had been given the small newspaper after the owner, a gambling opponent, was unable to cover his wagers.

With his father's blessing, William Hearst quickly transfigured the newspaper into something closer to the New York *World.* He added a superb writing staff, including guest contributors such as Mark Twain. In three short years, circulation increased from 5,000 to 80,000.

As soon as Hearst established a comfortable customer base in San Francisco, he turned his attention to New York. On November 8, 1895, he acquired the New York *Journal,* a newspaper that had been founded by Joseph

Pulitzer's estranged brother, Albert. Suddenly, Hearst was in competition with the newspaper that, years earlier, he had concluded to be the best in the world.

By applying the same formula for growth he had used in California, Hearst was able to increase circulation from 30,000 to 100,000 in a matter of weeks. The success soon led to the launching of a third newspaper, the *Chicago American,* on July 4, 1900. Three years later, he married Millicent Willson. While honeymooning in Europe, Hearst picked up *The Car,* a magazine so intriguing that, upon his return, he was prompted to found *Motor* magazine, a success to this day.

Hearst next launched an aggressive, but rather unsuccessful, run for political office. In 1904, he was defeated in his attempt to run as the Democratic candidate for president. The following year, he lost his bid for mayor of New York.

While Hearst continued to mix politics with business, his strength was in publishing. In 1905, he purchased *Cosmopolitan* magazine, which had been held by a number of owners, including Ulysses S. Grant Jr., since its founding in 1886. Six years later he acquired *Good Housekeeping.* A year after that, he established another newspaper, the *Atlanta Georgian,* and acquired yet another magazine, *Harper's Bazaar.*

Entering the 1920s, Hearst owned 13 newspapers, 6 magazines, the International News Service, King Features Syndicate, and a motion picture production company. One of his earliest film successes was a 21-week serial that he named *The Perils of Pauline.*

William Randolph Hearst died on August 14, 1951, at the age of 88. All five of his sons, William Randolph Jr., Randolph, George, John, and David, followed their father into the media business. Today, The Hearst Corporation is a highly diverse media organization with 12,000 employees.

SOURCES: The Hearst Corporation archives; James F. O'Donnell, *Hearst: A Century in Journalism, 1887–1987,* The Hearst Corporation, 1987

Gottlieb Heileman

[G. Heileman Brewing Company]

Gottlieb Heileman was born in the southern German province of Württemberg on January 6, 1824. His parents, Casper and Fredricka Heilemann (the original spelling of their last name had a double *n*), had eight children, but only three lived to adulthood.

While living in Germany, Heileman received considerable training as both a brewer and a baker. However, he was not interested in serving an extended European-type apprenticeship and set his sights on the "New World." Heileman immigrated to America in 1852, living first in Philadelphia, then moving to Milwaukee, Wisconsin, where he established a bakery with Gottlieb Maier. Five years later, he sold his share of the venture and moved to La Crosse, Wisconsin, where he worked in local breweries. He also wed Johanna Bandle, a marriage that would produce eight children.

In November 1858, Heileman and partner John Gund established The City Brewery, which lasted until 1872. On the flip of a coin, Heileman retained the brewery and Gund took possession of the other property the two had acquired over their 14-year partnership. Heileman renamed the business G. Heileman's City Brewery.

Gottlieb Heileman died on February 19, 1878. He is buried in Oak Grove cemetery in La Crosse, not far from his old partner, John Gund. Upon his death, his wife Johanna assumed the role of president, one of the first women in the entire country to reach such a level in business. She remained active in the business until her death on January 5, 1917, at the age of 85.

During the 1880s, Heileman started to package its beer in bottles, a departure from the pitch-lined oak kegs. In 1890 the company introduced a 64-ounce picnic bottle. That same year the company was incorporated as the G. Heileman Brewing Company.

The company survived Prohibition by producing and marketing nonalcoholic beer, soda, and malt extract. Shortly after Prohibition ended, Heileman started packaging beer in steel cans, which were replaced by aluminum cans in the 1970s.

In 1959, Heileman ranked 39th in the country in terms of beer sold. Through strong management and a public stock offering in 1973, Heileman was able to expand rapidly through internal growth and acquisitions. Among the companies bought were Blatz, Pabst, Lone Star, C. Schmidt & Sons, and several smaller breweries. Heileman itself was acquired by Hicks, Muse & Company, a Dallas investment firm, in 1993. Today, Heileman is the nation's fifth-largest brewer.

SOURCE: Heileman archives

Henry J. Heinz

[H. J. Heinz Company]

Henry John Heinz was born on October 11, 1844, the first of eight surviving children of Henry and Anna M. (Schmitt) Heinz, both immigrants from southern Germany who first met in Birmingham, Pennsylvania, across the Monongahela River from Pittsburgh. Six years after Henry was born, the family moved to nearby Sharpsburg, where his father had purchased a brickyard.

The property that surrounded the new family residence was ideal for Anna's vegetable gardening. Young Henry not only helped his mother with the garden, he also took to the streets to sell the excess vegetables. This sideline proved so successful that he was able to purchase a horse and cart. The energetic 12-year-old also found time to work in his father's brickyard and to help at a neighboring potato farm.

At age 15, Henry enrolled in Duff's Mercantile College and assumed bookkeeping responsibilities for his father. He also became quite interested in

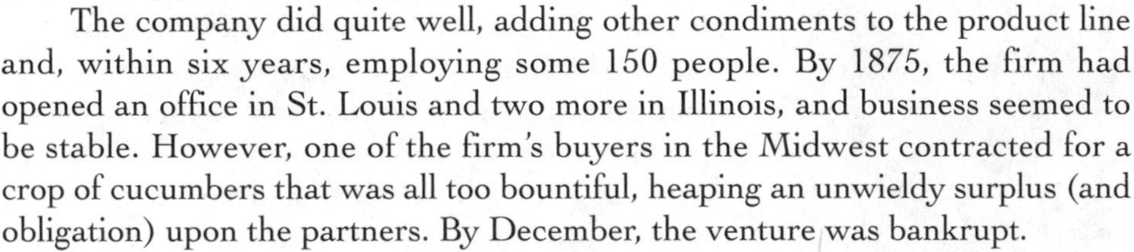

his mother's homemade horseradish. Commercial varieties were often produced with cheap fillers, such as turnips, that discolored the horseradish. To cover up this flaw, it was frequently packed in jars made of colored glass.

The horseradish that came from Anna's kitchen was pure, and to offer proof Henry packed it in clear jars, which he sold to restaurants, grocers, and even directly to households. The product sold so well that Henry purchased half interest in his father's brickyard and built a new home for his parents.

In 1869, Henry and a neighbor launched a partnership, Heinz and Noble, to sell bottled and canned food under the Anchor brand name. Their first product, of course, was the Heinz family horseradish. Later that same year, Henry married Sarah "Sallie" S. Young, a daughter of Irish immigrants.

The company did quite well, adding other condiments to the product line and, within six years, employing some 150 people. By 1875, the firm had opened an office in St. Louis and two more in Illinois, and business seemed to be stable. However, one of the firm's buyers in the Midwest contracted for a crop of cucumbers that was all too bountiful, heaping an unwieldy surplus (and obligation) upon the partners. By December, the venture was bankrupt.

Henry J. Heinz was not only disappointed with the fate of his company, he was also quite upset with the fact that creditors were left unsatisfied. He referred to these debts as his "Moral Obligations," and as soon as he was once again making money, he paid all of his creditors in full.

After the failure of his first venture, it was only a matter of months before Heinz rebounded and, with his brother John and cousin Frederick, launched the F&J Heinz Company. While the product line was similar to that offered by his first business, he made an important addition: ketchup. The ambitious Heinz faced his past failure squarely: He adopted the pickle, which is a processed cucumber, as his logo.

In 1888, Henry Heinz bought out his brother and cousin and renamed the venture the H. J. Heinz Company. Two years later, he moved his operations from downtown Pittsburgh to the city's north side. By 1896, his company was marketing more than 60 products. However, while riding a train in New York City, Heinz spotted an advertisement boasting "21 styles of shoes." For some reason, he took a shine to the number 57, which he expanded to "57 Varieties."

Henry J. Heinz died of pneumonia in 1919 at the age of 75. At the time of his death, his company employed more than 6,000 people at more than two dozen factories and seed farms. Henry was succeeded by his second son, Howard C. Heinz. Today, the H. J. Heinz Company markets 4,000 varieties of food products, employs nearly 43,000 people, and has annual sales in excess of $9 billion.

SOURCES: H. J. Heinz Company archives; Eleanor Foa Dienstag, *In Good Company: 125 Years at the Heinz Table,* Warner Books, copyright by Heinz Company, 1994

John Hendricks

[Discovery Communications]

John Hendricks grew up in Huntsville, Alabama, with a fascination for science and discovery. He grew up near the NASA facility that developed the engines for Saturn 5. He still remembers how his house shook when they test-fired the rockets. He was a kid who built his own telescope and watched documentaries.

Hendricks graduated from the University of Alabama in Huntsville with a B.S. in history in 1973. Shortly after graduating, he founded the American Association of University Consultants, a private consulting organization specializing in television distribution and marketing of educational programs and services.

In 1982, John Hendricks incorporated Cable Educational Network. This positioned him to launch The Discovery Channel in June 1985. This was the first cable network designed to provide world-class documentary programming on topics such as nature, science and technology, history, human adventure, and world exploration. Within one year, the network had signed up seven million subscribers. Two years later, the subscriber base exceeded 30 million.

It was not all smooth sailing. Six months into the network's first season a major investor pulled out of the project, and in February 1986 Hendricks had $27,000 in the company's bank account and was facing a $26,200 payroll, along with $2 million in accounts payable. His solution was to form an alliance with TIC, Cox Cable Communications, United Artists Entertainment, and Newhouse Broadcasting, all companies that wanted to provide their customers with access to the Discovery Channel. The badly needed equity infusion launched the company past the lean years, and Hendricks hasn't looked back.

In October 1991, Discovery Communications purchased The Learning Channel, which offers children and adults enjoyable, entertaining educational programming.

John Hendricks continues to serve as Chairman and Chief Executive Officer of Bethesda, Maryland–based Discovery Communications, Inc., which operates four distinct business units:

- Discovery Networks, U.S., consisting of Discovery Channel, The Learning Channel, Animal Planet, and the recently launched package of Discovery digital services: Discovery Kids Channel, Discovery Science Network, Discovery Travel & Living Network, and Discovery Civilization: The History and Geography Channel.
- Discovery Networks International, consisting of 19 different feeds of 15 separate Discovery networks transmitted worldwide in 18 languages.

- Discovery Enterprises Worldwide, consisting of Discovery Channel Multimedia, Discovery Channel Online, Discovery Channel Video, Discovery Channel Publishing and Discovery Channel Education.
- Discovery Retail, consisting of 113 stores of The Nature Company, 16 Discovery Channel stores, and three Scientific Revolution stores.
- DCI also operates a wholly owned subsidiary, Your Choice TV, Inc.

SOURCES: Discovery Communications archives; *CableVision* magazine, June 18, 1990; "The Brains Behind Smart TV," *Los Angeles Times*, June 18, 1995.

William R. Hewlett, David Packard

[Hewlett-Packard Corporation]

Not long after they played together for the Stanford University football team, William Hewlett and David Packard launched a company that built electronic components for the movie industry. Soon they expanded into defense and commercial electronics products. Today, Hewlett-Packard is a leading producer of computer and electrical products.

William R. Hewlett was born on May 20, 1913, in Ann Arbor, Michigan. He received a bachelor of arts degree from Stanford University in 1934, followed by a master's degree in electrical engineering from the Massachusetts Institute of Technology in 1936, then a second degree in engineering from Stanford in 1939.

While playing football for Stanford, Hewlett met Packard and built a close friendship. David Packard was born on September 7, 1912, in Pueblo, Colorado. He received a bachelor of arts degree in 1934 and a master's degree in electrical engineering in 1939.

From 1936 to 1938, Packard was an engineer with General Electric Company's plant in Schenectady, New York. In 1938, he returned to California and, with a capitalization of $538, launched a partnership with Hewlett. The two flipped a coin to determine which name would be first in their company name.

They leased a small garage in Palo Alto, California, and started to build their first product, a resistance-capacitance audio oscillator. They labeled their device as the 200A Audio Oscillator, hoping that the "200" would make customers think they had been established for some time and had earlier models already on the market.

Their credibility received a major boost when the Walt Disney Studios purchased eight of their model 200B oscillators. These were used to produce the stereophonic sound in the successful Disney film *Fantasia*. After adding other products, including a wave analyzer, the founders and their 60 employees moved to newer quarters when World War II erupted.

William Hewlett entered the U.S. Army in 1941 while Packard stayed behind to manage the company. During the war, Hewlett-Packard built microwave products and oscilloscopes for radar-jamming equipment. By the end of the 1940s, Hewlett-Packard was introducing as many as 20 new products each year. Growth in the following decades was impressive, and by 1976 annual sales reached $1 billion. Two years later, they nearly doubled.

William Hewlett retired from active service in 1964. David Packard remained with Hewlett-Packard until 1993, when the 81-year-old founder finally retired. David Packard died on March 26, 1996, at the age of 83. Today, annual sales at Hewlett-Packard are nearly $30 billion.

SOURCE: Hewlett-Packard archives

Frank Hickingbotham

[TCBY—The Country's Best Yogurt]

One fateful holiday season, Frank Hickingbotham met his wife, Georgia, at Neiman-Marcus for a snack. Georgia ordered her favorite treat, peach yogurt, which Frank declined. After pressure from Georgia, Frank finally took a bite and said: "This can't be yogurt."

The couple felt certain that they could market yogurt to a health-conscious America. Through some inquiries, they found that the store was supplied by Daniel Brackeen, a yogurt producer from Dallas, Texas. His company, Americana Foods, was nestled inside an unattractive warehouse that was home to several companies—mostly meat cutters. The Hickingbothams traveled to Dallas and entered into an agreement with Brackeen's company for his yogurt mix.

Hickingbotham then arranged for space in a Little Rock, Arkansas, shopping center for the first store, named appropriately "This Can't Be Yogurt." Georgia designed the first store's interior. On September 23, 1981, the store opened its doors and, at the end of the day, sales totaled about $153.00.

The traffic picked up, however, and by the end of their first week in business, sales exceeded $2,400. They doubled the following week, pushing the Hickingbothams into a new dilemma. People (mainly ice cream competitors) started digging through their trash to find out where they purchased their supplies. To maintain secrecy, the family loaded trash into a van owned by Georgia's brother and drove directly to the dump.

By the end of the first year, Hickingbotham had opened six stores in the Little Rock area. The next year, the couple started offering franchises for $15,000. The rapid success allowed Hickingbotham to take the company public in 1984, just three years after opening for business. That year, the company sought a name change, but wanted to retain the initials TCBY. Georgia came up with the new name: The Country's Best Yogurt.

The rapid growth continued. In 1985, 140 new stores were opened, and by 1988 more than 1,000 TCBY stores were in business. The first international store was opened in Canada in 1987.

Prior to the election of Bill Clinton as president of the United States, TCBY enjoyed the services of current political celebrities Hillary Rodham Clinton and Thomas "Mack" McLarty, who served on TCBY's board of directors before departing for Washington, D.C., where McLarty joined the Clintons as the White House chief of staff.

Today, TCBY has nearly 3,000 stores operating throughout the world. Annual sales and franchising revenues are more than $200 million.

SOURCE: TCBY archives

Stephen C. Hilbert

[Conseco, Inc.]

Realizing that his marketing niche was in insurance, Stephen Hilbert had a discussion with the founder of one of the insurance companies he worked for. The man described the steps he took to establish the company, and Hilbert thought to himself, "I can do that." He formulated a strategy for building an insurance empire from existing companies and launched Conseco, Inc., which today is a $29 billion insurance company.

Stephen C. Hilbert was born on January 23, 1945, in North Terre Haute, Indiana. His father worked in the maintenance department of an aluminum factory and his mother was a telephone operator.

Hilbert attended Indiana State University while selling Grolier's encyclopedias door-to-door. After being recognized as the national sales leader, he quit school to accept a full-time position with Grolier. He then enlisted in the U.S. Army from 1966 through 1969. Upon discharge, he worked as a marketing representative for R. J. Reynolds Tobacco Company.

Hilbert's next moves led him into a profession that he eventually mastered. In 1973, he joined Aetna Life & Casualty, followed by positions with Franklin National Life and United Home Life Insurance Company, then a return tour with Aetna. During this time, he recognized an opportunity to capitalize on the changes occurring within the life insurance industry.

Specifically, he determined that a holding company using a centralized management structure could acquire existing insurance companies and enhance their value by streamlining and consolidating administrative functions, refocusing marketing efforts, and improving investment yields. And he decided to act on his vision to build the insurance company of the future, the company that would later become Conseco.

Starting with $10,000 of their own money, Hilbert and a partner set out to raise capital, selling stock door-to-door. Their market was everyone who lived within reasonable driving distance because they couldn't afford hotel rooms. The effort paid off. Between 1979 and 1982, they were able to raise $326,000 selling stock at $1 per share.

On February 2, 1982, the company made its first acquisition. The following year they formally organized under the name Conseco, Inc., and made a public offering of their stock two years later. By that time, corporate assets reached $100 million.

The formula for growth has been simple. Buy promising insurance companies, cut their costs, and integrate them into an efficient, streamlined operation. Then provide a solid management team that can increase penetration of the market served by that company.

Hilbert has made at least a dozen more major acquisitions over the past decade. The company has grown from 20 employees and $4 million in assets in 1982 to more than 3,700 employees and nearly $24 billion in assets today. In 1996, Conseco merged with Life Partners Group and acquired the remaining interest in American Life Holdings and Bankers Life Holdings that it did not already own. The company also acquired two leading providers in the long-term care and cancer insurance industries. These moves, combined with strong growth in existing operations, advanced the company to the Fortune 500 list.

SOURCE: Conseco, Inc., archives

John A. Hillenbrand

[Hillenbrand Industries]

In the mid-1800s, the German immigrant family of John Hillenbrand settled in Cincinnati, Ohio, attracted in part by the city's large German-speaking population. Tragically, 16-year-old John and his infant sisters were orphaned and his only asset was the family's unprofitable farm.

He looked across the state line to the rolling hills and abundant forests surrounding Batesville, Indiana, and became intrigued with the regional demand for good wood and cleared farmland. He purchased land, initially in small parcels, then cut and sold the trees. The remaining cleared land was sold for farms. By the time that the industrious Hillenbrand was 18 years old, he owned 16 sawmills throughout southeastern Indiana.

John Hillenbrand's son, John A. Hillenbrand, was the founder of the company known today as Hillenbrand Industries. By the time young Hillenbrand reached adulthood, the Hillenbrand name was already well known throughout the region. Building on his father's success, Hillenbrand established a number of enterprises, including a bank, three furniture companies, a general store, and a newspaper.

In 1906, Hillenbrand acquired a struggling local firm known as the Batesville Coffin Company, which had been established in 1884. By employing skilled German craftspeople, he was able to produce high-quality coffins. As the region's population grew, Hillenbrand's casket company sustained respectable growth over the next three decades.

By the 1940s, Batesville Casket Company had innovated a protective metal burial casket, which resisted corrosion and the entry of air and water. The company also developed mass-production techniques for metal caskets, which were less expensive than handcrafted wooden caskets. This fueled the subsequent rapid growth of the company.

All four of John's sons became active in the business. John W. Hillenbrand, the oldest, served as president and chairman of the board until 1972. William A. Hillenbrand founded the Hill-Rom Company in 1929 to make hospital beds. As with the caskets, the hospital beds were initially made of wood by master craftspeople. After World War II, the company expanded its product line to include other hospital furniture.

The Hillenbrand holdings were eventually reorganized under Hillenbrand Industries, Inc., which now includes Batesville Casket Company, the world's largest manufacturer of caskets, and Hill-Rom Company, the world's largest manufacturer of hospital beds. Hillenbrand employs nearly 10,000 people worldwide and has annual sales of more than $1.6 billion.

SOURCE: Hillenbrand Industries archives

J. F. Hillerich, John A. "Bud" Hillerich, Frank W. Bradsby

[Hillerich & Bradsby]

After watching a struggling baseball superstar break his bat, 18-year-old John "Bud" Hillerich invited the player back to the family woodshop to fashion one that would help him out of the slump. After working all night, the player had a perfect day at the plate, and the Hillerich family started making Louisville Slugger baseball bats. They later added a marketing whiz named Frank Bradsby, and Hillerich & Bradsby went on to become one of the most famous sporting goods companies in history.

In 1842, J. Michael Hillerich (pronounced hill-rick) and his family left Baden-Baden, Germany, and immigrated to the United States, eventually settling in Louisville, Kentucky. In 1859, his son, J. Fredric Hillerich, established a small woodworking business making roller skids, bedposts, tenpins, duckpins, wooden bowling balls, handrails, and decorated porch columns.

In 1880, John A. "Bud" Hillerich went to work in his father's shop at the age of 14. On a fateful day four years later, Bud skipped work to attend a professional baseball game of the Louisville Eclipse. The team's star player, Pete "The Old Gladiator" Browning, was not only in a slump, he also shattered his favorite bat.

When the game was over, Bud struck up a conversation with Browning and invited him to the shop to get a new bat made. Later that day, Bud and Browning selected a piece of white ash and Bud went to work. They worked all night long, with Browning taking practice swings periodically until the bat felt perfect. The next day, Browning went three for three with the bat, and the Hillerich family found a new market niche.

Bud's father, J. F. Hillerich, initially balked at the opportunity, regarding the venture as trivial. Nonetheless, Bud persisted, and bat making soon dominated the business. By 1894, the firm called their bats Louisville Sluggers.

The firm had several professional ballplayers as clients. Bud and his coworkers committed the weight, length, and style of each of the players to memory, and the Hillerich employees and their clients became close friends. Bats were distributed to the general public through the Simmon's Hardware Company of St. Louis.

In 1897, J. F. Hillerich granted a partnership in the firm to 31-year-old Bud and changed the company name to J.F. Hillerich & Son. The bat business continued to grow. In September 1905, the great ballplayer Honus Wagner entered into an endorsement contract with Hillerich, granting permission to use his autograph on Louisville Slugger bats. This started a trend that later included Ty Cobb, Babe Ruth, Ted Williams, Mickey Mantle, and many others.

The company made another important addition in 1912. Frank W. Bradsby, a young buyer from Simmon's Hardware in St. Louis, was recruited to join the firm and manage sales. Bradsby quickly established himself as a dominant figure in the sporting goods industry. His impact was so great on the firm that, in 1916, the name was changed to Hillerich & Bradsby Company.

The company responded to other opportunities in the sporting goods industry. In 1916, it began making golf clubs. By 1934, it introduced the PowerBilt line of clubs that is still in existence today. Later, in 1966, the company bought Wally Enterprises of Ontario, Canada, and entered the hockey stick business.

Hillerich & Bradsby continued to expand its baseball presence, as well. In 1975, the company introduced a line of baseball gloves, which eventually opened the door for other accessories to be added. Responding to a new trend, Hillerich & Bradsby contracted with Alcoa in 1970 to manufacture aluminum bats, purchasing that business line from Alcoa eight years later.

The 1930s and 1940s brought unusual challenges to Hillerich & Bradsby. The flood of 1937 caused considerable damage to the administrative and manufacturing facilities of the company. During the war years of 1941 to 1945, the company shifted production to the manufacture of M1 carbine stocks and tank pins.

Frank Bradsby was active in managing the company until his death in 1937. Bud Hillerich continued to serve as president until his death in 1946 at the age of 80. He was on the way to Los Angeles, California, to attend the annual professional baseball meeting when he died. He was succeeded by his older son Ward, who died in 1949, then his younger son Frank, who died in 1969. John A. Hillerich III was then appointed to the post.

Today, the company continues to manufacture more than 1 million wood Louisville Slugger bats annually. Some are still made by hand for professional baseball players, who each use, on average, more than 70 bats per season. The company also manufactures more than 1.5 million aluminum bats at its Ontario, California, plant and continues to offer a variety of sporting goods products.

SOURCE: Hillerich & Bradsby archives

Austin H. Hills, Reuben W. Hills

[Hills Bros. Coffee]

In 1638, Joseph Hills left his home in Kent, England, and immigrated to Malden, Massachusetts to start a new life. The Hills family subsequently grew and moved throughout New England. Descendant Austin Hills, born in 1823, settled in Thomeston, Maine. He and his wife had three sons, including Austin Herbert Hills, born on March 30, 1851, and Reuben Wilmarth Hills, born on May 25, 1856.

Austin Hills, Sr., traveled with friends in 1863 to California to search for gold. However, he had to settle for a job as a shipwright, building ferryboats that worked the San Francisco Bay. Over the next ten years he made several trips to visit his family in Maine. Finally, in 1873, with the opening of the transcontinental rail service, his wife and sons moved to San Francisco.

Austin Hills (shown at right), age 22, became a skilled machinist and found a job in San Francisco servicing White sewing machines. In 1875, he opened his own business selling dairy products in a public market. Seventeen-year-old Reuben worked odd jobs for local grocers for two years. Then, on February 14, 1878, Austin and Reuben Hills established a partnership known simply as Hills Bros. to retail dairy products at San Francisco's Bay City Market.

In 1881, the brothers purchased a coffee store known as the Arabian Coffee & Spice Mills, where they sold roasted coffee beans, teas, and eventually spices and flavoring extracts. Three years later they moved to larger quarters, and in 1886 they dropped their retail operations to focus on the wholesale trade.

As the market for Hills Bros. products grew among San Francisco merchants and five western states, their wholesale dairy division started looking for a new way to pack butter for export. About 1898, Norton Brothers, a Chicago can company, had just patented a process for vacuum-packing foods, and in 1899 Hills Bros. obtained exclusive rights to the process over the entire Pacific Coast. Subsequently, Hills Bros. butter became the first food product to be vacuum-packed in a can.

Encouraged by the success of the vacuum-sealed can for butter, Reuben Hills (shown at right) sensed that the process might also work well for coffee. After considerable testing, his theory was proven true, and in July 1900 Hills Bros. introduced its original vacuum-packed coffee. By extending the shelf life of coffee, the brothers revolutionized their industry.

Their business rapidly expanded over the next several years until 1906, when the great San Francisco earthquake and fire destroyed the Hills Bros. plant and offices. The brothers moved their dairy business to a temporary location in one direction and their coffee operations to temporary space in another direction. Still, it took them two years to fully recover.

Once they had their facilities under one roof, they resumed their rapid expansion. Soon their fresh, vacuum-packed coffee was being stocked in 11 western states. They officially incorporated as Hills Bros. in 1914, then changed the name to Hills Bros. Coffee, Inc., in 1929. By then, they had moved into their own seven-story building along the San Francisco Bay waterfront.

Reuben's three sons and Austin's son joined the company and played a key role in expanding sales into the Midwest. Austin Hills died in 1933, and his brother Reuben died one year later. The third generation of Hills family members later joined the company and introduced Hills Bros. coffee to the eastern seaboard.

Hills Bros. grew to be the third-largest coffee roaster in the United States until 1976, when it was sold to a Brazilian cooperative. Six years later, a private San Francisco investment group acquired the firm, and they in turn sold it to Nestlé Holdings, Inc. in 1985, to become a part of Nestlé USA.

SOURCE: Hill Bros. Coffee, Inc. archives

Conrad N. Hilton

[Hilton Hotels]

When his family needed money during the panic of 1907, Conrad Hilton suggested they rent some of the family bedrooms to travelers. Eventually, Hilton purchased his own hotel, a seedy property that served the Texas oil fields. After barely surviving the Great Depression, Hilton went on a buying and selling binge, building the Hilton Hotel chain into one of the world's most respected hospitality companies.

Conrad Nicholson Hilton was born on December 25, 1887, in San Antonio, New Mexico Territory, the second of eight children born to August and Mary Hilton. August, an immigrant from Norway, had built and lost several fortunes in speculative ventures. His flagship business was a general store in San Antonio, which enabled him to build a large home with several bedrooms.

During the panic of 1907, money was scarce. At young Conrad's suggestion, the Hilton family transformed their home into a modest inn. Each night, Conrad went to the train station to drum up business, and for $1 travelers were given a clean room, meals cooked by Mary Hilton, and good hospitality.

Hilton was educated at St. Michael's College, the New Mexico Military Institute, and the New Mexico School of Mines. Upon completion of his education, he worked at his father's business until being elected to the first New Mexico state legislature after statehood was awarded in 1912. While young Hilton was serving in the U.S. Army during World War I as a second lieutenant in Europe, his father died in an automobile accident.

After the war, Hilton returned to New Mexico and sought to establish his own business. He was intrigued with banking after being involved with bank leg-

islation during his earlier term in office. Following a failed San Antonio banking venture, Hilton headed for Texas in 1919 with his $5,000 savings and inheritance to buy another bank.

That bank deal didn't materialize. When Hilton walked into the lobby of the rundown Mobley Hotel in Cisco, Texas, he was amazed at the line of oil field workers looking for rooms. The hotel's owner told Hilton that no rooms were available and, apparently overwhelmed with the business, said that he would like to sell the hotel. With his own $5,000 plus $20,000 borrowed from a bank and $15,000 borrowed from friends, Conrad Hilton purchased his first hotel.

Hilton skillfully managed his Cisco hotel and, over the next six years, acquired several other properties. In 1925, he made a major commitment to build a Hilton Hotel in Dallas. The project did not go smoothly, and Hilton ran out of funds before the hotel was built. Additional investors were found, and the hotel did get built, but Hilton lost ownership of the property.

More problems followed. The Depression brought havoc to the hotel industry, with more than 80 percent of all properties being forced into bankruptcy. Hilton was not exempt, losing three of his eight hotels and falling $500,000 in debt with no source of income. The pressure also cost him his marriage.

Hilton, a strong Roman Catholic, maintained his faith. Slowly he pulled himself through the Depression and launched a series of deals, buying hotels at low prices and selling them at a profit. In 1938, he acquired the Sir Francis Drake in San Francisco, followed by the Town House in Los Angeles, the Stevens in Chicago, and the Roosevelt and the Plaza in New York.

In 1949, Hilton achieved world recognition when he purchased the famed Waldorf-Astoria Hotel in New York City. Five years later, he paid $111 million for the entire chain of Statler Hotels. He also launched his international operations in 1949, opening the 300-room Caribe Hilton in San Juan, Puerto Rico.

Hilton became known as an enthusiastic deal maker in the hotel industry. One New York executive noted in a Hilton biography: "Hilton is notorious for walking around and around a hotel he wants to acquire. He studies everything; how many men and women come in and out, how many are smiling. . . . If there are 64 lightbulbs framing the marquee, how many are burned out."

By the mid-1960s, Hilton had about 40 hotels in America and about 40 more in international cities such as Caracas, Barbados, Rome, and London. His success enabled Hilton to lead the life of a celebrity. He was married briefly to actress Zsa Zsa Gabor. Coincidentally, his son Nickie was actress Elizabeth Taylor's first husband.

Conrad Hilton died on January 4, 1979, at the age of 91.

SOURCE: Hilton Hotels archives

Benjamin F. Hirsch

[Turtle Wax]

Ben Hirsch was an energetic entrepreneur and entertainer. Early in adulthood he was a professional magician in the Chicago area. During the late 1940s, he came across the idea of a car polish, and he and his wife Marie perfected the formula for their Plastone brand wax in their home. With a total investment of $500, the couple regularly made batches of their wax in the family bathtub.

Once it was bottled, Hirsch would hop a Chicago streetcar and roam the city in search of buyers. He became famous for waxing the fenders of cars sitting in parking lots, then waiting until the owner returned. The couple also maintained a small storefront on Chicago Avenue.

Hirsch didn't limit his product line to car waxes. He also experimented with a shoe polish, marketed as Penny Shine, and a floor polish. He even developed a line of toppings for cakes and desserts, as well as Angel Rinse cold wash detergent.

By the early 1950s, Hirsch was peddling his wax to neighboring states. On one particular trip to Beloit, Wisconsin, he came across a stream called Turtle Creek. He reflected on the name, associating the hard shells of turtles with the strength of his car wax, then coined the name Turtle Wax for the business and Super Hard Shell for the polish.

The name took hold, resulting in more than one humorous consequence. The marketing department once received the following note: "To whom it may concern: I just wanted you to know I love your new product, Turtle Wax II. My turtles haven't shined like this in years . . ."

Upon his Hirsch's death in 1966, his daughter Sondra assumed the position of chairman of the board of directors. Her husband, Denis Healy, serves as president.

Today the company continues to be based in Chicago. It also maintains a plant in Skelmersdale, England, to serve the international market. Turtle Wax also operates several state-of-the-art car washes and detailing centers in the Chicago area.

SOURCE: Turtle Wax archives

Leon C. Hirsch

[United States Surgical Corporation]

Leon C. Hirsch was born on July 20, 1927, in Bronx, New York, the youngest of three children of Isidore and Roslyn Hirsch. As a child, young Hirsch spent most of his free time outdoors. Fascinated with ecology as a teenager, he often hitchhiked to neighboring Westchester County to collect salamanders, frogs, snakes, fish, and butterflies. When not outdoors, he was building thermostats for his aquarium where the array of animals and insects he collected would reside.

His passion for nature later drew him to the Bronx School of Science, where he studied science, mechanical drawing, and design. After serving for two years in the U.S. Army, Hirsch enrolled in a three-month advertising course at the City College of New York in 1947. Upon completion, the 20-year-old worked at a firm for only one year before launching his own company, eventually known as Lebow, Hirsch and Windley.

In 1955, he established New Jersey Standard Food, Inc., a home food distributor service, where he served as company president and secretary until 1959. Hirsch's desire to pursue new ventures led to another enterprise, Tenax, Inc., a company engaged in the manufacturing of coin-operated dry-cleaning machinery.

In 1964, he was in a business broker's office when he noticed an odd-looking device sitting nearby. He was told that it was a surgical stapling device called a Von Petz clamp and that the broker had been retained by the Soviet government to try to sell surgical staplers in America. Hirsch poured over the project's "sell book" and immediately contacted Dr. Mark Ravitch, professor of surgery at Johns Hopkins University, who thought the concept of using a mechanical device instead of sutures had much to offer the patient and the surgeon, but that the Russian staplers, as designed, were merely a medical curiosity.

Hirsch took the instrument home and came up with the idea of simplifying the function of the device by machine-loading the staples into a cartridge that could be easily slipped into the stapler like a razor blade into a razor. He constructed a little balsa wood model and showed it to Ravitch, who thought it was a terrific solution that could make the instrument practical. From that balsa wood model, United States Surgical Corporation (USSC) was born.

Hirsch's life savings of $50,000 were quickly exhausted. However, one of the surgeons who liked the prototype knew of a wealthy lawyer named Zanvyl Kreiger, part owner of a major league baseball team, the Baltimore Orioles. Intrigued, Kreiger agreed to contribute $2 million in loans to the company.

It took more than three years and $3 million to develop the first series of AUTO SUTURE staplers, which came to market in 1967. These instruments were much more user-friendly than their predecessors because they utilized disposable loading units, which eliminated the tedious hand loading of minute staples. Surgical stapling was now able to increase speed, precision, and overall reliability in the operating room.

In 1987, the company introduced a device called a *trocar,* which was capable of making tiny puncture incisions to serve as entry ports for minimally invasive instruments. This device launched USSC's entry into the laparoscopic or minimally invasive surgical market. Their laparoscopic clip applier made possible a revolutionary new technique for gallbladder removal, with such dramatic results that approximately 90 percent of the 600,000 gallbladder removals performed annually in the United States have been converted to this technique.

Today, USSC is the world's largest manufacturer and marketer of surgical staplers, with approximately a 60 percent share of the market and approximately a 50 percent share of the laparoscopic market. USSC continues to develop its product line through new areas of research and development, including cardiovascular, urologic, and orthopedic surgery, as well as women's health care. In 1967, in its first year as an operating business, USSC posted sales of just over $350,000. Fourteen years later, annual sales surpassed $100 million, and revenues in 1992 reached $1 billion.

SOURCE: United States Surgical Corporation archives

William H. Hoover

[The Hoover Company]

William H. Hoover was born in the heart of Pennsylvania Dutch country and raised in Stark County, Ohio. As a young adult, Hoover joined with his brothers to purchase the family tanning business. Over time, he bought out his two brothers, and in 1875 he moved the operation to North Canton, Ohio—called New Berlin at the time—where he expanded into the saddlery business. In 1908, he obtained rights to a "suction sweeper" that was invented by his wife's cousin. Quickly, the Hoover sweeper was refined and the business grew into one of the world's most popular vacuum manufacturers.

William Henry Hoover was born on August 18, 1849, in Lancaster County, Pennsylvania, to Daniel and Mary (Kryder) Hoover. In 1866 he attended Mount Union College in Alliance, Ohio. In 1870, he and his two brothers purchased the family tannery from their father. One year later, Hoover married Susan Troxel, and the couple eventually had six children.

In 1875, Hoover purchased the John Lind tannery in present-day North Canton, Ohio, where he relocated his family and business, which was eventually renamed the W.H. Hoover Company. The company's earliest successful product was a line of horse collars. By the mid-1880s, he had expanded into the saddlery business. Having bought out his brothers' share of the business, "The Boss" (which became an affectionate nickname) had a total of 55 employees. By 1887, he discontinued his tanning operations to focus on saddlery.

In 1907, Hoover made a decision that changed the shape of his company. Susan Hoover's cousin, Murray Spangler, was the night janitor at a Canton department store. Afflicted by asthma, Spangler set out to find a way to keep from raising dust while he was sweeping floors. With a tin soap box, a fan, a pillowcase, and a broom handle, he fashioned a crude, 40-pound device that pulled the dust away from him while he swept.

Spangler approached the Hoovers for financial backing to build and market the device. After Susan tried the device in the family home, she gave it her endorsement. In 1908, William Hoover purchased the patent from Spangler and incorporated The Hoover Suction Sweeper Company. Spangler was retained as plant superintendent to help build manufacturing operations, and in the first year six employees built and sold nearly 350 suction sweepers.

Hoover developed an ingenious marketing idea for his sweepers. He placed an ad in *The Saturday Evening Post* offering a free ten-day trial to anyone who submitted a written request. Rather than send the sweeper directly to those who answered the ad, Hoover sent the sweeper to a reputable store near the requester's home. He included a note asking the store to deliver it to the person; if a sale was made, the store could keep the commission. This not only secured a considerable amount of direct sales, it helped Hoover quickly establish a large network of retailers.

Word of Hoover's sweeper spread beyond America. In 1911, he opened a Canadian assembly plant. Eight years later, he began a sales organization in England. By the early 1920s, Hoover's sweepers were being sold around the world. In 1919, the saddlery business was discontinued, and Hoover focused on making improvements to the sweeper.

William Hoover was a man of strong religious convictions and community pride. In 1877, Hoover became active in the Christian church. By 1882, he was an ordained minister. He was also active in local politics, serving on the school board, and in 1905 he was elected mayor. Soon after he launched the sweeper business, he challenged his sons and employees to develop a product "that made cleanliness next to Godliness."

William Henry Hoover died on February 25, 1932. In 1985, Hoover was acquired by Chicago Pacific Corporation, which itself was acquired by the Maytag Corporation in 1989. The Hoover brand name continues to be one of the most recognized names in the floor-care industry. The company's main manufacturing facility is at the same site as William Hoover's first leather goods factory.

SOURCE: Hoover Company archives

George A. Hormel

[Hormel Foods Corporation]

Christian Hormel brought his family, including three-year-old John George Hormel, to Buffalo, New York, from Germany in 1833. John grew up an adventurous young man and, at age 19, took a job on a Mississippi riverboat. He later returned to Buffalo and went to work in a tannery. In 1856, he married Susanna W. Decker, who had also made the trip from Germany to Buffalo, where her father had established a successful meatpacking business.

George A. Hormel was born on December 4, 1860, the third of 12 children born to John G. and Susanna Hormel. When young George was five years old, the family moved to Toledo, Ohio, where his 35-year-old father and a partner launched a tanning business. When the panic of 1873 struck, the tannery closed down and 12-year-old George went to work at a variety of jobs—including lathe worker, meat market helper, dockworker, and lumberyard worker—to help support the family

At age 15, Hormel moved to Chicago to work for his Uncle Jacob—his mother's youngest brother—who had established a meatpacking company. The work was hard, at least 14 hours daily, and the pay was a mere $10 per month plus room and board. The experience proved valuable, but short-lived. Within two years, the shop was closed and Hormel was back in Toledo. Jacob later reopened the business, and Hormel joined him briefly before heading for Kansas City.

At age 19, Hormel took the $5 train trip to Kansas City in search of a new opportunity. Initially, the best he could do was wash dishes, but he soon was hired as a wool buyer. He quickly caught on and was granted a raise. Upon return from his next trip, however, he was shocked to find out that his employer absconded with $100,000 obtained through fraudulent sales.

Hormel returned to Chicago and landed a job with a large dealer in hides, wool, and furs. He at first performed general labor, but was soon promoted to buyer in the company's Des Moines, Iowa, office. As he traveled through his new territory, he was struck by the beauty and charm of the countryside. He became particularly fond of Austin, Minnesota, where he developed several close friendships.

In 1887, a fire burned down the building of Hormel's best customer in Austin. The owner built a new shop, but wanted to retire. He offered half interest each to his son and to George Hormel. In October of that year, the partnership of Friedrich & Hormel opened for business.

After four years of successful growth, the owners came to a crossroads. The production end of the business, which was handled by Hormel, had grown into a sizable operation. Friedrich, however, was content with the retail end of the business and was apparently not interested in pushing for further growth. In 1891, they parted company, and Hormel started operating under the name "Geo. A. Hormel & Co." George Hormel, with help from his only employee, built the company's first building by hand.

In 1892, Hormel married Lillian Belle Gleason, and within a year their only son, Jay C. Hormel, was born. Help for the business started to arrive when two of George Hormel's brothers moved to Austin in 1893. Eventually, his parents and other brothers also relocated, providing George with strong family support.

Company records captured the astonishing growth of Hormel's company. In his first year of business, 1892, he processed 610 hogs. By 1897 the number rose to nearly 9,000, and five years later it stood at 42,500. In 1912, the company processed more than 265,000 hogs. Sales were made by bicycle and horse-drawn carriages.

While the company experienced rapid growth, it was not always comfortable growth. George Hormel became adept at creative financing, which was necessary in this capital-intensive industry. The company nearly collapsed in 1921 under financial difficulties. The detective work of Jay Hormel uncovered the embezzlement of more than $1 million of company funds by a trusted employee. Facing $3 million in outstanding loans, George and Jay Hormel were able to negotiate an extension, and the company was soon profitable.

In 1929, George Hormel retired from active service with the company and assumed the role of board chairman. His son Jay was named president. George Hormel died on June 5, 1946, at the age of 85, two days after he suffered a stroke.

SOURCES: Geo. A. Hormel & Co. archives; Richard Dougherty, *In Quest of Quality: Hormel's First 75 Years*, Geo. A. Hormel & Co., 1966; *The Hormel Legacy: 100 Years of Quality*, Geo. A. Hormel & Co., 1991

Henry O. Houghton, George H. Mifflin

[Houghton Mifflin Company]

Henry Oscar Houghton was born on April 30, 1823, in Sutton, Vermont, the 11th child of William and Marilla (Clay) Houghton. Henry was the grandson of Revolutionary War veteran Captain James Clay and a descendant of John Houghton, who in 1653 was the first family member to immigrate to America from his native Lancaster, England.

At age 13, Henry Houghton went to work as an apprentice at the *Burlington Free Press*. After learning the craft, he set out for Nunda, New York. While riding the stagecoach, he became acquainted with another passenger, who happened to own a printing shop. He went to work for the man and attended school until 1842, when he returned to his old job in Burlington and enrolled at the University of Vermont.

Upon graduation, Houghton moved to Worcester, Massachusetts, and was hired by the *Daily Evening Traveler* at $5 per week. Several other printing jobs followed over the next two years, which provided funds to pay off his college debts and to become connected in the printing industry.

In 1848, Houghton was offered half interest in a profitable Boston printing shop for $3,100. After he raised the funds, he and his partner, Charles Bolles, moved their printing shop to Cambridge because of lower rent and less competition. Bolles and subsequent partners either retired or left, and the company moved to new quarters along the Charles River, where it was renamed H. O. Houghton & Company, and later Riverside Press.

The Riverside Press did a good deal of printing for the Boston book publisher Ticknor & Fields, founded in the 1830s. Ticknor & Fields assembled problably the most distinguished collection of writers ever associated with one American publishing house, including Henry Wadsworth Longfellow, Oliver Wendell Holmes, John Greenleaf Whittier, Ralph Waldo Emerson, Harriet Beecher Stowe, Nathaniel Hawthorne, Henry David Thoreau, and Mark Twain. By 1880, when Houghton Mifflin was formed, the two firms had merged into one successful printing/publishing company.

Houghton landed a desirable contract in 1863 to print and bind George and Charles Merriam's fourth revision of *Noah Webster's Unabridged Dictionary*.

Within four years the firm was printing, in addition to the dictionary, nearly 12 newspapers and magazines and more than 30 books. Houghton became printer *and* publisher of one of the magazines, *The Atlantic Monthly,* when its owners couldn't repay debts to Riverside Press.

As the business continued to grow, Houghton started to look for an assistant, but when a good candidate presented himself, Houghton balked.

George Harrison Mifflin came from a wealthy family, graduated from Harvard, and traveled extensively. While on a trip to Paris, he attended an exposition at which Riverside Press was presented with an award. Mifflin remembered reading Houghton's books as a child, and, anxious to pursue a rewarding profession, he returned to Massachusetts to look up the printer.

Young Mifflin not only asked to be part of Houghton's company, he offered to make an investment. The experienced Houghton turned him down, explaining that because of his privileged lifestyle Mifflin was not at all prepared for the rigors of the printing trade. Mifflin persisted and, in 1868, made a $15,000 investment and went to work for Riverside Press.

Mifflin was first assigned to bookkeeping, then later was put in charge of binding. In November 1871, Houghton was convinced of Mifflin's skills and determination. He promoted him to full partner and eventually renamed the firm Houghton, Mifflin, & Company.

The company grew rapidly over the next two decades, bolstered by the demand for textbooks. In 1882, the firm introduced the *Riverside Literature Series,* unabridged American masterpieces, complete with study guides, that were sold to schools for 15¢ each. Over 100,000 were sold in five short years.

Henry O. Houghton died on August 25, 1895. George Mifflin was 50 years old at the time. He and Houghton had been partners for fully half of his life. Mifflin died in 1921. The two partners came from very different backgrounds, yet worked well together for 25 years. Mifflin, indeed, finished the job that Houghton started.

Houghton Mifflin remains a leading publisher for the educational market. They also offer an extensive line of reference publications, fiction, and nonfiction for adults and young readers, and software for the educational and consumer markets.

SOURCE: Ellen B. Ballou, *The Building of the House: Houghton Mifflin's Formative Years,* Houghton Mifflin, 1970

Howard R. Hughes

[Hughes Aircraft Company]

Of all twentieth century entrepreneurs, perhaps the most famous is movie producer, aviator, engineer, financier, and industrialist Howard Hughes. He inherited a fortune and, over the next several decades, transformed it into one of the most diverse empires built by any American businessman.

Howard Robard Hughes was born on December 24, 1905, in Houston, Texas, the only child of Howard and Allene (Gano) Hughes. The elder Hughes was once an attorney, but later entered the Texas oil business. In 1908, he was granted a patent on a revolutionary drill bit that efficiently bore through hard rock. Income from the device enabled Howard Sr. to launch the Hughes Tool Company in 1913.

As a youngster, Hughes exhibited a strong curiosity for electronics and adventure. At age 11, he built a ham radio from scratch. Later, he rigged up a small gasoline engine to his bicycle, giving him one of Houston's first motorcycles. Perhaps the most significant event in his childhood was a short flight arranged by his father on a Glen Curtiss seaplane. This stirred a fascination with aerospace in young Howard that eventually transformed the industry.

After the death of Hughes's mother in 1922, he and his father moved to Los Angeles, California, where his Uncle Rupert had become a successful screenwriter. Young Hughes was soon introduced to some of Hollywood's biggest stars. When his father died two years later, Hughes inherited his 75 percent stake in Hughes Tool and quickly acquired the other 25 percent.

At the age of 20, while Hughes was making about $2 million annually from the family business, he decided to enter the movie industry. His first film, *Swell Hogan,* was never released, but by 1928 his film *Two Arabian Knights* won an Academy Award. His $4 million film *Hell's Angels,* released in 1930, became a classic, as did another of his early films, *Scarface.*

While making the 1940 movie *The Outlaw,* Hughes was dissatisfied with the effect created by the brassiere worn by the film's star, Jane Russell. By combining his knowledge of structural engineering with his director's eye, Hughes designed a new brassiere that not only enhanced the film, it started a nationwide trend.

Filmmaking was not the only pursuit of Howard Hughes. The Hughes Tool Company continued to be a money machine that fueled his interests. He accumulated real estate, thousands of acres at a time, but seldom sold any. He purchased controlling interest in Trans World Airlines (TWA). He even purchased the brewery adjoining the Hughes Tool Company.

Hughes organized Hughes Aircraft Company in 1932 as a division of Hughes Tool. Starting in a hanger in Burbank, California, Hughes and his team initially modified military aircraft for racing and recreation. He eventually designed, built, and piloted his own plane, the H-1, which set a world speed record of 352 miles per hour in 1935.

In 1938, one year after Amelia Earhart's plane disappeared, Hughes and a four-member crew, piloting a Lockheed Model 14, set an around-the-world flight record of three days, 19 hours, and 14 minutes. The crew was greeted by more than 1 million people who attended a New York City ticker-tape parade.

During World War II, Hughes teamed up with Henry Kaiser to build a "flying ship" to help ward off Nazi submarine attacks. The result was the famous Spruce Goose, the world's largest aircraft. Kaiser eventually dropped out of the venture, and after cost and schedule overruns, the plane didn't make its first voyage until 1947, well after the war ended.

Hughes nearly lost his life in 1946. While testing his XF-11 military plane, the aircraft went into a spin and crashed into a Beverly Hills home. A passing Marine pulled Hughes from the burning structure. Later, it was determined that he had more than 100 broken bones. The accident didn't slow him down. One year later he flew the maiden flight of the second XF-11 model, and later piloted the first flight of the Spruce Goose.

In 1953, Hughes Aircraft was incorporated as an independent entity and severed ties to Hughes Tool Company. By the mid-1950s, Hughes's companies employed 50,000 people and generated sales of $1 million per day. In 1955, he sold his Hollywood production company, RKO Studios, for $25 million, the largest cash deal in the history of the movie industry. Ten years later, he sold his stake in TWA for $546 million.

Hughes moved into the Desert Inn Hotel and Casino in Las Vegas in 1966. One year later, he bought not only the Desert Inn, but also the Sands, Castaways, and the Frontier, giving him 2,000 Las Vegas hotel rooms. He acquired a television station, Alamo Airways, and the NLV airport, motel, and restaurant.

He also purchased 25,000 acres of ranches, estates, and residential property surrounding Las Vegas. This was followed by more casinos, including the Silver Slipper, the Landmark, and Harold's Club-Reno. He sold Hughes Tool in 1972 for $150 million, but folded Hughes Helicopter (which was later sold to McDonnell Douglas) into his Las Vegas and mining holdings.

Because of his high-visibility success and renowned wealth, it is not surprising that Hughes spent many years dodging the public spotlight. In his later years he became something of a recluse and his business activities were often veiled in secrecy. His airplane accident had left him in pain for the rest of his life, and many rumors surfaced regarding his use of painkillers.

Hughes later moved to the Bahamas and, in failing health, relocated again to Acapulco, Mexico. When his condition worsened, an airplane was dispatched to fly Hughes to Houston. On April 5, 1976, 70-year-old Howard R. Hughes died from kidney failure while in flight.

While in his 20s, Howard Hughes became obsessed with the idea of creating a medical research institute. In 1952, Hughes spun off his Aircraft division from Hughes Tool, then donated the entire corporation to his Medical Institute. In 1985, the Howard Hughes Medical Institute sold the Hughes Aircraft Company to General Motors for $5.2 billion.

SOURCES: Hughes Aircraft Company archives; L. A. "Pat" Hyland, *Call Me Pat,* The Donning Company, Virginia Beach, VA, 1993

H. Wayne Huizenga

[Waste Management, Inc.; Blockbuster Video]

Harry Wayne Huizenga was born in 1937 in Evergreen Park, Illinois. He grew up in the tight-knit Dutch Reform community attending church but forbidden to read comic books. At age 14, he went to work for his father, Harry Huizenga, an aggressive building contractor.

In 1953, Harry moved his family to Fort Lauderdale, Florida, where he continued to build houses. Wayne attended Pine Crest High School, where he played on the school's first football team. When the name of the team was up for a vote, young Huizenga supported the name Panthers, which eventually was adopted by the team. The name would come up again later in Huizenga's life.

Upon graduation, Huizenga moved back to the Chicago area, where he drove a bulldozer and worked odd jobs. He later enrolled in Calvin College in Michigan, only to drop out two years later. He married and returned to Florida.

One day, in a local restaurant, Huizenga and his father bumped into an old friend from Chicago who was operating a small garbage-hauling business in Florida. By the end of the meal, Wayne Huizenga had been appointed the new manager of the fledgling business. Thereafter, he was supervising the crews of the three company trucks in the morning and knocking on doors for new accounts in the afternoons.

Eventually, Huizenga bought a garbage truck and launched his own $500-per-month route. His daily routine grew even longer: awake at 2:30 A.M., service accounts until noon, change clothes and solicit more business the rest of the day. By 1968, his business, Southern Sanitation Company, had 20 trucks and was serving clients from Fort Lauderdale to Key West.

Later, in 1971, he merged with Ace Scavenger Service, a Chicago garbage hauler founded in 1894 by Huizenga's grandfather. The new venture was named Waste Management. The company grew fast enough to go public later that same year, providing Huizenga with sufficient capital to make other acquisitions. Within a decade, annual sales exceeded $1 billion and the company was recognized as the largest waste hauler in the world.

Huizenga wasn't comfortable building just one empire. In the mid-1980s, he started looking for a new opportunity to replicate his success with Waste Management. Then he met David Cook, who had launched a small video rental company in Dallas called Blockbuster Video. Cook had established eight of his video superstores and felt that the concept had strong potential. Huizenga agreed and put together an $18 million equity infusion.

Cook left Blockbuster within several months of the deal and Huizenga launched an aggressive expansion. By the end of the year, 133 stores had been opened. At one point he was opening the doors to a new store every 17 hours, and in 1989, the company passed the 1,000-store mark. In 1992, he diversified the company by launching Blockbuster Music Plus stores, and one year later he acquired a majority interest in Spelling Entertainment, producers of a number of hit television shows.

Huizenga also entered the sports market in a big way. He purchased the Miami Dolphins football team and Joe Robbie Stadium. He brought professional baseball and hockey to south Florida by franchising the Florida Marlins and the Florida Panthers, which he named in honor of his high school football team.

By 1994, there were nearly 4,500 Blockbuster Video stores and nearly 500 Blockbuster Music Plus stores. The company caught the eye of Sumner Redstone, owner of the media giant Viacom, who made an offer of $8.4 billion, which Huizenga couldn't pass up. Blockbuster was sold to Viacom, and Huizenga agreed to stay on to help the transition for the next nine months.

Today, Huizenga is chairman and co-CEO of Republic Industries, a holding company with subsidiaries operating in the automotive retailing, automotive rental, automotive financial services, solid waste services, and electronic security services industries.

SOURCES: Huizenga archives; D. M. Anderson, M. Warshaw, and M. Mulvhill, "Blockbuster Video's Wayne Huizenga," *Success* magazine, March 1995

J. B. Hunt

[J. B. Hunt Transport]

Being born in rural Arkansas two years before the Great Depression didn't dampen the spirit of Johnnie Hunt. Starting at age 12, he worked in a variety of jobs that provided just enough money for food and shelter. After losing his first business venture, Hunt found success, first by developing an innovative packaging method for rice hull and next by establishing J. B. Hunt Transport, one of America's largest trucking companies.

Johnnie Bryan Hunt was born in 1927 in Cleburne County, Arkansas, the third of seven children born to Walter and Alma Hunt. Discouraged with work in the oil fields, Walter Hunt moved his family to Mississippi County in eastern Arkansas, where they rented land and began sharecropping.

Because of the Depression, J.B. quit school after the seventh grade and, at the age of 12, went to work in his uncle's sawmill, earning $1.50 per 12-hour workday. By 1945, he was old enough to enlist in the U.S. Army, after which he resumed his position at the lumber mill. He and his brothers also started hauling and selling lumber throughout Arkansas, Missouri, and Illinois. As a second sideline, he bought and transported chickens.

In 1948, Hunt attended auctioneering school in Mason City, Iowa. Upon completing school, he returned to Heber Springs, Arkansas, and borrowed enough money to buy a local livestock auction barn. The business failed, and Hunt was nearly $4,000 in debt. Convinced that opportunity existed in the big city, Hunt borrowed $10 and took a bus to Little Rock, Arkansas, where he rented a room at the local YMCA.

Motivated by his debt and and the fact that his girlfriend, Johnelle DeBusk, was waiting for him back home, Hunt quickly found a job with a Texarkana trucking firm. He saved most of his $40-per-week salary, and within a year he and Johnelle were married. Not long after that, he found a better job driving for Superior Forwarding Company, where he worked for the next seven years. When asked by a friend how he stayed awake all night driving trucks, Hunt replied: "I just think about all the people I owe money. I keep slapping my leg and keep on driving."

In the late 1950s, Hunt's route took him through the Stuttgart, Arkansas, region, where he frequently witnessed rice hulls burning in the fields. He recalled his early lumber mill days, when chicken farmers hauled off wood shavings for use as base litter in their poultry houses. Hunt had always felt that the rice hulls would make a superior poultry litter if only a good packaging system could be developed.

Hunt devised a system that would work and, by 1960, found an interested venture-financing partner, who encouraged him to sell stock to the eventual end users. J.B. took a one-week vacation from his job to travel through poultry country, calling on businesses such as Tyson Foods. By the end of his vacation, he had secured the necessary backing.

One year later, the J. B. Hunt Company broke ground for its rice hull packing plant. The family had sold their home, invested the proceeds into the venture, and the 34-year-old Hunt quit his secure truck driving job to devote his full attention to the business. At the end of the first year, the company showed a loss of nearly $20,000.

Deep in debt and with nowhere to turn, Hunt kept the factory going. At the end of the second year, it showed a small profit, and the following year ended with an even bigger profit. Eventually, the firm grew to be one the largest and most profitable rice hull providers in the country.

Revenues from the business enabled J. B. Hunt to participate in other investments. In 1969, he purchased a small trucking company whose assets included five old trucks, seven worn-out refrigerated trailers, and a hauling contract with Ralston Purina. Hunt drew upon both his trucking and business experience, and by 1982 J. B. Hunt Transport was the 129th-largest carrier in America. In 1990, it became the first trucking company in the country to reach $1 billion in annual sales.

In 1988, J. B. Hunt appeared on the *Forbes* magazine list of the 400 wealthiest Americans. He was one of only nine people on the list who had never received a high school diploma.

SOURCES: J. B. Hunt Transport archives; Marvin Schwartz, *J. B. Hunt: The Long Haul to Success,* The University of Arkansas Press, 1992

Jon M. Huntsman

[Huntsman Corporation]

While working for an egg distributor in the early 1960s, Jon Huntsman devised a plastic carton that would protect the eggs from breaking. This success convinced him to launch his own plastics company in 1970. His new product, a lightweight plastic clamshell container for food products, was adopted by McDonald's restaurants. Today, the Huntsman Corporation is the largest privately owned chemical company in the world.

Jon Huntsman was born in 1937 in Blackfoot, Idaho, the second of three sons of a music teacher and his wife. As a child he picked tomatoes, started his own lawn-mower service, and worked at J.C. Penney to earn money. He was granted a scholarship to attend college, and graduated from the Wharton School of Finance at the University of Pennsylvania. Upon graduation, he served in the U.S. Navy as a gunnery officer.

In 1961, Huntsman worked in the food distribution business, where he developed a polystyrene carton that would protect eggs better than the cardboard containers. The product was commercialized by Dow Chemical. By 1969, Huntsman was ready to strike out on his own. He formed Huntsman Container, where he invented the clamshell container that was used by McDonald's restaurants for many years. He then started producing a host of other plastics products, including bowls and plates for use in hospitals.

The first 20 years of the business were rough, particularly the 1973 oil crisis that dramatically increased the cost of polystyrene. Facing bankruptcy, Huntsman scoured the globe, buying and trading to acquire polystyrene. The experience prompted him to purchase the polystyrene business from Shell.

Huntsman hated to build from scratch what he could buy for half the cost. Most of the growth of the company occurred through the acquisition of firms that were at low ebbs in their business cycles. Huntsman would then cut operating costs, integrate the new addition into the corporation, and rebuild the business.

Huntsman and his family are members of the Mormon Church. In fact, one of Huntsman's earliest mentors was another Mormon entrepreneur, J. W. Merriott. Jon and his wife Karen have nine children and nearly 30 grandchildren. Karen has been a vice president in the company since the day it was founded. The children have been a part of the business their entire lives. Once each week, the family assembled to discuss business and vote on decisions, even when the children were as young as seven years old.

The family is very generous. Even when Huntsman was in the Navy making $220 per month, he contributed $50 of it to Navy charities. More recently, Huntsman provided the funds to help rebuild Armenia after the 1988 earthquake.

In October 1995, Huntsman made a $100 million donation to the University of Utah for cancer research, and he helped raise an additional $50 million from other donors. Both of Huntsman's parents died of cancer, and Huntsman himself has had personal battles with prostate cancer and mouth cancer.

Today, the Huntsman Corporation is the largest privately held chemical company in the United States, with revenues of approximately $5 billion annually and nearly 10,000 employees. Jon Huntsman continues to serve as chairman and chief executive officer.

SOURCES: Huntsman Corporation archives; Andrew Wood, "Blending Business and Benevolence," *Chemical Week* magazine, February 7, 1996

Michael Ilitch, Marian Ilitch

[Little Caesars Pizza]

In 1959, Michael and Marian Ilitch founded their first Little Caesars Pizza restaurant in Garden City, Michigan. Maintaining a focus on quality products, clever marketing, franchising, and diligent financial management, they have built a billion-dollar pizza empire. In addition, they own the Detroit Tigers (baseball), Detroit Red Wings (hockey), Detroit's Fox Theatre, and several other sports, entertainment, and food service organizations.

The couple met on a blind date in 1954 that was arranged by Mike's father, Sotir Ilitch, a Macedonian immigrant who became a tool-and-die worker for Chrysler. At the time, Mike was playing minor league baseball in the Detroit Tigers farm system and Marian was a Delta Airlines reservation clerk. Less than a year later they were married.

Mike's three-year minor-league career was interrupted with leg injuries. During one stretch, he made pizzas to support himself. Despite another attempt to make the big leagues, the Tigers relegated him once again to the minors, and Mike left baseball.

He worked for a cement company, then sold dinnerware and aluminum awning door-to-door. Eventually, he entered into a three-way partnership in an awning business that thrived. One day Mike returned home from work with devastating news—the other two partners had announced that they were buying out Mike's share. Marian offered cautious comfort that things have a way of working out for the best.

In 1959, the Ilitches saw opportunity in a food that was essentially a snack item for younger consumers—pizza. Confidant that a broader market existed, they launched their first Little Caesars Pizza restaurant in a Garden City, Michigan, strip mall. Mike made the pizza in the back and conceived marketing strategies, while Marian worked the cash register in the front and kept the books.

Their growth strategy focused on franchising. Their first franchise opened for business in 1962, and they diligently followed their plans for the next 18 years. By 1980, there were 200 restaurants, and the Ilitches were in a position to accelerate their activities.

The pizza business continued to be at the heart of their entrepreneurial ventures. Mike developed a brilliant marketing plan in the mid-1970s: Offer two pizzas for one low price. He called it "Pizza! Pizza!"® and with the help of his marketing department and advertising agency, has delivered humorous television commercials ever since.

Today, there are more than 4,000 Little Caesars in all 50 states as well as several foreign countries. More than 20 percent are company-owned. The Ilitches maintain 100 percent ownership of the privately held company, which now has annual sales of nearly $2 billion, making it one of the top three international pizza chains (along with Pizza Hut and Dominos).

Now in his mid-60s, Mike actively runs the company and continues to experiment with recipes in the company kitchen. Marian still controls the cash register. As treasurer for the company, she maintains a watchful eye on cash flow.

The entrepreneurial flair of the Ilitches isn't limited to pizza. In 1982, the couple purchased the Detroit Red Wings franchise of the National Hockey League, as well as Olympia Entertainment, Inc., the management company for Joe Louis Arena (the Red Wings' home ice), and other sports and entertainment facilities. Their management philosophy has kept the Red Wings among the league's most valuable franchises and a frequent contender in the Stanley Cup playoffs.

However, Mike's most satisfying sports venture had to be the 1992 acquisition of the Detroit Tigers, the professional baseball team that a few decades earlier had turned back his efforts to play major league ball. The couple added to their sports holdings by purchasing the Detroit Rockers of the National Professional Soccer League in 1993.

The Ilitches have also invested heavily in the cultural rebirth of downtown Detroit. In 1987 they purchased the 5,000-seat Fox Theatre and restored it to its original splendor. It features top-name national touring entertainers, an annual Broadway series, and classic films. They also opened The Second City Detroit Comedy Theatre in 1993, which is adjacent to the Fox Theatre. The Ilitch investment in downtown Detroit has exceeded $200 million since 1982.

In May 1996 the Ilitch family created Olympia Development, Inc., a real estate and entertainment development company to focus on downtown Detroit projects.

Despite being ranked in the Forbes 400 as one of the richest men in America, Mike Ilitch has not lost his humble disposition. Acquaintances characterize him as "a guy you'd like to drink a beer with." Marian Ilitch has managed the family's billion-dollar budgets while raising seven children. Predictably, she has been named by *Working Woman* magazine and the National Foundation for Women Business Owners as one of the "Top 50 Women Business Owners" in the country for the past several years.

SOURCES: Little Caesar Enterprises archives; Michael Oneal, " 'Pizza Pizza' and Tigers, Too," *Business Week,* September 14, 1992; Adam Bryant, "He's Marketing, She's Finance: A $2 Billion Mom-and-Pop Shop," *The New York Times,* Sunday, December 6, 1992

Walter L. Jacobs, John D. Hertz

[Hertz Corporation]

Walter L. Jacobs (photo below) was born in Chicago, Illinois, in 1898, the son of a tailor. Walter worked in the clothing trade with his father for a time, then took other jobs as a mechanic and a salesman.

In September of 1918, Jacobs borrowed $2,500 to establish the Rent-A-Ford car rental company. Starting with 12 Model T Fords, he leased cars for $10 per day plus mileage, and the first 100 miles were free. Unable to afford expensive advertising, Jacobs spread word about his company with handwritten penny postcards. Within five years, his fleet had grown to 600 cars. To sustain the capital-hungry venture, Jacobs turned to John Hertz in 1923.

John D. Hertz was an enterprising man. He started selling newspapers on a Chicago street corner. Later, he landed a job at the sports news desk. Restless with journalism, Hertz launched his Yellow Cab Manufacturing Company and, looking for a way to expand his business, agreed to acquire Jacobs's car rental agency with the understanding that Jacobs would remain at the helm.

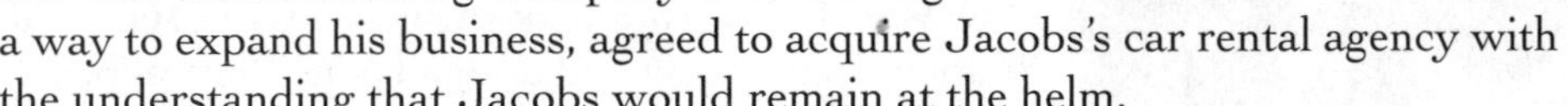

Hertz quickly learned that car rental customers were interested in comfortable touring vehicles, not bulky taxicabs. Undiscouraged, he launched a national advertising campaign and started a network of franchisers of the Hertz DrivUrSelf System. He also changed the company's color to yellow, which Hertz was obviously quite fond of.

In 1926, Hertz sold the car rental agency to General Motors. In 1953, Hertz was purchased from GM by the Omnibus Corporation, which took the company public a year later. By 1955, there were 1,000 Hertz locations worldwide. In the early 1960s, its fleet of cars numbered 85,000.

Walter Jacobs retired from his position as president and chief operating officer in 1960. He remained on the board of directors another seven years. He died in 1985.

Hertz went through a series of ownership changes until 1994, when it became a wholly owned subsidiary of Ford. Today, Hertz operates a fleet of 450,000 vehicles from nearly 5,300 locations in 140 countries.

SOURCES: Hertz archives; *DrivUrSelf Hertz,* company book, 1993

Roy Jacuzzi

[Jacuzzi Whirlpool and Spa]

Roy Jacuzzi led his family-owned business to international prominence after he invented the hydromassage bathtub. After 30 years of continuous improvements and the introduction of new products, Jacuzzi is a household name throughout the world.

In the early 1900s, seven brothers by the name of Jacuzzi left their native Italy and settled in California. The entrepreneurial family entered the aviation industry, carrying both U.S. mail and passengers. While in business, they built the first enclosed-cabin monoplane.

But their ingenuity wasn't limited to aeronautics. They later became involved with agricultural pumps, and in the 1950s one of the second-generation members of the Jacuzzi family adapted one of the company's pumps for home use in response to a medical problem. From this chance application, the family identified an opportunity: providing portable pumps to hospitals and schools.

Roy Jacuzzi (pictured here) was a third-generation family member who started working in the family business at age 12. Sensing an opportunity in the growing health and fitness trend in America, Roy developed the first self-contained, fully integrated whirlpool bath in 1968. His first model, named the Roman Bath, allowed bathers to enjoy hydromassage without placing a pump inside the tub.

Roy personally took his whirlpool to country fairs and trade shows. The public quickly accepted the stylish tubs, and more innovations followed. Larger units that would accommodate several people were built, and special heating and filtration systems that permitted water to be recycled were added.

By 1988, Roy was named president and chief executive officer of the family business. Always conscious of public trends, Roy responded to a fast-paced, shower-oriented society in 1990 with the announcement of the J-Dream. This is a self-contained whirlpool-shower combination with built-in vertical hydrotherapy. In essence, it is a Jacuzzi shower, complete with steam bath, overhead cascading water, and an optional built-in CD player with four speakers.

Even though he was responsible for running the company, Roy never stopped innovating. He is legendary for conceiving an idea while dining with his family and the following day handing Jacuzzi engineers a napkin with a prototype design. In all, Roy holds more than 250 patents related to whirlpool design and technology.

The Jacuzzi family sold the company several years ago, but Roy continued to serve as the top officer. In 1995, Jacuzzi became part of U.S. Industries, listed on the New York Stock Exchange, and Roy was named chairman of the corporation. However, it appears that Roy will be the last Jacuzzi to be associated with the company. He encourages his children to follow their own paths, and none seem to lead to Jacuzzi headquarters.

Today, Jacuzzi employs more than 2,200 people in facilities in California, Arkansas, Italy, England, Germany, France, Brazil, and Chile. Under Roy's leadership, the company remains the world's largest producer of whirlpool baths.

Roy Jacuzzi is not a typical entrepreneur. Unlike many (perhaps most) entrepreneurs, he continues to serve as head of the company, even though ownership has been sold. He also has avoided diversification, even into complementary lines such as toilets and sinks. He has made a conscientious decision to focus on what Jacuzzi does best—whirlpool baths, spas, and showers.

SOURCE: Jacuzzi Whirlpool and Spa archives

Andrew Jergens, Charles H. Geilfus

[Andrew Jergens Company]

In 1882, Andrew Jergens (shown below) and Charles Geilfus formed a partnership in Cincinnati, Ohio, to make soap. Through steady growth and key acquisitions, the company grew from a one-kettle operation to an internationally recognized provider of health and beauty products, most notably Jergens Lotion and Woodbury Soap.

Georg Jürgens brought his family to the United States in 1860 from their native Danish village near Rensburg, Schleswig-Holstein. After landing in New York, they ventured down the Ohio River, settling on a rented farm in Perry County, Indiana.

The middle of the three Jergens sons was Andrew. He was born in Denmark on March 2, 1852, and was age eight when the family landed in America. Young Andrew moved to Cincinnati and became an accomplished wood grainer by the age of 20. In 1876 he married Anna Schwenkmeyer, and the couple had three daughters and a son, Andrew Nicholas Jergens.

With $5,000 of his savings, Jergens established a soapmaking company with Charles Geilfus. Born on October 29, 1856, Geilfus was the youngest of four children born to German immigrants Louis and Appolonia Geilfus who came to Cincinnati through New Orleans. The family operated a grocery store.

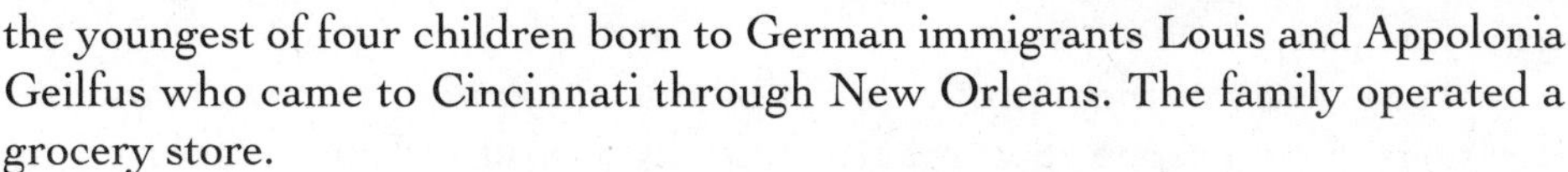

Geilfus worked in several trades, as confectioner, mantle ornament maker, marbleizer, and traveling agent. He married Ella Pelling shortly before entering his venture with Andrew Jergens, and the couple eventually had seven children.

The partners launched the Andrews Soap Company in 1882. Both manned the soap kettle in the early days; however, in time Geilfus took charge of administrative affairs and Jergens oversaw production. By 1885 they had about a dozen employees and were gaining regional popularity.

The plant was in an ideal location. Cincinnati at that time was known as "Porkopolis" because of the thriving livestock industry that grew around this river port city. The by-products from slaughterhouses provided the fats essential to the production of soaps and candles. In addition, the large German population, with a strong European work ethic, provided an excellent labor force.

Jergens and Geilfus dutifully plowed their profits back into the business and devoted most of their waking hours to the growing company. In the 1890s, cosmetics became a growing market, and Jergens successfully produced face powders, perfumes, face creams, and hand lotions.

In 1901, the company formally incorporated as The Andrew Jergens Company, with their stated purpose being: "To manufacture, buy, sell, trade and deal in soaps, oils, candles, chemicals, flavoring extracts, perfumery, cosmetics, toilet articles, and glycerine." Despite its history of successful manufacturing for nearly 20 years, the company would become famous for two products originated by other companies.

John H. Woodbury, a successful dermatologist in New York City, had devised a line of skin-care products. Woodbury advertised the wonders of his soap in the *Boston Store Catalogue,* no. 40, fall and winter 1891–1892:

> Woodbury's Facial Soap for the scalp, skin and complexion. Prepared by a Dermatologist with Twenty Years' Experience. Highly endorsed by the medical profession. Unequaled as a remedy for Eczema, Scaldhead, Oily Skin, Pimples, Flesh Worms, Ugly Complexion, etc. Indispensable as a Toilet Article, and a sure preventative of all Diseases of the Skin.

Woodbury contracted with Jergens to manufacture the soap and ship directly to the retailers. Two weeks before their formal incorporation in 1901, Jergens purchased all rights to manufacture and sell Woodbury's Soap, allowing Woodbury to devote his time to other interests.

Jergens acquired another famous product at about the same time. The Robert Eastman Company of Philadelphia was a small manufacturer of specialty creams, perfumes, and lotions. Jergens was interested in the Eastman perfume line and subsequently purchased the company, retaining Eastman and most of his talented employees.

One of the employees, Charles Conover, had developed a smooth hand cream that became an immediate hit. Thus, Jergens Lotion joined Woodbury's Soap to become the cornerstone products of a rapidly growing Andrew Jergens Company.

The success of these products can be traced to two important marketing decisions. First, despite concerns from the always frugal Andrew Jergens, the company launched a national advertising campaign. While this was an accepted practice with most national companies, it was cautiously adopted by Jergens, who only committed additional advertising money after increased sales were demonstrated.

The second strategy was much bolder. During the early part of the twentieth century, most manufacturers of health and beauty aids distributed their products only through drugstores. By the 1920s, Jergens had placed its products in discount chains and supermarkets. The fact that competitors balked at this practice enabled Jergens to gain a strong foothold in these mass-merchandising stores.

Charles Heinking Geilfus died August 1, 1914. None of his seven children became involved with the company. However, his sister's son, Frank Adams, was quite active with the company, particularly with advertising Woodbury Soap and Jergens Lotion. Frank served as corporate secretary from 1909 through 1929 and as vice president from 1929 through 1939.

Andrew Jergens died in Sarasota, Florida, on January 11, 1929, at the age of 74. His son, Andrew N. Jergens, became the corporation's second president in 1929, a post he held until his death on February 22, 1967.

SOURCES: Jergens family archives; Paul F. Erwin, *With Lotions of Love,* News Gazette Printing Company, Lima, OH, 1965

Steven P. Jobs, Steve Wosniak

[Apple Computer]

Steven Paul Jobs, an orphan, was adopted by Paul and Clara Jobs of Mountain View, California, in February 1955. The family later moved to Los Altos, where he attended Homestead High School. Jobs worked as a summer employee at Hewlett-Packard in Palo Alto and during the school year frequently attended lectures at the facility. There he met another counterculture electronics whiz kid, Steve Wosniak.

After graduating from high school in 1972, Jobs enrolled at Reed College in Oregon, but dropped out after one semester. He worked as a video game designer at Atari until he saved enough money to backpack through India. In late 1974, he returned to California and started attending meetings of the "Homebrew Computer Club" founded by Wosniak.

Jobs and Wozniak designed and built their first computer at Jobs's house. When a local electronics store ordered 25 of their computers, they raised $1,300 start-up capital by selling Jobs's Volkswagen microbus and Wozniak's Hewlett-Packard scientific calculator. Reminiscing on fond memories of a summer job in an Oregon orchard, Jobs dubbed the venture Apple Computer.

The founders sold their first Apple I in 1976, and within a year sales approached $800,000. The next year they designed their advanced Apple II, which, because of its advanced features and open architecture, developed something of a cult following. With the help of some industry insiders, including Nolan Bushnell (Jobs's old boss at Atari), they raised significant funding from the Rockefeller family venture firm.

Within three years, Apple had earnings of nearly $150 million. In 1980 the company went public, and the founders were suddenly worth more than $100 million. They next rolled out a flop (the Apple III), followed by another winner—the Macintosh. Wosniak became disenchanted with big business, left the company, and returned to college to work on his degree. Jobs stayed on, but professional managers pushed the entrepreneur into the background and, eventually, out the door of the company he had founded in his garage.

With a padded bank account and a lot of free time, Jobs made two key moves that would eventually pay off. His first was to launch another computer company, which he named NeXT, that would focus on high-end desktop computing in primarily academic environments. With early financial backing from H. Ross Perot and Canon, Jobs spent the next eight years trying to get NeXT hardware and software onto the market. Curiously, the hardware never quite caught on, but the specially developed software did.

Jobs second move was the 1986 purchase of Pixar Animation Studios, a George Lucas company located in Richmond, California. After paying Lucas $10 million for the company, Jobs reportedly invested an additional $50 million over the next decade. The company's first real success was the 3-D animation movie *Toy Story,* released and distributed by Disney in November 1995, which has grossed over $300 million. When Pixar was offered to the public in November 1995, Jobs's 80 percent share was valued at over $1 billion.

In one of the most interesting developments in Silicon Valley history, Steve Jobs announced in December 1996 that he was selling NeXT Computer to Apple Computer for $400 million and that he would be an active member of Apple's management team.

SOURCE: Pixar Animation Studio archives

George F. Johnson

[Endicott Johnson]

George Francis Johnson was born on October 14, 1857, in Milford, Massachusetts, the son of Frank and Sarah Jane (Aldrich) Johnson. At age 13, Johnson quit school to work at the Seaver Brothers Shoe Factory in Ashland, Massachusetts. Like his father, Johnson then moved from town to town, working for various shoe and boot manufacturers.

In 1881, Johnson became a foreman for George and Horace Lester's shoe manufacturing business in Binghamton, New York. Ten years later, the company's chief creditor, Henry B. Endicott, assumed control of the company and retained Johnson as the plant manager.

Johnson built the company into a strong market position and, in 1909, was made a partner in the venture. Ten years later, the company was rechartered as the Endicott-Johnson Shoe Corporation, having a listed capital of nearly $30 million. When Henry Endicott died the next year, Johnson was named president.

In 1930, Johnson was named board chairman. The company had grown to 18,000 employees in 28 plants, making 45 million pairs of shoes each year, ranking it among the world's largest shoemakers.

George Johnson was married twice. His first wife, Lucie (Willis) Johnson, died at an early age. The couple had six children, two of whom died in childhood. He and his second wife, Mary (McGlone) Johnson, had one daughter. George F. Johnson died on November 28, 1948, at the age of 91.

SOURCE: EJ Footwear archives

John H. Johnson

[Ebony]

John Harold Johnson was born on January 19, 1918, in Arkansas City, Arkansas. His father died when John was only six years old, and after his mother remarried the family moved to Chicago seeking work. However, none was to be found, and the family was forced to live on welfare. The experience inspired him to aim for success, and the book he read most in high school was Dale Carnegie's *How to Win Friends and Influence People.*

Upon graduation from high school, Johnson was unable to afford college and found a job as an office boy at the minority-owned Supreme Life Insurance Company of America. One of his duties was to read through literally hundreds of publications and summarize important events in the African-American community to the president. Eventually, Johnson felt that a high-quality magazine focusing on African-Americans was sorely needed.

In 1942, Johnson founded *Negro Digest,* a monthly magazine that condensed articles of interest and importance to African-Americans. To cover start-up expenses, Johnson's mother took out a $500 loan, guaranteed with her furniture. Johnson then conducted a direct mailing to 20,000 Supreme Life policyholders offering charter subscriptions for $2 to his (yet unpublished) magazine. Three thousand people responded, and the resulting $6,000 launched his magazine.

Johnson overcame immense obstacles, including the lack of interest in his magazines by advertisers. To fill ad space, Johnson founded a number of mail-order businesses, selling everything from wigs and dresses to vitamins and hair-care products. Eventually, he was able to demonstrate the value of the African-American market, and the advertising dollars rolled in.

Within three years, Johnson started his second magazine, *Ebony,* originally conceived as an African-American version of *Life.* The first press run in 1945 of *Ebony* magazine totaled 25,000 copies. By the mid-1980s, it had increased 100-fold to more than 2.5 million. This was followed by the 1951 debut of *Jet,* a pocket-sized, celebrity-oriented publication.

Johnson has been quick to respond to opportunity. In the early 1970s, the company sponsored a touring fashion show called *Ebony* Fashion Fair. One of the problems encountered by the models was finding makeup in dark shades. Johnson approached some of the better-known cosmetics firms to develop a new line, but none expressed interest. So, in 1973, Johnson founded Fashion Fair Cosmetics, run by Johnson's wife, Eunice. Today the cosmetic line accounts for nearly one-third of company revenues.

In the 1980s, he entered the radio market with the acquisition of WJPC in Chicago and WLOU in Louisville, Kentucky. He also started a television show, *Ebony/Jet Showcase.*

Johnson's adopted son, John H. Johnson Jr., died in 1981 at the age of 25 after a long bout with sickle-cell anemia. His daughter, Linda Johnson Rice, actively runs the company with her father.

SOURCES: Johnson Publishing archives; "Ebony Interview with John H. Johnson," *Ebony* magazine, November 1985

Joseph Johnson, William Seidemann

[Snap-on Tools]

Joseph Johnson was born on June 27, 1894, in Milwaukee, Wisconsin, the oldest of six children born to Norwegian immigrants Edward and Hildur (Mathisen) Johnson. At the age of 14, young Joseph left school to help support the family. He worked first as an errand boy, then later as a clerk. In 1913, he became a clerk with the Milwaukee Corrugating Company, then was appointed the Nebraska sales representative.

In 1918, Johnson went to work for the American Grinder Manufacturing Company in Milwaukee, which produced grinders and pumps for the automotive industry. The following year, he was promoted to manager of the newly formed wrench and tool division. During his short time with American Grinder, he became friends with William Seidemann, who also had recently joined the company.

William Seidemann was born on March 23, 1893, on a farm near Newburg, Wisconsin, the grandson of a German immigrant. Throughout his childhood, he demonstrated a remarkable mechanical aptitude with farm machinery. In 1910, he was hired as a cost accountant for a Milwaukee manufacturer of bottle-washing equipment. Over the next eight years, he served in various capacities with the company and studied accounting at a local commercial college. In 1918, he went to work for American Grinder.

Soon after Johnson was assigned to the new wrench division, he contemplated improvements. Each type of socket was permanently attached to different types of handles, resulting in a considerable expense to mechanics. He believed that a mechanic could benefit from ten types of sockets and five types of handles, and that if they were separate components, then these 15 items could be configured 50 different ways.

With Seidemann's help, Johnson fine-tuned the idea and presented it to the management of American Grinder, who promptly dismissed it. The pair decided to pursue the idea in their spare time. Working weekends in a shop owned by one of Johnson's relatives, they prepared a sample set that exceeded their expectations. They next prepared 2,000 advertising brochures with a picture of the set and the slogan "five do the work of fifty." They also added a name: Snap-on.

Johnson and Seidemann believed that mechanics would be their best customers, and they convinced a tire salesman to show their sample set and take orders. They built a second set and recruited a second salesman to do the same. Soon, 500 COD orders were delivered to the founders, who had neither working capital nor production facilities.

An attorney acquaintance was consulted, and he introduced the men to investors who were impressed by the orders. They agreed to provide start-up funding, and on April 8, 1920, the Snap-on Wrench Company was incorporated. Johnson and Seidemann quit their jobs and started operations in a 2,500-square-foot shop. Six months later, all 500 orders had been filled.

In 1921, Snap-on had sales of nearly $100,000. Within two years, sales increased to over $400,000. By 1925, the company had 17 branches and 165 salespeople. By the end of the decade, the company had consolidated its manufacturing shops into a new plant at Kenosha, Wisconsin. Shortly thereafter, it was reorganized as Snap-on Tools, Inc.

The company pulled through the Depression, and by 1940 sales reached $2 million. At the close of World War II, sales were nearly $10 million. William Seidemann retired from the company in 1954 and passed away on October 14, 1969, at the age of 77. Joseph Johnson retired from operations in 1960 and died on October 15, 1986, at the age of 92. Snap-on sales reached $670 million the year of his death. Today, Snap-on is a $1.5 billion company.

SOURCE: Snap-on Tools archives, history by Richard H. Keehn

Robert L. Johnson

[Black Entertainment Television]

Robert L. Johnson was born on April 8, 1946, in Hickory, Mississippi. While he was still a child, his family relocated to Freeport, Illinois. He graduated from the University of Illinois with a bachelor's degree in history in 1968 and four years later was awarded a master's degree in public affairs from the Woodrow Wilson School at Princeton University. While working on his education, Johnson also was building a family. He married Sheila Crump, and the couple eventually had two children.

Upon graduation from Princeton, Johnson landed a job as a public affairs officer with the Corporation for Public Broadcasting. Over the next several years, he worked in a variety of positions, including communications director for the Washington, D.C., office of the Urban League, followed by prominent appointments to Washington city government. In 1976, he was named vice president of the National Cable Television Association (NCTA).

Three years after his arrival at NCTA, Johnson became involved in a project to help launch a television network directed at senior citizens. The more he learned about the project, the more he became convinced that the African-American market was virtually untapped, and he quickly laid out a plan for the venture.

Johnson knew that, because of the magnitude of the business, he would have to leave NCTA. The organization, however, was supportive of his plan and offered him a $15,000 consulting contract, which he used as collateral for a start-up loan. After several disappointing attempts to raise the necessary money, TCI founder John Malone provided a combination debt and equity financing package that would not only help launch the new network, it would enhance TCI programming, especially in African-American markets.

In 1980, the Black Entertainment Television (BET) network made its debut, sharing a channel used by other broadcasters. Initially, programming was limited to a two-hour weekly broadcast. Within two years, the network was broadcasting classic movies, music videos, and new shows such as *Black Showcase* six hours daily.

Poised for expansion, Johnson raised considerable equity financing over the next few years from Taft Broadcasting and Home Box Office (HBO). By 1985, the company had more than 8 million subscribers in 40 states, and four years later the total nearly tripled to 23 million subscribers.

Buoyed by his success in the late 1980s, Johnson took two major steps in 1991. First, he broadened the reach of BET as a media venture by introducing *YSB* (Young Sisters and Brothers) magazine, which quickly developed a strong circulation base. Next, he took BET public, making it the first firm controlled by African-American stockholders to be traded on the New York Stock Exchange.

SOURCES: Black Entertainment Television archives; *Current Biography Yearbook 1994,* The H.W. Wilson Company, New York

Lou Johnson, Harry Johnson, Julius Johnson, Clarence Johnson

[Johnson Motor Company]

In 1843, 11-year-old Søren Johnson immigrated to America from Aalborg, Denmark. He later married Chicago-born Bertha Lawson, and the couple had seven children, five of whom lived into adulthood. Søren was a skilled blacksmith and railroad employee who moved frequently. Eventually, the family settled in Terre Haute, Indiana, in 1898.

The four Johnson brothers, Lou (born in 1881), Harry (1884), Julius (1886), and Clarence (1895) were destined to work together most of their lives. In 1902, they built an 18-foot rowboat in their father's barn and spent many of their days rowing on the Wabash River. A year later, Lou Johnson built a 150-pound, 3-horsepower motor that propelled their boat at a modest speed. This led to an improved engine and several orders from neighbors. By 1905, they were operating a growing business from the two-story barn.

In 1908, they moved into a small plant in Terre Haute, where their modest manufacturing business continued to grow. By 1911, the Johnson brothers diversified their operation by building a small airplane that Lou was able to fly. Over the next two years, the brothers shuttled their airplane to fairs and exhibitions and even established a flying school.

However, a tornado on Easter Sunday 1913 leveled the Johnson plant. The next day, the Wabash River flooded and washed away most of the rubble. The Johnson brothers were effectively out of business. Starting from scratch, they designed and built a small engine that could be attached to bicycles. Their "motor wheel" prototype was ready in 1917, and the brothers formed the Johnson Motor Wheel Company in South Bend.

The motor wheel was an instant success, and soon 17,000 units were on the market. It wasn't a hurricane, however, that ended the venture, but the Ford Model T. Adults quickly traded in their bicycles for the inexpensive, mass-produced cars. Coupled with the recession of 1921, the Johnson brothers were once again out of business.

The Johnsons turned back to their roots: the marine industry. In 1921, Lou Johnson completed design of the first Johnson outboard motor. By the end of the year, the Johnson Motor Company was in business in South Bend and its first motor had been built. The following year, more than 3,500 of the sleek, lightweight motors were sold. Growth was so rapid that, in 1927, the Johnson brothers opened a sprawling, $1 million factory at Waukegan, Illinois.

The company went public in early 1929 and used nearly half the proceeds to underwrite an extensive advertising campaign. The strategy probably would have worked if not for the stock market crash later that year and subsequent Great Depression. Within two years the company was trapped in debt while demand sunk.

The investment banking firm that handled the stock offering put the company in receivership and, in 1935, decided to sell it to the highest bidder. The eventual buyer was the Outboard Marine Company, which had only recently been formed through a merger of the two companies founded by Ole and Bess Evinrude.

SOURCES: Outboard Marine Corporation archives; Jeffrey L. Rodengen, *Evinrude Johnson and the Legend of OMC,* Write Stuff, FL, 1992

Jerral W. Jones

[Dallas Cowboys]

Jerral Wayne "Jerry" Jones was born on October 13, 1942, in Los Angeles, California. His father, J. W. "Pat" Jones, was successful in supermarket and insurance industries. Soon after Jerry was born, his father moved the family to North Little Rock, Arkansas. After attending local public school and working in his father's grocery stores, Jerry accepted a football scholarship to the University of Arkansas.

In 1964, he was the team's cocaptain for the 11–0 Razorbacks, which were named national champions after defeating the University of Nebraska in the

Cotton Bowl. While at school he sold shoes from the back of his car and operated a taxi service to shuttle wealthy Razorback fans between the stadium and the local airport.

Jones earned his MBA from the University of Arkansas in 1965, then joined his father's insurance firm, Modern Security Life in Springfield, Missouri. Five years later, he entered the oil and gas exploration business in Oklahoma and added to his astonishing success. He expanded his empire to include poultry, real estate, and banking.

In 1989, Jones purchased the Dallas Cowboys professional football club franchise for $140 million. In his first season as owner, the club turned in a dismal 1–15 season. However, it took Jones and his management team only three years to climb from the basement to the top, capturing the Super Bowl championship after the 1992 season. The following year, they became only the fifth team to win back-to-back Super Bowls.

While they fell short of the "Big Dance" in 1994, Jones and the Cowboys made history in 1995 by winning their third Super Bowl in four years. The win also marked the fifth team Super Bowl, tying a league record. It marked the club's eighth trip to the Super Bowl, also a record.

Jones and his wife, Gene, a former Arkansas beauty queen, live in Dallas. They have three children, all whom are involved with the Cowboys organization. In addition to the Cowboys, Jones continues to operate nearly a dozen companies that employ nearly 3,000 people in banking, poultry processing, and energy.

SOURCES: Dallas Cowboys archives; Paul Attner, "The Ringmaster," *The Sporting News*, March 13, 1995

Henry J. Kaiser

[Kaiser Aluminum and Chemical Corporation]

Henry John Kaiser was born on May 9, 1882, in Sprout Brook, New York, one of four children born to German immigrant parents. His father, Francis J. Kaiser, was a shoemaker and his mother, Mary (Yops) Kaiser, was a practical nurse. Young Henry quit school at age 13 to work in a Utica dry goods store. After hours, he made extra money taking photographs.

Kaiser later moved to Lake Placid, New York, where he approached the owner of a photography studio with an offer: Kaiser would work for free, but at the end of the year he would get half the profits if he were able to double sales. By year end, sales had tripled and 22-year-old Kaiser was made a partner. The following year, he bought out the founder and soon established stores at Daytona Beach and Miami, Florida, and at Nassau.

By 1906, Kaiser had moved to Spokane, Washington, and entered the hardware business. In 1914, at age 32, he established a construction business named the Henry J. Kaiser Company, Limited, at Vancouver, British Columbia. For the next seven years, he was awarded numerous road-paving contracts in Canada, Washington, and Idaho. He later attributed the early success to using machinery instead of horses.

When Kaiser learned of a large road contract up for bid in California, he hopped a train for Redding. However, along the way he found that Redding wasn't a scheduled stop. So, when the train slowed for a mail drop, Kaiser jumped from the train and walked to Redding, where he submitted the successful bid. As a result, he established his headquarters in Oakland, California, in 1921, which remained the center of his diverse empire for the rest of his life.

While paving a road in 1923 between Livermore and Pleasanton, California, Kaiser decided to establish a sand and gravel business. As with many of his ventures, the aggregate plant became one of the largest in northern California.

Kaiser, who landed several dam contracts through the 1930s, was one of the so-called Six Companies, Inc., that built the Hoover Dam. While building the Shasta Dam, Kaiser was awarded the contract for 6 million barrels of cement. From this first plant, the Kaiser Cement Corporation grew to be the largest cement company in the western United States.

When World War II erupted, Kaiser moved into the shipbuilding business. The Kaiser shipyards, at their peak, were turning out an average of one ship each day and one aircraft carrier each week. Altogether, they built nearly 1,500 vessels during the war. He also operated the largest artillery shell operation in the United States and even joined with Howard Hughes in the development of his *Spruce Goose.*

As the war scaled down, Kaiser determined that the greatest needs of the country would be metals, building materials, homes, and automobiles. He had already established Kaiser Steel at Fontana in southern California. Additionally, he felt that aluminum would be a successful product, so he leased surplus manufacturing plants from the War Assets Administration and went into the aluminum business. His subsequent success with Kaiser Aluminum today is, perhaps, his best-known achievement.

He also launched the Kaiser-Frazer Corporation in 1945 to manufacture cars. Ten years and 750,000 Kaiser automobiles later, he withdrew from the passenger car market and focused on producing Jeeps. In the 1950s, he built manufacturing facilities in South America through two new companies: Willys-Overland do Brasil and Industrias Kaiser Argentina.

One of Kaiser's favorite projects was the development of the Kaiser-Permanente Medical Care Program, which he established in 1945. It originated when Kaiser established a health care system for his employees, first at remote locations where dams and highways were being built, then later in his shipyards and steel mills. Eventually, the program proved so successful and efficient that it was opened for public enrollment.

Henry Kaiser moved to Hawaii in 1955 and promptly built the 1,100-room Hawaiian Village Hotel, a cement plant, a hospital, radio and television facilities, and the community of Hawaii Kai. Henry John Kaiser died in Hawaii on August 24, 1967, at the age of 85. By the time of his death, he had founded more than 100 companies that employed more than 90,000 people in 33 states and 41 countries.

SOURCE: Kaiser Aluminum and Chemical Corporation archives

Will K. Kellogg

[Kellogg Company]

John Preston Kellogg became disenchanted with modern medicine by 1850, having already lost his wife and two-year-old daughter, and found comfort in the Seventh-Day Adventist church. When the church later established a publishing business in Battle Creek, Michigan, Kellogg, who had remarried, moved his family there from Flint.

In 1866, the church opened the Western Health Reform Institute in Battle Creek, and two of Kellogg's sons, including John Harvey Kellogg, joined the staff. John eventually was named head of the institute and built it into a world-renowned health spa that was renamed the Battle Creek Sanitarium.

John P. Kellogg's seventh son was Will Keith Kellogg, born on April 7, 1860. Young Will was a rather shy boy who barely survived malaria. Since his parents believed the end of the world was at hand, education wasn't stressed. At age 14, Will was sent to Dallas, Texas, to help another church member establish a broom factory.

By 1880, Will (or W.K., as he preferred to be called) returned to Battle Creek and quickly earned a certificate in accounting and bookkeeping at the Parson's Business College at nearby Kalamazoo and was hired by his eldest brother, John, at the sanitarium. With his comfortable $6 per week salary, W.K. married Ella Osborn Davis in November 1880, and the couple eventually had five children, three of whom lived beyond childhood.

In search of a digestible alternative to bread, John and W.K. Kellogg (photo below) conducted numerous experiments, including the boiling of wheat. One day, a batch of boiled wheat was inadvertently left standing. The mixture dried and broke into flakes—*cereal* flakes—which were served to sanitarium patients. Eventually, the flakes became popular and, long after discharge, former patients were ordering the cereal by mail.

The cereal was named *Granose* and, to keep up with the demand, the brothers launched the San (short for sanitarium) Food Company. In 1894, John Kellogg was granted a patent for his flaked cereal, which was distributed in 10-ounce packages for 15¢ each. Eventually, W.K. convinced the board to construct a two-story factory for the growing cereal business.

W.K. Kellogg soon broke ties with the sanitarium and devoted his time to the cereal venture. Through experimentation using boiled corn, he was able to produce a new cereal that he called *corn flakes*. Eventually, Kellogg had his cereal packages include the following warning in bold red letters: *Beware of imitations. Non genuine without this signature: W. K. Kellogg.*

In 1906, W.K. posed an interesting question to a business colleague: "What would you think of calling these flakes Kellogg Corn Flakes instead of Sanitas Corn Flakes, then adding my signature to the package? The response was encouraging and W. K. Kellogg incorporated the Battle Creek Toasted Corn Flake Company, raising $35,000 working capital from former sanitarium patients.

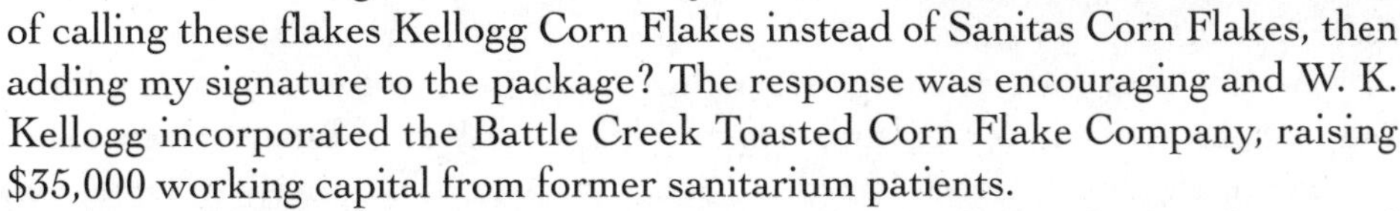

The company's rapid growth was fueled by Kellogg's faith in his cereal and his strong belief in advertising. Samples were delivered door-to-door from 1903 until World War I. By the mid-1920s, the name of the company was changed to the Kellogg Company.

W. K. Kellogg died on October 6, 1951, at the age of 91. Today, the Kellogg Company is a diversified food service company with annual sales of nearly $7 billion.

SOURCES: Horace B. Powell, *The Original Has This Signature—W. K. Kellogg,* W. K. Kellogg Foundation, 1989; *I'll Invest My Money in People,* W. K. Kellogg Foundation

Edwin S. Kelly, Arthur W. Grant

[The Kelly-Springfield Tire Company]

James Kelly, a Scotch immigrant who served under Washington at Valley Forge, moved to Springfield, Ohio, in 1808. His son, Oliver S. Kelly, ventured to California in search of gold, then later returned to Springfield and manufactured farm implements. His firm, The O. S. Kelly Company, later became a piano plate manufacturer.

Edwin S. Kelly was born on April 17, 1857, the son of Oliver and Ruth (Peck) Kelly. After graduating from Wooster College in 1878, Kelly entered the coal business. Ten years later his venture became The Springfield Coal and Ice Company. Kelly sold his company in 1894 so he could concentrate on a new venture with a man named Arthur Grant.

Arthur W. Grant was born on May 22, 1859, on a farm in Monroe County, Michigan. A few years after his birth, his father was killed in battle in the Civil War, and the family moved to Toledo, Ohio. After graduating from public school, Grant served in a number of positions with machine and automotive companies, eventually being named superintendent of the Gendron Iron Wheel Company. During his career, Grant developed and was given a patent for rubber tire manufacturing, which caught the attention of Edwin Kelly.

In July 1894, Kelly and Grant launched The Rubber Tire Wheel Company at Springfield. Their first product was a carriage tire that improved the ride and was held to the wheel by wires. Within four years, 45,000 sets of carriage tires had been produced, and their Springfield tire became a world standard.

By the end of the decade, Kelly and Grant sold the company to other investors, who changed the name to The Consolidated Rubber Tire Company. Kelly continued to remain somewhat active in the company that, in 1914, was renamed The Kelly-Springfield Tire Company. Three years later, the company established its primary manufacturing plant at Cumberland, Maryland. Today, Kelly-Springfield remains one of America's best-known tire companies.

After selling the tire company, Arthur Grant retired to his 500-acre farm and became active in agriculture. He and his wife, May (Mailey) Grant, had one daughter, Grace Alberta, born in 1886. However, Edwin Kelly was not yet ready for retirement.

In 1899, Kelly founded The Home Lighting, Heating and Power Company of Springfield, which later became part of the Ohio Edison Company. He had earlier acquired the local newspaper and, through consolidation, established the *Daily Times,* which he sold in 1903. However, he retained a key subsidiary, The Kelly-Springfield Printing Company, which held key railroad and government printing contracts. He also purchased The Oscar Lear Motor Truck Company of Columbus in 1908, which he resold four years later.

Kelly and his wife, Patti (Linn) Kelly, had four children. Edwin S. Kelly died on May 15, 1935, at the age of 78.

SOURCE: The Kelly-Springfield Tire Company archives

James S. Kemper

[Kemper Insurance Companies]

James Scott Kemper was born on November 18, 1886, in Van Wert, Ohio, the son of an attorney and a sixth-generation descendant of a colonial Virginia settler. After graduating from high school in 1905, he went to work as an office boy for the Central Mutual Insurance Company in Van Wert, earning $1 per day. His specialty became fire insurance, and he traveled the country processing claims, including a trip to San Francisco after the 1906 earthquake.

In 1911, Kemper was assigned to Chicago to investigate numerous lumberyard fires. In response to the problem, he innovated a program to reduce claims by stressing prevention and safety policies. That same year, he launched his own insurance company, which he called Lumbermens & Manufacturers Insurance Agency of Chicago. He traveled the Chicago area by horse and buggy, selling policies by day and writing them out at night.

Kemper quickly established a good reputation in the insurance industry. When the Chicago Lumbermens Association and the Illinois Lumber Merchants Association set their sights on a property-casualty insurance firm called Lumbermens Mutual Casualty Company, they asked 25-year-old Kemper to organize it.

When the company was less than six months old, Kemper started offering automobile insurance, in spite of reservations from his board of directors regarding the unknown risks of such policies. Four years later, he formed the Central Automobile Safety Committee to crusade against auto accidents. His interest in automotive safety prompted Kemper and his brother, Hathaway Kemper, to help establish the Northwestern University Traffic Institute in 1936, which to this day is the premiere traffic safety training and education center for police officers.

Company legend has it that the name of the company was switched to Kemper Insurance because a switchboard operator grew tired of answering the phone using the original name: Lumbermens Mutual Casualty Company.

James Kemper retired as chairman and chief executive officer in 1979, but remained active with the company until his death on September 17, 1981, at the age of 94.

SOURCE: Kemper archives

Robert S. Kerr, Dean A. McGee, James L. Anderson

[Kerr-McGee Corporation]

Robert Samuel Kerr was born on September 11, 1896, in Indian Territory near Ada, Oklahoma. His parents had moved from Texas to the Cherokee Nation a year earlier and supported their family of seven children through corn, cotton, and fruit farming. After high school, Kerr attended East Central State College for two years, then the University of Oklahoma at Norman until the money ran out.

Upon discharge from the service after World War I, Kerr married Reba Shelton and formed the Kerr-Dandridge Produce House with a partner. Two years later, the business burned to the ground and Kerr was $10,000 in debt. Reba taught school while Kerr completed college, and in 1922 he passed the bar exam and started practicing law. Tragedy struck again in 1924 when Reba and their son died during childbirth. While he rebuilt his life, Kerr was approached by his brother-in-law with an intriguing opportunity.

James LeRoy Anderson was born on September 29, 1884. At age 16, he left his family's Tennessee farm to join an older brother in the oil business in California. After working in the oil fields and saving money, he returned to Tennessee and graduated from Maryville Presbyterian College in 1906. For the next 17 years he held a wide range of positions in numerous oil fields, both in and outside of the United States. In 1923, he moved to Tennessee and married Mildred Kerr, Robert Kerr's younger sister, whom he had met while working in Oklahoma four years earlier.

In 1926, Anderson was working for Bert and William Dixon, two brothers who were active in various oil properties. The Dixons were interested in getting some of their idle equipment back into service and, on Anderson's recommendation, they hired Robert Kerr part-time to obtain contracts. Through his numerous political, military, and business contacts, Kerr was quite successful, and within two years another opportunity was presented: The Dixon brothers offered to sell their business to Kerr and Anderson.

In 1929, the Anderson & Kerr Drilling company assumed the Dixon holdings. Kerr had remarried by this time to Grayce Breene, and the couple had three sons and a daughter. Anderson managed their small oil business while Kerr split his time between the company and his law practice.

In 1932, growth opportunities in gas and oil operations led the owners to incorporate the venture as A & K Petroleum Company, and stock was offered to the public. By 1937, Anderson retired from the business, and the name of the company was changed to the Kerlyn Oil Company. Kerr decided it was time to hire a good geologist.

Dean Anderson McGee was born on March 20, 1904, at Humbolt, Kansas, to George G. and Gertrude H. (Sayre) McGee. His father was an oil wildcatter, and the family lived near the oil field, which provided an exciting playground for Dean. His interest in geology carried through school, and he graduated from the University of Kansas in 1926 with a mining engineering degree.

Over the next ten years, McGee worked in various capacities for Phillips Petroleum and, in 1935, was named the company's chief geologist. His position was secure, but McGee was restless to play a stronger role in building a company. When Kerr presented him with the chance to join Kerlyn, McGee accepted.

McGee joined the small company at a critical time. A & K Petroleum had been drilling a well near Magnolia, Arkansas, without luck. Soon, the money ran out and a loan couldn't be found. The workers stuck around the site only because they had no place else to go, and Dean McGee wondered what he had gotten himself into. Kerr eventually found enough money to resume drilling. On March 5, 1938, oil shot through the derrick.

During the 1940s, Robert Kerr's political career skyrocketed. He was elected governor of Oklahoma in 1942 and, in 1948, was elected to the U.S.

Senate. Dean McGee led the company through rapid growth, sparked by the 1945 purchase of a Wynnewood, Oklahoma, oil refinery and offshore drilling in the Gulf of Mexico. In 1946, the name of the company was changed to Kerr-McGee Oil Industries, Inc.

By the early 1950s, Kerr-McGee expanded its energy business by acquiring uranium mining and milling properties in New Mexico and Arizona. The following decade, the company moved into chemicals and forest products.

Robert S. Kerr died on January 1, 1963. McGee was elected board chairman, a post he held until his retirement in 1983 after 46 years of leadership. Dean A. McGee died on September 15, 1989, at the age of 85. Today Kerr-McGee has nearly 6,000 employees and annual sales approaching $4 billion.

SOURCE: Kerr McGee Corporation archives

Martin L. Keyes

[Keyes Fibre Company]

Martin L. Keyes was born on October 25, 1850, in Lempster, New Hampshire, the son of a sawmill operator and carriage maker. Young Martin inherited his father's flair for invention, building his own fishing rod and designing furniture.

After his father died, Keyes and his brother ran the family business. Then, in 1884, Keyes accepted the position of superintendent of the Indurated Fibre Company at Gorham, Maine, a manufacturer of papier-mâché tubs and pails. When the plant burned three years later, Keyes moved to another of their company mills in northern New York.

Over the next ten years, Keyes experimented with new ways to make plates and dishes with compressed papier-mâché. Initially, he steamed veneer and formed it into plates, but he later switched to forming pulp by using a special mold. He secured a patent and, by 1903, had arranged for the necessary equipment to be placed in a Shawmut, Maine, mill.

On August 29, 1903, the Keyes Fibre Company was formally incorporated. The first carload of finished plates left the mill on June 24, 1904, consisting entirely of pie plates for bakers. However, the orders were slow, and competing, lower-priced products were affecting profit margins. One of the original stockholders even tried to sell off his shares at a discount, but could find no takers.

Keyes persisted by stepping up marketing efforts and improving his packaging. In 1906, the company received a big boost when a major shipment was ordered in San Francisco immediately following the great earthquake. Within two years, a new mill was built and employment stood at 34.

In 1911, Keyes severed ties with his previous sales agent, who had sold the plates under his own name, and started marketing his products under the Keyes label. His new, aggressive, Chicago-based sales agent started to market the plates and other products throughout the country, providing an almost immediate increase in sales.

Martin Keyes died on November 19, 1914, and His son-in-law, Dr. George Averill, assumed the post of president. Over the following decades, the company expanded into other lines, including egg trays, bottle packs, containers for lightbulbs, fruit trays, and household paper plates. To better reflect its product line, Keyes Fibre changed its name to The Chinet Company.

SOURCE: The Chinet Company archives

Peter Kiewit

[Peter Kiewit Sons', Inc.]

In 1857, Johannes de Kiewit left difficult economic conditions in his native Holland and immigrated to America. After arriving in New York, he Americanized his first name to "John," hopped a train, and rode it until the tracks ended in Cincinnati, Ohio. He then traveled on a riverboat to Keokuk, Iowa, where he worked as a teamster on a wagon train supplying frontier outposts with supplies.

John married another Dutch immigrant, Katherine Blom, and the couple eventually had ten children. They named their fourth child, born in 1862, Peter, and he was destined to become the first of four generations of Kiewit men named Peter. By the time trains displaced wagon trains, Peter, now a teenager, convinced John to move the family to the bustling city of Omaha, Nebraska, and establish a brickyard business.

In 1884, 22-year-old Peter and his brother Andrew established their own business, named Kiewit Brothers, and built brick foundations for an Omaha homebuilder. Two years later, Peter married Anna Barbara Schleicher, a native of Germany who had immigrated to America with her widowed mother. Andrew soon left the partnership, and Peter, now sole proprietor, built a respectable enterprise.

On September 12, 1900, the fifth of six Kiewit children was born to Peter and Anna. He was given the name Peter, after his father, who then became known as Peter Kiewit Senior. This second Peter Kiewit, who was better known as "Pete," is the man who built Peter Kiewit Sons' to national prominence. (The second Peter Kiewit later had a son who was named Peter Kiewit Jr., which naturally complicated matters even further. Peter Jr., who was actually the *third* Peter Kiewit, eventually had a son who was named Peter Kiewit IV.)

In 1912, Peter Kiewit Sr. brought his two older sons, Ralph and George, into the partnership, which was renamed Peter Kiewit & Sons. Pete Kiewit, at age 12, was too young to lay bricks, but he was able to land a job lighting neighborhood gas lamps each evening, then extinguishing the flames at daybreak. In 1914, Peter Kiewit Sr. died after suffering from phlebitis and emphysema. Ralph and George assumed control of the business, and young Pete was soon assigned his first tasks with Peter Kiewit & Sons.

After graduating from high school, he enrolled at Dartmouth University. However, anxious to rejoin his brothers at the family business, he quit after one year and returned to Omaha. He quickly earned his bricklayer's union card and was named a partner. In 1922, he married Mary Drake, and the couple had two children, Jeanne in 1923 and Peter Jr. three years later.

George Kiewit left the family business in 1924, followed by Ralph seven years later. In 1931, Peter was left alone with the family construction business, which he reorganized as Peter Kiewit Sons' Company. He quickly hired a full-time salesman and starting bidding on larger jobs. Despite the Depression, the company was able to grow beyond the Omaha region by the end of the decade.

World War II provided a springboard for Pete Kiewit. He was tapped by the U.S. Army to build barracks at Fort Lewis, Washington. The original contract called for 760 buildings, but that was later doubled to 1,540 buildings—with no change in the timetable. Up until then, the maximum number of Kiewit employees was about 200. Suddenly, there were 10,000 workers. Kiewit not only survived the challenge, he successfully fulfilled other military contracts during the war.

Kiewit was well positioned to participate in the postwar building boom. During the 1950s, he was pulled once again into service for the military, sending 5,000 workers to the Arctic Circle in Greenland to build an air base and antimissile system. However, he didn't limit his endeavors to the construction industry. In 1962, he paid $40 million for Omaha's newspaper, *The World-Herald*.

Pete Kiewit died on November 2, 1979, at the age of 79. He had built Peter Kiewit Sons' from a small, regional firm to one of the largest construction companies in America. By the time of his death, the company had 33 subsidiaries. The construction business alone had nearly two dozen offices in the United States and Canada.

SOURCES: Peter Kiewit Sons, Inc. archives; Hollis J. Limprecht, *The Kiewit Story,* The Omaha World-Herald Company, 1981

Richard King, Henrietta C. King

[King Ranch, Inc.]

Richard King—river man, steamboat captain, livestock capitalist, and founder of the King Ranch—was born in New York in 1824. At age nine, he was indentured to a jeweler in Manhattan, but broke his apprenticeship in 1835 and stowed away on a vessel sailing for Mobile, Alabama. For most of the following six years, King pursued steamboating on the Alabama rivers and, at age 16, acquired his pilot's license.

In 1842, King enlisted for service in the Seminole War in Florida. There he met Mifflin Kenedy, who became his lifelong friend and business mentor. In 1845, King joined Kenedy on the Rio Grande for service in the Mexican War.

After that war, he remained in the region and became a partner in the Kenedy's steamboat firms, which dominated trade on the Rio Grande for more than two decades.

King was an innovator who designed specialty boats for the narrow beds and fast currents of the Rio Grande. He also came to appreciate the potential in the undeveloped land of South Texas. While traveling to the Lone Star Fair in Corpus Christi, he became so taken with the area surrounding the Santa Gertrudis creek that he began buying large tracts of land. He made two major purchases of nearly 70,000 acres in 1853 and 1854, which became the nucleus for the King Ranch.

Soon after the acquisitions, King married Henrietta Morse Chamberlain, who was born in 1832 in Boonville, Missouri, daughter of the Reverend Hiram Chamberlain and his first wife, Maria Morse. Following two years at the Holly Springs (Mississippi) Female Institute, Henrietta joined her family in 1849 and traveled to Brownsville, Texas. There her father established the first Presbyterian church on the Rio Grande. The following year, she met Richard King, and the two were married in December 1854. The couple eventually had five children.

Richard King traveled into Mexico in search of stock for his ranch and came across a village that was being ravaged by one of the periodic droughts that plagued the area. Cattle were dying from lack of water and forages, and King bought the cattle and invited the people of the village to work for him at his ranch. The entire village followed him back into Texas, becoming a workforce known as *los Kineños,* or King's men, that has become the backbone of the King Ranch through six generations.

When the Civil War broke out, King and his partners placed their steamboat interests under Mexican registry and moved their operations into Matamoros. King Ranch became a major depot on the Cotton Road over which hundreds of thousands of bales of cotton were shipped. In addition, King and Kenedy supplied Confederate troops on the Rio Grande.

In 1868, King and Kenedy dissolved their partnership, and as individual proprietors went on to build their own separate ranches. Flush with war profits, they revolutionized the economics of South Texas ranching with the introduction of fencing; cattle drives to northern markets; large-scale cattle, sheep, mule, and horse raising; and scientific livestock breeding. Between 1869 and 1884, King sent more than 100,000 head of livestock to northern markets, thus helping to stock the developing ranges of the American West and to establish the American ranching industry.

King's access to capital fueled his drive for expansion in land and cattle. He also began investing in outside endeavors, including railroads (especially the Corpus Christi, San Diego, and Rio Grande Narrow Gauge Railroad), packing houses, ice plants, and harbor improvements at Corpus Christi. He added to his fortune by developing a market for his commodity, including production volumes, and controlling transportation and markets.

By the time of his death in 1885 from stomach cancer, King had made over 60 major land purchases totaling some 614,000 acres. Under the terms of his will, the entire estate was left to Henrietta, who chose to personally manage the family empire. By the time of her death in 1925, the King Ranch covered nearly 1.2 million acres.

Along with her successful business dealings, Henrietta King's crowning achievement was the founding and development of Kingsville, originally a raw site on the prairie that had been her home for almost half a century. In 1903, she deeded nearly 77,000 acres along a proposed railroad route between Corpus Christi and Brownsville to the Kleberg Town & Improvement Company. From this, 853 acres were surveyed and divided into the town of Kingsville. Henrietta King and the King Ranch were principals in most of the town's early ventures, including the Kingsville Lumber Company, the Kingsville Ice & Milling Company, the Kingsville Publishing Company, and many other ventures.

King family members continued to expand the Ranch's operations over the decades. By the early 1970s, the King Ranch controlled more than 11 million acres of ranchland worldwide. However, much of it has since been sold off. Today, the nearly 1,300-square-mile King Ranch is still operated by descendants of Richard and Henrietta King.

SOURCE: King Ranch, Inc. archives

George R. Kinney

[Kinney Shoe Corporation]

George Romanta Kinney, founder of the pioneering retail shoe chain that bears his name, was the son of a merchant in Candor, a small country town in upstate New York. His father fell into financial difficulty after extending too much credit to local farmers, and upon his untimely death, nine-year-old George vowed to someday pay off the debts.

At age 17, Kinney found employment with a Binghamton, New York, manufacturer and wholesaler of boots and shoes. In 1885 he changed employers and started a ten-year career with the Lestershire Shoe Company, where he acquired a thorough knowledge of the shoe industry. He also used his paychecks to support his mother and sister back in Candor, and he paid off all of his father's debts.

In 1893, Kinney's employer went bankrupt, and control of the company was assumed by Henry B. Endicott. The following year, Kinney elected to use his life savings to purchase the Lester retail outlet in Waverly, New York. The 28-year-old widower and father of a young son then purchased inexpensive leather goods in large quantities directly from factories, passing on the savings to his customers. Recalling his father's troubles, Kinney also instituted a "cash only" policy.

His approach to retailing proved popular, and over the next several years he acquired a number of stores throughout New York and Pennsylvania. In 1895, Kinney moved to Wilkes-Barre, Pennsylvania, and had two desks placed in his shoe store, which served as corporate headquarters. He hired a secretary named Ella Mae Cook who, five years later, became his second wife.

Kinney's approach to growth was rather unique. While he maintained majority interest in his ventures, each store was treated as a distinct partnership. Managers held shares and were responsible for the expenses and management of their own stores. Kinney served as head buyer for all the stores and pioneered his concept of a family shoe store that offered "shoes for every member of the family from the cradle to the grave."

By 1903, Kinney had expanded to 15 stores and moved his headquarters to Manhattan. He continued to expand operations and, in 1917, replaced his various partnerships with a single corporation—G. R. Kinney & Company, Inc.—which by that time included 56 stores. Two years later, George Kinney died of a heart attack at age 53.

When Kinney Shoes celebrated their 50th anniversary in 1944, the company employed nearly 5,700 people in 338 retail stores, four manufacturing plants, and corporate headquarters. In the mid-1970s, the company entered the specialty athletic shoe market by introducing Foot Locker stores and, later, Lady Foot Locker.

SOURCES: Kinney Shoe Corporation archives; Kathleen McDermott, *Retail Revolutionary: Kinney Shoe Corporation's First Century in Footwear,* Kinney, 1994

John M. Kohler

[Kohler Co.]

Kohler Co. has been privately held for nearly 125 years by three generations of the Kohler family. It has been headed primarily by four family members: founder John Michael Kohler; his two sons, Walter Jodok Kohler and Herbert Vollrath Kohler Sr.; and his grandson, Herbert V. Kohler Jr., who currently serves as president and chairman.

John Michael Kohler was born on November 3, 1844, in Austria. His family immigrated to the United States ten years later, settling on a farm near St. Paul, Minnesota. When he was 18 years old, Kohler set out on his business career, serving in various capacities such as delivery wagon driver, wholesale grocery salesman, and furniture salesman.

On July 5, 1871, Kohler married Lillie Vollrath, and the couple made their home in Sheboygan, Wisconsin, where Lillie's father, Jacob J. Vollrath, owned a foundry that made plows, horse troughs, and small castings. John Kohler purchased the Sheboygan Union Iron and Steel Foundry from his father-in-law in 1873. His primary business was agricultural implements, but he eventually expanded into enamelware.

In 1883, he took one of his products, called a *horse trough/hog scalder,* heated it up to 1700°F, and applied some enamel powder. He then pictured it in his catalog with a suggestion: "A horse trough/hog scalder when furnished with four

legs will serve as a bathtub." He traded one of his new devices to a local farmer for a cow and 14 chickens, and John Kohler was in the plumbing business.

Lillie Kohler died in 1883, leaving John to care for their six children. Four years later, in 1887, John married Lillie's sister, Wilhelmina "Minnie" Vollrath. This marriage produced one son, Herbert Vollrath Kohler, born in 1891.

In 1887, John incorporated his foundry as the Kohler, Hayssen & Stehn Manufacturing Company, recapitalizing the venture at $75,000. This enabled the construction of a new, large plant that soon employed several hundred workers, while manufacturing continued at the original Sheboygan plant as well. John not only firmly entrenched his plumbing business, he also set a family standard of community service by serving in various public positions, including mayor of Sheboygan.

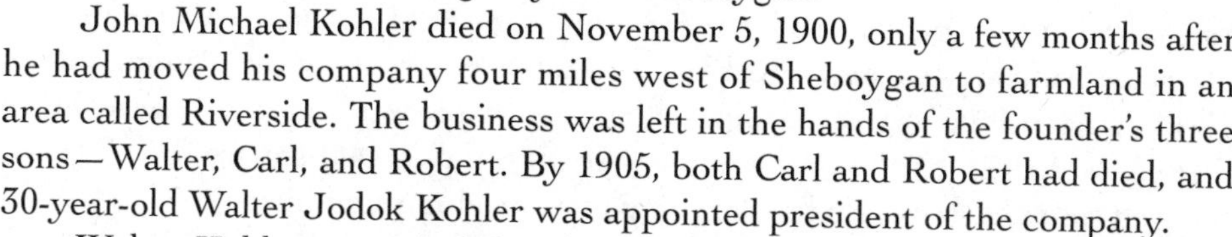

John Michael Kohler died on November 5, 1900, only a few months after he had moved his company four miles west of Sheboygan to farmland in an area called Riverside. The business was left in the hands of the founder's three sons—Walter, Carl, and Robert. By 1905, both Carl and Robert had died, and 30-year-old Walter Jodok Kohler was appointed president of the company.

Walter Kohler expanded the company from a short-line manufacturer of enameled cast-iron products to a full-line company that additionally offered vitreous china fixtures, brass fittings, heating equipment, and electric generators. He was a pioneer in designing, engineering, and manufacturing products such as the one-piece, built-in bathtub, the one-piece lavatory, the one-piece kitchen sink, and the "electric sink" (forerunner of today's dishwasher). He also pioneered the use of matching colors in iron and china bathroom fixtures.

Walter Kohler served one term as governor of Wisconsin from 1929 through 1931 while continuing to manage his company. (His son, Walter J. Kohler Jr., would later serve three terms as governor, from 1951 through 1957.) In addition to expanding the company, Walter became noted for his lifelong interest in the development of the Village of Kohler. With the assistance of the Olmsted Brothers firm—whose founder Frederick Olmsted planned and developed New York City's Central Park—Walter transformed Riverside into a beautiful shaded-garden paradise of parks, streets, churches, schools, and houses that has since served as the center of both the Kohler family and the Kohler Company.

Herbert Vollrath Kohler Sr., the only child from John Kohler's second marriage, was 16 years younger than his half-brother Walter. Herbert was appointed president of Kohler Co. in 1937 and, after the death of Walter J. Kohler in 1940, assumed the post of chairman. In addition to introducing vibrant accent colors in bathroom design in the 1960s, he expanded the company beyond the borders of Kohler, Wisconsin. The company became a leading manufacturer of four-cycle cast-iron engines and generators, with plants in Mexico and Canada.

Upon Herbert's death on July 28, 1968, the future of Kohler Co. was in question. Stock of the company was held by nearly 400 separate stockholders, not all of whom were family members. Herbert V. Kohler Jr., the oldest child of Herbert Sr., assumed control of the company by 1974 and quickly declared a 1-for-20 reverse stock split, forcing holders of fractional shares to sell them back to the company or come up with additional cash. Most sold, and the number of stockholders dropped to about 250, with Kohler family members holding 96 percent of the voting stock.

Herbert also retooled manufacturing operations and expanded the business, acquiring five diverse plumbingware companies and combining them into the Sterling Plumbing Group. Sterling quickly grew to become the third-largest full-line plumbing company in the United States. He also acquired a number of other complementary, well-known firms, including Ann Sacks Tile & Stone; Kallista bathroom and kitchen fixtures and faucets; and Canac kitchen cabinets; as well as furniture manufacturers Baker, Knapp & Tubbs, Inc., and McGuire Furniture.

There has also been continued investment in the Village of Kohler. The American Club, a former residence for immigrant workers, has been converted into a luxurious resort hotel. Kohler hospitality businesses now also include a world-class 36-hole championship golf course, a spa and fitness center, a shopping center called The Shops at Woodlake, and the 36,000-square-foot Kohler Design Center, a showcase for the company's products and history.

Today, Kohler Co. has sales of nearly $2 billion annually, well ahead of its chief rivals. It has about 15,000 associates worldwide, 7,000 of whom work in Kohler, Wisconsin. John Kohler's direct descendants still live in the Village of Kohler—population nearly 2,000—and still own and operate the business, is now valued at about $1 billion.

SOURCE: Kohler Co. archives

James L. Kraft

[Kraft Foods, Inc.]

James Lewis Kraft was born on December 11, 1874, in Fort Erie, Ontario, Canada, one of eleven children born to George F. and Minerva (Tripp) Kraft, early Canadian pioneers. The Kraft family were Mennonites, and young Kraft grew up with strong religious convictions that he carried through his entire life.

At the age of 16, Kraft quit school to sell eggs to hotels and stores in Buffalo, New York. Within two years he helped his family pay off their farm mortgage, but because of newly imposed tariffs on products crossing the border he abandoned his venture.

He next took some courses at a Buffalo business school, performing janitorial work in exchange for tuition. He also worked in an Ontario grocery store until he saved enough money to launch an ice company. Unfortunately, due to a mild winter, little ice formed on Lake Erie. He then invested in a Buffalo cheese business, but his partners eased him out of the company.

In 1903, Kraft moved to Chicago, where he took his remaining $65 savings, rented a horse and wagon, and launched another cheese business. Each morning, he went to the city's warehouse district, bought a supply of cheese, then resold it to area merchants. The business was so successful that by 1909 several of his brothers had joined the company, which was renamed J. L. Kraft & Brothers.

James Kraft had married Pauline Elizabeth Platt on June 2, 1910, and the couple had one daughter, Edith Lucile.

Within a few years, the company was distributing more than 30 varieties of cheese under the Kraft and Elkhorn labels. Through pasteurization and air-tight packaging, Kraft was able to distribute his cheese throughout the nation and, by 1915, was selling abroad.

In 1928, Kraft acquired the Phenix Corporation, and its famous Philadelphia Brand Cream Cheese was added to the Kraft product line. By the following year, Kraft owned more than 50 subsidiaries throughout the world.

Kraft served as president of the company until 1943, at which time he became board chairman, a post he held until 1951. James L. Kraft died in Chicago on February 16, 1953.

The Postum Company purchased the Jell-O Company in 1925, Baker's Chocolate in 1927, Maxwell House Coffee and Log Cabin Syrup in 1928, and Birds Eye Frozen Foods in 1929. Later in 1929, Postum changed its name to General Foods. General Foods made several subsequent acquisitions, including Oscar Mayer & Company in 1981. By 1989, Philip Morris Companies had acquired both General Foods and Kraft and had merged them into Kraft General Food, renamed Kraft Foods, Inc., in 1995.

SOURCE: Kraft Foods, Inc. archives

John H. Krehbiel Sr.

[Molex, Inc.]

John Hammond Krehbiel was born on August 14, 1906, in Hinsdale, Illnois, the son of Frederick A. and Lucille (Pemberty) Krehbiel. The Krehbiel family, devout Swiss Mennonites, had moved to America from Germany in the early 1800s and established a wagonmaking enterprise in Newton, Kansas. John's grandfather was one of the three founders of Bethel College.

When he graduated from high school, Krehbiel's father handed him $2,000 and told him that it would cover four years of college, but that John was free to use the money in any manner he wished. An acquaintance advised him to put the money into the commodities market because wheat was about to go through the roof. Krehbiel invested in the ill-fated 1928 stock market, and two weeks later the money was gone for good.

Krehbiel did attend several college classes at the Robie Institute (now the Illinois Institute of Technology) and the University of Chicago. However, rather than pursue a particular degree, he took classes that provided special insight into work-related topics. For instance, when he started working with explosive materials, he took classes in chemistry to help him understand the properties of chemicals and to be able to speak intelligently with chemists who were involved with the project.

His next endeavor was with a small, ready-mix concrete company, where Krehbiel took a low-paying job with the understanding that once he reached a certain sales quota he'd be given one-fourth stake in the company. Within 18 months he fulfilled his part of the agreement, but the owners never delivered on their promise.

Fortunately, friends at Commonwealth Edison, the local utility, told Krehbiel they were looking for a supplier of fireproofing compound. He quickly negotiated a contract for 100,000 pounds of the material and, at age 26, launched the J. H. Krehbiel Company. A rocky start grew worse in 1932 when the utility, a victim of the Depression, used Krehbiel's material at a much slower pace than he envisioned. However, other markets were identified and the company survived.

Krehbiel's next venture was even more volatile than the stock market. A neighbor owned a successful company that required nitrocellulose, a form of gunpowder, in one of its processes. To supply his plant, Krehbiel and the owner's son launched Illinois Manufacturing Chemists, despite the fact that the factory blew up not once, but twice.

John Krehbiel's father, Frederick, was himself quite an enterprising engineer and entrepreneur, launching several ventures over the course of his lifetime. None, however, was more important than Molex, which he founded in the 1930s. During World War I, the elder Krehbiel had been called upon to design a coal-refining plant. He observed a plasticlike by-product that came to be known as *molex*.

Twenty years later, Krehbiel started making pipes, flowerpots, and even toys with the substance. Frederick convinced John to join the enterprise during World War II, and the younger Krehbiel adapted the material to terminal blocks and boards that were used in home appliances, automobiles, and televisions. By the 1950s, father and son introduced their own line of connectors and terminals.

John H. Krehbiel Sr. died on November 12, 1993, at the age of 87. He had not only led the company through phenomenal growth, but he also continued to innovate products, as evidenced by his 14 patents. Today, Molex employs over 10,000 people in 46 plants, with annual sales in excess of $1.2 billion.

SOURCES: Molex, Inc. archives; Ed Linn *A Great Connection,* Molex, Inc.

Bernard H. Kroger

[The Kroger Co.]

At age ten, John Henry Kroger and a friend left their native Germany for America. Young John wanted to pursue opportunities in the Ohio valley that other German pioneers had described in their letters to families who remained behind. He worked in exchange for passage on a sailing vessel bound for Baltimore, Maryland. Upon arrival, he traveled by foot to Pittsburgh, Pennsylvania, where he caught a flatboat on the Ohio River.

Eventually, he landed at Covington, Kentucky, with about 6¢ left in his pocket and soon found a job in a cracker factory. He married Mary Schlebee, whose family had immigrated from Germany when she was only three years old, and the couple moved to Cincinnati, Ohio, and established a dry goods store. They had ten children, the fifth being Bernard Henry Kroger, born on January 24, 1860.

In 1873, a financial panic swept the country, forcing John Kroger out of business. Young Bernard, only 13 years old, quit school and went to work, first at a pharmacy, then on a nearby farm where he lived in a small, unheated loft above a shed. The following year, he contracted malaria and returned home on foot to save the train fare.

When his health was restored, he applied for a job with the Great Northern and Pacific Tea Company, which consisted of one small store. The owner hired him, gave him a quick course on door-to-door selling, then sent him off with a sample case of coffee, tea, and sugar. Kroger was too intimidated to knock on any doors, so he wandered aimlessly until coming upon a bakery, where he ordered some rolls.

When he was done eating, he found the courage to show his products to the owner, who promptly placed a large order. Encouraged with his first sale, Kroger took to the streets knocking on doors; at the end of the day, he had piled up orders totaling $35. His first week's commission of $7 was more than he had ever made in his life. For more than two years, Kroger continued his successful venture, eventually driving a delivery truck.

Soon after joining the Imperial Tea Company, Kroger was promoted to manager and asked to turn around the financially troubled business. By the end of the first day, he had discharged all the employees except a delivery boy, hired a new cashier, and acquired a cash register. Before a year passed, Kroger had the store operating with an impressive profit. He requested that the two owners give him a full partnership, but they declined, prompting Kroger to move on.

His experience at Imperial convinced Kroger that he was capable of owning his own grocery store. Lacking capital, he recruited a friend, B. A. Branagan, to join him in the business. With a little over $700, the two rented a store in Cincinnati, purchased a delivery wagon and a horse named Dan, and on July 1, 1883, opened their store.

Misfortune quickly struck. Dan was killed when horse and wagon were struck by a train. Next, the Ohio River flooded and destroyed the partners' entire inventory. Then one of Kroger's brothers died in another state and he had to absorb the costs of transportation and a funeral. However, Kroger was able to still manage a profit of more than $2,000 in his first year and promptly bought out his partner for $1,500.

Within two years he had opened three more stores. He continued to personally deliver groceries to the Jansen family across the Ohio River, as he had his eye on their daughter Mary Emily. They were married in 1886 and had seven children over the next 12 years. Tragically, Mary died from an overdose of ether while having minor surgery in the hospital.

Kroger coped with his loss by throwing himself into his work. The number of stores, which had grown to 17 by the early 1890s, increased quickly. By 1908, he had 136 stores in operation. Through unheard-of innovations such as selling baked goods and meats, Kroger's quickly became popular wherever a new store was established.

In 1928, Kroger sold his interest in the chain for a reported $28 million. Bernard Kroger died on July 21, 1938, at the age of 78, at his summer home on Cape Cod. Today the company operates more than 1,350 food stores in 19 states, has annual sales of more than $25 billion, and employs nearly 190,000 people.

SOURCES: The Kroger Co. archives; George Laycock, *The Kroger Story: A Century of Innovation,* The Kroger Co., 1983

Edward H. Lane

[Lane Furniture]

Altavista, Virginia, was established in 1907 by John Edward Lane and his brothers, owners of a successful railroad development company. When they learned that a forthcoming railroad line would cross the main line of the Southern Railway, they purchased 2,000 acres at the junction and founded the new town.

Five years later, John Lane acquired a small packing-box plant for $500 at a bankruptcy auction at Altavista. His 20-year-old son, Edward Hudson Lane, had shown promise in managing the family business interests, including farms and a sawmill, and he had taken courses in woodworking, foundry, and machine shop at what is now Virginia Tech in Blacksburg.

Edward Lane and a former teacher visited the company and found relatively few pieces of useful equipment. They made a list of needed equipment, which they ordered from the supplier that offered the most attractive credit terms. Lane focused production on cedar chests, which was the most profitable line produced by the company. He calculated that the plant could make 10 or 15 chests daily.

Lane renamed the venture The Standard Red Cedar Chest Company and, with five employees, started building chests. His first problem was finding cedar suppliers willing to extend credit. Drawing from his past experiences, he was able to establish his own small sawmill, which not only solved the supply problem, but also enabled him to pass along a 5 percent discount to buyers.

Sales, which were made through commissioned salespeople, were slow. Lane later recalled being "one jump ahead of the sheriff most of the time." When a local banker informed him that his chest company was insolvent, young Lane asked him what that meant. "Never mind," the banker told him, "You probably would be better off to remain ignorant of its meaning."

After the first three years, sales started to increase. World War I caused a brief interruption, but Lane weathered the war by building pine ammunition boxes. By 1922, the company changed its name to the Lane Company and launched an extensive advertising campaign. The product line was expanded to include chests made from mahogany and walnut.

The company remained essentially a chest maker through World War II. By the early 1950s, Lane was making television cabinets for General Electric. The experience convinced Edward Lane to expand into other lines of furniture. In 1956, he acquired the Bald Knob Furniture Company of Rocky Mount, Virginia, thus adding case goods to the product line. Within a decade the company was making tables and accent furniture.

In 1967, Edward Lane purchased the well-known Hickory Chair Company. The following year, he took the company public, providing capital to orchestrate more acquisitions. In 1969 the company purchased the Clyde Pearson Company, Hickory Tavern, and Bruington Furniture Companies. Action Industries and the Royal Development Company were acquired in 1972. These acquisitions positioned Lane as one of the country's leading manufacturers of wood and upholstered furniture.

Edward H. Lane died on May 19, 1973, just as his company was reaching annual sales of $100 million. Two of his sons continued to hold executive positions within the company.

SOURCE: Lane Furniture archives

William P. Lear Sr.

[LearJet, Inc.]

Starting his own business at the age of 20, William Lear proved to be one of America's finest inventors/entrepreneurs. After developing radio technology that helped launch Motorola, Lear invented and built numerous aerospace products. By the early 1960s, he had established LearJet, Inc., maker of America's premiere business jet.

William Powell Lear Sr. was born June 26, 1902, at Hannibal, Missouri. In 1922, after serving in the U.S. Navy, Lear established his own business. By the late 1920s, he had invented the first practical automobile radio, which was commercialized by Galvin Manufacturing (later Motorola).

Lear spent the next 30 years building Lear, Inc., with innovations in the aerospace and electronics industries. In 1942, Lear married Moya Olsen, daughter of Ole Olsen of the Broadway comedy team Olsen and Johnson. His wife was active in business activities while raising their four children.

In the late 1950s, Lear had become captivated with the sleek Swiss fighter-bomber known as the P-16, which he believed could be the model for a high-performance business aircraft. After studying the craft and working with Swiss designers, Lear moved back to America in 1962 and sold his interest in the company to the Siegler Corporation, which became known as Lear Siegler. At the time, Lear had grown to $100 million in annual sales and had more than 5,000 employees.

By 1963, the Lear family was living in Wichita, Kansas. Lear obtained space at the Wichita Municipal Airport and set out to build his business plane. Within nine months, the LearJet Model 23 flew into the Wichita sky. It became the first production aircraft to be completely financed by one man, and it soon set the standard for business jet travel.

During this same time, Lear established the LearJet Stereo Division. Through this company, Lear pioneered the development of eight-track stereo-cassette technology, which soon became a popular format for recorded music. In 1967, Lear sold the entire company (jets and stereos) to The Gates Rubber Company of Denver, Colorado.

However, even though Lear was in his 70s, he kept busy. He next designed a 12-seat business jet that he called the LearStar 600. He sold the design to Canadair, who built it under the Challenger name.

During his next venture, he became afflicted with leukemia, and on May 14, 1978, William Lear died at the age of 75. Lear had been awarded nearly 150 patents for a wide range of designs and inventions that affected nearly everyone in America.

SOURCES: LearJet, Inc. archives and Lear family archives

Henry D. Lee

[Lee Apparel Company]

Henry D. Lee was born on December 9, 1853, in West Randolph, Vermont, one of nine children born to Michael and Mary Ann (Cunningham) Lee. When he was only four years old his father died, leaving young Lee to be farmed out to another family until he was 11.

At age 13, he left his native Vermont and moved to Galion, Ohio, where he worked as a hotel night clerk. Within three years, he had built a savings of about $1,200. In 1875, he used his savings and a $50,000 bank loan to purchase a small oil company that was in bankruptcy. Soon, he was selling kerosene throughout north-central Ohio.

By the early 1880s, Lee sold half interest in his business to John D. Rockefeller's Standard Oil. Because of poor health, Lee later sold the remainder to Rockefeller and headed for Kansas.

In the fall of 1889, Lee arrived in Salina, Kansas, and quickly established a general store known as the H. D. Lee Mercantile Company. He launched several other local ventures as well, including the Lee Hardware Company, the Kansas Ice and Storage Company, the Farmers' National Bank of Salina, the H. D. Lee Flour Mills Company, and the Harvester Building Company.

After ten years in business, Lee's mercantile business had become something more than a grocery store. He offered stationery and school supplies, furnishings, and clothing, including work overalls. In time, he opened similar stores in other locations, including Kansas City; South Bend, Indiana; Waterbury, Connecticut; Trenton, New Jersey; and Minneapolis, Minnesota.

Lee was one of the first people in Salina to purchase an automobile. In the early days, there were no repair garages, and car manufacturers had to send mechanics to car owners to fix problems. While servicing Lee's car one day, a mechanic asked if the store could order or make a special coverall that he could wear over his clothes while working on cars.

Lee studied the opportunity and quickly designed such a garment, not only for mechanics, but also for farmworkers. He called his new coveralls Lee Union-Alls and launched a modest marketing effort. By 1911, Lee became so angry over delays in receiving shipments of the overalls and other clothing that he decided to establish a manufacturing plant. By 1915, a factory was opened in Kansas City, Kansas, and the H. D. Lee apparel line included overalls, work jackets, and blue denim pants.

During World War I, a supply officer from nearby Camp Funston happened to be in the store and spotted the Union-Alls. Lee was given an open order from the U.S. Army for all the overalls he could make, and it quickly became the fatigue uniform for the doughboys.

Over time, the company's clothing became quite popular among ranchers and cowboys. From this association, Lee developed a commitment to authentic Western wear, built strong to withstand the rigors of farmwork and rodeos. The company's line of Lee Riders have been popular since their introduction during World War II.

Henry D. Lee died on March 15, 1928. He was succeeded as president by Leonard C. Staples, the husband of Lee's niece. The H. D. Lee Company was very diversified: As well as manufacturing overalls, Western wear for the rodeo crowd, and other clothing, the company sold a brand of groceries under the Lee label. However, the company had such success in the apparel manufacturing field that the grocery section of the business was sold in the 1950s to Consolidated Foods.

Lee Company became a wholly owned subsidiary of VF Corporation in August 1969. Today, VF Corporation, with over 64,000 employees, is an international apparel company that produces Lee, Wrangler, Riders, Vanity Fair, Jantzen, and many other lines.

SOURCE: Lee Apparel Company archives

Dave Lennox, David W. Norris

[Lennox Furnace Company]

Dave Lennox was born on April 15, 1855, at Detroit, Michigan, the son of an expert railroad mechanic. Young Lennox grew up exposed to the work and tools of his father, who passed along the craft to his curious son.

Just before the first shots of the Civil War, the Lennox family moved to Aurora, Illinois. When the war started, the elder Lennox enlisted for a three-month tour of duty. When his time was up, he enlisted for a second tour. He never returned.

The Lennox family next moved to Chicago, where his mother managed a grocery store and young Dave worked in various machine shops. In 1888, he hopped a train to find opportunities further west and landed in Marshalltown, Iowa. He rented a 20- by 20-foot shop for $7 per month and established a small machine shop.

In 1895, Ernest Bryant and Ezra Smith from nearby Oskaloosa, Iowa, came into the shop. They had developed a new furnace that used an innovative mix of riveted steel and iron castings. Lennox, who was quite busy with other projects, reluctantly agreed to build a prototype furnace.

After Lennox invested his own time and materials, the two men were unable to raise investment funds for their furnace. Lennox then assumed ownership of Bryant and Smith's patents and stubbornly pursued completion of a prototype. After design revisions, considerable sweat, and more money, he was able to produce a working furnace. Once it was placed on the market, it quickly became popular, and his shop was soon overrun with orders.

By 1904, Lennox grew tired of the furnace business and sold it to a group of investors, including his son-in-law, David Windsor Norris, who owned the local newspaper. During the first year under new ownership, the Lennox Furnace Company sold 600 furnaces. Norris was so encouraged with the development that, at the close of World War I, he purchased the remaining shares of the company from the other investors.

In the early 1920s, Norris expanded by opening first a warehouse, then a manufacturing plant at Syracuse, New York. Sales continued to be promising, but the business was given a boost through the research and development efforts of Norris's son, John Norris, a graduate of the Massachusetts Institute of Technology.

Working in a quiet corner of one of the company's warehouses, young Norris fashioned a quiet, forced-air furnace with compact, enamel cabinets. He also switched the source of heat from coal to oil and natural gas. As the Depression came to an end, David Norris, who had originally opposed the new furnace technology, embraced his son's work.

The company built a new factory in 1940 at Columbus, Ohio. By the onset of World War II, Lennox had become a major force in the heating industry. When David W. Norris died in 1949, he was succeeded by his son, John. The following decade, young Norris changed the name of the company to Lennox Industries and led the company into the air-conditioning market.

In the early 1990s, the company consolidated its operations in a new world headquarters facility in Richardson, Texas.

SOURCE: Lennox International archives

Colonel Eli Lilly

[Eli Lilly & Company]

In 1789, Gustave Lilly brought his family from England to the United States, settling near Ellicott City, Maryland. One of his four sons, Eli, built a successful tavern business and later established a successful country plantation. His son, Gustavus, married Esther Elizabeth Kirby, and the couple eventually had 11 children. Their firstborn, Eli, would one day build one of America's largest pharmaceutical companies.

Eli Lilly was born on July 8, 1838, on his family's Baltimore County plantation. The Lilly family later moved to Kentucky, then to Indiana in the early 1850s. Lilly chose not to follow his father into the carpentry business. While visiting his uncle and aunt in Lafayette, Indiana, he became intrigued with a neighborhood apothecary called the Good Samaritan Drug Store.

The drugstore was owned by Henry Lawrence, a respected businessman who was happy to give young Lilly an apprenticeship. After spending months of studying and modest responsibilities, Lilly was handed a pestle and mortar to mix his own compounds. Lawrence also taught him the business of running a retail drugstore.

In 1858, Lilly went into a brief partnership at another drugstore, and the following year he became a clerk for Perkins and Coons, an Indianapolis retail drug business. In 1860, he returned to his family home in Greencastle, Indiana, where he established his own drugstore and married Emily Lemon.

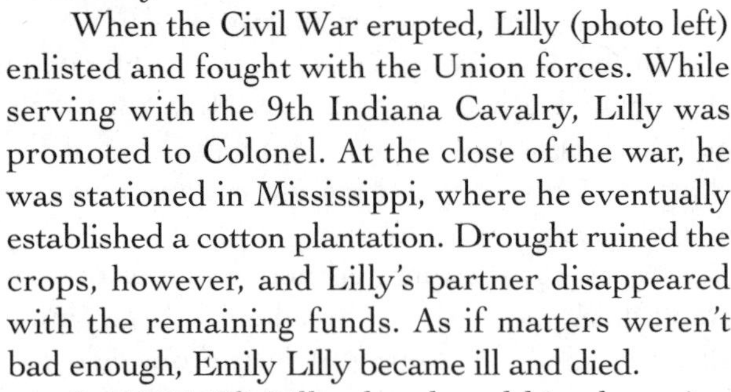

When the Civil War erupted, Lilly (photo left) enlisted and fought with the Union forces. While serving with the 9th Indiana Cavalry, Lilly was promoted to Colonel. At the close of the war, he was stationed in Mississippi, where he eventually established a cotton plantation. Drought ruined the crops, however, and Lilly's partner disappeared with the remaining funds. As if matters weren't bad enough, Emily Lilly became ill and died.

In 1866, Eli Lilly abandoned his plantation and, with his son, Josiah Kirby, moved back to Indiana. He worked for the next three years at a wholesale drugstore. Then, in 1869, he and a partner opened a drugstore in Paris, Illinois. The store was successful, but Lilly's heart was in manufacturing. In 1873, he returned to Indianapolis and, with a partner, opened a small laboratory.

The partnership lasted about three years and then was dissolved. Eli's share of the company was some equipment, some cash, and several gallons of finished fluid extracts. Discouraged, he approached Augustus Kiefer, another drugstore owner, for a job. Kiefer reminded him of his talent in manufacturing and encouraged him to start another company. The pair found several other Indianapolis druggists who were willing to commit to Lilly. So, with $1,400 and some supplies, the 38-year-old Lilly opened for business on May 10, 1876, in a small alley shop under the sign Eli Lilly, Chemist.

At the end of eight months in business, sales totaled nearly $4,500. Second-year sales grew to $11,318, and third-year sales skyrocketed to more than $48,000. In 1882, his son graduated from the Philadelphia College of Pharmacy and joined the firm as the superintendent of the laboratories.

Colonel Eli Lilly died on June 8, 1898. He was succeeded by his son, Josiah K. Lilly. Josiah's sons, Eli Lilly and Josiah Lilly Jr., each served later as company president. Today, Eli Lilly & Company employs about 26,000 people worldwide.

SOURCE: Eli Lilly & Company archives

J. Spencer Love

[Burlington Industries, Inc.]

James Spencer Love was born on July 6, 1896, in Cambridge, Massachusetts. His parents had moved from North Carolina to Cambridge when his father, James Lee Love, accepted a position as mathematics professor at Harvard University. Young Spencer attended Cambridge Latin School, moved on to Harvard, where he completed his bachelor's degree in three years, then continued his education at the Harvard Business School.

In 1917, Love enlisted in the U.S. Army and, shortly after his 21st birthday, was commissioned a first lieutenant. He went overseas during World War I with the 78th Division, achieving the rank of major by the time he turned 23.

After the war, Love was unable to find work in the Boston area. He later recalled: "I was a bit shocked to find that no one gave much of a damn about my brand-new Harvard degree or even my war record." Concluding that he could do better in the South, Love took his $3,000 in savings and moved to Gastonia, North Carolina, where his uncle gave him a job as a payroll clerk for the Gastonia Cotton Manufacturing Company. The job paid $120 a month.

When the plant became available for sale, Love assembled a group of investors, including his father, who pooled their resources to acquire a controlling interest of the business. Love was appointed secretary-treasurer and chief executive officer. Unfortunately, the cotton business subsequently went soft, and Love muddled on until 1923, when he was able to auction off the building and equipment for $200,000.

Love and most of his machinery then moved to Burlington, North Carolina, where a group of businesspeople feared that the local textile industry was facing collapse. They took a gamble on Love because of his ambition, business know-how, and machinery, and through their sponsorship, the first plant of the new Burlington Mills Company opened in October 1924.

His first plant, which employed 200 workers, was built in the middle of a cornfield, and textile operations started before the building was completed. Only half the weave room had a floor—the other half was mostly dirt. The company's first products were all made of cotton and included flag cloth, bunting, cotton scrims, curtain and dress fabrics, and "birdseye" (a diaper cloth).

The cotton textile market was challenging, and the new company struggled. Almost in desperation, Love experimented with a new synthetic fiber called *rayon,* which was criticized as being too shiny, too flimsy, and cheap-looking. Nonetheless, Love used it to make bedspreads, which became big sellers in the marketplace because of their low cost.

A second plant was built in 1926, and a New York sales office was opened three years later. Despite the Great Depression, Burlington Industries expanded. In 1935, headquarters moved to Greensboro, North Carolina, which afforded direct rail access to New York. The company was reorganized as Burlington Mills Corporation in 1937 and that year made its first appearance on the New York Stock Exchange. (It was later renamed Burlington Industries.)

By the late 1940s, *Forbes* magazine described Burlington as "one of the largest fabricators of man-made yarns in the world with a total of 75 plants, 12 located abroad." At the time, the company employed 22,000 workers and had annual sales of nearly $200 million. During this postwar boom, Burlington experienced such rapid growth that new plants were built with one wooden wall, which could be torn down quickly to expand the size of the plant.

J. Spencer Love died unexpectedly on January 20, 1962. At the time of his death, he presided over a company with 65,000 employees and more than

130 plants in 16 states and seven foreign countries. By the end of that year, Burlington became the first textile organization to ever surpass $1 billion in annual sales.

Today, Burlington Industries is one of the largest and most diversified manufacturers of textile products in the world with 23,000 employees and annual sales in excess of $2.2 billion. Major products include yarns, apparel fabrics, carpets, and home furnishings.

SOURCE: Burlington Industries archives

George Lucas
[Lucasfilm Limited]

George Lucas was born on May 14, 1944, in Modesto, California. After attending Modesto Junior College, he received a bachelor of arts degree from the University of Southern California School of Cinema and Television. In 1965, his thesis film won first prize in the Third National Student Film Festival.

In 1970, he was given the opportunity to direct a feature-length version of the film, titled *THX 1138,* which was produced by Francis Ford Coppola. Encouraged by the experience, Lucas formed his own film company, Lucasfilm Limited, the following year in San Rafael, California.

In 1973, Lucas cowrote and directed *American Graffiti,* an award-winning classic. Four years later, he wrote and directed *Star Wars,* a film that broke all box office records and was awarded seven Academy Awards. He completed the trilogy by writing and executive-producing sequels *The Empire Strikes Back* and *Return of the Jedi.*

Lucas became involved in another famous trilogy in 1980 when he served as executive producer of *Raiders of the Lost Ark,* directed by his longtime friend Steven Spielberg, which won five Academy Awards. He was coexecutive producer and creator of the sequel, *Indiana Jones and the Temple of Doom,* which was awarded two Academy Awards. More film credits followed, including *Captain EO, Willow, Tucker: The Man and His Dream,* and *Indiana Jones and the Last Crusade.*

The company established by George Lucas in 1971 has evolved into three operations. His first company, Lucas Digital, actually has two highly successful operations—Industrial Light & Magic and Skywalker Sound. Industrial Light & Magic (ILM) has played a key role in 8 of the top 15 box office hits of all time and has been awarded 14 Academy Awards for Best Visual Effects as well as eight Technical Achievement Awards. Skywalker Sound, has won ten Academy Awards for Sound Design. The laboratories of these two divisions brought to life the enormously successful film *Jurassic Park.*

His second company is LucasArts Entertainment Company, a leading international developer and publisher of entertainment software. Its games have won international acclaim and are consistently on the best-seller lists. The runaway hit *Rebel Assault* has sold more than 1,000,000 copies.

His third company is Lucasfilm Limited, which includes all of his feature films, television production, and licensing activities. It also includes the THX Group, which was created to define and maintain the highest-quality standards possible in motion picture theaters and home theater systems. Lucas is also the founder and chairman of the board of The George Lucas Educational Foundation.

SOURCE: Lucasfilm Limited archives

Rebecca W. Pennock Lukens

[Lukens Steel]

Rebecca Webb (Pennock) Lukens was born on January 6, 1794, the second child born to Isaac and Martha Webb Pennock, at Fallowfield, Pennsylvania. Her father's family had been given a land grant directly from William Penn, a portion of which had filtered down to Isaac. Rather than work the land, however, Isaac Pennock established the Federal Slitting Mill and made iron products.

The Pennocks were Quakers and therefore believed that their daughters should have the same educational opportunities as their sons. Not only was Isaac Pennock frequently accompanied by young Rebecca at the iron mill, but he also sent her to an exclusive boarding school.

In 1810, Pennock and a partner purchased a significant tract of land from the Coates family, founders of Coatesville, that included a modest iron mill known as the Brandywine Iron Works and Nail Factory. In 1813, Rebecca married Dr. Charles Lloyd Lukens, and four years later the couple entered into a lease with Isaac Pennock for the former Coates house and the Brandywine factory.

The Brandywine mill was in poor condition, and over the next several years Charles Lukens busied himself fixing old equipment and, as possible, adding new equipment. He also became engaged in manufacturing iron plates for boilers as substitutes for the expensive copper plates that were in common use. The idea was sound, and business grew quickly.

At the same time, the Lukens family was growing. Their first child, Martha, was born in 1814. Next came Elizabeth in 1817, Charles Edmund in 1818, Isaac (who died in infancy) in 1821, and Isabella in 1822.

Just as it seemed success was at hand, a series of disasters struck. Isaac Pennock died in 1824 and didn't specifically leave the Brandywine property to Rebecca and her husband. Rebecca's mother, with whom she did not have a good relationship, insisted that the Lukens compensate the other Pennock children for the property they had been renting for years, as well as the equipment that they had already purchased.

Then, in the summer of 1825, Charles Lukens himself died at the age of 39, leaving Rebecca financially crippled and pregnant. Having no alternatives,

Rebecca Lukens delegated supervision of the mill operations to her brother, while she took charge of the business and administrative duties. In the midst of the chaos, she delivered her sixth child, Charlesanna.

It took Rebecca Lukens nine years, but by 1834 the debts associated with rebuilding the mill were repaid and her mother's claims against her had been satisfied. She opened a store, warehouse, and freight agency at the new Coatesville railroad depot. However, she still was not free from the tragedies that haunted her life. In 1832, her second daughter, Elizabeth, died at the age of 15.

During the 1840s, Rebecca's daughters started to marry, resulting in a new generation of leadership at the mill. A final challenge was presented to Rebecca in 1849, when her youngest daughter Charlesanna died while giving birth. For the next six years, Rebecca raised her infant granddaughter while studying the Bible. On December 10, 1854, Rebecca Webb Pennock Lukens died at the age of 60.

Lukens remained in the hands of family members and related partnerships until 1890. It maintained consistent growth, eventually joining the ranks of the Fortune 500 list of America's largest industrial companies. Today, Lukens remains the oldest continuously operating steel mill in America.

SOURCE: Lukens, Inc. archives

W. Bruce Lunsford

[Vencor, Inc.]

W. Bruce Lunsford was born on November 11, 1947, and was raised on the family's 120-acre farm in rural Kenton County. Upon graduation from the University of Kentucky in 1969, he went to work for a Cincinnati accounting firm while attending night classes at the Salmon P. Chase College of Law. After he graduated in 1974 with a J.D. degree and went to work at a Cincinnati law firm.

In 1979, a fraternity brother invited him to become involved with the election campaign of Kentucky Governor John Y. Brown. Within 70 days, Lunsford was the state Democratic treasurer. Shortly thereafter, at age 33, he was appointed secretary of commerce.

Public servants, particularly those involved with business and industry, are exposed to a barrage of ideas, and Lunsford was no exception. A respiratory therapist named Michael Barr approached Governor Brown with an idea about specialty hospitals for patients dependent upon life-supporting ventilators. Brown passed him on to Lunsford, who patiently listened to the pitch.

Barr was confident that a focused-care facility that didn't provide a range of money-losing services would be able to provide superior services at a lower cost. Despite a lack of medical experience, Lunsford saw potential, and within 90 days a new venture was organized under the name Vencare, with Lunsford serving as CEO and Barr as COO. The partners soon acquired a financially distressed hospital in Lagrange, Indiana, and had it running in the black within months.

Lunsford started acquiring other distressed properties that were available at good prices. He structured a care-giving system that reduced paperwork and nonmedical personnel so that the company could provide care for a ventilator patient for about $750 per day, less than half the industry standard.

Lunsford and his wife, Becky, have three children. Today, Vencor owns or leases 38 hospitals throughout the country and provides subacute services to hundreds of nursing homes. Annual revenues exceed $2.5 billion.

SOURCES: Vencor, Inc. archives; Andrew Wolfson, "Health-care Titan," *Courier-Journal,* Louisville, KY, February 5, 1995

Bernard Marcus, Arthur M. Blank

[The Home Depot]

After being fired from their jobs at another home improvement supply chain, Bernard Marcus and Arthur Blank raised enough capital to launch their own retail chain. Today, The Home Depot is America's largest home-center retailer, with annual sales in excess of $12 billion.

Bernard Marcus was born May 12, 1929, in Newark, New Jersey, the son of a Russian cabinetmaker. He received his bachelor of science degree in pharmacy from Rutgers University. He served for ten years as vice president of Hard Goods Merchandising at Vornado, Inc., a discount retail chain, before joining Handy Dan Improvement Centers, a home-center retail chain. From 1972 to 1978, Marcus served as chairman and president of Handy Dan.

Arthur M. Blank was born in Flushing, New York. He grew up in Queens, New York, where his father owned a small drugstore and pharmacy supply business. When Arthur was 15, his father died of a heart attack, and the family eventually sold the business to Los Angeles–based Daylin, Inc. Arthur went to work for Daylin, and wound up working at its Handy Dan Home Improvement Center chain. That's where he met Bernard Marcus.

In April 1978, a man charged with reorganizing Handy Dan's parent company, Daylin, fired the chain's chairman and president, Bernard Marcus, and corporate controller, Arthur Blank. Five days later, Marcus was on the phone with an investment banker describing a new retail store that would focus on low prices, high volume, and high-quality service. They eventually raised $2 million.

On June 22, 1979, Marcus and Blank opened their first two Home Depot stores in Atlanta. They opened a third store in August 1979 and a fourth in February 1980. Employees in those early days fondly recall stacking empty cardboard boxes and paint cans on top shelves to make the stores "look full."

The partners' next venture was into the Miami market, opening two stores in September and two more in November of 1981. On November 22 they took the company public, and both investment and profits soared. Originally projecting per-store sales of $9 million, the founders and investors were delighted to see average sales exceed $17 million per store.

Today, The Home Depot is America's largest home-center retailer. It employs 80,000 people and operates nearly 400 warehouse-style home centers in 31 states and 19 stores in Canada. Gross sales for 1994 exceeded $12.4 billion. Stores are being added so fast that the company estimates 850 stores will be open by the end of fiscal year 1998.

There are many explanations for the phenomenal success of the company. Marcus insists his consumer research involves walking among customers and asking if they are finding the products they are looking for. The company offers free clinics for shoppers on all aspects of home remodeling and repair. Following the lead of Sam Walton, Home Depot prices are constantly the lowest possible, and special sales are avoided.

Employees are carefully selected, and the company tends to hire only full-time employees looking for a career. Only 1 in 50 applicants land a job, and the company keeps a sharp eye out for honest, extroverted people who do not require close supervision. "We have lots of entrepreneurial folks here that think futuristically, that are not afraid to push the envelope," says Marcus.

No one works on commission because, according to Marcus, it gives the impression that small purchasers don't count. However, bonuses are regularly distributed, and most management-level employees receive lucrative stock options.

But there is something more at work at The Home Depot. The company has managed to strike a careful balance between creative entrepreneurship and responsible financial management. The two founders are referred to by everyone in the company as simply Bernie and Arthur. More often than not, Bernie walks through the stores minus a coat and tie. Bruce Berg, president of the five-state southern division, drives a pickup and wears Reeboks. "I'm just not much of a necktie guy," says Berg.

Arthur and Bernie insist that the key to employee relations is humility. After their treatment at their prior jobs, Bernie says, "We vowed we'd never treat anyone like that. A lot of people that run major corporations today, they lack humility. And that's something that we have in abundance."

Bernie Marcus has served as chairman and chief executive officer since the company was founded in 1978. Arthur Blank, 13 years Bernie's junior, has always served as president and chief operating officer. Neither has imminent retirement plans.

Bernie serves on the boards of the National Foundation for the Centers for Disease Control and Prevention and of the Shepherd Center in Atlanta. He and his wife, Billi, have three children. He and his wife founded the Marcus Center in 1991, which provides support services for persons with developmental disabilities and their families.

Arthur Blank received his bachelor of science degree in business administration from Babson College. He serves on the boards of many community groups, including North Carolina Outward Bound School, Emory University, USA/Mobile Indoor Track & Field Championships, and the National Conference of Christians and Jews. He and his wife Stephanie have three children.

SOURCES: The Home Depot archives; *Georgia Trend,* March 1993, July 1994; Patricia Sellers, "Companies That Serve You Best," *Fortune* magazine, vol. 127, no. 11, July 31, 1993

Herbert Marcus Sr., Abraham L. Neiman, Carrie Marcus Neiman

[Neiman Marcus]

In 1905, an enterprising trio from Dallas, Texas—Herbert Marcus Sr., his sister, Carrie Marcus Neiman, and his brother-in-law, Abraham L. Neiman—

moved to Atlanta, Georgia, and established a sales promotion business. Within two years the venture was so successful that they were approached with offers to sell the business. They narrowed their options to two choices—sell for $25,000 in cash, which would provide them with capital to return to Dallas and start another venture, or obtain the Missouri franchise for a new soft drink called Coca-Cola.

Marcus and the Neimans elected to take the money, and in 1907 they returned to Dallas and opened a new department store named Neiman Marcus. They differentiated their store by offering a wide variety of exclusive products, spiced up with occasional exotic or unconventional items. Their two-story store was laid out so that customers weren't overwhelmed with merchandise.

Despite the nationwide panic of 1907, Neiman Marcus experienced steady growth until 1913, when the entire building and inventory was destroyed by a spectacular fire. However, it took the families only two weeks to reopen in temporary space until a new building was ready the following year.

With the exception of the fire, the first 20 years of Neiman Marcus was characterized by growth through innovative marketing. However, the second half of the 1920s proved challenging for the store. Abraham and Carrie Neiman divorced in 1926, and the Marcus family purchased Abraham's share of the business. The store also launched major building expansion that was completed in time for the Great Depression.

The addition of Herbert Marcus's four sons to the business during these years helped the company survive the rigors of the Depression. While catalogs were prepared by the store as early as 1909, Neiman Marcus became fully committed to catalog sales beginning in 1939. The Neiman Marcus Christmas Book quickly became the most celebrated of the store's mail-order catalogs.

Herbert Marcus Sr. died on December 11, 1950. Upon his death, Carrie Neiman was elected chairman of the board of directors and Stanley Marcus, Herbert's son, was named president and chief executive officer. Carrie Marcus Neiman remained active with the company until her death on March 8, 1952.

Neiman Marcus didn't open a second store until 1951. During the next two decades, several other stores were opened and several additions were made to the flagship store in downtown Dallas. In 1968, Neiman Marcus merged with Broadway Hale Stores, Inc., which is now known as Carter Hawley Hale Stores, Inc. Today, Neiman Marcus is a thriving retail chain of 28 stores and a flourishing mail-order business.

SOURCE: Neiman Marcus archives

Christian F. Martin Sr.

[The Martin Guitar Company]

Christian Frederick Martin was born on January 31, 1796, in Mark Neukirchen, Saxony, Germany, the son of Johann Georg Martin, a successful guitar maker. After learning the guitar-making trade, Christian moved to Vienna, Austria, was hired by Johann Stauffer, a well-known guitar maker, and rose to the position of foreman.

Martin next worked for Karl Kuhle and soon married his daughter, Ottilie Lucia Kuhle, a harpist and singer. The couple had one child, Christian F. Martin Jr., who was born on October 2, 1825, in Vienna. Soon afterward, the family moved to Germany.

The first three decades of the 1800s were marked by considerable tension between the Violin Makers Guild and the Cabinetmakers Guild, both of whom crafted guitars. The violin makers claimed that only they were prepared to design and build such a fine musical instrument. The cabinetmakers, on the other hand, pointed to the pioneering success of their own Johann Martin and others. In 1832, the authorities clearly sanctioned the making of guitars by both groups.

For Martin and many of his colleagues, however, the harm had been done. As cabinetmakers, they were free to practice their craft. Yet the jealousy and pressures remained, and Martin moved his family to the United States, where his work would be appreciated and his business might prosper.

The Martin family arrived in New York City in 1833, where Christian quickly established a full-line music store. Over the next five years, the family developed friendships with many Moravian families in the small town of Nazareth in eastern Pennsylvania.

Convinced that the town offered happiness and continued opportunity, the Martin family purchased land in Nazareth and built a house. By this time, two more children had been born, and after the move another two arrived, bringing the total to five.

Throughout the next 20 years, Martin's guitar business grew. It was also a period of experimentation, during which he innovated the use of "X bracing" in his guitars. His progress was documented in a Baltimore newspaper in 1850 which read: "C. F. Martin, Guitar Maker, respectfully informs the musical public generally, that the great favor bestowed on him has induced him to enlarge his factory, in order to supply the increasing demand for his instruments."

Martin's business slowed somewhat in the period just before the Civil War, but curiously, sales improved during the war. In 1867, Christian Frederick Martin Sr. brought his son, Christian Jr., and his nephew, Christian Frederick Hartman, into the business as partners. Hartman, who made both guitars and violins, had also immigrated to America from Germany.

Christian Frederick Martin Sr. died on February 16, 1873, at the age of 77. His son, Christian Jr., assumed control of the business, and upon his untimely death on November 15, 1888, the responsibility for the company passed to his 22-year-old son, Frank Henry Martin. He was succeeded by his son, C. F. Martin III, in 1948, who was then succeeded by his son, Frank Herbert Martin. Today, Christian Frederick Martin, IV, born July 8, 1955, serves as chairman and CEO.

SOURCE: "The Martin Family History," excerpted from *Martin Guitars: A History,* by Mike Longworth

Anthony A. Martino
[MAACO, Inc.]

Anthony A. Martino was born on January 7, 1933, in Philadelphia, Pennsylvania. Martino did not follow the family tradition of working for the railroad because he found that he liked cars better than trains. He left high school and went to work at a neighborhood automobile body repair shop.

In the late 1950s, automatic transmissions were becoming popular, and many of the older mechanics were hesitant to work with the new technology. In 1959, he decided to open a shop that would specialize in automatic transmissions. With a $3,000 loan from his father, he founded AAMCO Transmissions, an acronym of his initials (the Anthony A. Martino Company).

Martino was soon was deluged with work from auto dealerships and other mechanics. As the business poured in, he plowed the profits into advertising and quickly opened five more locations. In 1962, he and franchise expert Robert Morgan started offering franchises, and within five years more than 550 AAMCO centers were in business, generating more than $100 million in sales.

That's when 33-year-old Martino elected to retire from the business a wealthy man. He was not, however, a man of leisure. In 1972, he established MAACO, another play on his initials, to take advantage of the void in high-quality, reasonably priced painting and body work. Encouraged by the success of his first shop in Wilmington, Delaware, Martino and partner Daniel Rhode took to the road pushing franchises.

The first franchise opened in Tucson, Arizona, later that year. Seven more were added in 1973, and within two years MAACO had expanded to more than 200 centers. Today, MAACO has grown to nearly 500 franchise centers with annual sales in excess of $300 million.

Martino and Rhode also teamed up in 1982 to launch Sparks Tune-Up centers. After it had grown to 125 locations within five years, the chain was sold to GKN, the British company that also owns Meineke Muffler.

With his two major successes—AAMCO and MAACO—Martino moved the art of franchising into new territory. Both enterprises involved a franchised system that provides highly customized service. Every customer that came through the door had a unique problem that required a unique solution.

When Martino first offered AAMCO franchises, there was considerable skepticism about franchising customized automotive repair. Curiously, there was even wider skepticism when he announced his plans to franchise MAACO. The success of both ventures has opened the door for creative franchising in a wide range of industries that rely on custom solutions.

In 1988, Martino took note of the shortage of quality child care throughout the country and formed a partnership with Joseph Scandone, owner of the Goddard School in Malvern, Pennsylvania. They established a franchised chain of centers, called the Goddard Early Learning Centers. To date, more than 30 franchises have been sold.

Longtime associate and MAACO cofounder Daniel Rhode died in 1993 at the age of 57. He was in the process of building another franchise known as Hometown Auto Service.

SOURCE: MAACO Enterprises, Inc. archives

Ernest W. Maryland

[Conoco, Inc.]

After achieving success in the coal and oil business, 32-year-old Ernest Whitworth Maryland moved from Pennsylvania to West Virginia to try his luck. While drilling for coal seams, he inadvertently discovered oil. Later, in 1907, he struck a sizable gas reserve near the border town of East Liverpool, Ohio, and he entered an agreement to serve the town. However, the 1907 financial panic left him $150,000 in debt, and he had to forfeit his contract.

The following year, Maryland relocated to the Ponca City, Oklahoma, area looking for new opportunities. Although he was educated as a lawyer, Maryland was also a clever geologist and became convinced that a property known as the 101 Ranch would be an ideal place to drill. He secured a lease and founded the 101 Ranch Oil Company.

Despite several dry holes and poor financing, Maryland held to his conviction that oil was somewhere on the property. Finally, he made the first hit near an Indian burial ground.

Maryland then spent considerable time in the field making investments and upgrading his holdings throughout Oklahoma, Louisiana, Colorado, California, and Mexico. In 1923, J. P. Morgan personally met with Maryland and asked to be included in the venture. Thereafter, Maryland issued 3 million shares of stock, which Morgan purchased for $90 million.

In 1979, the corporate name was changed to Conoco, Inc. Today, Conoco is an integrated, international petroleum company employing 16,000 people and operating in 30 countries around the world. Headquartered in Houston, Texas, Conoco is the energy subsidiary of DuPont.

SOURCE: Conoco archives

Oscar F. Mayer

[Oscar Mayer & Company]

Oscar F. Mayer was born in 1859 in Bavaria. After immigrating to the United States at age 14, he spent nearly a decade learning the meat business, first as a Detroit butcher's boy and later as a worker in Chicago's stockyards and retail markets.

In 1883, Mayer leased a failing meat market in Chicago and, along with his brothers Gottfried and Max, returned it to such success that the owner resumed control of the business when the five-year lease ran out. So, in 1888, the Mayers found another location, complete with living quarters on the second floor. With a $10,000 loan, they leased the property, purchased equipment, and started over again.

Their first-day sales of Old World sausages and Westphalian hams totaled $59. Soon, salesmen were peddling Oscar Mayer meats in wicker baskets throughout Chicago and its suburbs. At the turn of the century, there were 43 employees, including five wagon salesmen, one pig-head-and-feet cleaner and cooker, and two stablemen to care for the delivery horses. In fact, as many as 80 horses were once kept in the company stables.

Mayer had four daughters and one son, Oscar G. Mayer, who joined the company in 1909 after graduating from Harvard. While visiting his fiancée in Madison, Wisconsin, in 1918, young Mayer learned of a small farmer's cooperative meat packing plant that was for sale, and the company quickly arranged its acquisition. The plant eventually became one of the largest and most efficient meat processing plants in the country and headquarters for the entire company.

Oscar F. Mayer was a stickler for a good product. Once, while on a tour of the Chicago plant, he tasted some of the wieners and said that they tasted good, but not good enough. In other words, they were not to be delivered. When his brother Gottfried, who was the plant manager, informed Oscar that the wieners were due in the Chicago Cubs baseball park the next day, he just shrugged. The batch of wieners was scrapped and a new one was made before game time.

In 1929, Oscar Mayer started banding its wieners with a yellow paper ring that carried the company name and the U.S. government inspection stamp. By introducing name differentiation in an industry that previously operated in anonymity, the company positioned itself for name-brand advertising.

When Oscar F. Mayer died in 1955 at the age of 95, annual sales were exceeding $220 million. The company remained an independent, family-owned business for nearly a century. In 1981, the company was sold to General Foods Corporation, which in 1989 was merged with Kraft Foods.

SOURCE: Kraft Foods, Inc. archives

Frederick L. Maytag

[The Maytag Company]

Upset that fellow farmhands received serious injuries during harvest season, Frederick Maytag launched a company to manufacture safe, automatic equipment. After establishing a reputation for high-quality products, Maytag started building washing machines in 1907 to keep workers busy during slow periods. Within nine years, washing machines built by The Maytag Company were outselling its farm implements. Today, Maytag is recognized as one of America's most dependable home appliance lines.

Frederick Louis Maytag was born July 14, 1857, near Elgin, Illinois. As a teenage farmhand, Maytag was affected by the number of farmworkers who were injured feeding the coarse threshing machines.

In 1892, Maytag and his two brothers-in-law were approached by George Parsons to help build and market a safe threshing machine feeder that Parsons had invented. The four men each contributed $600 and founded the Parsons Band Cutter and Self-Feeder Company. Their first factory was an abandoned building in Newton, Iowa.

Soon after the company achieved success, Maytag became alarmed over the incidence of equipment breakdowns. He was also struck by the fact that equipment problems were rare in the Austin, Minnesota, region, which was serviced by an able mechanic named Howard Snyder. Maytag brought Snyder to Iowa and put him in charge of all manufacturing, with instructions to build the most reliable equipment available.

By 1902, the company had become the largest feeder manufacturer in the world. Three years later, the company diversified its product line by introducing the Success Corn Husker and Shredder. Then, in 1907, Maytag started building a line of wooden-tub washers, known as The Pastime, to keep his workers busy during the off-season for farm implements.

Maytag's spirit of adventure even took him into the automobile business. Joined by his two sons, Elmer Henry and Lewis Bergman Maytag, the family established the Maytag-Mason Car Company in 1909. The venture lasted only two years, as Maytag became more focused on his rapidly growing washing machine business.

In 1909, Frederick Maytag assumed complete control of the company and renamed it The Maytag Company. The company soon unveiled its first power machine, the Hired Girl, which could draw power from any farm motor, including a tractor. In 1915, he introduced the gasoline-powered Multi-Motor model, which was targeted toward homes that didn't have electricity. Within one year, 16,000 units of the model were sold and, for the first time in the history of the company, the washing machine division outperformed the farm implement division.

By 1920, the company had perfected a method to cast an aluminum tub washer. This model sold at an astonishing pace, prompting Maytag to drop the farm implement line completely. The company then launched an innovative marketing campaign. For example, Maytag washers were provided to the "domestic science" department of every school with enrollment over 300. The company also started printing its brochures in several foreign languages.

Maytag's sons assumed more control of the company through the 1920s. Frederick Maytag died on March 26, 1937, at the age of 79. He was widely respected not only for his high-quality products, but for community services as well, having served in the Iowa Senate (1902 to 1912) and as Newton's mayor (1923 to 1925).

Frederick Maytag's sons and grandson continued to run the company until 1960, when the first nonfamily member was appointed president. Today, the Maytag Corporation offers consumers several brands of major appliances, including Maytag, Jenn-Air, Admiral and Magic Chef, as well as Hoover brand floor-care products and Dixie-Narco vending machines. The company has approximately 16,000 employees worldwide.

SOURCE: The Maytag Company archives

Craig McCaw

[McCaw Cellular Communications]

The McCaw family of the Seattle, Washington, area has emerged as one of America's wealthiest entrepreneurial families. At the forefront of this private family is Craig McCaw who rallied the family after his father's untimely death. However, the McCaw family was not an overnight success story.

J. Elroy McCaw, the son of a civil engineer, moved to Centralia, Washington, in the 1940s, where he founded radio station KELA. There he met an enterprising woman named Marion Oliver. The two were married and started a family, eventually having four sons. After serving with the Army Air Corps in intelligence during World War II, McCaw steadily acquired ownership in several other radio stations.

The most lucrative deal that the elder McCaw made was the 1953 acquisition of WINS radio in New York for $450,000, with only $60,000 up front. He sold the station in 1962 to Westinghouse Broadcasting for $10 million. (He sent his 12-year-old son, Craig, into the bank alone to deposit the $10 million check.) He nearly doubled his income from the deal by selling the accompanying property.

McCaw used his windfall to invest in an array of other ventures, especially in media, as well as to acquire the 20,000-square-foot mansion formerly owned by the Boeing family. Some investments didn't work out, including a small television station in Tacoma and a Canadian steel mill that went bankrupt.

In August 1969, Elroy and Marion McCaw were scheduled for a trip to France, but Elroy backed out at the last minute and one of Marion's friends went in his place. While she was gone, 19-year-old Craig walked into his father's bedroom and found Elroy dead from a massive stroke. As the shock of his death sank in, the family received another jolt: The family fortune was not in good shape, and creditors and lawyers came calling.

Craig McCaw orchestrated a response. He and his three brothers had been given a small cable-TV company in Centralia that employed only 10 people and served 4,000 homes. The Seattle Times Company offered to buy the business, but the brothers, who had worked there as teenagers, opposed the idea. So Craig finished classes at Stanford and moved to Centralia to manage the station.

Marion McCaw sold the mansion, settled the accounts with creditors, and eventually remarried. Her attorney through the process was the father of one of Craig's high school friends, Bill Gates. With the distractions addressed,

Craig and his brothers—Bruce, John, and Keith—were clear to expand the remaining business holdings.

Craig McCaw, with the full support of his brothers, then orchestrated a series of aggressive acquisitions. At the time, banks were offering favorable loans to cable operators and were generally willing to lend four or five times the annual cash flow. McCaw was able to make a down payment of perhaps $500,000 for a cable station that had an annual cash flow of $2 million, then turn around and obtain a loan for as much as $10 million. This in turn was used to acquire other cable stations.

By the early 1980s, the cable market had matured and banks were less willing to lend. The growth of the McCaw brothers was stymied, and suddenly their considerable empire was cash-hungry. They partnered with Affiliated Publications, owner of the *Boston Globe,* and the business stabilized. However, the rapid-growth days were over.

Craig McCaw turned his attention to another new field. The U.S. government was giving away large blocks of airwave spectra for cellular phone technology. The "portable" telephone he was using cost more than $3,000. However, he watched comparable electronics merchandise become more affordable and was convinced the same would happen with cell phones.

The McCaw family once again hit the pavement, gobbling up all the cell phone bandwidth they could reach. Once they had the licenses, they needed cash to open operations. One of their earliest backers was the E. W. Scripps Company. Also, Michael Milken, the legendary junk bond trader at Drexel Burnham Lambert, raised more than $1 billion, allowing McCaw Cellular Communications to become the premiere service provider in the country.

Eventually, the McCaw brothers had to decide which business they were in. They chose cellular communications, prompting two moves. First, they sold off their cable empire to Jack Kent Cooke for about $750 million. Second, they took McCaw Cellular public, raising more than $2 billion. In 1994, they sold the company to AT&T for cash and stock worth several billion dollars.

In 1995, Craig McCaw led a family investment in Nextel Communications, a wireless communications service that started as a dispatch service for trucking companies. Today the company has national coverage and provides truly integrated service of digital cellular, paging, and two-way radios. Also, McCaw and Bill Gates cofounded Teledesic Corporation, a satellite communications company that plans to launch a constellation of low-earth-orbit satellites to act as an "Internet in the sky."

SOURCES: AT&T Wireless Communications archives; O. Casey Corr, "The McCaw Fortune," *Seattle Times/Seattle Post-Intelligencer,* four-part series beginning April 4, 1993

Mark H. McCormack

[IMG]

Mark Hume McCormack was born and raised in Chicago, Illinois. At age six, he was struck by a car and suffered a fractured skull, which prevented him from participating in contact sports throughout childhood. An athlete at heart, McCormack channeled his energy into golf. McCormack graduated from the College of William and Mary, then earned his law degree from Yale University.

After a stint with the U.S. Army, McCormack took a job with a large law firm in Cleveland, Ohio. In 1960, he combined his legal skills and love of golf by entering into an agreement to represent a young golfer named Arnold Palmer, whom he had met while playing college golf. He soon added two more players, Gary Player from South Africa and Jack Nicklaus, who had just turned professional.

From his initial three successful clients, McCormack's company, International Management Group (IMG), has become the world's largest athlete-representation firm, with clients such as Andre Agassi, Joe Montana, Wayne Gretzky, and many, many more.

However, IMG has grown far beyond athlete representation. The firm promotes, manages, and owns hundreds of sports events and classical music events worldwide. One example is the *Stars on Ice* tour, launched in 1986 on the heels of Scott Hamilton's gold medal performance in the 1984 Olympics at Sarajevo. IMG picked up the tab to test the concept. One year later, Discover Card offered to fill the title sponsorship, a commitment it has maintained for nearly a decade.

An IMG subsidiary, Trans World International, has grown to become the largest independent producer of sports programs in the world. The company produces nearly 1,500 hours of original programming annually and has built an archive of nearly 250 different sports in over 100 countries.

In addition, McCormack is an accomplished author. His first book, *What They Don't Teach You at Harvard Business School,* was released in 1984. He has since published several other books, including *The 110% Solution, Hit the Ground Running,* and the first of an ongoing series of business books, *McCormack on Negotiating, McCormack on Selling,* and *McCormack on Managing.*

In 1991, the London Sunday *Times* named McCormack as one of the 1,000 people who have most influenced the twentieth century. He has three children from his first marriage, all of whom work at IMG. In 1986, he married Betsy Nagelsen, a veteran tennis professional who holds Wimbledon and U.S. Open titles. Today, IMG has more than 2,000 employees and maintains 73 offices in 28 countries.

SOURCE: IMG corporate literature, *Mark H. McCormack: The Man Behind the Legends*

Willoughby M. McCormick

[McCormick & Company, Inc.]

After developing an interest in producing food and drug products, young Willoughby McCormick moved to Baltimore and, in 1889, started supplying local grocers with a variety of products from fruit juice to insecticides. The company enjoyed sustained growth and eventually added spices to its

product line. Today, McCormick & Company is the largest spice company in the world.

Willoughby M. McCormick (photo at right) was born on July 12, 1864, on a farm in Dover, Virginia. At the age of 14, he moved to Texas, where he lived with relatives while working as a clerk in a country general store. It was here that young McCormick developed an interest in producing goods for the food and drug market.

In his early 20s, McCormick moved to Baltimore, Maryland, one of America's busiest distribution centers. Throughout 1888 and 1889, he established relationships with a number of local grocers. By the end of the second year, 25-year-old McCormick launched his manufacturing business in a modest space that included a small room, a cellar, and a small backyard storage area.

The early product line offered by McCormick was quite diverse. He made flavoring extracts, root beer, fruit syrups and juices, insecticides, and some basic pharmaceutical mixtures, as well as Uncle Sam's Nerve and Bone Liniment ("for man or beast") and Iron Glue ("sticks to everything but the buyer"). He later added spices to his product line when, in 1896, he purchased the F. G. Emmett Spice Company of Philadelphia and moved the business to Baltimore.

Each morning, McCormick drafted the work plan for his two female employees. Then he took to the streets with his samples to obtain more orders. His efforts were quite successful, and the company moved into larger quarters seven times between 1891 and 1903. In 1904, tragedy struck. McCormick and other residents stood helplessly as the great Baltimore fire ravaged the city's business section, leveling McCormick's building and destroying all company records.

The fire dealt a double blow to the company. Ninety-eight percent of his customers were wholesalers who applied their private label to McCormick's products. As a result, there was no name-brand recognition or product differentiation. The wholesalers simply found other manufacturers to supply their goods. McCormick became convinced that he needed to create customer demand by selling all his products under his own label.

By the end of 1904, a new McCormick & Company plant was built, a five-story building that consumed nearly an entire city block. However, this venture was to focus on his Bee Brand and other labels. McCormick had earlier selected the Bee Brand name because of his fascination with bees. He thought them to be the cleanest, most courageous, and most industrious of all insects.

Having no sons of his own, McCormick drafted his nephews Charles P. (bottom photo, preceding page) and Hugh P. McCormick into the business in 1912. Hugh became a leading authority on spices and made a strong contribution to the company's product line. Charles eventually took the helm of the company, despite the fact that his Uncle Willoughby fired him at least seven times during arguments over the treatment of employees.

The company operated in good financial shape until the late 1920s. Then, faced with the crash of the stock market, McCormick was forced to make deep cuts in his costs. In 1932, while in New York trying to raise money for the firm, Willoughby McCormick died of a heart attack at the age of 69. He had served as the president and dominant force of McCormick & Company for 42 years.

His nephew, 36-year-old Charles P. McCormick, succeeded him as president. Charles was an energetic leader who launched a series of initiatives to get the company moving again. He assembled a group of younger men and appointed them to a "junior board of directors." Within a year, the company regained much of the market lost during the Depression.

Charles remained active with the company until his retirement in 1969, a year before his death. His son, Charles McCormick Jr., was elected president and chief executive officer in 1987 and currently holds the position of chairman emeritus. Today, McCormick & Company has annual sales of nearly $2 billion.

SOURCE: McCormick & Company archives

J. F. McCullough, Alex McCullough

[International Dairy Queen]

J. F. McCullough, known affectionately as "Grandpa" McCullough, and his son Alex had been in the ice cream business since 1927. In the early 1930s they decided to move their business, the Homemade Ice Cream Company, from Davenport, Iowa, to the small town of Green River, Illinois. The small plant was housed in a closed cheese plant, next door to a blacksmith's shop, and Grandpa McCullough purchased a small store building across the street and converted it into his living quarters.

Their first employee, Herb Klavohn, lived on a nearby farm. His job was to collect milk and cream from local farmers in 10-gallon cans and then, after dropping his haul at the plant, deliver tubs of ice cream to stores throughout the region. The ice cream was frozen for the convenience of handling, not to preserve the taste. In fact, McCullough was quite aware that colder ice cream numbed the taste buds, robbing the customer of flavor.

The father and son team were intrigued with the idea of a soft ice cream that could hold its shape. However, the obstacle they faced was not how to produce soft ice cream, but how to keep it at the appropriate temperature, given the limitations of existing freezers. Setting aside the latter issue, the McCulloughs wanted to test public opinion of soft ice cream and convinced one of their customers, Sherb Noble, to hold a special sale in his ice cream store at Kankakee, Illinois.

On August 4, 1938, 67-year-old Grandpa McCullough and his 40-year-old son, Alex, scooped their first batch of soft ice cream from 5-gallon tubs at Noble's store. After two hours, more than 1,600 cones had been sold. Encouraged by the success, they conducted a similar sale a few weeks later in another customer's store in Moline, Illinois, with the same results.

Grandpa and Alex were convinced that their soft ice cream would become a big hit if they could find the right freezer. They approached two manufacturers of dairy equipment who weren't particularly interested. By chance, Alex was in Chicago and noticed a sign in front of a frozen custard stand promising "ice cream frozen seconds before you eat it."

Alex went in and found a machine that was quite similar to what he felt was needed for his soft ice cream. A few days later, his father noticed an advertisement in the *Chicago Tribune* for a frozen custard machine. They tracked down the manufacturer, Harry M. Oltz, and entered into a deal to use and manufacture his patented freezer. They contracted with a Wisconsin company to manufacture the first modified version of the freezer for a little over $1,000.

Grandpa McCullough named the venture Dairy Queen, because he felt his soft serve was the "queen" among dairy products. Alex McCullough personally towed the two new freezers on a trailer from Wisconsin to Joliet, Illinois, where Sherb Noble had the honor of opening the very first Dairy Queen. A second store was opened in Moline, Illinois. One week later, Noble opened the third Dairy Queen in a converted Shell Oil gas station in Aurora, Illinois.

By the end of World War II, Dairy Queen was positioned for growth. America was rebuilding, investment money flowed freely, and soldiers were reunited with their families. By then Grandpa McCullough had met Harry Axene, who had a golden touch for franchising. In 1945, there were eight Dairy Queens in operation. One year later the total increased to 17, and by the end of 1947 more than 100 Dairy Queen stores had been opened.

Once Dairy Queen was in the safe hands of Axene, Grandpa McCullough retired to Davenport, where he lived with his daughter until his death in 1963. Alex and his family moved to Casa Grande, Arizona, in the early 1950s. Alex McCullough died in 1975.

By the early 1950s, more than 1,400 Dairy Queen stores had been opened. Ten years later, that figure more than doubled. Today, Dairy Queens have been opened in more than 5,200 locations worldwide.

SOURCE: *The Cone with the Curl on Top,* International Dairy Queen, 1990

Eugene B. McDermott, J. Clarence Karcher

[Texas Instruments Inc.]

After being raised on an Oklahoma farm, John Clarence Karcher, born in the 1890s, graduated from the University of Oklahoma with degrees in both electrical engineering and physics. From his academic life emerged an interest in using seismic waves to map structures below the earth's surface.

Karcher was provided with several key opportunities to refine his theory. While working for the U.S. Bureau of Standards during World War I, he was loaned to the U.S. Navy to locate enemy artillery by timing air and seismic waves that were created by shell explosions. He included geophones as part of the experiment, and drawing on advice he was given during a brief association with Thomas Edison, he noted the signals echoed from below the earth's surface.

At the end of the war, Karcher continued to pursue his Ph.D. while considering the use of his reflection seismograph to locate oil and gas reservoirs. Encouraged by academic mentors and successful experiments, he attempted to adapt his ideas to the commercial market through the Geological Engineering Company, which was formed by two of his professors. His early equipment worked, but in 1921 two major oil strikes in Oklahoma glutted the market, and there wasn't much interest in a device that would help find more oil. Karcher put his equipment in storage and soon went to work for the Western Electric Company, developing improvements for ocean floor telegraph cable.

By 1925, the oil industry was once again profitable, and Karcher was recruited to a new venture called the Geophysical Research Corporation. Armed with a $300,000 research budget, he hired a young graduate student named Eugene McDermott, whom he had supervised one summer at Western Electric.

Eugene McDermott (pictured alone) was born on February 12, 1899, in Brooklyn, New York. After graduating from the Stevens Institute of Technology in 1919 with a master's degree in engineering, he enrolled at Columbia University and was awarded an M.A. in physics in 1925, at which time he was recruited by Karcher.

Karcher and McDermott worked night and day to equip both refraction and reflection crews. By the end of their first year, the company was able to lease its first crew. Within six months, three refraction crews were under contract to survey salt domes along the Texas and Louisiana coasts. More experimentation followed, and in 1928 the first oil was discovered as a result of structure-mapping the data obtained using the reflection seismograph.

In 1930, the two men struck out on their own, launching Geophysical Service Inc., with an office in Dallas, Texas, and a modest research laboratory in Newark, New Jersey. Within six months Karcher had 11 crews under contract with oil companies in Houston, Dallas, and Tulsa. By 1934, more than 40 crews were working the fields, and the research lab was moved to Dallas from New Jersey. The company was renamed Coronado Corporation in 1939, and Geophysical Service Inc., became a wholly owned subsidiary.

To eliminate the possible appearance of a conflict of interest, Karcher headed the corporate prospecting efforts and McDermott led the prospecting efforts for others. Standoline Oil acquired Coronado Corporation in 1941, but was not interested in the Geophysical Service Inc. subsidiary, which was sold to McDermott, J. Erik Jonsson, Cecil Green, and Dr. H. Bates Peacock on December 6. The day after the purchase, Pearl Harbor was attacked.

Over the next two decades, the company successfully expanded into the electronics industry. In 1951, the name of the company was changed to General Instruments Inc., to better reflect its product line. Due to a conflict with another company's name, the name was soon changed again to Texas Instruments Inc.

Eugene McDermott died on August 24, 1973, at the age of 74. Dr. John Clarence Karcher died on July 13, 1978, at the age of 84. Today, Texas Instruments employs more than 59,000 people and has annual sales of nearly $10 billion.

SOURCE: Texas Instruments archives

James S. McDonnell, Donald W. Douglas

[McDonnell Douglas Corporation]

There are few men who have had a stronger impact on the aerospace industry than James McDonnell and Donald Douglas. Both men led very similar lives—attending the same college, working for the same aerospace legend, starting companies from scratch—but their companies grew quite independently, not merging forces until both were giants in the aerospace industry.

Donald Wills Douglas was born on April 6, 1892, in Brooklyn, New York. While vacationing with his family in Riverside, Connecticut, in 1904, 12-year-old Douglas picked up a magazine and read about the Wright brothers' flight at Kitty Hawk a year earlier. Four years later, he was in a crowd at Fort Myer, Virginia, watching Orville Wright climb into his plane and fly into the sky.

In 1911, the U.S. Navy purchased its first three airplanes, equipped with floats instead of wheels, which were operated from the Severn River in Annapolis. From his barracks, Midshipman Donald Douglas was able to watch them take off and land. The following year, he left Annapolis and enrolled at the Massachusetts Institute of Technology.

Douglas graduated from MIT with a bachelor's degree in mechanical engineering and was appointed to a new position at the school: assistant in aeronautical engineering. The following year he accepted a job with aviation pioneer Glenn Martin, builder of the Martin Marietta empire.

When America entered World War I, the 25-year-old Douglas (pictured at right) left Martin to accept an aeronautical engineering post with the Army Signal Corps, where he was responsible for coordinating the development of America's airplane manufacturers. He then returned to Martin, where he was responsible for the design of what became the *Martin Bomber*.

In 1920, Douglas struck out on his own with a $1,000 savings account and an office in the rear of a barber shop. He soon found an investor and organized The Davis-Douglas Company. His first plane was the Cloudster, the first plane that was able to lift a payload that exceeded its own weight. The plane became the basis for a successful Navy torpedo bomber, and the company was renamed the Douglas Aircraft Company.

More successes followed. In 1924, several Douglas World Cruisers became the first airplanes to fly around the world. His first commercial airliner contract was awarded by an aggressive new company named Transcontinental and Western Air. Douglas built a 14-passenger, two-engine plane that was dubbed the DC-1 (DC as in Douglas Commercial). The new plane ushered in the age of commercial air travel.

Meanwhile, another aviation empire was being built.

James Smith McDonnell (photo at left) was born on April 9, 1899, in Denver, Colorado, and was raised in Little Rock, Arkansas. As a young man, he delivered newspapers by horseback. He was also interested in radio and filled the attic of the family home with ham radio equipment.

After graduating from high school in 1917, McDonnell enrolled at Princeton University, where he studied physics and was active with the Reserve Officers Training Corps. He developed an interest in airplanes and, upon graduation, enrolled at the Massachusetts Institute of Technology, the only school in the country in 1921 that offered a degree in aeronautical engineering.

McDonnell was called to active duty after graduating from MIT in 1923 and commissioned a lieutenant in the Army Air Corps Reserve. Upon discharge he held several jobs with organizations such as the Huff Daland Airplane Company of Ogdensburg, New York, and the Hamilton Aero Manufacturing Company of Milwaukee. In 1928, he launched his own consulting business in Milwaukee and built a tandem two-place low-wing monoplane, which he christened the *Doodlebug*.

By 1931, however, McDonnell was unable to attract financing for his airplane venture, and he went to work for the Great Lakes Aircraft Corporation in Cleveland, Ohio. Two years later he went to work for Glenn Martin, who by this time had moved his company to Baltimore, Maryland. He stayed with Martin for five years, working on projects such as the Martin B-10 and B-12 bombers.

In 1938, McDonnell left Martin and shopped for opportunities and backers. In July 1939, he incorporated the McDonnell Aircraft Corporation in St. Louis, Missouri, with $35,000 of his own money and another $135,000 in loans and investments. By this time, Douglas had established a strong reputation in the aircraft industry, and during World War II McDonnell's firm worked on several Douglas subcontracts. McDonnell was also awarded contracts for planes such as the FH-1, the company's first Phantom fighter.

The two companies continued to grow independently, building military and commercial aircraft as well as working on other aerospace and defense technology. In 1966, Douglas experienced a financial crisis that appears to have come about because of too much work. The cost of tooling for the company's vast backlog of orders was overwhelming, and Douglas started to look for partners.

In April 1967, McDonnell and Douglas merged. James McDonnell became chairman and CEO. Donald Douglas retired from active service, but was named honorary chairman of the board of directors, a post he held until his death.

James Smith McDonnell died on August 22, 1980, at the age of 81. Donald Wills Douglas died less than six months later, on February 1, 1981. Today, McDonnell Douglas has annual sales of about $15 billion. On December 15, 1996, the company announced its plans to merge with The Boeing Company.

SOURCE: McDonnell Douglas Corporation archives

Philip M. McKenna, Alex G. McKenna

[Kennametal, Inc.]

The story of Philip and Alex McKenna must begin with Robert McKenna, an Irish coppersmith who immigrated to Pittsburgh, Pennsylvania, in 1832. Upon his death in 1852, his three sons—Alexander, John, and Thomas—reorganized the family business, which eventually ended up in the hands of Thomas's seven sons. They reorganized the firm as McKenna Brothers Brass Company and extended their markets into cutting tools. The McKenna clan also became the majority stockholders of Vanadium Alloys Steel Company, established in 1910 in Latrobe, Pennsylvania.

Philip Mowry McKenna was born on June 16, 1897 to Alexander and Eliza DeHaven (Mowry) McKenna. His great-grandmother's sister happened to be the mother of another great entrepreneur, Andrew Carnegie, and both men were influenced by some of the same family members. Following in his father's footsteps in metallurgy, Philip received his first of 35 patents at the age of 16 while still in high school. Three years later, he was granted a second patent and became the vice president of Chemical Products Company while completing his B.S. degree in chemistry at George Washington University.

After serving in various business and research positions, Philip moved to Latrobe in 1928 and went to work at the Vanadium organization established by his cousins. During the 1930s, Philip discovered the intermetallic compound tungsten-titanium carbide, for which he received a patent in 1938. Used in metal-cutting tools to machine steel, McKenna's alloy lasted four to five times longer than the tools it replaced and provided a significant boost for industrial productivity.

To capitalize on this breakthrough material, which he dubbed Kennametal, Philip launched his own business, McKenna Metals Company. From the beginning, Philip was able to draw from an able companion, his cousin Alex McKenna.

Alex G. McKenna was born on December 9, 1914, in Crafton, Pennsylvania, to Charles H. and Jennie Elliott McKenna. While still a high school student, Alex assisted his cousin Philip with the experiments that led to the discovery of Kennametal.

While Alex completed his degree in metallurgy at Carnegie Tech (now Carnegie Mellon), he worked closely with Philip. When Philip established his company in 1938, Alex joined him and a few other family members. From the start, Philip served as chief executive officer, while Alex filled the role of chief operating officer. First-year sales were an encouraging $30,000, and the company relocated to a renovated garage. Sales increased rapidly, reaching $3.5 million by 1942 and one year later exceeding $7.5 million. In 1943, the partnership was formally organized as Kennametal, Inc.

The cousins adapted their Kennametal to applications beyond metal-cutting tools. They found an eager market in the mining industry for their superstrong carbide-tipped drilling bits. It was also used in carbide sealing rings, bearings, and nozzles. They also developed Kengrip brand tire studs and, at one point, manufactured more than half of all tire studs sold in America.

Philip McKenna died on August 16, 1969, at the age of 72. By that time, Kennametal had annual sales in excess of $70 million and more than 3,000 employees. Alex McKenna died on December 5, 1995, at the age of 80. In 1996, Kennametal surpassed the $1 billion sales mark.

SOURCE: Kennametal, Inc., archives

John McKesson

[McKesson Corp.]

John McKesson, a fourth-generation descendent of a Scottish immigrant, launched his pharmaceutical career in New York City in 1821, when he joined a drugstore known as J. M. Bradhurst & Company. In January 1833, McKesson left that business and, with Charles Olcott, established a new apothecary venture known as Olcott & McKesson.

Two years later, they purchased another drugstore. By 1842, they had acquired yet another pharmacy and had grown so large that they required a new building. McKesson and his partner built a flourishing business. A great deal of their trade included the import and sale of therapeutic drugs and chemicals, much of which came to New York by way of tall-masted clipper ships. They also bought medicinal herbs, roots, and spices from Shaker colonies in nearby Pennsylvania.

The 1850s brought challenges to McKesson's firm. The building, complete with inventory, burned to the ground in 1850. Not long after the partners rebuilt their business, Charles Olcott died. McKesson moved forward, adding four new partners, including his son, John McKesson Jr., and Daniel Robbins, who had walked from Poughkeepsie, New York, to respond to a McKesson job advertisement.

By this time the company was doing business well beyond New York City. It was distributing products in 17 states and territories stretching from Vermont to California. "Fancy goods" were added to the product line, including exotic oils, perfumes, and sponges. Its stock of bristle brushes was said to be the largest single supply in the country. In 1855, McKesson started to manufacture drugs, and its fluid extracts, tinctures, pills, and tablets soon became known throughout the land.

Among those who distributed McKesson products were H. C. Kirk, Charles Langley, and Augustus Hogge, who set out for San Francisco with a supply of McKesson & Robbins products. Not only did they sell products along the way, they helped establish the McKesson name in the boomtown of San Francisco.

Daniel Robbins died in 1888 at the age of 73. Five years later, John McKesson died at the age of 87. They had built an amazing distribution network for their wholesale goods throughout the country and laid the foundation for what would become one of America's largest companies.

Following the death of John McKesson Jr. in 1926, McKesson Corp. was sold to a private investor for $1 million. In 1939, one of the most bizarre incidents in American business history unfolded at McKesson. The investor, who was caught embezzling money from the company, turned out to be a convicted business swindler. When authorities went to arrest him, he committed suicide.

McKesson quickly recovered from the incident and continued its phenomenal growth. Today, McKesson Corp. is a leading provider of health care products and services, as well as health and beauty care, specialty foods, and general merchandise. Annual sales are $14 billion.

SOURCE: McKesson Corp. archives

Daniel E. Mead

[Mead Paper Company]

Daniel E. Mead was born in 1817 in Cooperstown, New York, where he spent his youth. His father, Anzel Mead, later moved his family to present-day Meadville, Pennsylvania. Daniel elected to continue west and, in 1841, settled in Dayton, Ohio, where he obtained a job as a bookkeeper in a hardware store. He was soon granted a partnership in the company.

In 1846, 29-year-old Mead cofounded Ellis, Chafflin & Company, the predecessor of the Mead Company. Over the next 20 years, the company continuously adapted the rapidly changing papermaking technology. It also went through several reorganizations and partnership changes, becoming Weston and Mead (1856), Mead and Weston (1860), Mead and Nixon (1866), and the Mead & Nixon Paper Company (1873).

Finally, in 1881, Mead bought out his partner and established the Mead Paper Company with initial capital of $150,000 and total assets of nearly $400,000. At the time, the plant employed 125 people at a total annual payroll of $40,000. The company recorded profits of $22,000 in 1881, $30,000 in 1882, and $50,000 by 1891.

Mead started to grow through expansion. Recognizing the rapid increase in popularity of books, magazines, and newspapers, he helped many publishers finance their early purchases of Mead paper. This built a loyal following among many ventures that later grew into successful publishing houses.

In December 1890, Daniel Mead was traveling through Chillicoth, Ohio, when his train stopped for a lunch break. He noticed a crowd gathered near the train station and, upon joining them, found it to be an auction of the Ingham & Company paper mill, with which he was well acquainted. By the end of the lunch break, Mead had submitted a high bid of $30,000 for the business, and Mead Paper Company became a two-plant organization.

Daniel Mead died on November 10, 1891. He left an estate valued at $500,000, and the company was operating at a comfortable level. Sadly, Daniel's sons elected to be absentee owners who drew funds from the business for personal matters. By 1905, the company went into trusteeship.

George H. Mead, a grandson of Daniel Mead, led the reorganization of the company in 1905, forming The Mead Pulp and Paper Company. George Mead was quite enthusiastic about the prospects of the company and soon returned Mead to profitability. Today, Mead is one of the largest manufacturers of paper in the world, with annual sales of $5 billion and more than 15,000 employees.

SOURCES: Mead Paper Company archives; *In Quiet Ways: George H. Mead, the Man and the Company,* The Mead Corporation, 1970

George J. Mecherle

[State Farm Insurance]

In the 1850s, Christian and Friedrich Mecherle left their native Germany and immigrated to the United States, where they spent six years traveling through the Midwestern wilderness. Eventually, the brothers settled in McLean County, Illinois, where in 1862 Christian married Susanna Johnson, a Quaker schoolteacher.

George Jacob Mecherle was born on June 7, 1877, the sixth of seven children born to Christian and Susanna. Having a schoolteacher for a mother proved beneficial for young Mecherle, who passed his teacher's certificate exams when he was only 13 years old.

Despite the credentials, Mecherle elected to remain a farmer. He married Mae Edith Perry, a neighbor's daughter, in 1901, and the couple maintained a family farm and raised five children over the next 18 years. By 1918, however, Mae was suffering from painful rheumatism, and the family moved to Florida. When it became apparent that the change of climate didn't help, they moved back to Normal, Illinois.

Mecherle, retired and in his early 40s, became restless and took a job with the Union Automobile Indemnity Association of Bloomington. He soon left over a disagreement with management and was hired by the Illinois Tractor Company. He was soon selling tractors faster than they could be built and delivered, leading once again to a dispute with management and a resignation letter.

During these sales ventures, Mecherle was developing a blueprint for his own business. His plan was to establish an insurance company that would cater to farmers and, by eliminating high-risk markets, offer reasonable rates. In July 1922, a license was issued, enabling the 45-year-old Mecherle to open his one-room office in Bloomington, Illinois. By December, he had written 1,300 policies.

The company had nearly 70,000 active policies in 1927, allowing the young company to reach the $1 million mark in annual sales in five short years. The following year, Mecherle opened his first branch office in Berkeley, California. He was ambitious and aggressively sought more policies. "A million or more by '44" became the motto, and in March of 1944 the company did indeed have more than 1 million policies in effect.

George J. Mecherle died on March 9, 1951, at the age of 74. At the time, nearly 2.2 million policies were in effect, and income from membership reached $120 million. Today, State Farm has nearly 17,000 agents and 69,000 employees who service 66 million insurance policies.

SOURCES: State Farm Insurance Company archives; Karl Schriftgiesser, *The Farmer From Merna,* Random House, 1955

Frederick Mellinger

[Frederick's of Hollywood]

Frederick Mellinger was convinced that all women were not created equal, and he gave considerable thought to a venture that would accentuate (and supplement) the female figure. During his three-year tour with the U.S. Army, he shared his thoughts with other servicemen and was encouraged by their reaction.

In 1946, Mellinger established Frederick's of Fifth Avenue in New York City, which was actually a modest loft far from the fashionable sections of Fifth Avenue. It had one desk, from which he processed orders. With these humble beginnings, Mellinger was determined to outfit American women in sexy, glamorous fashions and undergarments.

His initial move was to market black lingerie, including panties, bras, nighties, and peignoirs. Today this may seem tame, but in the 1940s it sparked an uproar in conservative circles, where white cotton bloomers were the accepted custom. At the end of his first year, Mellinger had sold about $46,000 worth of merchandise.

In 1947, Mellinger decided he would do better on the West Coast. He opened Frederick's of Hollywood with an expanded line of merchandise that quickly became fashionable, especially among the country's leading entertainers. One year after opening his new store, Mellinger introduced his first push-up bra, dubbed the Rising Star. Encouraged by the success, he frequently made other innovations that would enhance the appearance of clients, such as padded girdles and body shapers.

By the 1950s, Frederick's was offering everything a woman needed for a total makeover, including false eyelashes, wigs, padding for "every purpose," and even skyscraper high heels. Outerwear was fair game, too, as Mellinger introduced America to the French bikini. Even though it featured a 6-inch panty and full bra, the bare midriff was so scandalous, even in California, that an early customer was arrested for wearing one on a public beach.

The public was buying up Mellinger's new concepts as fast as he made them. Innovations like the front-hook bra and colorful bustiers became commonplace. "No matter how beautiful the outergarment," Mellinger said, "without the right foundation, the look will be wrong." He then took the concept even further, introducing unique, sexy designs in sleepwear, gowns, loungewear, hosiery, swimsuits, and even intimate daywear.

In November 1989, Frederick's opened the world's first Lingerie Museum at its flagship store in Hollywood. Each year, more than 80,000 visitors are greeted by exhibits from Madonna, Zsa Zsa Gabor, the Pointer Sisters, and many more celebrities.

Frederick's of Hollywood was first listed on the American Stock Exchange in 1981 and, ten years later, was listed on the New York Stock Exchange. Today, the company has annual sales of nearly $150 million generated by more than 200 retail stores and 50 million catalogs.

SOURCE: Frederick's of Hollywood archives

Edward G. Melroe

[Melroe Company]

Edward Gideon Melroe was born on April 23, 1892, to Oluf and Kari (Ellefson) Mollerud, Norwegian immigrants who Americanized their family name to "Melroe." He attended as much school as was available in Gwinner, North Dakota, then went to work full-time on the family farm. He later attended classes on steam and gas engines, as well as auto mechanics.

Edward, or "E.G." as he came to be known, married Mabel Petterson in 1917, and the couple eventually had five children. While working on the family farm during the 1920s, E.G. started experimenting with farm machinery design. He built a tractor specially adapted to grain farmers, but it had just enough flaws to remain obscure.

Undaunted, he next designed and fabricated an improved windrow pickup to help harvest grain. This device was used on combines to efficiently pick up windrows of grain with a minimal loss of kernels. The neighbors were so impressed that they recruited Melroe to modify their equipment.

Farming continued to be the family business through World War II, even though Melroe had built a substantial sideline business. In 1947, he formally organized the Melroe Company. From this modest plant, he started to mass-produce his Melroe Windrow Pickup and, a bit later, his Melroe Harrowweeder.

The company remained focused on these two products through the 1950s. The family and the company suffered a painful loss with the death of E.G. on April 30, 1955, seven days after his 63rd birthday. However, his sons Lester, Clifford, Roger, and Irving and son-in-law Eugene Dahl regrouped and kept the company going.

In 1957, Cyril and Louis Keller, two brothers who maintained a blacksmith shop in Rothsay, Minnesota, met with the Melroes. They were trying to build a loader that could easily maneuver in barns and other farm buildings. Their prototype was a three-wheeled loader powered by a 6-horsepower engine with a rope starter. It was crude, but the Melroes recognized the potential and purchased the rights to build the equipment in 1958.

The brothers quickly built an improved model that was able to turn 360 degrees in its own length. In 1959, another model was released, this time with the Melroe logo prominently displayed. By 1962, the brothers wanted to find a catchy name for their innovative loaders. An employee suggested *Bobcat,* after the prairie animal that was tough, quick, and agile.

The 1960s proved to be a decade of rapid growth for Melroes. Their Bobcat loaders were being adapted to use on farms, fertilizer plants, building and road construction sites, foundries, and municipal governments. Sales rose from less than $5 million in 1963 to nearly $17 million in 1967.

In 1969, the Melroe brothers sold their firm to Clark Equipment Company of Michigan. Clark was purchased in 1995 by Ingersoll-Rand Company of Woodcliff Lake, New Jersey. Today, the Melroe Company is North Dakota's largest manufacturer. Of the more than 1,800 people employed by Melroe, over half work at the Gwinner plant. Annual sales exceed $600 million.

SOURCE: Melroe Company archives

Franklin L. Miles, Albert R. Beardsley, George E. Compton

[Miles, Inc.]

Franklin Lawrence Miles was born on November 15, 1845, in Olmsted Falls, Ohio, to Charles and Electra A. (Lawrence) Miles. Charles answered the call of the 1849 gold rush, while his wife and two young children remained in Cincinnati. When the venture proved unsuccessful, Charles moved on to the Hawaiian Islands.

Tragedy struck in 1855 when his wife and young daughter died during an epidemic, which left young Franklin in the care of an uncle. Eventually, Charles returned for his son and opened a drugstore in Elkhart, Indiana. A decade later, Charles died at the age of 44 from pneumonia after fighting a fire in the winter cold. At age 19, Franklin Miles had lost his entire family.

Miles first pursued a legal career, using his inheritance to attend Yale and Columbia. By 1871, he had a change of heart and transferred to the University of Michigan to study medicine. He later moved to Chicago and was granted his M.D. by Rush Medical College in 1874. There, he met another medical student named Ellen Douglas Lighthall, and the two were married.

Franklin briefly maintained a practice in Chicago while Ellen completed school, and they then moved to Elkhart, where Franklin opened an office. The couple had three children over the next seven years while Miles's practice grew. Tragedy visited Miles once again in 1881, when Ellen died, leaving him to raise their three young children.

In addition to maintaining his practice, Franklin Miles experimented with various medicines in his home. His early formulas included Dr. Miles' Nervine for "disorders of the nerves," Dr. Miles' Heart Treatment, Dr. Miles' Tonic, Dr. Miles' Laxative Tablets, and many others. In 1884, he founded the Dr. Miles Medical Company to produce and market his medicines, but the firm had little activity during the early years. In 1887, his two founding partners sold their interest to George Compton, who had previously provided the small company with working capital.

George Emmett Compton was born on August 5, 1849, on a farm near Elkhart, Indiana, to Ezekiel and Frances (Ward) Compton. Ezekiel, a local home builder and farmer, died only three years after George's birth. When George reached his teens, he left home to become a clerk apprentice in Elkhart, eventually launching his own store. By 1877, his business was sufficiently secure to allow him to marry Elizabeth Price Ames.

Throughout the 1880s, Compton became associated with several Elkhart businesses, including a flour mill and a knitting company, as well as banking and real estate ventures. His association with Franklin Miles, however, proved to be his most successful move over the long term. He is not only credited as the chief financial backer and organizer of the company, he also convinced Miles that the venture could grow only under proven manufacturing and administrative leadership.

In 1889, the founders found the man they were looking for. Albert Raper Beardsley was born on November 7, 1847, in Dayton, Ohio. His father, Elijah, was a successful wagonmaker and a descendant of another Elijah Beardsley, who was an active participant at the Boston Tea Party. Young Albert left the family farm at age 14 to live with an aunt in Elkhart. Three years later he launched his mercantile career at a dry goods store and was soon operating his own ventures. Business was good, and in 1872 he married Elizabeth Baldwin. By 1882, he was the president of seven starch companies.

With a solid team at the top, the Dr. Miles Medical Company launched an aggressive advertising campaign that covered several states. The partners' flair for promotion was facilitated by a sophisticated printing operation they maintained, which produced almanacs filled with medical advice (and advertisements), promotional calendars, and much more. By 1900, the company employed 100 workers, a figure that doubled within four years.

In addition to the Dr. Miles Medical Company, Franklin Miles founded the Grand Dispensary in 1890, a curious venture that was both a group practice and a mail-order dispensary service. Advertisements encouraged readers to submit their medical complaints by mail, complete with an examination chart that the patient used to mark the locations of aches and pains. The incoming mail was then divided among Elkhart physicians for personal responses.

In 1893, Miles moved to Chicago and took the Grand Dispensary with him. Two years later, he married his second wife, Elizabeth N. State, and they eventually had two children, one of whom died at birth and the other at age nine. They later adopted a three-year-old daughter.

In 1902, Miles moved the Grand Dispensary back to Elkhart, where it was put under the management of his oldest son, Charles F. Miles. Suffering from bronchial problems, the 61-year-old Miles and his wife relocated to Florida in 1906. There, he developed an interest in agriculture and amassed more than 16,000 acres of land on either side of the Caloosahatchee River. He and his neighbor, Thomas Edison, developed a close friendship and spent considerable time together. Franklin Lawrence Miles died on April 1, 1929, at the age of 83.

The Dr. Miles Medical Company grew under the watchful eyes of the founders and their family members. Andrew Hubble "Hub" Beardsley, nephew of one of the founders, became the driving force of the company through the first part of the twentieth century. As the company struggled through the Great Depression, Hub Beardsley led the development of an effervescent cold formula that they named Alka-Seltzer, which launched the company to international prominence in a matter of years. Other products, including One-A-Day and Chocks vitamins, soon followed.

Miles, Inc., was acquired by Bayer AG of Leverkusen, Germany, in 1978. In April, 1995, Miles, Inc., was renamed the Bayer Corporation.

SOURCE: William C. Cray, *Miles 1884–1984: A Centennial History,* Prentice-Hall, 1984

Frederick E. J. Miller

[Miller Brewing Company]

Frederick Edward John Miller was born on November 24, 1824, in Riedlingen, Germany, to Thaddeus E. and Maria L. (Zepfel) Miller. At age 14, young Miller was sent to France for seven years of study, after which he extensively toured Europe. While returning to Germany, he visited an uncle in Nancy, France, who operated a brewery, and decided to stay with him to learn the trade.

Eventually, Miller was hired as the brewmaster at a brewery in a castle owned by the Holtenzollerns, Germany's royal family. In 1853, he married Josephine Miller, daughter of Franz and Maria Miller. Their first son, Joseph Edward Miller, was born the following year. That same year, political unrest in Germany prompted the young family to immigrate to the United States, bringing with them about $9,000 in gold.

The family lived in New York City for about one year as Frederick Miller toured the country in search of an ideal place to establish his brewery. Eventually he settled on Milwaukee, in part because of the city's magnificent harbor. In 1855, he purchased the idle Plank-Road Brewery, located several miles west of Milwaukee in the Menomonee Valley near a reliable water source and rich farmland. Since the brewery was so far from town, he also opened a boarding house next door for his unmarried employees.

As his business grew, Miller opened a 20-acre park, or "sommer-garten," near the brewery. Built in stages over 20 years, the beer garden became a summer attraction because of its expansive gardens, cool shade trees, picnic and recreation grounds, and musical entertainment. Two years after opening the brewery, Miller also opened a beer hall in downtown Milwaukee.

However, the 1860s were difficult. Predictably, beer sales were low during the Civil War. Miller himself delivered beer by horse and wagon to St. Louis during these lean years. There was tragedy at home, too. Josephine Miller died, leaving behind their older son and a two-year-old daughter, Louisa (several other Miller children had died in infancy). The loss devastated Miller, who managed to maintain his faith. Miller later married Lisette Gross, and they, too, had several children who died in infancy, as well as five who survived: Ernst, Emil, Fred, Clara, and Elise.

By 1870, the company had resumed its strong growth, and Miller replaced the Plank-Road Brewery with a new building that featured steam power. The increased capacity positioned the company for rapid growth in the following decade. In 1882, Miller started bottling his own beer. Two years later, he purchased property near Bismarck in Dakota Territory and started building a brewery. However, residents voted to prohibit alcohol and the venture was eventually abandoned.

Frederick Miller died on June 11, 1888, at the age of 63 and was succeeded by his son, Ernst. His descendants continued to operate the brewery for the next several decades, introducing highly successful labels such as Miller High Life beer, launched in 1903. By 1954, under the leadership of Frederick's grandson, Frederick C. Miller, the company had become the ninth-largest producer in the industry.

In 1966, the W.R. Grace Company acquired controlling interest in Miller Brewing Company, which they sold to Philip Morris three years later.

In 1970, a private foundation connected to Miller family heirs sold the remaining interest to Philip Morris. Today, Miller has emerged as the second-largest brewery in the country (third largest in the world). Its best selling product is Miller Lite, which was the first commercially successful low-calorie beer on the market.

SOURCE: Company brochures, *Miller History* and *Facts About Beer: The Brewing Industry & Miller Brewing Company*

Howard C. Miller

[Howard Miller Clock Company]

Howard C. Miller was born on April 4, 1905, in Grand Rapids, Michigan. While he was still a boy, the family moved to Zeeland, Michigan, where young Miller was raised. Miller learned to make clocks from his father, Herman Miller, and later spent a year in the Black Forest region of Germany studying the craft of clockmaking.

In 1926, he launched his company—originally named the Herman Miller Clock Company after his father—and started to manufacture chiming wall and mantel clocks. The company grew and was reorganized under the name Howard Miller during the Great Depression.

By the end of the 1930s, Miller had established a renowned reputation for producing high-quality clocks. The 1939 World's Fair at New York provided an excellent opportunity to showcase his products to an international audience, and his reputation grew around the globe.

World War II interrupted the growth of the Howard Miller Clock Company. The firm converted its manufacturing facilities to help the war effort by producing antiaircraft covers for airplanes built by the Ford Motor Company. At the end of the war, Miller turned his attention back to clockmaking. During the 1960s, the company focused on grandfather clocks.

During the 1970s and 1980s, Howard Miller adjusted to a changing market by producing digital and alarm clocks. Toward the latter part of this period, the company started to expand through acquisition. In 1983, the company purchased Hekman Furniture of Grand Rapids. This was followed by the acquisition of the Kieninger Clock Company of Germany, Woodmark Originals furniture company of North Carolina, and the Brookley Furniture Company of Mobile, Alabama.

Howard C. Miller died on September 21, 1995, at the age of 90. He is survived by his wife, Martha, and three children. Today the company is the largest clock manufacturer in the United States and the world's largest manufacturer of grandfather clocks. The company employs 1,500 people in eight manufacturing plants.

SOURCES: Howard Miller Clocks archives; Steve Kaskovich, "Changing Times," *The Detroit News*, October 30, 1989

George P. Mitchell

[Mitchell Energy & Development Company]

George Mitchell's father, Savvas Paraskevopoulos, an uneducated Greek goatherd, immigrated to the United States in 1901. He worked on a railroad crew and was renamed Mike Mitchell by the Irish timekeeper who found the name Parakevopoulos too much to handle. When George Phydias Mitchell was born on May 21, 1919, the family lived on Galveston Island in Texas. By this time, Mike ran a pressing shop and shoeshine parlor. Money was tight, but George flourished in the warmth of a tight-knit family.

As with most immigrant families of the time, the Mitchells promoted strong education to their children, and George, his two brothers, and sister all received college degrees. George's mother wanted him to become a doctor. However, his brother Johnny helped him get a summer job as a roustabout, and George was soon hooked on the romance and opportunity of oil.

While Mitchell completed his studies at Texas A&M University, he waited on tables and sold stationery and candy. He also became captain of the tennis team and commander of his cadet battalion. Upon graduating in 1940 with a degree in petroleum engineering, he joined Amoco. His career was short-lived, however, due to World War II, during which Mitchell served as a captain with the Army Corps of Engineers.

Upon discharge, Mitchell established an engineering and geology consulting business in Houston and soon bought out the interests of one of his clients in a small wildcat oil well. Through several carefully orchestrated moves, the company has evolved into Mitchell Energy & Development Corporation.

His breakthrough came in 1952. Mitchell and two college buddies drilled on a promising parcel in northern Texas. Not only did the first well produce, but the next ten were also successful. The partners were convinced that a huge stratigraphic trap lay under the area, and within three months Mitchell secured leases on 400,000 gas-prospective acres. His total gas production from that site now totals 1.5 trillion cubic feet, and the area still accounts for half of the company's gas production.

His next major accomplishment started in 1964, when he became involved with the real estate market. After learning that 50,000 acres of heavily forested land north of Houston was for sale, he struck a deal without having anything specific in mind for the property. Subsequently, he had occasion to tour two of the most depressed neighborhoods in the country—Watts in Los Angeles and Bedford-Stuyvesant in New York. He found the middle-class flight from inner cities disturbing and decided to use the property to create a model city.

The development, known as The Woodlands, opened in 1974. The profusely treed natural beauty of the land has been carefully preserved. The community is home to a new regional mall, excellent schools, a growing community college, and an outdoor entertainment pavilion that is summer home to the Houston Symphony. The population, currently near 50,000, is expected to reach 150,000 by the year 2025.

Mitchell, intense and insightful, remains chief executive of Mitchell Energy & Development. He's recognized as an all-American wildcatter, having been involved in drilling 8,000 wells, including 1,000 wildcats. Annual revenues for the company exceed $1 billion.

SOURCE: Mitchell Energy and Development Corporation archives

Arthur B. Modine

[Modine Manufacturing Company]

Arthur B. Modine was born on October 27, 1886, in Chicago, Illinois, one of five children born to Swedish immigrants John August and Amanda (Linstrum) Modin. Of the five children, only Arthur (who later added an *e* to his last name) and a sister survived childhood. As a boy, Arthur often accompanied his father, a successful Chicago contractor, to job sites, where he had his first exposure to large machinery.

Young Modine was so intrigued with his shop class in high school that he obtained an apprenticeship as a toolmaker at a rate of 12½¢ per hour. In 1903, he decided to pursue an education in engineering, first at the Armour Institute, then later at the University of Michigan. He graduated in 1908 with a degree in mechanical engineering.

Modine's first job was with People's Gas, Light, and Coke Company as an inspector. However, he resigned from the job after several incidents of passing out from gas fumes while conducting underground inspections. In 1910, Modine had only $400 and a secondhand Maxwell roadster when he answered a partnership opportunity in an automotive sheet metal and radiator repair shop.

Modine and his partners moved their business to Racine, Wisconsin, and by 1915, their Perfex Radiator Company had monthly sales exceeding $30,000. Over the next year, four other developments changed Modine's life: He married Margaret Bartlett; he filed for his first U.S. patent; he sold his share of Perfex Radiator; and, on June 23, 1916, he launched the Modine Manufacturing Company.

The company started with six employees in a shop with about 10,000 square feet of floor space. There, he conducted experiments with radiator design that would enable an efficient transfer of heat away from an engine. Eventually, he patented his Spirex radiator, and by 1918 the majority of leading tractor manufacturers were using Modine radiators. With America embroiled in World War I, the radiator was also adapted to military tractors.

In 1917, Modine first approached Henry Ford, who agreed to test his radiators. Unfortunately, the Spirex radiators lacked a critical flat steel member that Ford used in its radiators, and as a result they couldn't withstand the road test. Modine was called to the Iowa assembly plant to view firsthand the pile of scrapped radiators. The experience was followed by a downturn in the economy during the early 1920s, and Modine's helpers were forced to sell their inventory out of a Model T in neighboring villages.

Soon Modine developed an improved radiator called the Turbotube, which Ford agreed to look at. This time, it passed the road tests and, in 1925, was adopted as standard equipment for the Model T. Ford's initial order was for 150,000 radiators. Modine's enthusiasm took another dip three months later when Ford announced the discontinuation of the Model T. However, the relationship survived, and Modine negotiated a contract to supply half of Ford's radiators. The bond was strengthened in 1935 when Modine was named sole supplier of radiators for all Ford trucks.

The Heating Division of Modine was formally organized in 1928, but it traced its roots to the company's first shop, where Arthur Modine rigged fans behind steam pipes to provide heat for his assemblers. Eventually, the company applied principles similar to its radiator technology to produce heating systems for buildings. The idea was expanded during the 1930s with the development of the Modine Ice Fan, an air-conditioning unit that consisted of an ice-storage cabinet, a blower fan, and an adjustable air deflector.

Modine retired from the company in 1972. Altogether, 120 patents were issued in his name. Ironically, the Perfex Radiator Company went through reorganization in the early 1920s, and the Modine Manufacturing Company acquired the Perfex name and product line in the mid-1980s.

Arthur B. Modine died on June 11, 1981, at the age of 95. He was survived by his second wife, Hazel, whom he married in 1971, and two daughters. He was preceded in death by his first wife, Margaret, and his son, Thomas. Today, Modine employs more than 7,500 people worldwide and has annual sales of nearly $1 billion.

SOURCE: Modine Manufacturing Company archives

Thomas S. Monaghan

[Domino's Pizza]

Thomas Stephen Monaghan was born on March 25, 1937, in Ann Arbor, Michigan. After his father died four years later, young Monaghan and his brother were placed in a series of foster homes and orphanages. Finally, in 1956, he escaped a life of turmoil and uncertainty by enlisting in the U.S. Marine Corps, which he credits for tearing him down and rebuilding him in the proper mold.

In the Marines, Monaghan was stationed on the Pacific Ocean island of Okinawa. He became a passionate reader, and he was especially drawn to the writings of Norman Vincent Peale and Dale Carnegie. Upon discharge from Camp Pendleton in California in 1959, he invested his $2,000 savings and last Marine paycheck in a get-rich-quick scheme that soured.

With only $15 left, Monaghan hitchhiked back to Ann Arbor and enrolled at the University of Michigan. The 22-year-old Monaghan supported himself by delivering newspapers to homes, then later by buying a small newsstand. One year later, his brother Jim, a mail carrier, suggested the two of them buy a small Ypsilanti pizza store, called DomiNick's, that was for sale. The brothers

quickly borrowed $900 and were in the pizza business.

Within a year, Jim lost interest and traded his share of the business to Tom (pictured at right) for his Volkswagen Beetle. By late 1965, Tom had met with modest success and opened two more stores. An employee coined the name "Domino's" for the business, and the company decided to mount lighted roof panels featuring a domino on delivery vehicles. The domino had three white dots, representing the first three stores at Ypsilanti, Ann Arbor, and Mt. Pleasant.

Initially, Domino's found a receptive market in college towns and near military bases. Tom issued his first franchise agreement in 1967, and the following year, despite a devastating fire at the company's offices, the first out-of-state Domino's was opened—in Vermont. By 1969, he had a dozen stores in operation and another dozen in development.

The rapid expansion almost destroyed the company. Debt increased faster than Monaghan could keep up, resulting in the closing of several stores. The experience led to a more careful site-selection process, but the growth soon accelerated again, and by 1980 nearly 300 stores had opened.

Monaghan, a devout Catholic, married Marjorie Zybach in 1962, who he met while making a pizza delivery, and they now have four grown daughters. Today, there are more than 5,500 Domino's Pizza stores throughout the world. Annual sales exceed $2.8 billion.

SOURCES: Domino's Pizza archives; Ellen Stern, "Tom Monaghan Kneads the Dough," *Gentlemen's Quarterly,* July 1989; *1990 Current Biography Yearbook,* The H. W. Wilson Company, New York

Robert Mondavi

[Robert Mondavi Winery]

After helping to establish the family winery business, Robert Mondavi launched his own venture in 1966. Over the past three decades, the Robert Mondavi Winery label, along with his Woodbridge label, has become a national favorite.

Cesare and Rosa Mondavi immigrated from the Marche region of Italy in 1910 to the town of Virginia, Minnesota, where their son Robert was born on June 18, 1913. Cesare became involved with shipping grapes to other Italian immigrants in Minnesota, a job that frequently took him to California. Eventually, Cesare moved his family to the Napa Valley region of California, where he launched a grape-shipping company.

After Robert Mondavi graduated from Stanford University in 1936, he joined his father in the operation of a small winery. Young Robert quickly adapted to winemaking and helped the company prosper. In 1943, the family purchased the well-known Charles Krug Winery, and Robert launched a successful national marketing campaign.

In the early 1960s, Robert went to Europe to study winemaking. There, he found that wineries preferred small oak barrels instead of the 5,000-gallon redwood vats used in California. Mondavi appreciated the more robust flavor provided by the small French barrels and immediately incorporated them into the family operation.

In 1966, Mondavi left the family business and launched the Robert Mondavi Winery. Using his time-tested winemaking skills, his small French barrels, and a keen sense of management, Mondavi quickly established an international reputation for fine wines.

The Robert Mondavi Winery has experienced significant growth through acquisition. In 1979, he purchased the highly popular Woodbridge Winery from the Felice family. After Woodbridge, Mondavi acquired the Vichon Winery (1985) and the Byron Vineyard & Winery (1990). Mondavi also is the half owner with Baroness Philippine de Rothschild of the high-end Opus One.

Along with Julia Child, Robert is the founding cochairman of the American Institute of Wine and Food. In 1988, he launched The Robert Mondavi Mission Program designed to educate Americans about wine and its role in society. Robert and his wife, Margrit Biever Mondavi, have established the Great Chefs program at the Robert Mondavi Winery and various annual cultural events. Their children, Michael (president and CEO), Marcia (board member), and Timothy (managing director and winegrower), have been an integral part of the winery since its founding.

Today the family produces 750,000 cases of wine annually under the Robert Mondavi label and 4.5 million under the Woodbridge label. Total annual sales are nearly $250 million. Now in his 80s, Robert Mondavi continues to hold the position of chairman of the board of directors. He is universally recognized as the leading citizen and champion of the Napa Valley, and he can often be seen by tourists strolling the family vineyards.

SOURCE: Robert Mondavi Winery archives

John Moody

[Moody's Investors Service]

John Moody, born to a poor Scottish clerk, went to work on Wall Street at an early age in the late 1800s. By the time he was 30, he had advanced from errand boy to head of the statistical department of Spencer Trask & Company, a private banking organization.

Early in his career Moody learned the importance of factual information. After a hasty delivery of bonds to the great investor J. P. Morgan, Moody forgot to note the value of his shipment. When asked the value later, Moody stated the bonds totaled between $50,000 and $55,000. When pressed for the exact amount, he admitted that he didn't remember.

"Don't remember?!" bellowed the tough Morgan, who proceeded to chew him out and lecture him at the same time. The incident stayed with Moody his entire life, and by all accounts he never again made a similar mistake.

Moody was discouraged by the secrecy that surrounded companies. There was no Securities and Exchange Commission to mandate the release of critical information. Thus, investors had very little concrete information on which to make investment decisions.

Moody was convinced that good market information would sell. While keeping his job with Trask, spent all his free waking hours assembling an information manual for investors and preparing a "prospectus" of his forthcoming publication. A local printer agreed to print the prospectus on credit with the condition that he be given the job of printing the manual as well.

Once the prospectus was complete, Moody made his only investment in the company, $200 for postage, and mailed it to 5,000 bankers, brokers, and insurance agencies. He arranged to have his mail delivered to a secondhand bookstore at 6 Wall Street, an address that further enhanced the prospectus. Within two weeks, several hundred orders were returned with payment enclosed. In 1900, the 32-year-old Moody released his book, *Moody's Manual of Industrial and Miscellaneous Securities.* Within months, the book sold out.

The business expanded, and the Moody's name became well recognized. Encouraged by the growth on Wall Street, Moody introduced a monthly publication, *Moody's Investors Magazine,* in 1905. He also decided that his printing volume was sufficient to establish his own print shop, which he did in Elizabeth, New Jersey. Unfortunately, the magazine became a money-loser and the printing plant wasn't able to handle the job. When the panic of 1907 struck, Moody was deep in debt and lost control of his company.

Moody was able to quickly rebound. In 1909, he introduced his *Railroad Manual,* which analyzed railroad reports and rated their bond issues. Later that year, he launched *Moody's Weekly Review of Financial Conditions.* Five years later, he launched Moody's Investors Service.

By the mid-1920s, Moody's was well established, with annual sales in the $1.5 million range. Predictably, the Great Depression had a disastrous effect on the company, but in the long run it didn't prove fatal. By the late 1930s, the company was once again flourishing. In 1962, Moody's Investors Service was acquired by Dun & Bradstreet.

SOURCES: *Dun & Bradstreet and the Rise of Modern Business;* "A Fifty Year Review of Moody's Investors Service," prepared by John Moody, chairman

John L. Morris

[Bass Pro Shops]

John L. Morris founded Bass Pro Shops in 1971. The company started by offering specialized bass-fishing tackle that wasn't available in the Springfield, Missouri, area, especially the new high-tech tackle being used by the leading professional anglers. A lifelong lover of the outdoors, especially fishing, Morris was able to talk with anglers one-to-one to develop an understanding of the products that they needed.

His retail venture was so successful that Morris entered the direct mail-order business in 1974, distributing a 180-page catalog of 1,500 items to anglers in 20 states. Today, the mail-order catalog has grown to 400 pages, and Bass Pro Shops stocks and sells more than 30,000 items. Hundreds of its products are manufactured exclusively for the company.

Morris next established American Rod & Gun, a wholesale company. Then, in 1978, he offered the Tracker Marine aluminum Bass Tracker fishing boat package, providing a "fish ready" outfit complete with motor, trailer, and an assortment of accessories. Bass Tracker boats quickly became America's number one–selling fishing boats, and the line has been expanded to include a wide variety of aluminum fishing boat models, pontoon boats, and high-performance fiberglass Nitro fishing and ski boats.

In 1981, Morris opened the doors to his new Outdoor World national headquarters showroom in Springfield, a virtual superstore for fishing and outdoor equipment. Inside the facility is Hemingway's (a fresh-seafood restaurant), a McDonald's restaurant, the Tall Tales Barbershop, and a shooting range. The store includes the 250-seat Uncle Buck's Auditorium and conference room, where regularly scheduled seminars are presented by America's leading outdoor experts. In 1993, he added a 17,000-square-foot Wildlife Museum.

More than 4 million people visit Outdoor World each year, making it the number one tourist attraction in Missouri. Morris provides additional hospitality to visitors at his Big Cedar Lodge resort on Table Rock Lake in nearby Branson, Missouri. Opened in 1988, the facility includes the 51-room Valley View Lodge, 65-room Falls Lodge, 17-room Spring View Lodge, 41 private cabins, and two cottages scattered over 850 acres, close to Branson's famous entertainment and, of course, fishing.

In 1993, Morris entered into a partnership with Gaylord Entertainment Company, the nation's largest founder of live country music entertainment, to expand Bass Pro Shops' various outdoor sporting goods businesses. Altogether, Morris's businesses employ more than 3,600 people.

SOURCE: Bass Pro Shops archives

Harry W. Morrison, Morris H. Knudsen

[Morrison Knudsen Corporation]

Harry Winford Morrison was born on February 23, 1885, near the homestead farm of his grandparents in Kenney, Illinois. His grandfather was a successful farmer and miller who became a leader in the regional farmers cooperative. When Morrison was only four years old his mother fell ill, and some of the family members took her to the creek and baptized her. The exposure to the water gave her pneumonia, which caused her death.

A few months after his mother's death, young Morrison contracted a form of appendicitis and underwent surgery at the family farmhouse. He survived the episode but had a very slow recovery. When the doctor said that the boy should get air and sunshine, his father built a cot with wagon wheels that he could easily push outside.

As Morrison regained his strength, his father took him to his grandfather's home. Nearby, the Bates and Rogers construction company was building a railroad bridge, and Morrison's father propped up the boy's cot-wagon near the site so he could pass the time watching the construction activities. The superintendent of the job site noticed the boy, and the two soon became friends.

When the boy got older, his father sent him to a private school where the students were separated by their ability to pay. Since the Morrison family was unable to pay the full tuition, young Harry washed dishes and performed janitorial duties. Since he wasn't entitled to have butter with his meals, Harry would scramble to be first in line with the poor boys so that he could get the butter that the wealthier boys left behind on their plates.

Following these school years, the construction superintendent who befriended him years before gave him a job and sent him to a Reclamation Service project at the Minidoka Dam on the Snake River in Idaho. He was later hired as an inspector with the Reclamation Service.

In time, he concluded that better opportunities existed for contractors than for inspectors. He approached 50-year-old Morris Hans Knudsen, a contractor in Boise, Idaho, who had a modest road-building business. "I'd like to go into business with you," Morrison said. When Knudsen asked him what he had to offer, Morrison replied, "Plenty of guts."

"No," said Knudsen, "I mean how much money?"

"No money, just guts," repeated Morrison.

In 1912, they formed a partnership with Knudsen's $600 and a team of horses. They called themselves the Morrison Knudsen Company and quickly were granted a contract to build an irrigation pumping station on the Snake River.

Morrison worked hard to develop his management skills. Since he never finished high school, he educated himself by taking correspondence courses and attending night school. He once commented to his secretary that he built his vocabulary by working on crossword puzzles.

When the Bureau of Reclamation was soliciting bids for the construction of the Hoover Dam, Morrison organized six large Western construction companies, including his own, to provide a joint bid as the "Six Companies." The group was awarded the contract and completed the huge construction project ahead of schedule.

Morris Knudsen retired in 1939, turning full control of the organization over to Morrison. Four years later, Knudsen died.

By the 1950s, Morrison Knudsen was clearly the largest heavy-construction company in the world. *Time* magazine declared that Harry Morrison was "the man in history who has done the most to change the face of the earth." Morrison served as president of Morrison Knudsen until 1960, when he withdrew from active management and became chairman of the board of directors. He continued in that capacity until 1968, when, in declining health, he was granted the title founder-chairman.

Harry W. Morrison died on July 19, 1971, at the age of 86. His first marriage to Anna Daly in 1914 had produced no children. After Anna died in 1957, Morrison married Velma V. Shannon, who had a son and daughter from a previous marriage.

Today, Morrison Knudsen is a major international engineering and construction company with annual revenues of nearly $2 billion and 10,000 employees.

SOURCE: Morrison Knudsen Corporation archives

Charles H. Murphy Sr., Charles H. Murphy Jr.

[Murphy Oil Corporation]

Having already achieved success in Arkansas lumber and banking endeavors, Charles H. Murphy Sr. drilled his first oil well in 1907. Oil became the central focus of the Murphy family business some 30 years later, and today Murphy Oil Company is a Fortune 500 company listed on the New York Stock Exchange.

Charles Murphy's ancestors began arriving in America in about 1750. Their best-known relative was Lord Baltimore (Calvert), the founder of Maryland and the city of Baltimore. The Calverts and the Murphys moved through several states—including North Carolina, Georgia, and Alabama—before settling in southern Arkansas and northern Louisiana. George Murphy established his home near the Ouachita River in northern Louisiana, and his grandson, Charles H. Murphy Sr., soon began to run the family steamboat landings.

Charles Sr. lived a colorful early life, at one point serving as the sheriff of Union Parish. Eventually, he left public service to help build the Murphy family businesses, moving to El Dorado, Arkansas, when his uncle, Fletcher Sample, passed away. Sample had named Charles Sr. executor of the family's banks, and Murphy soon expanded them to include 13 in Arkansas, Louisiana, Mississippi, and the Indian territory.

All the banks made it through the 1907 panic, but after the panic was over Charles Sr. vowed to never again run a bank that he couldn't see every day. He promptly sold all the banks except the one in El Dorado, Arkansas, a town in which he had taken up residence.

Charles Sr. then reinvested his money in land and in sawmill businesses. Ultimately, oil was found below their land. It was at this point that the family's spirit of innovation, business, and leadership became apparent.

When Charles Murphy Sr.'s son, Charles Jr., was a young boy, he didn't have many friends his age to play with, so he spent his time with his father and with the caretakers and the cowboys who worked the family lumber and oil businesses. They talked about their work, and young Charles quickly developed the opinion that mineral rights were as important (if not more important) than surface rights.

Charles Sr. was 50 years old when his son was born, and he was in his 70s by the time Charles Jr. reached his 21st birthday in 1941. That year, Charles Sr. suffered a stroke, and while he recovered, he turned over control of the company to his son.

Charles Jr. maintained control of the family businesses from that point on, except for a brief stint in the service during World War II. Charles Sr. chose to remain in the background; only once did he overrule his son: He directed that the company purchase 40,000 acres of land in Louisiana, although Charles Jr. wasn't interested in the land. In 1944, in a joint venture with Sun Oil Company, the Delhi field—arguably the most important discovery in Murphy Oil history—was found on the land that Charles Jr. didn't want.

Charles Jr. did have a mind for business, though. At that time, C.H. Murphy & Company was a collection of eight partnerships and one small corporation. In 1950, Charles Jr. brought them together as the Murphy Corporation, headquartered in El Dorado, Arkansas. The company was capitalized at $1 million and boasted a reserve of 30 million barrels of oil and about 100 billion feet of natural gas. By January 1, 1996, those reserves had reached 226.7 million barrels of liquid oil and 642.8 billion cubic feet of natural gas.

Murphy Oil Corporation, as the company is now named, has entered into numerous historic agreements since its 1950 incorporation. Charles Murphy Jr. orchestrated investments in the Poplar, Sassan, and Ninian oil fields, all momentous occasions within Murphy Oil and the oil industry as a whole.

Charles Murphy Jr.'s company also jointly formed the Ocean Drilling & Exploration Company (ODECO) in 1954 and soon created Mr. Charlie (named after Charles Murphy Sr.), the prototype for all submersible drilling rigs. Mr. Charlie recently became the home of an international oil museum in Morgan City, Louisiana.

In 1991, ODECO became Murphy Exploration & Production Company, headquartered in New Orleans. Today, the other primary subsidiaries of the company are Murphy Oil USA, Inc., which includes the U.S. refining and marketing operations; Murphy Oil Company Limited in Calgary, Alberta, Canada; and Murphy Eastern Oil Company in London, England.

Under Charles Murphy Jr.'s direction, the enterprise also continued land and timber investments, eventually venturing into real estate. In 1988, the Murphy subsidiary, Deltic Farm & Timber Co., Inc., established Chenal Valley, a 7,000-acre Little Rock, Arkansas, development of homes, a country club, and a 36-hole golf course. Murphy Oil spun off the Deltic subsidiary in December 1996, enabling both companies to more fully realize their value.

After 57 years of service and leadership, Charles H. Murphy Jr. retired from the board of directors in October 1994.

SOURCE: Murphy Oil Corporation archives

Joel N. Myers
[AccuWeather, Inc.]

As a young boy, Joel Myers was fascinated by the weather. He parlayed this into a successful academic career and a successful business venture called AccuWeather, which today is the largest commercial weather forecasting organization in the world.

While growing up in Philadelphia, Pennsylvania, Joel Myers knew in his heart that his future was in predicting the weather. At age seven, he began recording the daily weather conditions in a journal. By age 11, he was making plans to trade in his paper route and start a business that predicted the weather.

Upon graduating from high school, Myers entered the meteorology program at Penn State University, where he went on to obtain bachelor's (1961), master's (1963), and Ph.D. (1971) degrees in meteorology. After obtaining his undergraduate degree in 1961, Myers started up the business he had dreamed about for more than ten years. His first customer, Columbia Gas, was signed in November 1962. The company paid $50 per month to receive forecasts during the winter months, providing AccuWeather a total first-year income of $200.

While he pursued graduate study, Myers started working with ski resorts to determine optimum times to turn on their automatic snowmaking equipment. Soon he had 50 ski resorts as clients, and AccuWeather had found a niche. He then applied the same technology to help government officials order and use winter supplies such as road salt. Along with his teaching and business responsibilities, Myers broadcast weather forecasts on radio and television for 18 years.

In the classroom, Myers continued to teach at Penn State, which was graduating one of every five meteorologists in the country. When he retired from an active teaching schedule in 1981, it was estimated that he had taught weather forecasting to nearly 17 percent of the practicing meteorologists in the entire country.

Myers had developed and refined some of the world's most important forecasting tools. In 1979, the company unveiled a state-of-the-art meteorological database that today is known as AccuData®. This supplies real-time weather information to thousands of subscribers. In 1983, Myers started sharing his full-color weather graphics, which today are used by CNN, CBS, and more than 200 local television stations.

AccuWeather later developed the MacWeather™ system of providing newspapers with camera-ready weather pages. It also innovated FirstWarn™, which automatically generates a "crawling" message over a television station's broadcast signal to notify the public the instant an official warning is issued.

Today, AccuWeather is the largest commercial weather service in the world. Its 300 employees serve more than 10,000 clients around the world. Myers has also launched another venture called Weather Prophets, Inc.

SOURCE: AccuWeather, Inc., archives

Lane Nemeth

[Discovery Toys, Inc.]

Frustrated with the inability to buy high-quality educational toys, Lane Nemeth contacted suppliers and asked how families could purchase the same toys that were found in schools and day-care centers. After being told that retailers just wouldn't carry such products, she founded Discovery Toys and established a large sales network that today sells close to $100 million worth of educational and developmental toys, books, games, and software.

Lane Nemeth was born Lane Perlowin in New York City in 1947. After graduating from high school, she received a B.A. from the University of Pittsburgh and an M.A. from Seton Hall University.

While running a children's day-care center in Martinez, California, Nemeth was intrigued with the unique toys that were purchased by the school. They were durable and seemed to encourage learning, yet they were not commercially available. Upon the birth of her daughter Tara in 1975, Nemeth's interest was even more pronounced. "Why can't I buy these kinds of toys for Tara?" she asked. "Where can I go to get them?"

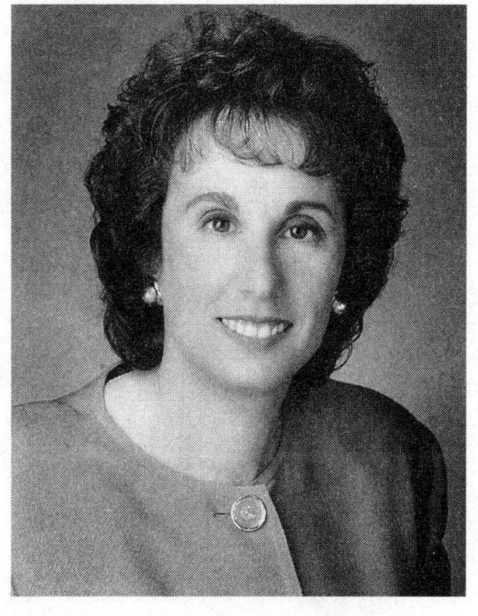

Nemeth approached the suppliers who distributed their products directly to schools and day-care centers, asking why their toys weren't available in retail stores. She quickly discovered that mainstream retailers were interested in glitzy, glamorous, shoot-'em-up toys and anything famous athletes and cartoon characters were selling. There was no shelf space for educational toys.

Spotting an opportunity, Nemeth developed a plan to offer inexpensive, high-quality toys, books, and games for children. She borrowed money from her friends and family, cashed in her savings, and launched Discovery Toys in 1978. Her office and warehouse was the back of the garage in her modest Martinez, California, home.

The suggestion to sell directly to consumers came from Nemeth's husband. She conceived a sales force of "Educational Consultants," most of whom were young mothers interested not only in earning extra money, but also emotionally invested in providing high-quality educational products to responsible families.

Her first-year sales reached $275,000. In four short years she surpassed the $10 million mark. The company moved to Benicia, then to Concord. Discovery Toys now occupies a new building in Livermore. Sales will break the $100 million level in 1997 and are projected to reach $250 million near the turn of the century.

Today, more than 35,000 educational consultants, mostly young mothers working part-time, market the company's products by demonstrating them in the homes of consumers. About one-third of the product line is composed of items that have been completely designed and developed by the company. In 1995, the company released Discovery Quest, a line of educational and developmental computer software.

SOURCE: Discovery Toys, Inc., archives

Edgar A. Newell, Lawrence F. Cuthbert

[Newell Companies]

In the late 1890s, the Linton Company was a small manufacturer of curtain rods in Providence, Rhode Island. The firm moved to Ogdensburg, New York, in 1903, enticed in part by a $1,000 loan from the Ogdensburg Board of Trade.

The president of the board was a successful local merchant named Edgar Newell, whose firm—The Edgar A. Newell Company—was organized in 1891. In addition to providing money, Newell personally guaranteed a loan to Linton. Newell had been born and raised in Ogdensburg. While not counted among the town's elite, he built a successful business that provided his sons, Albert and William Allan Newell, with college degrees.

When the company fell into financial distress and the note was called, Newell found himself the owner of a small manufacturing company whose product, curtain rods, he knew nothing about. The rods were made from brass tubes that were cut to length and had ornamental finials attached.

By 1907, Edgar had renamed the firm the Newell Manufacturing Company, Inc., and established a subsidiary across the border in Prescott, Canada. For several years the company remained predominantly a local supplier of curtain rods and fixtures, employing about 20 people and generating annual sales of nearly $50,000.

In 1912, the Newell Mfg. Co. brought in a new employee named Ben Cuthbert. Lawrence Ferguson "Ben" Cuthbert was born and raised on a farm near Hammond, New York. After studying accounting at Albany Business College, the 20-year-old graduate founded a small bank in Hammond. He was recruited to Newell, where, at age 23, he was given charge of the Canadian plant. There he started producing new products such as towel racks and ice picks.

At the U.S. plant, Edgar Newell's son Allan was given more responsibility. As the company expanded its market, innovations allowed Newell to manufacture curtain rods with new types of finishes. One innovation in particular led to a significant amount of business with the Woolworth discount store.

Edgar A. Newell died on August 20, 1920, leaving the U.S. plant to his older son, Albert, who returned from his Kansas City law practice to oversee operations. He left Allan his share of the Canadian plant, the balance of which was owned by Cuthbert. Eventually, Cuthbert and the Newell brothers divided ownership of both plants among themselves, and Cuthbert emerged as the active leader who orchestrated the continued growth of the company.

Newell remained a small drapery hardware manufacturer until the late 1960s, reaching annual sales of about $20 million. Since then, the company has acquired more than 50 companies, including Anchor Hocking glassware, Bernz-Omatic propane torches, Bulldog hardware, Holson Burnes and Intercraft picture frames, Levolor window treatments, and many more. Annual sales now approach $3 billion.

SOURCE: William R. Cuthbert, *Newell Companies—A Corporate History,* 1983

Arthur C. Nielsen Sr.

[A.C. Nielsen Company]

Arthur C. Nielsen graduated from the University of Wisconsin with a degree in engineering. In 1923, the 26-year-old Nielsen launched his first venture, selling engineering surveys. He would analyze products like drill bits and provide information to end users, such as how many holes the drill bits would be able to make before becoming dull. The business did well, but by 1930 the Depression had all but ruined his client base.

Noting that food and drugs continued to sell during the Depression, Nielsen turned his attention toward consumer-oriented markets. In 1933, he produced his first *Retail Drug Index* to track the sale of drugstore products. Initially, the manufacturers balked, until Nielsen was able to predict their own sales to within 1 percent. Impressed, they quickly subscribed to his services in order to track their competitors.

However, Nielsen found that at the end of the first year of service, virtually none of his clients renewed their contracts. Upon further analysis, he determined that they found the information interesting, but didn't really know what to do with it once they read the reports. Nielsen once again moved into action, providing seminars on how clients could use market information to their advantage. Slowly, he regained his lost customer base. He also added a *Food Index* and a *Department Store Index.*

In 1936, Nielsen became interested in the marketing aspects of radio. He acquired a machine that could maintain a minute-by-minute record of the dial settings of radios, allowing an analysis of listening patterns. By 1949, his *Radio Index* provided market-share information to potential advertisers. One year later, he purchased his biggest radio ratings competitor, Claude Hooper.

Nielsen then turned his attention to television. By 1953, he was tracking the television viewing habits of 700 families. As the market grew, Nielsen dropped the radio ratings business to focus on television.

In 1984, the A.C. Nielsen Company merged with Dun & Bradstreet. In 1996, the company spun off as an independent public corporation renamed ACNielsen, which today employs 17,000 people in 93 countries.

SOURCE: *Dun & Bradstreet and the Rise of Modern Business,* Dun & Bradstreet

Glenn E. Nielson

[Husky Oil Company]

Glenn E. Nielson was born on May 26, 1903, in Aetna, Alberta, Canada, the son of James E. and Margaret (Pilling) Nielson. His father was the son of Danish immigrants who, after joining the Mormon church, moved to Utah. His mother, a Canadian, met his father at Brigham Young University. The couple married and established a successful grain and sheep ranch in Canada.

As a child, Glenn Nielson lived a comfortable farm life. However, one year after venturing to England on his first church mission, he was called home to care for his dying father. After his death, Glenn managed the family ranch and, in 1928, married his high school sweetheart, Olive Wood. The couple had two sons and three daughters.

The Nielson ranch included 1,000 acres and 2,000 sheep, all debt free. With an eye toward expansion in 1929, Nielson borrowed $7,000 for seed and equipment. Shortly thereafter, the stock market crash ushered in the Great Depression, and he found himself behind on taxes and in debt. Still, the family managed to survive and Nielson was even able to earn a degree in agriculture from the University of Alberta.

In 1934, Nielson moved his sheep into Montana pastureland. However, the following year there was an outbreak of hoof-and-mouth disease, and Canada wouldn't permit him to move the sheep back to Canada. Moreover, the United States government wouldn't let him sell the sheep in America. When he was finally granted permission to move the herd back to Canada, most were lost after a massive snowstorm.

Nielson managed as best he could, hauling grain and hay while his wife cooked for harvest laborers. He slowly paid off his debts and restored his credit. In 1936, he came across an opportunity. The owners of the small refinery where Nielson purchased his gasoline offered him $5 a day plus a quarter-cent-per-gallon commission to sell gas and oil to his farm customers. Nielson made substantial sales, but the refinery owners reneged on the promised commission and he quit.

Not long afterward, Nielson accepted a job with Val Kirk, the owner of a small refinery called Husky Refining in Cody, Wyoming. After the Nielsons moved to Cody in 1937, Kirk offered to sell him the company for $500,000. He raised the $200,000 down payment from a farmers' cooperative and a Montana contractor. On January 1, 1938, the 34-year-old Nielson took control of the 18-employee, 900 barrel-per-day operation.

Within four years, Kirk was paid off and the business was slowly growing. However, in 1943, a West Coast oil company offered to buy Husky for $1.3 million. The farmers' cooperative, which would realize about $800,000 from the sale, was anxious to accept the offer. However, Nielson balked. He felt the company held too much potential, and the cooperative gave him 60 days to match the offer.

Nielson visited the big city banks, but none would lend him the money. He did get support, however, from several leading businessmen in Cody, including Milward Simpson, who later became governor and U.S. senator. Nielson's backers rallied the residents, and the results were amazing. He later observed that the money came from "ranchers and gamblers, saloonkeepers and lawyers, even a fellow who ran slot machines. People pulled money out of their socks and from under the floorboards."

With a final loan from Peter Kiewit, the successful contractor from Omaha, Nebraska, Nielson raised the money and bought out the farmers' cooperative. From that point forward, Husky grew and expanded throughout the United States and Canada.

By the late 1970s, annual sales at Husky Oil surpassed $600 million. By then, Nielson was in his 70s and was easing into retirement while retaining the title of board chairman. In addition to oil holdings, the company was a major asphalt producer, a steel fabricator, a coal briquette producer, and restaurant chain (Husky House) operator.

SOURCE: "The Man Who Founded Husky Oil," *The Denver Post, Empire Magazine,* September 24, 1978

Quintin G. Noblitt, Frank H. Sparks, Albert G. Redmond

[Arvin Industries, Inc.]

Quintin G. Noblitt was born on October 11, 1882, in Ohio Township in Bartholomew County, Indiana, the fourth of nine children who were raised on the peaceful family farm. Throughout childhood, he exhibited ingenuity on the farm, inventing a weed puller that worked without having to bend over, among other things. His father commented, perhaps half seriously, that he was only trying to avoid hard work.

At age 17, Noblitt moved to Columbus, Indiana, and worked as a machinist for four years. This was followed by nearly ten years of job-hopping in Indianapolis, Indiana, and Flint, Michigan. One of the jobs was with Carl Fisher's automobile company, where he first met Frank Sparks. The two became friends and crossed paths again while working for the Haywood Tire and Equipment Company. By 1916, they decided to start a business together.

Frank Hugh Sparks was born on January 11, 1891, near Culver, Indiana. Like so many other farm children, he raised and sold produce. But this natural-born salesman had an edge over competitors. After picking his vegetables, he'd wash them, dress in good clothes, and peddle his clean produce in the nicer neighborhoods.

Carl Fisher, the automotive magnate, who maintained a summer home in the area, took a liking to young Sparks and hired him at his Indianapolis garage during summers and after graduation. There and at a subsequent job at Haywood, he became close friends with Noblitt. Both men were restless to start their own business.

In 1916, Noblitt and Sparks invested $3,000 each and opened the Indianapolis Motor School to provide training for automobile mechanics. Sparks was an excellent salesman and quickly filled the classroom. Noblitt was experienced in all phases of automobile mechanics and proved to be an excellent teacher.

However, neither man anticipated the impact of World War I, and their classroom soon emptied. The partners closed the doors to their business and went to work for the war effort, but were soon planning their next venture. This time, they brought in a third partner, Al Redmond.

Albert G. Redmond was the youngest of the three partners, born at Indianapolis in 1894. His father died when Al was only six years old, and young Redmond never had the opportunity to complete high school. Instead, he was hired as a grease monkey at Carl Fisher's automobile company, where he met Noblitt. Redmond became something of an understudy to Noblitt, and when Noblitt changed jobs, Redmond usually went with him.

In 1919, Noblitt, Sparks, and Redmond decided the world could use a reliable tire pump. They each put up $1,000, rented an empty grocery store for $10 per month, and launched the Indianapolis Air Pump Company. Once Noblitt was able to design an efficient tire pump, Redmond quickly built them and Sparks sold them. At the end of their first year, they counted a $10,000 profit.

Encouraged and enriched by their early success, the partners became acquainted with a man named Richard Hood Arvin who had designed a crude but workable automobile heater. Since Arvin had no money to build and market his heater, he agreed to establish a separate company, the Arvin Heating Company, which he owned jointly with Noblitt, Sparks, and Redmond. In turn, the Indianapolis Air Pump Company built and sold the heaters, then paid a royalty to the Arvin company.

In 1922, Al Redmond decided to leave the organization and establish his own company. He sold his share of the business to Noblitt and Sparks for $10,000, then moved to Michigan and was soon granted 35 patents. In 1925, he established the A. G. Redmond Company which, by 1945, employed more than 2,000 people and built as many as 18,000 motors per day.

Richard Arvin opted out of the business in 1923, selling his stock and assets to Noblitt and Sparks for $2,000. However, the name Arvin had become known to customers, so the two remaining partners decided to keep it on their products. By 1950, the company itself was renamed Arvin Industries.

The company grew rapidly. Sales in 1924 reached $700,000. By 1927, sales had more than tripled, and the company name was changed to Noblitt-Sparks Industries. As with so many business ventures of the time, growth was steady until October 29, 1929, the day the stock market crashed. Two months later, Frank Sparks left the company to go to college.

The Depression was particularly harsh on the automotive industry, but by 1932 Noblitt announced that the rate of losing money was slowing. When Roosevelt closed the banks in 1933, Noblitt told his employees to stay home because he couldn't pay them, but they still came to work. By World War II, the company had regained its health, and in 1944 Noblitt retired as president. Quintin G. Noblitt died on July 3, 1954.

Frank Sparks was pushing 40 when he enrolled in college. After he was awarded a bachelor's degree from Butler University in 1935, he moved to the West Coast and enrolled at the University of Southern California. He was awarded his master's degree two years later. Despite the death of his wife, he moved into the doctoral program, and in 1941 he was awarded his Ph.D. He subsequently remarried and was chosen from a field of 72 candidates to serve as the eighth president of Wabash College. Frank H. Sparks died on December 30, 1964.

Al Redmond sold his company to Singer in 1945 and, in his 50s, enrolled at Michigan State University, where he even joined a fraternity. Four years later, he graduated with honors in the same class as his son. Albert G. Redmond died on May 7, 1986, at age 90.

Today, Arvin is a Fortune 1,000 company that employs 13,000 people.

SOURCES: Arvin Industries, Inc., archives; Coke Coons, *Arvin . . . The First Seventy Years*, Arvin Industries, 1989

John W. Nordstrom, Carl F. Wallin

[Nordstrom, Inc.]

Johan W. Nordstrom was born on February 15, 1871, in Alvik Neder Lulea, Sweden. His father, a blacksmith and wagonmaker, died when Johan was only eight years old, and three years later he had to quit school to work on the family farm. At age 16, he took his inheritance of a little over $100 and, with two friends, set out for America.

After arriving in New York, Nordstrom boarded a train for Stambaugh, Michigan, where a family member was living. With only $5 remaining in his pocket and hampered by his poor English, he settled for a job loading iron ore into railroad cars, earning $1.60 for each ten-hour day. Over the next five years, he worked his way toward the Pacific Northwest, working in Michigan and California logging camps, Colorado gold and silver mines, and various other demanding jobs.

In 1896, Nordstrom purchased a 20-acre potato farm near Arlington, Washington. The following year, gold was discovered in Canada's Yukon Territory and the adventurous Nordstrom was soon on a coal freighter heading north. Within two years he had staked a claim, sold it for $13,000, then moved back to Seattle where he married Hilda Carlson, a fellow Swedish immigrant.

While searching for gold, Nordstrom had met Carl F. Wallin, a Seattle shoe repairman. After Nordstrom returned to Seattle, Wallin encouraged Nordstrom—who had changed his first name from Johan to John—to join him in the shoe business. Nordstrom contributed $5,000, Wallin pitched in $1,000 and his expertise, and in 1901 they opened the doors of Wallin & Nordstrom.

While the first day's receipts only totaled $12.50, they were soon selling $100 worth of shoes on their busy Saturdays. They soon expanded their line and added larger sizes, primarily to fit their sturdy Scandinavian clientele. By 1905, annual sales were nearly $50,000 and the partners moved into larger quarters by purchasing the store and inventory of another shoe store.

For nearly two decades, the founders continued to increase their sales and inventory. Each time they outgrew a store, they simply traded up for a larger one. Their constant focus was value and selection, and store ambiance took a backseat. By 1915, two of Nordstrom's five children were working at the store—12-year-old Everett and 11-year-old Elmer—which charted the future course of the successful shoe store.

In 1923, Wallin & Nordstrom opened a second store, and Everett, who had just graduated from the University of Washington, was named manager. Within five years, John Nordstrom retired from the business and sold his share to Everett and Elmer. One year later, Wallin retired and also sold his shares to the Nordstrom sons, who were joined by a third brother, Lloyd, in 1933.

The Nordstrom brothers built the company into the largest independent shoe chain in the country. Their downtown Seattle store grew to become the largest shoe store in America. In the 1960s, the Nordstroms diversified their business with the purchase of Best Apparel, a Seattle-based clothing store.

By the early 1970s, control of the company was passed to a third generation of Nordstroms. As they passed the $100 million annual sales mark, the company was taken public. Today, several fourth-generation Nordstroms manage the company, which has annual sales in excess of $4 billion and more than 80 stores.

SOURCES: Nordstrom archives; Robert Spector and Patrick McCarthy, *The Nordstrom Way*, John Wiley & Sons, New York, 1995

John K. Northrop

[Northrop Aircraft Company]

John "Jack" Knudsen Northrop was born in 1895. Upon graduation from Santa Barbara (California) High School in 1913, he went to work as an architectural draftsman. During his school years he had worked for an auto mechanic and, more important, witnessed firsthand an airplane demonstration by French aviator Didier Masson.

In 1916, 21-year-old Northrop landed a job with Allan and Malcolm Loughead (pronounced, and later spelled, Lockheed), who had just opened up a local factory. One of Northrop's first assignments was the development of a Curtiss-designed seaplane for the U.S. Navy.

At the end of World War I, the Loughead brothers switched to sports planes. But surplus war planes flooded the market and the company folded. Northrop went to work in the construction business until 1923, when he was hired by Donald Douglas at Santa Monica. Soon, he was working on Douglas planes that eventually circled the globe.

The Douglas Company was primarily interested in military aircraft. Northrop's interest lay in commercial applications and in his spare time he designed a plane called the Vega, the prototype of which was built in his backyard. He approached Allan Loughead, who was then selling real estate in Hollywood, and asked if he was interested in getting back into the airplane business.

Loughead indeed was interested and, in 1927, launched the Lockheed Company that survives to this day. The first Lockheed Vega was quickly built and successfully flown on July 4, 1927. That same year, Northrop was consulted on the design of Claude Ryan's *Spirit of St. Louis*.

About one year after Lockheed was formed, Northrop left the company and formed Avion Corporation. His first project was the design of the Alpha, one of the first planes to incorporate metal components. William Boeing was so impressed with the plane that he bought the company from Northrop and renamed it Northrop Aircraft Company. Northrop remained with the company until 1932, at which time he returned to Douglas Aircraft.

In 1939, Northrop moved out on his own again, establishing Northrop Aircraft at Hawthorne, California. The company's earliest work involved subcontracts for other aircraft companies. As World War II approached, the company found itself quite busy. The Norwegian government ordered 24 patrol bombers, called the N-3PB. When England came under attack, Northrop quickly designed and built the famed P-61 Black Widow, the first plane designed for night combat.

Jack Northrop retired from active service in November 1952. He died on February 18, 1981. In 1994, the Northrop Corporation acquired Grumman, forming Northrop Grumman Corporation. The company, based in Los Angeles, California, has annual sales of $8 billion and employs 47,000 people.

SOURCE: Northrop Grumman archives

John H. Noyes, Pierrepont B. Noyes

[Oneida Limited]

The makers of Oneida silverware trace their roots to one of the many utopian communities that emerged in America in throughout the eighteenth and nineteenth centuries. In 1848, the Oneida Community from Oneida, New York, was founded on the principle of spiritual equality and forbade ownership of personal property. Children were in their mothers' care until age two and were then raised communally. This freed the women to join the men in the manufacture of various products, which eventually included animal traps and chains, as well as silver knives, forks, and spoons.

Under the guidance of founder John Humphrey Noyes, the Oneida Community grew steadily during its 31-year existence. However, in 1879, social pressures brought the experiment to an end. Members agreed to convert the nearly $600,000 in assets into a joint stock company, with ownership distributed according to original contribution and length of service. The new company was originally named the Oneida Community, Limited, a name that was later shortened to Oneida Limited.

Under new leadership, the company slowly slipped into financial difficulties over the next 15 years. But in January 1894, Pierrepont Burt Noyes, son of the community's founder, returned to Oneida after spending time out in "the World," as members referred to anything beyond their walls.

The younger Noyes proved even more capable than his father. He was appointed superintendent of the Niagara Falls plant and, within five years, led it to unprecedented profitability. By the age of 30, Noyes was the general manager of all the company's divisions—canning and manufacturing of tableware, traps, chains, and silk thread—and pioneered the use of advertising and marketing.

Like his father, Noyes wanted to create a utopian environment at Oneida and focused on fair wages, comfortable working conditions, and employee wellness and recreation. Eventually, the chain, silk, and trapping businesses were sold, while the canning business was discontinued, leaving the company completely dependent on the manufacture of silverware.

In 1926, Noyes appointed his son-in-law, Miles Robertson, to the post of general manager. Over the next several decades, Oneida gradually became more integrated with "the World" as outsiders joined the company. World War II provided an economic boost to the company. In addition to making tableware and surgical instruments for the military, the company manufactured rifle sights, parachute releases, hand grenades, shells, bayonets, aircraft fuel tanks, and engine components.

Pierrepont's son, Pierrepont Trowbridge "Pete" Noyes, was named president of Oneida in 1960. He led the company into the development of ornate stainless steel flatware, eventually capturing more than half of the domestic market. He continued to serve as chairman until 1981. The company later expanded through its 1983 purchase of Buffalo China, Inc., followed by several other key acquisitions. Today, Oneida has more than 4,000 employees and annual sales in excess of $375 million.

SOURCES: Oneida Limited archives; Walter D. Edmonds, *The First Hundred Years*, Oneida Ltd., 1958

Daniel J. O'Conor, Herbert A. Faber

[Formica Corporation]

After working in various roles at Westinghouse Corporation in Pittsburgh, Pennsylvania, Daniel O'Conor and Herbert Faber decided to strike out on their own. They set up a modest shop in Cincinnati, Ohio, in 1913, and made electrical insulators using a material that O'Conor invented. The new product, which they named *Formica,* became a core product that was eventually used in making laminates for homes and businesses. Today, Formica Corporation is one of the most recognized names in home products in the entire world.

In 1913, O'Conor (shown upper right) developed a new material that proved to be ideal for electrical insulation. The material replaced *mica,* from which O'Conor and Faber formed the name *Formica* for their new product. The 31-year-old O'Conor and the 30-year-old Faber (lower right) quit their jobs and moved to O'Conor's hometown of Cincinnati to established their business.

The assets of the new venture included homemade presses, an old boiler, and a small stove—but no money. Business picked up quickly, primarily from the growing automobile industry, and within five months they employed 18 people. This opened the door for private investors, and by the end of the year they had reorganized as The Formica Insulation Company.

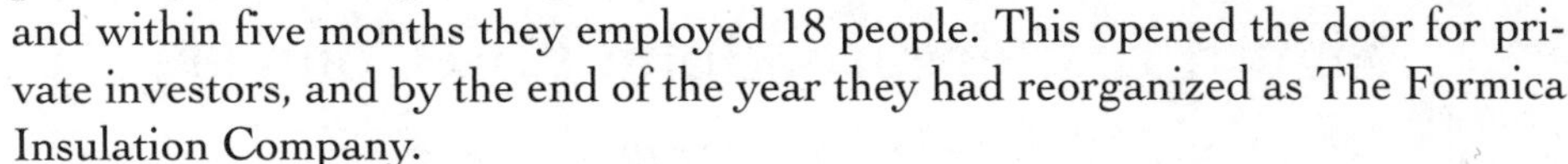

During the early years, both men worked long hours, often with makeshift or borrowed tools. O'Conor's clothes permanently reeked of the phenol used in making plastic laminates. The regulars at the neighborhood lunch counter thought the smell reminded them of a hospital, so they nicknamed O'Conor "Doc."

Over the next four years, the company grew despite the lack of capital. But the founders didn't want to dilute their ownership, so they borrowed heavily. At one point, a lender from Chicago grew tired of waiting for repayment of a $10,000 note and sent someone to Cincinnati. After meeting with O'Conor and Faber, the man returned to Chicago with great news: He had loaned them another $10,000.

Business boomed after World War I broke out. Formica was overwhelmed with orders for insulators for radios and a new product: pulleys for control cables in aircraft. Sales rose to $75,000 in 1917, then nearly doubled the following year. After the war, the company made automotive gears. By 1932, they were producing 6,000 gears each day for Chevrolet, Buick, Pontiac, and several of the other major automakers.

The real innovation at Formica Corporation came in the late 1920s. The company started making laminates with wood-grain patterns that radio manufacturers used for casing. This opened a new market in decorative laminates for residential and commercial use. During the Depression, this new product line filled the void left by the lack of demand for their core business products. Contractors, restaurants, and even the builders of railroad cars and the luxury liner *Queen Mary* were specifying Formica® brand laminates.

World War II once again provided a boost to Formica Corporation. This time, the company made burster tubes for bombs, as well as machine tool parts, insulators, and, of course, laminates. The postwar boom proved even more profitable. Americans had put off building houses and schools for five years. This led to explosive growth not only in American homes, but also in the 200,000 new classrooms that were built over the next four years. By 1948, the Formica Company dropped "Insulation" from its name.

In 1957, Formica Corporation was sold to American Cyanamid, opening the company to considerable financial and marketing resources. In 1985, American Cyanamid sold the company to Formica executives. In 1995, BTR Nylex, an Australian-based company, bought Formica.

SOURCE: Formica Corporation archives

Sigurd L. Odegard, John F. O'Connell
[GTE Corporation]

After Alexander Graham Bell's patent expired in the mid-1890s, independent telephone companies appeared throughout the country. By the turn of the century, more than 6,000 such ventures were launched, many competing head-to-head with Bell. As World War I raged, the market had matured somewhat, but still offered opportunities to newcomers.

Sigurd L. Odegard and John F. O'Connell were ambitious sons of Norwegian and Irish immigrant families. Both had worked in the accounting and statistical department of the Wisconsin Railroad Commission while earning their degrees at the University of Wisconsin.

In 1918, 33-year-old Odegard, 26-year-old O'Connell, and a third partner pooled their resources and, with $33,500, purchased the Richland Center Telephone Company in southern Wisconsin. They expanded the hours from daylight-only to 24-hours-per-day service while making other improvements. Two years later, they incorporated the venture as the Commonwealth Telephone Company and acquired three additional independent phone companies near the state capital of Madison.

Encouraged by their initial success, the founders raised additional capital and, through acquisitions, entered markets adjoining Wisconsin. They also purchased two small electric utility companies in Wisconsin.

While on vacation in California in 1926, Odegard secured an option to purchase the Associated Telephone Company of Long Beach. Building on the successful expansion model that evolved in Wisconsin, the new owners quickly purchased five additional telephone companies near Los Angeles. The Wisconsin-based enterprises were then folded into Associated, and by 1930 the company had revenues of $17 million and served nearly 500,000 telephones.

The next 15 years proved to be challenging for the rapidly growing company. Sigurd Odegard suffered a fatal heart attack in 1934 and died at the age of 49. John O'Connell died in 1945 at the age of 53 following a long illness. As for the business, the Great Depression had forced Associated into bankruptcy in 1933. Two years later, it emerged as the General Telephone Corporation.

By the end of World War II, General Telephone had increased the number of telephones it serviced to more than 700,000, and the company prospered in postwar America, both in terms of new acquisitions and expansion of existing holdings.

In 1955, General Telephone merged with Theodore Gary and Company, founded by Theodore Gary in 1897. Starting with a small telephone company in Macon, Georgia, Gary built an impressive empire that included not only telephone companies, but the Automatic Electric Company, makers of automated switching equipment. As a result of the merger, General Telephone served more than 2.5 million telephones and had annual revenues exceeding $350 million.

General Telephone made another key move in 1959 when it merged with Sylvania Electric Products. That company traces its roots to 1901 in Middleton, Massachusetts, where Frank Augustus Poor purchased the Merritt Manufacturing Company with $3,500 earned in his hay and grain business. Poor and his brothers expanded the lightbulb recycling business with expansions and acquisitions, eventually becoming a major manufacturers of lamps, televisions, and other consumer products.

After the merger with Sylvania, the company reorganized as the General Telephone and Electronics Corporation (GT&E) and later as simply GTE. Today, GTE is one of the world's largest telecommunications companies, with annual sales in excess of $21 billion.

SOURCE: Thomas McCarthy, *The History of GTE,* GTE Corporation, 1990

William F. O'Neil

[General Tire, Inc.]

In 1851, James and Catherine O'Neil immigrated to New York City from their native Ireland. The youngest of their nine children, Michael, had been born only one year earlier. When James died, 16-year-old Michael started his first in a series of jobs that eventually led into the Irish lace import business at Cape Cod, Massachusetts.

By 1877, he was both successful and restless. He and his wife, Patience, moved to Akron, Ohio, a promising city at the junction of two busy canals, where he established a dry goods business. Twelve years later, the store moved into a new four-story building in the heart of Akron. During these years Michael and Patience had seven children, the oldest being William Francis O'Neil.

Upon graduation from Holy Cross in 1907, William O'Neil moved to Denver, where he held a number of sales jobs. Upon learning of an open territory in Kansas City with Firestone, O'Neil sent a letter to the company inquiring about the opportunity. The people at Firestone, being quite familiar with the O'Neil family through the Akron business community, enthusiastically invited him to serve as their independent agent for the available territory.

Since O'Neil didn't have any experience in the management of the rubber business, it was suggested that he take a partner, and Winifred E. Fouse, a Firestone employee, was highly recommended. So, in 1908, 23-year-old O'Neil and 31-year-old Fouse established their tire distributorship in Kansas City, Missouri, named Western Rubber & Supply Company.

Like O'Neil, Fouse was a native of the Akron area. After graduating from high school, Fouse accepted a teaching position until he saved enough money to attend the Eastman Business College in Poughkeepsie, New York. He then went to work as an accountant with the Diamond Rubber Company in Akron, then later moved to Firestone.

The partners quickly built a brisk trade throughout their vast territory. However, as time passed, Firestone started to reduce their territory in favor of company-owned dealerships. In order to stabilize their income, O'Neil and Fouse opened a small support plant that manufactured tire patches, reliners, and other accessories. Within two years their plant employed 100 workers and had $500,000 in annual sales. When Firestone announced another major territorial reduction in 1914, the partners severed the relationship and laid plans to manufacture their own tires.

O'Neil returned to Akron to raise money for the venture. By this time, his father had sold his department store to the May Company, and Nate Dauby, president of May, became the first stockholder in the new venture. O'Neil's father and several other Akron businessmen signed on, as well, and in 1915 the General Tire and Rubber Company was incorporated. At the time, there were at least 350 other tire manufacturers in the country, and with the average age of the company's leadership being about 30, the industry joke was that no one at General Tire and Rubber was old enough to be a General.

O'Neil moved his Kansas City operation to Akron, and it quickly picked up where it left off. He also introduced innovative tires, such as his Jumbo line. By 1923, annual sales topped the $1 million mark. He developed an extra-heavy-tread tire for trucks, which by the 1930s helped General to become a market leader. A decade later, wartime production of tires provided a major boost to the company.

O'Neil and his wife Grace had six children. One son died during military service and three of the remaining four sons eventually held posts at the company. In 1987, Continental AG of Hannover, Germany, purchased General Tire.

SOURCES: General Tire, Inc. archives; Dennis O'Neill, *A Whale of a Territory: The Story of Bill O'Neil,* McGraw-Hill, 1966

Merritt J. Osborn

[Economics Laboratory, Inc.]

After spending nearly three decades working for and owning a diverse group of businesses, Merritt Osborn set out to find a good carpet cleaner. Once a formula was proven successful, he added a cleaner for homes. His company, Economics Laboratory, has grown into ECOLAB, an international multibillion-dollar company.

Merritt J. Osborn was born on February 14, 1879, in Buchanan, Michigan, the youngest of ten sons and one daughter born to a furniture manufacturer whose health failed him at an early age. Wearing hand-me-down clothes from his older brothers, Merritt had to quit high school after only two years to go to work.

At the age of 16, he moved to Chicago, where his brother had arranged a job for him with a drug wholesaler. Two years later, he went to work for another pharmaceutical company as a "drummer"—a commissioned salesman who scoured the countryside by horse and buggy. When the venture failed, he worked for Parke-Davis Pharmaceuticals in Indiana for five years, where he met and married Susan Bartley.

He then worked for Eli Lilly, who transferred him to San Francisco, then to St. Paul, Minnesota. Unhappy with being uprooted, Osborn left Lilly and went to work for the Hamm Brewing Company, marketing a medicinal malt extract called Digesto. In 1910, he went to work for Herbert Bigelow, a specialty advertising manufacturer who had decided to build trucks.

The venture didn't last long, but Osborn had learned enough about automobiles to become a dealer for the White Motor Truck, the White Steamer Touring Car, the Willys-Overland car, and the Willys-Knight car. After World War I ended, Osborn secured first a dealership, then the Northwestern distributorship, of the Ford Motor Company. His hopes proved to be overly optimistic, however, and the expense of maintaining too large an inventory forced him out of business.

In 1923, the 44-year-old entrepreneur was down to his last $5,000. While considering his next venture, he recalled his hotel experiences while traveling on business. Many times hotels would have to close for several days while their carpets were being cleaned. He quickly hired a chemist to develop a formula for carpets, rented three small rooms in the Endicott Building in St. Paul, and Economics Laboratory, Inc., was in business.

His first product, designed for carpet cleaning, was named Absorbit. By using it, hotel owners could have their carpets cleaned and their rooms back in service within a matter of hours. His earliest employees were George Meixner, a burly man who mixed the cleaning formula in a mortar box, and two young girls who made evening sales calls to hotels. If a manager agreed to buy Absorbit, the girls provided the first cleaning that very night.

While Absorbit did catch on, the volume of use was relatively low. Osborn switched his attention to the home market, developing a strong cleaner he named Soilax. The early success from his two cleaning products attracted the attention of local investors, and soon Osborn had the capital he needed to expand his company.

Larger quarters and better equipment were secured. Osborn was soon joined by his two sons, Edward B. and Stephen A. Osborn. Young Edward, known as E.B., became sales manager and revolutionized the company's marketing plans. Soon, the company was serving the restaurant market, where its dishwashing soap, under the label Electrasol, became especially popular.

Merritt J. Osborn died on January 16, 1960, at the age of 80. His son, E.B., assumed the post of president and led the company through further growth, including the establishment of dairy and food processing markets. The company, which had gone public in 1957, changed its name to ECOLAB, Inc., in 1986.

Today, the St. Paul–based company employs more than 13,500 people worldwide and has annual sales of more than $2.2 billion.

SOURCE: *Economics Laboratory, Inc.: The First Forty Years,* ECOLAB, Inc., 1964

George S. Parker

[Parker Pen Company]

George Parker left his family's Iowa farm to study telegraphy at a small school in Janesville, Wisconsin. The school soon offered its prize student a teaching position. Young Parker supplemented his modest salary by selling pens to his students. Frustrated with the poor quality, Parker designed and patented his own ink pen and launched the Parker Pen Company.

George Safford Parker was born on November 1, 1863, in Shullsburg, Wisconsin. His parents, of English descent, migrated by covered wagon from New England to Fayette, Iowa, where young Parker grew up on the family farm. When not planting, harvesting, or tending to other farm chores, Parker completed school and attended Upper Iowa University.

While in college, Parker developed an interest in pursuing a railroad career. An advertisement for the Valentine School of Telegraphy in Janesville, Wisconsin, caught his eye, so he saved up the $55 tuition and moved to Janesville. He excelled in his studies and within one year was given a job teaching classes. To supplement his low salary, Parker became a distributor for a Cincinnati fountain pen company.

Many of Parker's pen customers were also his students, and when the pens malfunctioned, which they frequently did, Parker felt obligated to repair them. Even though he was not formally trained, he soon learned how to take one apart, diagnose the problem, and make the proper repairs. As word spread that Parker could be counted on to fix the pens he sold, other students started buying them. This, in turn, led to even more repair work for Parker.

Frustrated with the poor quality of pens, Parker decided to design a pen that wouldn't require significant maintenance. With his scroll saw, files, and other tools, he was able to fashion a reliable ink feeder and holder. The 26-year-old Parker invested $85 to obtaining a patent, which was awarded on December 10, 1889.

At first, Parker subcontracted the manufacture of his pens to another company. Although it didn't yield high profit margins, he was happy to sell pens that were not only reliable, but also had *George S. Parker* stamped on them. Living in a boardinghouse, he was able to expand his sideline business by enticing the traveling salesmen who passed through town to add Parker pens to their product lines.

One such businessman was W. F. Palmer, an insurance salesman who approached Parker about a policy. Parker couldn't afford insurance, but the discussion turned to Parker's fountain pens, which intrigued Palmer. The two men struck a deal to establish a company to manufacture and sell the pens. Since Parker didn't have any capital, he sold one-half interest in his patent to Palmer, who made out the $1,000 check to The Parker Pen Company.

George Parker married Martha M. Clemens on November 23, 1892, and the couple had three children, Russell, Kenneth, and Virginia. The company grew steadily in the following years, during which Parker introduced several clever improvements. In 1898, while the Spanish-American War raged, Parker was granted a patent for an outer cap that slipped snugly over the barrel. One year later, he patented a jointless pen that addressed the problem of ink leakage.

In 1904, Parker introduced his most important product: the self-filling Parker Fountain Pen. Prior to this, pens had to be filled with eyedroppers. This new device used a special lever that allowed the ink to be drawn into the chamber. This was complemented with other improvements, such as the "spearhead feed" that prevented excess ink from flowing onto the writing point.

During World War I, Parker devised a special pen that was used by soldiers in the field. The pen handle contained a chamber in which "ink tablets" were stored. When they wanted to use the pen, they dropped a tablet into the pen barrel and filled it with water. After the war, however, sales at The Parker Pen Company started to decline.

A Parker salesman from Spokane, Washington, suggested that Parker make an oversize fountain pen that would hold a considerable reserve of ink. Further, he suggested that it sell for about $7.00, well above the $2.75 average pen cost. The salesman even suggested a name: the Parker Duofold. The pen quickly carried the company to international prominence.

By the early 1930s, George Parker assumed the role of chairman and elevated his son, Russell, to the position of president. Russell had joined the company in 1914 and worked his way through ranks. His brother, Kenneth, started working at Parker Pen in 1919, having first worked at the advertising agency Lord & Thomas. The founder's grandsons, Daniel and George, also joined the family business.

Tragically, Russell Parker died in early 1933, and George never fully recovered from the grief over the loss of his son. George Safford Parker died on July 19, 1937. Today, Parker Pen is a subsidiary of The Gillette Company, which, through its Paper Mate, Parker, and Waterman product lines, is the world's leading supplier of writing instruments. Parker pens are still manufactured in Janesville, Wisconsin.

SOURCE: Parker Pen Company archives

Antonio Pasin

[Radio Flyer]

Following in the footsteps of his father and grandfather, Antonio Pasin became a skilled wood craftsman near his hometown of Venice, Italy. His dream of pursuing opportunities in America was made possible when his family sold their mule to pay for his trip.

Arriving in Chicago penniless, 16-year-old Pasin worked several jobs, from water boy for a sewer-digging crew to piano finisher. Eventually, he accumulated enough woodworking equipment to begin making small wooden wagons for children. Working from a rented one-room shop, he made wagons each night and peddled them the next day.

Eventually, Pasin earned enough money to hire an assistant. In 1923, he organized his venture as the Liberty Coaster Company, named in honor of the Statue of Liberty. Seven years later, he incorporated the company as the Radio Steel & Manufacturing Company.

By the late 1920s, Pasin borrowed the metal-stamping technology from the automotive industry that enabled him to mass-produce stamped-steel wagon bodies. Following the lead of one of his heroes, Henry Ford, Pasin developed an efficient production line that rivaled any Ford plant.

Pasin's company weathered the Depression surprisingly well. In fact, even at the depths of the Depression, the factory produced 1,500 wagons daily. Pasin participated in the 1933 World's Fair by building a 45-foot-tall "Coaster Boy" exhibit, depicting a child kneeling in one of his wagons. The exhibit brought international attention to his company and a significant increase in orders.

World War II presented the company with a challenge. Most of the basic parts of Pasin's wagons were made with steel, which became an essential material for the war effort and, therefore, was in short supply. To compensate, Pasin landed a military contract to build a familiar piece of military equipment—the "Blitz Can"—the 5-gallon fuel cans that were mounted on the backs of Jeeps, trucks, and tanks.

After the war, Americans enthusiastically migrated into the suburbs to start new lives. Neighborhoods filled with children began to spring up around every city in the country, and Pasin worked hard to put a wagon in every driveway. At the same time, Pasin's son Mario graduated from Notre Dame and joined the family business. He spotted another interesting trend—lawns. Soon, the company was manufacturing a line of garden carts and wheelbarrows.

Throughout his life, Pasin provided job opportunities for people in the Chicago area as well as his native Italy. Many immigrants were not only given jobs at his factory, but were given interest-free loans to buy homes and even provided with tutors to help them learn English.

In 1987, the company took the name of its most popular product, Radio Flyer. Today, the company is owned and managed by three of Pasin's grandchildren. They continue to produce new wagons that combine the Radio Flyer tradition with the demands of the 1990s.

SOURCE: Radio Flyer, Inc., archives

Stanley C. Pearle

[Pearle Vision Center]

Stanley C. Pearle was born in 1918 in Pittsburgh, Pennsylvania, one of three boys, including an older brother, Lester, and a twin brother, Merle, who, like Stanley, is also an optometrist. Pearle graduated from high school in 1936 during the Great Depression and went to work as a sales trainee for Grafner Brothers, a Pittsburgh wholesale jeweler that was partly owned by Pearle's scoutmaster.

The job required Pearle to travel to jewelry stores throughout western Pennsylvania. In those days, many jewelry stores had optical departments staffed by optometrists, and Pearle became intrigued with the profession. He decided to attend optometry school, despite his boss's offer to double his salary if he stayed with the company.

Pearle worked his way through the Northern Illinois College of Optometry in Chicago, attending classes in the morning while working the night shift as a hotel clerk. Upon graduation in 1940, he returned to Pennsylvania and sat for the State Board of Optometry exam. However, he learned it would take two months to learn the results of the test—an eternity for an ambitious young man—so a fellow optometrist candidate and he scraped together the money to take a train to Texas, where they could receive their test results one day after completing the three-day exam.

After successfully passing the exam, Pearle immediately launched his career in Texas, where he remained even after learning that he passed the Pennsylvania exam. He did return to Pittsburgh long enough to marry his high school sweetheart, Elsie Cohen. The couple eventually had four children and remained happily married until Elsie's death in 1996.

In 1943, Dr. Pearle entered the U.S. Navy for a tour of duty. When World War II ended in 1945, he returned to private practice in Corpus Christi, Texas. He joined Lee Optical as a junior partner in 1948 and remained with them for ten years, during which time he helped open stores throughout southern Texas.

In 1958, the 40-year-old optometrist decided it was time to start his own optical company. His goal was to build attractive, modern optical stores in convenient locations, offering a good selection of high-quality products and services at competitive prices. This concept of one-stop total eye care came to life in 1961 with the opening of the first Pearle Vision Center in Savannah, Georgia, a site selected because it offered less competition than Texas.

The number of Pearle Vision Center stores grew rapidly through the 1960s and 1970s as optical advertising regulations eased and fashionable eyeware styles emerged. Pearle Vision quickly dominated the optical retail industry as the only national chain that advertised on national television. The organization began franchising stores in the 1980s and continued to grow by opening new stores and acquiring several large companies, including Rogers Optical in Pennsylvania, Hillman Kohan in New Jersey, and the Eyelab superstores.

Today, Pearle has nearly 700 locations in the United States, with the typical store featuring from 500 to 1,300 frames. Ownership has changed over the years, and in 1996 Pearle was acquired by Cole National Corporation of Cleveland, Ohio, a company focused on the optical retail business. Dr. Stanley Pearle continues to serve as an active consultant to the company. Over the past few years, he has become prominently featured in Pearle Vision advertising and merchandising, which has brought him celebrity status.

SOURCE: Pearle, Inc., archives

Richard S. Perkin, Charles W. Elmer

[The Perkin-Elmer Corporation]

Richard Scott Perkin was born on October 17, 1906, in Brooklyn, New York, the first of three children born to Richard W. and Mary Perkin. The elder Perkin was enthusiastic about the impact of technology on society and frequently lectured on the historical significance of science. When young Richard Perkin was nine years old, his parents presented him with a telescope—a gift that would shape his life.

Throughout his childhood, Perkin showed inventive genius. The telescope supported his fascination with astronomy, and soon he was fashioning more powerful homemade telescopes. His scientific interests led him to build a telephone system and even to mix up a batch or two of trinitrotoluene, better known as TNT. He was also a ham radio enthusiast and built much of his own equipment.

In 1924, Perkin enrolled at the famed Pratt Institute, but family finances and the death of his father forced him to withdraw after only one year. He then held a number of jobs, including electronics repairman, lineman, and office assistant. In the late 1920s he worked in various positions in New York's Wall Street district. During this time he met Gladys F. Talmage. The couple married in 1930 and eventually had four children.

The Great Depression played havoc with Wall Street during the early 1930s, and Perkin started considering other careers. He never lost his love for astronomy, and while attending a meeting of world-renowned astronomers at Harvard in 1936, Perkin decided he could earn a living from his hobby. Coincidentally, he bumped into an old friend, Charles Elmer, who felt the same way.

Charles Wesley Elmer was born on May 22, 1872, in Nelson, New York, the son of Theodore and Josephine (Darrow) Elmer. As a young adult, Elmer worked for the railroad, a job that led him to Panama. In 1898, he married May Custer, a niece of the famed General George Custer. The couple moved to New York City, where Elmer became a court recorder.

One evening, the Elmers were strolling in Manhattan when they dropped 10¢ in a vendor's sidewalk telescope and gazed into the sky. Intrigued with Saturn's rings, the couple spent more and more time with their hobby. They moved to Long Island, which afforded a better view of the sky, and filled their home with telescopes. Elmer became active with other amateur astronomers at The Brooklyn Institute of Arts and Sciences, where he befriended Richard Perkin.

Even though Perkin was 30 years old and Elmer was 64, neither seemed to care. As they conversed at the Harvard conference, it became clear that both were interested in filling the void of American optics' manufacturers. With a handshake, they decided to change that. Each man put up $5,000, another $10,000 was borrowed, and Perkin-Elmer was launched.

In 1938, they mailed a 16-page booklet, titled *How Optical Consulting May Help You,* to potential clients. Soon they were doing work for clients such as the National Geographic Society, Fairchild Aerial Camera Company, and Pioneer Instruments, a manufacturer of gunsights.

Not long after World War II erupted, government buyers visited Perkin and Elmer. The immense volume of military work forced the company to find new manufacturing space, and they moved to Glenbrook, Connecticut. When the war ended, the company had a healthy backlog of orders, but the founders knew the loss of military contracts would be painful.

Perkin-Elmer turned its attention to the business, medical, and academic markets. Nearly every field of technology was adapting to a growing consumer and educational market, and the founders uncovered considerable opportunities, especially when the space exploration program grew.

Charles Wesley Elmer died on December 7, 1954, at the age of 82. Perkin continued to lead the company into new markets throughout the world. Richard Scott Perkin died on May 22, 1969, at the age of 62. Today The Perkin-Elmer Corporation has annual sales of about $1.2 billion.

SOURCES: The Perkin-Elmer Corporation archives; Thomas Fahy *Richard S. Perkin and The Perkin-Elmer Corporation,* The Perkin-Elmer Corporation, 1987

H. Ross Perot

[Electronic Data Systems, Inc.]

Henry Ross Perot was born on June 27, 1930, at Texarkana, Texas, one of two children born to Gabriel Ross and Lulu M. (Ray) Perot. His birth name was actually Henry Ray Perot, but because an older brother named Ross died and his parents wanted to keep the name Ross in the family, they changed Henry Ray to Henry Ross.

Perot's family descended from French traders. His great-grandfather had drifted into Texas from Louisiana before the Civil War and established a general store. His grandfather, too, was an active merchant as well as a cotton trader, and his father Gabriel was also in the cotton business in Texarkana.

As a boy, Perot held a variety of jobs, including breaking horses, selling Christmas cards and magazines, buying and selling horses and calves, and delivering newspapers. He attended Texarkana Junior College and, being both patriotic and practical, later got an appointment to the U.S. Naval Academy, where *they* paid *him* to attend college. Upon graduation in 1953, Ensign Perot was assigned to the USS *Sigourney* and, within two years, was elevated to chief engineer.

In 1956, Perot married Margot Birmingham, and the couple eventually had five children. One year later, his tour of duty ended and Perot landed a job in Dallas with IBM. There, Perot quickly emerged as a top salesman of computer systems. In fact, it is rumored that he was so successful that a new commission structure was instituted, which discouraged Perot.

Perot became convinced that he could start his own business and provide software development services to owners of large IBM equipment. With $1,000 from his wife's savings account, he launched Electronic Data Systems Corporation (EDS) on June 27, 1962, his 32nd birthday. He was able to land a consulting contract with Blue Cross/Blue Shield of Texas, which provided him with office space. He handled their work each morning, then spent the afternoon chasing new business.

After making nearly 100 calls, Perot discovered that Collins Radio Company in Cedar Rapids, Iowa, needed additional computer access. Perot contacted an insurance company he had worked with at IBM, that had excess capacity and struck a deal. In four months, Perot was able to pocket $100,000 for his service.

In February 1963, Perot landed a contract with the Frito-Lay company for programming services, and the EDS concept was quickly proven successful. By the following year, the firm had 15 employees, four major accounts, and revenues of $500,000. Four years later, he made his first public stock offering.

Perot sold EDS to General Motors in 1984 for $2.5 billion and was appointed to the automaker's board of directors, but Perot resigned two years later after GM purchased his remaining holdings for $700 million. Two years after that, he launched Perot Systems, which today has grown to nearly 4,300 employees and annual revenues of nearly $350 million.

In 1992, Perot became a third-party candidate for the presidency of the United States. His supporters came together under an organization called United We Stand, and Perot received nearly 20 percent of the popular vote. His bid in the 1996 presidential race also fell short, but his impact on American business and politics have been legendary. With his typical patriotic candor, Perot summed up his life: "In 1936, I didn't think I could own a car. In 1986, I was the largest shareholder in General Motors. That's the kind of thing that can happen in America."

SOURCES: Todd Mason, *Perot,* Business One Irwin, Homewood, Illinois, 1990; *Colliers Encyclopedia,* 1996; *Ross Perot for President,* biography

Joseph N. Pew

[Sun Oil Company]

The first members of the Pew family immigrated to Virginia in the early 1600s, settling near Jamestown and Williamsburg. The family moved westward into West Virginia, and eventually some members settled in western Pennsylvania. John and Elizabeth Pew, along with their 15 children, were among the earliest settlers in Mercer, Pennsylvania.

One of his sons, also named John, married Nancy Glenn and established a farm about two miles south of Mercer, where they raised their ten children. Their youngest son, Joseph Newton Pew, was born on July 25, 1848. Throughout his childhood, he worked with his brothers and sisters on the family farm. The Pew family held strong antislavery sentiments and participated in the so-called underground railroad. Young Joseph was frequently called upon to help with a midnight dinner or a wagon ride to the north.

After attending college at nearby Edinboro, Pennsylvania, Pew taught school and opened up a real estate venture in Mercer. Soon he set his sights higher, moving to nearby Titusville, Pennsylvania, still bustling from the town's oil boom ten years earlier. Pew established a real estate, insurance, and loan business and within two years built a small $40,000 fortune. He married Mary Catherine Anderson, and the couple eventually had five children.

As Pew's business reputation grew, he became more active with local investments. Unfortunately, some of his oil ventures proved costly, and in 1875 he not only lost all of his money, he fell deeply in debt. Discouraged but not beaten, he moved to Bradford, Pennsylvania, the following year and became involved in natural gas wells. He found success once more and retired all his debts.

In 1877, Pew and Edward Emerson, a Titusville banker, organized the Keystone Gas Company and supplied Olean, New York, with natural gas. Encouraged by the success, they launched the Penn Fuel Company to pipe natural gas from Murrysville, Pennsylvania, to nearby Pittsburgh. As a result, Pittsburgh was the first major American city to be supplied with natural gas for home and industrial use.

Pew and Emerson sold Penn Fuel to a group led by George Westinghouse in 1883, but they organized another utility, the Peoples Natural Gas Company, which continues to serve the Pittsburgh region today. By the mid-1880s, Pew and Emerson were highly respected businessmen with diverse energy interests. Not surprisingly, the discovery of oil and natural gas near Lima, Ohio, attracted their attention.

In 1886, Pew and Emerson paid $4,500 for two oil leases near Lima. The venture became successful, and in 1889 they incorporated the Sun Oil Line Company to acquire pipelines, leases, storage tanks, and tank cars. One year later, they incorporated their oil drilling and refining activities under the name Sun Oil Company of Ohio.

In the late 1890s, Emerson sold all his interests to Pew, who accelerated the growth of the company. Sun Oil Company of New Jersey was launched in 1901. To support activities in the east, Pew purchased land in Marcus Hook, Pennsylvania (near Philadelphia), and established a major refinery. He also purchased oil-producing property in Texas, and he expanded into other products, such as petroleum asphalt.

Joseph Newton Pew suffered a major heart attack at his office and died at his desk on October 10, 1912, at the age of 64. His 30-year-old son, John Howard Pew, was promptly elected president. Over the subsequent decades, Sunoco grew into one of the world's most successful energy companies.

SOURCE: Sun, Inc., archives

Frank Phillips, Lee E. Phillips

[Phillips Petroleum]

Frank Phillips was born on November 28, 1873, in Greeley County, Nebraska, to Lewis and Lucinda Phillips. When a grasshopper infestation forced them from their family farm, Lewis moved his family to southwestern

Iowa. On a trip into Creston, the Union County seat, young Frank spotted one of the town's barbers wearing the flashy, striped pants that were popular during that era, and he declared that someday he'd make enough money to wear pants like that every day.

He decided to make it cutting hair, and at the age of 14 he became an apprentice barber. Soon he was one of the town's more popular barbers and was able to buy his own shop. Not long after that, he owned all three of the town's barbershops and was able to wear striped pants every day. He was also able to afford marriage and exchanged vows with Jane Gibson in 1897.

At the urging of his father-in-law, Phillips started selling bonds throughout the New England and Chicago regions. While returning from a business trip in 1903, Phillips visited the St. Louis Exposition and bumped into an old friend who was serving as a missionary to the Indians in Oklahoma. He shared glowing reports of the booming oil industry and the immense fortunes that were being made.

Later that year, Phillips and his father-in-law visited Bartlesville, Oklahoma, and were so impressed with the opportunities that they and Phillips's younger brother, Lee Eldas Phillips, launched the Anchor Oil and Gas Company. After selling considerable stock, the company drilled its first well in 1905, hitting a small but encouraging pocket of oil and gas. The next two wells were dry.

With the company nearly out of money, the fourth well, Anna Anderson Number 1, proved to be a gusher. It was the first of 80 consecutive producing wells, and money was no longer an issue. The brothers launched another oil venture, named the Lewcinda Oil Company, and established the Citizen's Bank and Trust in Bartlesville.

The Phillips brothers continued to increase both their oil and bank holdings, but they were more interested in banking. Just as they were about to sell off their oil and gas holdings, World War I erupted. The subsequent demand for oil drove prices (and profits) quite high, and they decided to remain in the energy business. In 1917, they consolidated their holdings—$3 million in assets and 27 employees—under an umbrella corporation named the Phillips Petroleum Company.

By 1921, the company owned or had a partnership in more than 900 producing wells. Three years later, Phillips had become the country's largest producer of natural gas liquids, with assets of over $100 million. As the country moved through the 1920s, the Phillips brothers felt a change was near. Henry Ford had sold 15 million Model Ts, and the brothers didn't want to lose an opportunity.

In November 1927, the Phillips brothers opened their first refinery. Eighteen days later, their very first service station opened in Wichita, Kansas. They selected the trade name Phillips 66 for their gasoline. There are many legends about the choice, but the most reliable seems to trace back to a discussion about the power of the fuel. An employee remarked that the car he was riding in (tanked up with Phillips gasoline) was doing 60 miles per hour, to which another replied, "Sixty, nothing, we're doing sixty-six!" The incident happened near Tulsa on Highway 66.

The brothers were so encouraged by the results of their first service station that they quickly opened three more. By the end of 1928 they had 1,800 service stations, and two years later the number had soared to nearly 7,000. They also diversified into the propane market, and by 1929 they were servicing 8,000 customers. Despite the financial devastation of the Great Depression, the Phillips brothers were able to survive and restore the company to profitability.

Frank Phillips retired as chairman of the board in 1949 and died a year later at the age of 76. Today the company has annual revenues in excess of $13 billion and employs more than 17,000 people worldwide.

SOURCE: Phillips Petroleum archives; *Phillips: The First 66 Years,* 1983

Frank N. Piasecki

[Piasecki Aircraft Company]

Frank Nicholas Piasecki was born on October 24, 1919, in Philadelphia, Pennsylvania, to Nikodem and Emilia Piasecki. After attending public school in Philadelphia, he studied mechanical engineering at the Towne School of the University of Pennsylvania while working at the Kellet Autogyro Company and the Aero Service Corporation. In 1940, he earned a B.S. in aeronautical engineering from the Guggenheim School of Aeronautics of New York University.

Upon graduation, Piasecki became a designer at Platt-LePage Aircraft Corporation, then later became an aerodynamicist for the Aircraft Division of the Edward G. Budd Manufacturing Company. During these years he founded and headed the PV-Engineering Forum, a research group that focused on vertical takeoff and landing (VTOL) aircraft, better known as helicopters. He piloted the group's PV-2 in 1943, which was only the second successful helicopter to fly in America.

The technical advances made by the group caught the attention of the U.S. Navy, which awarded Piasecki a contract for the construction of his proposed tandem helicopter capable of carrying large payloads in a big, enclosed cabin. In March 1945, he produced the first tandem rotor helicopter, which quickly became nicknamed "the Flying Banana."

In 1946, the PV-Engineering Forum was reorganized as the Piasecki Helicopter Corporation, and Piasecki was named chairman and president. The company then introduced a series of new helicopters for the U.S. Army, Navy, and Air Force; the Royal Canadian Navy and Air Force; and the French Navy.

The Piasecki Helicopter Corporation was eventually sold to the Boeing Airplane Company and was renamed the Vertol Division. After the sale, Piasecki and his colleagues formed the Piasecki Aircraft Corporation to continue with research and development of new VTOL aircraft. By 1966, one of the company's experimental helicopters recorded the amazing speed of 225 miles per hour.

Piasecki introduced the Heli-Stat in 1986, a hybrid dynamic-static heavy-lift craft that at the time was the largest flying aircraft ever built. As recently as

1994 he was working on improvements of the AH-64 Apache and the AH-1W SuperCobra helicopters.

Piasecki was the first man in history to qualify with the Civil Aeronautics Administration (now the Federal Aviation Administration) as a helicopter pilot before receiving his fixed-wing pilot's license. To date, he has been awarded 22 patents for products and improvements in VTOL aircraft technology. In 1958, Piasecki married Vivian O'Gara Weyerhaeuser. The couple has two daughters and five sons.

SOURCE: Piasecki Aircraft Company archives

Arthur H. Pitney, Walter H. Bowes

[Pitney Bowes Corporation]

After working independently for many years to develop and gain approval for an automatic postage-stamping machine, Arthur Pitney and Walter Bowes were introduced to one another at the recommendation of the post office. Working together, the inventive Pitney and the flamboyant Bowes were able to establish Pitney Bowes Corporation as the most successful postage metering company in the world.

Arthur H. Pitney was born in 1882. By the time he reached adulthood, he was convinced there was a market for a machine that would automatically apply postage stamps to envelopes. In 1902, he was granted his first patent on his double-locking, hand-cranked "postage stamp device" and launched a company called the Pitney Postal Machine Company. The following year, he convinced the United States Post Office to review his machine.

Confident that the post office would embrace his device and approve the concept of metered mail, he rented larger office quarters and started to promote the idea to businesses. However, he would soon be disappointed. The post office decided to seek the advice of the U.S. attorney general to make sure they had jurisdiction to approve the matter. The following year, the postmaster announced that bulk mailings of identical pieces of mail could be sent using bulk permits instead of stamps. But nothing was said of Pitney's machine.

More time passed, and Pitney took a job with a wallpaper company to support his family. There were false alarms and false hopes, but with each new promise came another delay. In 1910, Pitney renamed the firm the American Postage Meter Company and launched another attempt at approval, but the venture only ended in disappointment.

Walter Harold Bowes was born in 1882, one of twelve children born to Thomas Bowes and his wife in England. In 1893, the family immigrated to Boston, and Walter grew to be an adventurous young man, mixing a successful career in sales with a passion for sports, such as sailing. He frequently consummated deals at a considerable profit, only to spend the money during a period of intense recreation.

In 1909, Bowes was offered a business that manufactured check-endorsing machines. With $1,000 down payment, he purchased the Universal Stamping Machine Company and proceeded to build up the business while he developed a second product—a machine that the post office could use to cancel postage stamps. He later identified another attractive market—developing a machine that could both affix and cancel postage automatically.

In 1918, a former post office employee named Harry Seger, who was working with Pitney, had a discussion with a newly appointed assistant postmaster general about the virtues of Pitney's machine. Seger was told of a company in New York City run by a man named Bowes who would be interested in Pitney's work. The same man conveyed a similar suggestion to Bowes regarding Pitney.

Arthur Pitney made his first visit to Bowes's facility in Stamford, Connecticut, in October 1919. The two agreed to form Pitney Bowes Postage Meter Company, which would be based in Connecticut since Bowes already had a manufacturing company in place. Finally, on September 1, 1920, after nearly 18 years of effort on the part of Arthur Pitney, the U.S. Post Office opened the door for private postage meter companies.

Within two years, the U.S. Post Office was selling $4 million in postage through Pitney Bowes equipment. That same year, the company launched expansion into international markets. Arthur Pitney died on September 18, 1933. Walter Bowes died on June 24, 1957. Today, Pitney Bowes continues to be the dominant company in metered postage equipment, with annual sales well in excess of $3 billion.

SOURCES: Pitney Bowes, Inc., archives; William Cahn, *The Story of Pitney-Bowes*

Ralph L. Polk

[R.L. Polk & Company]

Ralph Lane Polk was born in 1849 at Bellefointaine, Ohio, the youngest of seven children born to Reverend David Polk Jr. and Mary Charlotte Polk. His father died eight years after his birth, and his mother moved the family to Trenton, New Jersey.

When he was 14, Polk quit school to help support the family. One year later, in 1865, he enlisted as a drummer boy with the Union forces and was present at the battle of Petersburg, the fall of Richmond, and the surrender at Appomattox. After the Civil War, Polk took a variety of jobs. While selling medicine, he met a man who was collecting names and addresses for a city directory. The work appealed to him, and he became an enumerator for $2 per day.

By 1870, Polk had worked for several publishers and settled in Detroit, Michigan. He wanted to establish a railroad directory that would serve all the towns along the Detroit-Milwaukee Railway. He formed a partnership with Nathan Burch, and subsequently Burch & Polk produced a city directory for

Evansville, Indiana. In 1871 they produced a directory for Lafayette, Indiana, and in 1872 they published a directory for towns along the Toledo, Wabash, & Western Railway.

At age 23, Polk was building a lucrative publishing business. He purchased half interest in the J.W. Weeks & Company directory for Detroit. Several years later, in 1885, R.L. Polk & Company was formally incorporated, and the directories were thereafter published under the Polk Company name.

Polk proceeded to acquire interests in several other directory publishers throughout the United States. Eventually, R.L. Polk & Company became one of the largest city-directory publishers in the world.

Ralph Lane Polk died in 1923 from complications of pneumonia. He was succeeded by his son, Ralph L. Polk II, who had joined the company in 1900 at the age of 18.

SOURCE: R.L. Polk Company archives

Kenneth N. Pontikes

[Comdisco, Inc.]

Kenneth N. Pontikes was born in 1940 in Chicago, Illinois, the son of Greek immigrants who operated a modest grocery store on the city's south side. He graduated in 1963 from Southern Illinois University with a B.A. degree in economics and marketing.

Upon graduation from college, Pontikes went to work for the Information Records Division of the IBM Corporation, where he sold punch-card tabulating machines. In the five years that he worked for IBM, he noticed that business organizations were interested in staying on top of the rapidly growing computer technology, but they were reluctant to commit large amounts of money to equipment that was quickly obsolete.

Pontikes decided that a broker/dealer of used computer equipment could find a market niche. In 1969, at the age of 29, he borrowed $5,000 from his father and launched the Computer Discount Corporation (later renamed Comdisco, Inc.).

By 1971, Comdisco generated annual revenue in excess of $5 million with a staff of only six people working in two rooms furnished with used office furniture. Soon, Comdisco was the largest dealer of used IBM equipment in the entire country. Over the next several years, Pontikes noticed that businesses were more inclined to lease equipment, which further reduced their capital commitment. By the late 1970s, Comdisco was not only providing the equipment, but was also writing the leases.

In the 1980s, Comdisco started leasing non-IBM equipment. At first, the company focused on telecommunications equipment, but later added computer equipment built by other manufacturers. By the end of the 1980s, approximately half of the company's income was derived from non-IBM products.

Recognizing another opportunity, Comdisco entered the disaster-recovery market, soon becoming the leader, re-creating the flow of information within and among organizations, primarily through subscription-based recovery services and fee-based consulting services.

Kenneth Pontikes was diagnosed with colon cancer in 1993. He died on June 24, 1994, at the age of 54, and was survived by his wife, Lynne, and three children. Today, Comdisco has annual revenues exceeding $2 billion and more than 2,000 employees.

SOURCE: Comdisco, Inc., archives

Leonard P. Pool

[Air Products and Chemicals, Inc.]

Leonard Parker Pool was born on November 5, 1906, in Minneapolis, Minnesota, eldest child of Leonard J. and Emma E. (Ludford) Pool. His father was employed in various railroad positions, requiring the family to move frequently. They moved to Deer Lodge, Montana, where Emma Pool, in her 40s, gave birth to two more children. They next moved to Meadville, Pennsylvania, where Emma had yet another child.

Young Leonard proved to be a good student. However, after he entered high school in 1920, his father's health deteriorated, and Leonard had to help support the family. He eventually dropped out of school and went to work on the Erie Railroad, where he was introduced to the new metalworking skills of oxyacetylene cutting and welding.

In 1925, Leonard's father died with essentially no estate, leaving the young man responsible for the support of the family. The family returned to Minneapolis, where Leonard found work, first at a service station repairing automobiles, then as a salesman for the Pillsbury Flour Company. When offered his choice of sales territories, Pool selected Detroit because it was home to a growing automobile industry, and in his estimation, autoworkers would eat a lot of pancakes.

Pool was still attracted to the welding industry and soon joined the Dockson Company in Detroit, which assembled and sold welding equipment made from components manufactured elsewhere. He experimented with other ventures, including a junkyard, then went to work for another company selling welding and cutting equipment. He also married Dorothy Rider, a French teacher in the Detroit school system.

As the Great Depression subsided, Pool once again focused on his own business. In 1936, after raising about $78,000, he launched the Acetylene Gas and Supply Company. From his small warehouse, he purchased oxygen from major suppliers and resold it in used tanks to small welding and machine shops. Soon, the company built an impressive client list and accepted a buyout offer from Compressed Industrial Gases.

While looking for a new opportunity, Pool struck upon a novel idea in 1939. Major manufacturers were using oxygen and other gases that were generated at the centrally located plants of major oxygen providers. Pool conceived a system that would generate oxygen at each customer's plant site, thereby avoiding the costly shipping charges. The plan would produce two revenue streams—one from the leases for the oxygen-producing plant and one from the sale of oxygen that was produced.

In 1940, Pool incorporated the Industrial Gas Equipment Company, which later that year was changed to Air Products. Pool accepted various contract jobs, boosted by World War II, which provided a cash flow to support the development of his oxygen plants. He also moved the company, first to Chattanooga, Tennessee, then to the Lehigh Valley region of Pennsylvania.

Pool took the company public in 1946, and Wall Street was intrigued with his idea for developing oxygen-generating plants on-site at the manufacturers' facilities. He started placing the equipment in a host of settings, from Ohio valley steel mills to foreign countries. Leonard, joined by his brother, George, accelerated his marketing efforts and, by the mid-1950s, was a dominant force in the market. In the following decade, the company moved into the chemicals market, which was reflected in its name change to Air Products and Chemicals.

George Pool died in 1973. Two years later, on December 27, 1975, Leonard Pool died. Today, Air Products and Chemicals has annual revenues of nearly $4 billion.

SOURCES: Air Products and Chemicals, Inc., archives; Andrew Butrica, *Out of Thin Air: A History of Air Products and Chemicals, Inc.*, Praeger Publishing, 1990 (copyright by Air Products and Chemicals)

Charles W. Post

[Postum Cereal]

Charles William Post was born on October 26, 1854, in Springfield, Illinois. Upon graduation from high school, he took military courses at the University of Illinois and later helped maintain order in Chicago while it was under martial law following the great fire of 1871.

As a young man, Post entered the hardware business in Independence, Kansas, and later traveled several western states selling agricultural equipment. He served as a plant manager for a farm implement factory in Kansas City and eventually helped organize the Springfield Plow Works in his native Illinois.

His ventures took both a physical and financial toll. In 1891, he traveled to Michigan where he was admitted to Kellogg's famous Battle Creek Sanitarium. To settle his accounts, the 37-year-old Post, broken both physically and financially, auctioned off his personal belongings on the steps of Battle Creek's city hall.

While recovering at the sanitarium, Post was served a caramel-flavored breakfast drink developed by Dr. John H. Kellogg. When his health was restored the following year, Post elected to remain in Battle Creek. His creativity was also restored, and he was able to structure a deal to purchase a nearby 15-acre farm and open his own modest sanatorium called La Vita Inn. Convinced of its health value and market potential, Post experimented with his own cereal drink.

By January 1895, Post had perfected his beverage. He spent about $70 to obtain the necessary equipment and supplies, including wheat, bran, and molasses, to launch his venture on a small barn on his property. He took his first batch of Postum cereal to the largest grocery store in Grand Rapids, where he was promptly dismissed. Eventually, Post convinced the grocer to accept a case on consignment, which quickly sold.

The value of the company reached nearly $40,000 by the fall of 1896, when Post officially named his venture the Postum Cereal Company. Post was happy with the progress of the company, but noted the product's cyclical nature. He decided that a granulated food that he made for himself, baked like breadsticks and then dried and ground in a coffee grinder, might sell well in the summer. By the following year, he introduced Grape-Nuts, so named because he felt that grape-sugar was formed in the baking process and that the product had a nutty taste.

By 1906 the company had undergone tremendous growth. Nearly 600 people worked at the cereal plant. Revenue was brisk, and Post purchased a tract of 200,000 acres of land in Garza County, Texas, near Lubbock, which became the foundation for the city of Post. That same year, he introduced a new cornflake cereal that was originally called Elijah's Manna, but was later changed to Post Toasties.

Charles W. Post died on May 9, 1914, at the age of 59. The ownership of the company passed to his daughter, Marjorie M. Post, who maintained an active role in management and was eventually appointed to the board of directors.

The Postum Company purchased the Jell-O Company in 1925, Baker's Chocolate in 1927, Maxwell House Coffee and Log Cabin Syrup in 1928, and Birds Eye Frozen Foods in 1929. Later in 1929, Postum changed its name to General Foods. General Foods made several subsequent acquisitions, including Oscar Mayer & Company in 1981. By 1989, Philip Morris Companies had acquired both General Foods and Kraft and had merged them into Kraft General Foods, renamed Kraft Foods in 1995.

SOURCE: Kraft Foods, Inc., archives

Harry V. Quadracci

[Quad/Graphics, Inc.]

In 1906, Virgilio Quadracci immigrated to the United States from his native Italy, settling in Racine, Wisconsin. Tragically, his wife and daughter died during a flu epidemic, leaving Virgilio to care for his remaining three small children while working the night shift at a local foundry. Virgilio eventually saved enough money to open a small grocery store, which grew quite successful until forced into bankruptcy during the Great Depression.

Virgilio's son, Harry R. Quadracci, stepped up to help the family. In 1930, at age 16, he established a small printing company in a garage behind his father's store and supplemented the family income by fulfilling local print jobs. Four years later, he sold the printing equipment to another printer, William A. Krueger, and helped him launch W. A. Krueger, Inc., which later became the largest publicly held printing company in America.

Harry's son, Harry V. "Larry" Quadracci, was born in 1936 in an apartment above the grocery store, which the family had been able to restore to profitability. By age six, Quadracci was stocking the shelves of the family store, and at age 15 he went to work part-time at W. A. Krueger.

Upon graduation from high school in Milwaukee in 1954, Quadracci attended Regis College in Denver, Colorado. After earning his B.A. in philosophy three years later, he attended Columbia University School of Law and was granted his Juris Doctor in 1960. He remained at Columbia briefly, then returned to Wisconsin and entered private practice. He soon concluded that business was more exciting than law and went to work once again for the W. A. Krueger printing company.

Quadracci held various positions during his career at W. A. Krueger, and he was eventually named vice president and general manager of the Wisconsin printing division. In 1969, however, he became frustrated by the lack of cooperation between management and labor. Convinced that he could create a more effective work environment, he left the company, mortgaged his house, and launched Quad/Graphics.

His first plant was a 20,000-square-foot building in Pewaukee, Wisconsin, in which he set up a leased printing press and a borrowed binder. Quadracci scoured first the region, then the entire country, to pick up the few jobs that were available. Every time a potential customer visited the plant, the 11 employees quickly fired up the press and looked as busy as possible until the visitor left.

Slowly the jobs picked up. By 1973 employment had doubled to 25 and annual sales were nearly $3 million. Encouraged by the increase in business from throughout the country, Quadracci opened sales offices in New York and Los Angeles two years later. The company that needed to accept any job it could get soon became known as the company that could do anything, and by 1982 employment exceeded 620.

Betty Quadracci, Harry's wife, is the publisher of *Milwaukee Magazine.* The couple has four children.

Quadracci's innovative management style has been heralded by prominent business journalists such as Robert Levering and Milton Moskowitz, authors of *The 100 Best Companies to Work for in America.* At annual company events, it's not unusual to find Quadracci making his entrance on top of an elephant or in front of a marching band. Today, the company has nearly 9,000 employees and annual sales of over $1 billion.

SOURCE: Quad/Graphics archives

Henry G. Reed, Charles E. Barton

[Reed & Barton]

In the early 1800s, Isaac Babbitt operated a small store in Taunton, Massachusetts, repairing watches and selling pewter gifts. As Babbitt's business grew, he renovated a small shed behind his store and started experimenting with various metal alloys.

In 1824, he hit upon a new alloy, called *Britannia,* that proved to be superior to pewter in luster, strength, and durability. Through the success of his Britannia, Babbitt soon outgrew his quarters and acquired another building. He recruited talented artisans, and within ten years his Taunton Britannia Company was producing award-winning silverware.

Two of Babbitt's most talented and committed employees were a metal spinner named Henry G. Reed and a solderer named Charles E. Barton. When Babbitt's venture encountered financial difficulties during the 1830s, these two friends formed a partnership to manage the company. They handled all administrative (and most manufacturing) matters for the firm and marketed their silverware under the Reed & Barton label.

Henry Reed was the driving force of the small company. In all, he worked for the company for 73 years, from 1828 through 1901. He served as president of the firm for 66 of those years. During the 1850s he innovated the electroplating method of silverplating, and in the 1860s he formed a separate food-service division that focused on fine hotels.

The company was nearly dealt a fatal blow with the 1859 discovery of the Comstock lode silver mine. The silver-rich strike was so large that the price of silver actually went down, threatening the value of the high-end Reed & Barton silver products. Rather than discounting prices, however, the company stood firm with its pricing strategy. Discriminating customers remained loyal to Reed & Barton, and the company actually expanded sales throughout the nation at the close of the Civil War.

Reed & Barton, still privately owned, is more than 170 years old, making it one of the oldest companies in America. The company has sales of more than $60 million annually through five operating divisions: Reed & Barton Silversmiths, The Eureka Manufacturing Company, the New England Collectors' Society, Reed & Barton Housewares, and The Sheffield Silver Company.

SOURCE: Reed & Barton archives

Frederick B. Rentschler

[Pratt & Whitney]

Frederick Brant Rentschler was born in Ohio in 1887. After graduating from Princeton in 1909, he returned to Ohio to work in his father's manufacturing plant. When America entered World War I, he enlisted in the U.S. Army and was assigned to supervise aircraft engine manufacturing.

Upon discharge in 1919, he helped organize the Wright Aeronautical Corporation of New Jersey, and was soon appointed president. Despite the success of the venture, the members of Wright's board of directors were reluctant to reinvest profits into research and development, a position that Rentschler found unacceptable. He resigned the post in 1924 to devote all his attention to engine development under more favorable conditions.

Throughout the 1920s, airplanes were constantly being improved and required more and more powerful engines. Curtiss Aeroplane and Motor Corporation and Packard Motor Company were developing new liquid-cooled engines that could deliver nearly 500 horsepower, which was much more impressive than the air-cooled engines. However, Rentschler was convinced he could build a new air-cooled engine that would deliver similar power, but would be lighter in weight than the liquid-cooled engines.

He traveled to Hartford, Connecticut, to visit the facilities of the Pratt & Whitney tool company, which had space available that could be used by Rentschler. The company traced its roots to founders Francis A. Pratt and Amos Whitney (a relative of inventor Eli Whitney). During the early days of the Civil War era, these two craftsmen resigned their positions with Samuel Colt's pistol factory and launched their own machine shop. Over subsequent decades the company built a solid reputation and eventually became a subsidiary of Niles-Bement-Pond.

Rentschler struck a deal with Pratt & Whitney in 1925 to launch the Pratt & Whitney Aircraft Company, which was jointly owned by the existing company and the founding team of Rentschler and George Mead.

Their first engine, dubbed the Wasp by Rentschler's wife, was submitted for Navy testing in 1926 and passed with flying colors. Within six months the engine was being installed in a variety of planes and was soon setting performance records in land planes and seaplanes. With the release of a sister engine, the Hornet, Pratt & Whitney helped elevate the United States to a higher standard of aircraft excellence.

After receiving an initial order for 200 Wasps from the U.S. Navy, Pratt & Whitney engines were soon installed in a variety of planes, including Boeing. To take advantage of opportunities in commercial air service, Rentschler and Edward Boeing orchestrated the 1928 consolidation of Pratt & Whitney, Boeing Airplane Company, Chance Vought Aircraft Corporation, and eventually several other manufacturers. The new organization, the United Aircraft and Transport Corporation, launched a passenger service group named United Air Lines.

The venture was short-lived. In 1934, the federal government ordered the breakup of the company on the grounds that it included both airlines and aircraft manufacturers. As a result, three separate corporations were formed: United Aircraft, the Boeing Airplane Company, and United Air Lines Transport. Rentschler retained the position of chairman of United Aircraft, which changed its name to United Technologies Corporation in 1975.

Frederick Brent Rentschler died in 1956. Today, Pratt & Whitney remains a leading company in the design, manufacture, and support of airplane engines and space propulsion systems. The company has 30,000 employees and annual revenues in excess of $6 billion. Its parent company, United Technologies, is one of the 50 largest corporations in the United States, with annual sales exceeding $22 billion and more than 170,000 employees worldwide.

SOURCE: Pratt & Whitney archives, *The Pratt & Whitney Story*

Richard S. Reynolds

[Reynolds Metals Company]

At the end of the Civil War, a 17-year-old veteran named Abram David Reynolds returned to his homeland in Tennessee and, with his father and brother, Richard J. Reynolds, resumed farming. After the death of their father, Richard moved to North Carolina and established the R. J. Reynolds Tobacco Company. Abram stayed in Tennessee, married Senah Hoge, and started a family.

Richard Samuel Reynolds was born on August 15, 1881, in Bristol, Tennessee, to Abram and Senah Reynolds. After graduating from the University of Virginia in 1902, Richard went to work for his uncle, R. J. Reynolds, who had built a successful tobacco empire. After developing the successful chewing tobacco called Prince Albert, Richard Samuel was prepared to launch a new cigarette that he called Kaiser William, in honor of the German leader, but his uncle R. J. persuaded him to name it Camel instead.

Richard S. Reynolds left the company after ten years for two reasons. First, he wanted to start and build his own company. Second, he was newly married to Julia Louise Parham, and the couple were starting a family that eventually included four sons. He knew that the R. J. Reynolds company would be passed on to his uncle's children, and R. S. wanted to establish something for his own children.

Reynolds moved back to Tennessee and established the Reynolds Corporation to manufacture soap, soap powder, window cleaner, and similar supplies. After his plant burned to the ground, he bought another property in Louisville, Kentucky, and resumed operations. Then World War I broke out and his products were classified as "nonessential," forcing him to close the business. After experimenting with asphalt and waterproof paper products, he turned his attention to aluminum.

Reynolds was familiar with tinfoil from his days with R. J. Reynolds Tobacco. In 1918, using his plant at Louisville, he launched the United States Foil Company and started producing foil for cigarettes, candy, and chewing gum. The company grew quickly and established several plants in the eastern United States. He also invested in railroads, mines, and several businesses, including a majority stake in the Eskimo Pie Company.

In 1926, Reynolds saw the benefits of aluminum foil over tinfoil, and switched production. Two years later, the 49-year-old owner organized Reynolds

Metals Company as a subsidiary of U.S. Foil, and although the company made an array of products, its chief product through the Great Depression was Reynolds Wrap Aluminum Foil.

Reynolds started looking toward Europe in the late 1930s for aluminum pig, the primary material used to produce aluminum products. He witnessed firsthand the efforts of Hitler to stockpile aluminum, leading Reynolds to conclude that the Nazis were planning to use the lightweight material in combat airplane production. Reynolds returned to the United States and quickly supervised the acquisition of as much aluminum as possible, resulting in nearly 1 billion pounds of aluminum production during the war.

In 1948, Reynolds was named chairman of the board of directors, and his oldest son, Richard, was named president. He died on July 29, 1955, at the age of 73. Today, the Reynolds Metals Company has annual sales of about $7 billion.

SOURCE: Reynolds Metals Company archives

Robert E. Rich Sr.

[Rich Products Corporation]

Rich's father, Paul Rich, operated a successful dairy business in the Buffalo area in the early 1900s. After selling the business in 1910, Paul and his wife established what eventually grew into Buffalo's largest independent ice cream company.

After graduating in 1935 from the University of Buffalo with a B.S. in business administration, Robert Rich borrowed $5,000 from his father and established his own dairy business, Wilber Farms Dairy. However, the father of three soon grew restless, complaining the only way to differentiate himself from competitors was to keep his milk trucks washed.

During World War II, he served with the War Food Administration, devising ways to ship dairy products to the front line. While there, he heard about research sponsored by Ford Motor Company to find uses for soybean, particularly as a nondairy whipping cream. Rich was fascinated by the potential of the soybean research and promptly established his own research team, which produced the company's first product: Rich's Whip Topping.

Rich went to New York City to demonstrate his whipped topping to a gathering of food buyers. As he stood before the filled room, Rich poured his miracle soybean mixture into a bowl and whipped and whipped and whipped some more. Nothing happened. He excused himself, stating he had to get a different bowl from the kitchen. He left the room, then bolted out the door. The following morning, he regained his nerve and was given another audience with some of the buyers. This time, the whipping worked to perfection, and Rich picked up some good customers.

His second sales trip was even more eventful. While riding in a railroad sleeping car with his cream packed in dry ice, Rich dozed off and the cream froze. When he went to demonstrate the product, he calmly borrowed a jackknife and chopped off a chunk. The frozen cream whipped up just as well as the liquid, and Rich had found his niche. First-year sales totaled $28,000. One year later, they reached nearly $500,000.

In 1961, Rich again led an aggressive research initiative to find a nondairy coffee cream. The result was Coffee Rich, a low-fat soybean product. Consumer demand exploded, sparking tremendous corporate expansion. Over the past three decades, Rich's has made a considerable number of acquisitions, including bakeries, frozen food companies, and dessert manufacturers.

The Rich family entered the sports market with the 1983 acquisition of the Class AAA Buffalo Bisons baseball franchise. One year later, they purchased the Class AA Wichita Wranglers. In 1994, they added the Class A Jamestown (New York) Jammers. The family has also paid to use their name for Rich Stadium, home of the Buffalo Bills. They own the Palm Beach National Golf and Country Club in West Palm Beach, Florida, as well.

Rich Products surpassed the $1 billion annual sales level in 1995. Today, the company is one of the largest family-owned manufacturers of frozen food in the world, employing more than 7,000 people in over 30 plants and offices. Robert E. Rich Jr. now serves as company president.

SOURCES: Rich Products Corporation archives; Theresa Howard, "Robert Rich Sr.," *Nation's Restaurant News* magazine, January 1995

Steve Robertson, Randy Ward

[This End Up Furniture]

In 1974, Steve Robertson and Randy Ward faced a dilemma. One night, Ward's friends ruined his furniture during a spirited party. The two men discussed the problem at Robertson's apartment, which was filled with shipping crates from his recently completed two-year sailing venture.

Finally, the two friends were struck with a clever idea. They tore the front and top off one of Robertson's shipping crates and, using old cushions, fashioned it into a sofa. The furniture quickly became a curiosity among their acquaintances, so the two men experimented with other pieces of furniture.

In December of that same year, Robertson and Ward decided to make a complete set of furniture for sale to raise money for Christmas. They built a sofa, chair, ottoman, cocktail table, and end tables and towed them to a Raleigh, North Carolina, flea market. Not only did they sell their set, they received orders for eight more sets.

For the next six months, the pair took orders at weekend flea markets, then built the furniture in a friend's basement during the day and made deliveries in the evening. Soon, they had enough business to rent an abandoned Raleigh florist shop.

In 1975, Robertson approached his sister and brother-in-law, Libby and Stewart Brown, about opening a retail outlet. Cautiously, they opened a shop in the historic district of Richmond, Virginia. The venture was so successful that Stewart quit his stockbroker job and the couple devoted themselves full-time to their This End Up furniture stores.

In 1985, Robertson, Ward, and the Browns sold the company to Melville Corporation of Rye, New York. Citicorp Venture Capital signed a definitive purchase agreement to acquire This End Up in 1996. Today, This End Up ranks among Americas top twenty furniture retailers.

SOURCE: This End Up archives

John D. Rockefeller

[Standard Oil Company]

After a rapid rise in the commission business, young John Rockefeller invested in a Cleveland oil refinery. Several years later, with Henry Flagler, he founded the Standard Oil Company of Ohio, which quickly became the world's dominant oil refiner. He eventually amassed a large number of oil-related businesses that he combined under Standard Oil of New Jersey.

The Rockefeller family can be traced back to France, when the Rockefeller or Rockquefeuille family moved to Germany to escape persecution of the Huguenots. In 1740, Diell Rockefeller, John Rockefeller's great-great-grandfather, immigrated to New Jersey from Germany.

John Davison Rockefeller was born on July 8, 1839, in Richford, New York. His family moved to Strongsville, Ohio, in 1853 and sent young John to high school in Cleveland. After two years of business education, he went to work for the wholesale commission firm of Hewitt and Tuttle as an office boy. One year later, he was promoted to bookkeeper and, by the end of his second year of employment, had saved $800 from his modest salary.

By 1859, the 20-year-old Rockefeller had launched his own commission house with M. B. Clark. As a respected businessman, he was asked to visit Titusville, Pennsylvania, and to comment on the opportunities in the oil industry. Upon his return, Rockefeller stated that an oil venture seemed too risky an investment until a good refining system was developed.

Rockefeller became acquainted with Samuel Andrews, a local petroleum refiner, and eventually invested in Andrews refinery. Five years later, Rockefeller purchased Andrews's interest for $75,000 and joined forces with Henry M. Flagler, another Cleveland businessman. On January 10, 1870, they incorporated the Standard Oil Company of Ohio, which within ten years became the dominant organization in the oil industry, controlling more than 90 percent of the refining capacity in the entire world.

By 1899, Rockefeller had established Standard Oil of New Jersey, which served as an umbrella for more than 30 corporations. His fortune, by this time, exceeded $1 billion. In 1911, the venture was interpreted as a monopoly by the U.S. Supreme Court and ordered to be broken up into 39 separate and distinct companies. Rockefeller complied and, that same year, launched a number of philanthropic organizations, including the Rockefeller Foundation.

John D. Rockefeller died on May 23, 1937. His son, John D. Rockefeller Jr., continued to oversee Standard Oil of New Jersey while building Rockefeller Center in New York. He also donated the land in Manhattan on which the United Nations headquarters was built.

SOURCE: Standard Oil archives

Frederick H. Rohr

[Rohr, Inc.]

Frederick Hilmer Rohr was born on May 10, 1896, in Hoboken, New Jersey. His father had immigrated to the United States from Germany eight years earlier to establish a sheet metal business. When Frederick was two years old, his family moved to San Francisco, California, and opened a new shop. During young Rohr's childhood, he worked in the shop and eventually became a sheet metal apprentice.

During World War I, Rohr served as a quartermaster in the U.S. Navy. His father moved his shop to Fresno, California, and Frederick returned to the family business after the war. Rohr and his friends developed an interest in aviation and purchased several vintage World War I planes which were restored and flown in a nearby pasture. Sometimes, their flights weren't successful, and the owner of an adjacent orchard started to assess the young men $50 for each tree that they knocked down.

In 1924, Rohr left his father's shop and moved to San Diego, California, where he established his own firm, the Standard Sheet Metal Works. While looking for contracts, he learned that the Ryan Aircraft plant was looking for someone to fabricate fuel tanks. He visited the empty plant on a Sunday and persuaded an employee to provide the specifications for the tanks. He then returned to his shop, built the tanks, and carried them into the Ryan plant on Monday morning. Ryan's managers were so impressed they allocated space in their plant for Rohr to set up shop.

A young aviator named Charles Lindbergh called on the Ryan plant (by this time owned by Frank Mahoney) in 1927 and asked to have a special plane built that could carry him nonstop across the Atlantic. A team of workers at the factory, including Rohr, frequently worked on the project into the night, so they became known throughout the industry as the "Nighthawks." The plane, named the *Spirit of St. Louis,* did make the flight and became a centerpiece of aviation history.

Shortly thereafter, the plant moved to St. Louis. Rohr stayed behind and worked for Solar Aircraft. His high-quality craftsmanship became well known among airplane makers, and in 1932 he went to work for Boeing in Seattle. Then, in 1935, he returned to San Diego and rejoined Claude Ryan, who had reopened the Ryan Aeronautical Company.

In 1940, Rohr was comfortable with his reputation in the airline industry and decided to once again launch his own business, Rohr Aircraft, later renamed the Rohr Corporation. Work started in a garage in Rohr's backyard, but was soon moved to a three-story building in San Diego. With the onset of World War II, the small company was quickly engaged in military projects. First-year revenues were nearly $1.5 million, and a second factory and a two-story office building were added the following year.

The war years propelled Rohr into the national arena in the aerospace industry. Its "power package" (The motor mounts, cowl panels, cowl flaps, plumbing, electrical harness, and related accessories) for military and commercial aircraft was highly successful, with 38,000 of them built for both the B-24 Liberator bomber and the PBY series of flying boats. However, the end of the war caused the company to refocus on the commercial market.

Over the next two decades, Rohr grew to be a renowned and highly successful manufacturer. Frederick Rohr struck a good balance between his work and family life with wife Shirley and their two children. When his young son contracted polio in the early 1950s and became wheelchair-bound, Rohr spent considerable time inventing devices that would make life easier. Frederick Rohr died on November 8, 1965.

During the 1960s, the Rohr company diversified its operations, building satellite antennas, boats, rocket motor cases, nozzles, deep-submergence vessels, modular housing, and ground and transit vehicles. However, most of these ventures were later spun off. Today, Rohr is a leading supplier of nacelles and pylon systems to the world's major commercial airframe and engine manufacturers. The company designs, integrates, manufactures, sells, and supports aircraft engine nacelle systems and components for large commercial aircraft.

Rohr, Inc., is headquartered in Chula Vista, California, and has operations in the United States, Europe, and Asia. Annual revenues are nearly $800 million.

SOURCE: Rohr, Inc., archives

Warren W. Rosenthal

[Long John Silver's]

Warren W. Rosenthal grew up in the small town of Paducah, Kentucky. Following World War II, Rosenthal and his wife moved to Lexington so that he could attend the University of Kentucky. They rented an apartment from Jerome Lederer, a local businessman who owned three small but successful coffee shops called Jerry's, and the two men became friends.

Upon graduation from college, Rosenthal returned to Paducah and went to work in his father's dry goods store. However, when the elder Rosenthal died a few months later, Warren was unsure about the future. He went to New York City for a job interview and immediately knew the city was too big for him. On his way back home, he stopped in Lexington to visit Lederer, who invited him to become a partner in Jerry's.

The two men worked hard, reinvested profits, and soon were operating eight drive-in restaurants with curb service and inside dining. Rosenthal, owner of one-third of the business, was named chief executive officer and looked for more growth opportunities. In 1957, the company, by then operating under the name Jerrico, Inc., started to franchise.

Jerome Lederer died in 1963, and Rosenthal acquired the other two-thirds of the company. While continuing to build his Jerry's holdings, Rosenthal experimented with four other restaurant concepts, including a roast beef restaurant similar to Arby's. None of the four worked.

In 1969, Rosenthal was ready to try something creative again. He wanted to adapt the seafood concept to fast food and focused on fish and chips. Another restaurant, H. Salt Fish and Chips, appeared to be doing quite well, prompting Rosenthal to open his first Long John Silver's Fish and Chips. The building was patterned after a wharfside structure Rosenthal had seen in San Francisco.

Within four years, Jerrico had opened 104 Long John Silver's restaurants. For some reason, H. Salt started losing its customer base. Rosenthal reacted by taking down the "Fish and Chips" signs and replacing them with "Seafood Shoppes," which was more representative of the broader menu at Long John Silver's. The business continued to prosper, and by 1977 more than 600 restaurants were operating in 24 states.

Rosenthal stepped down as president of Jerrico in 1982, but remained chairman of the board. He retired from the chairmanship in 1989, and the publicly traded company was soon acquired in a leveraged buyout. The following year, the owners spun off the other restaurants owned by Jerrico, including Jerry's, and changed the company name to Long John Silver's Restaurants, Inc., reflecting their current focus.

SOURCE: Long John Silver's archives

Margaret Rudkin

[Pepperidge Farm, Inc.]

Margaret Rudkin was born into a comfortable, middle-class family in New York City in 1897. After completing school, she worked in New York's banking and brokerage sector.

In 1923, Margaret married Henry Rudkin. The couple soon purchased land in Fairfield, Connecticut, and built an impressive home among the orchards, barns, and stables. The land was rich with pepperidge trees, and their homestead was named "Pepperidge Farm."

The Rudkins led the good life in the country. However, in 1935, one of their three sons became afflicted with a serious asthmatic condition, resulting in a two-year quest to find an appropriate treatment. Eventually, Margaret was advised to put the boy on a nutritional diet of wholesome foods.

While researching old family cookbooks, Margaret found a recipe for whole wheat bread made from natural ingredients, including stone-ground wheat, molasses, yeast, and honey. Undaunted by the fact that she had never made a loaf of bread in her life, and ignoring many unsuccessful attempts, she was finally able to bake a loaf of the bread. It turned out to be both healthy and delicious.

Her son's condition improved. This intrigued his physician, and Margaret was soon baking bread for the doctor and his other patients. Encouraged by their reaction and with the support of her husband, 40-year-old Margaret decided to venture into the commercial market.

In August 1937, she walked into a local grocery store in Fairfield and handed a sample to the owner. Despite her insistence on a 25¢ retail price (commercial bread sold for a dime), the grocer bought the bread. By the time she arrived back home, the grocer had called to announce the bread was sold out and he wanted another order. Soon, grocers throughout the area were stocking bread from Pepperidge Farm.

Within six months, demand reached 1,000 loaves a week. Margaret hired her first employees and moved the baking operation from her kitchen to the garage, then later to the stables. In 1938, she made her first two major capital investments: a large-capacity mixer that cost $987 and a station wagon to make deliveries. She also expanded into New York City, where Henry would drop off some loaves at a store near Grand Central Station on his way to his office.

In 1939, *Reader's Digest* published an article called "Bread, de Luxe" that was very favorable to Pepperidge Farm. As a result, Margaret was flooded with requests. By the end of the year, volume had grown to 30,000 loaves per week.

Margaret moved the operations from the farm to a building in Norwalk, Connecticut, in 1940. She also added new products, including stuffing, pound cake, and melba toast. Growth was steady, even through World War II. On July 4, 1947, Margaret celebrated Independence Day by opening a modern factory in Norwalk that had 65,000 square feet and the capacity to make 4,000 loaves of bread an hour. Within two years the old plant was called back into service, and she opened another plant in Downingtown, Pennsylvania, to serve the mid-Atlantic market. By the end of the decade, she was filling 500,000 orders per week.

Margaret devised an enterprising distribution strategy during the 1940s. Being a staunch proponent of entrepreneurism, she developed a network of independent, self-employed distributors, each of whom had a vested interest in building profitable routes.

Throughout the 1950s, Pepperidge Farm continued to grow. Another plant was added in Downers Grove, Illinois, in 1953. Also, the product line was greatly increased. Cookies, biscuits, and other items were added, and the company became sophisticated at marketing and public relations. Urged by her sons, Margaret also expanded into frozen foods.

The rapid growth and high product quality of Pepperidge Farm did not go unnoticed. In 1961, the company merged with the Campbell Soup Company.

Pepperidge Farm maintained an independent structure, with Margaret serving as chairman of the board and son Bill as president.

In April 1966, Henry Rudkin died. Several months later Margaret, then in declining health, retired from the business, and on June 1, 1967, she died at the age of 69. Her kitchen business had grown into a $50 million bakery that produced 70 million loaves of bread annually.

Upon Margaret's death, Bill Rudkin was promoted to chairman of the board. The company has continued to grow and prosper under the Campbell Soup Company umbrella.

SOURCE: Pepperidge Farm, Inc., archives

Arthur Salomon, Herbert Salomon, Percy Salomon

[Salomon Brothers, Inc.]

Ferdinand Salomon, who immigrated from Alsace-Lorraine on the Franco-German border to America at a young age, had established a modest brokerage firm in New York during the late nineteenth century. He and his wife, Sophia, had four sons: Arthur born in 1880, Leo in 1881, Percy in 1882, and Herbert in 1884. By 1900, all but Leo were employed at their father's brokerage house.

When their father left Sophia and remarried, the boys left Ferdinand's firm. On January 3, 1910, with $5,000 in savings and a fourth partner named Benjamin Levy, they opened their own small office on Broadway under the name Salomon Brothers. Each morning, the brothers would call on banks to see who had surplus funds to lend. Within six months they had gained a good reputation for their work in the limited investment field.

The brothers expanded into the bond market with insurance companies, banks, and trust companies, but they lacked access to the New York Stock Exchange. Unable to afford their own seat, the brothers formed a partnership in 1910 with Morton Hutzler, who held a seat. The move helped advance the business modestly, but they still lacked capital. Advancement was further complicated by their Jewish lineage and their lack of educational credentials—none of the brothers had attended college.

The Liberty Loan Act of 1917, which opened up the investment market for wider participating, provided the brothers with the break they needed. Salomon Brothers and Hutzler quickly registered with the U.S. government and became authorized to deal with government securities. By the close of World War I, the firm was focused on primary and secondary markets in foreign debts, as well as short-term government notes.

By the early 1920s, the investment community was taking note of the Salomon brothers. By 1922 they had moved into an office on Wall Street and had opened branch offices in Boston, Massachusetts, and Chicago, Illinois. The brothers were even invited into several of J. P. Morgan's syndications.

The latter half of the decade was rocky. Arthur Salomon died on July 3, 1928, at the age of 48, and Herbert assumed leadership of the company. One year later, Wall Street was stunned by Black Friday and the subsequent Great Depression, forcing hundreds of investment companies to close or drastically reorganize. Fortunately, Salomon Brothers was active in the bond market, which became a popular alternative to the highly volatile stock market.

The company continued a moderate pattern of growth through the 1950s, with Percy's son, William Salomon, joining the firm. He became the first managing partner in 1963. The company started the 1960s with 19 active partners and about 424 employees. However, the next two decades brought rapid growth, buoyed by the firm's participation in two landmark financial rescues: New York City in the mid-1970s and Chrysler in the 1980s.

Today, Salomon Brothers has annual net revenues of nearly $4 billion, with 6,600 employees and 39 offices in 22 countries.

SOURCES: Salomon Brothers archives; Robert Sobel, *Salomon Brothers 1910–1985: Advancing to Leadership,* Salomon Brothers, 1986

Harland D. Sanders

[Kentucky Fried Chicken]

After his widowed mother remarried, 12-year-old Harland Sanders moved out of his family home and started the first of many jobs that included farmhand, railroad conductor, railroad fireman, insurance salesman, steamboat operator, and much more. Eventually, Sanders opened a successful service station from which he fed travelers his specialty, fried chicken, at a single table with six chairs. Later, he franchised his recipe to other restaurants. Today, Kentucky Fried Chicken operates nearly 10,000 restaurants worldwide.

Harland David Sanders was born on September 9, 1890, on a farm near Henryville, Indiana. When his father died six years later, Sanders's mother went to work as a seamstress while Harland cared for his younger brother and sister. His duties included cooking, and his mother taught the young boy the art of country cooking.

Not long after his mother remarried, 12-year-old Harland quit school and went to work as a farmhand. He then moved to New Albany, Indiana, and was hired as a streetcar conductor. At age 16, an Army recruiter convinced Sanders to lie about his age and enlist, which he did. He was promptly sent to Cuba.

Upon discharge from the service, Sanders moved in with relatives in Huntsville, Alabama, where he went to work for the railroad. When his mother separated from his stepfather, Sanders supported her and his brother and sister. At about the same time, he married Josephine King, who soon delivered the first of their three children.

Sanders had a hot Irish temper, and before long he lost his job at the railroad. He took several correspondence courses from LaSalle, including enough law classes to qualify him to practice in a justice of peace court. Once again, a dispute left him jobless. He returned to New Albany and worked on a railroad construction site by day and unloaded coal by night. He next worked as an insurance agent until a dispute over commissions left him fired from yet another job. Through these years he also operated a steamboat, made acetylene lighting systems for farmers, and sold automobile tires.

By this time, Sanders was convinced that he wasn't cut out to work for someone else. He moved to Nicholasville, Kentucky, and opened a service station.

Business was good until the Depression struck in 1929. Then, many of his clients were unable to pay their bills, and Sanders lost the station.

Sanders' next move proved to be his best. In 1930, at the age of 40, he moved to Corbin, Kentucky, and opened another filling station. He knew that owning a business during the Depression required extra special service. He washed windshields and filled the radiators of every car that stopped, even if people were just asking directions. If they gave him enough time, he swept their floors and checked the air in their tires.

Soon, many travelers between Detroit, Columbus, Cincinnati, Chattanooga, Atlanta, and other cities were stopping at Sanders's service station. To make extra money, he put six chairs around a table in a back room and started cooking meals for travelers. He found that he enjoyed cooking and experimenting with spices the way his mother had taught him, and the travelers enjoyed his panfried chicken, country ham, biscuits, and other specialties. Eventually, his little restaurant was listed in *Adventures in Good Eating,* a travel guide published by Duncan Hines.

By 1937, he had moved across the street into a restaurant that seated 142. He also added a small motel. He had perfected his "finger-lickin' good" chicken recipe of 11 herbs and spices, but struggled with the 30-minute preparation time. At about the same time, the governor of Kentucky honored him with a ceremonial Kentucky Colonel designation. By 1939, he had cut the preparation time to eight minutes by using pressure cookers to prepare his chicken.

It seems as though adversity was a constant companion of Sanders. In 1939, his rapidly growing business burned to the ground. Undaunted, Sanders built another restaurant and motel with a new twist: Anyone wishing to use the pay phones or ladies' restroom had to actually walk through a replica of one of his motel rooms. This room-sized advertisement helped keep his motel business thriving.

By the time Sanders was earning a comfortable living, another hardship was presented. A new highway bypass carried away most of his customers. Business soured quickly, and Sanders was forced to sell his business at an auction. The proceeds were just enough to cover his debts.

Harland Sanders was 66 years old and had nothing to show for nearly 55 years of labor. Rather than sit back and collect Social Security, he was determined to find another market niche. His most valuable asset was his secret chicken recipe, which he called "Kentucky Fried Chicken" to differentiate it from "Southern fried chicken." By 1956, Sanders was able to convince about a dozen restaurants to make and sell his chicken and pay him a 4¢ royalty on each piece they sold.

Buoyed by this modest success, Sanders packed his 1946 pickup truck with a 50-pound barrel of seasoning and a pressure cooker and took to the road to sign up more "franchises." By 1960, 400 restaurants in the United States and Canada were cooking Kentucky Fried Chicken. Within four years, the number of outlets approached 650, and annual sales reached $37 million.

That year, the 74-year-old Sanders sold the business to John Brown Jr., a 29-year-old lawyer who eventually became Kentucky's governor, and Jack Massey, a successful Nashville entrepreneur. The sales price was $2 million for rights to all but a few states, Canada, and England. In addition, the company kept Colonel Sanders on the payroll as a goodwill ambassador. Harland D. Sanders died on December 16, 1980, at the age of 90.

In 1971, Kentucky Fried Chicken was sold to Heublein, Inc., which later merged into R.J. Reynolds Industries. In 1986, it was sold to PepsiCo. Today, there are nearly 10,000 Kentucky Fried Chicken restaurants worldwide, with more than 200,000 employees and annual sales in excess of $8.2 billion.

SOURCE: Kentucky Fried Chicken archives

Jacob Sapirstein

[American Greetings Corporation]

Jacob Sapirstein was born on October 30, 1884, at Wasosz, Poland. When war broke out in 1904 between Russia and Japan, his widowed mother vowed to send her daughter and six sons to America, one at a time. With the help of the Hebrew Immigrant Aid Society, the 20-year-old Sapirstein immigrated to Boston in 1905.

After living in Chicago briefly, he moved to Cleveland, Ohio, to work for relatives in their card shop in the Hollenden Hotel. Postcards were gaining in popularity at the time and were often called "view cards" since they pictured panoramic views of cities.

In 1906, Sapirstein established his own business and started importing cards from Germany. He sold his products to candy stores, drugstores, and other retailers, making his rounds on a horse-drawn wagon. He was an innovative marketer who provided his customers not only with high-quality cards, but with attractive display racks as well.

Sapirstein married Jennie Kantor, another Polish immigrant, in 1908, and the couple had four children who joined the family business at an early age. Irving, their eldest son, started working at age five. In 1918, when an influenza epidemic swept through Cleveland, Jacob Sapirstein was too ill to work. Irving, by then age nine, filled all the Christmas orders and prepared the invoices.

By 1917, the company had outgrown the family's living room and moved into a rented garage on Cleveland's east side. Through the 1920s, Sapirstein and his sons continued to build their business. Finally, in 1932, Irving convinced his father that the family could do better printing their own line of greeting cards, and the orders poured in. Four years later, son Harry opened the first branch office in Detroit. Then, in 1938, the Sapirstein Greeting Card Company became American Greetings Publishers. (When the company went public in 1952, the name was changed again to American Greetings Corporation.)

The company introduced its first line of *Forget Me Not* cards in 1939, priced at a nickel each. The following year, annual sales topped $1 million for the first time in company history. That same year, the Sapirstein brothers—Irving, Morris, and Harry—changed their last name to Stone. (Sapirstein translates to "sapphire stone.")

By 1960, Jacob Sapirstein started to relinquish some of his responsibilities to his sons. Irving became president and has since led the company through exciting growth. Jacob, however, continued to visit the plant and keep his eye on finances. He became intrigued with computer technology, and for his 100th birthday told his family: "Get me another book on computers."

Jacob Sapirstein died on June 24, 1987, at the age of 102, two days before he was scheduled to retire from the board of directors of American Greetings. One year earlier, the company he had started with a horse and buggy surpassed $1 billion in sales. Always modest about his success, Sapirstein lived at the same house in University Heights, Ohio, for 55 years.

Today, American Greetings is the world's largest publicly owned creator, manufacturer, and distributor of greeting cards and related social expression products. The company's artists, writers, designers, and planners produce 22,000 new designs each year, which are sold in more than 100,000 retail outlets worldwide. Annual sales exceeds $2 billion.

SOURCE: American Greetings corporate archives

Alex Schulman

[A. Schulman, Inc.]

Alex Schulman was born on January 11, 1897, at Minsk, Russia, the youngest of four sons. Five years later, his family immigrated to the United States, settling in Akron, Ohio.

At age nine, Schulman established himself as Ohio's most successful newspaper salesman. He would awaken at four o'clock in the morning and walk several miles to Market and Howard streets, the choice corner in Akron, where he would literally have to fight off the competition. There, he would sell 1,000 newspapers before school started. After school, it was back on the corner with the afternoon edition.

After graduating from Akron's Central High School in 1916, Schulman went to work for Goodyear Tire & Rubber as an office boy. He later took a similar job with a scrap rubber company, a business that intrigued him. By the age of 23, Schulman was promoted to manager of the company's Akron branch.

In 1928, Schulman established A. Schulman, Inc., his own scrap rubber business. The company took old truck tires, ground off the bead and peeled the carcass into rubber ribbons. These strips were then used to make seals, mounts, and spacers for machines and automobiles, or converted into forklift tires and doormats.

After World War II, Schulman became active in the plastics industry, particularly with resin products. This resulted in the development of several proprietary compounds that were produced under the Schulman name. These are used by manufacturers to make plastics more rigid or flexible, stronger, and flame-retardant, as well as to add color.

Alex Schulman died in 1962, but his lifelong philosophy of finding the "best corner" continues at his company. Today, A. Schulman, Inc., employs more than 2,000 people in 11 manufacturing plants, and annual sales are nearly $750 million.

SOURCE: A. Schulman archives

Howard Schultz

[Starbucks Coffee Company]

Howard Schultz was raised in federally subsidized housing in Brooklyn, New York. His father held a variety of jobs, including cab driver, diaper-service truck driver, and laborer in a paper factory. His mother worked as an office receptionist.

Schultz earned his B.S. degree in business from Northern Michigan University in 1975. He spent the next three years in sales and marketing positions with Xerox Corporation, then joined Hammarplast, USA, a U.S. subsidiary of Perstorp, AB, a Swedish housewares company, rising to the position of vice president and general manager.

In 1982, Schultz became the director of operations and marketing for the Starbucks Coffee Company, a small chain of coffee houses in Seattle, Washington, named after the first mate in *Moby Dick.* The company's first store had opened in 1971 in Seattle's Pike Place Market. By the time Schultz joined the company 11 years later, three more stores had been added.

While visiting Italy in 1983, Schultz was intrigued with the vast number of successful espresso bars. He envisioned a similar concept being embraced by American culture. Schultz returned to Seattle and presented the concept to the Starbucks owners, who did not share his vision. Confident that the idea would work, the 30-year-old Schultz left Starbucks and launched his own coffee shop, Il Giornale, which served Starbucks coffee.

Over the next three years, Schultz's venture grew slowly. However, he continued to build a strong investor base and, in 1987, acquired the Starbucks stores for a little less than $4 million. Combining the companies gave him 11 stores, about 100 employees, and an American culture that still centered on supermarket coffee. Over the next two years, the company opened dozens of stores with faith that the concept would catch on. In 1989, the company posted a $1 million loss. One year later, the loss was even greater.

However, Schultz continued to follow his vision. Slowly, Americans became familiar with *latte, barista, decaf doppio,* and an assortment of other new terms. Eventually it became fashionable to drink coffee in coffee shops, and Starbucks was the rising star. By 1991, Schultz had the company in the black and had expanded the store count to 116.

Over the next five years, Schultz moved his stores beyond the Western states and was soon a recognized national brand. He took the company public in 1992 and, within two years, had expanded to 425 stores with sales in excess of $400 million. In 1996, Starbucks opened up its 1,000th store and was on its way to becoming a billion-dollar company.

SOURCES: Starbucks Coffee Company archives; Jim Morrison, "Howard's Trend," *Southwest Airlines Spirit* magazine, September 1995

Charles Schwab

[Charles Schwab & Co., Inc.]

Charles Schwab was born in 1937 at Sacramento, California, and raised in nearby Woodland, where his father served as the district attorney in Yolo County. Charles was an industrious boy, picking English walnuts and selling them in 100-pound sacks for $5 and, at the age of 12, selling his chickens' eggs door-to-door. At 14, he was a golf caddy, and through his college years he worked at such diverse jobs as sugar beet picker, life insurance salesman, and bank teller.

Schwab also became interested in stocks at an early age. After graduating from Stanford with a bachelor's degree in economics, he went to work at a small investment advisory service while attending graduate school. Soon after receiving his MBA in 1961, he was promoted to vice president. A year later, he and two partners launched a newsletter for investors.

The company grew quickly and soon included a $20 million mutual fund. However, in addition to the market decline in the late 1960s, the state of Texas ordered the company to stop soliciting investments by mail. After court battles, Schwab was $100,000 in debt and in divorce court.

Schwab quickly recovered. He borrowed money from relatives and founded an investment brokerage firm that he named First Commander. In 1974, a high school buddy suggested he look into discounting his rates. When the Securities and Exchange Commission abolished fixed commissions a year later, his business took off, and all his past debts were retired.

In 1983, Schwab started to look for capital to expand. He raised $55 million by selling the company to BankAmerica. Within five years, BankAmerica was experiencing financial pressures and Schwab was frustrated with the complex banking regulations. He packaged a buyout (actually, a buyback) package valued at nearly $325 million. After a public stock offering six months later, the firm was valued at more than $400 million, with Schwab's personal holdings worth nearly $120 million.

Today, The Charles Schwab Corporation, primarily through its subsidiary Charles Schwab & Co., Inc., is one of the nation's largest brokerage firms, serving nearly 4 million active investors. The company employs 10,000 people, maintains nearly 250 branch offices, and has annual revenues of nearly $2 billion.

SOURCES: Charles Schwab & Co., Inc. archives; Terence Pare, "How Charles Schwab Wins Investors," *Fortune* magazine, June 1992; Charles Schwab, *Charles Schwab: How to Be Your Own Stockbroker,* Dell Publishing, 1984

Edward W. Scripps

[The E. W. Scripps Company]

James Mogg Scripps, a widower with six children, immigrated from England in 1844 and settled on a farm in Illinois. He later married a second wife, Julia A. Osborne. Scripps was an enterprising man, and in the coming years he worked as a leather bookbinder, founded an icehouse, invented a corn-planting machine, and established a lumber mill and brick kiln.

Edward W. Scripps, was born on June 18, 1854, in Rushville, Illinois, one of five children born to James and Julia. At the age of 18, E. W. Scripps moved to Chicago and took a clerk's job in a drugstore. Next, he and his older half-brother, James E. Scripps, started a small newspaper called the *Detroit News.* At 2¢ per copy, the newspaper circulated well.

Through the Detroit experience, Edward Scripps not only gained editorial experience, but he also drew some conclusions about what makes a newspaper successful. He later moved to Cleveland, Ohio, where he established the *Penny Press,* which later became the *Cleveland Press.*

Scripps formula for a successful newspaper was really quite simple. First, he insisted that everyone who worked for the paper, including himself, operate at arm's length from outside influences. To do so, he had to be financially independent from anyone who might wish to influence what was reported. Second, the paper had to have mass appeal, meaning that it had to be clearly written, inexpensive, and interesting. Scripps concluded that if he worked hard at the second issue, the paper would sell well and provide a good income, which would take care of the first issue.

His approach to managing the newspaper worked quite well, and soon Scripps had money in the bank. While looking for investment opportunities in coal, someone suggested that he keep his money in the market that he knew best—journalism. Scripps agreed and launched the Cincinnati *Penny Paper,* which later became the *Cincinnati Post.*

Scripps was aware that access to national and international news was crucial, and he owned several Associated Press franchises. He also started his own service and, after making several acquisitions of small agencies, dropped his affiliation with Associated Press. His new organization grew to become United Press International, which today is no longer part of the Scripps empire.

In 1908, 54-year-old Edward Scripps started the process of retirement. Succession proved a difficult issue. After a policy dispute, his oldest son James left the organization and operated several West Coast newspapers until his death at age 35. His second son, John, died tragically at age 26. His third son Edward had already died at age 7. That left Robert, who was the only son to outlive E. W. Scripps.

Concurrently, a journalist named Roy W. Howard had worked his way through the ranks of United Press, becoming president in 1912. In 1922, Edward Scripps emerged from retirement to reorganize the media empire, and renamed it Scripps-Howard. Roy Howard was appointed president, a post he held until 1952.

Edward W. Scripps died on March 12, 1926, while aboard his yacht off the coast of Africa, and was promptly buried at sea. At the time of his death, Scripps-Howard owned 25 daily newspapers. Today, The E. W. Scripps Company is America's tenth-largest newspaper publisher. The company also owns nine television stations, several cable companies, and an entertainment production company. Annual revenue exceeds $1.2 billion.

SOURCES: The E. W. Scripps Company archives; company handbook, *Scripps-Howard Handbook,* 3rd edition, 1981

Richard W. Sears, Alvah C. Roebuck

[Sears, Roebuck and Co.]

Richard Sears and Alvah Roebuck were raised in separate states, but they lived very similar lives. Both went to work at an early age to support their families; both became intrigued with watches; and both headed to Chicago to find an opportunity, Sears from Minnesota and Roebuck from Indiana. Soon after Roebuck responded to an employment ad placed by Sears, the pair incorporated Sears, Roebuck and Co., one of the world's best-known retail stores.

Richard Warren Sears (pictured left) was born December 7, 1863, at Stewartville, Minnesota, to James Warren and Eliza Sears, both of English descent. Although Sears's father was a successful blacksmith and wagonmaker, he eventually lost his money in a stock-farm venture. Consequently, Richard started working at an early age to help support his parents and two younger sisters.

After learning telegraphy, Sears went to work for the railroad, where he soon became the station agent at North Redwood, Minnesota. He also supplemented his salary by selling lumber and coal to local residents. One day, a shipment of watches came through the station addressed to a Redwood Falls jeweler, who promptly refused delivery.

Sensing an opportunity, Sears received permission from the manufacturer to try to sell the watches, and he sold them to other railroad employees for a nice profit. Encouraged by the response, he ordered and sold another shipment. In 1886, at the age of 22, he established the R.W. Sears Watch Company in Minneapolis.

One month after the birth of Richard Sears, Alvah Curtis Roebuck (pictured below) was born on January 9, 1864, in Lafayette, Indiana, to English parents. Three years after his birth, his family moved to a farm outside the city. His father died in 1876, and his mother assumed management of the family farm.

Roebuck displayed a strong mechanical aptitude and, by the age of 16, had become a proficient watchmaker. By the time he was 22, he was employed in a small jewelry store in Hammond, Indiana, but he soon grew restless and headed for Chicago in search of a better opportunity.

One year after Richard Sears established his watch business, he decided to move his one-man company to Chicago. Soon after he arrived, he placed the following ad in the Chicago *Daily News:* "Wanted: Watchmaker with reference who can furnish tools. State age, experience and salary required." Alvah Roebuck read the ad on April 1, 1887, and submitted a response. Two days later, Sears hired him. In 1893, they incorporated the firm as Sears, Roebuck and Co.

The company was strictly a mail-order business for many years. People living in rural America welcomed the Sears, Roebuck catalogs with open arms. Transportation, even into small towns, was a difficult proposition, and patrons from across the country placed their orders from the catalog, which by 1895 included 532 pages of merchandise. Sales that year exceeded $750,000.

The company also experienced big changes in 1895. Julius Rosenwald, a Chicago clothing manufacturer, was recruited to serve as vice president. The rapid growth of the company created enormous organizational problems, and Rosenwald was the right man to solve them.

That same year, Alvah Roebuck sold his interest in the company because of ill health. However, he continued to oversee the division that handled watches, jewelry, and optical goods. Roebuck later established a manufacturing company and a motion picture equipment company, which he sold in 1924.

Sears and Rosenwald continued to guide the growth of the company. In 1896, they moved to a six-story headquarters building in Chicago. Ten years later, they opened a 40-acre, $5 million mail-order plant and office building on Chicago's West Side. When it opened, it was the largest business building in the world. They also opened an office in Dallas that same year.

In 1906, Richard Sears reflected on the lack of sales to city residents. He wrote: "We do comparatively very little business in cities, and we . . . assume the cities are not at all our field—maybe they are not—but I think it is our duty to prove they are not . . ."

Sadly, Sears didn't get an opportunity to test his theory. Ill health forced Sears into retirement in 1908 while he was in his early 40s. His 22-year-old company had sales of $40 million that year. Richard Sears died on September 28, 1914, at the age of 50.

Sears did enter the cities in a very big way. The company's first retail store opened in 1925 and was an immediate success. Within two years there were 27 stores in operation, and by 1931 retail stores outsold the mail-order division. That same year, Sears established Allstate Insurance Company as a wholly owned subsidiary.

In 1933, Alvah Roebuck rejoined Sears as a company historian. One year later, a store manager asked him to make a public appearance, which led to several successful years of touring the retail stores and meeting the public. Roebuck remained at corporate headquarters until his death on June 18, 1948.

Today, Sears is one of the world's leading retailers, with annual sales in excess of $35 billion and nearly 300,000 employees in 800 department stores and 1,800 other retail stores.

SOURCE: Sears, Roebuck and Co. archives

Samuele Sebastiani

[Sebastiani Vineyards]

Samuele Sebastiani was born in Tuscany, Italy, and raised in a family of sharecroppers who maintained a modest winemaking business. By the age of 18, his ambitions as a winemaker exceeded the opportunities in Italy, so his parents bought him a boat ticket to New York in 1895, where he worked until he raised enough money for a ticket to California. Finding no jobs when he arrived in San Francisco, Sebastiani worked for free in the artichoke and cabbage fields of Colma, just to demonstrate what a hard worker he was. Eventually, he was put on the payroll, and by 1896 he had earned enough money to purchase a wagon and four horses. The 22-year-old then quarried the mines of Sonoma, cutting cobblestones and chopping wood, then hauling his cargo to San Francisco.

In his free time, Sebastiani would relax by playing boccie at the Lone Star Saloon. One day, he met a man named Ted Riboni who owned the Burgess Winery. When Riboni learned that Sebastiani worked the grapes in Italy, he offered him a job. Sebastiani accepted, and worked for Riboni until a tragic fire destroyed the distillery in 1903.

Sebastiani returned to the quarry with a bigger and better team of horses. However, he soon met a man named Milani who owned a winery at the northeast corner of Sonoma. By chance, Milani wanted out of the business and, on a handshake, turned the operation over to Sebastiani in exchange for his promise to pay for the winery after he sold his first batch of wine. In 1904, the Sebastiani Vineyards opened for business.

The first batch of wine was zinfandel, which he made with an antique crusher, a basket press, and a 500-gallon redwood tank. Sebastiani made his deliveries by horse and wagon, selling not only his wine, but coal and lumber as well. The venture provided him with enough income to marry Elvira Eraldi, daughter of the Lone Star's saloonkeeper.

By 1909, he had retired his debt to Milani and acquired another property, the Vallejo ranch, which had been originally farmed by the Franciscan Fathers, who planted the first vines in 1825. In 1911, he built an impressive stone addition onto the winery and, shortly thereafter, added brandy to his product list. Over the next five years, he added two impressive 65,000-gallon tanks on the premises.

The onset of Prohibition in 1919 provided a challenge to the young winery. Sebastiani initially maintained sales by shipping his grapes in refrigerator cars to the East, where people, predominantly immigrants, were making small batches of wine for personal consumption. By 1924, he was shipping "medicinal" wine—port and sherry—to eastern warehouses. This new market prompted him to buy the Woodbridge Winery in 1926, despite the continued pressures of Prohibition.

Samuele Sebastiani died in 1944. Today, third-generation family members continue to produce their popular wine under the Sebastiani and Woodbridge labels.

SOURCE: Sebastiani Vineyards archives

Joseph M. Segel

[QVC Network]

Joseph M. Segel was born in 1931. In 1951 he received a bachelor of science degree in economics at the University of Pennsylvania's Wharton School of Business and Commerce. Over the past 50 years, he has founded 19 different companies in publishing, giftware marketing, minting, photographic preservation, charter aviation, software testing, television, and the hospitality industry.

In 1964, he founded his first public company, the Franklin Mint, which became a preeminent producer of high-quality collectible items, as well as the only private mint commissioned by foreign countries to produce coin of the realm. Segel retired as chairman of the company in 1973, and Franklin Mint was acquired by Warner Communications, which later sold it to a private group.

Segel founded his second public company in June, 1986. The QVC Network, dedicated to 24-hour television shopping, registered record-breaking sales of $112 million in its first year of operation. The West Chester, Pennsylvania–based company now reaches over 55 million American homes, employs 7,000 people, and has annual sales of over $1.6 billion. Segel retired as chairman in 1993, but continues to serve as chairman emeritus.

From 1970 to 1990, Segel and his family were the principal owners of Le Mirador Hotel in Mont Pelerin, Switzerland. In 1990, Segel sold it to a Japanese company, but three years later reacquired the property and immediately launched a $20 million restoration project.

SOURCE: QVC Network archives

Franklin A. Seiberling, Charles W. Seiberling

[The Goodyear Tire and Rubber Company]

After the depression of the 1890s wiped out their family business interests, Frank and Charles Seiberling looked for a new business opportunity. In 1898, Frank purchased an abandoned building and, with his brother, established a rubber business. Although he never met Charles Goodyear, inventor of the vulcanized rubber process, Frank named his start-up company The Goodyear Tire and Rubber Company.

Franklin Augustus Seiberling was born at Western Start, Ohio. At age six, his family moved to nearby Akron, Ohio, where his father, who was an active entrepreneur and inventor, established several companies. When the elder Seiberling gained control of the Akron Electric Street Railway, Frank and his brother, Charles Williard Seiberling, were put in charge.

The depression in the early 1890s claimed most of the Seiberling's business ventures. In 1898, Frank was offered a small, vacant plant in East Akron for $13,500. Out of work, he agreed to buy the site, borrowing $3,500 from his brother-in-law for a down payment.

The next day, he decided to establish a rubber business at the site, and he named his new company after Charles Goodyear, who had died 40 years earlier. For his logo, Seiberling turned to Mercury, the Roman messenger of the gods. He selected Mercury's winged foot to symbolize the carrying of good tidings to tire users around the world.

With 13 employees, the Seiberling brothers commenced to manufacture bicycle and carriage tires, horseshoe pads, and poker chips. First-year sales were impressive, nearly $500,000.

Several innovations followed, and by 1900 Goodyear was manufacturing automobile tires. In 1903, it was granted a patent for the tubeless tire. Six years later, the company introduced pneumatic tires for airplanes. Frank Seiberling personally invented several machines for use in the tire and rubber manufacturing process. He also brought German zeppelin interests to the United States in 1910. Under his leadership, the country's first airship, *Akron,* was built.

By 1916, less than 20 years after its founding, Goodyear had become the world's largest tire company. One year later, annual sales topped the $100 million mark.

The Seiberling brothers left Goodyear in 1921 and, six months later, founded the Seiberling Rubber Company in nearby Barberton, Ohio. Charles Seiberling died in 1946. Frank Seiberling served as president until 1938 and as chairman of the board until he retired in 1950 at the age of 90. He died five years later.

SOURCE: The Goodyear Tire and Rubber Company archives

Walter A. Sheaffer

[Sheaffer Inc.]

After successfully building the family jewelry, organ, and sewing machine business, Walter A. Sheaffer founded the Sheaffer Pen Company in 1912. The pen that he invented in 1907 launched an enterprise that became the industry leader in a dozen short years. The Sheaffer fountain pen was, and even today continues to be, the hallmark for quality in the pen industry.

Walter A. Sheaffer was born in Bloomfield, Iowa, on July 27, 1867. His father, Jacob Sheaffer, had left behind his Pennsylvania Dutch roots in Lancaster County, Pennsylvania, to stake his claim in the California gold rush. After fortune eluded him, he returned east as far as Bloomfield, Iowa, and built a successful jewelry store and insurance business.

Unfortunately, his insurance business was tied to the Great Western Insurance Company of Chicago. The catastrophic Chicago fire of 1871 drained the insurance funds, and, because stockholders were personally liable for excess losses, Jacob was forced to sell off the jewelry store.

Young Walter Sheaffer inherited his father's entrepreneurial flair. At age 11, Walter started working in a print shop for $1 per week. Soon he was netting nearly $75 per month operating his own peanut stand. By age 13, he quit high school and accepted a job with a Centerville, Iowa, jeweler. He was paid $15 per month plus board and lodging. Lodging consisted of sleeping space under a store counter.

Jacob Sheaffer opened another jewelry store, although this time he was considerably less successful. In 1888, Walter answered his father's appeal for help and the two entered into a partnership. Competition from two new mail-order businesses, Sears Roebuck and Montgomery Ward, was quickly identified as the problem. These high-volume competitors were selling watches, silverware, and other products for almost the same price that the Sheaffers had to pay for them wholesale.

Walter's response would become the foundation for his business legacy. He abandoned the low-cost, low-quality product lines in favor of higher-cost, higher-quality goods. He started displaying 17-jewel Hamilton watches alongside those selling for $3.95. He commissioned a line of high-quality Sheaffer silverware. Most important, he implemented a new marketing strategy that focused on quality and long-term value.

Walter saw additional opportunities. He started selling pianos and organs. Not only did he show them in the center of the jewelry store, he personally carted them by horse and wagon to surrounding farmhouses (and back again that same night if he was unable to make a sale). It is well documented that Walter's musical instruments could be purchased with cash, credit, and occasionally a horse.

In his memoirs, Walter recalled those early days:

> If we went to a farmer and he was husking corn, we would agree to husk corn for one or two hours if he would agree to talk with us for that same length of time. We would start right in and help him and that would put him in a good frame of mind. If he was harvesting, we would help him harvest; or the man I had with me would take the place of the man I wanted to sell to.

Walter and his wife Nellie had two children, Clementine and Craig. The Sheaffers purchased their first house for $460 and a colt. They acquired their second home from Walter's grandfather for $10 monthly payments, investing the $750 cash raised from the sale of their first home into the business.

Walter traded this home for an 8-acre property. After planting and raising a successful peach orchard on the land, he traded the property for a run-down 188-acre farm, which he promptly renovated. Then, in 1906, Walter traded the farm plus $300 cash for a jewelry store and inventory in Fort Madison, Iowa.

In 1907, Walter Sheaffer, entrepreneur and horse trader, became Walter Sheaffer, inventor. After dwelling on the awkwardness of filling ink pens with eyedroppers, he designed a pen that was refilled with a lever and a small deflatable rubber sac. A 10- by 14-foot workshop in the back of his jewelry store became the laboratory to build a prototype. Within a year, Sheaffer secured U.S. Patent No. 896,861 for his new fountain pen.

During the next several years Sheaffer improved the pen—although he didn't actively seek to market it. He was somewhat intimidated by competition in the fountain pen market, which included more than 50 companies, some of which were quite large. He also was admittedly comfortable with his $12,000 annual income from the jewelry store.

Nonetheless, in 1912, at age 45, Sheaffer took out a second patent on an improved pen and converted the small workshop into a pen factory. Seven employees, including his young son Craig, manufactured the pens while two outside salesmen collected orders.

In 1913, the W. A. Sheaffer Pen Company was formally incorporated, capitalized with a total investment of $35,000. Walter owned 51 percent of the stock and was named the company's first president. At the end of the first year of operation, the company reported sales of $100,000 and a profit of $17,500, or 50 percent of the original investment. Despite enormous competition, Sheaffer had captured 3 percent of the writing-instrument market.

By 1917 the company employed 100 people and was producing 100,000 pens per year. By 1920 sales reached $1.5 million. That same year Walter introduced a pen with a new type of 14-karat-gold point, priced at $8.75—three times the cost of competitive products. He backed the pen with a lifetime guarantee, and it quickly became the nation's best-seller.

Other major innovations directed by Walter included the introduction of the pen-and-pencil gift set in 1919, SKRIP ink in 1922, and pens made with a colorful, tough new plastic in 1924. By 1925, Sheaffer achieved industry leadership, controlling 25 percent of the market.

The company was listed on the New York Stock Exchange in 1928. Despite the stock market crash in 1929, sales in 1930 were nearly $7 million. The Depression eventually caught up with the Sheaffer Pen Company, reducing employees to three-day workweeks. Walter and son Craig mortgaged their homes to keep the operations financed.

In 1938, at the age of 71, Walter passed the responsibilities (and title) of the company presidency to his son, Craig. However, he retained his position as chairman of the board. On June 19, 1946, Walter died at the age of 78. Local stores and the city hall in Fort Madison were closed for his funeral, which was attended by more citizens than any other in the history of Fort Madison.

Craig Sheaffer died in 1961. Five years later corporate stockholders voted to sell the company to Textron, Inc., which merged it in 1976 with another subsidiary to form the Sheaffer Eaton Division. In 1987, Textron sold the company, which is now operating as a separate Delaware corporation named Sheaffer Inc.

SOURCE: Sheaffer Inc. archives

Henry A. Sherwin, Edward P. Williams

[Sherwin-Williams]

Quitting school at an early age, Henry Sherwin went to work in a Vermont general store. He later moved to Cleveland, Ohio, where he soon was a partner in a paint and glass venture. When his partners wanted to pursue other opportunities, Sherwin took on two new partners, Edward Williams and Alanson Osborn. Sherwin, Williams & Company was soon producing one of America's most popular lines of paint.

Henry Alden Sherwin was born on September 27, 1842, in Baltimore, Vermont, the son of Alden W. and Rachel Bachelder Sherwin. He quit school at age 13 to work in a local general store, where he slept in a room on the second floor. His first business venture was as an itinerant photographer.

In 1860, Henry's uncle, Nelson Sherwin, a Cleveland attorney, convinced the boy to move to Ohio. He first worked as a wrapping boy in a dry goods store. When the company's bookkeeper joined the military in 1863, Henry took his place, and eventually moved on to a wholesale grocery store. He later turned down an offer to become a partner because the store sold liquor, which was against his principles.

On September 27, 1865, Sherwin married Frances Smith of Cleveland, and the couple eventually had three daughters. The following year, Sherwin was presented with three interesting career choices: bank cashier job, partner in a wholesale drugstore, or partner in a paint and glass company. Intrigued with the notion of manufacturing something, he invested his $2,000 savings in the paint venture. In 1870, Sherwin's partners left the company to pursue the manufacture of linseed oil, so he invited his friend, Edward Williams, to join the paint company.

Edward Porter Williams was born on May 10, 1843, in Cleveland, Ohio, the son of William and Laura Fitch Williams. He was the second youngest of eight children, the first two of whom were from William's first marriage to Laura's sister, Lucy Fitch Williams.

Williams graduated from Cleveland High School in 1859 and went on to graduate from Hudson College (which later became Case Western Reserve) with a bachelor's degree in 1864 and with a master's degree in 1869. While attending school, he and his brother Charles served in the 85th Ohio Volunteer Infantry until the close of the Civil War.

After the war, Williams moved to Kent with family members and cofounded a glass manufacturing company. However, it wasn't large enough to support the entire family, so he returned to Cleveland. In 1870, Williams and another acquaintance, Alanson T. Osborn, each invested $15,000 into the paint venture owned by Henry Sherwin.

Sherwin, Williams & Company had impressive first-year retail sales of more than $420,000. The following year, the company started manufacturing its own coatings, and by 1874 the factory employed nearly 20 people.

Sherwin and a company engineer soon developed a new type of stone-grinding mill that produced "pigments ground to extraordinary fineness and uniformity." Patented in 1876, the mill enabled the development of a ready-mixed coating. They were so confident of the quality of this new coating that they backed it with a guarantee, offering to "forfeit the value of the paint and the cost of applying it if in any instance it is not found to be as above represented."

Sherwin also received a patent in 1877 on a reclosable can, and the following year the company released its first ready-mix interior coatings. However, Sherwin's genius wasn't limited to product promotion. He was an active supporter and practitioner of advertising and good marketing practices. He personally designed the company's first trademark, a chameleon on a palette, which was officially adopted in 1884.

Williams's talents were applied in the direction of sales and human relations. The company's first traveling salesman was hired in 1876. Within four years, four representatives were covering states stretching from the Atlantic coast to the Mississippi River, from Florida to Minnesota, as well as all of Canada.

In 1888, the company made its first acquisition, the Calumet Paint Company of Chicago, previously owned by the Pullman Standard Car Company, maker of the well-known railroad sleeping cars. Calumet sold coatings for railroad cars, carriages and buggies, manufacturing equipment, ships and marine equipment, and commercial buildings, and Sherwin-Williams couldn't have picked a better time to enter those markets.

In 1890, the company surpassed $1 million in annual sales for the first time. One year later, the partners arranged their first exclusive dealership in Worcester, Massachusetts. Local dealerships were established at a furious pace, and by the turn of the century, distribution and marketing functions throughout North America were well organized.

Edward Porter Williams died on May 4, 1903. He was survived by his wife, Mary Louis Mason Williams, and four children. His son, Edward Mason Williams, was active in the company business until 1913, and he served on the board of directors until his death. Henry Alden Sherwin died on June 26, 1916. His grandson, John Prescott, joined the company in 1923 and retired as a director in 1969.

Today, Sherwin-Williams has annual sales of nearly $3 billion and operates over 2,000 retail stores.

SOURCE: Sherwin-Williams archives

William G. Shortess

[Federal Paper Board Company]

William G. Shortess was born in Pennsylvania in 1871, the youngest of six children. He developed his interest in paperboard products at an early age and, as a young man, went to work for W. J. Alford, owner of the Continental Paper Company.

One of Shortess's early assignments was to manage Alford's Haverhill Box Board Company near Boston, Massachusetts. When Alford acquired the Traders Board Company in Bogota, New Jersey, Shortess was given the management responsibility at that plant as well. Two years later, the Thames River Specialties Company mill in eastern Connecticut was added to the list, and Shortess commuted to the three sites by train. In his spare time, Shortess operated his own small mill in Reading, Pennsylvania, that he purchased in 1909.

While Shortess rose to serve as one of three members of the board of directors, Alford was reluctant to grant him an equity stake in the company. In March 1916, Shortess grew tired of waiting and resigned. He raised money and launched the Federal Paper Board Company across the railroad tracks from his old employer. Being no stranger to the industry, Shortess generated about $460,000 in sales his very first year.

People inside the industry joked that Will Shortess couldn't drive by a paperboard mill without buying it. Less than six months after opening for business, he bought a second mill at Versailles, Connecticut. By the late 1920s, he owned and operated eight mills. Most he bought at a discount and, after modernizing equipment, led to impressive levels of productivity. When he acquired his Steubenville, Ohio, plant in 1928, it still had a dirt floor. Within years it not only had a concrete floor, it became one of his key plants.

Shortess was widely saluted as a visionary and gambler, but was less heralded as a financial manager. Throughout his life with Federal he could be characterized as one step ahead of his creditors. If a promising plant was on the market, Shortess bought it and worried about paying for it later. Through his 1920s buying spree, the interest payments on previous obligations were left unattended.

Finally, in January 1929, creditors seized control of the business and made him submit a letter of resignation, which they could accept later if they so elected. Not long after, the country entered the Great Depression, further eroding the power base of Shortess. Yet Shortess, full of optimism and energy, cut his costs and stopped buying mills for a full five years. He repaid all his debts, and the creditors tore up his resignation letter.

In 1935, Shortess purchased the S-C-S Box Company of Palmer, Massachusetts. The company made egg cartons, clothing boxes, and bakery boxes, and when orders were slow they made jigsaw puzzles. So successful was this plant that, in the 1970s, it was the sole Federal Paper Board mill operating that had been acquired by Shortess.

Will Shortess died on February 4, 1942, at the age of 71. His wife, Joanna Shortess, assumed ownership of the company. Inexperienced at business, the 74-year-old Joanna first thought about running the company herself. She later dropped that idea and sold the company to the three top executives: J. R. Kennedy, Shortess's assistant, Guy Freas, manager of the Steubenville plant, and Howard Brown, manager of the Versailles plant. Will and Joanna, with no children of their own, considered these three men as their extended family.

Today, Federal Paper Board Company is a diverse, international operation with annual sales of nearly $1.5 billion. In March 1996, Federal Paper Board became part of International Paper Company.

SOURCES: Federal Paper Board Company archives; Richard Blodgett, *Federal Paper Board at Seventy-Five,* Greenwich Publishing Group, 1991

Mo Siegel

[Celestial Seasonings, Inc.]

Mo Siegel was born in Salida, Colorado. When he was two, his mother died tragically following an automobile accident. His entrepreneurial father—who sold military surplus, real estate, and other merchandise, as well as operating a dairy farm and pharmacy—remarried two years later.

The family then moved to the small town of Palmer Lake, Colorado. There, he developed an appreciation for the mountains and the great outdoors. He also had to learn to live with asthma, which spurred an interest in healthy eating and living that eventually led to a job with a health food store in Aspen, Colorado.

In 1960, the 19-year-old Siegel was living in Boulder, where friends and family would pick herbs in the hills for tea. Soon, the group was selling their natural teas, packaged in hand-sewn tea bags, through local health food stores. The venture was named Celestial Seasonings, in honor of the nickname of one of the founders, and the tea was called MO's 36 Herb Tea. The company operated from an old barn outside of Boulder.

In 1970, the six-employee company established a new line: Sleepytime Herb Tea. One year later, Celestial moved into larger facilities, and Siegel started purchasing herbs from around the world. In 1972, Red Zinger Herb Tea was introduced, and within two years annual sales topped $1 million.

Siegel established the Red Zinger Bicycle Classic race in 1975. He later sold sponsorship of the event to Coors, and today the event is known as the Coors Bicycle Classic. Employment and sales at Celestial grew steadily over the next nine years, and in 1984 the company was sold to Kraft.

Within two years, Siegel left the company to pursue other interests, including a company that grows algae that produces a chemical that may treat heart disease. He also worked with singer/musician John Denver on his Windstar Foundation. Then Siegel launched Earth Wise, a company that manufactures a line of environment-friendly cleaning products.

In 1991, Celestial asked Siegel to return as the head of the company he had founded more than 20 years earlier. Within two years he took the company public and introduced *American Casuals Black Teas,* which featured packaging that included essays from celebrity writers. That year, sales increased to nearly $60 million.

Today, annual sales at Celestial is nearly $70 million. Mo, now in his late 40s, and his wife, actress Jennifer Cooke, have two children. He also has three children from his first marriage.

SOURCES: Celestial Seasonings archives; Jeffrey Leib, "Celestial's Soul," *The Denver Post Magazine,* February 27, 1994

Melvin Simon, Herbert Simon

[Simon Property Group]

After graduating from the Bronx High School of Science, Melvin Simon earned a B.S. degree in accounting and an MBA at the City College of New York. While serving in the U.S. Army, Melvin was transferred to Fort Benjamin Harrison in Indianapolis, Indiana. Upon discharge, he remained in Indianapolis and went to work for a local shopping center developer.

In 1960, Melvin's brothers, Herbert and Fred, joined him in Indianapolis, and the three of them launched their own development company: Melvin Simon & Associates. They developed shopping centers around one or two key anchor tenants and then sold them to investors.

The company's early projects were modest, usually involving grocery stores and drugstores. Soon the brothers were building Kmarts throughout the Midwest. Their first enclosed mall, the University Mall in Fort Collins, Colorado, was built around an existing Montgomery Ward store. By 1967, the brothers owned and operated more than 3 million square feet of retail space, and were adding more than 1 million square feet annually.

By the early 1980s, the company was opening as many as four new enclosed malls each year. In the late 1980s, Simon & Company featured innovative urban development projects, such as O'Hare International Center and Riverway next to O'Hare Airport in Chicago; The Fashion Centre at Pentagon City in Arlington, Virginia; and the Newport Centre Mall project in Jersey City, New Jersey. The company also developed A&S Plaza, a nine-story "vertical mall" in midtown Manhattan.

The 1990s brought even bolder property development projects. In partnership with The Gordon Company, the brothers opened The Forum Shops at Caesars, between Caesars Palace and The Mirage hotels in Las Vegas, Nevada. In August 1992, Simon and its partner, Triple Five Corporation, opened the Mall of America in Bloomington, Minnesota.

On December 14, 1993, the Simon Property Group went public, raising nearly $840 million, qualifying it as the largest publicly held real estate investment trust. The growth didn't stop there. In 1996, the company merged with part of the holdings of the Edward J. DeBartolo Company of Youngstown, Ohio, a $3 billion marriage. Today, Simon DeBartolo controls 110 million square feet of space in 32 states, a total of about 7 percent of all shopping mall space in America.

Herbert and Melvin also own the Indiana Pacers basketball franchise. Melvin Simon's son, David, now serves as CEO of the company.

SOURCE: Simon archives

John R. Simplot

[J.R. Simplot Company]

John Richard "Jack" Simplot was born on January 4, 1909, in Bunkin, Iowa, the third of six children born to Charles and Dorothy Simplot. Shortly after his birth the family moved to Washington, then a year later to a farm at Burley, Idaho. When he was eight years old, the family moved to Venice, California. Young Simplot became a newspaperboy, and rather than fight other boys for strategic street corners, he walked the hallways of office buildings and sold to customers before they reached the street.

The family later moved to Santa Rosa, California, where Simplot found a way to beat his competition in another field. A local golf course offered opportunities for boys to caddie, but Simplot's young age put him at a disadvantage with the older boys. His solution was to hitch rides with the golfers as they drove to the course, and during the ride he would bargain with them for caddie services.

In 1922, the family moved back to Idaho, settling on the family's farm at Declo, and young Simplot spent most of his time engaged with rugged chores.

One year later, at age 14, he decided to leave the farm and pursue other opportunities. He dropped out of school, earned $80 selling his lambs, and found a variety of jobs sorting potatoes, digging irrigation ditches, and even trapping muskrat.

After three years, Simplot returned to the family farm and launched another venture. The hog market was depressed and he was able to purchase about 500 head for $1 each. To fatten them up, he built an enormous vat into which he dumped water, discarded potatoes, hay, barley, and horsemeat and cooked the mixture over fires fueled by sagebrush and used tires.

A few months later, he was able to sell the entire herd for about $7,800, yielding him a considerable profit. This provided the capital he needed to establish his own farming business, and he purchased farm equipment, horses, seed potatoes, and a used car. By 1927, Simplot was farming potatoes on 120 acres of rented land.

In 1930, Simplot was introduced to a machine that automatically sorted potatoes. He and another farmer split the $254 purchase price of the machine and not only used it on their own farms, but they also leased it to other farmers. When they had a dispute about clients, Simplot suggested they flip a coin and the winner gets the machine. Simplot won the toss.

With clear title to his sorting machine, Simplot organized the J.R. Simplot Produce Company and started acquiring potato-packing warehouses. By 1940, the 31-year-old Simplot was operating 32 packing warehouses and was the largest single shipper of Idaho potatoes, shipping 10,000 railroad carsful that year.

That same year he was presented with another opportunity. An onion processor in Berkeley, California, was delinquent in paying an $8,500 bill to Simplot. When Simplot visited the man, he met another client who was also upset because the processor was behind on delivery. The two men talked and drafted a contract on an envelope for Simplot to deliver 200,000 pounds of onion flakes and 300,000 pounds of onion powder. Simplot returned to Idaho and, after finding someone who knew how to make onion flakes and onion powder, fulfilled the contract.

During World War II, Simplot's potato empire grew through huge contracts to supply dried potato products to the military. As the war wound down, he knew that he'd have to find new markets to maintain the same level of sales. The solution came from one of his own researchers, who developed a method of frying and freezing cut potatoes—french fries. The new product quickly caught on, and Simplot became one of the driving forces behind (and primary suppliers of) McDonald's french fries.

Simplot has been twice married. He and his first wife had three sons and a daughter. He and his second wife, Esther, did not have any children. Jack Simplot retired from active management of the privately held company which bears his name. The agribusiness firm today has nearly $3 billion in annual sales and 13,000 employees. Today Simplot serves on the board of directors of Micron Technology, a large manufacturer of computer chips.

SOURCES: J.R. Simplot Company archives; Harold R. Bunderson, Idaho Entrepreneurs—Profiles in Business, Boise State University, Boise, ID

Solomon G. Simpson

[Simpson Timber Company]

Raised along rough Canadian rivers, Solomon "Sol" Simpson spent his teenage years moving logs along the water. He immigrated to Nevada in search of gold, but instead made his money in logging and road-plowing ventures. He followed the lumberjacks to the Washington forests, where he established the Simpson Logging Company, which grew into one of America's premiere forest products companies.

Solomon Grout Simpson was born in 1843 in St. Charles, Quebec, Canada. His parents, Joseph and Caroline Grout Simpson, had immigrated to Canada from Yorkshire, England, in the early years of the nineteenth century. While a teenager, young Simpson worked as a timber raftsman, floating spruce and fir logs along the Ottawa and St. Lawrence Rivers.

In 1865, 22-year-old Simpson moved to Carson City, Nevada, in search of gold. When his luck and money ran out, he started logging and grading roads. During this venture, he married Mary James Macon Garrard, great-granddaughter of William Garrard, the first elected governor of Kentucky. The couple later had two daughters.

After losing their Carson City home to creditors, Sol and Mary moved to the boomtown of Seattle in Washington Territory. With modest funds, the couple established residence and Simpson launched another road-grading venture with horse-drawn scrapers. Soon, Captain William Renton, founder of the Port Blakely Mill Company, became familiar with Simpson's work and hired him to clear railroad beds for the Seattle & Eastern Railroad.

As logging towns sprouted along the railroad tracks, Simpson diversified into log hauling with teams of horses. To provide a source of feed, he cleared some land near the tracks and raised hay, turnips, and carrots. Then, in 1889, Port Blakely awarded him the contract to harvest and deliver logs and hand-hewn ties to market. One year later, Simpson officially organized S. G. Simpson & Company, listing his primary assets as road graders and horses.

In 1895, Simpson and his investors incorporated the Simpson Logging Company for "land development, operation of canals and railroads, stage lines, wagon roads, logging roads, plank roads, tramways, operation of logging camps, telegraph and telephone lines, dealing in assorted merchandise, and carrying on a general mercantile business." Within three years, he was operating eight logging camps and 80 miles of railroad track.

Simpson's camps attracted many Scandinavian and Finnish immigrants. As they arrived at Simpson's headquarters, their assigned camp numbers were printed in blue chalk on the backs of their shirts. The men would then ride a flatbed car 25 miles into the forest to their quarters. Simpson also hired several family members and other promising managers. One talented man who Simpson hired as a foreman, Mark Reed, eventually married Simpson's oldest daughter, Irene.

When gold was discovered in Alaska, Simpson expanded his holdings into that territory. He invested in retail, banking, and transportation ventures. In

1900, he launched the White Star Steamship Company with C. D. Lane, owner of Nome's richest gold mine.

Then tragedy struck. One of the White Star steamers, with Irene aboard, disappeared at sea. Although the distressed ship (and its crew and passengers) was later recovered, a barrage of lawsuits and damage awards nearly bankrupted Simpson. Oddly, the only asset he was able to retain was his interest in Simpson Timber, which his creditors felt had little value.

Shortly after the Alaska incident, Simpson contracted a form of leukemia. He died on May 5, 1906, during a visit with Mark and Irene Reed. Upon his death, Alfred H. Anderson, one of the company's investors, became president of Simpson Logging. However, Mark Reed essentially ran the company and, upon Anderson's death in 1914, was named president.

Today, Simpson is a multifaceted forest-product conglomerate with holdings in both lumber and paper. It is still privately owned by Sol Simpson's descendants and is directed by members of the Reed family.

SOURCES: Simpson Timber Company archives; Robert Spector, *Family Trees: Simpson's Centennial Story,* Simpson Timber Company, 1990

Jacob A. Slosberg

[Stride Rite Corporation]

Jacob A. Slosberg's family immigrated to America in 1887 when the boy was only 12 years old. Five years later, young Jacob went to work for a Lynn, Massachusetts, shoe company. After learning the retail end of the business, he went to work for a shoe manufacturer, then two other shoe companies. Finally, he was hired at The Thomas Plant Company, where he spent the next 20 years.

Thirty years after Slosberg entered the shoe industry, he had saved enough money to launch his own company. He and partner Philip Green opened the Green Shoe Manufacturing Company in a converted stable in Boston, Massachusetts, in 1919. Soon, nearly 100 employees were turning out up to 1,000 pairs of children's shoes each day.

In the early 1920s, Slosberg's sons, Sam and Charles, joined the company. Shortly thereafter, Slosberg and his partner had a disagreement over the direction of the company. Slosberg wanted to produce higher-quality, higher-priced shoes, while Green favored bargain shoes. Eventually, Green sold his share to a local banker.

Slosberg's entry into the higher-quality shoe market was successful, and by 1924 the company outgrew its plant and moved into new facilities nearby. Business was brisk, and the Slosbergs purchased full ownership of the company ten days before the stock market crashed in 1929. Despite economic hardship, the company was able to not only survive the Depression, but to actually grow in size.

In 1933, Slosberg wanted to unite his Green-Flex, Mo-Debs, Junior Arch Preservers, and Shirley Temple Shoes under a single trade name. A former shoe manufacturer who owned the trade name *Stride Rite* was hired into the sales department. The Slosbergs liked the name and purchased it for $1,000, although the name of the company was not changed to Stride Rite until 1972.

At the start of World War II, the company was producing more than 3,000 pairs of shoes daily and employed nearly 500 people. In the decade following the war, employment quadrupled and annual production reached nearly 18,000 pairs of shoes. Jacob A. Slosberg died on September 9, 1953, at the age of 78.

In 1969, Stride Rite acquired Uniroyal's shoe division, including the Keds and Sperry Top-Sider footwear trademarks. Keds had been developed by the U.S. Rubber Company in 1916. The name was chosen because it sounded like *peds,* the Latin word for foot. In 1967, U.S. Rubber changed its name to Uniroyal. Sperry Top-Sider shoes were developed by yachtsman Paul Sperry in 1935, and Sperry sold his company to U.S. Rubber in 1941.

SOURCE: Stride Rite Corporation archives

Horace Smith, Daniel B. Wesson

[Smith & Wesson]

Horace Smith was born on October 28, 1808, in Chesire, Massachusetts. At the age of four, his father, Silas Smith, moved the family to Springfield, Massachusetts, where he had taken a job at the Springfield Armory. When Horace turned 16, he followed his father into the Armory, entered an apprentice program, and was initially assigned to assist a bayonet forger. He later became an accomplished gunsmith and is credited with several innovative improvements in machinery and weapons.

Smith left the Armory in 1842 and moved to Connecticut, first to Newton, then to New Haven, where the 34-year-old craftsman went to work for famed inventor Eli Whitney. Within two years he had moved to Norwich, Connecticut, where he was employed by a weapons manufacturer known as Allen & Thurber. While with this firm, Smith built whaling guns and barrels and invented an exploding bullet used to kill whales.

By 1852, Smith had changed employers again and was working for the tool company Allen, Brown & Luther in Worcester, Massachusetts. During this time he became interested in "repeating" firearms (guns that didn't need to be reloaded after each shot) and, that same year, established a partnership with Daniel Wesson to pursue that market.

Daniel Baird Wesson was born on May 18, 1825, in Worcester, Massachusetts, to Rufus and Betsey (Baird) Wesson. He lived on his family farm until 1842, when he entered an apprenticeship in gunmaking under his older brother, Edwin Wesson, who owned a shop in Northboro, Massachusetts. The business did quite well until Edwin's sudden death in 1849. Creditors eventually took over the business, leaving Daniel with very little, not even his personal tools.

Wesson and his wife moved back to Worcester, where he once again went to work for a gunmaker. The job put him in contact with Horace Smith, and the two men shared a vision for improvements in weapons. In 1852, they launched a partnership at Norwich, Connecticut. However, the venture ran into financial difficulties, and in 1855 the partners lost the business. Smith then returned to his hometown of Springfield and opened a livery stable with his brother-in-law. The following year, Wesson moved to Springfield, and the Smith & Wesson partnership was revived in October 1856.

The founders soon introduced their Model 1 revolver, which featured a .22-caliber rimfire cartridge. The business expanded rapidly, and in 1859 they moved their 25 employees to a new factory near the center of Springfield. By the early years of the Civil War, demand was so heavy and the backlog of orders so large that they refused to even accept new orders.

Sales dropped to a trickle in the postwar economy, so Smith and Wesson took their show to Europe and Russia, which proved quite successful. In fact, the first significant customer for their Model 3 .44-caliber revolver was the Russian military, which placed an order for 20,000 in 1881.

Horace Smith died in 1893, and Daniel Baird Wesson died on August 4, 1906. A series of successful new weapons has led Smith & Wesson through the twentieth century as a major manufacturer of military, law enforcement, and sports weapons. After undergoing a number of ownership changes, Smith & Wesson was acquired by Tomkins plc of London, England, in 1986.

SOURCES: Smith & Wesson company archives; Roy G. Jinks, *History of Smith & Wesson*

O. Bruton Smith

[Charlotte Motor Speedway]

After building a successful career selling automobiles and promoting car races, O. Bruton Smith and a partner built the Charlotte Motor Speedway. Opened in 1960, the poorly financed track couldn't attract large crowds and within two years was bankrupt. Smith left the state and built several more successful automobile and insurance businesses, using his profits to repurchase stock in the speedway. Eventually, he regained control and, through Speedway Motorsports, Inc., has acquired or built several more tracks.

O. Bruton Smith is a native of Oakboro, North Carolina. By the 1950s, he became a successful car dealer and promoter of regional stock car races in the North Carolina area.

In 1959, Smith made public his plans to build a superspeedway in Charlotte. At about the same time, Curtis Turner, a successful lumber industry entrepreneur, announced his own plans to build a similar facility. Since the city couldn't logically support two speedways, Smith and Turner combined forces.

The project proved challenging. Neither man was able to raise the nearly $2 million required for construction, so they took to the road selling stock for $1 per share. Once financing was completed, the land they purchased for the track proved difficult to develop, and construction was hampered by unusually heavy rain.

Finally, Charlotte Motor Speedway opened its gates on June 19, 1960, for the inaugural World 600 race. Fans were disappointed to find a mountain of granite in the infield, left over from the construction. It was so high that viewers were unable to see the entire track. The track itself proved inadequate, as the surface cracked and potholes appeared during the race. Flying asphalt even punctured the gas tank of one of the racing cars.

The condition of the track hurt ticket sales. After the 1961 World 600 race, Smith and Turner filed for Chapter 11 bankruptcy protection and lost control of the speedway. It was a devastating blow to Smith, who had put his heart and soul, not to mention most of his money, into the project.

Smith took to the road and, over the next 13 years, established several new automobile dealerships and insurance agencies in Texas, Arizona, Illinois, and eventually back in North Carolina. He continued to amass Charlotte Motor Speedway stock while the team managing the track made small but continuous improvements.

Finally, in 1975, Smith had purchased enough stock to regain control of his speedway. He tapped H. A. "Humpy" Wheeler to serve as president and general manager, and the two men set out with a new vision for auto racing. Their first move was major landscaping that included a beautiful graniteless infield.

In 1977, they borrowed more than $2 million for major improvements that started with the women's facilities. (Research demonstrates that sports that attract women are more likely to survive tough economic times.) Women represented only 12 percent of the race crowd, and Smith wanted to improve his market. He next added 10,000 more seats, a new press box, and the track's first luxury suites.

These actions paid off. Attendance skyrocketed and Smith repaid the loan in three years. In 1984, he launched another expansion, this time at a cost of $20 million. He built the Chrysler Grandstand, bringing total seating to nearly 108,000. He also built 40 luxury, two-bedroom condominiums, but the centerpiece of the expansion was the seven-story Smith Tower that housed offices, a movie theater, and the Speedway Club, which featured a five-star restaurant.

The track became popular through several racing innovations, including lighting that facilitated the first-ever night race of The Winston Cup. The raceway also introduced the Legends series. Several movies, including *Stroker Ace* and *Days of Thunder*, were filmed at the track, as well as many commercials.

In 1990, Smith was ready to apply his racing expertise outside North Carolina. He established Speedway Motorsports, Inc., and acquired the Atlanta Motor Speedway. He doubled seating capacity, improved traffic and pedestrian flow, and built a 46-unit condominium complex, complete with clubhouse, tennis courts, and a swimming pool.

Smith took the company public in February 1995. In June of that year, Smith purchased 50 percent interest in the North Wilkesboro (North Carolina) Speedway. He next acquired the 70,000-seat Bristol (Tennessee) International Raceway from founder Larry Carrier in January 1996. Smith is also building the 150,000-seat Texas Motor Speedway near Fort Worth on land purchased from Ross Perot Jr.

SOURCE: Charlotte Motor Speedway, Inc., archives

Clarence W. Spicer

[Spicer Manufacturing Company]

Clarence Winfred Spicer was born on November 30, 1875, on his father's Illinois dairy farm. He displayed an early aptitude for farm machinery and was given responsibility for keeping it in good running order. Spicer received his bachelor of science degree from Alfred University in 1899, then later studied engineering at Cornell.

While at Cornell, he became focused on the problem of providing power for the propulsion of automobiles. As part of his research, he designed and built his first "horseless carriage," which included a universal joint–propeller shaft drive. Soon, automobile manufacturing companies sought rights to his patented universal joint.

Several other inventions, improvements, and patents soon followed, including a machine for producing welded tubing, a railroad generator drive, a safety clutch, and a method for easily erecting a wire fence. Altogether, more than 40 patents were awarded to Spicer.

In 1904, Spicer formally launched his company in Plainfield, New Jersey. A local manufacturer of printing presses was too busy to build the universal joints for Spicer, but the company offered him space in its factory, where "C. W. Spicer, the universal joint man" (as his advertising literature proclaimed), went to work with his three employees. One year later, the company was formally incorporated as the Spicer Universal Joint Manufacturing Company.

Gradually, the business grew. When Plainfield residents complained about the noise of hammers coming from the company's plant, a separate forge shop was built in South Plainfield in 1910. By 1914, the company was in need of additional capital. Charles A. Dana then took control of the firm and, in 1916, reorganized it as the Spicer Manufacturing Company. Spicer was appointed vice president, and, free from financial matters, he concentrated on product innovation and improvement.

Among his other achievements were the development of hydraulic presses, a gear drive for railway car lighting, and air-conditioning equipment. Spicer and his wife, Anna O. (Burdick) Spicer, had four sons. Clarence Spicer died on November 21, 1939, at the age of 63.

SOURCE: Dana Corporation archives; The History Factory

Joseph Spiegel

[Spiegel, Inc.]

Moses Spiegel was a respected teacher and rabbi of the small community of Abendheim, Germany, during the mid-1800s. His eldest son, Marcus, was a part of the poorly organized German Republican Army that struggled in vain against the superior Prussian forces. In 1848, the Spiegel family was forced to flee the country to New York, leaving Marcus behind to fight a war that could not be won.

Among the Spiegel children who did make the trip was young Joseph. The family settled into a modest Manhattan home, where Moses provided a modest living by selling sewing and household goods by day and serving as the neighborhood rabbi by night. Eventually, Marcus was able to elude the Prussians and join the family in New York.

The oldest Spiegel child was Sara, who had married Michael Greenebaum and moved to Chicago, where her husband established a small tinsmith shop. Marcus, always looking for adventure, also moved to Chicago. He married and was living in Ohio by the time the Civil War erupted. Predictably, he enlisted with the Union forces, was commissioned a lieutenant, and rounded up his own troops.

Joseph Spiegel, in his late teens, eventually joined his brother in the Ohio Volunteers. By May 1864, the brothers were aboard a transport boat in Texas when the boat came under Confederate attack. Marcus Spiegel was killed in the battle. Joseph was one of the 270 survivors who were taken prisoner and marched to the rebel prison camp at Fort Camp, Texas.

Upon his release a year later, Joseph Spiegel traveled to Chicago, where another sister, Theresa, lived with her husband, Henry Liebenstein, who was a successful furniture wholesaler. The couple was anxious to help Spiegel establish a furniture store, and in April 1865, J. Spiegel and Company opened its doors. For the next five years, Liebenstein taught Spiegel the furniture business, and the small store grew steadily.

In 1870, Spiegel married Mathilde Liebenstein, the niece of his brother-in-law. Their first son was born the following year, Modie J. Spiegel. He was originally named Moses after Joseph's father, but an adenoidal aunt who tried to say "Moses" would instead say "modie," which was a treat for the Spiegel family. Thus, Moses became Modie.

The year 1871 brought another challenge when a fire broke out, possibly in the O'Leary cowshed, that spread through most of Chicago. Spiegel was able to save most of his merchandise, but he lost the small store that he had worked so hard to build. He soon opened in another location and, after weathering the depression of 1873, established a new partnership called Spiegel and Cahn, Retail Furniture Dealers.

Upon retirement of his partner in 1879, the firm again became J. Spiegel and Company. Two more sons were born as the company continued to grow and prosper. By the 1890s, however, the store faced another challenge. Its product line was always high quality and high priced, and the wealthy Chicago residents started to move away from the downtown shopping district. Joseph Spiegel remained adamantly opposed to carrying lower-quality merchandise and, for that matter, refused to extend credit terms.

By this time, Modie was active in the business, and when the company policies translated into financial hardship he was able to convince Joseph to carry additional product lines that appealed to a broader customer base. Joseph also agreed to offer credit. The switch worked, and the store regained its momentum.

During the first decade of the twentieth century, Spiegel extended its reach when it entered the mail-order business. This caught the eye of Aaron Waldheim, president of May, Stern and Company. Soon the two firms joined forces and established the Spiegel, May, Stern Company. The flagship store, by then known as Spiegel House Furnishings, resumed operation as a retailer.

Spiegel eventually closed its Chicago stores and, by the 1930s, focused on its catalog business. By the 1960s, Spiegel had become one of the dominant retailers in America—without operating a single retail outlet.

SOURCES: Spiegel, Inc. archives; James Cornell Jr., *The People Get the Credit,* Spiegel, Inc., 1964

Steven Spielberg

[Amblin Entertainment]

Steven Spielberg invested all of his childhood energy into making home movies in his neighborhood. After producing his first acclaimed movie at age 21, he dropped out of college and launched a series of blockbuster movies that have made him arguably the greatest director in the history of the film industry. Spielberg has recently teamed up with several other great American entrepreneurs in a blockbuster multimedia venture named DreamWorks SKG, into which he merged his film company, Amblin Entertainment.

Steven Spielberg was born on December 18, 1946, in Cincinnati, Ohio. His father, an electrical engineer, and mother, a concert pianist, moved the family frequently, and Spielberg spent most of his childhood in Haddonfield, New Jersey, and Scottsdale, Arizona. In Scottsdale, he made home movies while in grammar school and, at age 12, made his first film with actors.

As a teenager, he continued making amateur films and, upon graduation from high school, enrolled in the film department at California State University, Long Beach. After making five short films, his 22-minute film about hitchhikers, titled *Amblin* (which he later named his production company), was shown at the 1969 Atlanta Film Festival.

Based on the success of *Amblin,* the 21-year-old Spielberg was given a seven-year contract with Universal Pictures, making him the youngest director ever to land a long-term deal with a major studio. In 1973, after directing several television shows, including episodes of *Night Gallery, Marcus Welby,* and *Columbo,* Spielberg directed a feature-length, made-for-television movie titled *Duel.* One year later, Spielberg made *The Sugarland Express.*

In 1975, Spielberg spent less than $10 million to make his first blockbuster film, *Jaws,* which quickly made more than $100 million at the box office. At age 26, Steven Spielberg was the most sought-after director in Hollywood. His amazing ability to develop movies of mass appeal led to several other blockbusters, including *Close Encounters of the Third Kind* (1977), *Raiders of the Lost Ark* (1981), *E.T. The Extra-Terrestrial* (1982), *Indiana Jones and the Temple of Doom* (1984), *Indiana Jones and the Last Crusade* (1989), *Jurassic Park* (1993), and *Schindler's List* (1993). He also made several other critically acclaimed movies, including *1941, The Color Purple, Empire of the Sun,* and *Always.*

In 1984, Spielberg established his own production company, Amblin Entertainment, which has been instrumental in the development of several other well-known films, including *Gremlins, Goonies, Back to the Future* (I, II, and III), *Who Framed Roger Rabbit, An American Tail, The Land Before Time, The Flintstones, Little Rascals, Little Giants, Casper, The Bridges of Madison County, How to Make an American Quilt,* and *Twister.* Amblin also produces several television shows, including *ER, Tiny Toons Adventures,* and *Animaniacs.*

Throughout his career, Spielberg has undertaken projects in collaboration with other highly talented entrepreneurs. Many of his early films were made with his close friend George Lucas. More recently, Spielberg merged Amblin Entertainment into DreamWorks SKG, a venture he cofounded with moviemaker Jeffrey Katzenberg and record entrepreneur David Geffen. Microsoft cofounder Paul Allen later became an investor in the company, and Bill Gates recently announced a joint venture between Microsoft and DreamWorks.

SOURCE: Amblin Productions archives

Frederick T. Stanley

[The Stanley Works]

After gaining skills as a shopkeeper and Yankee peddler, Frederick Stanley joined his brother in establishing a small manufacturing business. In 1852, the company was formally incorporated as The Stanley Works, which has grown to be one of the best-known hardware manufacturers in the world.

Frederick Trent Stanley was born on August 12, 1802, in New Britain, Connecticut, the grandson of a celebrated Revolutionary War hero. At the age of 16, Stanley completed his schooling and moved to New Haven, Connecticut, where he became a store clerk.

After his father drowned at sea, the 21-year-old Stanley moved to Fayetteville, North Carolina, and invested his modest inheritance in his own store. He selected this southern town because most of the northeast was already saturated with shops and traveling salesmen, and he was convinced that better opportunities could be found in the "frontier" regions, where he didn't have to compete with Yankee peddlers.

Soon, young Stanley's store was successful. He often packed his goods on a wagon and sold them in the surrounding countryside. He frequently found that, in order to secure a sale of hinges, he had to agree to do the installation as well, a service he readily provided.

Stanley sold his North Carolina business after three years and returned to New Britain. He soon invested in a general store, as well as in a small company that made suspenders. He also became interested in iron, which by this time was replacing brass in many products. His brother, William Stanley, had become a partner in a small iron works, and in 1830 Frederick bought out the other partners, leaving the two brothers as owners.

At about the same time, Frederick and William installed a steam engine to provide power to their manufacturing business, giving them a competitive advantage over the shops that relied on water or horses. The small company was able to maintain a modest profit by selling its hinges and other hardware to peddlers for resale.

In 1835, Frederick, William, and a few other partners invested $18,000 to launch a lock company. The company quickly prospered and, through ownership changes, became known as Stanley, Russell & Company. In 1839, Frederick and William sold their share in the venture, which then became Russell & Erwin, forerunner of the American Hardware Corporation.

After another two-year merchandising excursion in the South, Frederick and his brother decided to return to manufacturing. They purchased an abandoned New Britain armory in 1842 and moved their dormant steam engine to the new site. Soon they were fashioning wrought-iron bolts, doors, and chest handles. Because of increased access to western markets through the growing canal, river, and railroad networks, the company grew quickly. In 1852, the venture was formally incorporated as The Stanley Works.

The Stanley family of New Britain was quite large and very industrious. On another side of town, two of Frederick's cousins established a partnership with Thomas Conklin to manufacture rulers. Eventually the business was folded into The Stanley Rule & Level Company, manufacturer of rules, levels, tri-squares, and other measuring instruments. Throughout the next several decades, Henry Stanley was able to guide the venture through numerous acquisitions and considerable growth.

The Stanley Works, under the leadership of Frederick Stanley and an enterprising manager named William H. Hart, also experienced astonishing growth through acquisitions and clever innovations. For example, Stanley and Hart determined that shopkeepers wasted time finding screws to fit the hinges customers picked out, so they started packaging screws and hinges together.

Frederick T. Stanley died in 1883 and was succeeded by his cousin Henry, who died three months later. William Hart then assumed the position of president and led the company into the twentieth century. In 1920, The Stanley Rule & Level Company formally merged with The Stanley Works, creating one of America's leading hardware manufacturing companies.

Today, The Stanley Works employs more than 18,500 people and has annual sales exceeding $2 billion.

SOURCE: The Stanley Works archives

Ellsworth M. Statler

[Statler Hotels]

As a young boy, Ellsworth Statler was captivated by the impressive five-story hotel that sat across the river from his Ohio home. In 1876 at age 13, he convinced the owners to hire him as a bellboy, and soon was running a billiard room and bowling alley on the premises. A chance trip through Buffalo, New York, led to the opening of a restaurant and, eventually, his first hotel. The Statler Hotels soon became the premier properties in several American cities.

German-born William Jackson Statler immigrated to Somerset County, Pennsylvania, in 1850, where he met and married Mary Ann McKinney of Scotch-Irish descent. Statler was a merchant and part-time preacher who was much more interested in heavenly rewards than in earthly possessions. Thus, he never displayed much interest in material wealth.

Ellsworth Milton Statler was born on October 26, 1863, in Somerset, Pennsylvania, one of eleven children born to William and Mary Ann. In 1869, William Statler moved his family to Bridgeport, Ohio, to assume management of a general store. The small Ohio River town sat directly across from Wheeling, West Virginia, a busy transportation hub in post–Civil War America.

To help with family finances, nine-year-old Ellsworth joined his brothers working at a local glass factory. His heart, however, lay across the river. Each day young Statler would stare at the five-story McLure House hotel, the tallest building in Wheeling. He begged his mother to let him apply for a bellboy position that paid $6 per month. She forbid it, and when he pressed for a specific age that would be old enough, she vaguely answered that he would have to wait until he was "in his teens."

In 1876, 13-year-old Ellsworth Statler stepped off the ferry in Wheeling and walked directly to the McLure House. He entered and announced to the young clerk on duty that he was interested in a job as a bellboy. The clerk quickly dismissed Statler, informing him that no jobs were available and that the boy was too young. The following night, Statler appeared again before the clerk, who again dismissed him. Each night, Statler reappeared, until the clerk finally gave him a chance when a regular bellboy didn't show up for work.

Unlike the other bellboys, Statler proved to be energetic and diligent with his responsibilities. When his father died two years later, Ellsworth told the owners that he was ready for more responsibility (and money), and the 15-year-old boy was promptly promoted to head bellboy. He started carrying a notebook, which became a lifelong habit, in which he noted ways to improve efficiency. When it became apparent that the owners didn't care for tedious bookkeeping chores, Statler assumed the responsibility.

After a major remodeling project, the owners gave Statler the right to operate the hotel's billiard room. A traveling billiard salesman arranged for his company to finance the new tables, and Statler was soon operating a first-rate hall. He also opened up a bowling alley, snack shop, and railroad ticket counter at the McLure House. Soon, he was pocketing $10,000 annually.

When returning from a fishing trip in Canada, the 31-year-old Statler came across a large building under construction in Buffalo, New York. He was captivated by the immense size of the block-long Ellicott Square structure, which promised to be "The Biggest Office Building in the World."

Statler decided on the spot that he would open a restaurant in this fine building. He signed an $8,500 per year lease, raised some operating money (including $10,000 of his own savings), and, with his new bride, Mary Manderbach Statler, moved to Buffalo. On July 4, 1895, his Ellicott Square Restaurant opened for business.

Every conceivable detail of the venture was addressed, except one. The people in Buffalo weren't interested in going to the downtown district to eat meals. The beautiful, highly efficient restaurant was a little bit emptier each night, until Statler's attorney recommended bankruptcy.

Statler fought back. He called all his creditors to a meeting and sat before the semicircle of unhappy merchants. Statler simply leaned forward and said: "If you men give me a year, every one of you will get every dollar I owe. If you don't, you may wind up not getting one cent." With that, he left the room. The next day, he was told that he'd be given his year.

That day, he fired his expensive chef imported from New York and hired a cheaper one from Buffalo. He also fired several staff members and personally assumed their duties. Still, he needed to bring in customers.

Fate came to the rescue. The veterans organization, the Grand Army of the Republic, announced that their annual convention would be held in Buffalo. When their members reached town, they were handed flyers announcing Statler's buffet meal for 25¢ per person. The crowd of visitors swamped the restaurant, and by the time the convention ended local patrons filled the seats.

When a consortium of local business leaders announced the Pan-American Exposition celebration in Buffalo, Statler saw his chance to build a hotel—sort of. The city couldn't support the event without more hotel rooms, but no one, including Statler, could afford to build a hotel for a single event.

Statler's solution was to build a "temporary" hotel of more than 2,000 rooms from wood and plaster. The exposition turned into a total failure, capped by the September 6, 1901, assassination of President McKinley after he addressed visitors. However, even though Statler's occupancy projections were not met, he was able to show a slight profit from the venture.

Three years later, Statler built another temporary hotel at the St. Louis (Missouri) World's Fair, this time netting a profit of more than $360,000. The venture had a tragic side, however, as hot coffee from an exploding urn scalded 80 percent of Statler's body. It took months for him to recover, and his health was unstable for the rest of his life.

In 1908, the 45-year-old Statler opened the doors to his first permanent hotel, The Statler Hotel, located in Buffalo, New York. Statler was involved in every phase of design, insisting (over the objections of the architects) that every room have a private bath and a closet. The 13-story, 300-room hotel became an immediate success.

On October 12, 1912, he opened his second hotel: the 16-story, 800-room Cleveland Statler Hotel. This was followed by the Detroit Statler, the St. Louis Statler, and the Pennsylvania Hotel in New York City. In 1923, he built a new Statler Hotel in Buffalo, renaming his flagship property the Hotel Buffalo. Next came the Boston Statler in 1927.

Statler and his wife, Mary, had no children of their own. In 1925, Mary died of cancer, leaving Ellsworth to look after their four adopted children. Two years later, without fanfare, Statler married Alice Seidler, his longtime secretary. In April 1928, Statler fell ill with pneumonia. Because of the scar tissue from the St. Louis accident, he was unable to fight the disease. On April 16, 1928, Ellsworth M. Statler died at the age of 64.

Upon his death, Alice Statler assumed the position of board chairman and, for the next 26 years, led the Hotels Statler Company, Inc., through considerable growth. In 1954, Conrad Hilton bought the Statler chain of hotels.

SOURCES: Statler Foundation archives; Floyd Miller, "Buffalo's Fabulous Hotelman," *Buffalo Evening News*, 12-part series starting July 20, 1968

Henry E. Steinway Sr.

[Steinway & Sons]

The piano, which traces its roots to the early 1700s, soon caught the fancy of skilled artisans throughout Europe, including Heinrich Engelhard Steinweg of Germany. Born in 1797, Heinrich's mother died while the family was hiding from Napoleon's forces in the mountains. Not many years later, he and his father were part of a group that was struck by lightning, and Heinrich was the only survivor.

By 1836, Steinweg was an accomplished craftsman and musician. He built his first grand piano in the kitchen of his Seesen home and presented it to his wife, Julianne Theimer, as a wedding present. Eventually Steinweg's five sons joined him in the music and piano manufacturing business.

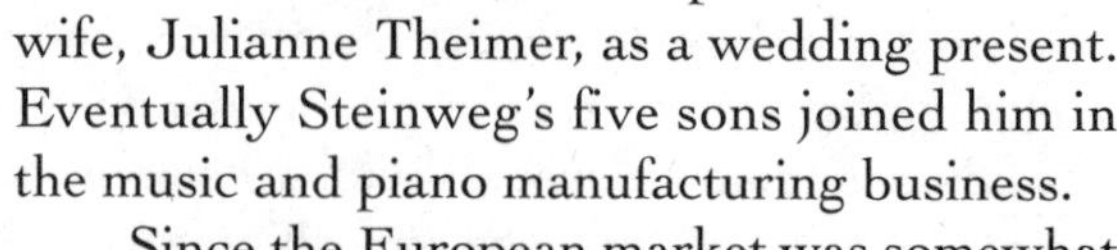

Since the European market was somewhat depressed in 1849, Heinrich's son Charles immigrated to the United States and soon found work as a cabinetmaker. The following year, Charles was joined by Heinrich and Julianne, his three sisters, and three of his four brothers—William, Henry Jr., and Albert. Heinrich's fifth son, Theodore, stayed behind to continue the family business in Germany.

To adapt to his new country, Steinweg Americanized his name to Henry Steinway (picture shown here). For their first three years in New York, the Steinways worked at other piano companies to learn American business practices. By 1853, however, they felt comfortable enough to launch their own firm, and Steinway & Sons was launched in a rented loft. The oldest daughter, Doretta, became their leading salesperson, often providing free piano lessons to customers.

Within two years, the company moved to larger quarters and successfully introduced its overstrung grand piano. By 1859, Steinway & Sons was selling nearly 500 pianos annually and had developed an international reputation for fine craftsmanship. In 1860, a new factory was opened on Fourth Avenue (now Park Avenue), where more than 350 employees were soon producing nearly 2,000 pianos annually.

Henry Jr. emerged as a highly talented designer and was responsible for all seven of the company's patents during its first 12 years. Tragically, he contracted tuberculosis and died in 1865 at the age of 35. Less than one month later, 36-year-old Charles died of typhoid while visiting his brother in Germany.

Because of the tragic losses, Albert's continued military service in the Civil War, and the declining health of 68-year-old Henry Sr., Theodore sold the family's holdings in Germany and joined his brothers in America. He and William then took charge of the company. In 1866, the family opened their first Steinway Hall, a 2,000-seat auditorium that became home to the New York Philharmonic symphony.

Henry E. Steinway Sr. died in 1871. Theodore and William continued the company's growth in the following decades. Control remained in the Steinway family until the company was sold to CBS in 1972. CBS, in turn, sold it to the Birmingham family in 1985. In 1995, Steinway & Sons and The Selmir Company merged to become Steinway Musical Instruments, Inc. The company went public the following year.

Steinway & Sons has been granted more than 110 patents in its nearly 145-year history. Curiously, the company has sold a total of less than 600,000 pianos—compared to the 200,000 some manufacturers produce *each year*. Yet, more than 90 percent of all piano concerts at major orchestra venues are performed on a Steinway.

Today, the company markets its pianos through less than 100 authorized dealers in the United States and 200 dealers worldwide. The Steinway plant in Queens, New York, produces about 2,500 pianos annually, a figure that has remained rather constant for the past decade. The company also maintains a manufacturing facility in Hamburg, Germany, that produces approximately 2,000 pianos each year.

SOURCE: Steinway & Sons archives

Thomas Stemberg

[Staples, Inc.]

After receiving his undergraduate degree (1971) and graduate degree (1973) from Harvard, Thomas Stemberg went to work for the Jewel Companies, eventually reaching the post of vice president for sales and merchandising of its Boston-based Star Markets subsidiary in 1980. His rapid rise was no accident. Stemberg displayed an early knack for opportunity. He was the first person in America to fashion a line of generic (unbranded) foods for price-conscious shoppers.

In 1982, Stemberg moved to First National Supermarkets in Connecticut as a senior vice president for sales and merchandising. One year later, he was named president of its Edwards-Finast division. There, he launched the company into a network of high-volume megastores that worked on one simple formula: cut costs, buy in volume, and cut prices. Despite his success, Stemberg found himself in a dispute with management and was fired.

At Star Markets, Stemberg's chief competitor was Purity Supreme, owned by Leo Kahn. By the time Stemberg was fired, Kahn had sold his food stores and was looking for another venture. He was quite familiar with Stemberg, and the two soon had breakfast, at which point Kahn offered to back Stemberg in a business venture. However, neither had a specific market niche in mind.

One Fourth of July weekend, Stemberg needed a printer ribbon for his computer. All the traditional stores were closed, at which point it dawned on him that office supplies were available only Monday through Friday, and even then they were overpriced. Suddenly, Stemberg and Kahn had a market niche. In 1986, they opened their first Staples store in Brighton, Massachusetts.

Originally, the low-priced office supplies sold well in the self-service warehouse. Over time, however, Stemberg modified his strategy to focus on building long-term relationships with customers. Today, sales personnel patrol store aisles, ready to assist all customers with any question about the company's products, especially the high-cost electronic equipment. Sales are tracked to specific customers, to whatever extent possible, enabling the store to provide customized services to repeat customers.

The company topped $1 billion in sales for the first time in 1993. Two years later, it topped $2 billion. Today, there are nearly 500 Staples stores in the United States and Canada. In 1996, the company acquired rival Office Depot through a $3.5 billion stock swap, creating a chain of 1,100 stores. Thomas Stemberg continues to serve as chief executive officer.

SOURCES: Staples, Inc. archives; *Boston Business Journal,* May 12, 1995; *Fortune* magazine, July 10, 1995

Levi Strauss

[Levi Strauss & Co.]

Levi Strauss was born on February 26, 1829, in Buttenheim, Bavaria, to Hirsch Strauss and his second wife, Rebecca. Levi, named "Loeb" at birth, had six older siblings. His sister Fanny was also born to his father's second wife. His three brothers, Jacob, Jonas, and Louis, and his two other sisters, Mathilde and Rosla, were from his father's first marriage.

In 1847, two years after their father died of tuberculosis, Rebecca Strauss and the children immigrated to New York City. Jonas and Louis had already established a dry goods store and they put their younger brother to work. At one point, Levi Strauss roamed the hills of Kentucky, selling thread, scissors, yarns, and bolts of fabric. In 1850, the founding year of Levi Strauss & Co., young Levi was already established in the dry goods business.

In 1853, Levi sailed to San Francisco and established a wholesale dry goods business. The waterfront location was convenient for receiving the shipments that arrived by boat from the Strauss Brothers store in New York. Levi's sister, Fanny, had married another dry goods merchant named David Stern, and they also moved to San Francisco to pursue opportunities presented by the California gold rush.

In 1872, Strauss received a letter from Jacob Davis, a Nevada tailor, who described his innovative use of metal rivets at pocket corners and the base of the button fly. These provided extra strength at the stress points.

Davis wanted to patent the process but had no money. He offered Levi half ownership if Levi would pay for the patent. Not only did Levi finance the patent costs, he brought Davis to San Francisco to oversee production. On May 20, 1873, the pants were officially protected with a U.S. patent. Later that year, the double Arcuate Stitching Design® was added to the hip pocket. In 1886, the Two Horse Design® leather patch was introduced, completing the basic components that are still found on every pair of Levi's jeans.

The initial production of the "waist overalls," as they were then called, was done by seamstresses working from their homes. Soon, orders were piling up, and Strauss opened a factory on Fremont Street to keep up with demand. In 1879, Strauss was selling his pants for $1.46 a pair.

By 1890, the 61-year-old Strauss officially incorporated his company. For efficiency in controlling inventory, lot numbers were assigned to all the store's products. His denim overalls were assigned lot number "501," a designation that remains to this day.

Although David Stern had died, his able sons were active in the business, so Strauss turned most of his attention to other business and philanthropic ventures. On September 27, 1902, Strauss died in his sleep. He had left the bulk of his $6 million estate to his four nephews.

On April 18, 1906, a massive earthquake struck San Francisco. The magnificent Levi Strauss & Co. headquarters and factory burned to the ground. However, rather than close their business, the Stern brothers quickly went to work and replaced the facilities. In 1919, Sigmund Stern invited his son-in-law, Walter A. Haas, to join the company. The Haas family has been instrumental in managing the company ever since.

The company referred to its product as "waist overalls" until about 1960, when the word *jeans* became the accepted term for riveted denim pants. The word possibly derives from the *Genoese,* referring to pants or fabric from the city of Genoa, Italy; another explanation of the origin is a fabric called *jean,* which was replaced by the more popular denim.

Today, Levi Strauss & Co. still markets its popular 501 Jeans®. The company employs nearly 35,000 people worldwide and has annual sales of about $6 billion.

SOURCE: Levi Strauss & Co. Archives

Justus C. Strawbridge, Isaac H. Clothier

[Strawbridge and Clothier]

Justus C. Strawbridge was born on January 11, 1838, near Reading, Pennsylvania, one of three sons born to Dr. George F. and Ann (Zelley) Strawbridge. Upon her husband's death, Ann, a strict Quaker, moved back to her hometown of Mount Holly, New Jersey.

After growing up on the family farm, 15-year-old Strawbridge went to work for Joshua Baily, a Philadelphia dry goods importer, for a $50 annual salary. Eight years later, in 1861, he and another salesman ventured out on their own in a store owned by Baily, who also agreed to be their chief supplier.

The store quickly prospered and Strawbridge bought out his partner within two years. One year after the store became J. C. Strawbridge & Company, he married Mary Lukens, a Quaker schoolteacher. The couple eventually had five sons. To help manage the growing enterprise, Strawbridge turned to his good friend and supplier, Isaac Clothier.

Isaac Hallowell Clothier was born November 5, 1837, in Philadelphia, Pennsylvania, to Quaker parents who were active in the antislavery movement. At age 17, Clothier went to work for George Parrish, an importer of British dry goods. He later established his own business and married Mary Jackson. The couple eventually had nine children.

On July 1, 1868, the two merchants, both 30 years old, formed Strawbridge & Clothier. They built a modern, five-story structure in the heart of Philadelphia and, for the first time, the city was offered all types of domestic and imported goods under a single roof. Strawbridge took charge of the silks and Clothier focused on the other yarn goods. Delivery was handled by horse and wagon during the winter, and boys on foot during the summer.

Their early success was reflected in their profits: $15,000 in the first year and nearly $42,000 in the second. Soon they expanded their line to included manufactured goods and ready-to-wear clothes. Employment at the store rose to nearly 300 people.

The founders were innovative merchandisers, as illustrated by their "Shawl Room." An early advertisement proclaimed:

> New Shawl Room. Now open for Business. This new room is handsomely carpeted and furnished, and is one of the best lighted, spacious and most cheerful salesrooms in Philadelphia. We cordially invite our Lady Customers to make use of this comfortable apartment on their visits to the city, whether to purchase or not.

Clothier retired in 1895, and Strawbridge retired five years later. On March 27, 1911, Justus C. Strawbridge died at the age of 73. Ten years later, Isaac H. Clothier died on January 15, 1921. Second- and third-generation family members assumed management of the store, which started building in additional locations in the 1950s. Today, Strawbridge & Clothier is part of the May Department Store organization.

SOURCES: Strawbridge and Clothier archives; Alfred Lief, *Family Business: A Century in the Life and Times of Strawbridge & Clothier*, McGraw-Hill, 1968

Frank C. Sullivan
[RPM, Inc.]

In May 1947, Frank C. Sullivan founded Republic Powdered Metals to provide economical, high-quality industrial maintenance products that would waterproof, rustproof, and protect customers' plants, property, and equipment. His first product, Alumanation #310, is a heavy-duty asphaltic aluminum coating that has remained in the company's product line for nearly 50 years.

Sales in the first year reached $100,000 and, within ten years, surpassed $2 million. The company started to expand in the 1960s. In 1961, Sullivan opened a plant in Gilroy, California. In 1966, with annual sales approaching $7 million, he made his first acquisition: the Bondex Company of St. Louis, Missouri, manufacturer of Bondo auto repair compounds. That same year, the company moved into a campuslike setting in Medina, Ohio, which remains its world headquarters.

Tragedy struck the company in its third decade of existence with the untimely death of Frank C. Sullivan on August 18, 1971, two years after his company went public. By the time of his death, he had led Republic Powdered Metals to annual sales of $11 million. His philosophy—go out and get good people, create the atmosphere to keep good people, and let them do their job—became the governing principle for corporate growth and expansion.

Republic Powdered Metals, now known as RPM, Inc., posted sales of $1.3 billion for the fiscal year ending May 1997, marking its' 50th consecutive record year in sales and earnings. More than half of RPM's growth has come through acquisition, including such well-known companies as the Rust-Oleum Corporation, which has helped make RPM the fifth-largest paint company in North America.

SOURCE: RPM, Inc. archives

William R. Sweatt, Harold W. Sweatt, Mark Honeywell
[Honeywell, Inc.]

By the 1880s, a Swiss immigrant and Civil War veteran named Albert M. Butz had made his way to St. Paul, Minnesota, where he became involved with developing fire extinguishing devices. He also engineered a device that could regulate the dampers on a coal stove with information provided from a thermostat. While the device was not especially sophisticated by today's standards, it was quite revolutionary at the time.

With supporters, the Butz Thermo-Electric Regulator Company was launched on May 4, 1886. However, Butz proved to be more innovating than enterprising, and his patents fell into the hands of his attorneys and some local businessmen, who renamed the firm the Consolidated Temperature Controlling Company. One of the officers in the firm, George Wilson, suggested to his son-in-law, W. R. Sweatt, that the company would make a good investment.

William Richard Sweatt was born in Iowa in 1867, the son of a Vermont banker who had moved his family west in search of better opportunities. The family later moved to Fargo, North Dakota. At age 24, William Sweatt moved to Minneapolis, Minnesota, where he married Jessie Wilson.

By 1893, Consolidated experienced financial difficulties, and Sweatt was persuaded to take control of the company. He was able to stabilize the venture, but the other stockholders lost patience with their stagnant investment and, in 1898, sold the entire company to Sweatt for $5,000. He then changed the name to the Electric Heat Regulator Company and started improving his product line.

Meanwhile, a talented inventor in Wabash, Indiana, named Mark Honeywell had launched his Honeywell Heating Specialty Company to build and market his pressurized water-heating system. During World War I, Honeywell diversified into a broader line of home heating controls, making him a direct competitor of Sweatt.

In 1913, Sweatt's 22-year-old son, Harold, graduated from the University of Minnesota and joined the company, which by this time was renamed the Minneapolis Heat Regulator Company. The company now employed nearly 50 people and had annual sales of about $200,000. Father and son were able to increase this to about $1 million annually by the end of the decade. Another son, Charles B. Sweatt, was later named advertising manager.

In 1927, William Sweatt and Mark Honeywell merged their companies, creating the Minneapolis-Honeywell Company. Honeywell was named president of the new firm, a post he held until 1934. The operation, based in Minneapolis, was well positioned for a series of key acquisitions through the 1930s. In 1934, the company established its first European subsidiary in the Netherlands. That same year, Mark Honeywell was named chairman and Harold Sweatt was elected president. William Richard Sweatt died three years later.

The younger Sweatt had the company well positioned by the outbreak of World War II. As a leading manufacturer of electronic controls, the company built a diverse range of instruments and control equipment for the war effort. The experience opened the door for Minnesota-Honeywell to become a prominent postwar defense contractor.

Harold Sweatt became the chairman of the board in 1953, and Paul Wishart was named the first president who was not a Sweatt or a Honeywell. Ten years later, the name of the firm was shortened to Honeywell, Inc. Today, Honeywell employs 50,000 people in 95 countries. Annual revenues are nearly $7.5 billion.

SOURCES: Honeywell, Inc. archives; Jeff Rodengen, *The Legend of Honeywell,* Write Stuff Syndicate, Inc., Fort Lauderdale, FL, 1995

Jokichi Takamine

[Takamine Laboratories]

Jokichi Takamine was born in 1854 at Takaoka City, Japan, to Seiichi and Yukiko Takamine. When he was 12, his family sent him to live with a Dutch family at Nagasaki, where he was taught the English language. He later studied in Kyoto and Tokyo. In 1879, he graduated from the University of Tokyo and went on to Glasgow University in Scotland for postgraduate study.

Takamine studied the manufacture of fertilizers in Europe for several years, then returned to Japan and went to work for the Department of Agriculture and Commerce. He was soon given an assignment in New Orleans, Louisiana, where he met Caroline Field Hitch, the daughter of a southern mother and a former colonel in the Union Army. Three years later, the couple married and moved to Japan, where they soon had two sons.

In Japan, Takamine established the Tokyo Fertilizer Company and conducted private research on the diastatic enzymes of fungi. He soon developed an enzyme that proved to be highly efficient in the process of distilling alcoholic beverages. In 1890, he moved his family to Peoria, Illinois, and launched the Takamine Ferment Company. His process was not welcomed by everyone, however, and manufacturers who felt threatened economically were able to wage a campaign of hatred against the Japanese immigrant. Not long after he patented his Taka-Diastase, his plant was burned to the ground.

Takamine soon licensed his enzyme to the pharmaceutical company Parke, Davis & Company and relocated to New York, where he launched another research project. While studying the adrenal glands of sheep, he and his researchers were able to crystallize the naturally produced drug epinephrine. He quickly patented this amazing discovery and, in 1898, launched the Takamine Laboratory at Clifton, New Jersey.

For more than two decades, the size and scope of Takamine's ventures grew. In addition to his New Jersey company, he founded Sankyo Pharmaceutical Company of Tokyo and the International Takamine Ferment Company of New York. He was also instrumental in exporting several products to Japan, including aluminum, asbestos, Bakelite, and caustic soda.

Takamine became well known in New York society and actively supported projects that would enhance relations between Japan and America. When President Taft's wife launched a beautification project along the Tidal Basin in Washington, D.C., Takamine helped arrange a gift of 3,000 cherry trees from the mayor of Tokyo. To this day, Washington's cherry trees are a major tourist attraction, each year announcing the arrival of spring.

Jokichi Takamine died on July 22, 1922, at the age of 67. He had secured nearly 50 patents for enzymes during his lifetime. He was succeeded by his sons, who continued to build the company as a producer of enzymes for commercial applications. In 1956, the company was acquired by Miles, Inc.

SOURCES: William C. Cray, *Miles 1884–1984: A Centennial History,* Prentice-Hall, 1984; J. W. Bennett, *Takamine: Documents from the Dawn of Industrial Biotechnology,* Miles, Inc., Elkhart, IN, 1988

Charles D. Tandy

[Tandy Corporation]

Charles David Tandy was born on May 15, 1918, in Brownsville, Texas, the second child of David and Carmen (McClain) Tandy. In 1918, David moved his family to Fort Worth, where he and a partner established the Hinckley-Tandy Leather Company, which sold shoelaces and shoe soles to small shoe repair shops. Carmen Tandy and her mother supported the business by selling shoe polish and other supplies door-to-door.

Young Charles was an enterprising child who, among other ventures, sold scrap-leather products to his classmates. When he was 18 years old, a famous Broadway showman assembled a spectacular stage show in Fort Worth, complete with 55 beautiful dancers who wore gold boots as part of their costumes. Five of the dancers were scheduled off each night, and Tandy and a friend secured a contract to repair their golden boots for $5 per pair.

After graduating from Texas Christian University, Tandy set his sights on Harvard. By the time World War II erupted, he was on active duty with the U.S. Navy as part of a deal that enabled him to attend the Harvard Business School. Unfortunately, the war kept him from completing his MBA, and in 1947 he returned to Fort Worth and entered the family business. With him came his new wife, Gwendolyn Purdy Johnston, a widow and mother of two children.

The Hinckley-Tandy Leather Company started to expand once Charles Tandy entered the business. In addition to shoe accessories, the company had achieved considerable success marketing leathercraft kits. After the war, Veterans hospitals incorporated these kits into their rehabilitation programs, which helped expand the market beyond schools and hobbyists. In 1950, the partners split the company, with David and Charles Tandy keeping the leathercraft business, which was renamed The Tandy Leather Company.

Charles Tandy became the driving force of the company. He believed there was an incredible opportunity for growth in markets that served hobby and crafts enthusiasts. In 1952, he orchestrated the company's first acquisition, the American Handicrafts Company of East Orange, New Jersey.

In 1955, Tandy orchestrated a merger with the publicly traded American Hide and Leather Company, establishing Tandy Industries as a wholly owned subsidy of American Hide. By 1959, Charles Tandy was appointed chairman of American Hide and Leather, which included the 109 company-owned Tandy stores.

Within three years Tandy acquired Cost Plus Imports, a specialty retailer that was established near Fisherman's Wharf in San Francisco. After opening several other Cost Plus stores, it became clear that this new group of stores would do better as an independent company, outside of the Tandy organization. The chain, which was renamed Pier 1, was subsequently sold off.

Also in the early 1960s, Tandy became interested in a Boston electronics retailer named Radio Shack. It had been founded by Theodore Deutschmann in 1921 as a source of radio and electronic components for ham radio enthusiasts. When Tandy was introduced to the company, it had nine retail outlets and a mail-order business with annual sales of about $14 million. It was also in serious financial trouble.

In 1963, Tandy reached a deal with Radio Shack. He felt that retail stores would provide a better long-term revenue stream than the mail-order business. After consulting with past mail-order sales records, he started opening stores in locations where the most mail orders originated, giving him access to clients who would instantly recognize the Radio Shack name. Within a year, 27 new stores were opened.

Tandy's first wife, Gwendolyn, had succumbed to cancer. In 1969, Tandy married Anne Burnett Windfohr who, like his first wife, was a widow. Charles David Tandy died on November 4, 1978, at the age of 60.

By the late 1960s, the number of Radio Shacks increased to nearly 250. In 1971, it had nearly 1,100 stores. In the mid-1980s, with more than 3,000 stores in business, the company rolled out its TRS-80 computer. Tandy Corporation, now one of the nation's largest retailers of consumer electronics, has nearly 7,000 Radio Shack stores and has established 92 domestic and foreign Computer City outlets. The company has annual sales of approximately $6 billion.

SOURCES: Tandy Corporation archives; Irvin Farman; *Tandy's Money Machine,* The Mobium Press, Chicago, 1992

R. David Thomas

[Wendy's International]

Dave Thomas was born on July 2, 1932, in Atlantic City, New Jersey. He was adopted six weeks later by Rex and Auleva Thomas of Kalamazoo, Michigan, and Thomas has never known his birth parents. When he was only five years old, Auleva died unexpectedly, resulting in several moves for the family as Rex Thomas sought work.

Despite the turmoil in his personal life (or perhaps because of it), Thomas sought work early. At age 10 he tended gas pumps. He next tried delivering newspapers, caddying at a golf club, and even setting pins at a bowling ally, but Thomas quickly lost interest in all of these pursuits.

In 1944, the Thomas family moved from Indiana to Knoxville, Tennessee. He lied about his age and landed a job at Walgreen's Drug Store where, in full uniform, he made milkshakes and ice cream sundaes behind the soda fountain. It was the first job that Thomas loved; however, the manager found out that Thomas was only 12 years old and promptly dismissed him.

His father overreacted to the news and screamed at young Thomas: "You'll never keep a job! I'll be supporting you for the rest of your life!" The experience made a lifelong impression on young Thomas and, lying once more about his age, he quickly found a job at the Regas Restaurant in downtown Knoxville. The owners were not only successful restaurateurs, but were also kind, patient employers who helped teach the business to young Thomas.

When he was 15, the family moved again, this time to Fort Wayne, Indiana. There, he went to work as a busboy at the Hobby House Restaurant. When his family prepared to move once more, Thomas chose to rent a room at the YMCA, drop out of high school, and work full-time at the Hobby House.

When he turned 18, he enlisted in the U.S. Army. After attending cooking school, he was shipped to Frankfurt, Germany, where he managed an enlisted men's club. Upon discharge from the military, Thomas returned to the Hobby House in Fort Wayne where he met and married one of the waitresses, Lorraine Buskirk, in 1954. The couple eventually had five children.

Two years later, the owner of the Hobby House met a fellow from Kentucky at a restaurant convention who wanted to sell him franchise rights for his special chicken. Thomas objected to the proposal, but his boss went ahead and made the deal with Colonel Harland Sanders to put his Kentucky Fried Chicken on the menu.

In the early 1960s, Thomas's boss offered him a chance to turn around four Kentucky Fried Chicken restaurants he had opened in Columbus, Ohio. Thomas cut the menu, focusing on chicken and side dishes, and struck ingenious deals, such as trading chicken for radio station advertisement time.

By 1967, Thomas was part owner of the Columbus franchise with its four stores, and later he opened a fifth. The next year, the owners sold them back to Kentucky Fried Chicken, netting Thomas his first $1 million. KFC then hired Thomas to serve as the regional director of franchises from Florida to Michigan.

Throughout most of his life, Thomas wanted to own his own restaurant. Although experts said America didn't need another hamburger restaurant, he opened the first Wendy's Old Fashioned Hamburgers restaurant on November 15, 1969, in Columbus, Ohio. He named it Wendy's, after the nickname given his daughter, Melinda Lou by her brother and sisters.

Encouraged by the success of the first restaurant, he opened a second one the following year and two more stores in 1971. In 1973, he started franchising his restaurants with astonishing results: More than 1,000 Wendy's were opened in the first 100 months.

Today, there are more than 5,000 Wendy's worldwide, employing over 130,000 people, with corporate headquarters at Dublin, Ohio.

SOURCES: Wendy's International, Inc., archives; R. David Thomas, *Dave's Way*, The Berkley Publishing Group, 1991, 1992

William B. Thompson

[Newmont Mining Company]

William Boyce Thompson was born on May 13, 1869, in a gold mining camp at Alder Gulch, Montana, where he grew up alongside prospectors and

Indians on the rough American frontier. When William reached high school age, his father relocated his lumber and carpentry business, as well as the family, to Butte, Montana.

The administrator of Butte's high school was struck by young Thompson's intelligence and convinced the boy's parents to send him to the Phillips Exeter Academy in New Hampshire. There, Thompson learned about life beyond the Montana mines and made several friends who later achieved outstanding success. He did not graduate from the academy, but the experience prepared him for his subsequent enrollment at the Columbia College of Mines in New York.

Thompson remained at Columbia only one year, but the opportunity to see Wall Street in New York City firsthand convinced him that the way to make money in mining was through the stock market and not working in the mines. Thompson returned to Montana and made several unsuccessful attempts to open a mine of his own.

He was, however, able to negotiate marriage to Gertrude Hickman, a childhood friend. The couple moved to Helena, Montana, where Thompson established a moderately successful lumber and coal business. He also made an unsuccessful run for political office.

In January, 1899, the 30-year-old Thompson announced that he was fed up with getting nowhere. He packed up his wife and daughter, along with a stack of mining stock certificates, and moved to a suite in the Waldorf-Astoria Hotel in New York City. He was able to solicit modest financial backing and eventually negotiated an agreement to manage the Shannon Mine in Arizona. By 1904, he was able to walk away from the mine with a $75,000 profit.

Two years later, Thompson helped raise $1.5 million toward the expansive Utah Copper Development near Salt Lake City. Also joining the operation was another renowned mining dynasty, the Guggenheim family. This was the first of several ventures, including the Cumberland Ely Copper Company, that Thompson presented to the Guggenheim interests. By age 37, Thompson was a millionaire.

Thompson orchestrated several other successful mining ventures over the next decade. In 1916, he decided to consolidate his promotional activities under a single company, incorporated as the Newmont Company. The name was a derivative of the two states that had the greatest effect on Thompson: New York, where he made his money, and Montana, where he was born.

World War I sparked a worldwide demand for copper, and Thompson was ready. He had earlier acquired the Magma Copper Company, which operated a copper mine near Superior, Arizona, and in 1914 he had stepped up activities at the mine. His interest in the mine proved to be a long-term success because, by 1970, Magma was to become Newmont's best-performing subsidiary.

William Thompson died on June 27, 1930, at the age of 61. By the time of his death, Newmont had added oil exploration to its list of activities. By 1939, the company was also operating a dozen gold mines in North America. Today, Newmont Mining Corporation, based in Denver, Colorado, has annual sales of nearly $640 million.

SOURCE: Robert H. Ramsey, *Men and Mines of Newmont: A Fifty-Year History,* Octagon Books, New York, 1973

Charles L. Tiffany

[Tiffany & Co.]

Charles Lewis Tiffany was born on February 15, 1812 in Killingly, Connecticut. In 1837, the 25-year-old Tiffany and his friend, John P. Young, borrowed $1,000 from Tiffany's father, Comfort Tiffany, to open a stationery and "fancy goods" store in New York City. Their first-day sales receipts totaled $4.98. By 1850, the original line of umbrellas, pottery, and similar items was expanded to include watches, clocks, silverware, and unique gifts.

Tiffany was a gifted merchant who catered to a diverse customer base. He even offered, at one time, souvenir 4-inch sections of the transatlantic cable. He later purchased and sold the "Girdle of Diamonds" that had belonged to Marie Antoinette.

In 1851, Tiffany teamed up with silversmith John C. Moore and started to manufacture his own products. Ten years later, he established a Swiss office to help access fine timepieces for his customers. Eleven years later, he opened a manufacturing plant in Geneva. Soon, he innovated the Tiffany Timer, which today is known as a stopwatch. The company cited several uses for the Timer in their advertising literature, including "railroad, engineering, racing, gunnery, and scientific purposes."

When Tiffany moved his growing company to 550 Broadway in 1853, he placed an imposing 9-foot bronze and wood statue of Atlas hoisting a 4-foot clock above the doorway. This famous Atlas clock was later moved to the current flagship store at 727 Fifth Avenue, and a likeness is found in all of Tiffany's locations.

In 1877, the Tiffany Diamond, one of the world's largest and finest yellow diamonds, was discovered in the Kimberley Mine in South Africa. Eventually, the 287-carat stone was cut to 128 carats to obtain the 90 precise facets that provided its brilliance.

Charles L. Tiffany died on February 17, 1902, two days after his 90th birthday. His oldest son, Louis Comfort Tiffany, became renowned for his work in stained and iridescent glass. Today, Tiffany & Co. is a publicly traded company with annual sales of nearly $570 million.

SOURCE: Tiffany & Co. archives

Doug Tompkins, Susie Tompkins

[Esprit de Corp.]

Doug Tompkins, the son of an antique dealer, was born in Ohio and raised in New York. From a very early age Tompkins was an avid sportsman, preferring the great outdoors to the classroom. After dropping out of high school, he spent the next several years rock climbing and working his way across the country doing odd jobs, such as climbing trees for timber companies. He even tried out for the U.S. Olympic Ski Team.

While hitchhiking near Lake Tahoe, California, one fateful day in 1964, Tompkins was given a lift by 21-year-old Susie Russell, a San Francisco native. Six months later, they were married, and Doug launched a ski shop in San Francisco called The North Face. He added outdoor clothing, and the company experienced modest success.

Three years later, Susie Tompkins and her friend, Jane Tise, designed what they later called "some funky 1940s dresses," which were quickly sold to a local department store. Encouraged by the prospects, Doug sold his store and joined Susie and Jane in forming the Plain Jane Dress Company. The Tompkins apartment served as the business office, and their station wagon served as showroom and delivery truck.

The company soon generated enough sales to afford larger accommodations, and in 1969 they moved into a small loft above a massage parlor in San Francisco's Mission district. The following year, they changed the name of the company to Esprit de Corp.—a play on the French term *esprit de corps,* denoting their common spirit of camaraderie.

By 1975, annual sales approached $100 million and operations had been moved to a converted winery. That same year, Doug and Susie bought out Jane and entered into several partnerships for production, sales, and distribution in Hong Kong and Düsseldorf. In 1980, they started shipping a large mail-order catalog that became a successful alternative to media advertising, and Esprit quickly became a household name. The catalog, which featured the company's own employees as models, was discontinued in 1984.

The founders later divorced, and in 1990 Susie and other partners bought out Doug and proceeded to redefine the company. Today, the company employs more than 5,000 workers worldwide. Esprit is sold in department stores, specialty stores, and more than 300 Esprit retail stores.

SOURCES: Esprit de Corp. archives; Paul McHugh, "Alone in the Wilderness," *San Francisco Observer,* April 28, 1996

Reuben N. Trane

[The Trane Company]

Reuben N. Trane was born on September 13, 1886, in La Crosse, Wisconsin. His father, James Trane, was a steamfitter who had immigrated from Norway in 1864 and opened his own plumbing shop the same year that Reuben was born.

After graduating from high school in 1905, Reuben worked for a year in his father's shop until he saved enough money for college. He then attended the University of Wisconsin and, in 1910, was awarded a bachelor of science degree in mechanical engineering. Upon graduation, he went to work as a sales engineer for a Milwaukee machine tool firm. Reuben married Helen Katherine Hood on May 13, 1912, and the couple eventually had three children.

In 1913, Reuben returned to La Crosse and, with his father, incorporated The Trane Company to produce steam valves and traps that his father had developed in connection with a vapor heating system. Despite the distractions brought on by World War I, the company grew and a new plant was built. By 1925, three additions had been made to the factory, and employment reached 100 workers.

Reuben Trane was an active inventor, and during the 1920s he developed a convector radiator—which he called a "heat cabinet"—to replace the old cast-iron radiators. It was made from thin aluminum or copper fins that helped spread the heat produced by copper tubing that carried steam or hot water. When the established manufacturers snubbed his invention, he decided to build and market the units himself. Soon, he added an electric fan to his device, creating a "unit heater" that became widely used in manufacturing plants and warehouses.

Like most U.S. companies, Trane was affected by the Great Depression, but investment in new products continued. In 1930, the company opened a new factory at La Crosse. Within two years, Reuben Trane's experiments with air-conditioning paid off, and the company was soon manufacturing refrigeration compressors.

During World War II, most of the company's activities focused on the war effort. Trane produced a number of heating, ventilating, and air-conditioning products, but perhaps the company's most significant contribution was a unique aluminum brazing process that resulted in a top secret product called the *aircraft intercooler,* which greatly enhanced the performance of Allied aircraft. This technology was later extended to the space program.

The postwar building boom fueled Trane's rapid growth, as the construction of new homes, office buildings, plants, and other structures flourished. Concurrently, Reuben Trane pioneered the use of mechanical refrigeration in a wide range of applications, including railroad freight cars and buses.

At work, the inventor had not only built a strong company that changed the environment in which people lived and worked, he also was granted 27 patents for his creative products. Reuben N. Trane died on September 5, 1954.

Today, The Trane Company employs more than 17,500 people worldwide, including nearly 3,000 in La Crosse, Wisconsin. Trane was acquired by American Standard, Inc., in February 1984.

SOURCE: The Trane Company archives

James Treybig

[Tandem Computers, Inc.]

James Treybig was born in 1940 in Clarendon, Texas, the son of a geophysicist. He graduated from Rice University with a B.A. in 1963 and a B.S. in electrical engineering in 1964. This was followed by an MBA from Stanford University in 1968.

From 1967 through 1973, he held various marketing positions with the Hewlett-Packard Company, then worked for the San Francisco venture capital firm of Kleiner & Perkins.

In the early 1970s, Treybig recognized that a growing number of companies needed to have reliable mainframe computer power that would not be compromised because of power outages, disk failures, and so forth. To guard against problems, banks and other users were buying two mainframes and running them side-by-side. If the first failed, the second would serve as a backup.

Treybig was convinced that a single computer could offer the same level of reliability if it had two (or more) of each critical component within a single machine. In 1974, he launched Tandem Computers, Inc., to manufacture these fault-tolerant machines.

Once his engineers started working on such a machine, they quickly realized that they could not only incorporate two each of the critical components, but could easily include three or more under one computer roof. The technology developed permitted them to build very powerful machines at a surprisingly low cost.

The company went public in 1977 and sales skyrocketed. In 1980, *Inc.* magazine named Tandem the fastest growing public company in America. By 1987, just 13 years after being founded, the company recorded its first $1 billion year. Today, Tandem has annual sales in excess of $2 billion and employs 8,500 people worldwide.

SOURCE: Tandem Computers, Inc., archives

Donald Trump

[The Trump Organization]

Fred Trump was born in New Jersey, the son of an immigrant from Sweden. He was only 11 years old when his father died and, as the oldest son, assumed responsibility to support the family doing odd jobs. After learning carpentry at school, Fred built garages for neighbors, charging $50 apiece. After graduating from high school in 1922, he was hired by a local homebuilder and was soon in business for himself.

In 1936, Trump married Mary MacLeod and the couple had five children, including son Donald Trump born in 1946. Young Donald was drawn to his father's business early and spent considerable time on job sites, often collecting empty soda bottles that he returned for the deposit. The aggressive and assertive youth, liked by some and despised by others, often found himself in trouble for "stirring things up."

At age 13, young Trump was enrolled in the New York Military Academy in upstate New York. The experience proved constructive, and he learned how to channel his aggressive nature into positive achievement. In his senior year, he was appointed both captain of the cadets and captain of the school's baseball team. Upon graduation in 1964, he attended Fordham University for two years, then transferred to the Wharton School of Finance at the University of Pennsylvania.

After graduating from college, Trump returned to New York and took a job with his father's construction business. He soon grew restless with the tight margins and rough nature of building homes in New York's outer boroughs. Donald had his sights set on higher goals: Manhattan.

His first venture wasn't even in New York, but in Cincinnati, where a 1,200-unit apartment building was available for $6 million. The construction costs were nearly twice that but, for several reasons, nearly 800 of the units sat vacant. After putting $800,000 in repairs, the building was fully occupied. A few years later, he sold the property for $12 million.

In 1971, Trump rented a modest studio apartment in Manhattan and worked his way into the social circles and exclusive clubs of New York's elite. He became intrigued with an abandoned railroad yard along the Hudson River and convinced the owner, Penn Central, to sell the property to what he called "The Trump Organization," which wasn't much of an organization but it sounded impressive. The deal was made and the name stuck.

Penn Central also owned a number of other properties throughout New York. One in particular, the Commodore Hotel, caught Trump's eye. The property had fallen into disrepair, but the location, close to Grand Central Station, was attractive. He recruited Hyatt Corporation as a managing partner and, in 1975, completed the deal. Within five years, the Grand Hyatt opened to rave reviews.

His next acquisition was the Trump Tower, which he converted into the largest residential building in New York City. With these and other successful real estate projects in hand, Trump established national credibility as a developer. He then turned his attention to Atlantic City, New Jersey, where gambling had recently been legalized.

In 1980, Trump acquired about 2½ acres of prime oceanfront property in Atlantic City and, with Holiday Inn as a partner, opened his first casino. In 1986, he bought out Holiday Inn and renamed the property Trump Plaza Hotel and Casino. Encouraged by the success, he later added Trump Castle and the Taj Majal casino to his Atlantic City operations.

By 1990, much of Trump's empire had become entangled in debt, which was estimated to be $5 billion. However, Trump pulled off an astonishing recovery. In addition to his continued interests in real estate and gambling, he purchased the Miss Universe, Miss USA, and Miss Teen beauty pageants in 1996.

SOURCE: Donald Trump with Tony Schwartz, *Trump: The Art of the Deal,* Random House, 1987

Earl Tupper

[Tupperware]

Earl Tupper was raised in a poor family from Berlin, New Hampshire, where he graduated from high school in 1926. In 1937, while working in a DuPont chemical plant, Tupper experimented with plastics.

Tupper became interested in using plastics for household use and, in 1938, launched the Tupper Plastics Company. In 1942, he purchased a manufacturing facility in Farnumsville, Massachusetts. To maintain revenue, he was able to pick up subcontract work from DuPont and, during the war, manufactured plastic parts for gas masks and Navy signal lamps.

As World War II came to a close, American families were buying electric refrigerators and freezers in record numbers. Unlike the old iceboxes, these modern appliances used dry, low temperatures. A distressing side effect was that food frequently dried out and lost flavor. Tupper believed that plastic food storage containers could solve the problem, especially if a good seal could be created.

Tupper continued his experiments to develop home products with plastics. Since materials were scarce due to the war, he had asked his former supervisors at DuPont to sell him leftover plastic scrap. They could only provide polyethylene slag, a hard, black waste product of the oil refining process.

Amazingly, Tupper discovered a way to purify the slag. His refining process produced a clear, flexible yet unbreakable, tasteless, odorless plastic that was lightweight and easy to clean. He then developed an injection molding machine to fashion his storage products and designed a lid that worked something like a paint can lid, but in reverse. By 1946, he was able to introduce his line of Tupper Plastics, a collection of unbreakable containers that kept food fresh.

Tupper proudly placed his products in hardware and department stores—where they sat on the shelves unsold.

Along came an ingenious woman from Detroit named Brownie Wise, who liked the product after taking three days to figure out how the seal worked. She was the single parent of a seriously ill young son, and supplemented her secretary's salary by hosting home sales parties for Stanley Home Products, West Bend appliances, and other goods. Convinced that the product would sell only when properly demonstrated to customers, Wise and a few others added Tupperware to their line, and Tupper could barely keep up with the orders.

In 1951, Tupper pulled his inventory from store shelves and hired Brownie Wise to develop a direct sales program. Wise, who had moved to Florida, hopeful that the change of weather would improve her son's health (it did), found a 1,300-acre site near Kissimmee, Florida, for the corporate headquarters.

The emergence of the Tupperware Home Parties played an interesting role in postwar society. Thousands of women who were unemployed or underemployed, including Brownie Wise, found an opportunity to enter the workforce and achieve financial independence. Their success vaulted Earl Tupper's company to success far beyond what he imagined when he first left DuPont.

In 1958, Brownie Wise left the business and Earl Tupper sold his company to the Rexall Drug Company. After changing its name to Dart Industries, then merging with Kraft in 1980, Tupperware became part of Premark International, which was launched from Kraft in 1986.

Today, the Tupperware sales force numbers nearly 1 million people in over 100 countries. Nearly 100 million people attend Tupperware parties and demonstrations each year, and annual sales are nearly $1.4 billion. In 1996,

Tupperware Corporation was spun off from Premark and is now an independent public company.

SOURCE: Tupperware archives

Gary Turner, Richard W. Long

[GT Bicycles]

Gary Turner professionally repaired custom trumpets and, in his spare time, drove race cars. In the early 1970s, these diverse talents frequently came in handy, since his son, a devout biking enthusiast, repeatedly roughed up his bicycle.

After one particularly bad bicycle accident, Turner borrowed a friend's tube-bending machine and reconstructed a bike frame that was more durable and stronger than conventional off-road frame designs. Soon, he was making bikes for the entire neighborhood in the garage of his Fullerton, California, home.

Turner became acquainted with Richard Long at a local bicycle motocross (BMX) track. Long owned a bicycle shop in Anaheim, California, and the two men became friends. Both shared a frustration with the bicycle products that existed, particularly for the upstart BMX market.

Eventually, the two friends developed a vision for a bicycle company that would meet the needs of all age groups, while at the same time providing the quality and durability necessary for BMX and mountain bike environments. Since the demand for Turner's home-built frames never subsided, the pair decided to launch their own company.

In 1979, Long sold his bike shop, and GT Bicycles, the initials of cofounder Turner, was in business. Throughout the next decade, the partners expanded their line beyond youth bicycles, with special emphasis on mountain bikes.

Long is credited with positioning GT Bicycles as a modern-day version of the legendary Schwinn bicycle company. The time-proven Schwinn formula involved the supply of a complete line of juvenile-to-adult bicycles which, ideally, leads to brand loyalty among satisfied customers. With GT having a 35 percent share of the juvenile market, chances are good that Long's strategy will have long-term benefits.

Long and Turner kept GT Bicycles private until 1993, when they sold majority interest to Bain Capital Company, which took the firm public in 1995. Today, the company makes GT, Powerlite, Robinson, and Dyno brand bicycles at factories in Santa Ana and Huntington Beach.

Tragically, 46-year-old Richard Long was killed in a traffic accident on July 12, 1996, just one week before a new GT racing bike was scheduled to debut for the U.S. Cycling Team at the 1996 Summer Olympics at Atlanta.

Today, GT Bicycles employs more than 700 people and has annual revenues approaching $200 million. Gary Turner is still active in the company with special design projects and promotional events.

SOURCE: GT Bicycles archives

Robert E. "Ted" Turner III

[Turner Broadcasting Corporation]

Robert Edward "Ted" Turner III was born on November 19, 1938, in Cincinnati, Ohio. At age nine, the family relocated to Savannah, Georgia. His father, Ed Turner, built a lucrative billboard business after the family lost its cotton farm during the Great Depression.

Young Turner grew up attending boarding schools and military academies. After leaving Brown University his senior year, Turner went to work in his father's business, Turner Advertising Company. Not long after the company had just made a large acquisition, the elder Turner committed suicide. Ted Turner, at age 25, was named president and chief operating officer in 1963 and was able to not only turn the company around, but to take it to new heights.

In 1970, Turner purchased WTCG, an Atlanta independent UHF television station. Six years later, he renamed the station WTBS and started transmitting programming to cable systems nationwide, establishing the "superstation" concept.

Turner moved into the sports market in the mid-1970s. Turner Broadcasting purchased the Atlanta Braves professional baseball franchise in 1976 and, the following year, purchased the Atlanta Hawks professional basketball franchise. In partnership with the former Soviet Union, he organized the Goodwill Games in 1985. The international event made its debut in 1986 in Moscow and has since been held every four years.

In 1980, Turner launched Cable News Network, better known as CNN—the first live, 24-hour news network. The first home for the CNN staff of 300 was a converted country club basement. Despite technical and logistic challenges, the network steadily grew. Encouraged by the success, he established a second news network, Headline News, two years later. Then, in 1985, CNN International was created as a 24-hour world news network primarily directed to viewers outside the United States.

In 1986, Turner acquired the MGM Entertainment Company, including its film library of over 3,300 feature films. This library provided the initial programming foundation for the TNT network, launched the following year. TNT provides original productions, classic films, and sports coverage.

In late 1991, Turner acquired the cartoon library and production facilities of Hanna-Barbera Productions. The following year, he launched the Cartoon Network, the world's first 24-hour, all-cartoon channel. In 1993, he acquired Castle Rock Entertainment, a major motion picture and television producer.

Turner Broadcasting merged with New Line Cinema, the leading independent producer and distributor of motion pictures, in 1994. That same year, Turner launched yet another 24-hour network, Turner Classic Movies.

In October 1996, Turner Broadcasting merged with Time Warner, creating the world's largest media company. Turner serves as Time Warner's vice chairman and largest individual shareholder. He oversees all the assets of Turner Broadcasting (including all CNN networks, TNT, TBS, Cartoon Network, and Turner Classic Movies), HBO, the Atlanta Braves, and the Atlanta Hawks.

Turner is married to actress Jane Fonda and has five children from two previous marriages. Turner's empire employs more than 7,500 people and earns annual revenues of nearly $3.5 billion.

SOURCES: Turner Broadcasting Systems, Inc., archives; "Man of the Year: CNN's Ted Turner," *Time* magazine, January 6, 1992

John Tyson, Don Tyson

[Tyson Foods]

John Tyson was born on July 26, 1904. As an adult, Tyson supported his young family during the Great Depression by hauling hay from his father's farm near Kansas City to markets and returning with loads of fruit. The work was seasonal, and to generate a steady income Tyson started carrying chickens. By 1931, he decided to concentrate on transporting chickens, so he moved his wife and one-year-old son, Don Tyson, to Arkansas.

Over the next several years, Tyson developed a profitable business hauling chickens to St. Louis and Kansas City. He was an innovative driver, one of the first to use a special feed and water distribution system on his truck, enabling him to travel farther distances. In the spring of 1936, he gambled nearly $2,000 on a shipment of chickens to Chicago, where he netted a profit of more than $200.

Encouraged by the premium return he was able to get from cities that weren't close to chicken farms, Tyson started servicing other markets from Cleveland, Ohio, to Houston, Texas. Money was still tight, and Tyson often arranged credit at gas stations along his routes, paying his bills as he returned from making sales.

As the transport business grew, many of the farmers had trouble obtaining enough baby chicks to keep up with the demand. This prompted Tyson to become a distributor, putting him in a unique relationship with chicken farmers: He sold them baby chicks and, when they were ready for market, he came back and picked them up. When his supplier couldn't provide chicks fast enough, Tyson established his own hatchery.

By World War II, Tyson had found a third business market: chicken feed. Originally he owned a dealership for Ralston Purina. However, as with the chick business, when his supplier couldn't provide feed fast enough to keep up with demand, Tyson started mixing his own brand with wheat bran, corn, and soybean meal. In 1947, he formally incorporated his operation under the name Tyson Feed and Hatchery.

John's son, Don Tyson (pictured with his father at right), was born on April 21, 1930. He joined the growing family business in 1952 after attending the University of Arkansas. The company employed about 52 people and had annual sales of about $1 million. Helen Tyson was still keeping the books for the business, and chicks were being delivered from the back of John's car.

At about the same time that Don Tyson became active with the firm, the market for chickens was changing dramatically. New technologies and improved transportation capabilities increased the pressure on the already competitive market. The younger Tyson was convinced that the only survival strategy involved industry consolidation.

John Tyson had already purchased a small chicken farm, but Don wanted to increase the role that the Tyson family played in farming operations. He also opened the company's first chicken processing plant in 1957. Over the next decade, Don led the company into new and diverse ventures, including the lucrative Cornish game hen market and the acquisition of several key companies.

In 1967, John and Helen Tyson died tragically when a train struck their car at a railroad crossing. Don had already been serving as corporate president and, despite the loss, was able to maintain the impressive rate of growth. By 1971, annual sales were nearly $72 million and, within two years, more than doubled to $162 million.

In the early 1990s, Tyson made an impressive entry into the seafood market with the acquisitions of Arctic Alaska Fisheries and Louis Kemp Seafood. Today, Tyson Foods, Inc., is the world's largest producer, processor, and marketer of chickens and poultry-based food products, with production of more than 35 million chickens each week. Tyson employs nearly 60,000 people worldwide and has annual sales of about $6.5 billion. Don Tyson now serves as senior chairman and his son, John H. Tyson, is the company's vice chairman.

SOURCES: Tyson Foods, Inc.; Marvin Schwartz, *Tyson: From Farm to Market,* The University of Arkansas Press, Fayetteville AR, 1991

William E. Upjohn

[The Upjohn Company]

The roots of the Upjohn family can be traced back several centuries to the Apjon family in Wales. Some members of the family made their way to England, where the name was changed to Upjohn. Upjohn family members arrived in New York City in the 1830s, where William and Uriah Upjohn graduated from the College of Physicians and Surgeons. Following the advice of a professor, they set out for Michigan Territory.

In 1837, Uriah settled near Kalamazoo and married Maria Mills. Between 1839 and 1858, the couple had 12 children, 11 of whom lived to adulthood. This included William Erastus Upjohn, born on June 5, 1853, in Richland, Michigan. After growing up with the rigors of farmwork, young William joined several brothers and sisters at the University of Michigan.

Upon graduation from medical school in 1875, Upjohn joined his Uncle William's practice in the small town of Hastings, Michigan. In 1878, he married Rachel Babcock, the daughter of a Kalamazoo pharmacist, and established an independent practice.

Like many other physicians of the time, Upjohn was frustrated with the quality and usefulness of pills. Many of the crude compressed tablets quickly dried out and became so hard that they wouldn't dissolve in the body. Upjohn started experimenting with new ways to produce and seal pills. Using powdered medicine, he applied a protective coating while agitating the pills in a revolving frying pan. When swallowed, his "friable" pills quickly dissolved.

In 1885, Upjohn was granted a patent for his pill-making process. He moved his wife and two children to Kalamazoo (two more children were born later) and, with several of his family members, established The Upjohn Pill and Granule Company. The company's first price list included nearly 200 pill formulas, and the friable pills became an instant hit with physicians, not only because they worked, but also because they were priced lower. First-year sales were an impressive $50,000.

By the 1890s, the product list exceeded 500 items, and William Upjohn aimed for a wider market. He established a New York City sales office, arranged for representation in England, and sent company sales reps to major conferences and expositions. By the turn of the century nearly 60 people were employed at Kalamazoo and the company was well known. However, sales were stagnant, and a newer type of pill was being introduced elsewhere. Clearly, the company, renamed The Upjohn Company, needed another ace product.

In 1907, Upjohn became interested in a substance called *phenolphthalein,* which was found to be a good laxative. Despite the failure of other companies to package and market the product, William Upjohn insisted that the product could be successful. He designed a pink, rectangular wafer, flavored with mint, that was scored down the middle so that it could be easily broken in half. Given the name Phenolax, the flavored laxative went on the market in 1908 and quickly became the star product Upjohn needed.

Other innovations followed, especially after Upjohn established a research department in 1913. By 1923, Upjohn was highly regarded internationally, and the 70-year-old founder was considering retirement. His son, Harold, who was running the company, was heir apparent. However, Harold died tragically after a hernia operation, and seven years later William Upjohn passed control of the company to his nephew, Dr. L. E. Upjohn, who had been managing the New York office since 1906.

Dr. William Erastus Upjohn died on October 20, 1932. His company had grown to employ nearly 1,200 people and his products were in use around the world. Today, the company is part of Pharmacia & Upjohn, formed in 1995 when Upjohn merged with Pharmacia of Stockholm. The organization is one of the world's largest drug companies, with annual revenues in excess of $7 billion.

SOURCES: The Upjohn Company archives; Robert Carlisle, *A Century of Caring: The Upjohn Story,* The Upjohn Company, 1987

Marcus L. Urann

[Ocean Spray Cranberries, Inc.]

Marcus L. Urann was born on October 2, 1873, in Sullivan, Maine. He graduated from the University of Maine in 1897 and received his LL.B. degree from the Boston University School of Law. He joined a law practice in Boston and soon became intrigued with the cranberry industry on Cape Cod.

In 1906, Urann purchased his first cranberry bog and established the United Cape Cod Cranberry Company. A year later, he cofounded the American Cranberry Exchange, a cranberry marketing cooperative. As his visibility increased, he became interested in selling cranberries in cans, which would mean customers could enjoy the fruit year-round. Unable to entice the other members to join him, Urann launched his own cranberry sauce canning operation in 1912 and selected the brand name Ocean Spray for his label.

For nearly two decades, Urann expanded his sale of cranberry products. As other growers took notice of his success, they, too, began preserving their crops in cans. By the end of the 1920s, three dominant companies emerged—Urann's Ocean Spray Preserving Company, the A.D. Makepeace Company of Wareham, Massachusetts, and the Enoch F. Bills Company of New Egypt, New Jersey, which was operated by Elizabeth F. Lee.

Urann suggested that the three merge their organizations. In 1930, they combined to become Cranberry Canners, Inc., and Urann was named president. Under his guidance, numerous small growers from Massachusetts and nearby states joined the rapidly growing organization. By 1940, growers in Wisconsin and Oregon started joining Cranberry Canners, and by the middle of World War II, Urann had consolidated owners of cranberry bogs from coast to coast, feeding 15 production facilities.

During World War II, sugar and can shortages affected the company's sales to the general public. What little cranberry sauce was available was packed in glass jars. To compensate, Urann directed the preparation of dehydrated cranberries for shipment to soldiers. He also experimented with a diversified product line, offering a cranberry-orange marmalade.

Following the war, the focus of the cooperative, which changed its name to the National Cranberry Association in 1946, shifted back to the consumer market. By 1950, nearly 2,000 growers had become part of the organization, and the association's first Canadian venture, Ocean Spray Limited of Canada, was launched.

In 1954, the 81-year-old founder retired from the National Cranberry Association. Five years later, the name of the organization was officially changed to Ocean Spray Cranberries, Inc., to reflect its familiar brand label. Marcus L. Urann died on April 3, 1963, at the age of 89. Today, Ocean Spray Cranberries, Inc., has annual sales in excess of $1 billion.

SOURCE: Ocean Spray Cranberries, Inc., archives

Gilbert Van Camp, Frank Van Camp, Gilbert C. Van Camp II

[Van Camp Seafood Company]

Gilbert Van Camp was an innovative Indiana businessman during the Civil War era. Gilbert and his son, Frank, produced Van Camp's Pork and Beans and other goods. After Gilbert's death, the company experienced financial difficulty and was acquired by the Stokely Company. Shortly thereafter, Frank's son, Gilbert Van Camp II, recruited his father into a tuna canning business venture. By the 1920s, the Van Camp Sea Food Company (as it was originally named) was a leading producer of seafood products, including Chicken of the Sea tuna.

Sometime after the Van Campen family immigrated to America in the seventeenth century, the Dutch family Anglicized their name to "Van Camp." Charles Van Camp, born on May 12, 1787, moved from New Jersey to Indiana Territory in 1804, and established himself as a farmer and wagonmaker. On December 12, 1816, one day after the region was granted statehood, Charles married Mary Halstead. On Christmas day of the following year, Mary gave birth to their son, Gilbert.

After growing up on his family's Indiana farm, Gilbert Van Camp left home at age 17 with $1 and a bundle of clothes. Four years later, in 1838, Gilbert established a tinsmith partnership with "a Mr. Fudge" and starting making stoves. Other business ventures followed, and in 1860 Gilbert moved his family to Indianapolis, where he designed and built a cold-storage warehouse for his food preservation company.

Two years later, while the country was in the midst of the Civil War, Gilbert was the owner of The Fruit House Grocery, where he also experimented with using tin cans to preserve food. That same year, his son Frank was born. In 1882, after Gilbert had built a national reputation as a canning expert, he formally launched the Van Camp Packing Company. Frank worked closely with his father and served as the company's general manager.

One of Frank Van Camp's best-known contributions came in 1891. While salvaging the plant after a devastating fire, Frank opened a smoke-covered bottle of ketchup and poured some over his beans and ham during a lunch break. He enjoyed the taste so much that he later bought 10¢ worth of beans and a slab of pork, mixed them with tomato sauce, and packed them in three sample jars. He then sent them with a salesman to Pittsburgh, who came back with an order for a carload. This was the beginning of Van Camp's Pork and Beans label, a product that launched the company into international markets.

Gilbert Van Camp died in 1900, but the company continued to grow under Frank's leadership. Its success with pork and beans was followed by canned milk. However, the company didn't fair as well with tomatoes, and tough times followed. Eventually, the company fell into receivership, was purchased by the Stokely company, and renamed Stokely-Van Camp. Frank paid off his remaining debts and gave his blessing to the westward move of his only son, Gilbert.

Gilbert C. Van Camp II was born on January 11, 1888, in Indianapolis, Indiana. Like his father, Gilbert entered the family business at an early age and became quite adept at the art of canning. He also attended the Wharton School of Business at the University of Pennsylvania. When control of the company left the family, Gilbert moved west and went to work for the California Gypsum Tile Company in the Mojave Desert.

Gilbert's love for fishing led to occasional trips to San Pedro, California, where he became intrigued with The California Tunny Canning Company. Being well versed in the science of canning, Gilbert imagined his family's mass-production techniques could be applied to tuna canning. He summoned his father, Frank, who arrived in 1914, and they came to terms to purchase the company. Undaunted by their previous failure, the Van Camps were once again in the canning business.

Gilbert, now 26 years old, immediately repaired or replaced old machinery, laid out a more efficient processing plant, and built a cold-storage warehouse. On June 6, 1914, the first catch of albacore was landed and packed. Soon, the Van Camps were buying all that the local fishermen could catch. In 1915, the Van Camps commissioned 15 new albacore boats and gave them to the local fisherman, greatly increasing their daily haul.

After World War I, Van Camp was the only profitable canner in the region. Several of the other companies approached Frank and Gilbert about a merger, which was completed on July 13, 1922, when the state issued a charter for the Van Camp Sea Food Company.

Disaster nearly struck the family again. In an attempt to offset the seasonal nature of fishing, the company started packing grapefruit, tomatoes, spinach, and olives. The venture turned into a debacle, and the company went into receivership. Fortunately, the company came across an abundant supply of sardines and was able to pay off its debts. In June 1925, Frank regained his position as president. That same year, Van Camp consolidated its tuna products under a single label, Chicken of the Sea.

Frank Van Camp died on November 23, 1937. Gilbert, who had been maintaining his own fresh fish company and insurance agency, assumed the post of president. In 1945, his son, Gilbert C. Van Camp III, joined the company after graduating from Occidental College and a tour in the armed forces. He assumed the role of president on July 16, 1957.

The Van Camp Sea Food Company was acquired by Ralston Purina in June 1963. In 1988, Van Camp Seafood was sold to a group of private investors who moved its corporate offices to San Diego, California.

SOURCE: Van Camp Seafood Company archives

Lillian M. Vernon

[Lillian Vernon]

Lillian Vernon was born in 1927 in Leipzig, Germany. Her family fled to Holland in 1933 after Adolf Hitler came to power. Four years later, the family immigrated to the United States, and her father established a leather goods business in New York City.

Lillian got married in 1949, and two years later the 24-year-old housewife, pregnant with her first child, decided she could supplement the family income by at least $75 per week by selling goods through the mail. Using $2,000 that she received from her wedding, Lillian purchased a modest inventory of purses and belts from her father. She set up shop in her kitchen and placed a $495 advertisement in *Seventeen Magazine,* offering to personalize the products by monogramming her customers' initials free of charge.

Success came quickly, as orders for her $2.99 purse and $1.99 belt poured in. Within weeks of the magazine's release, she received $32,000 worth of orders. In 1954, Lillian rented a storefront for her company, called Vernon Specialties after her home in Mt. Vernon, New York. Within two years she rented an additional building just for monogramming services, which had become a major marketing attraction.

Encouraged by her initial success, Lillian developed new marketing strategies. She started manufacturing and wholesaling custom-designed products for other well-known companies, including Max Factor, Elizabeth Arden, and Avon. The first Vernon mail-order catalog appeared in 1956. The 16-page black-and-white mailer was sent to 125,000 customers who had responded to her earlier advertisements.

In 1965, Lillian renamed her company the Lillian Vernon Corporation. (The mother of two sons legally changed her name to Lillian Vernon in 1994.) Annual sales surpassed $1 million in 1970. By the late 1980s, Lillian had taken the company public (American Stock Exchange) and built a sprawling, million-square-foot distribution center on a 62-acre site in Virginia Beach, Virginia.

Today, Lillian Vernon still heads the company that she founded in her kitchen more than 46 years ago. Lillian Vernon—headquartered in New Rochelle, New York—processes nearly 5 million orders annually, has revenues of $245 million, and employs over 3,500 people. Each year, the company produces 27 editions of its eight mail-order-catalog titles for a combined circulation of 180 million copies.

SOURCE: Lillian Vernon archives

Marion E. Wade

[ServiceMaster Company]

Marion E. Wade was born in 1898 at Pocahontas, Arkansas. After his father's dry goods business failed in 1905, the family moved to McAlester, Oklahoma, where Marion and his three older brothers helped with family finances by delivering newspapers. Marital problems plagued his parents, who eventually divorced, and Marion moved with mother to Oak Brook, Illinois, where they lived with family members.

Young Marion had two dominant influences during his early life: a strong Christian home life and baseball. After finishing grammar school in 1912, he was hired as an office boy at a wholesale paper company. He continued his education by taking evening classes in mathematics at the local YMCA. He even landed a roster spot on the Terre Haute minor league baseball team at the age of 14.

In the summer of 1917, Wade met his future wife, Lillian, on a tennis court, and the couple soon married, leaving him with both a mother and a wife to support. He spent the next several years selling insurance and aluminum cookware, but the family finances remained unstable.

Then, tragedy struck in March 1926. When Wade returned home one snowy night to the family's small basement apartment, he found that his wife and three-year-old daughter had fallen ill and had been rushed to the hospital. His daughter died, and Lillian's condition remained critical. Wade blamed himself and their poor financial condition, and he vowed to make a success of his life.

Wade did achieve nominal success over the next three years, but in 1929 his employer went bankrupt as the country entered the Great Depression. Unemployed, with a wife and children to support, he decided to launch his own mothproofing business. Over the next several years, he not only built his business, but he also innovated a new moth-killing product called Fumakill.

In 1945, Wade's modest company had six people on the payroll. That year, he moved the company to larger quarters, added carpet cleaning to his list of services, and hired Kenneth N. Hansen, a local minister. A new venture—Wade, Wenger and Associates—then absorbed Wade's modest business. Wade was happy to turn control of the finances over to Hansen with the simple instructions: "Pay our bills promptly. Give the employees the best wages possible. If there's anything left over after that, I'll get paid."

The company was renamed ServiceMaster, representing the founder's conviction that all men and women are in *service* to the *master,* Jesus Christ. A satellite operation was promptly opened in Milwaukee, Wisconsin, then shortly thereafter in other cities. In March 1952, the company signed its first franchise agreement.

After experiencing a heart murmur, Marion Wade stepped aside in 1965 and named Ken Hansen to the post of president and chief executive officer. Hansen phased out company-owned branches, relying completely on franchise operations. He also looked for expansion opportunities. In 1962, ServiceMaster entered the hospital-cleaning market. This activity grew so quickly that, by 1979, 95 percent of ServiceMaster's revenues were from hospital contracts.

The company also added laundry and linen service (1967), plant operations and maintenance (1971), clinical equipment management (1975), materials management (1977), and food service management (1981). In 1975, Ken Wessner was named chief executive officer.

By the early 1980s, the company found that the growth in the hospital and institutional market was slowing. Corporate strategy in the 1980s and 1990s has been directed more toward residential opportunities: Acquisitions have included Terminix pest control (1986), Merry Maids cleaning service (1988), American Home Shield maintenance service (1989), TruGreen lawn care (1990), and ChemLawn lawn care (1992).

SOURCES: ServiceMaster Company archives; Marion E. Wade and Glenn D. Kittler, *The Lord Is My Counsel*, Prentice-Hall, 1966

Charles R. Walgreen Sr.

[Walgreen Company]

Charles Rudolph Walgreen was born on October 9, 1873, on a farm near Galesburg, Illinois, to Swedish immigrants Charles and Ellen Walgreen. The elder Charles was a widower with two children when he married Ellen, with whom he had three children, including son Charles. When young Charles was 14, his father sold the farm and moved the family to Dixon, Illinois, a growing community on the busy Rock River. Three years later, Charles was working as a clerk at the town's largest general store, I. B. Countryman's.

Walgreen soon took another job at the Henderson Shoe Factory. After chopping off part of his finger on a stitching machine, Walgreen and a local physician developed a friendship. The doctor liked Walgreen and suggested he take a job with one of the local drugstores, which the physician could arrange. Walgreen finally agreed and became a $4-per-week clerk at Horton's Drug Store.

Restless in the small town, 19-year-old Walgreen borrowed $20 from his sister and boarded a train to Chicago. Upon arrival, he scanned the *Chicago Tribune* want ads and found a job at a city drugstore. Several jobs later, he went to work at William Valentine's drugstore for a monthly salary of $35 for a 79-hour workweek.

Dissatisfied with his employer's strict management style, Walgreen stepped up his pace and planned to quit the job as soon as he was recognized as a model employee, thus causing Valentine to regret the loss. However, Valentine quickly rewarded young Walgreen for the effort with a pay raise and provided something of an apprenticeship in drugstore management. The recognition and encouragement prompted Walgreen to accelerate his studies, and in 1897 he became a registered pharmacist.

In 1898, the United States went to war with Spain. Walgreen enlisted for a tour of duty and quickly found himself in charge of a dispensary in Cuba. While treating patients, Walgreen himself fell victim to yellow fever and malaria. At one point he was unconscious for so long that his name was placed on a list of deceased patients. His condition improved noticeably and he was discharged with a modest military pension.

Walgreen returned to Chicago and went to work at a small drugstore not far from Valentine's. By 1901, he was able to buy the store and quickly improved the level of service offered to customers. The success provided the means for him to marry Myrtle Norton in 1902, and the couple eventually had three children, one of whom died in infancy.

In 1907, Walgreen made the final payment on his drugstore and, two years later, purchased Valentine's store as well. He soon built a large soda fountain at the new location, and when the summer crowds subsided Myrtle started cooking hot meals for customers. At the end of the first year, he tallied $40,000 in sales at the store that he had purchased for $15,000.

Walgreen recognized opportunity in launching new stores and installing a trusted employee to manage each location. By 1916, he had nine stores doing nearly $300,000 annually in business. Ten more were added over the next three years. The 1920s brought considerable growth, with sales increasing from $1.5 million in 1920 to $9.3 million in 1925, then to $47 million five years later. By that time, nearly 400 drugstores carried the Walgreen name.

In 1939, Walgreen retired from the post of president and was succeeded by his son, Charles. Charles Sr.'s health deteriorated quickly, and two weeks before Christmas 1939, he died at the age of 66. Today, the Walgreen Company operates more than 2,200 drugstores with annual sales of nearly $12 billion.

SOURCES: Walgreen Company archives; Herman Kogan and Rick Kogan, *Pharmacist to the Nation: A History of Walgreen Company,* Walgreen Company, 1989

W. R. DeWitt Wallace, Lila B. Acheson Wallace

[Reader's Digest]

William Roy DeWitt Wallace was born on November 12, 1889, in St. Paul, Minnesota, the third son of James and Janet Wallace. He grew up a rather spirited young man with considerable interests in sports. He attended Macalester College, where his father served as a professor, but suddenly dropped out shortly after a cow was found in a third-floor chapel.

He spent the next year working at a Colorado bank, then moved to the West Coast and enrolled at the Berkeley campus of the University of California. During his summer vacation in 1911, Wallace traveled to Oregon, where he sold maps door-to-door. He became enthusiastic about selling and spent his evenings scouring magazines for helpful ideas.

Wallace became aware of both the vastness and importance of information. He dismissed newspaper articles as too "hasty" to be of lasting value, yet books required too much time to read in quantity. He enjoyed magazines, which provided a thorough, yet compact analysis of a topic. Wallace was fond of conversation with a wide range of people, and concluded that most people were interested in broadening their horizons with a reasonable investment of their time and attention.

Wallace returned to college briefly, then dropped out and returned to Minnesota. After being dismissed from the Webb Publishing Company, he published his own 128-page book, *Getting the Most Out of Farming*. He took to the highway in a used car and personally sold 100,000 copies of the book to banks, seed stores, and other businesses that gave them away to customers.

The experience with his book convinced Wallace that there was a market for a publication that would help readers keep up with information and improve their lives. The idea was reinforced during World War I, when Wallace was injured in combat. While in recovery, he spent his days reading magazines. Upon discharge, he returned to St. Paul and became a permanent fixture in the local library while he attempted to sell his idea to an existing publisher.

Wallace was never able to forget a classmate's sister named Lila Bell Acheson. He learned she was unmarried, working in New York City at a YWCA, and was active in improving working conditions for female factory workers. He immediately sent off a telegram to her that stated: "Conditions among women workers in St. Paul ghastly. Urge immediate investigation."

Lila Bell Acheson (Wallace), was born in 1889 in Virden, Manitoba, Canada, the third of five children born to Reverend T. Davis and Mary (Huston) Acheson. Shortly after her birth, her family moved to the United States, where she later graduated from high school in Lewiston, Illinois. After graduating from the University of Oregon, Lila taught school in Eatonville, Washington, and became active with the YWCA. After World War I, the Labor Department recruited her for outreach to female factory workers, first in New Orleans, then in New York City.

Once DeWitt caught up with Lila, it was only a matter of time before they were engaged. DeWitt next took a job as a writer with Westinghouse in Pittsburgh, Pennsylvania, but was let go in 1921 during a companywide cutback. Frustrated with the lack of interest from established publishers, DeWitt became convinced that the only way that his idea could be tested was by doing it himself.

DeWitt and Lila decided to get married and self-publish their periodical. Through exhaustive research and writing, the first edition was prepared. They also developed a subscription solicitation letter and built a mailing list. In late 1921, they sent off their solicitations and took a belated honeymoon. When they returned two weeks later, there were 1,500 subscription forms waiting for them. A few months later, 5,000 copies of *Reader's Digest,* volume one, number one were printed.

The periodical proved popular. By 1926, the couple had 30,000 subscribers. Three years later, the number reached nearly 300,000, and by 1939 circulation was over 3 million. The company's headquarters was moved to Chappaqua, New York, where the Wallaces replicated many of the amenities found in Williamsburg, Virginia, the couple's favorite holiday destination.

In the years that followed, the company grew to become a global publisher of magazines, books, and home entertainment products, and one of the world's leading direct-mail marketers. DeWitt and Lila Wallace retired from active management of *Reader's Digest* in 1973. Before his death in 1981 at the age of 91, and hers three years later at the age of 94, the Wallaces continued the philanthropic work they had started years earlier when their company proved so successful.

SOURCES: The Readers Digest Fund archives; Charles W. Ferguson, "Unforgettable DeWitt Wallace," *Reader's Digest,* February 1987

Robert L. Waltrip

[Service Corporation International]

Robert Waltrip, a graduate of the University of Houston, took over his family's funeral home in the 1950s. With an eye toward expansion, he had added two more funeral homes to his Heights Undertaking Company.

During his early years as a funeral director, Waltrip began to develop the concept of a "service center" approach to funeral home management. He was convinced that economies of scale could be realized by sharing facilities, equipment, personnel, and vehicles. Such a notion was revolutionary in the industry that was dominated by family-owned funeral homes.

In July of 1962, Waltrip launched Southern Capital Company as a vehicle to acquire funeral homes. He targeted well-established, high-volume funeral homes and, once acquired, operated them under their existing names to capitalize on their established reputation.

Waltrip made his early acquisitions inside Texas. In November 1968, the company moved outside Texas with the purchase of Drake and Son in Chicago,

Illinois. One year later, he changed the name of his venture to Service Corporation International and made his first Canadian acquisition.

By making stock available to the public in 1970, Waltrip was able to finance an aggressive acquisition program throughout the decade. By early 1980, he added International Funeral Industries, the second-largest consolidator in the country, with 91 funeral homes and 22 cemeteries.

The company expanded its international presence in 1993 with the acquisition of the Pine Grove Funeral Group in Australia. The following year it moved into England, France, Switzerland, Italy, Belgium, the Czech Republic, and Singapore.

Today, Service Corporation International is the largest death-service organization in the world, with 30,000 employees, 2,800 funeral homes, 324 cemeteries, and 138 crematoriums worldwide. In the United States, the company handles one out of every nine funerals. Annual sales exceed $1.6 billion.

SOURCE: Service Corporation International archives

Charles B. Wang

[Computer Associates International]

Charles B. Wang was born on August 19, 1944, in Shanghai, China, the second of three sons born to a justice on the Shanghai supreme court. Not long after the Communist revolution of 1949, the family was forced to flee China, and the Wang family, including eight-year-old Charles, immigrated to Queens, New York.

Wang received average grades while attending Brooklyn Technical High School and Queens College. Upon graduation, he studied the *New York Times* want ads and, impressed with several pages of job openings in the computer field, announced to his mother that he wanted to be a computer programmer. When she asked what that was, he replied: "I don't know, mom, but boy, they need 'em."

Determined to learn the computer field, Wang was able to land a job as a programmer trainee in the Electronic Research Laboratory at Columbia University. Over the next four years, he mastered the art of computer programming. His next stop was a company called Standard Data Corporation, where he and Russ Artzt, a friend from Columbia, were assigned the task of writing and marketing software to enhance IBM mainframes.

Wang spent a considerable amount of time in the field, and he witnessed firsthand that the needs of clients were actually a secondary concern and that new technology was driving the market. He became convinced that a software company sensitive to the needs of the client would be successful.

In the mid-1970s, Standard Data was approached by a Swiss company looking for an American distributor for CA-SORT, a software utility for IBM mainframes. Standard Data was not only disinterested, they had decided to abandon the software market completely. With Artzt and two others, Wang established Computer Associates International and negotiated the purchase of Standard's software division.

While the early days of the company were lean, Computer Associates was able to operate profitably. Within four years the company was grossing $13 million, and in December 1981 Wang took the company public. He then established a pattern of making key product and company acquisitions in the rapidly changing computer market and integrating them into existing Computer Associates products.

The results have been astonishing. Computer Associates surpassed $1 billion in annual sales by 1989. Today, the company has 10,000 employees serving 100,000 clients, with annual revenues of $4 billion.

SOURCES: Computer Associates International archives; Charles B. Wang, *Techno Vision,* McGraw-Hill, 1994

Aaron Montgomery Ward

[Montgomery Ward & Company]

After deciding that barrel and brick making were poor career choices, Aaron Montgomery Ward worked in various retail positions in the Chicago area. While traveling through the rural southern states, he devised a plan to distribute a general-merchandise catalog to rural families that would enable them to buy high-quality goods at reasonable prices. After overcoming several obstacles, Ward finally shipped his catalog, which became an instant success.

Aaron Montgomery Ward was born on February 17, 1844, in Chatham, New Jersey. His ancestors had served in both the American Revolution and the French and Indian War. Ward himself was named in honor of General G. Aaron Montgomery Ward, an army general who served under George Washington.

When Ward was nine, his father moved to Niles, Michigan. Ward quit school at age 14, working first in a barrel factory for 25¢ per day, then in a brick factory for 30¢ per day. Ward later commented, "I learned that I was not physically or mentally equipped for brick or barrel making."

Ward moved to St. Joseph and became a salesman in a general store for $6 per month plus board. Eventually, he worked at several retail jobs in Chicago, during which time he became accomplished at the art of selling.

Eventually, he was assigned a territory in the southern states. While traveling through the rural communities, Ward became intrigued with the potential of the market. Customers were looking for goods that were quite similar to what was sold in the cities. However, because of their remote location, their only suppliers were country storekeepers and salesmen who added large markups.

Ward devised a plan to sell to rural clients from a distance. He would supply a list of products from which the customers would submit orders. Ward could then ship the products to the nearest railroad station. He presented his plan to friends and coworkers back in Chicago, none of whom were interested.

Unable to secure investors, Ward saved his money and, in 1871, was able to acquire a small lot of merchandise and prepare a single-page price list. Just as he was about to send this to members of the National Grange, whose members were active lobbyists for fair business practices in rural America, the great Chicago fire of 1871 wiped out his inventory.

Undaunted, Ward was able to recruit two coworkers into his venture, and in 1872 the three men rented a small room on North Clark Street and sent out their one-page catalog of about 150 items. This price list is often credited as being the world's first general-merchandise mail-order catalog.

Ward's close friend, George R. Thorne, had also lost his general store in the Chicago fire and subsequently went into the lumber business. In 1872, Ward married Elizabeth Cobb, the younger sister of Thorne's wife. The following year, Ward's two partners left the venture and Thorne became Ward's new partner.

The Montgomery Ward catalog quickly grew in size and distribution. In 1875, Ward offered a money-back guarantee to dissatisfied buyers. This presented a threat to the rural storekeepers, who reportedly burned the Montgomery Ward catalogs in protest. By 1888, sales exceeded $1 million annually.

Aaron Montgomery Ward died of pulmonary edema on December 8, 1913, at the age of 69. He and his wife had no children of their own, but had adopted a daughter, Marjorie, who herself had no children. A large portion of his estate was passed on to Northwestern University and other educational institutions. George Thorne died in 1918, and his five sons were active in the business in the ensuing years.

Today, Montgomery Ward employs more than 50,000 people in nearly 400 retail stores, 21 distribution centers, and 105 product service centers. Annual sales now exceed $7 billion. In 1994, the company obtained Lechmere, a large, privately held retailer in New England.

SOURCE: Montgomery Ward & Company archives

Arthur P. Warner

[Warner Electric Brake Company]

Arthur Pratt Warner was born in 1870, the son of a Civil War veteran. While still a child, the Warner family moved to the Beloit, Wisconsin, area where young Arthur saw his first electric light at a circus in 1880. From that moment, his passion was electricity. At age 13, he built an electric motor for his mother's sewing machine along with a battery-driven power supply.

At age 18, Warner provided the first electricity service in Beloit when he built a dynamo for the Beloit Iron Works. Two years later, he built a second plant. Then, at age 21, he and a friend, Wilbur Wiley, launched the Wiley-Warner Electric Company to furnish electric power to the residents of Beloit.

In 1897, he accepted a job in Madison, Wisconsin, with a manufacturer of DC power equipment. While devising his winding for elevator motors, he developed an interest in building a device that would measure the turning speed of electric motors. He eventually built such an instrument that accurately measured acceleration and deceleration.

He took the idea to General Electric, who turned it down because they thought the market would be too limited. Undaunted, Warner and his brother, Charles, founded the Warner Instrument Company in Beloit in 1904. Their mission was to manufacture speed indicators, which they called "cut meters," for industrial machinery.

The rapid growth of Warner's firm can be attributed to two factors. First, he was willing to invest in advertising. Second, he continued to look for new applications for his product, which resulted, for example, in a spin-off product that could be used to measure the speed of automobiles. The success of this product surprised Warner, who later said: "We did not think the auto-meter had any great future. It was only a luxury gadget which we used to promote the cut meter."

However, once the popularity of the auto-meter was apparent, Warner made a major commitment to its development and marketing. He pushed the product in front of the automakers. The Overland was the first car to have the auto-meter as standard equipment. The Cadillac was the second.

To boost public awareness, Warner built a car with a large, visible speed indicator mounted high enough for everyone to see clearly. He then personally drove through major cities, collecting his share of speeding tickets for exceeding the 10-mile-per-hour limit. While driving through Washington, D.C., President Teddy Roosevelt came out of the White House and asked to be taken for a ride. At age 42, Warner sold his company to the Stewart Company of Chicago, which was reorganized as Stewart-Warner, a leading manufacturer of automotive instruments.

In the early 1900s, Warner developed an interest in airplanes. After meeting aviation pioneer Glen Curtiss in 1906, Warner helped form the Aeronautical Society of America. In 1909, he ordered an airplane, only the third built by Curtiss. While delivering the plane to Warner, Curtiss flew it in an exhibition in St. Louis. In the crowd below was a young boy named Charles Lindbergh who was so affected by the show that he followed a career in aviation.

Warner also founded the Warner Trailer Company, launched just before the start of World War I. His early products included a tourist trailer, forerunner to the modern recreational vehicles. However, his real growth was in industrial, military, and farm trailers. In 1929, he sold the trailer company to Fruehauf.

In 1927, Warner launched yet another company: the Warner Electric Brake Corporation. The young company, however, was quickly saddled with the Great Depression, which kept growth at a minimum. However, the company rebounded in the late 1930s, capturing nearly three-fourths of the country's house trailer market. When World War II broke out, its electric brake was fitted on a variety of military vehicles.

Warner's education was rather simple. He audited a course in electricity at Beloit College in 1885. Later, he took a correspondence course in electrical engineering. With so little formal schooling, it is astonishing that he was awarded nearly 100 patents on his various inventions.

Arthur P. Warner died in 1957. In 1985, with annual sales at $200 million, Warner Electric Brake was sold to the Dana Corporation.

SOURCE: Dana Corporation archives; The History Factory

William R. Warner, Jordan W. Lambert

[Warner-Lambert Company]

William Richard Warner was born in 1836 in Caroline County, Maryland. In the early 1850s, he was hired by a drugstore in Easton, Maryland, to perform some chores around the shop. He was paid in merchandise rather than cash, which the enterprising Warner sold door-to-door. The young man enjoyed the pharmacy business and attended the Philadelphia College of Pharmacy. Upon graduation in 1856, 19-year-old Warner opened his own drugstore in Philadelphia. He became well known as a pharmacist and, in 1860, served as a member of the committee to revise the nation's pharmacopoeia.

Warner's store grew steadily and he started experimenting with new formulas. In 1879, he conceived the idea that medicine administered in repeated doses would work better than medicine administered in a single dose. Most medicines tasted bad, and in response he established a tablet-coating process to apply a sugar shell to the unpleasant-tasting pills. He fashioned a large copper pan above the drugstore counter, which swung back and forth to provide an even distribution of the syrup over the pills.

By 1886, Warner abandoned his retail operations to concentrate on his successful drug manufacturing business. William R. Warner & Company moved into a new building and, two years later, released its first edition of the *Therapeutic Reference Book,* a compilation of medicines, poisons and antidotes, and other pertinent information.

At about the same time, Jordan Wheat Lambert—born in 1852 in Alexandria, Virginia—was in St. Louis, Missouri, working with a new antiseptic developed by Dr. Joseph Lawrence, based on the work of noted scientist Joseph Lister. In 1881, Lawrence transferred ownership of his antiseptic formula, which was called Listerine, to Lambert. The Lambert Pharmacal Company was then organized to produce Listerine for the medical profession.

Lambert died in 1889, and management of his company was passed to his son, Albert.

Albert Lambert expanded his market in 1895 by promoting Listerine to dentists as an oral antiseptic. By 1914, the product was so popular that he decided to market Listerine directly to consumers through the commercial market.

William Warner died in 1901, and control of the company passed to William R. Warner Jr., the oldest of his three sons. Seven years later, the company merged with St. Louis–based Pfeiffer Chemical Company, and in 1916 the corporate headquarters was moved to New York City.

In 1955, the Warner company merged with Lambert to form the Warner-Lambert Pharmaceutical Company. In 1970, the company merged with another pharmaceutical giant, Parke, Davis & Company.

SOURCE: Warner-Lambert Company archives

Cadwallader C. Washburn, John Crosby

[General Mills]

The first two members of the Washburn family to immigrate to America were passengers on the Mayflower, which marked the beginning of the family's long and distinguished service to the new country. Two members of the Washburn family later fought at Lexington, and one lost his life there. The other found his way into Washington's army until the battle of Yorktown brought the Revolutionary War to a close. He returned to New England and settled at Livermore, Maine.

One of his descendants, Israel Washburn, and his wife, Martha (Benjamin) Washburn, were the parents of 11 children, including Cadwallader Colden Washburn, who was born on April 22, 1818. After growing up on the family farm, young Washburn clerked in a general store and later in a post office. At the age of 20, he tried his hand at teaching, but soon grew tired of it and moved west. In 1842, he arrived in the pioneer town of Mineral Point, Wisconsin.

After several successful business ventures, Washburn and other investors formed the Minneapolis Milling Company to lease power rights to grain mill operators in 1856. He also became interested in politics and was elected to the U.S. Congress as a representative of Wisconsin, where he served alongside two of his brothers. When the Civil War erupted, he was appointed a colonel of a Wisconsin regiment and took part in several important campaigns.

After the war, Washburn served two more terms in Congress and a term as governor of Wisconsin. He also built, in 1866, the first Washburn flour mill in Minneapolis. Local residents, convinced that there wouldn't be sufficient demand for his flour, dubbed the venture "Washburn's Folly." However, Washburn had a plan.

In the mid-1800s, winter wheat was easily ground into white flour. This was preferred to spring wheat which, because of its darker bran content, generally ground into a grayish flour. Replacing his grindstones with steel rollers and adding new technology, Washburn was able to grind his spring wheat into a flour that was not only white, it offered superior baking qualities. This was not only good for his business, it helped to establish Minneapolis as a major milling center.

Washburn formed a partnership with John Crosby (pictured at right) in 1877. Like Washburn, Crosby was a native of Maine, born in 1829. He and his wife, Olive (Muzzy) Crosby, had two sons, both of whom were later active in the family business.

Despite a devastating flour-dust explosion that leveled their new plant, the partners were able to rebuild the facility and resume operations in time to enter their flour in the 1880 Millers' International Exhibition. The flours produced by the Washburn Crosby Company made a clean sweep, winning the bronze, silver, and gold medals. From that point forward, the company's highest-grade flour was marketed under the Gold Medal brand label.

In 1888, the company recruited a masterful marketing leader named James S. Bell to run the company. Bell led the company to phenomenal growth over the next three decades until his death in 1915. Washburn (pictured at right) resumed the top position of the company until 1925, when Bell's son, James Ford Bell, was named president. He was later succeeded by his son, Charles H. Bell, in 1952.

After World War I, the company experienced a steady increase in customer inquiries. In 1921, the company created a fictitious name, Betty Crocker, for its consumer response department. The name stuck, and soon the Betty Crocker Cooking School was broadcast over the radio. That same year, the company launched a new cereal named Wheaties that, through sponsorship of major league baseball, became known as the "breakfast of champions."

In 1928, James F. Bell consolidated Washburn Crosby and several regional millers under a single new company that was named General Mills. One year later, the Sperry Flour Company, largest miller on the West Coast, joined the venture, resulting in the largest flour miller in the world. Within five months, General Mills incorporated 27 associated companies in 16 states, giving it the size and strength to survive the Great Depression.

Today, General Mills remains one of the dominant food companies in the country. In addition to its vast cereal labels, Gold Medal flour, and Betty

Crocker products, the company markets several snack and convenience foods and owns the Red Lobster and The Olive Garden restaurant chains.

SOURCE: General Mills archives

Albert J. Weatherhead Jr.

[The Weatherhead Company]

Albert J. Weatherhead Jr., the eldest of six children, was born on June 26, 1892, in Cleveland, Ohio. In his childhood, young Weatherhead exhibited more fondness for sports than study. This prompted his father, the owner of a small manufacturing business, to enroll him in the University School with instructions to the headmaster to administer whatever discipline was necessary to improve his grades. The challenge worked and his grades improved, although Weatherhead still served as the football team captain.

Upon graduation in 1911, Weatherhead entered Harvard College to study engineering. He continued to pursue his love of sports, starring on the football team, serving as captain of the wrestling team, and boxing. After graduating from Harvard, Weatherhead took the job of history instructor and football coach at Bowdoin College in Maine. He later took a design engineer post in Buffalo, New York.

When World War I broke out, Weatherhead enlisted as an airplane pilot. He later received the Silver Star for exemplary combat service. In 1919, with $1,000 of accrued service pay, Weatherhead opened a modest shop in his native Cleveland and started making parts for the automotive market.

His break came with the release of his second product: radiator drain cocks. His first large order was from Stewart Warner for 182,000 drain cocks. This was followed by an order from Ford for 5,000 each month. By 1926, his 35 employees were manufacturing gasoline shutoff cocks, copper tubing connectors for carburetors, and boosters for vacuum tanks. Altogether, Weatherhead held nearly 70 patents.

Throughout the 1930s, Weatherhead continued to increase his service to the large automakers. He developed the hydraulic plumbing system, including fittings and hoses, for both General Motors and Ford. By 1934, he controlled 75 percent of Chrysler's hydraulic-line business. By 1937, he had moved into the defense business with precision-manufactured aircraft components and aircraft hydraulics systems. The growth continued through the 1940s and into the next decade, and in 1956 The Weatherhead Company was listed on the Fortune 500.

Albert and his wife, Dorothy (Jones) Weatherhead, had three sons. Dorothy passed away in 1959, and in 1963 Albert married Lillian (Izo) Weatherhead. Albert J. Weatherhead died on December 13, 1966, at the age of 74. He was still chief executive when the company neared $100 million in annual sales. The Weatherhead Company was acquired by the Dana Corporation in 1977.

SOURCE: Dana Corporation archives; The History Factory

Ernest T. Weir

[Weirton Steel Corporation]

At an early age, Ernest T. Weir purchased a small plant in Clarksburg, West Virginia, that had been sitting idle for several years. Through determined growth, the company established two other locations, one being in present-day Weirton, West Virginia, named in honor of Ernest. Weir eventually coordinated the merger of the Weirton Steel Company with two others to form the National Steel Corporation, which became America's fifth-largest steel producer.

Ernest Tener Weir was born on August 1, 1875, in Pittsburgh, Pennsylvania. Five years later his only sibling, David Manson Weir, was born. Their parents, James and Margaret Weir, were immigrants from Northern Ireland.

James provided a modest living through ownership of a livery stable near (the present) Schenley Park in Pittsburgh, renting horses and carriages. He also boarded and rented animals.

James Weir died when Ernest graduated from grade school. The company sold off the business, and 15-year-old Ernest, sole support of the family, obtained a job with a local wire company as an office boy and was paid $3.00 per week. In 1903, after holding various jobs in local steel mills, he was appointed general manager of a plant in nearby Monessen that was part of the newly formed United States Steel Corporation.

While serving in this capacity, Weir grew close to James R. Phillips, the district manager of operations. Both men were in good-paying, responsible positions at a young age and, more important, both were ambitious. Too ambitious, in fact, to wait until promotions moved them to the level of responsibility that they sought. Soon the men were planning their own company. They searched for an available location using false names, fearful that they would be fired if their employer learned of the plans.

They eventually came across an empty mill in Clarksburg, West Virginia, that was available at a bargain price of about $190,000. The two men combined their modest savings and found other private investors to reach a total capitalization of $250,000. In April 1905, the mill started operations as the Phillips Sheet and Tin Plate Company. Weir was in charge of all functions in Clarksburg, and Phillips, the senior and most visible partner, was responsible for sales.

Disaster struck only a month after operations began. James Phillips was killed in a train accident near Harrisburg, Pennsylvania, while returning from a sales trip. Weir, not quite 30 years old, was left with total responsibility for the speculative venture. He named a new plant superintendent and personally took to the road making sales. By 1908, the company had achieved stable earnings and steady growth, and Weir decided to expand the Clarksburg plant.

The automobile industry in Detroit was one of many new industries that needed steel. Weir was keenly aware of the opportunities for steelmakers and had his eye on growth. In 1909, he purchased a large tract of land along the Ohio River in an area that was then called Crawford's Crossing. By the end of the year he had ten mills operating at the plant. A year later he added ten more. In 1911, Weir purchased the Pope Tin Plate Company of Steubenville, Ohio, which sat directly across the river from his new plant. By 1915, Weir had built 50 hot mills in three plant locations and the annual output of his company was second only to United States Steel.

The plant built at Crawford's Crossing proved to be the most interesting of Weir's holdings. He strongly believed that mills should be built away from metropolitan areas so that laborers and managers would live together within communities. His new plant, built from scratch in farmland, resulted in the emergence of several small towns. To help entice people to relocate to this area, Weir's company had to form a real estate and building loan company.

Weir's strategy shifted to *integration.* Most steel plants during these times were small facilities dedicated to one or two functions, such as tin mills or coke ovens. Weir believed that steel production could be more cost-effective by integrating as many functions as possible at a single site. Thus, after 1915, the company acquired iron ore and coal properties and built coke ovens, blast furnaces, open-hearth furnaces, blooming mills, and rolling mills.

By 1918, Weir was satisfied with the integration. On August 1, 1918, on Weir's 43rd birthday, all three plants of the company were reorganized under the name of the Weirton Steel Company. For the next ten years Weir put his energies into keeping his plants modernized, increasing output, and expanding sales.

In the growing steel industry of the 1920s, bigger was better. Ernest Weir understood the benefits of company growth and economies of scale. In 1929, he forged a merger between Weirton Steel, the Michigan Steel Company, founded by George R. Fink, and the M.A. Hanna Company of Cleveland, whose chief executive officer, George M. Humphrey, was a mutual friend of Weir and Fink.

The new company was named the National Steel Corporation, of which Weirton Steel owned 50 percent. Ernest Weir was named chairman and chief executive officer. Despite the onset of the Great Depression soon after the merger, National Steel experienced continuous growth over the next several decades, eventually becoming the fifth-largest steel producer in America.

Armed with only an eighth-grade education, Ernest Weir built a steel empire. While his Weirton Steel plants were in West Virginia, he always maintained his residence in Pittsburgh. In fact, Pittsburgh became the headquarters for National Steel, although it required only modest office staff. In a display of gratitude, the communities that grew up around Weirton Steel consolidated into the City of Weirton, which at the time was West Virginia's fourth-largest city.

Ernest T. Weir died in June 1957 at age 81. His company is remembered as being charitable in the communities where plants were located. Weir himself was quite active in cultural, educational, and medical endeavors, primary in the Pittsburgh region.

The 1970s were very difficult for domestic steelmakers, and the company that was built by Ernest Weir was no exception. On March 2, 1982, National Steel announced, in effect, that it would no longer be making investments in its Weirton Steel division. Labor and management leaders reacted by forming an employee stock ownership plan, or ESOP, which took control of the mill on January 11, 1984. On that day, Weirton Steel became the world's largest wholly employee-owned company.

SOURCES: Weirton Steel Corporation archives; John D. Ubinger, "Ernest Tener Weir: Last of the Great Steelmasters," *The Western Pennsylvania Historical Magazine,* volume 58, numbers 3 and 4, July and October, 1975

Thomas B. Welch, Charles E. Welch

[Welch's Grape Juice Company]

Dr. Thomas B. Welch and his son, Dr. Charles E. Welch, were strong Christian Prohibitionists who set out to find an alternative to wine used in church services. They developed an unfermented wine that came to be known as Welch's Grape Juice and, in the process, created the fruit juice industry.

Thomas Bramwell Welch, the sixth of 15 children, was born on December 31, 1825, in Glastonbury, England. Six years later his family immigrated first to Canada, then to Hammond, New York, where his father, Abraham, opened a store and his mother, Mary, established a millinery shop.

Tom, described as both a dreamer and a doer, adopted a religious and a strong abolitionist fervor. At age 17 he joined the Wesleyan Methodist church and within two years was an ordained preacher. Throughout his late teens, Tom was active in the Underground Railroad that transported escaped slaves from the south into Canada.

In 1847, Tom married Lucy Hutt, a French-Canadian who had worked for Mary Welch as a milliner and a cook. After many moves, the couple landed in Waterton, New York, and Tom enrolled in the Syracuse Medical College. On March 2, 1852, the third of their seven children, Charles Edgar Welch, was born. Three months later, Tom graduated and established his medical practice.

Still restless, Tom again changed professions. In 1856, he moved the family to Minnesota and established a dental practice. Still later, the family moved to Vineland, New Jersey, and became quite active in the Methodist church and the temperance movement.

Tom also enjoyed creating new products. He developed a "stomach soother" that he named Dr. Welch's Neutralizing Syrup, dental alloys that he marketed as Dr. Welch's Dental Alloys, and he even took a stab at revising the dictionary with his *Dr. Welch's Sistem of Simplified Spelling.* He also established a magazine, *Items of Interest,* that became the second-leading dental journal in the country.

One day, a visiting minister with a weakness for sacramental wine stayed at the Welch home. An ugly episode of overindulgence by the minister led Tom to the conclusion that a nonalcoholic substitute was needed in the church. Following the process developed by Louis Pasteur, and working with Lucy and Charles in the family kitchen, Tom discovered a method of preparing a fruit juice from locally grown grapes that would not ferment into wine. While the experiment succeeded, Tom was disappointed to find resistance to his Dr. Welch's Unfermented Wine within the church.

At the age of 20, Charles Welch moved to Washington, D.C., studied dentistry, and established a practice. But the fruit juice experiments nagged at him, and in 1875 he returned to Vineland intent on finding a use for it. Tom, by then a successful Prohibition crusader, had all but abandoned the juice. He advised Charles, "Now don't think I'm trying to discourage your pushing the grape juice. It is right for you to do so, as far as you can, without interfering with your profession and your health."

Charles eventually moved his dental practice to Vineland and increased his attention to the juice business. In 1879, he married Jennie Ross, an early grape juice customer. While Tom, Charles, and their families continued to produce grape juice, they also opened the Welch's Dental Supply Company in Philadelphia, proof that their beverage business remained a sideline. Tragically, Jennie died in 1884, leaving behind two young children. Charles would later remarry and have three more children.

Charles had been more aware of other markets for the juice. Like his father, he had established a small periodical, *The Acorn,* in which he would advertise the family grape juice for use in the Sacrament (spiritual health) and for medicinal use (physical health). He later started another publication, *The Progress,* and directed much of his advertising toward physicians.

By 1889, Tom and Charles became caught up in the evangelism movement. After briefly considering a move to Africa, they instead chose to support the cause from America. Charles established yet another publication, *The African News,* and became closely aligned with a well-known Methodist evangelist, Bishop William Taylor. Charles also became convinced that the best way to support missionary work would be through personal philanthropy, which would be possible if the grape juice became profitable.

His marketing efforts, highlighted by a successful presence at the 1893 Chicago World's Fair, paid off. The Welch's Grape Juice Company had been officially launched, and Welch's Grape Juice was in such demand that the local farmers couldn't supply enough grapes.

Charles relocated the company first to Watkins, New York, where he converted an old flour mill into a juice factory, then later to the grape belt of Chautauqua County, New York, and Erie County, Pennsylvania. The soil and climate along Lake Erie already produced some of the finest Concord grapes in America.

The new plant in Westfield, New York, proved to be the turning point for the Welch's Grape Juice Company. Backed by modern manufacturing equipment, a good labor supply, and an abundant source of grapes, Charles was able to turn his attention to marketing matters. He vigorously pursued national markets, devoting a considerable portion of revenues to advertising.

Once again, advertising brought in orders that exceeded plant capacity. Soon the company had to look beyond Westfield for space. It purchased Walker Grape Juice Company, which maintained a large plant across the border in North East, Pennsylvania. Charles's four sons become involved with the expanding operations. In 1914, son Paul orchestrated the opening of the company's plant in Ontario, Canada.

Meanwhile, Charles pursued other investments. He became quite active in real estate acquisitions and was said to have invested in many of the farms that supplied his factory. When space in one of his buildings was vacant for too long, he decided to open his own restaurant, which was managed by his only daughter. On April 12, 1911, he placed this notice in the *Westfield Republican:*

> Name Wanted. There will be an up-to-date restaurant in the corner store of the Welch block. Ten dollars will be given for a better name than "Motor Inn." Dr. C.E. Welch.

Charles also had a political career, serving many terms as Westfield's mayor. In 1916, he was nominated by the Prohibitionist Party for the position of New York governor. While he didn't win, the experience did entrench him as a leader of the Prohibition movement.

Tom died on December 29, 1903, two days shy of his 79th birthday. By that time Charles had assumed the position of president. He held that post until his death on January 6, 1926. Thomas and Charles Welch created an entire beverage industry. Tom never received a penny in return for his investment. Charles and his family, however, did benefit from the venture and followed their hearts by donating large sums to church and youth causes.

Charles's son Edgar assumed presidency of the company after his father's death, and the Welch Grape Juice Company was sold to private investors in 1928. This syndicate was driven solely by profit, with little regard for the trust that Charles had established between employees and local farmers or for the manufacturing facilities. Eventually, the company stood at the brink of disaster, desperately needing capital improvements and strong leadership.

In June 1945, Jacob Merrill Kaplan purchased the company. A Welch's competitor for many years, Kaplan understood Welch's hold on the market. "What Ivory was to soap," Kaplan wrote, "Welch was to grape juice." An honorable and able man, Kaplan took sales from a little under $8 million in 1944 to $26 million in 1951.

In June 1952, Kaplan sold the company to the National Grape Cooperative Association, a consortium of the farmers who had supplied Kaplan and Welch's. Today this organization has 1,500 members and annual sales exceeding $550 million.

SOURCES: Welch's Grape Juice Company archives; William Chazanof, *Welch's Grape Juice: From Corporation to Co-operative,* Syracuse University Press, 1977; *Welch's: This Is Our Story,* Welch's Grape Juice Company

Henry Wells, William G. Fargo

[Wells Fargo & Company]

Henry Wells was born on December 12, 1805, in Thetford, Vermont, the fourth child of Shipley and Dolly (Randall) Wells. His father was a Presbyterian minister who also farmed and manufactured bricks. In 1814, the family moved to Seneca Falls in upstate New York. Seven years later, young Henry started an apprenticeship program as a tanner and shoemaker.

After completing the apprenticeship in 1826, Wells married Sarah Daggett and the couple eventually had four children. (Sarah died in 1859, and Wells later married Mary Prentice of Boston.) In the 1830s, Wells developed an interest in transportation and, by 1836, was a passenger and freight forwarder on the Erie Canal. Starting in 1841, he became involved with several partnerships that provided transportation services for goods, mail, and parcels.

William George Fargo was born on May 20, 1818, in Pompey, New York, the eldest of 12 children of William and Tracy (Strong) Fargo. Young William worked on the family farm until age 13, when he was hired to deliver mail on a 43-mile circuit surrounding Pompey. In 1840, Fargo married Anna H. Williams. The couple had eight children, only three of whom lived to adulthood.

After experimenting with innkeeping and grocery ventures, Fargo became a freight agent for the Auburn & Syracuse Railroad in New York. His demeanor and work ethic caught the eye of Henry Wells, the owner of an express transportation business, and in 1845 Fargo became a partner in a new venture, Wells & Company, that offered express service from Buffalo to Detroit and Chicago.

In 1850, Wells & Company joined with other principals to form the American Express Company, and Wells was named president. Two years later, Fargo suggested the partners extend service to California, and they formed Wells, Fargo & Company. Through the growth that soon followed, the Wells, Fargo office in western towns soon connected settlers to the rest of the world. With the 1866 acquisition of the Overland Mail Company, the company essentially controlled the nation's stagecoach industry.

By 1868, Wells had retired from active participation in the business and devoted himself to education. Specifically, he established Wells College in Aurora, New York, only the second college in America that was dedicated to the education of women. Wells provided a great deal of land and money to launch the school and for its support during the early years. Henry Wells died on December 10, 1878, in Glasgow, Scotland, two days before his 73rd birthday.

Fargo was appointed president of American Express in 1868 and, two years later, was named president of Wells, Fargo & Company. He also owned the *Buffalo Courier* and was even elected mayor of Buffalo in 1861. In 1871, the town of Fargo, North Dakota, was named after him. William George Fargo died on August 3, 1881.

In 1905, the San Francisco–based Wells Fargo Bank was spun off from other holdings and, through a series of mergers, is a major California bank. American Express has grown into a major credit card and financial services company.

SOURCES: Wells Fargo Bank archives; Robert Chandler, "Henry Wells" and "William George Fargo," Banking and Finance to 1913, *Encyclopedia of American Business History and Biography*

George Westinghouse

[Westinghouse Electric Company]

George Westinghouse was born on October 6, 1846, in Central Bridge, New York, the eighth of ten children born to a Vermont farmer. His father later moved the family to Schenectady, New York, where he built a successful business innovating and manufacturing farm machinery.

At age 17, George entered the service during the Civil War, first as a cavalry scout and later as a naval engineer. After the war, he briefly attended Union College at Schenectady, then went to work in his father's shop. His first invention, at age 19, was a small rotary engine for which he was granted the first of nearly 400 patents he would receive over his lifetime.

In 1869, 22-year-old Westinghouse innovated perhaps his best-known device: the air brake. The young inventor rode aboard the first train ever equipped with air brakes, which traveled from Pittsburgh, Pennsylvania, to Steubenville, Ohio. That same year, he founded the Westinghouse Air Brake Company. He soon became convinced that there was a need for improved railroad safety, and he developed an electric signaling system. By 1881, he had merged several businesses in the industry into the Union Switch and Signal Company.

Westinghouse's interest extended beyond railroads. He invented dozens of products related to the control and distribution of natural gas, and he established a gas company in Pittsburgh. By the mid-1880s, he became active in the electrical industry and applied similar principles of control and distribution. His work led to the standardization of alternating current in the United States, and in 1886 he founded the Westinghouse Electric Company.

By 1890, George Westinghouse had achieved sales of $4 million and had installed more than 300 central power stations. Three years later, he provided the power plant for the Chicago World's Fair, which literally showcased his work to the world. Shortly thereafter, he was contracted to provide three generators that would harness the power of Niagara Falls. His system produced so much power that lines were strung to nearby Buffalo, which became the model for modern power generation and distribution.

Westinghouse next obtained American rights for the steam turbine developed by Sir Charles Parsons in England. The device was initially used to supply power for the Westinghouse Air Brake plant. Then, in 1900, he installed a central station turbine generator at Hartford, Connecticut, to produce electricity for the city. The success demonstrated the superiority of steam-generated power plants, which became the standard throughout the country.

George Westinghouse died on March 12, 1914. Altogether, he established nearly 60 companies that have provided gainful employment for hundreds of thousands of men and women over the years. But far more jobs were created in the railroad, natural gas, and other industries that grew with the advent of convenient electric power.

In recent years, Westinghouse, which reported sales of $6.3 billion in 1995, has rapidly increased its communications and media activity. In 1995, Westinghouse acquired CBS, Inc., for $5.4 billion, forming the largest television and radio broadcaster in America. One year later, the company completed a $4.9 billion merger with Infinity Broadcasting Company.

SOURCE: Westinghouse Electric Company archives

Uncas A. Whitaker

[AMP, Incorporated]

Uncas Aeneas Whitaker was born on March 22, 1900, in Lincoln, Kansas, and was subsequently raised in rural Weaubleau, Missouri. He studied at Drury College in Missouri and Missouri School of Mines and Metallurgy before transferring to the Massachusetts Institute of Technology, where he was awarded a B.S. in mechanical engineering in 1923.

Upon graduation, Whitaker accepted a job with the Westinghouse Air Brake Company in Pittsburgh, Pennsylvania. There, he took night classes at the Carnegie Institute of Technology (now part of Carnegie Mellon University) and earned a second degree in electrical engineering.

By 1929, Whitaker had grown restless for a new opportunity and joined the Hoover Company. Within months, he was named director of development and design, and was charged with designing a reliable, low-priced sweeper. The result was the Hoover Model 150, a sweeper that kept Hoover profitable through the Depression years.

During Whitaker's years with Hoover, he kept himself busy with more than vacuum cleaners. He studied law at night at the Cleveland Law School. He also became a flying enthusiast, purchased an airplane, and acquired half interest in the small company that owned the hangar he rented. The experience provided Whitaker with valuable insight into running a business and, more specifically, contracting with the federal government.

After ten years with Hoover, Whitaker moved to New York City and took a job in 1939 with American Machine and Foundry as an engineer and business manager. Within two years he was able to successfully reorganize their engineering department. The experience, in a sense, rounded out an 18-year, hands-on education for the engineer, lawyer, inventor, and businessman.

In 1941, Whitaker became acquainted with Stephen Buchanan, founder of a company named Industrial Manufacturers. The firm had innovated a new type of solderless connectors and had attracted the interest of the Naval Bureau of Aeronautics. Whitaker and Buchanan joined forces and launched a new company called Aero-Marine Products, which was changed to Aircraft-Marine Products a few months later. One year later, Buchanan left the venture, leaving Whitaker in control.

World War II taxed America's manufacturing capacity, particularly in the aircraft industry, where President Roosevelt pushed for the completion of 125,000 new planes by 1943 to 1944. The solderless connections produced by Aircraft-Marine Products, or A-MP for short, dramatically reduced the time it took to assemble many aircraft components, and thus sale of the product fueled the company's rapid growth.

Whitaker decided to relocate his Elizabeth, New Jersey, plant in 1942. After exhaustive market research, he decided that central Pennsylvania provided an advantageous location and business climate. The following year, his plant was reopened in Harrisburg, Pennsylvania.

The end of World War II signaled a change in A-MP's market focus, requiring a rather drastic adjustment in its manufacturing strategies. The company, like many others who were so active in the supporting the war effort, had to refocus on the commercial market. To accomplish this, Whitaker drew on his experience at Hoover and its consumer-oriented product line. He also insisted that highly innovative employees be given considerable latitude at the company. As a result, the company had its share of eccentric personalities, even though Whitaker himself was quite grounded.

There were also changes in Whitaker's home life. In 1944, the 44-year-old founder married Helen Fisher, a former coworker at the Hoover Company. Two years later, Uncas and Helen adopted his sister's two teenage daughters following her unexpected death.

As the 1950s drew to a close, the company changed its name to AMP, Incorporated, and had become a 2,400-employee, $30 million company. By 1965, AMP produced 15,000 items, broke $100 million in sales, and was designated one of the 500 largest companies in the country.

Uncas A. Whitaker, an avid angler, died in September 1975, while vacationing in Maine. Today, AMP has annual sales of nearly $5.5 billion and has 45,000 employees worldwide.

SOURCES: AMP, Incorporated, archives; W. H. Cohn, *The End Is Just the Beginning: U. A. Whitaker, Biography of an Engineer,* Carnegie Mellon University, 1980; Bern Sharfman, *The AMP Story: Right Connections,* 1992

Charles Wiley, John Wiley

[John Wiley & Sons, Inc.]

The Wiley family has a long and prestigious history in New York City dating back to the successful rum-trading business maintained by a Captain John Wiley in the mid-1700s. His grandson, Charles Wiley, was born in New York

City in 1782. In 1805, he married Lydia Osburn, the proprietor of a small grocery store, and the couple eventually had five children, including John Wiley.

Charles Wiley opened his first printing shop in 1807 and, over the next five years, produced a number of books, many for the legal profession. In 1814, he established a partnership with a well-established printer, Cornelius Van Winkle. The pair, who maintained an office at No. 3 Wall Street, served as printer and publisher for a number of titles until 1818, when the partnership dissolved.

Wiley kept the Wall Street office and, with a partner, operated as a bookseller and publisher under the name Wiley & Company. Printing was contracted out. Later, he took another partner and changed the name to Wiley & Halstead. In 1822, Wiley was once again operating alone under the imprint of Charles Wiley. One of his authors was James Fenimore Cooper, often cited as America's first important novelist.

Charles Wiley died in 1826 at the age of 44. His 18-year-old son, John Wiley (pictured at left), assumed responsibility for the family business, where he had been working for the previous two years. Young John maintained the course set by his father while engaging in a series of partnerships, including one with George Palmer Putnam, father of renowned publisher George Haven Putnam. As his reputation grew, Wiley was able to produce works of many of the great writers of the time, including Edgar Allan Poe, Herman Melville, and Nathaniel Hawthorne.

In 1833, Wiley married Elizabeth B. Osgood, the daughter of a Springfield minister. The couple had 11 children, but only 5 lived beyond childhood. When his partnership with Putnam ended in the late 1840s, Wiley shifted his focus somewhat, publishing only proven authors and spending more time with imported titles, including Bibles, travel guides, and children's books.

John Wiley's oldest son, Charles, started working for the firm in 1850 when he was only 15 years old. In 1865, Charles was promoted to partner and the firm was renamed John Wiley & Son. Ten years later, John's son William had put in sufficient time with the company to warrant a partnership, and the firm became John Wiley & Sons. The addition of his sons energized the business, which had lost momentum after the Civil War. With the new generation came an emphasis on science, technical, and educational books.

John Wiley died in February, 1891, and was succeeded by his son William. Today, John Wiley & Sons is the oldest independent publisher in North America and is a global corporation, with operations in the United States, Canada, Europe, Asia, and Australia. The company has 11,000 active book titles and releases approximately 1,500 new titles each year. The company has 2,000 employees worldwide and annual sales of more than $400 million.

SOURCES: John Wiley & Sons, Inc., archives; John H. Moore, *Wiley: One Hundred and Seventy-five Years of Publishing,* John Wiley & Sons, 1982

Elmer L. Winter, Aaron Scheinfeld

[Manpower, Inc.]

Elmer L. Winter was born on March 6, 1912, in Milwaukee, Wisconsin, to Sigmund and May Winter. His father, an immigrant from Bohemia, operated a men's clothing store in Milwaukee. His mother was the daughter of a Hungarian immigrant. Upon graduation from high school, Elmer majored in economics at the University of Wisconsin and graduated from the university's School of Law in 1935.

In 1936, Winter was offered a job in the Chicago law firm owned by his brother-in-law, Aaron Scheinfeld, for $30 per month. The firm later expanded, and Winter became a partner, managing the Milwaukee office. In 1948, while working on an important legal case, the partners tried to find temporary help to ease the workload on their office staff, but were unable to locate any agency that provided such a service. Recalling a client who provided short-term laborers for unloading freight cars, they shared the idea of a temporary help firm with acquaintances, who readily agreed that such a venture would be well received.

Winter and Scheinfeld rented a small store in Milwaukee, hired a manager, and declared themselves to be in the business of providing temporary manpower to businesses. When they approached a colleague for a suggestion for a name for their "manpower operation," he replied, "There you have it: *Manpower.* That's the name of your company."

At the end of their first year in business, the company showed a $9,000 loss. The founders had a successful law practice and nearly abandoned their temporary-help venture, but decided to give it another year because the customers that they did serve were quite satisfied. At the end of the second year, they had made enough to cover their losses and expenses and even to show a small profit.

By 1956, Manpower had grown so successful that Winter and Scheinfeld retired from their law practice to devote full attention to their temporary-help venture. Prior to Manpower, companies generally employed workers either full-time or part-time, and most of the arrangements were between the employer and the applicant. Manpower added a new word to the workplace—*temp,* or temporary worker, which was help contracted through an agency that had a vested interest in providing enthusiastic, qualified workers on short notice.

The firm provided employment opportunities for a wide range of workers—women who were returning to the workforce after raising families, retired persons wanting to supplement social security income, and students working their way through college. In 1953, the founders started franchising Manpower, which fueled a rapid period of growth.

In 1976, Manpower was sold to the Parker Pen company. Today, the company maintains 2,000 offices in 38 countries, and annual sales approach $6 billion.

SOURCE: Manpower, Inc., archives

Frank W. Woolworth

[Woolworth Corporation]

The Woolworth family first came to America in 1678 when Richard Woolworth, a colonial weaver, left his native Wooley, England. Several generations later, Frank Winfield Woolworth was born on April 13, 1852, in Rodman, New York, to John H. and Fanny (McBrier) Woolworth. The family moved to Great Bend, New York, several years later, where Woolworth spent much of his youth on the family farm.

Anxious to leave the farm, young Woolworth offered to work for a retailer in nearby Watertown for free. Eventually he was added to the payroll with a $3.50 weekly salary for an 84-hour work week. His next job was with a local dry goods and carpet store. However, the move didn't work out and his employer lowered his wage from $10 per week to $8 because of poor sales. Subsequently, he became ill and lost his job.

Woolworth rebounded and, in 1876, married Jennie Creighton, a Canadian woman who worked as a seamstress in Waterton. Later that year, his first employer, who was always fond of Woolworth's talent in designing window displays, asked him to return to his old job.

In 1878, Woolworth was asked to launch a 5¢ counter promotion at the store. The event involved stocking a counter with nickel items that would attract shoppers to the store who would, ideally, also purchase other items. The owner of the store purchased $100 worth of notions that Woolworth arranged on a 10-foot counter fashioned from two sewing tables.

The 5¢ sale proved to be such a great success that Woolworth borrowed a little over $300 and established his own shop in 1879, called the Great 5¢ Store, in Utica, New York. The small, 14- by 25-foot store did a fair business but, despite Woolworth's handbill advertisements, proved to be in a poor location. Woolworth decided to search for a more attractive site.

A friend suggested to Woolworth that he open his discount store at Lancaster, Pennsylvania. Logic suggested that the thrifty Pennsylvania Dutch residents would appreciate a good bargain store, so he hopped a train to Lancaster and found the city streets filled with evening shoppers. Satisfied with the location, he quickly found an available store that rented for $30 per month.

On opening day, June 21, 1879, hundreds of shoppers converged on the store, which registered sales of nearly $130 on the first day, as almost one-third of the inventory was sold. The success continued, and soon the sign on the front of the store was changed to Woolworth's 5 and 10¢ Store. Encouraged by his success, he opened a second store in Scranton, Pennsylvania, in 1880.

By 1888, 12 stores were open. All of these early Woolworth's stores were opened under partner-manager arrangements, where Woolworth shared ownership and profits with the men who were managing them. However, from that point forward all the stores were owned exclusively by Woolworth.

Woolworth developed a fondness for buying trips and was soon introducing his customers to a wide range of inexpensive European-made goods. If he liked a particular product, it wasn't uncommon for him to negotiate purchase of the entire factory output, not only to provide an adequate inventory, but to keep competitors from stocking the same goods.

The corporate headquarters was moved to Manhattan in the 1880s, and in 1905 the founder formally incorporated his 120 stores under an umbrella organization, F. W. Woolworth & Company. By 1909, he took his "five and dime" concept to England, where it became the "three and sixpence" stores.

In 1913, President Woodrow Wilson flipped on the lights in the new Woolworth Building in Manhattan, a 60-story "cathedral of commerce" that, at the time, was the world's tallest skyscraper. Frank W. Woolworth died on April 8, 1919, five days short of his 67th birthday. At the time of his death, more than 1,000 Woolworth stores were in existence and annual sales were nearly $120 million.

SOURCES: Woolworth Corporation archives; John P. Nichols, *Skyline Queen and the Merchant Prince,* Simon & Schuster, 1973

Wilbur Wright, Orville Wright

[Wright Aeronautical Company]

The Wright brothers are generally celebrated for their pioneering research and innovation regarding flight and are credited with achieving the first sustained, controlled flight in an engine-propelled aircraft. However, throughout their careers the brothers founded and built a number of companies, one of which eventually became the Curtiss-Wright Corporation.

Wilbur Wright was born on April 16, 1867, in Millville, Indiana, the third son of Milton and Susan Wright. Milton Wright, a bishop in the Church of the

United Brethren in Christ, moved his family to Dayton, Ohio, in 1871, where Orville was born on August 19 of that year.

Wilbur and Orville Wright were hard workers and clever innovators, although neither graduated from high school. They developed an early venture printing local newspapers after they fashioned a crude printing press from lumber, a tombstone, and an old buggy. Curiosity brought them into the bicycle business, and they soon established a successful venture, the Wright Cycle Company, to build their own line of bicycles.

By 1899, the Wright brothers had developed a keen interest in aviation. That year, Wilbur wrote to aviation pioneer Samuel Langley, who provided him with considerable material on aeronautics. That same year he also struck upon one of the most important theories of wing control by means of devices known as *ailerons*. The brothers decided to test their airplane at Kitty Hawk, North Carolina, along the ocean on the Outer Banks, since the area provided strong winds to launch the plane and soft sand for landing.

Their first attempts to fly in 1901 were unsuccessful. They went back to the drawing board and designed a second model, which they were able to fly in 1902. However, their glider would quickly fall into a tailspin and crash. Eventually, Orville worked out the problem by making the tail a movable rudder. On December 17, 1903, the brothers were able to launch four successful, sustained flights, landing them a spot in aviation history.

The Wright brothers made a number of improvements to their equipment over the next few years and coaxed longer, more complex flights from their airplane. However, because patents were not quickly issued, the brothers dismantled their plane in 1906 and maintained an air of secrecy over their technology.

By 1908, the brothers and their airplane emerged again, as Orville pursued a military contract and Wilbur went to Europe to showcase their airplane. Orville's bid to capture a military contract proved disastrous. While flying with Lt. Tom Selfridge of the U.S. Army Signal Corps, a propeller accident caused the plane to crash, killing Selfridge and seriously injuring Orville.

Wilbur, however, was well received in Europe and solicited considerable business. And despite the earlier tragedy, the brothers were granted American military contracts. With an impressive backlog of orders, the Wright Company was launched in 1909.

As the industry grew, the Wrights became involved in a bitter patent dispute with Glenn Curtiss over similar aileron technology. On May 30, 1912, Wilbur Wright died of typhoid fever. Eventually, the courts ruled in Orville's favor, but the victory was short-lived. Curtiss, with the support of Henry Ford, baited Orville into reopening the suit, which became tied up in the courts until the onset of World War I, at which time patents were essentially meaningless.

Despite the bad blood, the Curtiss Aeroplane and Engine Company merged with the Wright Aeronautical Company in 1929, forming the Curtiss-Wright Corporation. Wilbur and Orville Wright were both lifelong bachelors. Orville Wright died on January 30, 1948.

SOURCE: Curtiss-Wright Corporation archives

William Wrigley Jr.

[Wm. Wrigley Jr. Company]

William Wrigley Jr. grew up in Philadelphia, Pennsylvania. His father was a soap manufacturer, and as a young boy William sold Wrigley's Scouring Soap from a basket in the streets of the city. When he reached his teens, he peddled the soap in outlying towns from a horse and wagon.

In 1891, the 29-year-old Wrigley moved to Chicago, Illinois, with $32 and the desire to establish his own business. He started doing what he knew best: selling Wrigley's Scouring Soap. As an incentive to grocers, Wrigley handed out baking powder. Soon, the baking powder became more popular than the soap, so he switched to the baking powder business.

By 1892, Wrigley started to offer two packages of chewing gum as a premium with each can of baking powder. Again, the premium became more popular than the product it was promoting, so Wrigley decided to go into the chewing gum business.

He immediately started to market the gum under his own name. His first two flavors were Lotta and Vassar, followed one year later with Juicy Fruit and Wrigley's Spearmint. Wrigley handled most of the sales himself, and despite strong competition and financial struggles, he was able to sustain a share of the market.

Wrigley's marketing strategy was to appeal to the consumer. He continued his practice of offering incentives with purchases, and he soon had an entire catalog of gift items. He also experimented with advertising in selected markets. Once he was convinced of the value of advertising, he launched successful media campaigns. On at least two occasions, he sent free chewing gum to every person listed in every telephone book in the United States. Eventually, customers across the nation were walking into their local stores asking for Wrigley's gum.

As the company grew, Wrigley added new products and markets. Wrigley's Doublemint gum was introduced in 1914. Wrigley started shipping to foreign markets, including Canada (1910), Australia (1915), and Great Britain (1927).

In addition to his chewing gum empire, Wrigley was active in two other highly visible ventures. For $2.5 million, he purchased Santa Catalina Island off the coast of Los Angeles. Investing nearly $20 million, he converted the island into one of America's best-known resorts.

The other venture was the Chicago Cubs professional baseball team. Wrigley first bought in to the Cubs in 1916, but it wasn't until 1924 that he acquired majority interest. From that point forward, he was quite actively involved with the team. Under his leadership, the team moved from last place to the World Series in five seasons. When the Cubs won the National League title in 1929, the proud owner told his players to go out and celebrate and that "no expense account under $50 would be honored."

William Wrigley Jr. died in January 1932. The business continued under the leadership of his son, Philip K. Wrigley, until his death in 1977. Philip's son, William, was named president and chief executive officer in 1961.

SOURCES: Wm. Wrigley Jr. Company archives; "William Wrigley, Jr., American," *Fortune* magazine, April 1932

Stephen A. Wynn

[Mirage Resorts, Incorporated]

Stephen A. Wynn was born on January 27, 1942, in New Haven, Connecticut. He received his B.A. in English literature from the University of Pennsylvania.

Wynn started his career in Las Vegas, Nevada, at the age of 25 as a part owner of the Frontier Hotel. In addition, he launched a wine and liquor import company in 1969. After completing a profitable real estate transaction with Howard Hughes, Wynn acquired control of the Golden Nugget, a small casino with no hotel rooms, in 1972. He established a series of aggressive expansion projects, and today the Golden Nugget has nearly 2,000 rooms and suites, elegant dining facilities, and, of course, a world-class casino.

In 1980, Wynn opened the Golden Nugget Hotel & Casino in Atlantic City, New Jersey, at a cost of $140 million. After the venture was sold to Bally seven years later for $440 million, Wynn turned his attention back to Las Vegas and orchestrated the design and development of the Mirage, a South Seas theme resort that he opened in November 1989 at a cost of $630 million.

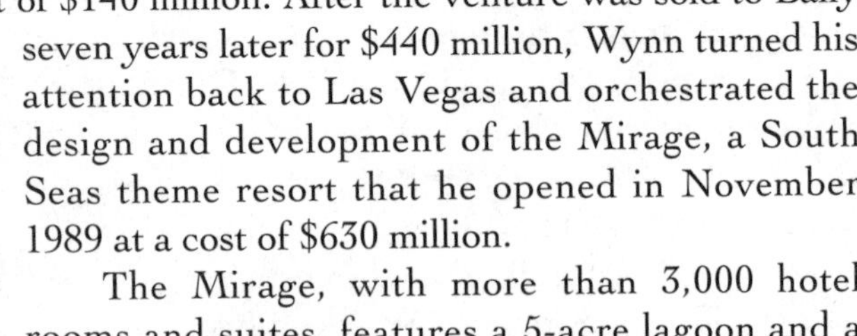

The Mirage, with more than 3,000 hotel rooms and suites, features a 5-acre lagoon and a fire-erupting volcano, a habitat for the Royal White Tigers used by Siegfried and Roy, a tropical rain forest, and much more. The Mirage has been acclaimed as the most successful hotel ever launched, not counting its gaming revenue.

In 1993, Wynn added to his Las Vegas holdings with the opening of the $475 million Treasure Island at the Mirage, a pirate-themed resort. That same year, the company acquired the 164-acre Dunes Hotel & Country Club for $70 million.

Wynn is currently developing two major sites. In Las Vegas, he is building Bellagio, a $1.4 billion, 3,000-room resort incorporating a traditional

European theme, which he promises will be the most romantic hotel in the world. He is also building Beau Rivage, a $475 million, 1,800-room resort in Biloxi, Mississippi.

Wynn and his wife, Elaine Farrel Pascal, married in 1963 and have two daughters, Kevyn and Gillian.

SOURCE: Mirage Resorts, Incorporated archives

George Zambelli

[Zambelli International Fireworks]

Marco Polo is renowned for his international travels and adventures, but he also is credited with playing a leading role in the development of the pyrotechny, or fireworks, industry. Continuing the time-honored tradition of Italian pyrotechny professionals, Antonio Zambelli left his native Italy in 1893 and immigrated to New Castle, Pennsylvania, where he became one of the area's many fireworks manufacturers.

Zambelli had three sons who later joined him in the business—Joseph, Louis, and George. While the children were young and the profits were low, Antonio worked in the local steel mills to support his growing family and business. George wanted the business not only to grow, but to become the greatest fireworks company in the world. He recognized the challenges that lay in his path and equipped himself with a degree from Duquesne University before taking the helm of the company.

After George Zambelli was named president of Zambelli International, he faced the challenge of combining the old ways of hand-packing fireworks with the newer technologies that became available. He also had to face the challenges of an industry in which the smaller companies were being weeded out or absorbed by the larger companies. New Castle was once home to one-fourth of all pyrotechny producers in the country. Today, only Zambelli remains in the area.

Through the years, Zambelli has developed an expertise base for planning and producing shows, including displays that are electronically synchronized with music and lasers. However, the secret is perhaps found in his approach to the market: No show is too big or too small: He has even accommodated churches that have approached him with a $150 budget.

He is best known, however, for shows on a grander scale, including most of the presidential inaugurations over the past four decades. One of his greatest honors was being named one of three pyrotechny firms to entertain the crowds at the Statue of Liberty celebration on July 4, 1986. Zambelli's firm shot off 26,400 shells at the site where, more than 90 years earlier, George's father caught his first glimpse of America.

Today, Zambelli International is the oldest and largest manufacturer of fireworks in America. The company remains based in New Castle and maintains branch offices at Boca Raton, Florida, and Shafter, California. Zambelli's wife, Connie, and three of his five children are involved with the business full-time. The company operates two manufacturing plants in the New Castle area, including its modern 400-acre Nashua Harbor Plant that includes more than 60 blockhouses.

SOURCES: Zambelli International Fireworks archives; Nan DeVincentis Hayes, "Zambelli: The First Family of Fireworks," *Italian Times*, winter 1988/89

Kurt Ziebart

[Ziebart International]

In 1950, Kurt and Edith Ziebart immigrated from Germany to the United States. In 1953, the family moved to Detroit, Michigan, where Ziebart, a master mechanic, was confident he could find work. They were so poor when they reached Detroit that Kurt had to borrow money from his uncle to pick up their luggage at the train depot.

Ziebart was hired as a mechanic at a local automobile dealership. However, he was frequently frustrated by the language barrier and often could not understand what the customers meant as they described their engine problems. Within a year, he moved to another job at a collision shop owned by Rudy Herman. Ziebart was much more comfortable with the job because problems such as damaged bumpers didn't require a detailed customer description.

In 1954, Ziebart switched jobs again, this time to a Packard dealership. He promptly purchased a new 1953 Packard from his employer at a very good price—since the car had been totally demolished in an accident. He then spent most of his spare time rebuilding the car.

The restoration of the car was tedious work, and Ziebart was determined to protect his investment from rust. He knew from experience that the most damaging rust started on the *inside* of the car, often in doors and rocker panels, and that it was expensive to repair the damage by the time it became visible.

His efforts to protect against rust, however, proved difficult. The major obstacle was finding an effective sealant that could be easily applied, but one that would withstand the movement and vibration of the car, as well as diverse temperature changes. Moreover, the areas that needed to be protected were difficult to reach with available sprayers.

After six years of experimentation, Ziebart perfected his systematic rustproofing process, which included drilling inconspicuous holes, inserting specially designed high-pressure sprayers, and injecting a reliable sealant. Once the process was perfected, the Packard dealership started offering the rustproofing service as an option.

In 1960, Ziebart was confident that his idea could stand alone and, with Rudy Herman and another partner, opened a small shop. The following year he received a contract from General Motors to rustproof 150 vehicles. The proceeds were used to launch an advertising campaign, and the company was soon booked weeks in advance.

The success of Ziebart's venture attracted others who expressed an interest in establishing a similar business, and in 1962 the first franchise was opened. By the end of the following year, 18 shops were in operation, including one in Canada. Ziebart and his partners elected to dissolve their partnership and sell the company to an investment group led by Roger Waindle, who renamed it the Ziebart Process Corporation. Kurt and Edith Ziebart then moved to northern Michigan and acquired a successful Mercedes Benz dealership.

Ziebart International acquired Tidy Car, an Ontario-based detailing franchise, in 1989. Today, Ziebart has more than 700 franchises in 41 countries, and annual revenue exceeds $155 million.

SOURCE: Ziebart International archives

Photo Credits

Page 11, photo courtesy of Carnival Cruise Lines.
Page 16, photo courtesy of Avery Dennison Corporation.
Page 32, photos courtesy of Baskin-Robbins.
Page 38, photo courtesy of Bausch & Lomb Inc.
Page 57, photo provided by and reproduced with permission of Binney & Smith, maker of Crayola products.
Page 67, photo courtesy of The Boeing Company.
Pages 70, 71, photos courtesy of Booz Allen & Hamilton, Inc.
Page 106, photo courtesy of United Parcel Service, © 1960 by Yousuf Karsch.
Page 107, photos courtesy of United Parcel Service.
Page 132, photo courtesy of Cray Research, a Silicon Graphics Co.
Pages 152, 153, photos courtesy of Brown-Forman Beverage Worldwide.
Page 169, photo courtesy of R.R. Donnelley & Sons Company Archives.
Pages 172, 173, photos courtesy of Dow Jones & Company.
Page 190, photo courtesy of Bob Evans Farms, Inc.
Page 204, photo courtesy of the Procter & Gamble Company.
Page 246, photo courtesy of Winnebago Industries, Inc.
Page 253, photo courtesy of H. J. Heinz Company.
Page 254, photo courtesy of Discovery Communications, © 1996 Rhoda Baer.
Page 261, © by Nestlé.
Page 263, photo courtesy of Hilton Hotels.
Page 266, photo courtesy of The Hoover Company.
Page 279, © 1997, by Hertz System, Inc. Hertz is a registered service mark and trademark of Hertz System, Inc.
Page 280, photo courtesy of Jacuzzi Inc.
Page 281, © 1997 by Andrew MacAoidh Jergens.
Page 293, photo courtesy of W.K. Kellogg Foundation.
Page 303, photo courtesy of Kohler Co.
Page 314, photo courtesy of Eli Lilly and Company Archives.
Page 327, photo courtesy of Maytag.
Page 331, photos courtesy of McCormick & Company, Inc.
Page 334, reprinted by permission of Texas Instruments.
Pages 335, 336, photos courtesy of McDonnell Douglas.
Page 346, photo courtesy of Miller Brewing Co.
Page 351, photo courtesy of Domino's Pizza, Inc.
Page 359, photo courtesy of Lourdes Rosado-Ford.
Page 369, photos courtesy of Formica Corporation.
Page 405, photo courtesy of Kentucky Fried Chicken (KFC) Public Affairs Department, circa 1968.
Page 410, photo courtesy of The Charles Schwab Corporation.
Pages 412, 413, photos courtesy of Sears, Roebuck and Company.
Page 414, photo courtesy of Sebastiani and Cuneo family.
Page 434, © 1993 Universal City Studios and Amblin Entertainment.
Page 438, photo courtesy of Steinway & Sons.

Page 447, photo courtesy of Wendy's International Inc.
Page 457, photo courtesy of Turner Broadcasting.
Page 459, photo courtesy of Tyson Foods, Inc.
Page 467, photo courtesy of Walgreen Co.
Page 469, © by Arnold Newman, The Readers Digest Fund.
Page 471, photo courtesy of Computer Associates International.
Page 477, photos courtesy of General Mills Archives.
Page 485, photo courtesy of Westinghouse Electric.
Page 488, photos courtesy of Photo Archives Dept.—John Wiley & Sons.
Page 493, photo courtesy of the Wm. Wrigley Jr. Company.
Page 494, photo courtesy of Mirage Resorts, Incorporated.

Index of Companies

Index of Entrepreneurs